Contents

3   Customer Information, Risk and Suitability, Product Information 73

Top-off General Securities Representative Exam

Series 7
1st Edition

Securities License Exam Manual

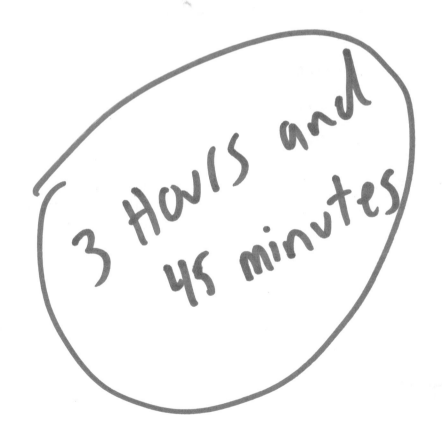

3 Hours and 45 minutes

At press time, this edition contains the most complete and accurate information currently available. Owing to the nature of license examinations, however, information may have been added recently to the actual test that does not appear in this edition. Please contact the publisher to verify that you have the most current edition.

SERIES 7 TOP-OFF GENERAL SECURITIES REPRESENTATIVE EXAM LICENSE EXAM MANUAL, 1ST EDITION
©2018 Kaplan, Inc.

Published in July 2018 by Kaplan Financial Education.

Printed in the United States of America.

ISBN: 978-1-4754-8149-5

Introduction

INTRODUCTION

Thank you for choosing Kaplan for your educational needs and welcome to the General Securities Representative Examination (Series 7) License Exam Manual (LEM). This manual applies adult learning principles to give you the tools you'll need to pass your exam on the first attempt.

Why Do I Need to Pass the Series 7 Exam?

The Financial Industry Regulatory Authority (FINRA), or another self-regulatory organization, requires its members and employees of its members to pass a qualification exam to become registered as a General Securities Representative. You must pass the Series 7 exam to be qualified to sell all types of securities.

Are There Any Prerequisites?

No. However, in order for a Series 7 registration to become effective, an individual must pass both the Series 7 qualification exam and the Securities Industry Essentials (SIE) exam.

What Is the Series 7 Exam Like?

The exam is administered via computer. A tutorial on how to take the exam is provided prior to taking the exam. Each candidate's exam includes 10 additional, unidentified pretest items that do not contribute toward the candidate's score. The pretest items are randomly distributed throughout the exam. Therefore, each candidate's exam consists of a total of 135 items (125 scored and 10 unscored). There is no penalty for guessing. Therefore, candidates should attempt to answer all items. Candidates will be allowed 3 hours and 45 minutes to complete the Series 7 exam.

What Score Must I Achieve to Pass?

All candidate test scores are placed on a common scale using a statistical adjustment process known as equating. Equating scores to a common scale accounts for the slight variations in difficulty that may exist among the different sets of exam items that candidates receive. This allows for a fair comparison of scores and ensures that every candidate is held to the same passing standard, regardless of which set of exam items they received. Be sure to check the Exam Tips and Content Updates link on your Dashboard for any updates to the passing requirement.

What Topics Will I See on the Exam?

The questions you will see on the Series 7 exam do not appear in any particular order. The computer is programmed to select a new, random set of questions for each exam taker, selecting questions according to the preset topic weighting of the exam. Each Series 7 candidate will see the same number of questions on each topic, but a different mix of questions. The Series 7 exam is divided into four major job function areas:

Four Major Job Functions	No. of Questions	% of Exam
F1. Seeks Business for the Broker-Dealer From Customers and Potential Customers	9	7%
F2. Opens Accounts After Obtaining and Evaluating Customers' Financial Profile and Investment Objectives	11	9%
F3. Provides Customers With Information About Investments, Makes Suitable Recommendations, Transfers Assets, and Maintains Appropriate Records	91	73%
F4. Obtains and Verifies Customers' Purchase and Sales Instructions and Agreements; Processes, Completes, and Confirms Transactions	14	11%
	125	100%

Write 3, 4, 5, 6

Test candidates should be aware that within each major job function, FINRA has identified tasks and knowledge statements that test questions are based on. The complete Series 7 General Securities Representative Qualification Examination Content Outline can be viewed on FINRA's website: www.FINRA.org.

When you complete your exam, you will receive a printout that identifies your performance in each of the four major job function areas.

PREPARING FOR THE EXAM

How Is the License Exam Manual Organized?

The License Exam Manual is organized in Units. There is a glossary that can help clarify unfamiliar terms you come across, and an index makes it easy to locate content within the LEM. In addition to the regular text, each Unit ends with a test. Look for unique features created to help you understand and comprehend the material. When additional emphasis is critical to your success, the following distinctions are made.

There is a PDF of the LEM on your dashboard. If you open the PDF, you can then search the LEM for key words by pressing Ctrl + F.

| TAKE NOTE | Each Take Note provides special information designed to amplify important points. |

| TEST TOPIC ALERT | Each Test Topic Alert! highlights content that is likely to appear on the exam. |

| EXAMPLE | Examples provide practical applications that convert theory into understanding. |

| QUICK QUIZ | Quick Quizzes are a quick interactive review of what you just read. These ensure you understand and retain the material. |

Additional Study Resources

To accompany and supplement your License Exam Manual, your study package may contain additional study resources. Be sure to spend some time on your homepage, view the best practices video, and understand all that is available to help you study.

SecuritiesPro QBank

Coordinating with the LEM, the SecuritiesPro™ QBank includes a large number of questions that are similar in style and content to those you will encounter on the exam. You may use it to generate tests by a specific Unit or combination of Units. The QBank also allows you to create Weighted Mock Exams that mimic your test. There is no limit on the number of QBank exams you can create.

One thing you should know about the SecuritiesPro™ QBank is that the answer choices are scrambled each time you take a test. That is, if the first time you saw a specific question, the correct answer was choice A, that statement might be choice D the next time. Please keep this in mind if you need to contact us regarding that question.

Practice and Mastery Exams

Depending on the study package purchased, you may also have a fixed Practice Exam or a fixed Practice and Mastery Exam. These exams are designed to closely replicate the true exam experience, both in terms of the degree of difficulty and topical coverage. They provide scores and diagnostic feedback, but you will not be given access to—nor will you be able to obtain from Kaplan—correct answers or question explanations. The Practice and Mastery Exams are sound indicators of potential actual exam scores—the better you do on these exams, the more likely you are to pass your actual exam. These may be taken just once each.

Video Library

You may also have access to various topics from our video library. These short, engaging videos cover key topics from your manual. If your package includes access to our video library, please review the topics as you complete your reading assignments in the study manual.

Exam Tips & Content Updates Link

Don't forget to monitor your Exam Tips & Content Updates. When rules and regulations change, or we want to share new information regarding your exam, it's posted there.

In addition, try as we may, in a text this large, errors are difficult to avoid. When we become aware of them, we acknowledge them in the Corrections tab, also located on your dashboard.

What Topics Are Covered in the Course?

The License Exam Manual consists of eight Units, each devoted to a particular area of study that you will need to know to pass the Series 7. Each Unit is divided into study sections devoted to more specific areas with which you need to become familiar.

The Series 7 License Exam Manual addresses the following topics:

Unit	Topic	Questions	Associated Function
1	Seeking Business for the Broker-Dealer from Customers and Potential Customers	9	Function 1
2	Opens Accounts After Obtaining and Evaluating Customers' Financial Profile and Investment Objectives; Retirement Plans	11	Function 2
3	Customer Information, Risk and Suitability, Product Information	91 total questions	Function 3
4	Options		Function 3
5	Direct Participation Programs		Function 3
6	Municipal Securities		Function 3
7	Margin Accounts	14 total questions	Function 4
8	Customers' Purchase and Sales Instructions, Processing Transactions and Complaint and Dispute Resolutions		Function 4

How Much Time Should I Spend Studying?

Plan to spend approximately 75–100 hours reading the material and carefully answering the questions. Spread your study time over the three to four weeks before the date on which you are scheduled to take the Series 7 exam. Your actual time may vary depending on your reading rate, comprehension, professional background, and study environment.

What Is the Best Way to Structure My Study Time?

The first thing you should do is create a study calendar. Information on the study calendar is located on your homepage.

The following schedule is suggested to help you obtain maximum retention from your study efforts. Remember, this is a guideline only, because each individual may require more or less time to complete the steps included.

Step 1. Read a Unit and complete all exercises. Review rationales for all questions whether you got them right or wrong (2–3 hours per Unit).

Step 2. In the SecuritiesPro™ QBank, create a minimum of two 40-question exams for each Unit as you go. Carefully review all rationales. Use the reference number to locate additional or related information on the test topic in your LEM if needed (2–3 hours per Unit).

■ Do not become too overwhelmed or bogged down in any one Unit. You don't want to lose sight of the finish line because you're having trouble with one hurdle. Keep moving forward. It's a steady pace that wins the race.

■ View rationales after each question initially, and spend time studying each rationale in order to learn the concepts. Later, you will want to create exam scenarios in which scores and rationales are viewed at the end of each exam.

■ Perfection is not the goal during the reading phase; scores in the mid- to high-60s are good initially.

Step 3. When you have completed all the Units in the License Exam Manual and their Unit Tests, using the SecuritiesPro™ QBank, concentrate on comprehensive exams covering all the material. With your comprehensive testing, it is best to view correct answers and rationales only after the test is completed. Plan to spend at least one week testing before a scheduled class (about 2 hours for every 100 questions).

■ You should complete at least 10 Weighted Mock Exams before class. Review your answers and rationales. Also, review your LEM and video library, as needed.

■ Your goal is to consistently score in the 80s.

Step 4. Complete online Practice and Mastery Exams. You should complete each exam, while observing the time limits for the actual exam. Upon completing the exam, you will receive a diagnostic report that identifies topics for further review (about 2 hours per exam). We recommend taking the Practice Exam before a scheduled class and the Mastery Exam afterward.

Note: After completing Practice, Mastery, and Mock Exams, be sure to review your Performance Tracker so you can identify areas of weakness. You can then create focused exams on topics as needed. Also, review your LEM and video library for additional help.

Remember, you will not see the answer key and rationale, but the detailed diagnostic breakdown will provide you with clear guidance on areas where further study is required.

How Well Can I Expect to Do?

The exams administered by FINRA are challenging. You must display considerable understanding and knowledge of the topics presented in this course to pass the exam and qualify for registration.

Our practice questions were carefully crafted to simulate the actual exam. In addition, weighting was considered (i.e., the number of questions likely seen on each topic). The wording must be somewhat different, but if you understand the subject matter, you will be able to find the correct response when you sit for the test. We often add new questions to refresh our question bank, sometimes with no direct supporting information pertaining to a specific question's subject in our LEM. In that case, there will be a thorough rationale to help you capture and retain the information you need. Because complex questions require you to link different concepts together to arrive at a correct answer, dealing with questions not directly addressed in the LEM will help develop that skill.

If you study diligently, complete all sections of the course, and consistently score at least 85% on the tests, you should be well prepared to pass the exam. However, it is important for you to realize that merely knowing the answers to our questions will not enable you to pass unless you understand the essence of the information behind the question.

TEST-TAKING TIPS

Passing the exam depends not only on how well you learn the subject matter but also on how well you take exams. You can develop your test-taking skills—and improve your score— by learning a few test-taking techniques:

- Read the full question
- Avoid jumping to conclusions—watch for hedge clauses
- Interpret the unfamiliar question
- Look for key words and phrases
- Identify the intent of the question
- Memorize key points
- Use a calculator
- Beware of changing answers
- Pace yourself

Each of these pointers is explained in the following, including examples that show how to use them to improve your performance on the exam.

Read the Full Question

You cannot expect to answer a question correctly if you do not know what it is asking. If you see a question that seems familiar and easy, you might anticipate the answer, mark it, and move on before you finish reading it. This is a serious mistake. Be sure to read the full question before answering it. Mistakes are often made when assuming too much (or too little).

Avoid Jumping to Conclusions—Watch for Hedge Clauses

The questions on FINRA exams are often embellished with deceptive distractors as choices. To avoid being misled by seemingly obvious answers, make it a practice to read each question and each answer twice before selecting your choice. Doing so will provide you with a much better chance of doing well on the exam.

Watch out for hedge clauses embedded in the question. (Examples of hedge clauses include the terms *if*, *not*, *all*, *none*, and *except*.) In the case of *if* statements, the question can be answered correctly only by taking into account the qualifier. If you ignore the qualifier, you will not answer correctly.

Qualifiers are sometimes combined in a question. Some that you will frequently see together are *all* with *except* and *none* with *except*. In general, when a question starts with *all* or *none* and ends with *except*, you are looking for an answer that is opposite to what the question appears to be asking.

Interpret the Unfamiliar Question

Do not be surprised if some questions on the exam seem unfamiliar at first. If you have studied your material, you will have the information to answer all the questions correctly. The challenge may be a matter of understanding what the question is asking.

Very often, questions present information indirectly. You may have to interpret the meaning of certain elements before you can answer the question. Be aware that the exam will approach a concept from different angles.

Look for Key Words and Phrases

Look for words that are tip-offs to the situation presented. For example, if you see the word *prospectus* in the question, you know the question is about a new issue. Sometimes a question will even supply you with the answer if you can recognize the key words it contains. Few questions provide blatant clues, but many do offer key words that can guide you to selecting the correct answer if you pay attention. Be sure to read all instructional phrases carefully. Take time to identify the key words to answer this type of question correctly.

Identify the Intent of the Question

Many questions on FINRA exams supply so much information that you lose track of what is being asked. This is often the case in story problems. Learn to separate the story from the question.

Take the time to identify what the question is asking. Of course, your ability to do so assumes you have studied sufficiently. There is no method for correctly answering questions if you don't know the material.

Memorize Key Points

Reasoning and logic will help you answer many questions, but you will have to memorize a good deal of information. Some memorization will be automatic as you go over the material and answer questions; some you will simply have to do systematically.

Use a Calculator

Most of the questions found on FINRA exams requiring calculations are written so that any math needed is simple in nature and function. However, using a calculator is recommended to ensure that common math errors do not lead you to incorrect answers. While test centers generally have calculators available for your use, you should have a simple function calculator with you, if needed in case of test center shortages. Test center staff will advise you as to whether or not you may use your own calculator.

Avoid Changing Answers

If you are unsure of an answer, your first hunch is the one most likely to be correct. Do not change answers on the exam without good reason. In general, change an answer only if you:

- discover that you did not read the question correctly; or
- find new or additional helpful information in another question.

Pace Yourself

Some people will finish the exam early and some do not have time to finish all the questions. Watch the time carefully (your time remaining will be displayed on your computer screen) and pace yourself through the exam.

Do not waste time by dwelling on a question if you simply do not know the answer. Make the best guess you can, mark the question for *Record for Review*, and return to the question if time allows. Make sure that you have time to read all the questions so that you can record the answers you do know.

THE EXAM

How Do I Enroll in the Exam?

To obtain admission to a FINRA-administered exam, your firm must electronically apply for and pay a fee to FINRA through its Central Registration Depository, better known as the Web CRD®. To take the exam, you must make an appointment with a Prometric Testing Center as far in advance as possible to get the date you would like to sit for the exam.

You may schedule, reschedule, or cancel your exam, locate a test center, and get a printed confirmation of your appointment 24 hours a day, 7 days a week.

- Prometric secure website at www.prometric.com, 1-800-578-6273

You must have your Central Registration Depository (CRD) number available when scheduling your exam. This unique personal identification number should be provided to you by your employing member firm. On a cautionary note, failure to show for an examination will be permanently recorded on your examination history on the Web CRD.

What Should I Take to the Exam?

Take one form of personal identification with your signature and photograph as issued by a government agency. No personal items, food, or drink, including coffee and water, are permitted inside the testing room. Personal items include, but are not limited to the following: pens, pagers, cellular phones, watches, hats, nonmedical electronic devices, outerwear, purses, and wallets. Personal items must be kept in your assigned locker or returned to your car before the start of your exam. Because the testing vendor is not responsible for any personal items, you are encouraged to bring only your identification into the Center.

Erasable note boards and pens will be provided to you upon admittance to the testing room. If you need additional note boards or pens, please alert your proctor. The note boards and pens must be returned at the end of your exam or continuing education session.

If you need a calculator for your testing session, please see the Test Center Administrator. You will be provided with a nonprogrammable, nonprinting calculator.

Additional Trial Questions

During your exam, you may see extra (generally 10 for the Series 7 exam) trial questions. These are potential future exam-bank questions being tested during the course of the exam. These questions are not included in your final score.

Exam Results and Reports

At the end of the exam, your score will be displayed, indicating whether you passed. The next business day after your exam, your results will be mailed to your firm and to the self-regulatory organization and state securities commission specified on your application.

1

Seeking Business for the Broker-Dealer From Customers and Potential Customers

I n placing investment, retirement, and variable contract securities in the hands of investors, the registered representative and broker-dealer must inevitably approach the public. The Financial Industry Regulatory Authority (FINRA) and other regulatory organizations formulate and enforce strict ethical rules regarding what is said to customers, who may in fact know very few of the details regarding how their investments work. Everything stated to a prospective customer must be strictly true, and no material fact may be omitted.

The Series 7 exam will include nine questions on the topics covered in this Unit. ◼

In this Unit you will learn to:

- **compare** the three main categories of types of communications with the public, their characteristics and definitions;

- **sort** other communications by characteristics and definitions;

- **classify** the required approvals of public communications including reviews and education of personnel;

- **identify** rules for product specific advertisements and disclosures required for public use;

- **determine** the application of investment company products and variable contracts communications to the public;

- **identify** characteristics of the primary market;

- **explain** the process for bringing new issues to market;

- **contrast** prospectus requirements;

- **differentiate** official statements, preliminary official statements (POS), and notice of sale for municipal securities; and

- **distinguish** exempt transactions rules and rules regarding restricted securities.

1. 1   TYPES OF COMMUNICATION

FINRA, as a **self-regulatory organization (SRO)**, has taken the federal requirements on communications with the public and expanded on them in its Conduct Rules. These rules require that all members observe high standards of commercial honor and just and equitable principles of trade. It is strictly prohibited to make use of any manipulative, deceptive, or other fraudulent devices or contrivances when conducting business with the public.

FINRA and Securities and Exchange (SEC) rules deal with communications concerning a member's investment banking or securities business. A principal must be familiar with the standards for content, supervisory review and approval, and recordkeeping for such material.

FINRA provides definitions and categories that differentiate the various types of communications for which the principal is responsible.

TAKE NOTE   General securities principals (Series 24) may review and/or approve communications for all securities except options. Limited securities principals (Series 26) may only review and/or approve communications for investment company products.

The definitions of communication with the public are classified into institutional communications, retail communications, and correspondence.

The application of the rules differs depending on the category of a particular communication. For this reason, the principal must be able to determine what fits where.

1. 1. 1   INSTITUTIONAL COMMUNICATION

Institutional communication is any written communication that is distributed or made available only to institutional investors but does not include a member firm's internal communications.

Keep in mind that when regulators talk about written communication, they always include electronic communications (e-comm), too.

Institutional communication is used exclusively with the following institutional investors:

■ Member firm or registered person of the member firm

■ Bank

■ Savings & loan

■ Insurance company

■ Registered investment company

■ Investment adviser

■ Any entity with $50 million or more of total assets, including natural persons

■ Governmental entity

■ Employee benefit plan that meets the requirements of Section 403(b) or Section 457 and has at least 100 participants

■ Person acting solely on the behalf of an institutional investor

Note that individual participants of employee benefit plans and qualified plans are not considered institutional investors.

If a member has reason to believe that a communication or excerpt of the communication intended for institutional investors will be forwarded to or made available to a person who is not an institutional investor, the communication must be treated as a retail communication until the member reasonably concludes the improper practice has ceased.

This definition is important because any entity that isn't an institutional is retail.

Each member must establish written procedures that are appropriate to its business, size, structure, and customers for the review of institutional communications used by the member and its associated persons by an appropriately qualified, registered principal. Such procedures must be reasonably designed to ensure that institutional communications comply with applicable standards. When such procedures do not require review of all institutional communications before first use or distribution, they must include provision for the education and training of associated persons as to the firm's procedures governing institutional communications, documentation of such education and training, and surveillance and follow-up to ensure that such procedures are implemented and adhered to. Evidence that these supervisory procedures have been implemented and carried out must be maintained and made available to FINRA upon request.

1. 1. 2   RETAIL COMMUNICATION

Retail communication is defined by FINRA as "any written (including electronic) communication that is distributed or made available to more than 25 retail investors within any 30 calendar-day period." What would commonly be thought of as "advertisements" and "sales literature" generally fall under this definition.

What is a retail investor? Any person—other than an institutional investor—regardless of whether the person has an account with the firm is considered a retail investor. An appropriately qualified registered principal of the member must approve each retail communication before the earlier of its use or filing with FINRA's Advertising Regulation Department.

The requirement to have a principal approve retail communication does not apply if, at the time that a member intends to distribute it:

- another member has filed it with FINRA's advertising department and has received a letter from the department stating that it appears to be consistent with applicable standards; and
- the member using it in reliance upon the letter has not materially altered it and will use it in a manner that is consistent with the conditions of the department's letter.

The requirement of prior principal approval generally will not apply with regard to what is posted to an online interactive electronic forum or any retail communication that does not make any financial or investment recommendation or otherwise promote a product or service of the member.

FINRA may also grant an exception from the approval rule for good cause.

Notwithstanding any other exception, an appropriately qualified registered principal of the member must approve each retail communication before the earlier of its use or filing with FINRA.

TEST TOPIC ALERT   Please note that the term *retail customer* refers to any customer, existing or prospective, that does not fit into the definition of institutional client.

1. 1. 3 CORRESPONDENCE

Correspondence is written or electronic communication that is distributed or made available to 25 or fewer retail investors within any 30 calendar-day period.

Similar to what was discussed earlier for institutional communications, each member must also establish written procedures that are appropriate to its business, size, structure, and customers for the review of incoming and outgoing correspondence with the public, including procedures to review incoming correspondence directed to registered representatives to properly identify and handle customer complaints and to ensure that customer funds and securities are handled in accordance with firm procedures. Procedures may allow for either pre- or post-review of correspondence by a principal. When pre-review is not required, the firm must include a provision for the education and training of associated persons as to the firm's procedures governing correspondence, documentation of such education and training, and surveillance and follow-up to ensure that such procedures are implemented and adhered to. Evidence that these supervisory procedures have been implemented and carried out must be maintained and made available to FINRA upon request.

QUICK QUIZ 1.A

Objective: Compare the three main categories of types of communications with the public, their characteristics and definitions

1. Which of the following are included in the rules on retail communications?
   I. A market research report ✓
   II. A public appearance
   III. A letter sent out to 10 customers
   IV. A website ✓

   A. I and III
   B. I and IV
   C. II and III
   D. II and IV

2. Institutional communication is defined as
   A. sales material received from a mutual fund or other institutional investor
   B. sales material sent only to an institutional investor
   C. sales material sent to both institutional investors and the general public
   D. sales material sent to an institutional investor for forwarding to its public clients

3. When comparing the types of communication, which of the following require prior principal approval before use?
   A. Sending a letter to a pension plan with a recommendation for the purchase of a security
   B. The broker-dealer sending a letter to all existing clients promoting a new service it offers
   C. Sending a summary of a recent meeting to an institutional client
   D. Notifying all existing clients of a change of location

All Quick Quiz answers are found at the end of their units.

1. 2   OTHER COMMUNICATIONS

In addition to the three kinds of communications with the public, there are several other types of communications you should be aware of.

1. 2. 1   PUBLIC APPEARANCE

Public appearance is participation in a seminar, webinar, forum (including an interactive electronic forum such as a chat room), radio or television interview, or other public appearance or public-speaking activity.

Each member must establish written procedures that are appropriate to its business, size, structure, and customers to supervise its associated persons' public appearances. Therefore, preapproval of a principal may be required but is not mandated. Such procedures must provide for the education and training of associated persons who make public appearances as to the firm's procedures, documentation of such education and training, and surveillance and follow-up to ensure that such procedures are implemented and adhered to. Evidence that these supervisory procedures have been implemented and carried out must be maintained and made available to FINRA upon request.

Any scripts, slides, handouts, or other written (including electronic) materials used in connection with public appearances are considered communications for purposes of this rule, and members must comply with all applicable provisions of this rule based on those communications' audience, content, and use.

If an associated person recommends a security in a public appearance, the associated person must have a reasonable basis for the recommendation. The associated person also must disclose any conflicts of interest that may exist, such as a financial interest in any security being recommended.

1. 2. 2   INDEPENDENTLY PREPARED REPRINT

An **independently prepared reprint (IPR)** consists of any article reprint that meets certain standards designed to ensure that the reprint was issued by an independent publisher and was not materially altered by the member. A member may alter the contents of an independently prepared reprint only to make it consistent with applicable regulatory standards or to correct factual errors.

An article reprint qualifies as an independently prepared reprint under the rules only if, among other things, its publisher is not an affiliate of the member using the reprint or any underwriter or issuer of the security mentioned in the reprint. Also, neither the member using the reprint nor any underwriter or issuer of a security mentioned in the reprint may have commissioned the reprinted article. IPRs must be preapproved by a principal and are exempted from the FINRA filing requirements.

1. 2. 3   RESEARCH REPORTS

A **research report** is a document prepared by an analyst or strategist, typically as a part of a research team for an investment bank or broker-dealer. The report may focus on an individual stock or sector of the economy and generally, but not always, will recommend buying, selling, or holding an investment.

FINRA has established rules designed to improve the objectivity of research reports and provide investors with more useful and reliable information when making investment decisions.

Chinese wall btwn I-Banks and research

Members must take steps to ensure that all research reports reflect an analyst's honest view and that any recommendation is not influenced by conflicts of interest, such as investment banking business with the issuer. If a member issues a report or a research analyst renders an opinion that is inconsistent with the analyst's actual views regarding a subject company, FINRA considers such action fraudulent.

To ensure the investing public receives objective information from the media and publications, the rule requires the following.

- Firms must clearly explain their rating systems, use rating terms according to their plain meaning, note the percentage of all ratings they have assigned to each category (e.g., buy/sell/hold), and document the percentage of investment banking clients in each category.

- Analysts' compensation may not be tied to the firm's investment banking revenues.

- Analysts must disclose in their research reports and public appearances whether they or any member of their households have a financial interest in the subject security and whether their employer firms owned 1% or more of any class of a subject company's equity securities at the close of the previous month.

Keeping Broker-dealer research separate from I-Bank in order to avoid conflicts of interest

- Research reports must disclose whether, within the last 12 months, the firm has received fees for investment banking services from—or managed or co-managed—a public offering for a company that is the subject of a research report. They must also disclose whether the firm expects to receive or intends to seek in the three months following publication of a research report any investment banking fees from any company that is the subject of a report.

- An investment adviser or a broker-dealer may not present to a client research reports, analyses, or recommendations prepared by other persons or firms without disclosing the fact that the adviser or broker-dealer did not prepare them. An adviser or a broker-dealer may base a recommendation on reports or analyses prepared by others, as long as these reports are not represented as the adviser's or broker-dealer's own.

1. 2. 3. 1   Quiet Period

A member must not publish or distribute research reports and research analysts may not make public appearances if the member has participated as an underwriter or a dealer in the IPO or, with respect to the quiet periods after a secondary offering, quiet periods of a minimum of 10 days following the date of an IPO, and a minimum of 3 days following the date of a secondary offering. FINRA interprets the date of the offering to be the later of the effective date of the registration statement or the first date on which the securities were bona fide offered to the public.

TAKE NOTE

The following items fall outside the definition of research reports:

- Discussions of broad-based indices

- Commentaries on economic, political, or market conditions

- Technical analyses concerning the demand and supply for a sector, index, or industry based on trading volume and price

■   Statistical summaries of multiple companies' financial data, including listings of current ratings

■   Notices of ratings or price target changes

1. 2. 4   ELECTRONIC COMMUNICATIONS WITH THE PUBLIC

Although not classified as a specific type of communication, with the growth of the internet and the rise of **electronic communications** in general, it has been necessary for FINRA to bring electronic communications in the securities industry into the regulatory framework.

Websites, whether sponsored by the company itself or set up by an individual registered representative, are considered retail communications and are subject to applicable filing and recordkeeping rules. They must be reviewed and approved by a principal prior to first use and must contain no exaggerated claims or misleading information, and if materially altered since the last filing, must be reapproved and refiled. There must also be nothing in the website that suggests business affiliation with or approval by FINRA.

Members may indicate FINRA membership on a member's website provided that the member provides a hyperlink to FINRA's homepage, www.finra.org, in close proximity to the member's indication of FINRA membership. This provision also applies to a website relating to the member's investment banking or securities business maintained by or on behalf of any person associated with a member.

Electronic bulletin boards are also considered retail communications, but a registered representative using one, or a chat room, need not identify himself as a registered person. Use of an online interactive forum by a registered representative must be approved by a principal, although each post does not require principal approval. The communications must be held to normal standards of accuracy and completeness.

Individual emails to customers fall under the definition of correspondence and are subject to the appropriate standards of conduct and supervision. Instant messaging could qualify as retail communication or correspondence, depending on the size and identity of the audience.

FINRA has released a notice dealing with the use of social media, such as Facebook, Twitter, and so forth. As of the date of this printing, there have been no cases and nothing practical has been determined. When and if the topic becomes eligible for exam questions, we will post a notice to the exam tips blog, located on the homepage of your Kaplan website.

TAKE NOTE

Regulations are clear; firms must have established procedures to maintain, review, and supervise communications transmitted via blogs, email, instant messaging, texts, Twitter, Facebook, and whatever new communication forum is coming our way.

Recently a firm and some representatives were fined when it was discovered that reps had used outside electronic sources for securities-related business. In other words, no supervision, no review, no record of the communication! FINRA does not look kindly on that.

1. 2. 5 GENERIC ADVERTISING (SEC RULE 135A)

Generic advertising promotes securities as an investment medium but does not refer to any specific security. Generic advertising often includes information about:

- the securities investments that companies offer;
- the nature of investment companies;
- services offered in connection with the described securities;
- explanations of the various types of investment companies;
- descriptions of exchange and reinvestment privileges; and
- where the public can write or call for further information.

All generic advertisements must contain the name and address of the sponsor of the advertisement but never include the name of any specific security. A generic advertisement may be placed only by a firm that offers the type of security or service described.

TAKE NOTE

Firms must have available for sale the type of security or service they advertise. For example, a brokerage firm is not permitted to advertise no-load mutual funds if it does not sell them.

QUICK QUIZ 1.B

Objective: Sort other communications by characteristics and definitions

1. Which of the following requires that the communication was issued by an independent publisher and not materially altered by the member?

    A. Research report
    B. IPR
    C. A website article
    D. A script for a public appearance

2. If the firm wanted to promote securities as an investment medium but does not refer to any specific security, it would likely use which of the following?

    A. Generic advertising
    B. An independent generic research report
    C. A generic website post
    D. A public correspondence

3. Company-sponsored websites, set up by an individual registered representative, are considered

    A. an advertisement
    B. speculative and may be preapproved by the rep prior to first use
    C. correspondence
    D. retail communication

All Quick Quiz answers are found at the end of their units.

REQUIRED APPROVALS OF PUBLIC COMMUNICATIONS

A principal of your firm may be required to approve or review communications to the public. Here are the requirements.

documented training and education

Institutional—No preapproval of a principal is required. When such procedures do not require review of all institutional communications prior to first use or distribution, they must include provision for the education and training of associated persons as to the firm's procedures governing institutional communications.

>25 Retail—Preapproval of a principal is required (prior to use).

<25 Correspondence—Pre- or post-review of a principal is required (reviewed before or after use)

Public appearance—Preapproval of a principal may be required but is not mandated.

Independently prepared reprints—IPRs must be preapproved by a principal if the communication meets the definition of a retail communication.

Research reports—Approval requirements are based on how they are defined (institutional, retail). Research reports must be preapproved by a principal if the communication meets the definition of a retail communication.

Electronic communications:

- Website preapproval of a principal required *~ website = retail*

- Electronic bulletin boards—Use of an online interactive forum by a registered representative must be approved by a principal, although each post does not require principal approval.

- Emails and instant messaging—Approval requirements are based on how they are defined (institutional, retail, or correspondence).

- Generic advertising—Preapproval of a principal is required.

1. 3. 1   FILING REQUIREMENTS

When a firm becomes registered with FINRA, during the first year of operation, FINRA will require the member to file any retail communication that is published or used in any electronic or other public media, including any generally accessible website, newspaper, magazine or other periodical, radio, television, telephone or audio recording, video display, signs or billboards, motion pictures, or telephone directories (other than routine listings) with FINRA at least 10 business days before first use (pre-filing).

After the first year of registration, a member firm, sometimes referred to as established, may file within 10 business days of first use (post-filing) retail communications relating to investment companies (including mutual funds, variable contracts, and UITs).

TEST TOPIC ALERT

Whether a first-year firm or not, retail communications for investment companies (including mutual funds, variable contracts, and UITs) that include a ranking or a comparison that is generally not published or is the creation of the investment company or the member must be filed with FINRA at least 10 business days before first use (pre-filing).

If the ranking or comparison is generally published or is the creation of an independent entity (e.g., Lipper or Morningstar), the usual filing rules for filing will apply (i.e., within 10 business days of first use [post-filing]).

Retail communications must be kept on file for three years from last use. This includes electronic securities business correspondence.

Objective: Classify the required approvals of public communications including reviews and education of personnel

1. Which of the following is NOT subject to preapproval by a principal prior to use?
   A. Research reports
   B. Independently prepared reprints
   C. A website
   D. A form letter to 20 prospective customers

(handwritten note: Correspondence — can be pre or post approved)

2. A registered representative wants to send out an independently prepared reprint to a prospective client. What guideline must be followed before sending the IPR to the prospect?
   A. The wording of the article may be changed so that it accurately fits the needs of the prospect as long as the general concept is intact.
   B. If a rule has changed that impacts the content of the article, it may not be sent.
   C. Preapproval of a principal is not required in order for the IPR to be sent to retail customers.
   D. Any inaccurate content of the article may be changed prior to delivery to retail customers.

3. A registered representative would like to speak at a conference next month. The conference is delivered in the form of a webinar, and there are over 500 people enrolled to attend. Which of the following accurately defines responsibilities regarding this speaking engagement?
   A. If the RR uses any handouts for the presentation, they must be reviewed by a principal.
   B. The RR must complete a training program prior to this type of activity.
   C. Recommending a security is prohibited at such an engagement.
   D. Preapproval of a principal may or may not be required, depending on the written procedures of the broker-dealer.

All Quick Quiz answers are found at the end of their units.

1. 4   PRODUCT-SPECIFIC ADVERTISEMENTS AND DISCLOSURES

All of a member's communications with the public—institutional, retail, and correspondence—must be based on principles of fair dealing and good faith and provide a sound basis for evaluating the facts in regard to any particular security or type of security, industry discussed, or service offered.

No material fact or qualification may be omitted if it could cause the communication to be misleading. Although most of these standards apply to all forms of communications with the public, the principal should be aware of the nuances.

Exaggerated or misleading statements are prohibited. In determining whether a communication is misleading, FINRA calls for consideration of the following.

Overall context of the statement—A statement that is misleading in one context may be appropriate in another. An essential test in this regard is the balanced treatment of risks and potential returns.

Different levels of explanation or detail may be needed depending on the audience and the ability of the member to control who might come in contact with the communication.

Overall clarity of the communication—FINRA warns that unclear statements can create serious misunderstandings to the point of constituting a rules violation.

EXAMPLE   Overly technical explanations or material disclosures buried in footnotes are likely to confuse the reader and could be construed as misleading.

1. 4. 1   USE OF INVESTMENT COMPANY RANKINGS IN RETAIL COMMUNICATIONS

For purposes of this Rule, the term "**ranking entity**" refers to any entity that provides general information about investment companies to the public, that is independent of the investment company and its affiliates, and whose services are not procured by the investment company or any of its affiliates to assign the investment company a ranking.

Members may not use investment company rankings in any retail communication other than:

- rankings created and published by Ranking Entities or
- rankings created by an investment company or an investment company affiliate but based on standard performance measurements.

1. 4. 1. 1   Required Disclosures of Investment Company Rankings

A headline or other prominent statement must not state or imply that an investment company or investment company family is the best performer in a category unless it is actually ranked first in the category.

Other disclosures include:

- the name of the category (e.g., growth);
- the name of the ranking entity and, if applicable, the fact that the investment company or an affiliate created the category or subcategory;
- criteria on which the ranking is based (e.g., total return, risk-adjusted performance);
- the fact that past performance is no guarantee of future results; and
- a ranking based on total return must be accompanied by rankings based on total return for 1 year, 5 years and 10 years, or since inception, if shorter.

1. 4. 2 REQUIREMENTS FOR THE USE OF BOND MUTUAL FUND VOLATILITY RATINGS

The term "**bond mutual fund volatility rating**" is a description issued by an independent third party relating to the sensitivity of the net asset value of a portfolio of an open-end management investment company that invests in debt securities to changes in market conditions and the general economy, and is based on an evaluation of objective factors, including the credit quality of the fund's individual portfolio holdings, the market price volatility of the portfolio, the fund's performance, and specific risks, such as interest rate risk, prepayment risk, and currency risk. These ratings may not describe volatility as a risk rating.

1. 4. 2. 1 Required disclosures of bond mutual fund volatility ratings

The name of the entity that issued the rating must be disclosed, along with:

- the date of the current rating;
- a link to a website that includes the criteria and methodology used;
- a statement that there is no standard method to determine the rating;
- a description of the types of risk the rating measures (e.g., short-term volatility); and
- a statement that there is no guarantee the fund will continue to have the same rating or perform in the future as rated.

1. 4. 3 SALES LITERATURE DEEMED TO BE MISLEADING

The Securities and Exchange Commission, under the Investment Company Act of 1940, addresses certain broad categories of investment company names that are likely to mislead investors about an investment company's investments and risks. The name rule requires a registered investment company with a name suggesting that the company focuses on a particular type of investment (e.g., an investment company that calls itself the ABC Stock Fund, the XYZ Bond Fund, or the QRS U.S. Government Fund) to invest at least 80% of its assets in the type of investment suggested by its name.

In addition, any advertisement, pamphlet, circular, form letter, or other sales literature addressed to or intended for distribution to prospective investors is considered materially misleading unless the sales literature includes the following information.

Sales literature for a money market (mutual) fund must include the following statement:

"An investment in the Fund is not insured or guaranteed by the Federal Deposit Insurance Corporation or any other government agency. Although the Fund seeks to preserve the value of your investment at $1.00 per share, it is possible to lose money by investing in the Fund."

With regard to a money market fund, for any quotation of yield, only current yield is required, unless it's a tax-free money market fund. In that case, both tax-equivalent and current yields are shown.

TAKE NOTE   Money market funds, which are composed of short-term, high-quality debt instruments are inappropriate for investors seeking long-term growth.

Disclosures

past performance does not guarantee future results

Any sales literature that contains performance data for an investment company, other than a money market fund, must include the following:

■ A legend disclosing that the performance data quoted represents past performance; that past performance does not guarantee future results; that the investment return and principal value of an investment will fluctuate so that an investor's shares, when redeemed, may be worth more or less than their original cost; and that current performance may be lower or higher than the performance data quoted. The legend should also identify either a toll-free (or collect) telephone number or a website where an investor may obtain performance data current to the most recent month-end unless the advertisement includes total return quotations current to the most recent month ended seven business days before the date of use.

sales fees

■ If a sales load or any other nonrecurring fee is charged, the maximum amount of the load or fee, and if the sales load or fee is not reflected, a statement that the performance data does not reflect the deduction of the sales load or fee, and that, if reflected, the load or fee would reduce the performance quoted.

must show 1, 5, 10 year returns

■ In any sales literature for an investment company, other than a money market fund, that contains performance data, average annual total return (after taxes on distributions, as well as after taxes on distributions and redemption) for 1-, 5-, and 10-year periods must be shown. If the fund has been in operation for a shorter period, the life of the fund must be used. Longer periods may be shown in five-year increments up to the life of the fund. If the sales literature refers to yield, it must include the total return figures and show the current yield in no greater size or prominence than total return. The quotation must also identify the length of the period quoted and the last day in the base period used in the computation.

Some municipal bond funds like to advertise a tax-equivalent yield. To do so, they must show both the current yield and total return as above in addition, and the tax-equivalent yield may be set out in no greater prominence. And, as stated previously, if the fund carries a sales load, performance data must indicate the effect of the load.

TAKE NOTE   Disclosure documents, such as a statutory prospectus, summary prospectus, or statement of additional information, are not prepared by member firms (they are prepared by the issuer) and as such are not subject to approval by a principal.

1. 4. 4   CIVIL LIABILITIES

If prospectus is wrong w/ contains false statements = ppl who signed it can be held liable

The seller of any security being sold by prospectus is liable to purchasers if the registration statement or prospectus contains false statements, misstatements, or omissions of material facts. Any person acquiring the security may sue:

■ those who signed the registration statement;

■ directors and partners of the issuer;

■ anyone named in the registration statement as being or about to become a director or partner of the company;

■ accountants, appraisers, and other professionals who contributed to the registration statement; and/or

■ the underwriters.

QUICK QUIZ 1.D

Objective: Identify rules for product specific advertisements and disclosures required for public use

1. All of a member's communications with the public must be based on which of the following?

    I.   The likelihood for acceptance
    II. Fair dealing
    III. Good faith
    IV. A good deal

    A. I and II
    B. I and IV
    C. II and III
    D. III and IV

2. When using performance data in an advertisement, which of the following is TRUE?

    A. Performance data does not include any sales load.
    B. 1-, 5-, and 10-year numbers must be shown or since inception if shorter.
    C. The advertisement must disclose that past performance is an indication of future performance.
    D. Performance data beyond 10 years is not allowed.

3. Which of the following statements is NOT true?

    A. Hedge clauses may be used as long as they are fully disclosed and not misleading.
    B. Recruitment advertising must disclose the name of the firm that is posting the advertisement.
    C. Offering 20% off to do someone's federal and state tax return in exchange for a referral (5 referrals and the tax return is free) is a violation of general communication standards.
    D. It is not permitted to state that if a mutual fund investment is held for more than 10 years, the investor will not lose its original principal in the investment.

All Quick Quiz answers are found at the end of their units.

1.5   COMMUNICATIONS REGARDING VARIABLE CONTRACTS

The following standards apply to all communications related to variable life and variable annuities, in addition to the general FINRA standards governing communications. These standards are applicable to advertisements and sales literature, as well as individualized communications such as personalized letters and computer-generated illustrations, whether printed or made available on-screen.

1. 5. 1   PRODUCT COMMUNICATIONS

[handwritten margin note: must say what product it is]

All communications must clearly describe the product as either variable life or a variable annuity, as applicable. Proprietary names may be used in addition to these descriptions. There may be no implication that the product being offered or its underlying account is a mutual fund.

1. 5. 2   LIQUIDITY

Because variable life insurance and variable annuities frequently involve substantial charges and/or tax penalties for early withdrawal, there may be no representation or implication that these are short-term, liquid investments. Any statement about the ease of liquidation of these products must be accompanied by the negative impact of factors such as contingent deferred sales loads, tax penalties, and impact on cash value and death benefits.

1. 5. 3   GUARANTEES

[handwritten margin note: Insurance guarantees do not apply to separate account]

Although insurance products contain a number of specific guarantees, the relative safety of the product from these guarantees may not be overemphasized because it depends on the claims-paying ability of the insurance company. There may be no representation or implication that a guarantee applies to the investment return or principal value of the separate account. Also, it may not be represented or implied that an insurance company's financial ratings apply to the separate account.

Although the rating firms we've mentioned before (Standard and Poor's and Moody's Investor Service) offer ratings on the financial health of insurance companies, the primary source used by almost everyone in the industry is A.M. Best. An A or an A+ rating from them signifies substantial ability to meet their claim obligations.

1. 5. 4   FUND PERFORMANCE PREDATING INCLUSION IN A VARIABLE PRODUCT

Illustrations are sometimes used to show how an existing fund would have performed as an investment option within a variable life or variable annuity policy. Performance that predates a fund's inclusion may be used only if no significant changes occurred to the fund at the time or after it became a part of the variable product.

1. 5. 5   SINGLE PREMIUM VARIABLE LIFE

Communications regarding single premium variable life may only emphasize investment features of this product if an adequate explanation of the life insurance features is also provided.

By definition, single premium life insurance is a modified endowment contract (MEC). Because MECs restrict access to cash values, few are issued.

Variable life insurance = life insurance policy that builds up with cash value and invests in a variety of mutual funds in separate accounts

1. 5. 6   HYPOTHETICAL ILLUSTRATIONS OF RATES OF RETURN IN VARIABLE LIFE INSURANCE

Hypothetical illustrations showing assumed rates of return may be used to demonstrate the performance of variable life policies. Rules that apply to the use of these illustrations include the following:

■ Hypothetical illustrations may not be used to project or predict investment results.

■ Illustrations may use any combination of assumed investment returns up to and including a gross rate of 12%, provided that one of the returns is a 0% gross rate. The maximum rate illustrated should be reasonable, considering market conditions and the available investment options.

■ Illustrations must reflect the maximum mortality and expense charges associated with the policy for each assumed rate of return illustrated. Current charges may also be illustrated.

In general, variable life product performance may not be compared with other investment products. However, comparison of variable life with a term insurance product is permitted to demonstrate the concept of tax-deferred growth resulting from investment in the variable product.

QUICK QUIZ 1.E

Objective: Determine the application of investment company products and variable contracts communications to the public

1. Under FINRA filing requirements and review procedures, which of the following statements are TRUE?

   I. A new member firm must file advertising with FINRA at least 10 days before use for the first year.
   II. An established firm must file investment company communications that include a ranking not independently prepared with FINRA within 10 days of first use.
   III. Retail communications must be kept on file for 2 years.
   IV. Retail communications must be kept on file for 3 years.

   A. I and III
   B. I and IV
   C. II and III
   D. II and IV

2. Your established firm wishes to promote a mutual fund it markets to the public. What approval and filing requirements apply to this communication?

   I. It must be filed with FINRA at least 10 days before first use.
   II. It must be filed with FINRA within 10 days of first use.
   III. It must be approved by an experienced registered representative.
   IV. It must be approved by a registered principal.

   A. I and III
   B. I and IV
   C. II and III
   D. II and IV

3. Communications related to variable life and variable annuities must meet specific standards. All the following standards are required EXCEPT

    A. all communications must clearly describe the product as either variable life or a variable annuity

    B. if so added as a feature of the product, there may be an implied guarantee within the communication of the principal value of the separate account

    C. hypothetical illustrations showing assumed rates of return may be used to demonstrate the performance of variable life policies

    D. communications regarding single premium variable life may only emphasize investment features of this product if an adequate explanation of the life insurance features is also provided

All Quick Quiz answers are found at the end of their units.

1. 6 PROCESS FOR BRINGING NEW ISSUES TO MARKET

Corporations issue equity and debt securities as a means of raising capital in order to implement ideas such as expanding operations or funding a merger or acquisition.

Investing in equity securities is perhaps the most visible and accessible means of creating wealth. Individual investors become owners of a publicly traded company by buying stock in that company. In doing so, they can participate in the company's success over time. They also share in the risk of operating a business; they can lose their investment.

When a corporation issues equity securities, it is conservative for the issuer and risky for investors; once the corporation has an investors' money, it is under no obligation to give any of it back.

On the other hand, when investors purchase a company's debt, they lend money to the company and as a creditor of the company, the company is obligated to pay investors back. Therefore, when a corporation issues debt, it is considered risky for the issuer and conservative for investors.

In general, securities are bought either as new issues from a corporation, municipality, or the federal government, or in the secondary market as trades between investors. This section begins the process for bringing new issues to market.

1. 6. 1 THE SECURITIES ACT OF 1933

Investigation of the conditions that led to the 1929 market crash determined that investors had little protection from fraud in the sale of new issues of securities, and rumors, exaggerations, and unsubstantiated claims led to excessive speculation in newly issued stock. Congress passed the **Securities Act of 1933** to require issuers of new securities to file registration statements with the SEC in order to provide investors with complete and accurate information in the form of a prospectus when soliciting sales. Think of the Securities Act of 1933 as the Paper Act because of the registration statement and prospectus. It will remind you of the paperwork requirements for full and fair disclosure.

New securities that are subject to the act's requirements are called nonexempt issues. Exempt securities are not subject to these requirements.

1. 6. 2   EXEMPT ISSUERS AND SECURITIES

The Securities Act of 1933 provides specific exemptions from federal registration provisions.

Among the exemptions are the following issuers:

- The U.S. government
- U.S. municipalities and territories
- Nonprofit religious, educational, and charitable organizations
- Banks and savings and loans
- Public utilities and common carries whose activities are regulated as to rates and other items by a state or federal regulatory body

The following securities are exempt from the Securities Act of 1933:

- Commercial paper—maturity less than 270 days
- Bankers' acceptances—maturity less than 270 days
- Securities acquired in private placements—restricted stock

[handwritten margin note: do not need to file prospectus w/ SEC w/ exempt]

1. 6. 3   STATE REGISTRATION *[handwritten: - how to / qualifications of registering w/ state]*

State securities laws, also called **blue-sky laws**, also require registration of securities, broker/dealers, and registered representatives. An issuer or investment banker may blue-sky an issue by one of the following methods.

- Qualification—The issuer files with the state, independent of federal registration, and must meet all state requirements. *[handwritten: - state]*
- Coordination—The issuer registers simultaneously with the state and the SEC. Both registrations become effective on the same date. *[handwritten: - SEC / state]*
- Notice filing—Securities listed on the major exchanges and on Nasdaq, as well as investment companies registered under the Investment Company Act of 1940, are known as federal covered securities. State registration is not required, but most states require the filing of a notice that the issuer intends to offer its securities for sale in that state and the state may assess a filing fee. *[handwritten: - already registered - file a notice saying you are going to offer securities for sale]*

1. 6. 4   PARTICIPANTS IN A CORPORATE NEW ISSUE

The main participants in a new issue are the company selling the securities and the broker-dealer acting as the underwriter.

1. 6. 4. 1   The Issuer

The issuer, or the party selling the securities to raise money, must file a registration statement with the SEC. This document requires that the issuer supply sufficient information about the security and the corporation and its officers to allow an investor to make a sound investment decision. When the SEC reviews this document, during what is known as the 20-day cooling-off period, it looks for sufficiency of investment information rather than accuracy, though upon completion of the review, it does not guarantee adequacy of the prospectus.

Near the end of the cooling-off period, the underwriter holds a **due diligence** meeting. The preliminary studies, investigations, research, meetings, and compilation of information about a corporation and a proposed new issue that go on during an underwriting are known collectively as due diligence.

The underwriter must conduct a formal due diligence meeting to provide information about the issue, the issuer's financial background, and the intended use of the proceeds. Representatives of the issuer and the underwriter attend these meetings and answer questions from brokers, securities analysts, and institutions.

As part of the due diligence process, investment bankers must:

- examine the use of the proceeds;

- perform financial analysis and feasibility studies;

- determine the company's stability; and

- determine whether the risk is reasonable.

TAKE NOTE

The issuer knows a lot about manufacturing, or accounting or software, or whatever it is they do. They don't know a lot about what it takes to sell securities to the public.

The issuer will place a notice in order to attract an underwriter.

1. 6. 4. 2 Underwriter

A business or municipal government that plans to issue securities usually works with an **underwriter** (investment bank) (a securities broker-dealer that specializes in underwriting new issues). An investment bank's functions may include:

- advising corporations on the best ways to raise long-term capital;

- raising capital for issuers by distributing new securities;

- buying securities from issuers and reselling them to the public;

- distributing large blocks of stock to the public and to institutions; and

- helping issuers comply with securities laws.

The investment banker who negotiates with the issuer is known as the **underwriting manager** or **syndicate manager**. The underwriting manager directs the entire underwriting process, including signing the underwriting agreement with the issuer and directing the due diligence meeting and distribution process. A syndicate may have more than one manager.

TAKE NOTE

Investment bankers help issuers raise money through the sale of securities. They do not loan money. They are also called underwriters. All underwriters of corporate securities must be FINRA member firms.

1. 6. 4. 3 Forming a Syndicate

Underwriting syndicate members make a financial commitment to help bring the securities public. In a firm commitment offering, all syndicate members commit to purchase from the issuer and then distribute an agreed-on amount of the issue (their participation or bracket). Syndicate members sign a **syndicate agreement**, or **syndicate letter,** that describes the participants' responsibilities and allocation of syndicate profits, if any. A syndicate and selling groups may be assembled either before or after the issue is awarded to the underwriter.

In a **negotiated underwriting**, the issuer and the investment banker negotiate the offering terms, including the amount of securities to be offered, offering price or yield, and underwriting fees.

Negotiated underwritings are standard in underwriting corporate securities because of close business relationships between issuing corporations and investment banking firms.

Competitive bid underwriting arrangements are the standard for underwriting most municipal securities and are often required by state law. In a competitive bid, a state or municipal government invites investment bankers to bid for a new issue of bonds. The issuer awards the securities to the underwriter(s) whose bid results in the lowest net interest cost to the issuer.

TAKE NOTE Syndicates are usually formed to spread the risk among several underwriters instead of one underwriter taking all the risk of an offering.

1. 6. 4. 4   Selling Group Formation

Although the members of an underwriting syndicate agree to underwrite an entire offering, they frequently enlist other firms to help distribute the securities as members of the selling group. **Selling group** members act as agents with no commitment to buy securities.

The managing underwriter is normally responsible for determining whether to use a selling group and, if so, which firms to include. If the securities to be issued are attractive, broker-dealers will want to participate. If the securities are not attractive, the manager may have to persuade broker-dealers to join.

Selling group members sign a **selling group agreement** with the underwriters, which typically contains:

- a statement that the manager acts for all of the underwriters;
- the amount of securities each selling group member will be allotted and the tentative public offering price at which the securities will be sold (this price is firmed up just before the offering date);
- provisions as to how and when payment for shares is to be made to the managing underwriter; and
- legal provisions limiting each selling group member's liability in conjunction with the underwriting.

TEST TOPIC ALERT Syndicate members take on financial liability and act in a principal capacity. Selling group members have no financial liability and act as agents because they have no commitment to buy securities from the issuer.

1. 6. 5   TYPES OF UNDERWRITING AGREEMENTS

An agreement among underwriters details each underwriter's commitment and liability, particularly for any shares that remain unsold at the underwriting syndicate's termination.

The agreement designates the syndicate manager to act on behalf of the syndicate members. The manager's authority to manage the underwriting, which includes establishing the offering price with the issuer, deciding the timing of the offering, controlling advertising, and making all required filings, comes via this agreement.

1. 6. 5. 1   Firm Commitment

The **firm commitment** is the most commonly used type of underwriting contract. Under its terms, the underwriter(s) (investment bank[s]) commit to buy the securities from the issuer and resell them to the public. The underwriters assume the financial risk of incurring losses in the event they are unable to distribute all the shares to the public.

A firm commitment underwriting can be either a negotiated underwriting contract or a competitive bid arrangement. Negotiated underwriting contracts are used in most corporate issues. The issuer selects an underwriter and negotiates the conditions of the underwriting contract. A competitive bid arrangement is the standard for new issue offering in the municipal securities market. The underwriting contract is awarded to the underwriter who presents the most competitive bid, or lowest net interest cost, to the issuer. Sales begin on the effective date of the offering.

TAKE NOTE

> In a firm commitment underwriting, the managing underwriter takes on the financial risk because he purchases the securities from the issuer. Because he purchases and resells the shares, he is acting in a principal (dealer) capacity.

1. 6. 5. 2   Standby

When a company's current stockholders do not exercise their preemptive rights in an additional offering, a corporation has an underwriter **standing by** to purchase whatever shares remain unsold as a result of rights expiring.

Because the standby underwriter unconditionally agrees to buy all shares that current stockholders do not subscribe to at the subscription price, the offering is a firm commitment.

TAKE NOTE

> By engaging a standby underwriter, an issuer is assured of selling all the shares being offered.

1. 6. 5. 3   Best Efforts

In a **best efforts** arrangement, the underwriter acts as agent for the issuing corporation. The deal is contingent on the underwriter's ability to sell shares to the public. In a best efforts underwriting, the underwriter sells as much as possible, without financial liability for what remains unsold. The underwriter is acting in an agency capacity with no financial risk.

1. 6. 5. 3. 1   All or None

In an **all-or-none (AON) underwriting**, the issuing corporation has determined that it wants an agreement outlining that the underwriter must either sell all of the shares or cancel the underwriting. Because of the uncertainty over the outcome of an AON offering, any funds collected from investors during the offering period must be held in escrow pending final disposition of the underwriting.

Brokers engaged in an AON distribution are prohibited from deceiving investors by stating that all the securities in the underwriting have been sold if it is not the case.

1. 6. 5. 3. 2   Mini-Max

A **mini-max offering** is a best efforts underwriting setting a floor or minimum, which is the least amount the issuer needs to raise in order to move forward with the underwriting, and a ceiling or maximum on the dollar amount of securities the issuer is willing to sell. The underwriter must locate enough interested buyers to support the minimum (floor) issuance requirement. Once the minimum is met, the underwriter can expand the offering up to the maximum (ceiling) amount of shares the issuer specified. Mini-max underwriting terms are most frequently found in limited partnership program offerings, and funds collected from investors during the offering period must be held in escrow pending final disposition of the underwriting.

TEST TOPIC ALERT

Be prepared for a question that requires an understanding of underwriter risk in firm commitment and best efforts underwriting.

In a firm commitment underwriting, the underwriter takes on the financial risk because the securities are purchased from the issuer. Because of this risk, the underwriter is acting in a principal capacity.

In a best efforts underwriting, the underwriter sells as much as possible, without liability for what cannot be sold. The underwriter is acting in an agent capacity with no financial risk.

For example, if a corporation plans to sell 100,000 shares of common stock, but after exerting its best efforts, the underwriter can only sell 80,000 shares, the underwriter has no liability for the remaining 20,000 shares.

- Firm commitment = principal capacity, underwriter has risk

- Best efforts = agency capacity, underwriter has no risk

Remember that a standby offering is a firm commitment offering involving unexercised preemptive rights.

1. 6. 6   REGISTRATION OF SECURITIES

The Securities Act of 1933 requires new issues of corporate securities to be registered with the SEC. The corporate issuer does so by filing a registration statement. Most of the registration statement becomes the prospectus.

1. 6. 6. 1   The Registration Process

After an issuer files a registration statement with the SEC, a 20-day **cooling-off period** begins. During the cooling-off period, the SEC reviews the security's registration statement and can issue a stop order if the statement does not contain all of the required information.

The Three Phases of an Underwriting

Issuer files registration statement with the SEC	Cooling-off period	Effective date—offering period may begin
Before the filing of the registration statement, no sales may be solicited and no prospectus may circulate.	No one may solicit sales during the cooling-off period, but indications of interest may be solicited with a red herring.	Sales may now be solicited, but the firm must use a final prospectus.

Red Herring. The **red herring (preliminary prospectus)** is used to gauge investor reactions and gather indications of interest for corporate securities. A registered representative may discuss the issue with prospects during the cooling-off period and provide them with preliminary information through the **red herring**. It must carry a legend, printed in red, that declares that a registration statement has been filed with the SEC but is not yet effective. The final offering price and underwriting spread are not included in the red herring.

Allowable Activity During the Cooling-Off Period

May:	May Not:
■ Distribute red herrings	■ Offer securities for sale
■ Publish tombstone advertisements	■ Distribute final prospectuses
■ Gather indications of interest	■ Disseminate advertising material
	■ Disseminate sales literature
	■ Take orders
	■ Accept postdated checks

SEC rules prohibit the sale of public offering securities without a prospectus, which means that no sales are allowed until the final prospectus is available.

Tombstone Advertisements. During the cooling-off period, sales of the security and related activities are prohibited. Nonbinding indications of interest may be gathered with a preliminary prospectus. In addition, tombstone advertisements are allowed to be published. These announcements, typically published after the offering has been cleared for sale, offer information to investors. However, they do not offer the securities for sale. Issuers are not required to publish tombstones, but they may appear either before or after the effective date of the sale.

TAKE NOTE

The term "tombstone advertisement" is derived from the bare-bones, minimum information they provide. Information found in a tombstone advertisement includes:

- name of issuer,
- type of security,
- underwriter,
- price, and
- effective date of sale.

What is in a tombstone ad

1. 6. 6. 2   Pricing the New Issue of Publicly Traded Securities

During the cooling-off period, the underwriter advises the issuing corporation on the best price at which to offer securities to the public. The following variables may be considered when pricing new issues:

Thoughts that go into pricing new security

- Indications of interest from the underwriter's book
- Prevailing market conditions, including recent offerings and the prices of similar new issues
- Price that the syndicate members will accept
- Price-to-earnings (PE) ratios of similar companies and the company's most recent earnings report (at what price the shares must be offered so that the PE ratio is in line with the PE ratios of other similar publicly traded stocks)
- The company's dividend payment record (if any) and financial health
- The company's debt ratio

An issue's price or yield must be determined by the effective date of the registration. The effective date is when the security begins to trade.

1. 6. 6. 3   Stabilizing Price   *— underwriter bids for shares in open market to stabilize bids*

In the case of a stock offering, when demand is considerably lower than supply for a new issue, the price in the aftermarket is likely to fall. Under these circumstances, the underwriter can stabilize the security by bidding for shares in the open market. These bids may be placed at or just below the public offering price. The managing underwriter can enter or appoint a syndicate member to enter stabilizing bids for the security until the end of the offering period.

1. 6. 6. 3. 1   Syndicate Penalty Bid

Stabilizing after an issue is sold out is not permitted. If syndicate members' clients turn in shares on a stabilizing bid after the issue is sold out, the syndicate manager will levy a syndicate penalty bid against those members.

· Syndicates clients cannot immediately sell new issue they bought.

TEST TOPIC ALERT

Stabilizing bids must not be made at a price higher than the public offering price (POP). Stabilization is not illegal; however, if the stabilization bid is made at a price higher than the public offering price, it is called pegging, or fixing, and is strictly prohibited. If public buying interest does not increase, the managing underwriter may have no choice but to abandon the POP, pull the stabilizing bid, and let the stock find its own price level.

1. 6. 7   UNDERWRITING COMPENSATION

The price at which underwriters buy stock from issuers always differs from the price at which they offer the shares to the public. The price the issuer receives is known as the **underwriting proceeds**, and the price investors pay is the **public offering price (POP)**. The **underwriting spread**, the difference between the two prices, consists of the:

■ **manager's fee**, for negotiating the deal and managing the underwriting and distribution process;

■ **underwriting fee**, for assuming the risk of buying securities from the issuer without assurance that the securities can be resold; and

■ **selling concession**, for placing the securities with investors.

TAKE NOTE

A member can grant discounts and other concessions only to other FINRA member firms. The only exception is that a member firm can grant concessions to a foreign nonmember firm that is ineligible for FINRA membership.

1. 6. 7. 1   Industry Standard Practices

The industry norm for allocating the spread for corporate equity issues is as follows.

Spread Allocation

Underwriting Component	Fee Range
Syndicate manager's fee	10–20%
Underwriting syndicate fee	20–30%
Selling concession	50–60%

Who Gets What in an Underwriting

New Issue
Incorporated
Common Stocks
1 Million Shares
Price $10

$10 million gross from the sale
of the issue to the public.
(1 million shares × $10 = $10 million)

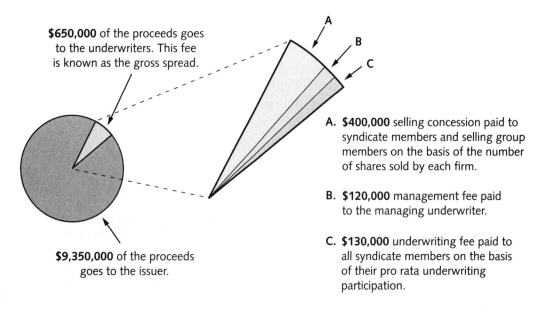

$650,000 of the proceeds goes
to the underwriters. This fee
is known as the gross spread.

A
B
C

A. **$400,000** selling concession paid to
syndicate members and selling group
members on the basis of the number
of shares sold by each firm.

B. **$120,000** management fee paid
to the managing underwriter.

C. **$130,000** underwriting fee paid to
all syndicate members on the basis
of their pro rata underwriting
participation.

$9,350,000 of the proceeds
goes to the issuer.

The amount of the spread varies by issue and can be influenced by any of the following:

■ Type of commitment—A firm commitment earns a larger spread than a best efforts agreement because of the risks the underwriter assumes.

■ Security's marketability—A bond rated AAA has a smaller spread than a speculative stock.

■ Issuer's business—A stable utility stock usually has a smaller spread than a more volatile stock.

■ Offering size—In a very large offering, the underwriter can spread costs over a larger number of shares; thus, the per share cost may be lower.

1. 6. 8   THE FINAL PROSPECTUS (EFFECTIVE, STATUTORY PROSPECTUS)

When the registration statement for corporate securities becomes effective, the issuer amends the preliminary prospectus and adds information, including the final offering price and the underwriting spread for the final prospectus. Registered representatives may then take orders from those customers who indicated interest in buying during the cooling-off period.

A copy of the final prospectus must precede or accompany all sales confirmations. However, if the prospectus has been filed with the SEC and is available through its website, access to the prospectus equals delivery of the prospectus.

The prospectus must include:

- a description of the offering;
- the offering price;
- selling discounts;
- the offering date;
- use of the proceeds;
- a description of the underwriting, but not the actual contract;
- a statement of the possibility that the issue's price may be stabilized;
- a history of the business;
- risks to the purchasers;
- a description of management;
- material financial information;
- a legal opinion concerning the formation of the corporation;
- an SEC disclaimer; and
- an SEC review.

SEC Disclaimer. The SEC reviews the prospectus to ensure that it contains the necessary material facts, but it does not guarantee the disclosure's accuracy. Furthermore, the SEC does not approve the issue but simply clears it for distribution. Implying that the SEC has approved the issue violates federal law. Finally, the SEC does not pass judgment on the issue's investment merit.

The front of every prospectus must contain a clearly printed SEC disclaimer specifying the limits of the SEC's review procedures. A typical SEC disclaimer clause reads as follows:

> *These securities have not been approved or disapproved by the Securities and Exchange Commission or by any State Securities Commission nor has the Securities and Exchange Commission or any State Securities Commission passed upon the accuracy or adequacy of this prospectus. Any representation to the contrary is a criminal offense.*

> *The information supplied to the SEC becomes public once a registration statement is filed.*

TEST TOPIC ALERT

Anything that says the SEC approves or disapproves an issue of securities is wrong. The SEC does not approve or disapprove—it clears or releases issues of securities for sale. When the SEC has completed its review, the registration becomes effective.

Issuers and underwriters are responsible for the information found in the prospectus and will conduct due diligence meetings to ensure that the prospectus is true and accurate.

1. 6. 9   SUMMARY PROSPECTUS—SEC RULE 498

A mutual fund can provide a **summary prospectus** to investors that may include an application investors can use to buy the fund's shares.

The summary prospectus is a standardized summary of key information found in the fund's statutory (full) prospectus. Investors who receive the summary have the option of either purchasing fund shares using the application found therein or requesting a statutory prospectus. An investor who purchases fund shares on the basis of the summary prospectus must be able to access a statutory prospectus online. Remember, customers can always request and receive a paper copy.

The summary must provide specific information in a particular sequence. Following is a list of required disclosures:

■ Risk/Return Summary: Investments, Risks, and Performance

■ Risk/Return Summary: Fee Table

■ Investment Objectives, Principal Investment Strategies, Related Risks, and Disclosure of Portfolio Holdings

■ Management, Organization, and Capital Structure

■ Shareholder Information

■ Distribution Arrangements

■ Financial Highlights Information

1. 6. 10   STATEMENT OF ADDITIONAL INFORMATION (SAI)

Although a prospectus is always sufficient for the purpose of selling shares, some investors may wish to have additional information not found in the prospectus. This additional information is not necessarily needed to make an informed investment decision but may be useful to the investor.

An SAI must be available to investors upon request without charge. Investors can obtain a copy by calling or writing to the investment company, via a company website, contacting a broker that sells the investment company shares, or contacting the SEC.

The SAI affords the fund an opportunity to have expanded discussions on such matters as the fund's history and policies. It will also typically contain the fund's consolidated financial statements.

1. 6. 11   TRUST INDENTURE ACT OF 1939

The Trust Indenture Act of 1939 applies to corporate bonds (nonexempt) with the following characteristics:

■ Issue size of more than $50 million within 12 months

■ Maturity of nine months or more

■ Offered interstate

[handwritten margin note: must be a trustee w/ these types of transactions (bonds)]

This act was passed to protect bondholders and requires that issuers of these bonds appoint a trustee to ensure that promises (covenants) between the issuer and the trustee who acts solely for the benefit of the bondholders are carried out. The document is filed at the office of a custodian so that investors may review it if they choose.

TEST TOPIC ALERT

The test might ask about the definition of a trust indenture. The best answer defines the trust indenture as a series of promises between the issuer and the trustee for the benefit of the bondholders.

1. 6. 12 OFFICIAL STATEMENTS, PRELIMINARY OFFICIAL STATEMENTS (POS), NOTICE OF SALE FOR MUNICIPAL SECURITIES

Municipal bonds are securities issued either by state or local government or by U.S. territories, authorities, and special districts. Investors that buy such bonds are loaning money to the issuers for the purpose of public works and construction projects (e.g., roads, hospitals, civic centers, sewer systems, and airports). Municipal securities are considered second in safety of principal only to U.S. government and U.S. government agency securities. The safety of a particular issue is based on the issuing municipality's financial stability.

Municipal securities are exempt from the filing requirements of the Act of 1933. However, like all other securities, they are subject to the anti-fraud provisions of the Securities Exchange Act of 1934. Therefore, a full and fair disclosure of material facts of the offering is still required.

The full and fair disclosure document for municipal securities is called the **official statement** (there is no prospectus). There is no preliminary prospectus either for municipal securities, but there is a **preliminary official statement**.

In addition, when a municipality wants to raise money through a bond offering, an **official notice of sale** is published in the Daily Bond Buyer. This is the notice that is used to obtain an underwriter for municipal bonds. Underwriters who are interested in bidding on municipal offerings will review the official notice of sale to determine if they would like to submit a bid to the issuer.

QUICK QUIZ 1.F

Objective: Explain the process for bringing new issues to market

1. All of the following are true statements EXCEPT

   A. prior to the filing of the registration statement, the SEC will set up a cooling-off period to ensure all registration requirements have been fully met
   B. the front of every prospectus MUST contain the SEC Disclaimer
   C. the preliminary prospectus may be used to gather indications of interest
   D. the Securities Act of 1933 required issuers of new securities to file registration statements with the SEC

2. Nonbinding indications of interest may be gathered with which of the following?

   A. A statutory prospectus
   B. The firm quote
   C. A tombstone ad
   D. A legal opinion

3. Because the firm commitment is the most commonly used type of underwriting contract, which of the following can be said of this type of underwriting?

    A. A firm commitment underwriting must be used with a negotiated underwriting contract.
    B. A firm commitment underwriting can be either a negotiated underwriting contract or a competitive bid arrangement.
    C. In a firm commitment all the underwriting risk is shifted to the issuer.
    D. A firm commitment may be added to a best efforts for the sake of securing the underwriting commitment.

4. The Securities Act of 1933 regulates all of the following activities EXCEPT

    A. delivery of prospectuses for full and fair disclosure
    B. registration of securities at the state level
    C. underwriting of new issues
    D. securities fraud in the primary market

5. Which of the following are characteristics of the Securities Act of 1933?

    A. Requires registration of exchanges
    B. Will approve certain securities to be sold to the public
    C. Requires full and fair disclosure of material facts
    D. Defines and regulates mutual funds

6. An underwriter has a firm commitment with an issuer to sell $5 million of common stock to the public. The underwriter has 4 selling groups. What is each selling group's responsibility for the sale?

    A. Each shares a firm commitment with the issuer to sell all the securities in the offering.
    B. Each selling group is responsible for $1 million of the $5 million offering.
    C. Selling groups take no financial responsibility in the offering.
    D. Selling groups only sell to institutional buyers.

All Quick Quiz answers are found at the end of their units.

1. 7   EXEMPT TRANSACTIONS

Securities offered by industrial, financial, and other corporations may qualify for exemption from the registration statement and prospectus requirements of the 1933 Act under one of the following exclusionary provisions:

- **Regulation A+**: small and medium corporate offerings
- **Regulation D**: private placements
- **Rule 147**: securities offered and sold exclusively intrastate
- **Regulation S**: offers and sales made outside the United States by U.S. issuers
- Other exempt transactions, including Rule 144, Rule 144a, and Rule 145

1. 7. 1   REGULATION A+: SMALL AND MEDIUM OFFERINGS

With the passage of the JOBs Act, a capital formation scheme was called for that would further ease the requirements for small- and medium-sized companies to raise capital. Previously known as Regulation A, the new rule is Regulation A+.

Regulation A+ provides two offering tiers for small- and medium-sized companies that will allow the companies to raise capital in amounts substantially more than the $5 million previously allowed under Regulation A.

(handwritten margin note: Small/medium companys can raise capital even w/ less filing?)

- **Tier 1**: Securities offerings up to $20 million in a 12-month period will be allowed. Of the $20 million, no more than $6 million can be sold on behalf of existing selling shareholders. The offering would be subject to a coordinated review by individual states and the SEC.
- **Tier 2**: Securities offerings up to $50 million in a 12-month period will be allowed. Of the $50 million, no more than $15 million can be sold on behalf of existing selling shareholders. These offerings are subject to SEC review only and none at the state level. Tier 2 offerings are still subject to rigorous disclosure requirements to the SEC including audited financial statements, annual, semi-annual and current reports.

Offerings under both tiers are open to the public and general solicitation is permitted for both tiers. However, Tier 2 investors must be "qualified" investors, and there are two ways to qualify:

- Be an accredited investor as defined in Rule 501 of Regulation D
- Limit the investment to a maximum of the greater of 10% of the investor's net worth or 10% of the investor's net income per offering. Note that self-certification for Tier 2 as to net worth and income is all that is required with no burdensome filings. Tier 1 has no investment limits.

Finally, remembering that the new Regulation A+ is intended for small- and medium-sized companies, the regulation specifically excludes investment companies (i.e., private equity funds, venture capital funds, and hedge funds).

In a Regulation A+ offering, the issuer files an abbreviated **notice of sale**, or **offering circular**, with the regional SEC office. Investors are provided with this offering circular rather than a full prospectus.

(handwritten margin note: files a brief offering circular/ notice of sale w/ SEC)

The cooling-off period is 20 days between the filing date and effective date, and the issuer need not provide audited financial information. Individuals buying securities in a Regulation A+ offering must receive a final offering circular at least 48 hours before confirmation of sale.

1. 7. 2   REGULATION D: PRIVATE PLACEMENTS   *(handwritten: — Hedge Funds)*

(handwritten margin note: not selling to open market)

The SEC does not require registration of an offering if it is privately placed with:
- accredited investors that do not need SEC protection or
- a maximum of 35 individual (nonaccredited) investors.

An **accredited investor** is defined as one who:
- has a net worth of $1 million or more, not including net equity in a primary residence; or
- has had an annual income of $200,000 or more in each of the two most recent years (or $300,000 jointly with a spouse) and who has a reasonable expectation of reaching the same income level during the current year.
- Officers and directors of the issuer are also accredited.

Purchasers must have access to the same type of information they would receive if the securities were being sold under prospectus in a registered offering. The amount of capital that can be raised is unlimited.

A private placement investor must sign a letter stating that he intends to hold the stock for investment purposes only. **Private placement stock** is called **lettered stock** due to this investment letter. The certificate may bear a legend indicating that it cannot be transferred without registration or exemption; therefore, private placement stock is also called **legend stock**.

The SEC requires that all companies raising capital in a nonpublic offering that qualify under the Regulation D exemption file the information on Form D electronically via the internet.

The SEC also specifies the instances when an amended Form D should be filed, such as to correct a mistake of fact or error or to reflect a change in information.

1. 7. 2. 1   General Solicitations and Advertising Private Placements

In order to solicit or advertise private securities offerings (private placements), a business will need to meet certain requirements regarding the intended investors. First, meeting the requirements assumes that the securities are in fact being offered under the Regulation D registration exemption. Beyond that assumption, the requirements are as follows:

■ All purchasers of the advertised securities must be accredited investors, or the business must reasonably believe that the investors are accredited investors at the time of the sale. In other words, while businesses may sell to up to 35 nonaccreditied investors, in order to solicit or advertise, all purchasers must be accredited.

■ The business must take reasonable steps to verify that all purchasers are accredited, considering background, relevant facts (such as reported income), and particular circumstances of each purchaser.

TEST TOPIC ALERT   Sometimes it is difficult to identify private placement stock in a question because of the many terms that can be used to describe it. Recognize all of the following terms as being synonymous with private placement stock:

■ Restricted (because it must be held for a six-month period)

■ Unregistered (no registration statement on file with the SEC)

■ Letter stock (investor agreed to terms by signing an investment letter)

■ Legend stock

In addition to previous exemptions, Regulation D under the Securities Act of 1933 allows the offer and sale of securities to accredited investors without registration under the act. These transactions are called private placements.

Under SEC **Rule 506**, the exemption can be approached in one of two ways:

■ The company cannot use general solicitation or advertising to market the securities and limits the number of nonaccredited investors to 35.

■ The company can advertise as long as it sells exclusively to accredited investors. (There are heightened verification rules regarding the accredited investor if advertising.)

Under SEC **Rule 501**, an accredited investor can be

1. an insider at the issuer;
2. a professional, sophisticated, or institutional investor; or
3. an individual who meets one of two criteria: at least $1 million net worth (excluding the net value of his primary residence) or at least $200,000 in adjusted gross income (AGI) for the last two years with good prospects of reaching that level in the current year ($300,000 if the investor is a married couple).

Note that assets held jointly with another person who is not the purchaser's spouse may be included in the calculation for net worth, but only to the extent of percentage of ownership.

TAKE NOTE   Just because an investor is accredited does not automatically qualify her for investing in a private placement or any other investment for that matter. Suitability must be determined prior to all recommendations.

1. 3. 1   RULE 147: INTRASTATE OFFERINGS

Under **Rule 147**, offerings that take place entirely in one state are exempt from registration when:

- the issuer has its principal office and receives at least 80% of its income in the state;
- at least 80% of the issuer's assets are located within the state;
- at least 80% of the offering proceeds are used within the state;
- a majority of the issuers' employees are based within the state; and
- all purchasers are residents of the state.

TAKE NOTE   To qualify under the Rule 147 exemption, only one of the three 80% tests noted above must be met.

Purchasers of an intrastate issue may not resell the stock to any resident of another state for at least six months after the purchase.

1. 3. 2   RULE 144

Rule 144 regulates the sale of control and restricted securities, stipulating the holding period, quantity limitations, manner of sale, and filing procedures.

Control securities are those owned by directors, officers, or persons who own or control more than 10% of the issuer's voting stock.

TAKE NOTE   If an unaffiliated individual owns 7% of the voting stock of XYZ, that person is not a control person. However, if that person's spouse owns 4% of the voting stock, then both would be considered control persons. In other words, if there is a 10% or more interest held by immediate family members, then all those family members owning voting stock are control persons.

Restricted securities are those acquired through some means other than a registered public offering. A security purchased in a private placement is a restricted security. Restricted securities may not be sold until they have been held fully paid for six months. According to Rule 144, after holding restricted stock fully paid for six months, an affiliate may begin selling shares but is subject to the volume restriction rules as enumerated below. In any 90-day period, an investor may sell the greater of:

- 1% of the total outstanding shares of the same class at the time of sale, or
- the average weekly trading volume in the stock over the past four weeks on all exchanges or as reported through Nasdaq.

After the six-month holding period, affiliated persons are subject to the volume restrictions for as long as they are affiliates. For unaffiliated investors, the stock may be sold completely unrestricted after the six-month holding period has been satisfied.

Selling shares under Rule 144 effectively registers the shares. In other words, buyers of stock being sold subject to Rule 144 are not subject to any restrictions if they choose to resell.

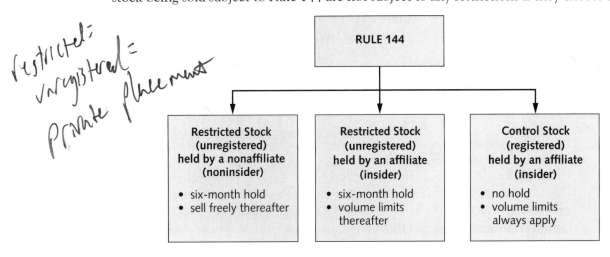

restricted = unregistered = private placement

TEST TOPIC ALERT

When you encounter a Rule 144 question, always look for two things:

What kind of stock is being sold? (Restricted or control)

Who is selling it? (Insider or noninsider)

Only restricted stock has a holding period. Control stock, unless it is restricted, can be sold immediately, but volume limits always apply.

1. 3. 3   RULE 144A

private placement security non-registered w/ SEC

Rule 144a allows nonregistered foreign and domestic securities to be sold to certain institutional investors in the United States without holding period requirements. To qualify for this exemption, the buyer must be a **qualified institutional buyer (QIB)**. One requirement of a QIB is a minimum of $100 million in assets.

1. 3. 4   ANTI-FRAUD REGULATIONS OF THE ACTS OF 1933 AND 1934

all information must be accurate

Although a security may be exempt from the registration and prospectus requirements, no offering is exempt from the anti-fraud provisions of the Securities Act of 1933 or any other securities act, including the Securities Exchange Act of 1934. The anti-fraud provisions of the Act of 1933 apply to all new securities offerings, whether exempt from registration or not. Issuers must provide accurate information regarding any securities offered to the public.

1. 3. 4. 1   Protecting the Public and Restricted Persons Prohibitions (FINRA Rule 5130)

members do not buy the IPO stock for their own benefit or bribe ppl. w/ it essentially no insider trading

The rule is designed to protect the integrity of the public offering process by ensuring that:

■ members make a bona fide public offering of securities at the public offering price;

■ members do not withhold securities in a public offering for their own benefit or use such securities to reward persons who are in a position to direct future business to the member; and

■ industry insiders, such as members and their associated persons, do not take advantage of their insider status to gain access to new issues for their own benefit at the expense of public customers.

The rule applies only to a new issue, which is defined to mean any initial public offering of equity securities. The rule does not apply to additional issue offerings, debt securities, restricted or exempt securities, convertible securities, preferred stock, investment company securities, offerings of business development companies, direct participation companies, and real estate investment trusts. Essentially, the rule applies to IPOs of common stock.

The rule prohibits member firms from selling a new issue to any account where restricted persons are beneficial owners. Restricted persons are defined as follows:

(restricted group)

1. Member firms

2. Employees of member firms

3. Finders and fiduciaries acting on behalf of the managing underwriter, including attorneys, accountants, financial consultants, and so on

4. Portfolio managers, including any person who has the authority to buy or sell securities for a bank, savings and loan association, insurance company, or investment company

5. Any person owning 10% or more of a member firm

Furthermore, any immediate family member of any person in 2–5 above is also restricted. Immediate family includes parents, in-laws, spouses, siblings, children, or any other individual to whom the person provides material support.

EXAMPLE   Aunts and uncles, as well as grandparents, are not considered immediate family. If, however, one of these individuals lives in the same household as a restricted person, that individual would be a restricted person.

Finally, there is a de minimis exemption. If the beneficial interests of restricted persons do not exceed 10% of an account, the account may purchase a new equity issue. In other words,

(handwritten margin notes:) restricted persons cannot buy their own IPO — & employees at XYZ (& who is IPO'ing cannot buy their shares)

restricted persons will be able to have an interest in an account that purchases new equity issues as long as no more than 10% of the account's beneficial owners are restricted persons.

Spinning is the practice of allocating highly sought after IPO shares to individuals who are in a position to direct securities business to the firm. This is why portfolio managers are categorized as restricted persons. These individuals are in a position to direct business to a firm and may be willing to do so on the basis of the size of their allocation.

Before selling an IPO to any account, representatives are required to obtain a written representation from the account owner(s) that the account is eligible to purchase a new common stock issue at the public offering price. All representations must be obtained within the 12-month period before the sale of the new issue and must be retained for at least three years following the new issue sale.

QUICK QUIZ 1.G   Objective: Distinguish exempt transactions rules and rules regarding restricted securities

1. ABC, Inc., will be offering $8 million of its common stock in its home state and in three other states. For the offering to be cleared for sale by the SEC, ABC must file
   A. an offering circular
   B. a standard registration statement
   C. a letter of notification
   D. nothing

2. Which of the following is NOT required in a preliminary prospectus?
   A. Written statement in red that the prospectus may be subject to change and amendment and that a final prospectus will be issued
   B. Purpose for which the funds being raised will be used
   C. Final offering price
   D. Financial status and history of the company

3. All of the following statements about a red herring are true EXCEPT
   A. a red herring is used to obtain indications of interest from investors
   B. the final offering price does not appear in a red herring
   C. additional information may be added to a red herring at a later date
   D. registered representatives may send a copy of the company's research report with it

4. If the SEC has cleared an issue for sale, which of the following statements is TRUE?
   A. The SEC has guaranteed the issue.
   B. The underwriter has filed a standard registration statement.
   C. The SEC has endorsed the issue.
   D. The SEC has guaranteed the accuracy of the information in the prospectus.

5. Which of the following is subject to the holding period provisions of Rule 144?
   A. A corporate insider who has held restricted stock for 2 years.
   B. A nonaffiliate who has held registered stock for 3 years.
   C. A nonaffiliate who has held control stock for 6 months.
   D. A nonaffiliate who has held restricted stock for 3 months.

All Quick Quiz answers are found at the end of their units.

QUICK QUIZ ANSWERS

Quick Quiz 1.A

1. **B.** Retail communication is defined as "any written (including electronic) communication that is distributed or made available to more than 25 retail investors within any 30-calendar-day period." A public appearance is not written and the letter sent out to 10 customers is correspondence.

2. **B.** Institutional communication is any written communication that is distributed or made available only to institutional investors.

3. **B.** Sending notification to existing clients at a broker-dealer would involve more than 25 retail investors in a 30-calendar-day period. This would define it as retail communication and require prior principal approval. It is the best answer from the choices given. The pension plan is an institution; a single letter is a correspondence and a communication that does not promote a product or service of the firm. Principal approval is not required for the other choices.

Quick Quiz 1.B

1. **B.** An independently prepared reprint (IPR) consists of any article reprint that meets certain standards designed to ensure that the reprint was issued by an independent publisher and was not materially altered by the member.

2. **A.** All generic advertisements must contain the name and address of the sponsor of the advertisement but never include the name of any specific security.

3. **D.** Websites, whether sponsored by the company itself or set up by an individual registered representative, are considered retail communications and are subject to applicable filing and recordkeeping rules.

Quick Quiz 1.C

1. **D.** A form letter to 20 prospective customers is a correspondence and, as such, may be pre- or post-reviewed by a principal.

2. **D.** IPRs may be altered to make it consistent with regulatory standards or make it consistent with correct factual errors. Preapproval is required for IPRs.

3. **B.** Before engaging in a public appearance, RRs must complete training on the firm's procedures and adhere to the firm's procedures.

Quick Quiz 1.D

1. **C.** All forms of communication from the member—institutional, retail, and correspondence—must be based on principles of fair dealing and good faith and provide a sound basis for evaluating the facts in regard to any particular security or type of security, industry discussed, or service offered.

2. **B.** 1-, 5-, and 10-year numbers must be shown or since inception if shorter. If the sales load is reflected, the communication must state that either the performance data does not reflect the sales load and therefore the performance data would be reduced or it does reflect the sales load and the performance data has been reduced.

3. **B.** There are many times the firm needs to recruit but may not wish its current reps to know of that fact. In those cases, a "blind ad" is permissible.

Quick Quiz 1.E

1. **D.** Established firms are firms that have been in business for more than a year. As such, they may post-file with FINRA within 10 days of first use. Preapproval is done by a registered principal.

2. **D.** If the firm were a new firm, it would have to file all retail communications at least 10 days before first use. Your firm is well established; this will be approved by a registered principal, and because it is for an investment company, the communication will be filed with FINRA within 10 days of first use.

3. **B.** There may be no representation or implication that a guarantee applies to either the investment return or principal value of the separate account.

Quick Quiz 1.F

1. **A.** The cooling-off period is effective only after the registration statement has been filed, not before. All the other statements are correct.

2. **C.** Nonbinding indications of interest may be gathered with a preliminary prospectus or a tombstone advertisements.

3. **B.** A firm commitment underwriting can be either a negotiated underwriting contract or a competitive bid arrangement.

4. **B.** The Securities Act of 1933 regulates federal registration of new issues with the SEC. The Uniform Securities Act regulates the registration of securities at the state level. Registering at the state level is called blue-skying the issue.

5. **C.** The Securities Act of 1933 regulates new issues of corporate securities sold to the public. The act is also referred to as the Full Disclosure Act, the Paper Act, the Truth in Securities Act, and the Prospectus Act. The purpose of the act is to require full, written disclosure about a new issue. The Securities Exchange Act of 1934 requires exchanges to register with the SEC, and the Investment Company Act of 1940 defines and regulates investment companies, including mutual funds.

6. **C.** Selling groups take no financial responsibility in an underwriting. They only get paid for what they sell. Selling groups are not limited to selling to institutional buyers.

Quick Quiz 1.G

1. **A.** In a Regulation A+ offering, the issuer files an abbreviated notice of sale, or offering circular, with the regional SEC office. Investors are provided with this offering circular rather than a full prospectus.

2. **C.** The fact that this is a preliminary prospectus, should remind you that there are two items specifically NOT in the preliminary prospectus—the effective date and the final offering price.

3. **D.** Because the preliminary prospectus may be used for gathering indications of interest only, it may not be used to solicit sales. No other form of communication may be attached to or accompany it.

4. **B.** The issuer, with the help of the underwriter, has filed a registration statement from which the SEC will determine if the issuer has fully disclosed all matters as dictated by the Securities Act of 1933.

5. **D.** Only restricted stock is subject to the six-month holding period for both affiliates and nonaffiliates; registered shares are not and control stock is not. The nonaffiliate in choice D, who has only held the shares for 3 months, will still be subject to the holding period until the 6-month requirement is met.

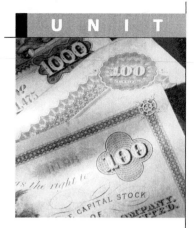

2

Opens Accounts After Obtaining and Evaluating Customers' Financial Profile and Investment Objectives; Retirement Plans

In dealing with customers and their accounts, the registered representative must be both honest with the customer and thorough with documentation from the time the account is opened, through all the dealings with the account. All account activity is documented and everything is done in the customer's best interest. Firms and associated persons will be accountable to FINRA and other regulatory bodies for strict ethics and honesty in dealing with the investing public.

In this unit, we will cover accounts, registrations, and gathering information, along with retirement plans.

The Series 7 exam will include 11 questions on the topics covered in this Unit. ■

In this Unit you will learn to:

■ **identify** characteristics of different types of accounts,

■ **compare** various account registration types,

■ **explain** requirements for opening customer accounts,

■ **contrast** qualified and nonqualified retirement plans,

■ **recall** characteristics of individual retirement plans,

■ **identify** characteristics of employer-sponsored plans, and

■ **define** ERISA and its application to private-sector retirement plans.

2. 1   TYPES OF ACCOUNTS

The two most common accounts offered by broker-dealers to their customers are cash and margin accounts.

2. 1. 1   CASH ACCOUNT

A **cash account** is the most basic investment account. Anyone eligible to open an investment account can open a cash account. In a cash account, a customer pays in full for any securities purchased.

Certain accounts must be opened as cash accounts, such as personal retirement accounts (individual retirement accounts and tax-sheltered annuities), corporate retirement accounts, and custodial accounts (Uniform Gift to Minors Act and Uniform Transfers to Minors Act accounts).

2. 1. 1. 1   Transfer on Death (TOD)

This is an account that allows the registered owner of the account to pass all or a portion of it, upon death, to a named beneficiary. This account avoids probate (having the decedent's will declared genuine by a court of law) because the estate is bypassed. However, the assets in the account do not avoid estate tax, if applicable.

TOD accounts are available for individual accounts and for certain joint accounts (joint tenants with rights of survivorship).

2. 1. 1. 2   Inheritance

When a person dies and leaves securities to heirs, the cost basis to the recipient is the fair market value on the date of the owner's death.

EXAMPLE

A father purchased $5,000 of ABC stock in 2005. When he died, the stock was valued at $10,000. If the stock was left to his children, they receive an automatic step up to the fair market value on the date of death ($10,000). Therefore, if the stock was sold for $10,000 after inheriting it, there would be no tax due on the sale.

2. 1. 2   MARGIN ACCOUNT

In a margin account, the customer can use some cash and some credit to purchase securities. This is a leveraged purchase of securities; investors can buy more securities with some cash and some credit than they can purchase with just cash. The firm can lend funds at the time of purchase, with the securities in the portfolio serving as collateral for the loan. This is called buying securities "on margin." The shortfall between the purchase price and the amount of money put in is a loan from the brokerage firm, and the customer will incur interest costs, just as with any other loan.

Margin transactions are not available for use within mutual funds, retirement accounts or in custodial accounts for minor children.

ETFs can use margin or can buy ETFs using margin

2. 1. 3   PRIME BROKERAGE ACCOUNT

A **prime brokerage account** is one in which a customer, generally an institution, selects one member firm (the prime broker) to provide custody and other services, while other firms, called executing brokers, handle all trades placed by the customer.

To open a prime brokerage account for a customer, a member (the prime broker) must sign an agreement with the customer spelling out the terms of the agreement, as well as names of all executing brokers the customer has contracted with. The prime broker will then enter into written agreements with each executing broker named by the customer. The customer receives trade confirmations and account statements from the prime broker, who facilitates the clearance and settlement of the securities transactions. Responsibility for compliance of certain trading rules rests with the executing brokers.

The key advantage of a prime brokerage account is that it usually provides a client with the ability to trade with multiple brokerage houses while maintaining a centralized master account with all of the client's cash and securities. A prime brokerage account often includes a list of specialized services, such as securities lending, margin financing, trade processing, cash management, and operational support. Prime brokerage accounts are likely to be offered to a broker-dealer's more active trading clients, like hedge funds, for example, who may require a number of executing broker outlets to conduct their transactions and who can benefit by having margin requirements that are netted across all of the prime broker's positions.

2. 1. 4   FEE-BASED ACCOUNT

Many firms offer investors **fee-based accounts** that charge a single fee (either fixed or a percentage of assets in the account) instead of commission-based charges for brokerage services. Fee-based accounts are not wrap accounts. **Wrap accounts** are accounts for which firms provide a group of services, such as asset allocation, portfolio management, executions, and administration, for a single fee. Wrap accounts are generally investment advisory accounts.

Fee-based accounts are appropriate only for investors who engage in at least a moderate level of trading activity. Accounts with a low level of trading activity may be better off with commission-based charges. Rules require that, before opening a fee-based account, investors be given a disclosure document describing the services to be provided and the cost.

2. 1. 4. 1   Advisory Account

An **advisory account** is an account through which a Registered Investment Adviser (RIA) or an Investment Adviser Representative (IAR) of the RIA provides investment advice to clients for a fee. It is important to understand that an advisory account is very different from a brokerage account. In a brokerage account, a fee is paid when transactions occur. In advisory accounts, a fee is paid for advice regarding the securities in the account. An RIA has a fiduciary obligation (is legally obligated) to act in the best interests of clients at all times. RIAs must provide clients with a Form ADV which describes how they do business, reveals any potential conflicts of interest, and clearly describes how they are compensated.

2. 1. 5   PAYMENT AND DELIVERY INSTRUCTIONS

After opening an account, the customer and the registered representative establish payment and delivery instructions. Although these instructions may be changed for individual transactions or at any time to be applied going forward, the customer selects any of the following when initially opening the account.

2. 1. 5. 1   Transfer and ship

Securities are registered in the customer's name and shipped to them.

2. 1. 5. 2   Transfer and hold in safekeeping

Securities are registered in the customer's name, and the broker-dealer holds them in safekeeping.

2. 1. 5. 3   Hold in street name

Securities are registered in the broker-dealer's name and held by the broker-dealer. Although the broker-dealer is the securities' nominal owner, the customer is the beneficial owner.

2. 1. 5. 4   Delivery versus payment (DVP)

DVP securities are delivered to a bank or depository against payment. Normally used for institutional accounts, this is a cash-on-delivery (COD) settlement. The broker-dealer must verify the arrangement between the customer and the bank or depository, and the customer must notify the bank or depository of each purchase or sale. In addition, the customer designates whether the broker-dealer should hold or forward any cash balance.

QUICK QUIZ 2.A   Objective: Identify characteristics of different types of accounts

1. An IRA account at a broker-dealer must be set up as

   A. a cash account
   B. a margin account
   C. a wrap account
   D. an advisory account

   D

2. A customer would like to use one broker-dealer to handle the administration of the account but various other broker-dealers to execute trades for certain types of securities. Which type of account would meet the customer's needs?

   A. Advisory account
   B. Prime brokerage account
   C. Fee-based account
   D. Wrap account

   B

3. A customer is an active trader within his securities account and does not like to pay for transactions individually. What type of account would be most appropriate for the customer?

   A. Cash account
   B. Margin account
   C. Wrap account — *fee based acct*
   D. Prime brokerage account

   C

market value is calculated at time of death on a TOD account.

D

4. The daughter of a deceased parent is named as the beneficiary of a TOD account. In the father's account is a security that was purchased for $10,000 15 years ago and is valued at $22,000 at the time of death. The security is valued at $21,000 when all paperwork is completed and she has access to the money. Which of the following statements are true regarding the security?

    A. The daughter's cost basis is $10,000.
    B. The daughter's cost basis is $21,000.
    C. If she sells the security for $21,000, she will realize a $12,000 capital gain.
    D. If she sells the security for $21,000, she will realize a $1,000 capital loss.

All Quick Quiz answers are found at the end of their units.

2. 2   REGISTRATION TYPES

There are many different registration types available when opening an account at a broker-dealer.

2. 2. 1   INDIVIDUAL ACCOUNT

A **single (individual) account)** has one beneficial owner. The account holder is the only person who may:

■ control the investments within the account, and
■ request distributions of cash or securities from the account.

2. 2. 2   JOINT ACCOUNTS

In a **joint account,** two or more adults are named on the account as co-owners, with each allowed some form of control over the account. In addition to the appropriate new account form, a joint account agreement must be signed

The account forms for joint accounts require the signatures of all owners. Joint account agreements allow any or all tenants to transact business in the account. Checks must be made payable to the names in which the account is registered and must be endorsed for deposit by all tenants (although mail need be sent to only a single address). To be in good delivery form, securities sold from a joint account must be signed by all tenants.

The suitability requirements for a joint account follow the same basic rules as all accounts—put the interest of the client first. Because a joint account is really nothing other than a collection of individuals, suitability information must be obtained on all of the account owners and any recommendations must be appropriate based upon that information. In other words, the suitability of recommendations must be based on the group, not on any individual within the group.

2. 2. 2. 1   Joint Tenants With Rights of Survivorship (JTWROS)

JTWROS ownership stipulates that a deceased tenant's interest in the account passes to the surviving tenant(s).

- JTWROS—all parties have an undivided interest in the account

- TIC—each party must specify a percentage interest in the account

Checks or distributions must be made payable to all parties and endorsed by all parties.

2. 2. 2. 2   Tenants in Common

Tenants in common (TIC) ownership provides that a deceased tenant's fractional interest in the account be retained by that tenant's estate and not passed to the surviving tenant(s). If one account owner dies or is declared incompetent, all pending transactions and outstanding orders must be canceled immediately.

EXAMPLE

If a TIC agreement provides for a 60% ownership interest by one owner and 40% ownership interest by the other, that fraction of the account would pass into the deceased owner's estate upon death. The TIC agreement may be used by more than two individuals.

2. 2. 2. 3   Community Property

Community property is a marital property classification recognized by some, but not all, states. In these jurisdictions, most property acquired during the marriage is considered to be owned jointly by both spouses and would be divided at the time of divorce, annulment, or death. Joint ownership is therefore automatically presumed by law in these jurisdictions, absent any specific evidence that would point to a contrary conclusion for any item of ownership. Exceptions are made for inheritances, gifts, or any property that is owned by one spouse before marriage, which is considered the separate property of that spouse, unless it was designated to be owned jointly by both spouses during the marriage.

It is important to know that laws in jurisdictions where community property is presumed differ from state to state. Additionally, community property can have certain federal tax implications. Generally, community property may result in lower federal capital gains taxes after the death of one spouse when the property is dissolved by the surviving spouse. Some states have created separate classifications called "community property with rights of survivorship" that are similar to joint tenancy with rights of survivorship property designations.

2. 2. 2. 4   Sole Proprietorship

This is the simplest form of business organization and is treated like an individual account. In a **sole proprietorship**, all income (or loss) is that of the individual. In fact, one of the risks of operating in this fashion, is that all the owner's assets are liable for the debts of the business— you can lose everything. Obviously, this is one of the major considerations when opening an account for this form of business.

This is an account that is easy to create and easy to dissolve.

2. 2. 2. 5   Partnership (Unincorporated Association)

A **partnership** is an unincorporated association of two or more individuals. Partnerships frequently open cash, margin, retirement, and other types of accounts necessary for business purposes.

The partnership must complete a **partnership agreement** stating which of the partners can make transactions for the account. If the partnership opens a margin account, the partnership must disclose any investment limitations.

An amended partnership agreement must be obtained each year if changes have been made.

2. 2. 2. 6   Corporate Accounts

A registered representative who opens a corporate account must establish:

■ the business's legal right to open an investment account;

■ an indication of any limitations that the owners, the stockholders, a court, or any other entity has placed on the securities in which the business can invest; and

■ who will represent the business in transactions involving the account.

When opening an account for a corporation, a firm must obtain a copy of the **corporate charter**, as well as a **corporate resolution**. The charter is proof that the corporation does exist, and the resolution authorizes both the opening of the account and the officers designated to enter orders.

2. 2. 2. 6. 1   Dividend Exclusion Rule

Dividends paid from one corporation to another are 50% exempt from taxation. A corporation that receives dividends on stocks of other domestic corporations, therefore, pays taxes on only 50% of the dividends received. This provision encourages corporations to invest in common and preferred stock of other U.S. corporations.

2. 2. 2. 7   Numbered Accounts

At a customer's request, his account may be identified by only a number or symbol. The customer must sign a form certifying that he owns the account(s) identified by the number or symbol and must supply other information identifying himself as the owner.

EXAMPLE   Celebrities sometimes use numbered accounts to preserve anonymity.

2. 2. 2. 8   Fiduciary and Custodial Accounts

When securities are placed in a fiduciary, or custodial, account, a person other than the owner initiates trades. The most familiar example of a fiduciary account is a trust account.

Money or securities are placed in trust for one person, often a minor, but someone else manages the account. The manager or trustee is a fiduciary.

In a fiduciary account, the investments exist for the owner's beneficial interest, yet the owner has little or no legal control over them. The fiduciary makes all the investment, management, and distribution decisions and must manage the account in the owner's best interests. The fiduciary may not use the account for his own benefit, although he may be reimbursed for reasonable expenses incurred in managing the account.

Securities bought in a custodial account must be registered in such a way that the custodial relationship is evident.

EXAMPLE

Marilyn Johnson, the donor, has appointed her daughter's aunt, Barbara Wood, as custodian for the account of Johnson's minor daughter, Alexis. The account and the certificates would read "Barbara Wood as custodian for Alexis Johnson."

The beneficial owner's Social Security number is used on the account.

A fiduciary is any person legally appointed and authorized to represent another person, act on his behalf, and make whatever decisions are necessary to the prudent management of his account. Fiduciaries include:

■ a trustee designated to administer a trust;

■ an executor designated in a decedent's will to manage the affairs of the estate;

■ an administrator appointed by the courts to liquidate the estate of a person who died intestate (without a will);

■ a guardian designated by the courts to handle a minor's affairs until the minor reaches the age of majority or to handle an incompetent person's affairs;

■ a custodian of a Uniform Gift to Minors Account (UGMA) or a Uniform Transfer to Minors Account (UTMA);

■ a receiver in a bankruptcy; and

■ a conservator for an incompetent person.

Any trades the fiduciary enters must be compatible with the investment objectives of the underlying entity.

2. 2. 2. 8. 1   Opening a Fiduciary Account

Opening a fiduciary account may require a court certification of the individual's appointment and authority. An account for a trustee must include a trust agreement detailing the limitations placed on the fiduciary. No documentation of custodial rights or court certification is required for an individual acting as the custodian for an UGMA or UTMA account. The registered representative for a fiduciary account must be aware of the following rules:

■ Proper authorization must be given—the necessary court documents must be filed with and verified by the broker-dealer.

■ Speculative transactions are generally not permitted.

■ Margin and option accounts are only permitted if authorized by the legal documents establishing the fiduciary accounts.

■ The prudent investor rule requires fiduciaries to make wise and safe investments.

■ Many states publish a legal list of securities approved for fiduciary accounts.

■ A fiduciary may not share in an account's profits but may charge a reasonable fee for services.

2.2.2.9   Death of an Account Holder

With regard to individual accounts, once a firm becomes aware of the death of the account owner, the firm must cancel all open orders, mark the account "deceased," and freeze the assets in the account until receiving instructions and the necessary documentation from the executor of the decedent's estate. If the account has a third-party power of attorney, the authorization is revoked.

TAKE NOTE   Discretionary authority ends at the death of the account owner.

Depending on the type of account, the documents necessary to release the assets of a decedent are:

■ a certified copy of the death certificate,

■ inheritance tax waivers, and

■ letters testamentary.

If one party in a JTWROS account dies, the account cannot be transferred to the name of the new owner (the other party) until a certified copy of the death certificate is presented to the member firm. The other documents noted above are not needed to transfer ownership at death in a JTWROS account.

If one party in a TIC account dies, the decedent's interest in the account goes to his estate. The executor for the decedent must present the proper documents before the assets belonging to the decedent can be released. In some states, the death of a tenant in a TIC account requires that the executor present an affidavit of domicile to the member that shows the decedent's estate will be handled under the laws of that state.

Also note that in TIC accounts, the death of a tenant requires that the member firm freeze the account and acceptance of orders until the required documents are presented. Compare this with a JTWROS account, for which the death of one tenant does not preclude the remaining tenant from entering orders.

With regard to partnership accounts, if one partner dies, the member needs written authority from the remaining partners before executing any further orders. This written authorization generally takes the form of an amended partnership agreement.

TEST TOPIC ALERT   Three basic steps apply at the death of a customer:

■ Cancel open orders

■ Freeze the account (mark it deceased)

■ Await instructions from the executor of the estate

| QUICK QUIZ 2.B | Objective: Compare various account registration types |

1. All of the following are true regarding community property EXCEPT

(handwritten: A)

   A. property acquired prior to marriage is considered to be jointly owned
   B. community property is considered to be owned jointly by both spouses and would be divided at the time of divorce, annulment, or death
   C. not all states are community property states
   D. an exception to community property is for property that was inherited

2. When an account is titled as tenants in common, which of the following will occur at the death of one of the joint tenants?

(handwritten: C)

   A. The decedent's interest in the account is passed on to the survivors of the account.
   B. Death dissolves the account, and all property is split according to proportionate interest.
   C. The decedent's interest in the account passes to the estate.
   D. Any outstanding orders that have been placed and not executed are allowed to be completed.

3. If opening an account for a sole proprietor, which of the following considerations would be the most important to convey?

(handwritten: personal assets at risk in sole proprietorship   A)

   A. The account is subject to the creditors of the business.
   B. It is treated like an individual account.
   C. Any gains and losses are taxed to the business, not the individual.
   D. It is an account that is easy to create and easy to dissolve.

All Quick Quiz answers are found at the end of their units.

2. 3   REQUIREMENTS FOR OPENING CUSTOMER ACCOUNTS

FINRA's suitability rule (FINRA Rule 2111) is based on a fundamental requirement to deal fairly with customers. Firms and their associated persons "must have a reasonable basis to believe" that a recommended transaction or investment strategy involving securities is suitable for the customer.

The more information a representative has about a customer's income, current investment portfolio, retirement plans, and net worth, as well as other aspects of his current financial situation, the better a recommendation will be. The more a customer knows about the risks and rewards of each type of investment, the better the customer's investment decisions will be. Both financial and nonfinancial information must be gathered before making investment recommendations.

2. 3. 1   NEW ACCOUNT FORM

Knowing your customer begins with the **new account form**. The SEC requires that brokerage firms create a record for each account with an individual customer that includes the following information:

■ Customer name
■ Tax identification number (e.g., Social Security number)
■ Address
■ Date of birth
■ Telephone number
■ Drivers license, passport information, or information from other government-issued identification
■ Employment status and occupation
■ Whether the customer is employed by a brokerage firm
■ Annual income
■ Net worth
■ Account investment objectives

Brokers must make a good-faith effort to obtain additional information. However, if the customer neglects or refuses to provide all the information, or is unable to provide it, then the rule excuses the broker from obtaining it.

TEST TOPIC ALERT   The customer's signature is not required on the new account form. The only signature required to open an account is a partner, officer, or manager (a principal) signifying that the account has been accepted in accordance with the member's policies and procedures for acceptance of accounts.

Accounts may be opened by any legally competent person above the age of majority. Individuals who have been determined legally incompetent may not open accounts.

Ideally, when opening an account, representatives should know all essential facts about a customer's current financial situation, present holdings, risk tolerance, needs, and objectives. Such information should be updated periodically as situations change.

There are four items that must be obtained on the new account form:

■ Name
■ Address (not a PO Box)
■ Social Security number or tax identification number
■ Date of birth

Must be obtained on new acct. form

If a customer only provides minimum information and refuses to provide all information requested, the account may still be opened if the firm believes the customer has the financial resources necessary to support the account. If sufficient information has not been received to determine suitability, recommendations cannot be made and only **unsolicited** trades may occur.

T A K E   N O T E   Trades that are initiated by the customer are **unsolicited**. When the registered representative initiates the trade, then the trade is **solicited**.

2. 3. 1. 1   Trusted Contact Person (Rule 4512)

If the person opening the account is age 65 or older, FINRA requires members to make reasonable efforts to obtain for noninstitutional customers the name of and contact information for a trusted contact person age 18 or older who may be contacted about the customer's account. Rule 4512 does not require a customer to provide trusted contact information.

Member firms may place a temporary hold on the distribution of funds or securities from the account of someone age 65 and older, or someone age 18 and older who has a mental or physical impairment that renders the individual unable to protect her own interests. The temporary hold is also allowed, in certain circumstances where the member reasonably believes that financial exploitation of the specified adult has occurred, is occurring, has been attempted or will be attempted.

2. 3. 1. 2   Updating Client Information

The completed form must be sent to the customer within 30 days. After that, account information must be updated no less frequently than every three years. Anytime the account is amended, an updated form must be sent to the customer within 30 days.

2. 3. 1. 3   Regulation S-P (Privacy Notices)

This regulation was enacted by the SEC to protect the privacy of customer information. In particular, the regulation deals with nonpublic personal information. Examples of nonpublic personal information include a customer's Social Security number, account balances, transaction history, and any information collected through an internet cookie. Your firm must provide a privacy notice describing its privacy policies to customers whenever a new account is opened and annually thereafter.

If your firm reserves the right to disclose to unaffiliated third parties nonpublic personal information, the notice must provide customers a reasonable means to opt out of this disclosure. Reasonable opt-out means include providing customers with a form with check-off boxes along with a prepaid return envelope, providing an electronic means to opt out for customers who have agreed to the electronic delivery of information, and providing a toll-free telephone number. Asking customers to write a letter to express their disclosure preferences or to opt-out would not be considered reasonable under Regulation S-P.

In addition, the regulation embodies the obligation of financial institutions to safeguard customer information as related to all forms of existing and developing technology. For example, this would include, but not be limited to, securing desktop and laptop computers and encrypting email.

2. 3. 2 CUSTOMER IDENTIFICATION PROGRAM (CIP)

Under provisions of the **USA PATRIOT Act**, broker-dealers are required to institute a **customer identification program (CIP)** designed to:

gov't issued IDs are required

- verify the identity of any new customer;
- for an individual, an unexpired government-issued identification such as a drivers license, passport, military ID, or state ID;
- for a person other than an individual, documents showing the existence of the entity, such as certified articles of incorporation, a government-issued business license, a partnership agreement, or trust instrument;
- maintain records of the information used to verify identity; and
- determine whether the person appears on the Office of Foreign Assets Control (FOCA) list of known or suspected terrorists or terrorist organizations.

These rules are designed to prevent, detect, and prosecute money laundering and the financing of terrorism.

As part of its customer identification program, a broker-dealer must, before opening an account, obtain the following information at a minimum:

Info needed before you open an account

- Customer name
- Date of birth (for an individual)
- Address, which shall be:

    — for an individual, a residential or business street address;

    — for an individual who does not have a residential or business street address, an Army Post Office (APO) or Fleet Post Office (FPO) box number, or the residential or business street address of a next of kin or another contact individual; or

    — for a person other than an individual (such as a corporation, partnership, or trust), a principal place of business, local office, or other physical location

- Social Security number for an individual or Tax ID number for a business entity
- For a non-U.S. person, one or more of the following: a taxpayer identification number, a passport number and country of issuance, an alien identification card number, or the number and country of issuance of any other government-issued document evidencing nationality or residence and bearing a photograph or similar safeguard. An exception is granted to persons who do not currently have, but who have applied for, a Social Security number. In this instance, the firm must obtain the number within a reasonable period and the account card must be marked "applied for."

The CIP must include procedures for responding to circumstances in which the broker-dealer cannot form a reasonable belief that it knows the true identity of a customer. These procedures should describe:

- when the broker-dealer should not open an account;
- the terms under which a customer may conduct transactions while the broker-dealer attempts to verify the customer's identity;
- when the broker-dealer should close an account after attempts to verify a customer's identity fail; and
- when the broker-dealer should file a suspicious activity report (SAR) in accordance with applicable law and regulation.

2. 3. 3   OPENING ACCOUNTS FOR OTHER BROKERS' EMPLOYEES

Regulatory bodies have rules and special procedures regarding the establishment of accounts for certain individuals, including:

- employees of broker-dealers, and
- spouses or minor children of broker-dealer employees.

2. 3. 3. 1   FINRA Requirements

The FINRA rule requires that a person associated with a member, before opening an account or placing an initial securities order with another member, notify the employer and the executing member (where the new account is to be maintained), in writing, of her association with the other member.

Before the account can be opened, the employing FINRA member firm must grant written permission. Prior written consent from the employer is specified within the rule.

Upon written request from the employing member firm, the executing member must supply to the employing member duplicate copies of confirmations, account statements, or any other account information requested.

Exceptions exist when the registered representative is limited to purchasing directly from investment companies, including variable contracts, and 529 plans.

2. 3. 4   ACCOUNT AUTHORIZATIONS

When opening a brokerage account, the customer opening the account will have final say on investment decisions unless they give someone else that authority, such as a registered representative.

2. 3. 4. 1   Discretionary Power

A customer can give **discretionary power** over his account(s) to someone else only by filing a trading authorization or a limited power of attorney with the broker-dealer. No transactions of a discretionary nature can take place without this document on file. Once authorization has been given, the customer is legally bound to accept the decision made by the person holding discretionary authority, although the customer may continue to enter orders on his own. Principal approval is required for a registered representative to have discretionary authority.

In addition to requiring the proper documentation, discretionary accounts are subject to the following rules:

- Each discretionary order must be identified as such at the time it is entered for execution.
- An officer or a partner of the brokerage house must approve each order promptly and in writing, but not necessarily before order entry.
- A record must be kept of all transactions.
- No excessive trading, or churning, may occur in the account relative to the size of the account and the customer's investment objectives.

To safeguard against the possibility of churning, a designated supervisor or manager must review all trading activity frequently and systematically.

If you are having difficulty identifying a discretionary order, try this method: An order is discretionary if any one of the three As is missing. The three As are:

- activity (buy or sell),

- amount (number of shares), and

- asset (the security).

An order that specifies time or price is not discretionary. In other words, if the customer states buy at the best price or sell at the best time; discretionary authority is not needed to execute the trade. This type of order is a **not held order**, or **market not held order** and is sent to the floor broker on the floor of the exchange for execution.

If a person not named on an account will have trading authority, the customer must file written authorization with the broker-dealer giving that person access to the account. This trading authorization usually takes the form of a power of attorney. Two basic types of trading authorizations are full and limited powers of attorney. Both would be canceled upon the death of either party.

2. 3. 4. 2   Full Power of Attorney

A **full power of attorney** allows someone who is not the owner of an account to:
- deposit or withdraw cash or securities, and
- make investment decisions for the account owner.

Custodians, trustees, guardians, and other people filling similar legal duties are often given full powers of attorney.

2. 3. 4. 3   Limited Power of Attorney

A **limited power of attorney** allows an individual to have some, but not total, control over an account. The document specifies the level of access the person may exercise. Limited power of attorney, also called limited trading authorization, allows the entering of buy and sell orders but no withdrawal of assets. Entry of orders and withdrawal of assets is allowed if full power of attorney is granted.

A durable power of attorney (POA) will survive a declaration of mental incompetence, but not death.

2. 3. 4. 4   Authorization Records for Negotiable Instruments Drawn From a Customer's Account

No member or person associated with a member may submit for payment a check, draft, or other form of negotiable paper drawn on a customer's checking, savings, or similar account, without that person's express written authorization, which may include the customer's signature on the negotiable instrument such as a check. If written authorization is separate from the negotiable instrument, the member must preserve the authorization for a period of three years following termination of the document.

2. 3. 4. 5   Approval and Documentation of Changes in Account Name or Designation

Before any customer order is executed, there must be placed upon the order form or other similar record, the name or designation of the account (or accounts) for which such order is to be executed. No change in such account name(s) (including related accounts) or designation(s) may be made unless the change has been authorized by a registered principal.

2. 3. 5   CUSTOMER INFORMATION AND SUITABILITY

Registered representatives must always know their client prior to making any recommendation. A customer's investment objectives may lead to a recommendation to buy, sell, or hold a security. All recommendations, even a hold recommendation, must be suitable for the client's situation.

Selecting suitable investments to meet investor needs is an art and a science, and negotiating the difference between what the representative considers suitable and what the customer wants is a legal, ethical, and personal dilemma.

If a customer asks a representative to enter a trade the representative feels is unsuitable, it is the representative's responsibility to explain why the trade might not be right for the customer. If the customer insists on entering the transaction, the representative should have the customer sign a statement acknowledging that the representative recommended against the trade, and the representative should mark the order ticket **unsolicited**.

Suitability issues can involve things like the source of the investor's funding. A customer may wish to liquidate some of the additional equity available on his home in order to invest in a security. The customer must be made aware of the substantial risks inherent in such a step.

2. 3. 6   TRANSFERRING CUSTOMER ACCOUNTS BETWEEN BROKER-DEALERS

When a customer, whose securities account is carried by a broker-dealer, wants to transfer the account to another broker-dealer, the **Automated Customer Account Transfer Service (ACATS)** automates and standardizes the procedure for the transfer. The customer signs a **Transfer Initiation Form (TIF)**, which is sent to ACATS by the receiving firm. For purposes of this rule, customer authorization could be the customer's actual signature or an electronic signature.

Once forwarded and received by the carrying firm, it has one business day to validate the securities listed on the TIF or take exception to the transfer instructions. If there are no exceptions, within three business days following validation, the carrying firm must complete the transfer of the account.

No member may interfere with a customer's request to transfer an account in connection with the change in employment of the customer's registered representative when the account is not subject to any lien for monies owed by the customer or other bona fide claim.

2. 3. 6. 1   Transferring Assets From One Broker-Dealer to Another

FINRA Rule 2273 requires registered reps, who move to a new firm and try to convince former customers to move with them, to provide educational material outlining things for the customer to consider, including financial incentives that could rise to a conflict of interest for the rep.

The FINRA-prepared educational communication highlights the following potential implications of transferring assets to the new firm:

■ Whether financial incentives received by the representative may create a conflict of interest

■ That some assets may not be directly transferrable to the recruiting firm and, as a result, the customer may incur costs to liquidate and move those assets or account maintenance fees to leave them with his current firm

■ Potential costs related to transferring assets to the recruiting firm, including differences in the pricing structure and fees imposed by the customer's current firm and the recruiting firm

■ Differences in products and services between the customer's current firm and the recruiting firm

The new rule states that a member that hires a registered person must provide to a former customer (a natural person), in paper or electronic form, the educational communication when:

■ the member, directly or through that registered person, individually contacts the former customer to transfer assets; or

■ the former customer, absent individualized contact, transfers assets to an account assigned to the registered person at the member.

The communication is required at the time of contact with a former customer by the registered person or the member firm regarding transferring assets.

Contacting the customer may be done with written, electronic, or oral communication. Electronic communication may include a hyperlink directly to the educational communication. If the contact is oral, the member or registered person must notify the former customer that an educational communication that includes important considerations in deciding whether to transfer assets to the member will be provided not later than three business days after the contact.

If a former customer attempts to transfer assets, but no individualized contact with the former customer by the registered person or member occurs before the former customer seeks to transfer assets, the member must deliver the educational communication with the account transfer approval documentation.

The delivery of the communication applies for three months following the date the registered person begins employment or associates with the member.

FINRA Rule 2273 is not applicable when a former customer is contacted to transfer assets expressly states that she is not interested in transferring assets to the member. If the former customer later decides to transfer assets to the new member without further individualized contact within the period of three months following the date the registered person begins employment with the member, then the educational material is required to be sent. This rule is also not applicable to institutional accounts rather solely for natural persons.

QUICK QUIZ 2.C

Objective: Explain requirements for opening customer accounts

1. When filling out a new account form, which of the following would NOT be required?

A. Date of birth
B. Physical address of where you live
C. Customer's signature
D. Principal's signature

2. As part of the requirement to verify the identity of the person opening an account, all of the following are true EXCEPT

A. the applicant must provide a valid government picture ID
B. determine if the applicant is on a list of known or suspected terrorist individuals and groups
C. until the customer identification is verified, no transactions are allowed in the account
D. a person that has applied for, but not yet received, a Social Security number may still open an account

3. When opening an account for a registered representative of another broker-dealer, which of the following is necessary?

A. The registered representative must obtain the consent of the employing broker-dealer prior to opening the account.
B. Duplicate account statements are automatically sent to the employing broker-dealer on a monthly or quarterly basis.
C. The registered representative must notify his employer, in writing, that a trading account was opened at another broker-dealer.
D. The notification requirements are not required if the registered representative is listed on a joint account and does not contribute money to the account.

4. When a registered representative opens a trading account at another broker-dealer, all of the following are required EXCEPT

A. the rep must obtain permission of the employing broker-dealer prior to opening the account
B. the rep must inform the broker-dealer where the account is being opened of their employment status at the employing broker-dealer
C. permission is not required of the employing broker-dealer if the registered representative is purchasing securities directly from an investment company
D. after the account is opened the employing broker-dealer must be informed of each transaction in the account

All Quick Quiz answers are found at the end of their units.

2. 4   RETIREMENT PLANS

An important goal for many investors is to provide themselves with retirement income. Many individuals accomplish this through corporate retirement plans, others set up their own plans, and some have both individual and corporate retirement plans.

[handwritten margin notes: qualified = pre-tax contributions / Non-qualified = post-tax contributions]

There are two basic types of retirement plans in the United States: qualified and non-qualified. Generally speaking, qualified plans allow pretax contributions to be made, while nonqualified plans are funded with after-tax money. Both plans can allow money to grow tax deferred until needed. There are exceptions to these basic characteristics.

Contribution limits for qualified retirement plans vary and are adjusted from time to time.

A taxable distribution from any retirement plan is taxed as ordinary income, never as a capital gain.

2. 4. 1 NONQUALIFIED PLANS

Nonqualified plans may be used to favor certain employees (typically executives) because nondiscrimination rules are not applicable to nonqualified plans.

2. 4. 1. 1 Deferred Compensation Plan

[handwritten margin note: defer part of salary to retirement and it is taxed / then]

A **nonqualified deferred compensation plan** is an agreement between a company and an employee in which the employee agrees to defer receipt of current income in favor of payout at retirement. It is assumed that the employee will be in a lower tax bracket at retirement age (persons affiliated with the company solely as board members are not eligible for these plans because they are not considered employees for retirement planning purposes).

Deferred compensation plans may be somewhat risky because the employee covered by the plan has no right to plan benefits if the business fails. In this situation, the employee becomes a general creditor of the firm. Covered employees may also forfeit benefits if they leave the firm before retirement.

When the benefit is payable at the employee's retirement, it is taxable as ordinary income to the employee. The employer is entitled to the tax deduction at the time the benefit is paid out.

TAKE NOTE Deferred compensation plans usually benefit highly compensated employees that are just a few years from retirement.

2. 4. 1. 1. 1 Section 457 Plan

Section 457 plans are nonqualified retirement plans set up by state and local governments and tax-exempt employers for their employees and independent contractors that work for those entities. They function as deferred compensation plans in which earnings grow tax deferred and all withdrawals are taxed at the time of distribution. Employees may defer up to 100% of their compensation, up to an indexed contribution limit.

2. 4. 1. 2 Payroll Deduction Plan

Payroll deduction plans allow employees to authorize their employer to deduct a specified amount for retirement savings from their paychecks. The money is deducted after taxes are paid and may be invested in any number of retirement vehicles at the employee's option.

TEST TOPIC ALERT

You might think of a 401(k) plan as a payroll deduction plan. For the FINRA exams, 401(k) plans are considered salary reduction plans, not payroll deduction plans. In exam questions, assume that payroll deduction plans are nonqualified. Also note that 401(k) plans are qualified plans, whereas payroll deduction plans are not.

QUICK QUIZ 2.D

Objective: Contrast qualified and nonqualified retirement plans

1. Generally speaking, nonqualified retirement plans
   A. are funded with after-tax dollars
   B. must have a trust agreement
   C. may not discriminate with regard to who can participate
   D. must have IRS approval

2. A deferred compensation plan
   A. must allow all eligible employees to participate
   B. is funded through a trust agreement that protects the employee in the event the company goes out of business
   C. may not protect the employee from losing the deferred compensation should the employee leave the company before retirement.
   D. typically benefits younger employees

3. A 457 plan
   A. is a type of deferred compensation plan for employees of state and local municipalities
   B. will distribute money to participants, but only the earnings will be taxed
   C. is a type of qualified plan
   D. allows employees to defer up to 50% of income within the plan

All Quick Quiz answers are found at the end of their units.

2.5   INDIVIDUAL PLANS

The U.S. government encourages individuals to save for retirement by providing tax benefits to those that contribute to individual retirement accounts (IRAs).

2.5.1   IRA

IRAs were created to encourage people to save for retirement in addition to other retirement plans in which they participate. The IRA discussed here is sometimes referred to as a **traditional IRA**. Anyone who has earned income and is under age 70½ is allowed to make an annual contribution of up to an indexed maximum ($5,500 in 2014) or 100% of earned income, whichever is less. Earned income is defined as income from work (e.g., wages, salaries, bonuses, commissions, tips, and, believe it or not, alimony). Income from investments is not considered earned income. If the contribution limit is exceeded, a 6% excess contribution penalty applies to the amount over the allowable portion (unless corrected shortly thereafter as defined by IRS rules).

2. 5. 1. 1   Contribution limits

Between January 1 and April 15 (the last legal filing date), contributions and adjustments may be made to an IRA for both the current year and the previous year. Contributions of earned income may continue until age 70½. Contributions are fully deductible, regardless of income, if the investor is not covered by a qualified employer plan or, in the case of a defined benefit plan, is ineligible for coverage. If covered or, in the case of a defined benefit plan, eligible for coverage, contributions are only deductible if the taxpayer's **AGI (adjusted gross income)** falls within established income guidelines (and those amounts are not tested).

Spousal option is available for a spouse who has little or no income. The same amount can be contributed to the individual account and the spousal IRA.

An additional catch-up contribution is available for those age 50 and older.

Excess contributions are subject to a 6% penalty. The excess contribution penalty can be avoided by removing the excess contribution (and any earnings) prior to the legal filing date.

Certain investments are not permitted for funding IRAs, including:

- collectibles (e.g., antiques, gems, rare coins, works of art, stamps),
- life insurance contracts, and
- municipal bonds (which are considered inappropriate because the benefit of their tax-free interest is lost within a retirement plan).

Certain investment practices are also considered inappropriate. Those that are not permitted within IRAs or any other retirement plan include:

- margin account trading,
- short sales of stock, or
- uncovered call options.

Covered call writing is permissible because it does not increase risk. A covered call occurs when an investor writes a call option against stock the investor already owns. If the call is exercised and the investor is obligated to sell the stock, they simply sell the stock they already own.

TAKE NOTE   Although life insurance is not allowed within IRAs, other life insurance company products, such as annuities, are. Annuities are frequently used as funding vehicles for IRAs. Following is a partial list of which investments are appropriate for IRAs:

- Stocks and bonds
- Mutual funds (other than municipal bond funds)
- Unit investment trusts (UITs)
- Government securities
- U.S. government-issued gold and silver coins

2. 5. 1. 2   Distributions

Distributions may begin without penalty after age 59½ and **required minimum distributions (RMDs)** must begin by April 1 of the year after the individual turns 70½. Distributions before age 59½ are subject to a 10% penalty, as well as regular income tax. The 10% penalty is not applied in the event of:

- death;
- disability;
- purchase of a principal residence by a first-time homebuyer (up to $10,000);
- education expenses for the taxpayer, a spouse, a child, or a grandchild;
- medical premiums for unemployed individuals;
- medical expenses in excess of defined AGI limits; and
- Rule 72t: substantially equal periodic payments.

If RMDs do not begin by April 1 of the year after the individual turns 70½, a 50% insufficient distribution penalty applies. It is applicable to the amount that should have been withdrawn based on IRS life expectancy tables. Ordinary income taxes also apply to the full amount.

2. 5. 2   ROTH IRA

Created in 1997, **Roth IRAs** allow the same contribution amounts as traditional IRAs. The maximum contribution is 100% of earned income up to an indexed maximum. Both the catch-up provision for those age 50 or older and spousal Roth IRAs are available. Earnings accumulate tax deferred.

Unlike traditional IRAs, contributions are nondeductible (after-tax), contributions can be made to a Roth IRA beyond the age of 70½, and withdrawals from a Roth IRA need not begin at age 70½.

Contributors who have too much adjusted gross income may not contribute (number not testable). The owner of a Roth IRA can withdraw contributions at any time without tax or penalty.

If initial contributions to the Roth IRA are less than five years before withdrawal, no matter at what age, earnings withdrawn will trigger ordinary income taxes plus a 10% penalty.

Before age 59½, if the account is held five years, contributions and earnings may be withdrawn tax free in the case of death, disability, or first-time home purchase (up to $10,000). Other than for these exceptions, for the withdrawal of earnings from a Roth IRA to be tax- and penalty-free, the owner must be over 59½ years old and initial contributions must also have been made five years before the date funds are withdrawn.

The biggest advantage of Roth IRAs is that distributions (including earnings) that satisfy holding period requirements are income tax free.

2. 5. 3   ROLLOVERS AND TRANSFERS

Individuals may move their investments from one IRA to another IRA or from a qualified plan to an IRA. These movements are known as rollovers or transfers. Assets may also be rolled over into an employer's retirement plan, provided the employer is willing to accept such deposits.

A **rollover** occurs when an IRA account owner takes temporary ownership of IRA account funds when moving the account to another custodian. One hundred percent of the funds withdrawn must be rolled into the new account within 60 days or they will be subject to tax and a 10% early withdrawal penalty, if applicable. An individual can make only one rollover from an IRA to another (or the same) IRA in any 365-day period (not per calendar year), regardless of the number of IRAs the individual may own. The limit will apply by aggregating all of an individual's IRAs, including SEP and SIMPLE IRAs, as well as traditional and Roth IRAs, effectively treating them as one IRA for purposes of the limit. However,

- trustee-to-trustee transfers between IRAs are not limited, and
- conversions from traditional to Roth IRAs are not limited.

IRA assets may be directly transferred from an IRA or qualified plan. A **transfer** occurs when the account assets are sent directly from one custodian to another, and the account owner never takes possession of the funds. There is no limit on the number of transfers that may be made during a 12-month period.

If a participant in an employer-sponsored qualified plan leaves his place of employment, he may move plan assets to a **conduit IRA**. If the employee takes possession of the funds through a rollover, 20% of the distribution will be subject to federal withholding tax (withheld).

TAKE NOTE   An employee leaves work and the company must distribute the balance of his 401(k) plan. If the proceeds are made payable to the employee, a 20% withholding applies. If the proceeds are sent to another plan trustee, there is no withholding. The 20% withholding only occurs on distributions from an employer's qualified plan made directly to the plan participant.

2. 5. 3. 1   Conversions and Recharacterization

The IRS, during specified periods, has allowed investors to convert one type of IRA to another. In addition, the IRS has allowed, under current tax code, investors the opportunity to treat a contribution allocated to one type of IRA as if it had been made to a different type of IRA. It is known as recharacterizing the contribution.

The most common case of recharacterization is when a traditional IRA has been converted into a Roth IRA, and the participant wishes to go back to the traditional IRA instead of remaining in the Roth. This would be accomplished by having the contribution transferred from the Roth IRA back to the traditional IRA in a trustee-to-trustee transfer. If the transfer is made by the due date (including extensions) for the individual's tax return for the year during which the contribution is made, the individual can treat the original conversion as if it never happened.

There are several reasons why individual might choose to recharacterize their contributions, but here are two of the most common:

- Exceeding the earnings limitation on contributing to a Roth IRA. Example: A Roth contribution might have been made early in the year. Due to larger than expected earnings by year-end, the investor's adjusted gross income exceeds the allowable limit. Recharacterization is a way to "undo" the Roth IRA contribution and put the money into a traditional IRA.

- A significant decrease in the value of the account since the original conversion. Example: A conversion of $100,000 in a traditional IRA to a Roth IRA takes place. The investor has until April 15, or any available extension time for filing, to decide what to do. If on that date, the value of the Roth is less than the original amount converted, the investor will still owe ordinary income taxes on the $100,000 converted. But if the individual were to recharacterize the entire account (worth less than the amount originally converted), the funds would be back in a traditional IRA, and no taxes would be due until the money is withdrawn.

Be aware of the rules regarding conversions and recharacterizations. You cannot convert and reconvert an amount during the same tax year or, if later, during the 30-day period following a recharacterization. If you reconvert during either of these periods, it will be a failed conversion.

QUICK QUIZ 2.E

Objective: Recall characteristics of individual retirement plans

1.   How often can an IRA be rolled over to another IRA?

  A.   Once every 60 days
  B.   Once every 90 days
  C.   Once every 12 months
  D.   There are no limits on how often a rollover can occur

2.   Allowable investments within an IRA include all of the following EXCEPT

  A.   investment company securities
  B.   corporate stocks and bonds
  C.   certain U.S. government–minted gold and silver coins
  D.   collectibles such as postage stamps

3.   The main difference between a traditional IRA and a Roth IRA is

  A.   the traditional IRA is funded with after-tax dollars and the Roth IRA is funded with before-tax dollars
  B.   the Roth IRA has higher contribution limits
  C.   if meeting the requirements, distributions from a Roth IRA are tax-free, while distributions from traditional IRA's are taxed as ordinary income
  D.   if the individual has too much adjusted gross income, contributions to a traditional IRA are not allowed; no such limitation exists for Roth IRAs.

All Quick Quiz answers are found at the end of their units.

2.6   EMPLOYER-SPONSORED PLANS

There are many types of retirement plans that corporate entities can provide employees to encourage saving for retirement.

2.6.1   CORPORATE RETIREMENT PLANS

Corporate retirement plans fall into two categories: defined benefit or defined contribution.

A **defined benefit plan** promises a specific benefit at retirement that is determined by a formula involving typical retirement age, years of service, and compensation level achieved.

The amount of the contribution is determined by the plan's **trust agreement** and uses actuarial calculations involving investment returns, future interest rates, and other matters. This type of plan may be used by firms that wish to favor older employees; a much greater amount may be contributed for those with only a short time until retirement.

Defined contribution plans are easier to administer. The current contribution amount is specified by the plan's trust agreement and individual employee accounts are created; however, the benefit that will be paid at retirement is unknown. These plans favor younger employees because they have more time for the money to grow.

Following are several types of defined contribution plans:

- **Money purchase plans** are the simplest of the qualified defined contribution plans. Any employer that meets funding requirements may offer such a plan. The employer simply contributes a specified fraction of the employee's compensation up to an indexed maximum.

- **Profit-sharing plans** are a popular form of defined contribution plan. These plans do not require a fixed contribution formula and allow contributions to be skipped in years of low profits.

TAKE NOTE

All defined benefit and defined contribution plans, other than profit-sharing plans, require an annual contribution. Employers may skip contributions to profit-sharing plans in unprofitable years.

- **401(k) plans**, the most popular form of defined contribution retirement plan, allow the employee to elect to contribute a specific percentage of salary to a retirement account. Contributions are excluded from the employee's gross income and accumulate tax deferred. Employers may make matching contributions up to a specified percentage of the employee's contributions. Additionally, 401(k) plans permit certain hardship withdrawals.

- **Roth 401(k)** plans are a relatively new plan option. Roth 401(k) plans are now available as a plan option. A Roth 401(k), like a Roth IRA, requires after-tax contributions but allows tax-free withdrawals, provided the plan owner is at least 59½—though unlike a Roth IRA, there are no income limitations on who may have such a plan. Like a 401(k), it allows the employer to make matching contributions, but the employer's contributions must be made into a traditional 401(k) account. The employee, who would thus have two 401(k) accounts, may make contributions into either, but may not transfer money from one to the other once it has been deposited. In contrast to a Roth IRA, the account owner must begin withdrawals by the age of 70½ (unless still working—see Required Beginning Date in the following topic).

- **Simplified employee pension plans (SEPs)** are qualified individual retirement plans that offer self-employed persons and small businesses easy-to-administer pension plans. SEPs allow an employer to contribute money to SEP IRAs that its employees set up to receive employer contributions.

  Self-employed individuals may contribute up to a maximum amount each year to a SEP IRA for themselves or employees. Catch-up contributions are generally not allowed for the self-employed person. However, if an employee is enrolled in a SEP and the SEP permits non-SEP-IRA contributions be made to the SEP account, they may also make additional catch-up contributions to the SEP account if they are age 50 or older.

Generally, an employer can take an income tax deduction for contributions made each year to each employee's SEP. Also, the amounts contributed to a SEP by an employer on behalf of an employee are excludable from the employee's gross income.

■ **Savings incentive match plans for employees (SIMPLEs)** are retirement plans for businesses with fewer than 100 employees that have no other retirement plan in place. The employee makes pretax contributions into a SIMPLE up to an annual contribution limit. The employer makes matching contributions. Matching contribution requirements and limits for employers are specified by the IRS and include catch-up contributions for those age 50 and older.

2. 6. 2   REQUIRED BEGINNING DATE

We have already covered the age at which minimum distributions must begin for IRAs. What about in the case of qualified corporate plans? The term used here is "required beginning date." A participant must begin to receive distributions from his qualified retirement plan by April 1 of the later of the following years:

■ The first year after the calendar year in which he reaches age 70½

■ The first year after the calendar year in which he retires from employment with the employer maintaining the plan

In other words, if you are still working for that employer and are over 70½, minimum distributions are not required until after you retire.

2. 6. 3   STOCK PURCHASE PLANS AND STOCK OPTIONS

Some publicly traded companies offer their employees the ability to purchase company stock. There are several ways this can be done, but haps the most straightforward method of employee stock ownership can be found in an **employee stock purchase program (ESPP)**. These plans provide a convenient method for employees to purchase company shares.

Employee **stock purchase plans** are essentially a type of payroll deduction plan that allows employees to buy company stock without having to effect the transactions themselves. Money is automatically taken out of a participant's paycheck on an after-tax basis every pay period and accrues in an escrow account until it is used to buy company shares on a periodic basis, such as every six months. These plans are similar to other types of stock option plans in that they promote employee ownership of the company but do not have many of the restrictions that come with more formal stock option arrangements. Plus, they are designed to be somewhat more liquid in nature.

Here are the basics:

■ Contribute from 1% to 10% of salary. The contribution is a payroll deduction. This is calculated on pretax salary but taken **after tax** (unlike with a 401(k), there is no tax deduction on ESPP contributions).

■ At the end of a "purchase period," usually every 6 months, the employer will purchase company stock for participants using contributions during the purchase period. There will be a discount on the purchase price. The employer takes the price of the company stock at the beginning of the purchase period and the price at the end of the purchase period, **whichever is lower**, and THEN gives a discount from that price.

■ Participants can sell the purchased stock right away or hold on to the stocks longer for preferential tax treatment.

h Can sell right away

An employer may also offer **stock options** that give an employee the right to purchase a specified number of shares of the employer's common stock at a stated price over a stated time period. Unlike qualified retirement plans there are no nondiscrimination requirements for these plans. For publicly traded stock, the "strike" price (also called the grant or exercise price) is usually the market price of the stock at the time the option is granted. In most cases, there is a minimum time the employee must remain with the company in order to be able to use the option (the vesting period). The hope of the employee is that the market price of the employer's stock will increase in value. Then, the employee will be able to purchase the stock by exercising the option (purchasing the stock) at the lower strike price and then sell the stock at the current market price. These are available only to employees of the issuing company. Most states require that the stock option plan be approved by the board of directors.

2. 6. 4   TAX-SHELTERED ANNUITIES (403(B) PLANS)

Tax-sheltered annuities (TSAs) are available to employees of:

■ public educational institutions,

■ tax-exempt organizations (501(c)(3) organizations), and

■ religious organizations.

In general, the clergy and employees of charitable institutions, private hospitals, colleges and universities, elementary and secondary schools, and zoos and museums are eligible to participate if they are at least 21 years old and have completed one year of service.

TSAs are funded by elective employee deferrals. The deferred amount is excluded from the employee's gross income, and earnings accumulate tax free until distribution. A written salary reduction agreement must be executed between the employer and the employee.

As with other qualified plans, distributions are 100% taxable, and a 10% penalty is applied to distributions before age 59½.

TEST TOPIC ALERT

You might see a question that asks if a student can be a participant in an educational institution's TSA. The answer is no, because the plan is only available to employees.

QUICK QUIZ 2.F

Objective: Identify characteristics of employer-sponsored plans

1. All of the following statements regarding required minimum distributions from a 401(k) are true EXCEPT

    A. minimum required distributions begin by April 1 of the year following the year in which the participant turns 70½

    B. required minimum distributions are not required if the participant is still working

    C. minimum distributions not taken are subject to a 50% penalty

    D. minimum required distributions taken after age 70½ are taxed at a more favorable long-term capital gains rate

2. One of the most important characteristics of a profit-sharing plan is that

    A. the employer is not required to make a contribution if the company has no profits
    B. it favors older employees
    C. the employer may pick and choose who participates and who doesn't
    D. contributions are made with after-tax dollars and therefore only the growth is taxed at distribution

3. A type of payroll deduction plan that allows employees to purchase the company stock at a discount from the purchase price is called

    A. stock options
    B. employee stock purchase plans
    C. profit-sharing plan
    D. money purchase plan

4. A married 72-year-old employee, whose spouse is 55, works for a manufacturing firm and has $1 million in the firm's 401(k) plan. What is accurate regarding the minimum required distribution (RMD) from the 401(k) at this point in time?

    A. RMDs should have begun by April 1 of the year following the year in which the participant turned 70½.
    B. There is no required RMD at this time because the spouse is under age 59½.
    C. RMDs will begin after the employee retires.
    D. Any required minimum distributions not taken at this time are subject to income taxes plus a 10% penalty.

All Quick Quiz answers are found at the end of their units.

2. 7   EMPLOYEE RETIREMENT INCOME SECURITY ACT OF 1974 (ERISA)

The **Employee Retirement Income Security Act (ERISA)** was established to prevent abuse and misuse of pension funds. ERISA guidelines apply to private-sector (corporate) retirement plans and certain union plans—not public plans like those for government workers. Significant ERISA provisions include the following.

■ **Participation:** This identifies eligibility rules for employees. All employees must be covered if they are 21 years or older and have performed one year of full-time service, which ERISA defines as 1,000 hours or more.

■ **Funding:** Funds contributed to the plan must be segregated from other corporate assets. Plan trustees must administer and invest the assets prudently and in the best interest of all participants. IRS contribution limits must be observed.

■ **Vesting:** Vesting defines when an employer contribution to a plan becomes the employee's money, such as an employer matching contribution to a 401(k) plan. ERISA limits how long the vesting schedule can last before the employee is fully vested. Note that an employee is always fully vested in her own contributions to a plan.

■ **Communication:** The plan document must be in writing, and employees must be given annual statements of account and updates of plan benefits.

■ **Nondiscrimination:** All eligible employees must be treated impartially through a uniformly applied formula.

■ **Beneficiaries:** Beneficiaries must be named to receive an employee's benefits at death.

TEST TOPIC ALERT

You may see a question that asks for the type of plans that ERISA regulates. ERISA applies to private-sector plans (corporate) only. It does not apply to plans for federal or state government workers (public sector plans). Nor is it applicable to non-qualified plans.

QUICK QUIZ 2.G

Objective: Identify characteristics of employer-sponsored plans

1. ERISA rules and regulations include all of the following EXCEPT

    A. ERISA protects participants in private-sector retirement plans such as a pension from the creditors of the corporation
    B. a retirement plan covered by ERISA may not discriminate against who is eligible to participate in the plan
    C. it defines when employer contributions become the employee's money
    D. ERISA allows the corporation to be the beneficiary of plan benefits for employees before their retirement

2. Which of the following plans are covered by ERISA?

    A. A defined benefit plan offered by a manufacturing company to employees
    B. A pension plan offered to employees of the City of Detroit, Michigan
    C. A deferred compensation plan offered to select employees of a CPA firm
    D. A 457 plan

3. Which of the following ERISA rules ensure that a retirement plan is able to meet current and future obligations?

    A. Beneficiary rules
    B. Vesting rules
    C. Funding rules
    D. Participation rules

All Quick Quiz answers are found at the end of their units.

QUICK QUIZ ANSWERS

Quick Quiz 2.A

1. **A.** Retirement accounts must be set up as cash accounts. All trades must be paid for in full.

2. **B.** A prime brokerage account is one in which a customer, generally an institution, selects one member firm (the prime broker) to provide custody and other services, while other firms, called executing brokers, handle all trades placed by the customer.

3. **C.** A wrap account would allow the customer to bundle services of the broker-dealer, including trades, for a periodic fee (i.e., quarterly).

4. **D.** When inheriting securities, the recipient gets an automatic step up in cost basis to the current market value at the time of death ($22,000). Therefore, if she sells the stock for $21,000 she will realize a $1,000 capital loss.

Quick Quiz 2.B

1. **A.** Property acquired before marriage is considered to be owned separately, not jointly as stated in the answer choice.

2. **C.** In a tenants-in-common account, when one of the parties dies, the decedent's interest in the account passes to their estate.

3. **A.** With a sole proprietorship, because the businessowner is subject to unlimited liability, the account is subject to the creditors of the business.

Quick Quiz 2.C

1. **C.** The only signature required on a new account form is a principal's signature. Customers are not required to sign the new account form.

2. **C.** Until the customer identification is verified, transactions may be allowed in the account, not that no transactions are allowed in the account as stated in the answer choice.

3. **A.** Prior to opening an account at another broker-dealer, the registered representative must obtain the consent of the employing broker-dealer.

4. **D.** The broker-dealer where the account is held is not required to inform the employing broker-dealer of each transaction in the account but is required to provide duplicates of trades if requested.

Quick Quiz 2.D

1. **A.** Generally speaking, nonqualified retirement plans are funded with after-tax dollars.

2. **C.** A deferred compensation plan may not protect the employee from losing the deferred compensation should the employee leave the company prior to retirement.

3. **A.** A 457 plan is a type of deferred compensation plan for employees of state and local municipalities.

Quick Quiz 2.E

1. **C.** An IRA can be rolled over to another IRA once every 12 months.

2. **D.** Collectibles such as postage stamps, art, baseball cards, and the like are not allowable investments for retirement accounts.

3. **C.** If meeting the requirements, distributions from a Roth IRA are tax-free while distributions from traditional IRA's are taxed as ordinary income.

Quick Quiz 2.F

1. **D.** Minimum required distributions taken after age 70 ½ are taxed, as are all taxable distributions from retirement accounts, as ordinary income.

2. **A.** One of the most important characteristics of a profit-sharing plan is the employer is not required to make a contribution if the company has no profits.

3. **B.** A type of payroll deduction plan that allows employees to purchase the company stock at a discount from the purchase price is called an employee stock purchase plan.

4. **C.** A participant is not required to take minimum distributions from the employer's 401(k) while still working. After retirement starts, RMDs from a qualified retirement plan must begin by April 1 of the first year after the calendar year in which the plan participant retires from employment with the employer maintaining the plan.

Quick Quiz 2.G

1. **D.** ERISA does NOT allow the corporation to be the beneficiary of plan benefits for employees before their retirement.

2. **A.** A defined benefit plan offered by a manufacturing company to employees is covered by ERISA. Only private-sector plans are covered by ERISA, not state or local government plans (public sector plans).

3. **C.** Funding rules ensure that a retirement plan is able to meet current and future obligations under ERISA.

3

Customer Information, Risk and Suitability, Product Information

An important part of a registered representative's work is to identify the customer and understand financial needs. Only with a thorough knowledge of the customer's financial and nonfinancial information and tax status can the representative make suitable investment recommendations and provide appropriate information for the customer to use in making investment decisions. The representative must also understand the various forms of investment risk and the relationship between risk and reward inherent in securities investment. This gathering and processing of information is covered in this unit and will include portfolio theory, fundamental analysis, and product selection based on objectives of the customer.

The Series 7 exam will include 91 questions on the topics covered in units 3, 4, 5, and 6. (Function 3 of the FINRA exam). ■

In this Unit you will learn to:

- **apply** financial and nonfinancial information to know your customer before making recommendations;

- **match** customer objectives to types of products;

- **identify** various types of risk;

- **summarize** portfolio analysis and modern portfolio theory;

- **distinguish** the characteristics of fundamental analysis;

- **distinguish** the characteristics of technical analysis;

- **distinguish** characteristics, risks, and recommendations of common stock;

- **distinguish** characteristics, risks, and recommendations of preferred stock;

- **define** options and characteristics;

- **describe** the use of debt securities based on different investment objectives;

- **identify** various money market securities and risks;

- **compare** the different types of investment companies;

- **compare** the recommendations of mutual funds to investor objectives;

- **compare** share classes, pricing, and expenses of mutual fund shares;

- **summarize** voluntary accumulation plans;

- **define** annuities and their characteristics;

- **compare** the different ways to distribute money from an annuity;

- **recall** suitability considerations of annuities;

- **distinguish** the characteristics of variable life insurance and its suitability; and

- **define** the general characteristics of Education Savings Accounts.

3. 1   KNOW YOUR CUSTOMER

The *Know Your Customer* (KYC) rule places an obligation on the firm and associated person to seek information from customers. Customers are not required to provide all information asked; therefore, the KYC rule provides some flexibility when information is unavailable despite the fact that the firm or the associated person asked for it.

In this case, when some customer information is unavailable despite a firm's request for it, the firm may narrow the range of recommendations it makes. The rule does not prohibit a firm from making a recommendation in the absence of certain customer-specific information, if the firm has enough information about the customer to have a reasonable basis to believe the recommendation is suitable based on what the firm knows. The significance of specific types of customer information will depend on the facts and circumstances of the particular case. Of course, the firm itself may require, in order for customers to receive recommendations, that customers provide certain types of information.

Both financial and nonfinancial information must be gathered before making investment recommendations.

3. 1. 1   CUSTOMER PROFILE: FINANCIAL INVESTMENT CONSIDERATIONS

Before making a recommendation for a new customer, a representative must try to find out as much about that person's financial and nonfinancial situation as possible. Financial investment considerations can be expressed as a sum of money. Financial questions have answers that show up on a customer's personal balance sheet or income statement. Asking a customer, "When would you like to retire?" is not a financial question; it is nonfinancial. The answer does not show up on the customer's personal balance sheet or income statement.

3. 1. 1. 1   Customer Balance Sheet *- get understanding of customers Assets and liabilities*

$$A - L = E$$

An individual, like a business, has a financial balance sheet—a snapshot of his financial condition at a point in time. A customer's net worth is determined by subtracting liabilities from assets (assets – liabilities = net worth). Representatives determine the status of a customer's personal balance sheet by asking questions similar to the following.

- What are the values of tangible assets? Home? Car? Collectibles?
- What are your liabilities? How much do you owe on your mortgage? Car? Outstanding Loans?
- What are the values of securities you currently own?
- Have you established long-term investment accounts, and what are the values of those accounts? Do you have an IRA, corporate pension, or profit-sharing plan; and what are the values of those plans? What is the cash value of your life insurance?
- What is your net worth? How much of it is liquid?

3. 1. 1. 2   Customer Income Statement

To make appropriate investment recommendations, representatives must know the customer's income situation. They gather information about the customer's marital status, finan-

cial responsibilities, projected inheritances, and pending job changes by asking the following questions:

- What is your total gross income? Total family income?
- How much do you pay in monthly expenses?
- What is your net spendable income after expenses? How much of this is available for investment?

TAKE NOTE   Before recommending any investment to a customer, a representative must, at a minimum, make a reasonable effort to obtain information concerning the customer's financial status, tax status, and investment objectives.

3. 1. 1. 3   Customer Profile: Nonfinancial Investment Considerations

Once representatives have an idea of the customer's financial status, they gather information on the nonfinancial status. A nonfinancial investment consideration is one that cannot be expressed as a sum of money or a numerical cash flow (risk tolerance, or tax bracket, for example). Nonfinancial considerations often carry more weight than the financial considerations and include the following:

- Age
- Marital status
- Number and ages of dependents
- Employment
- Employment of family members
- Current and future family educational needs
- Current and future family health care needs
- Risk tolerance
- Attitude toward investing
- Tax status

No matter how much an analysis of a customer's financial status tells the representative about the ability to invest, it is the customer's emotional acceptance of investing and motivation to invest that mold the portfolio.

To understand a customer's aptitude for investment, the representative should ask questions similar to the following.

- What kind of risks can you afford to take?
- How liquid must your investments be?
- How important are tax considerations?
- Are you seeking long-term or short-term investments?
- What is your investment experience?
- What types of investments do you currently hold?
- How would you react to a loss of 5% of your principal? 10%? 50%?
- What level of return do you consider good? Poor? Excellent?
- What combination of risks and returns do you feel comfortable with?

- What is your investment temperament?
- Do you get bored with stable investments?
- Can you tolerate market fluctuations?
- How stable is your income?
- Do you anticipate any financial changes in the future?

TAKE NOTE

A representative's job is to assist customers in meeting their financial objectives. Responsible reps must learn all about the customers' financial situations. Securities laws prohibit unsuitable recommendations.

If a customer contacts a registered representative and wants to purchase securities that the rep feels are not suitable for the client, the registered representative has a responsibility to tell the customer that she feels the trade is not suitable. If the customer insists on the purchase, the RR should place the order and mark the trade unsolicited.

QUICK QUIZ 3.A

Objective: Apply financial and nonfinancial information to know your customer before making recommendations

1. All of the following are financial considerations in a customer profile EXCEPT

    A. 401(k) balance
    B. wanting to retire at age 65
    C. annual income
    D. amount of mortgage on home

2. A retail investor opens an account at your firm but only provides minimum information and that she wants to invest for retirement in 20 years and is willing to take moderate risk. Which of the following statements best describes the responsibilities of the registered representative handling the account?

    A. Recommendations cannot be made because the customer refuses to provide income information, personal assets and liabilities, or how much can be invested.
    B. The account cannot be opened without financial and nonfinancial information.
    C. Only unsolicited trades can be made in this account.
    D. The representative is limited to what can be recommended to the customer based on the information that was provided.

3. Which of the following would be considered nonfinancial investment considerations on a customer profile?

I. Total fixed assets
II. Attitude toward risk
III. Monthly income available for investment
IV. Tax bracket

A. I and II
B. I and III
C. II and IV
D. III and IV

All Quick Quiz answers are found at the end of their units.

3. 2 CUSTOMER INVESTMENT OBJECTIVES

People have many reasons for investing. Most customers claim that they invest so that their money will grow. With careful questioning, however, representatives may learn that because of tax status, income, or other events, some growth investments are appropriate while others are not. Some basic financial objectives that customers have are discussed in the following sections.

If a customer wants to invest but does not have a solid foundation to build an investment portfolio, the foundation should be solidified first. Consider the following before investing:

■ Are insurance needs met?

— Life, health, disability

■ Are there sufficient cash reserves (typically three to six months of living expenses) in the event of

— job loss,

— medical emergencies, and

— major home or car repairs?

A prospective investor who does not have a solid foundation from which to invest really should not be investing money. Consider a $5,000 investment in equity securities when sufficient cash reserves are not in place. Six months after the investment the furnace needs to be replaced and the equity securities must be liquidated to pay for a new furnace. However, the $5,000 investment isn't worth $5,000 anymore because of a downturn in the market; it is only worth $4,000.

3. 2. 1 PRESERVATION OF CAPITAL

For many people, the most important investment objective is to preserve their capital. In general, when clients speak of safety, they usually mean **preservation of capital**. Recommendations may include the following:

■ Money market securities
■ Money market mutual funds

- Certificates of deposit (CDs)
- Government securities
- Principal-protected funds may also be appropriate if they are looking to invest for a longer time horizon

3. 2. 2 CURRENT INCOME

Many investors, particularly those on fixed incomes, want to generate additional **current income.**

- Traditional debt securities such as corporate, government, municipal bonds, and agency securities may provide steady interest income.
- Equity securities may be purchased for the dividends they produce; these include preferred stocks, utilities, and blue-chip stocks that have a solid dividend paying history.
- Many pooled investments can provide income as well, such as income-oriented mutual funds.

TAKE NOTE

to receive security's
dividend = must purchase
before ex-div date

- If needed, the declaration date, ex-date, record date, payable date, and settlement date are defined in your glossary.

- Dividends are not guaranteed and must be declared by the board of directors. In order to be entitled to a dividend, the stock must settle no later than the record date.

- Regular way settlement for corporate securities is trade date plus 2 business days (T+2).

- The first day an investor can trade for a security and not receive the dividend is called the ex-date or ex-dividend date.

- The value of the security is reduced by the amount of the distribution on the ex-date.

3. 2. 3 CAPITAL GROWTH (CAPITAL APPRECIATION)

Capital growth refers to an increase in an investment's value over time. This can come from increases in the security's value. Growth-oriented investments are equity oriented.

EXAMPLE

When an investor has a time horizon that is 7-10+ years away, such as retiring or funding a college education, investing for capital appreciation is appropriate. When investors want growth, equity securities, specifically common stock, is appropriate.

Generally speaking, common stock with earnings momentum, a high price/earnings ratio and low dividend payout ratio are considered growth oriented.

3. 2. 4   TAX ADVANTAGES

Investors often seek ways to reduce their taxes. Some products, like individual retirement arrangements (accounts) (IRAs) and annuities, allow interest to accumulate tax deferred (an investor pays no taxes until money is withdrawn from the account). Other products, like municipal bonds, offer tax-free interest income.

TAKE NOTE   Municipal bonds, which provide federally tax-free income, are not suitable for retirement accounts. The federally tax-free interest income will be fully taxable upon withdrawal.

3. 2. 5   PORTFOLIO DIVERSIFICATION

You know the saying "Don't put all your eggs in one basket!" Investors with portfolios concentrated in only one or a few securities or investments are exposed to much higher risks. For them, portfolio diversification can be an important objective. Mutual funds, by their nature, tend to be diversified. An asset allocation fund includes stocks, bonds, cash, and perhaps hard assets and real estate, making it a good option when it comes to diversification. Also, consider a foreign, international, or global fund to increase **diversification** for a portfolio that is domestic in nature.

3. 2. 6   LIQUIDITY

Some people want immediate access to their money at all times. A product is liquid if a customer can sell it quickly at face amount (or very close to it) or at a fair market price.

Remember that a liquid investment does not mean you won't lose money on your investment. It simply means you can get the current market value of the investment quickly.

Liquid investments include:

- securities listed on an exchange or unlisted Nasdaq securities;
- mutual funds;
- exchange-traded funds; and
- real estate investment trusts (REITs).

Illiquid investments include:

- annuities, when initially purchased and/or when the annuitant is under age 59½;
- real estate;
- direct participation programs;
- hedge funds; and
- funds of hedge funds.

EXAMPLE

An investor buys $10,000 of a listed security on the New York Stock Exchange (NYSE). The value drops to $9,000 and the investor sells the security and receives $9,000 when the trade settles two business days later. The investor lost money on the investment, but the investment was liquid because when he sold it, the current market value was received quickly.

TEST TOPIC ALERT

Annuities, particularly when issued, are not considered liquid. Most annuities have a surrender penalty that may last 7-10 years or longer. In addition, there are taxes and a 10% tax penalty for withdrawals before 59½ years of age.

3. 2. 7   SPECULATION

A customer may want to speculate—that is, try to earn much higher-than-average returns in exchange for higher-than-average risks. Investors who are interested in speculation may be interested in:

- option contracts;
- high-yield bonds;
- unlisted or non-Nasdaq stocks or bonds;
- sector funds;
- precious metals; and
- special situation funds.

As a registered representative, one must always determine the suitability of such recommendations.

TEST TOPIC ALERT   A number of exam questions will require you to analyze a customer's situation and select an appropriate recommendation. Here are some guidelines:

Investor Objective	Recommendations
Preservation of Capital/Safety	CDs, money market mutual funds, fixed annuities, government securities and funds, agency issues, investment grade corporate bonds and corporate bond funds
Growth	Common stock, common stock mutual funds
(Balanced/moderate growth)	Blue-chip stocks, defensive stocks
(Aggressive growth)	Technology stocks, sector funds
Income	Bonds (but not zero coupons), REITs, CMOs
(Tax-free income)	Municipal bonds, municipal bond funds, Roth IRAs
(High-yield income)	Below investment grade corporate bonds, corporate bond funds
(From stock portfolio)	Preferred stocks, utility stocks, blue-chip stocks
Liquidity	Securities listed on an exchange, Nasdaq stocks or bonds, mutual funds, publicly traded REITS
Portfolio Diversification	Mutual funds, in general; more specifically, asset allocation funds and balanced funds
	For equity portfolios, add some debt and vice versa
	For domestic portfolios, add some foreign securities
	For bond portfolios, diversify by region/rating
Speculation	Option contracts, DPPs, high-yield bonds, unlisted/non-Nasdaq stocks or bonds, sector funds, precious metals, commodities, futures

QUICK QUIZ 3.B   Objective: Match customer objectives to types of products

1. When filling out a customer profile, you discover that the only security this investor owns is a listed NYSE stock now valued at $100,000 that was inherited from the customer's father 10 years ago when it was valued at $40,000. Which of the following should be discussed with her?

    A. This stock has performed exceedingly well and, depending on her investment objectives, should not be touched.
    B. You understand the sentimental value of this investment, but there is a risk when all your money is tied to one security. It may make sense to diversify the money based on an asset allocation model, depending on her investment objectives.
    C. This stock has liquidity risk and should be sold and placed into a more liquid position.
    D. The stock should be combined with a bond in order to diversify her portfolio.

(handwritten) doesnt talk about domestic/international or risk criteria but answer fits this all into account   C

2. A customer owns an equity income fund, an equity growth fund, and a corporate bond fund. She is looking to add a level of diversification and growth. Which of the following choices would be most appropriate for you to recommend?

   A.   An international stock fund
   B.   A value managed equity growth fund
   C.   A high-yield bond fund *(handwritten)* ~ more div't than govt bond and not present
   D.   A government bond fund

3. A couple in their early 30s has been married for 4 years. Both work and have no children, so their disposable income is relatively high. They live in the suburbs and are planning to buy a condominium downtown. They need a safe place to invest the amount they have saved for about 6 months for their down payment. Which of the following mutual funds is the most suitable for these customers?

(handwritten) B̶ C

   A.   ATF Capital Appreciation Fund
   B.   ABC Growth & Income Fund
   C.   LMN Cash Reserves Money Market Fund
   D.   XYZ Investment-Grade Bond Fund

(handwritten) money market: good, safe, short term

All Quick Quiz answers are found at the end of their units.

3. 3   ANALYZING FINANCIAL RISKS AND REWARDS

Because all investments involve trade-offs, the representative's task is to select securities that will provide the right balance between investor objectives and investment characteristics.

New financial instruments, new classes of mutual funds, and new forms of variable contracts are also constantly being developed. The fact that something is the newest does not make it a good investment for a customer. **Risk factors** and suitability requirements apply to new investment instruments just as much as those that have been around for centuries.

3. 3. 1   INVESTMENT RISKS

In general terms, the greater the risk the investor assumes, the greater the potential for reward. Representatives should consider all potential risks in determining the suitability of various types of investments. Following are the most common risks. Those that affect all investments are called **systematic risks**. Those that affect some and not others are **unsystematic risks**.

(handwritten) Systematic = unavoidable through diversification

3. 3. 1. 1   Business Risk

Whether caused by bad management or unfortunate circumstances, some businesses will inevitably fail, even more so during economic recessions. Typically when a business fails, it liquidates (sells off its assets) in a bankruptcy, pays its creditors from the proceeds, and pays whatever is left, if anything, to its shareholders. **Business risk** is a form of unsystematic risk, it affects companies and industries individually. Business risk can be reduced by diversifying investments.

(handwritten) i.e. risk you dont get paid back by company you invested in or loaned $ to when they go bankrupt

---

EXAMPLE   A large manufacturer has just been charged with a major accounting scandal by
the SEC. As a result, the company's stock price falls significantly. The scandal does not
impact the stocks of other manufacturers in the industry.

3. 3. 1. 2   Inflation Risk

Also known as **purchasing power risk** or **constant dollar risk**, **inflation risk** is the effect
of continually rising prices on investments, resulting in less purchasing power as time goes on.

A client who buys a fixed return security such as a bond, fixed annuity, or preferred stock
may not see the investment keep pace with inflation.

3. 3. 1. 3   Capital Risk

Capital risk or **principal risk** is the potential for an investor to lose all his money (invested
capital) under circumstances either related or unrelated to an issuer's financial strength.

3. 3. 1. 4   Timing Risk

Even an investment in the soundest company with the most profit potential might do
poorly simply because the investment was timed wrongly. The risk to an investor of buying or
selling at the wrong time and incurring losses or lower gains is known as **timing risk**.

EXAMPLE   Short-term investors are subject to timing risk. When investing on the absolute
worst day to invest each year (in other words, at the very top of the market before it
fell), the average time to make your money back has been three years.

3. 3. 1. 5   Interest Rate Risk

Interest rate risk refers to the sensitivity of an investment's price or value to fluctuations
in interest rates. The term is generally associated with debt (i.e., bonds, bond funds) and preferred stocks because their prices are interest rate sensitive. An inverse relationship exists with
these securities; as yields go up, prices go down, and vice versa.

Know that the longer a bond's maturity (or duration), the more volatile it is in response to
interest rate changes compared with similar short-term bonds. For bonds with short maturities,
the opposite is true. Their prices remain fairly stable because investors generally will not sell
them at deep discounts or buy them at high premiums.

EXAMPLE   If interest rates go up, the overall price of debt securities, no matter how diversified the debt portfolio is, will decline. Therefore, we can define interest rate risk as a
type of systematic risk.

TEST TOPIC ALERT

Short-term interest rates are more volatile than long-term interest rates because they change more frequently. The federal funds rate is considered volatile because it changes daily. Make sure you differentiate between the question that is asking about interest rate volatility (short term is more volatile) versus price volatility (long term is more volatile).

3. 3. 1. 5. 1   Duration

Duration is another useful tool in bond calculations; it is a measure of the amount of time a bond will take to pay for itself. Each interest payment is taken to be part of a discounted cash flow, so there is more to the calculation than simply adding up the interest payments. For the Series 6, remember that duration is often used to assess the sensitivity of a bond in response to interest rate changes—the longer the duration, the greater the sensitivity, and thus greater interest rate risk in an environment of changing interest rates. Remember also that the duration of an interest-paying bond is always shorter than the time to its maturity because the interest payments can be reinvested and earn additional interest. By way of comparison, the duration of a zero-coupon bond is always equal to the time to its maturity because there is only one payment—the one made when the bond matures.

3. 3. 1. 6   Reinvestment Risk

When interest rates decline, it is difficult for bond investors to reinvest the proceeds from investment distributions and maintain the same level of return at the same level of (default) risk. **Reinvestment risk** is mostly associated with bonds that mature or when a bond or preferred stock is called by the issuer.

EXAMPLE

In 1979, an investor purchased a 12%, 30-year Treasury bond and earned 12% for 30 years. But when that bond matured in 2009, interest rates had dropped to below 5%. The investor could not reinvest his Treasury bond proceeds and get 12% with no default risk anymore.

3. 3. 1. 7   Market Risk — Systematic

Both stocks and bonds involve some degree of **market risk**—the risk that investors may lose some of their principal due to price volatility in the overall market (also known as systematic risk).

An investor cannot diversify away market risk. If the entire market is in a tailspin, all of the investor's securities will likely decline.

EXAMPLE

If the S&P 500, an index of 500 large-cap stocks, drops in value by 10%, it is highly likely that every investor that owns a stock portfolio has lost money as well, even if that stock portfolio was composed of many different stocks in many different industries.

TEST TOPIC ALERT   Market risk is a type of systematic risk.

3. 3. 1. 8   Credit Risk

Credit risk, also called financial risk or default risk, involves the danger of losing all or part of one's invested principal through an issuer's failure. Credit risk is associated with debt securities, not equity securities, and varies with the investment product.

Bonds backed by the federal government or municipalities tend to be very secure and have low credit risk. Long-term bonds involve more credit risk than short-term bonds because of the increased uncertainty that results from holding bonds for many years.

Bond investors concerned about credit risks should pay attention to the ratings. Two of the best-known rating services that analyze the financial strength of thousands of corporate and municipal issuers are Moody's Investors Service and Standard & Poor's Corporation.

To a great extent, a bond's value depends on how much credit risk investors take. The higher the rating, the less likely the bond is to default and, therefore, the lower the coupon rate. Clients seeking the highest-possible yields from bonds might want to buy bonds with lower ratings; higher yields reward investors for taking more credit risk.

There is also a variable price difference between speculative and investment-grade debt, other things such as maturity date being equal. During times of confidence in the economy, the price of a AAA bond and that of a BB bond, for example, will be closer together than during periods of economic uncertainty. This reflects investors' reduced willingness to take risks during periods of uncertainty: speculative debt is discounted more than during periods of confidence.

Bond Ratings

Standard & Poor's	Moody's	Interpretation
Bank-grade (investment-grade) bonds:		
AAA	Aaa	Highest rating. Capacity to repay principal and interest judged high.
AA	Aa	Very strong. Only slightly less secure than the highest rating.
A	A	Judged to be slightly more susceptible to adverse economic conditions.
BBB	Baa	Adequate capacity to repay principal and interest. Slightly speculative.
Speculative (noninvestment-grade) bonds:		
BB	Ba	Speculative. Significant chance that issuer could miss an interest payment.
B	B	Issuer has missed one or more interest or principal payments.
C	Caa	No interest is being paid on bond at this time.
D	D	Issuer is in default. Payment of interest or principal is in arrears.

3. 3. 1. 9   Liquidity Risk

The risk that a client might not be able to sell an investment and receive its current market value quickly is known as **liquidity risk**.

The marketability of the securities you recommend must be consistent with the client's liquidity needs.

EXAMPLE

It is not always easy or quick to turn real estate, or thinly traded securities, into cash. Unlisted, non-Nasdaq securities are considered thinly traded.

For debt securities, the higher-quality, shorter-term debt will be more liquid than longer-term, lower-quality debt.

3. 3. 1. 10   Legislative/Political/Social Risk

Legislative risk exists because federal and state legislatures have the power to change laws and this can impact securities (companies) negatively and result in capital loss for investors.

Risk associated with the possibility of unfavorable government action or social changes resulting in a loss of value is also called **social risk** or **political risk**. Political risk is an important risk to discuss when recommending foreign or international investments because governments outside the United States may not be as stable as ours.

3. 3. 1. 11   Call Risk

Related to reinvestment risk, **call risk** is the risk that a bond might be called by the issuer before maturity, and investors cannot reinvest their principal at the same or a higher rate of return. When interest rates are falling, bonds with higher coupon rates are most likely to be called.

Investors concerned about call risk should look for **call protection**, a period of time during which a bond may not be called. Corporate and municipal issuers generally provide some years of call protection.

TAKE NOTE

Bond funds can't be called, but the bonds within the bond fund's portfolio can be called.

3. 3. 1. 11. 1   Advantages of a Call to the Issuer

Callable bonds can benefit the issuer in many ways.

- If general interest rates decline, the issuer can redeem bonds with a high interest rate and replace them with bonds with a lower rate.
- The issuer can call bonds to reduce its debt any time after the initial call date.
- The issuer can replace short-term debt issues with long-term issues and vice versa.
- The issuer can call bonds as a means of forcing the conversion of convertible corporate bonds.

3. 3. 1. 12 Currency Risk

This is the risk that changes in the rate of exchange will adversely affect an investment. As a rule of thumb, an investor who purchases an international fund (e.g., a foreign bond fund) will lose if the U.S. dollar appreciates against the foreign currency. The investor will profit if the U.S. dollar weakens (depreciates) against the foreign currency.

QUICK QUIZ 3.C

Objective: Identify various types of risk

1. Investors cannot diversify away which of these risks?

   A. Business risk
   B. Default risk
   C. Legislative risk
   D. Market risk

2. A conservative customer is invested in a large-cap, value-managed equity fund. The stock market drops 10% due to a poor economic forecast for the country. Your customer is upset that his conservative mutual fund lost almost as much as the stock market. What risks does your customer need to understand?

   I.   Business risk
   II.   Market risk
   III. Systematic risk
   IV.   Unsystematic risk

   A. I and III
   B. I and IV
   C. II and III
   D. II and IV

3. All of the following would be appropriate for a conservative investor seeking income EXCEPT

   A. an immediate fixed annuity
   B. an investment-grade corporate bond fund
   C. a high-yield bond fund
   D. a utility fund

4. Which of the following would an issuer most likely call?

   A. High-interest bond, callable at a premium
   B. High-interest bond, callable at par
   C. Low-interest bond, callable at a premium
   D. Low-interest bond, callable at par

All Quick Quiz answers are found at the end of their units.

3. 4 PORTFOLIO OR ACCOUNT ANALYSIS AND ITS APPLICATION TO PRODUCT SELECTION

By analyzing an investment portfolio and analyzing an account, products may be selected to fit the needs of the customer. One of the important items to consider is the performance of various securities that are recommended.

The securities and performance measures will depend on the information gathered and the customer's investment experience. Aggressive investors may try timing the market and seek capital appreciation.

EXAMPLE

A customer may like moving in and out of the market. If trading a lot, it would be important to know whether market prices are going up, have started to slide, or seem to have reached a plateau. On the other hand, a buy-and-hold investor may be more concerned about the stock's value 15 or 20 years in the future, and is likely to be more interested in whether it has a pattern of earnings growth and seems to be well positioned for future expansion.

With a conservative investor or one who is approaching retirement, the primary concern may be the income your investments provide. An examination of the interest rate that bonds and certificates of deposit (CDs) are paying in relation to current market rates would be important. Also, an evaluation of the yield from stock and mutual funds bought for the income they provide is important. Of course, if market rates are down, reinvestment opportunities may disappoint as existing bonds mature. There may be a temptation to buy investments with a lower rating in expectation of getting a potentially higher return. In either event, a performance measure that assesses the risk to the results would be helpful when making investment decisions.

In **measuring investment performance**, be sure to avoid comparing apples to oranges. Finding and applying the right evaluation standards for investments is important. Otherwise, the wrong conclusions may result.

EXAMPLE

There's little reason to compare yield from a growth mutual fund with yield from a Treasury bond because they don't fulfill the same role in a portfolio. Instead, measure performance for a growth fund by the standards of other growth investments, such as a growth mutual fund index or an appropriate market index. Here are some concepts to consider when evaluating the performance of your investments including yield, rate of return, and capital gains and losses.

3. 4. 1 DIVERSIFICATION

Diversification, with its emphasis on variety, allows the spreading of assets around. In short, don't put all your investment eggs in one basket.

3. 4. 1. 1   Asset Allocation

Asset allocation (more accurately, but rarely stated, asset class allocation) refers to the spreading of portfolio funds among different asset classes. Proponents of asset allocation feel that the mix of assets within a portfolio, rather than individual stock selection or marketing timing, is the primary factor underlying the variability of returns in portfolio performance. There are three major types (each with subclasses) of asset classes:

- Stock, with subclasses based on market capitalization, value versus growth, and foreign equity
- Bonds, with subclasses based on maturity (intermediate versus long-term), and issuer (Treasury versus corporate versus non-U.S. issuers)
- Cash, focusing mainly on the standard risk-free investment, the 90-day Treasury bill, but also including other short-term money market instruments

In some instances, tangible assets, such as real estate (usually in the form of REITs), precious metals and other commodities, and certain collectibles (think fine art), are part of the asset allocation because these types of assets tend to reduce inflation risk. Increasingly, institutional investors (and some very high net worth individuals due to the high cost of entry) are using such alternative investment asset classes as hedge funds, private equity, and venture capital.

3. 4. 1. 1. 1   Strategic Asset Allocation

Strategic asset allocation refers to the proportion of various types of investments composing a long-term investment portfolio.

EXAMPLE

A standard asset allocation model suggests subtracting a person's age from 100 to determine the percentage of the portfolio to be invested in stocks. According to this method, a 30-year-old would be 70% invested in stocks and 30% in bonds and cash; a 70-year-old would be invested 30% in stocks with the remainder in bonds and cash.

Over time, the portfolio is **rebalanced** to bring the asset mix back to the target allocations. If the stock market should perform better than expected, the client's proportion of stocks to bonds would be out of balance. So, on some timely basis (perhaps quarterly), stocks would be sold and bonds would be purchased (or funds would be placed in cash) to bring the proportions back to the desired levels.

3. 4. 1. 1. 2   Tactical Asset Allocation

Tactical asset allocation refers to short-term portfolio adjustments that adjust the portfolio mix between asset classes in consideration of current market conditions.

EXAMPLE   If the stock market is expected to do well over the near term, a portfolio manager may allocate greater portions of a portfolio to stocks. If the market is expected to decline, the portfolio manager may allocate greater portions of the portfolio entirely to bonds and cash.

3. 4. 2   MODERN PORTFOLIO THEORY

Managing risk is about the allocation and diversification of holdings in a portfolio. Investments should be chosen with an eye to what is already owned and how the new investment helps achieve greater balance.

For example, an investment strategy might include some investments that may be volatile because they have the potential to increase dramatically in value, when other investments in your portfolio are unlikely to have the same potential.

Modern portfolio theory, (MPT, portfolio theory) employs a scientific approach to measuring risk and, by extension, to choosing investments. It involves calculating projected returns of various portfolio combinations to identify those that are likely to provide the best returns at different levels of risk. It is the concept of minimizing risk by combining volatile and price-stable investments in a single portfolio.

Harry Markowitz, the founder of MPT, explained how to best assemble a diversified portfolio and proved that the portfolio with a lower amount of volatility would do better than a portfolio with a greater amount of volatility.

Modern portfolio theory focuses on the relationships among all the investments in a portfolio. This theory holds that specific risks can be diversified away by building portfolios of securities whose returns are not correlated. MPT seeks to reduce the risk in a portfolio while simultaneously increasing expected returns.

Holding securities that tend to move in the same direction as one another does not lower an investor's risk. Diversification reduces risk only when assets whose prices move inversely, or at different times, in relation to one another are combined.

In other words, MPT wants securities in a portfolio to have **negative correlation**, not **positive correlation**. Perfect negative correlation is − 1.0 and would indicate that if one security goes up, the other security would go down the same amount. Obviously, this is not an exact science, but it is an indication of the movement of the portfolio.

Some analysis tools that are used in modern portfolio theory include the following terms.

3. 4. 2. 1   Capital Asset Pricing Model (CAPM)

The CAPM is used to calculate the return that an investment should achieve based on the risk that is taken. The more risk taken, the higher the potential reruns. Investors should be rewarded for the risk they take. CAPM calculates a required return based on a risk multiplier called the beta coefficient.

A portfolio's **total risk** is made up of unsystematic risk and systematic risk. If an investor has a diversified portfolio, unsystematic risk is reduced to almost zero. Therefore, the only real risk is systematic risk and this is the risk that needs a required return.

Investors with a well-diversified portfolio will find that the risk affecting the portfolio is wholly systematic (markets moving together). Individual investments have both systematic and unsystematic risk; however, in a portfolio that is diversified, only the systematic risk of a new security would be relevant.

In other words, if an individual investment becomes part of a well-diversified portfolio, the unsystematic risk can be ignored.

2   Beta Coefficient

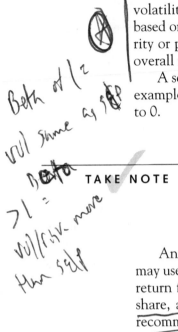

Beta and **beta coefficient** mean the same thing. In the securities industry, coefficient is ordinarily dropped for purposes of convenience. A stock or portfolio's beta is a measure of its volatility in relation to the overall market (systematic risk). The overall market is typically based on the S&P 500. A security that has a beta of 1 moves in line with the market. A security or portfolio with a beta of greater than 1 is generally going to be more volatile than the overall market. The reverse is true when the beta is less than 1.

A security that does not move in relation to market movement would have a beta of 0. For example, a money market security or money market mutual fund would have a beta of close to 0.

Beta = 0 = very low risk money market

Beta of 1 = vol same as S&P

Beta >1 = vol/risk more than S&P

TAKE NOTE   If the S&P 500 rises or falls by 10%, a stock with a beta of 1 rises or falls by about 10%, a stock with a beta of 1.5 rises or falls by about 15%, and a stock with a beta of .75 rises or falls by about 7.5%.

Analysts advise when to buy, sell, or hold securities. The CAPM is a method that analysts may use to make these decisions. An analyst would calculate the expected return and required return for the security. By subtracting the required return from the expected return for each share, analysts calculate the alpha for the security. A positive alpha would indicate a buy recommendation.

3. 4. 2. 3   Alpha — *return above a benchmark (S&P 500)*

Alpha is the extent to which an asset's or portfolio's actual return exceeds or falls short of its expected returns. A positive alpha rather than a negative one is desirable.

actual return – expected return

EXAMPLE   If an investment has a beta of 1.5, it is 50% more volatile than the market is. Therefore, if the market goes up 10%, it is expected that the investment with a beta of 1.5 will go up 15%.

However, if the investment only goes up 11%, the investor took a greater risk for less return on their money.

So the actual return of 11% is less than the 15% expected return (negative alpha).

If the investment increased by 17%, the investor received a greater return than the risk taken.

So the actual return of 17% is greater than the expected return of 15% (positive alpha).

The CAPM calculation of alpha would replace the expected return with the required return.

QUICK QUIZ 3.D

Objective: Summarize portfolio analysis and modern portfolio theory

1. Which of the following would be inappropriate for a registered representative to present to a customer?

   A. Comparing an equity growth fund's performance with a government bond fund in hopes of selling the equity growth fund
   B. Presenting an equity income fund and a bond fund to a customer that is looking to generate income
   C. Presenting an asset allocation model and explaining the theory behind the different asset classes relationships
   D. Presenting a money market mutual fund with the understanding that this is a liquid investment

2. A beta coefficient can best be described as all of the following EXCEPT

   A. a measurement of volatility
   B. a way to compare performance of a security against the stock market as a whole
   C. a way to reduce risk in a portfolio of securities
   D. it narrows the types of investments to present to a conservative or aggressive investor

3. When looking at the alpha of a particular investment, you notice it is a negative number, and that indicates

   A. the investment lost money
   B. the investor took more risk that the return received
   C. the investment is not volatile
   D. a very efficient portfolio manager

4. Which of the following types of risk cannot be eliminated through diversification under the modern portfolio theory?

   A. Interest rate risk
   B. Systematic risk
   C. Business risk
   D. Liquidity risk

All Quick Quiz answers are found at the end of their units.

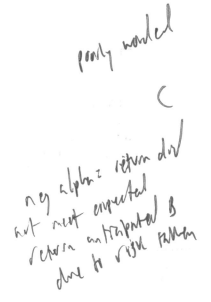

3.5 FUNDAMENTAL INVESTMENT ANALYSIS

Fundamental analysis is the study of the business prospects of an individual company within the context of its industry and the overall economy. They do this by examining the company in detail, including the **financial statements** and company management. We could compare this to an individual receiving a full physical examination that, in addition to all kinds of tests, would include a detailed family medical history. With a company, the financial statement analysis is like the blood tests, x-rays, stress test, and so forth, and the evaluation of the company's management is like the medical history.

3. 5. 1   BUSINESS CYCLE

Because **business cycle phases** have different effects on different industries, fundamental analysts look for companies in industries that offer better-than-average opportunities within the current business cycle.

The Four Stages of the Business Cycle

Peak

Expansion   Contraction

Trough

It is useful to distinguish between the four types of industries:

- Defensive
- Cyclical
- Countercyclical
- Growth

3. 5. 1. 1   Defensive Industries

Defensive industries are least affected by normal business cycles. Companies in defensive industries generally produce nondurable consumer goods, such as

- food,
- pharmaceuticals,
- tobacco, and
- utilities.

Public consumption of such goods remains fairly steady throughout the business cycle.
During economic contraction, including recessions and bear markets, stocks in defensive industries generally decline less than stocks in other industries. During expansions and bull markets, defensive stocks may advance less. Investments in defensive industries tend to involve less risk and, consequently, lower investment returns.

The terms of bull and bear (markets) are defined in your glossary.

Those using **sector rotation** will "rotate" into defensive issues when it appears the business cycle is headed into the contraction phase. They then rotate into cyclical issues when the economy is in the expansion phase. This is also called **segment rotation**.

3. 5. 1. 2   Cyclical Industries

Cyclical industries are highly sensitive to business cycles and inflation trends. Most cyclical industries produce

- steel,
- heavy equipment (such as tractors, airplanes, cranes),
- auto industry, and
- capital goods (such as washers and dryers).

durable consumer goods

During recessions, the demand for durable goods declines as manufacturers postpone investments in new capital goods and consumers postpone purchases of automobiles.
Cyclical industries perform better in expanding economies.

3. 5. 1. 3   Countercyclical Industries

Countercyclical industries, on the other hand, tend to turn down as the economy heats up and to rise when the economy turns down. Gold and gold mining stocks have historically been a countercyclical industry.

3. 5. 1. 4   Growth Industries

Every industry passes through four phases during its existence: introduction, growth, maturity, and decline. An industry is considered in its growth phase if the industry is growing faster than the economy as a whole because of technological changes, new products, or changing consumer tastes.

Technology associated with computers and bioengineering are considered **growth industries.** Because many growth companies retain nearly all of their earnings to finance their business expansion, growth stocks usually pay little or no dividends. *– question seen on this*

3. 5. 1. 4. 1   Special Situation Stocks

Special situation stocks are stocks of a company with unusual profit potential resulting from nonrecurring circumstances, such as new management, the discovery of a valuable natural resource on corporate property, or the introduction of a new product.

3. 5. 2   FINANCIAL STATEMENTS

A corporation's **financial statements** provide a fundamental analyst with the information needed to assess that corporation's profitability, liquidity, financial strength (ability of cash flow to meet debt payments), and operating efficiency. By examining how certain numbers from one statement relate to prior statements and how the resulting ratios relate to the company's competitors, the analyst can determine how financially viable the company is.

Companies issue quarterly and annual financial reports to the SEC. A company's balance sheet and income statement are included in these reports.

3. 5. 2. 1   Balance Sheet

The balance sheet provides a snapshot of a company's financial position at a specific point in time. It identifies the value of the company's assets (what it owns) and its liabilities (what it owes). The difference between these two figures is the corporation's owners' equity, or net worth.

The balance sheet equation is:

assets = liabilities + owners' equity; or

assets – liabilities = owners' equity.

Although it is useful in determining a company's current value, the balance sheet does not indicate whether the company's business is improving or deteriorating. The balance sheet gets its name from the fact that its two sides must balance. The balance sheet equation mathematically expresses the relationship between the two sides of the balance sheet. Simply stated, everything that is owned (assets) minus everything that is owed (liabilities) is equal to the net worth (owners' or shareholders' equity) of the entity.

3. 5. 2. 2   Assets

Assets appear on the balance sheet in order of liquidity, which is the ease with which they can be turned into cash. Assets that are most readily convertible into cash are listed first, followed by less liquid assets. Balance sheets commonly identify three types of assets: current assets (cash and assets easily convertible into cash), fixed assets (physical assets that could eventually be sold), and other assets (usually intangible and only of value to the corporation that owns them).

3. 5. 2. 2. 1   Current Assets

Current assets include all cash and other items expected to be converted into cash within the next 12 months, including the following:

- Cash and equivalents include cash and short-term safe investments, such as money market instruments that can be readily sold, as well as other marketable securities.
- Accounts receivable include amounts due from customers for goods delivered or services rendered, reduced by the allowance for bad debts.
- Inventory is the cost of raw materials, work in process, and finished goods ready for sale.
- Prepaid expenses are items a company has already paid for but has not yet benefited from, such as prepaid advertising, rents, insurance, and operating supplies.

3. 5. 2. 2. 2   Fixed Assets

Fixed assets are property, plant, and equipment. Unlike current assets, they are not easily converted into cash. Fixed assets, such as factories, have limited useful lives because wear and tear eventually reduce their value. For this reason, their cost can be depreciated over time or deducted from taxable income in annual installments to compensate for loss in value.

3. 5. 2. 2. 3   Other Assets

Intangible assets are nonphysical properties, such as formulas, brand names, contract rights, and trademarks. Goodwill, also an intangible asset, reflects the corporation's reputation and relationship with its clients.

TAKE NOTE   Although intangible assets may have great value to the corporation owning them, they generally carry little value to other entities.

3. 5. 2. 3   Liabilities

Total liabilities on a balance sheet represent all financial claims by creditors against the corporation's assets. Balance sheets usually include two main types of liabilities: current liabilities and long-term liabilities.

3. 5. 2. 3. 1   Current Liabilities

Current liabilities are corporate debt obligations due for payment within the next 12 months. These include the following:

- Accounts payable—amounts owed to suppliers of materials and other business costs
- Accrued wages payable—unpaid wages, salaries, commissions, and interest
- Current long-term debt—any portion of long-term debt due within 12 months
- Notes payable—the balance due on equipment purchased on credit or cash borrowed
- Accrued taxes—unpaid federal, state, and local taxes

3. 5. 2. 3. 2   Long-Term Liabilities

Long-term liabilities are financial obligations due for payment after 12 months. Examples would include bonds and mortgages.

TAKE NOTE   Long-term debts include mortgages on real property, long-term promissory notes, and outstanding corporate bonds.

TEST TOPIC ALERT   Under current accounting practice, deferred tax credits are treated as a liability.

Sample Balance Sheet

Balance Sheet
Amalgamated Widget
as of Dec. 31, 2018

ASSETS			
Current assets	Cash and equivalents	$ 5,000,000	$ 40,000,000
	Accounts receivable	15,000,000	
	Inventory	19,000,000	
	Prepaid expenses	1,000,000	
	Total current assets		
Fixed assets	Buildings, furniture, and fixtures	$40,000,000	
	(at cost less $10 million accumu-	15,000,000	$ 55,000,000
	lated depreciation)		
	Land		
	Total fixed assets		
Other (intangibles,		$5,000,000	
goodwill)			$100,000,000
Total assets			
LIABILITIES AND NET			
WORTH	Accounts payable	$5,000,000	$ 10,000,000
Current liabilities	Accrued wages payable	4,000,000	
	Accrued taxes payable	1,000,000	
	Total current liabilities		
Long-term liabilities	8% 20-year convertible		$ 50,000,000
Total liabilities	debentures		$ 60,000,000
Net worth	Preferred stock $100 par ($5	$20,000,000	
	noncumulative convertible	1,000,000	
	200,000 shares issued)	4,000,000	
	Common stock $1 par	15,000,000	
	(1 million shares)		
	Capital in excess of par		
	Retained earnings		
Total net worth			$ 40,000,000
Total liabilities and net			$100,000,000
worth			

3. 5. 3   SHAREHOLDER EQUITY

Shareholder equity, also called net worth or owners' equity, is the stockholder claims on a company's assets after all its creditors have been paid. Shareholder equity equals total assets less total liabilities. On a balance sheet, three types of shareholder equity are identified: capital stock at par, capital in excess of par, and retained earnings.

TAKE NOTE   net worth = assets – liabilities

3. 5. 3. 1   Capital Stock at Par

Capital stock includes preferred and common stock, listed at par value. Par value is the total dollar value assigned to stock certificates when a corporation's owners (the stockholders) first contributed capital. Par value of common stock is an arbitrary value with no relationship to market price.

3. 5. 3. 2   Capital in Excess of Par

Capital in excess of par, often called additional paid-in capital or paid-in surplus, is the amount of money over par value that a company received for selling stock.

could be proceeds from an IPO

3. 5. 3. 3   Retained Earnings

Retained earnings, sometimes called earned surplus or accumulated earnings, are profits that have not been paid out in dividends. Retained earnings represent the total of all earnings held since the corporation was formed less dividends paid to stockholders. Operating losses in any year reduce the retained earnings from prior years.

3. 5. 3. 4   Capital Structure

A company's **capitalization** is the combined sum of its long-term debt and equity securities. The **capital structure** is the relative amounts of debt and equity that compose a company's capitalization. Some companies finance their business with a large proportion of borrowed funds; others finance growth with retained earnings from normal operations and little or no debt.

Looking at the balance sheet, a corporation builds its capital structure with equity and debt including the following four elements:

■ Long-term debt
■ Capital stock (common and preferred)
■ Capital in excess of par
■ Retained earnings (earned surplus)

EXAMPLE

(See the table below for reference and explanation of the following terms.) The total capitalization on the sample balance is $90 million ($50 million in long-term debt, $20 million in preferred stock, and $20 million in shareholders' equity). Remember, common stock + capital surplus + retained earnings equals net worth (shareholders equity).

LT debt		$50 million
+	Pfd.	$20 million
+	Common	$ 1 million
+	Cap. surplus	$ 4 million
+	Ret. earnings	$15 million
Total capitalization		$90 million

If a company changes its capitalization by issuing stock or bonds, the effects will show up on the balance sheet.

3. 5. 4   FINANCIAL LEVERAGE

Financial leverage is a company's ability to use long-term debt to increase its return on equity. A company with a high ratio of long-term debt to equity is said to be highly leveraged.

Stockholders benefit from leverage if the return on borrowed money exceeds the debt service costs. But leverage is risky because excessive increases in debt raise the possibility of default in a business downturn.

In general, industrial companies with debt-to-equity ratios of 50% or higher are considered highly leveraged. However, utilities, with their relatively stable earnings and cash flows, can be more highly leveraged without subjecting stockholders to undue risk. If a company is highly leveraged, it is also affected more by changes in interest rates.

3. 5. 5   BALANCE SHEET COMPUTATIONS

The following computations help a financial analyst compare different companies within an industry under current economic conditions when making a recommendation to customers.

3. 5. 5. 1   Working Capital

Working capital is the amount of capital or cash a company has available. Working capital is a measure of a firm's liquidity, which is its ability to quickly turn assets into cash to meet its short-term obligations.

The formula for working capital is:

$$\text{current assets} - \text{current liabilities} = \text{working capital}$$

Factors that affect working capital include: increases in working capital, such as profits, sale of securities (long-term debt or equity), and sale of noncurrent assets; and decreases in working capital, such as dividends declared, paying off long-term debt, and net loss.

3. 5. 5. 2   Current Ratio

Knowing the amount of working capital is useful, but it becomes an even better indicator when paired with the **current ratio**. This computation uses the same two items, current assets and current liabilities, but expresses them as a ratio of one to the other. Simply divide the current assets by the current liabilities and the higher the ratio, the more liquid the company is.

3. 5. 5. 3   Quick Asset Ratio (Acid Test Ratio)

Sometimes it is important for the analyst to use an even stricter test of a company's ability to meet its short-term obligations (as such, "pass the acid test"). The quick asset ratio uses the company's quick assets instead of all of the current assets. Quick assets are current assets minus the inventory. Then divide these quick assets by the current liabilities to arrive at the quick ratio.

TAKE NOTE   Liquidity measures a company's ability to pay the expenses associated with running the business.

3. 5. 5. 4 Debt-to-Equity Ratio

The best way to measure the amount of financial leverage being employed by the company is by calculating the **debt-to-equity ratio**. It is really a misnomer—it should be called the debt-to-total capitalization ratio because that is what it is. For example, using the numbers in the capitalization chart in the previous example, we see that the total capital employed in the business is $90 million. Of that, $50 million is long-term debt. So, we want to know how much of the $90 million total is represented by debt capital. The answer is simple: $50 million of the $90 million, or 55.55%. That is the debt-to-equity ratio.

3. 5. 5. 5 Book Value per Share

A fundamental analyst is described as one who focuses on the company's books. Therefore, one of the key numbers computed is the **book value per share**. The calculation is almost identical to one we have already studied—net asset value (NAV) per share of an investment company.

In the case of a corporation, it is basically the liquidation value of the enterprise. That is, let's assume we sold all of our assets, paid back everyone we owe, and then split what is left among the stockholders. But, remember, before we can hand over anything to the common shareholders, we must take care of any outstanding preferred stock. So, from the funds that are left after we pay off all the liabilities, we give the preferred shareholders back their par (or stated) value and the rest belongs to the common stockholders.

But, there is one more thing. In the case of liquidation, some of the assets on our books might not really be worth what we're carrying them at—in particular, those that are known as intangible assets (goodwill, patents, trademarks, copyrights, etc.). That is why the analyst uses only the tangible assets, computed by subtracting those intangibles from the total assets. Expressed as a formula, book value per share is:

$$\frac{\text{tangible assets} - \text{liabilities} - \text{par value of preferred}}{\text{shares of common stock outstanding}} = \text{book value per share}$$

3. 5. 6 BALANCING THE BALANCE SHEET

Balance sheets, by definition, must balance. Every financial change in a business requires two offsetting changes on the company books, known as double-entry bookkeeping. For example, when a company pays a previously declared cash dividend, cash (a current asset) is reduced while dividends payable (a current liability of the same amount) is eradicated. This results in no change to working capital or net worth because each side of the balance sheet has been lowered by the same amount.

3. 5. 6. 1   Depreciating Assets

Because fixed assets (e.g., buildings, equipment, and machinery) wear out as they are used, they decline in value over time. This decline in value is called depreciation. A company's tax bills are reduced each year the company depreciates fixed assets used in the businesses.

Depreciation affects the company in two ways: accumulated depreciation reduces the value of fixed assets on the balance sheet, and the annual depreciation deduction reduces taxable income on the income statement.

Companies may elect either straight-line or accelerated depreciation. By use of the straight-line method, a company depreciates fixed assets by an equal amount each year over the asset's useful life. A piece of equipment costing $1 million with a 10-year useful life will generate a depreciation deduction of $100,000 per year.

Accelerated depreciation is a method that depreciates fixed assets more during the earlier years of their useful life and less during the later years.

TAKE NOTE
> Compared with straight-line, accelerated depreciation generates larger deductions (lower taxable income) during the early years and smaller deductions (higher taxable income) during the later years.

3. 5. 7   FOOTNOTES

Footnotes to the financial statements identify significant financial and management issues that may affect the company's overall performance, such as accounting methods used, extraordinary items, pending litigation, and management philosophy.

Typically, a company separately discloses details about its long-term debt in the footnotes. These disclosures are useful for determining the timing and amount of future cash outflows. The disclosures usually include a discussion of the nature of the liabilities, maturity dates, stated and effective interest rates, call provisions and conversion privileges, restrictions imposed by creditors, assets pledged as security, and the amount of debt maturing in each of the next five years.

Also disclosed in the footnotes would be off-the-books financing arrangements, such as debt guarantees.

TEST TOPIC ALERT
> Footnotes are generally found on the bottom of the financial statements and can be several pages long.

TAKE NOTE
> The balance sheet reports what resources (assets) a company owns and how it has funded them. How the firm has financed the assets is revealed by the capital structure—for example, long-term debt and owners' equity (preferred stock, common stock, and retained earnings).

3. 5. 8 INCOME STATEMENT

revenue V.
expenses

The **income statement**, sometimes called the profit and loss or P&L statement, summarizes a company's revenues (sales) and expenses for a fiscal period, usually quarterly, year to date, or the full year. It compares revenue against costs and expenses during the period. Fundamental analysts use the income statement to judge the efficiency and profitability of a company's operation. Just as with the balance sheet, technical analysts generally ignore this information—it is not relevant to their charting schemes.

3. 5. 8. 1 Components of the Income Statement

The various operating and nonoperating expenses on the income statement are discussed below.

Rev
- COGS (labor, material,
production)
———
Gross profit (sales)
- rent, utilities, etc.
———
Net profit (EBIT)

Revenues indicate the firm's total sales during the period (the money that came in).

The **cost of goods sold (COGS)** is the costs of labor, material, and production (including depreciation on assets employed in production) used to create finished goods. Subtracting COGS from revenues shows the gross operating profit. The two major methods of accounting for material costs are the first in, first out method (FIFO) and last in, first out method (LIFO). Under LIFO accounting, COGS normally will reflect higher costs of more recently purchased inventory (last items in). As a result of higher reported production costs under LIFO, reported income is reduced. The opposite is true if the FIFO method is used.

Pretax margin is determined by subtracting COGS and other operating costs (rent and utilities) from sales to arrive at net operating profit. The resulting figure is earnings before interest and taxes (EBIT).

operating
income - interest
expenses = pretax
income

Interest payments on a corporation's debt is not considered an operating expense. However, interest payments reduce the corporation's taxable income. **Pretax income**, the amount of taxable income, is operating income less interest payment expenses.

If dividends are paid to stockholders, they are paid out of net income after taxes have been paid. After dividends have been paid, the remaining income is added to retained earnings and is available to invest in the business.

Pretax income - taxes = Net income (profit to go to retained earnings)

TEST TOPIC ALERT

Please note the three terms above that we have put in boldface for you. Revenue (or sales), cost of goods sold, and pretax income are the three primary components of an income statement.

Think of it simply like this: the income statement shows (1) what came in, (2) what went out, and (3) how much is left (before taxes).

TAKE NOTE

Interest payments reduce a corporation's taxable income, whereas dividend payments to stockholders are paid from after-tax dollars. Because they are taxable as income to stockholders, dividends are taxed twice, whereas interest payments are taxed once as income to the recipient.

• Interest payments aren't taxable as an "operating expense" for a corp. - reduce taxable income

• Dividends are taxed twice - as a corp and as a recipient

3. 5. 8. 2 Accounting for Depreciation

As mentioned earlier, when reviewing the balance sheet, fixed assets are shown at their cost minus accumulated **depreciation**. For these assets, which wear out over a period of time, tax law requires that the loss of value be deducted over the asset's useful life, longer for some assets, shorter for others (you won't have to know depreciation schedules). On the income statement, the allowable portion for the year is shown as an expense and, for our purposes, will generally be part of COGS. Remember, if the company uses accelerated depreciation, the expenses will be higher in the early years resulting in lower pretax income (and lower income taxes) but higher income later on.

3. 5. 9 INCOME STATEMENT COMPUTATIONS

There are a number of important ratios that can be computed using information from the income statement. We'll take a look at several of them.

3. 5. 9. 1 Earnings Per Share (EPS)

Among the most widely used statistics, EPS measures the value of a company's earnings for each common share:

$$EPS = \frac{\text{earnings available to common}}{\text{number of shares outstanding}}$$

Earnings available to common are the remaining earnings after the preferred dividend has been paid. Earnings per share relates to common stock only. Preferred stockholders have no claims to earnings beyond the stipulated preferred stock dividends.

Simplified Income Statement

Net Revenues (Sales)	$10,000,000
− Cost of Goods Sold (including $500,000 of depreciation)	5,500,000
= Gross Profit	4,500,000
− Other Operating Expenses (rent, utilities)	500,000
= Operating Profit (EBIT)	4,000,000
− Interest Expense	750,000
= Income after Interest Expense (Pre-tax Income)	3,250,000
− Income Tax	1,000,000
= Net Income	2,250,000
Earnings per Share (1,000,000 common shares outstanding)	2.25
Dividends per Share ($1.50)	1,500,000
Credited to Retained Earnings	750,000

3. 5. 9. 2   Earnings per Share After Dilution

EPS after dilution assumes that all convertible securities, such as warrants and convertible bonds and preferred stock, have been converted into the common. Because of tax adjustments, the calculations for figuring EPS after dilution can be complicated and will not be tested.

3. 5. 9. 3   Current Yield (Dividend Yield)

A common stock's **current yield**, like the current yield on bonds, expresses the annual dividend payout as a percentage of the current stock price:

$$\text{current yield} = \frac{\text{annual dividends per common share}}{\text{market value per common share}}$$

3. 5. 9. 4   Dividend Payout Ratio

The **dividend payout ratio** measures the proportion of earnings paid to stockholders as dividends:

$$\text{dividend payout ratio} = \frac{\text{annual dividends per common share}}{\text{earnings per share (EPS)}}$$

Vt.1.tes pay high ↓ vidends

In general, older companies pay out larger percentages of earnings as dividends. Utilities as a group have an especially high payout ratio. Growth companies normally have the lowest ratios because they reinvest their earnings in the businesses. Companies on the way up hope to reward stockholders with gains in the stock value rather than with high dividend income.

3. 5. 9. 5   Statement of Cash Flow

The **statement of cash flow** reports a business's sources and uses of cash and the beginning and ending values for cash and cash equivalents each year. The three components generating cash flow are:

■ operating activities,
■ investing activities, and
■ financing activities.

TEST TOPIC ALERT

Most financial professionals add revenues and expenses that do not involve cash inflows or outflows (e.g., cost allocations, such as depreciation and amortization) back to the company's net income to determine the cash flow. As described previously, the cash flow statement will also reflect money from operations, financing, investing, but not accounting changes.

add back depreciation and amortization to companys net income to come up w/ cash flow #

3. 5. 9. 6   Cash Flow From Operating Activities

[handwritten: — income statement items]

[handwritten left margin: cash - in 4 out day-to-day cash flows 4 interest +4 N payments]

Operating activities (all transactions and events that normally enter into the determination of operating income) include cash receipts (money coming in) from selling goods or providing services, as well as income from items such as interest and dividends. Operating activities also include cash payments (money going out) such as cost of inventory, payroll, taxes, interest, utilities, and rent. The net amount of cash provided (or used) by operating activities is the key figure on a statement of cash flows. Even though it would seem that interest and dividends would belong in investing activities, the accounting gurus put them here.

EXAMPLE

[handwritten left margin: add back depreciation to get true cash flow 4]

Sometimes using some numbers makes this concept much easier. If you take a look at the income statement we reviewed a few pages ago, you will see that this company's net income (bottom line, to use the vernacular) was $2,250,000. Among the $6 million in expenses deducted from the total revenues was $500,000 of depreciation. However, the company never "wrote a check" for that money; it is the amount of the original cost that it is allowed to be written off as an expense each year as the fixed assets wear out. So, not only does the company have the net income remaining after all expenses and taxes, but also it actually had another $500,000 in funds it could use, giving the company a total cash flow of $2,750,000.

3. 5. 9. 7   Cash Flow From Investing Activities

Investing activities include transactions and events involving the purchase and sale of securities, land, buildings, equipment, and other assets not generally held for resale as a product of the business. It also covers the making and collecting of loans. Investing activities are not classified as operating activities because they have an indirect relationship to the central, ongoing operation of the business (usually the sale of goods or services).

3. 5. 9. 8   Cash Flow From Financing Activities

[handwritten: — balance sheet items]

[handwritten left margin: any cash flows for debt 4 equity financing]

All **financing activities** deal with the flow of cash to or from the business owners (equity financing) and creditors (debt financing). For example, cash proceeds from issuing stock or bonds would be classified under financing activities. Likewise, payments to repurchase stock (treasury stock) or to retire bonds and the payment of dividends are also financing activities.

TEST TOPIC ALERT   Cash flow from operations will only use items from the income statement, while cash flow from financing activities will use balance sheet items. Make sure you know which one the question is asking about.

3. 5. 9. 9   Earnings Before Interest and Taxes (EBIT)

EBIT helps a fundamental analyst to evaluate a company's performance without incorporating interest expenses or income tax rates. Without accounting for interest or taxes that are variables for every company, the fundamental analyst can focus on operating profitability as a single measure of success.

This is very important when comparing companies within an industry that have different debt obligations or tax obligations.

It is calculated from information found on the income statement.

Example: ABC Corp.	
Sales revenue	$10,000,000
Expenses	8,000,000
Earnings before interest and taxes	2,000,000
Interest paid	500,000
Earnings before taxes	1,500,000
Income taxes	60,000
Net Income	$1, 440,000

3. 5. 9. 10   Earnings Before Taxes (EBT)

With EBIT, the analyst has taken out the tax structure when evaluating a company in an industry—once again, making it easier to compare companies within an industry. Note that a highly leveraged company will have a relatively higher interest expense, and a lower EBT to a company with less debt obligations.

bpay more interest if you are a highly levered company

QUICK QUIZ 3.E

non-cyclical branches of non-durable consumer goods

Objective: Distinguish the characteristics of fundamental analysis

1. During an economic downturn, a fundamental analyst may be interested in what industry?

    A. Producers of capital goods such as washers and dryers
    B. Technology industry
    C. Steel industry
    D. Food industry

2. If a company has the following items on their balance sheet; what is the net worth of the company?

    - Current assets of $1 million
    - Inventory of $300,000
    - Fixed assets of $2 million
    - Liabilities of $2 million

    3.) A - L = E mm assets

    A. $5,300,000
    B. $1,000,000
    C. $1,300,000
    D. $300,000

    3.3 - 2 = Equity aka net worth

    = 1.3mm

    retained equity earnings

3. Which of the following items would NOT be important to a fundamental analyst when reviewing a possible investment?

   A. What phase the business cycle is in
   B. The quality of management
   C. The company's market share of its core business
   D. The stocks trading range over the last 12 months ← *technical*

4. The difference between current assets and current liabilities is called

   A. net worth
   (B) working capital
   C. cash flow
   D. quick assets   ← *(current assets – inventory) – liability*

5. Potential litigation for patent infringement would appear on a corporation's

   A. balance sheet as a deferred asset
   (B) footnotes
   C. income statement as an expense
   D. statement of potential litigation

All Quick Quiz answers are found at the end of their units.

3. 6   TECHNICAL ANALYSIS

Both technical and fundamental analyses attempt to predict the supply and demand of markets and individual stocks. **Technical analysis** attempts to predict the direction of prices on the basis of historic price and trading volume patterns when laid out graphically on charts.

Fundamental analysts concentrate on broad-based economic trends; current business conditions within an industry; and the quality of a particular corporation's business, finances, and management.

3. 6. 1   MARKET AVERAGES AND INDEXES

Stock prices tend to move, or **trend**, together, although some move in the opposite direction. The average stock, by definition, tends to rise in a bull market and decline in a bear market. Technical analysts chart the daily prices and volume movements of individual stocks and market indexes to discern patterns that allow them to predict the direction of market price movements.

3. 6. 1. 1   Trading Volume

Market trading volume substantially above normal signifies or confirms a pattern in the direction of prices. If overall volume has been listless for months and suddenly jumps significantly, a technical analyst views that as the beginning of a trend.

3. 6. 1. 2   Support and Resistance Levels

Stock prices may move within a narrow range for months or even years. The bottom of this trading range is known as the **support level**; the top of the trading range is called the **resistance level**.

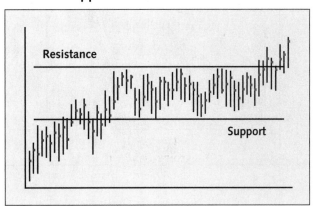

Support and Resistance Levels

When a stock declines to its support level, the low price attracts buyers, whose buying supports the price and keeps it from declining farther. When a stock increases to its resistance level, the high price attracts sellers, whose selling hinders a further price rise. Stocks may fluctuate in trading ranges for months, testing their support and resistance levels. If a particular stock's price penetrates either the support or the resistance level, the change is considered significant.

A decline through the support level is called a **bearish breakout**; a rise through the resistance level is called a **bullish breakout**. Breakouts usually signal the beginning of a new upward or downward trend.

3. 6. 1. 3   Advances/Declines

The number of issues closing up or down on a specific day reflects **market breadth**. The number of advances and declines can be a significant indication of the market's relative strength. When declines outnumber advances by a large amount, the market is bearish even if it closed higher. In bull markets, advances substantially outnumber declines. Technical analysts plot daily advances and declines on a graph to produce an **advance/decline line** that gives them an indication of market breadth trends.

3. 6. 2   CHARTING STOCKS

In addition to studying the overall market, technical analysts attempt to identify patterns in the prices of individual stocks.

3. 6. 2. 1   Trendlines

Although a stock's price may spike up or down daily, over time its price tends to move in one direction. Technical analysts identify patterns in the **trendlines** of individual stocks from graphs as they do patterns in the overall market. They base their buy or sell recommendations on a stock's price trendline. An upward trendline is bullish; a downward one is bearish.

Upward and Downward Trendlines

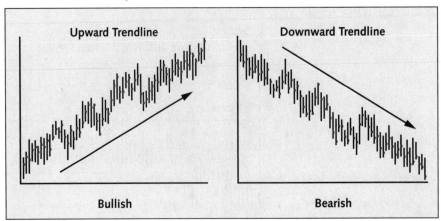

A trendline connects the lows in an uptrend and the highs in a downtrend. Three common patterns in stock price trendlines are consolidations, reversals, and support and resistance levels.

3. 6. 2. 1. 1   Consolidations

If a stock's price stays within a narrow range, it is said to be **consolidating**. When viewed on a graph, the trendline is horizontal and moves sideways, neither up nor down.

3. 6. 2. 1. 2   Reversals

A **reversal** indicates that an upward or a downward trendline has halted and the stock's price is moving in the opposite direction. Between the two trendlines, a period of consolidation occurs, and the stock price levels off. A genuine reversal pattern can be difficult to recognize because trends are composed of many rises and declines, which may occur at different rates and for different lengths of time.

Because of its gently curving shape, an easily identifiable reversal pattern is called a **saucer** (reversal of a downtrend) or an **inverted saucer** (reversal of an uptrend). A similar reversal pattern is the **head-and-shoulders** pattern, named for its resemblance to the human body.

The **head-and-shoulders top** pattern indicates the beginning of a bearish trend in the stock. First, the stock price rises, then it reaches a plateau at the neckline (left shoulder). A second advance pushes the price higher, but then the price falls back to the neckline (head). Finally, the stock price rises again, but falls back to the neckline (right shoulder) and continues downward, indicating a reversal of the upward trend.

When reversed, this pattern is called a **head-and-shoulders bottom**, or an **inverted head and shoulders**, and indicates a bullish reversal.

Head-and-Shoulders Top and Bottom Trendlines

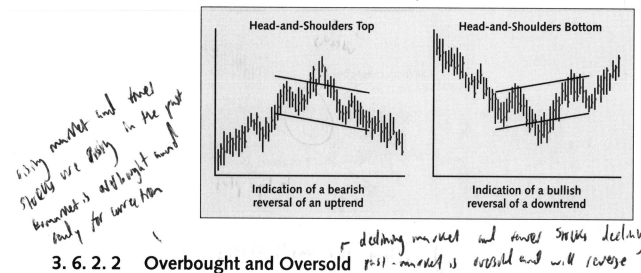

(handwritten margin note, left): rising market and there we going in the past / slowly market is overbought and / only for correction

3. 6. 2. 2   Overbought and Oversold

(handwritten note above section): declining market and fewer stocks declining than / past - market is oversold and will reverse

If market indexes such as the S&P 500 and the Dow are declining, but the number of declining stocks relative to the number of advancing stocks is falling (fewer stocks declining), the market is said to be oversold and is likely to reverse itself.

Conversely, if market indexes are rising, but the number of declining stocks relative to the number of advancing stocks is rising (fewer stocks rising), the market is said to be overbought and is ready for a correction.

3. 6. 3   TECHNICAL MARKET THEORIES

Technical analysts follow various theories regarding market trends. Some of them are outlined next.

3. 6. 3. 1   Dow Theory

(handwritten): 3 types of timelines of changes in stock prices

Analysts use the **Dow theory** to confirm the end of a major market trend. According to the theory, the three types of changes in stock prices are **primary trends** (one year or more), **secondary trends** (3-12 weeks), and **short-term fluctuations** (hours or days).

In a bull market, the primary trend is upward. However, stock prices may still drop in a secondary trend within the primary upward trend, even for as long as 12 weeks. The trough of the downward secondary trend should be higher than the trough of the previous downward trend. In a bear market, secondary upward trends may occur, but the highs reached during those secondary upward movements are successively lower.

According to the Dow theory, the primary trend in a bull market is a series of higher highs and higher lows. In a bear market, the primary trend is a series of lower highs and lower lows. Daily fluctuations are considered irrelevant.

A primary upward trend interrupted by secondary downward movements is shown in the following chart. The chart illustrates a series of successively higher highs and lows, conforming to the definition of a primary upward trend.

Any change in direction is considered deceptive unless the Dow Jones Industrial and Transportation Averages reflect the change. However, using this average lacks precision and is sometimes slow in confirming changes in market trends.

(handwritten margin note, lower left): Primary trend / 1 year ↑ / Bull - higher / highs / lower lows / Bear - lower / highs / lower lows

Dow Theory of Market Trends

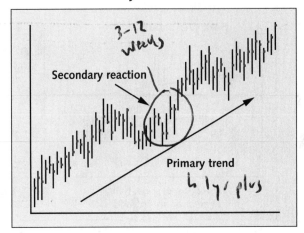

3. 6. 3. 2   Odd-Lot Theory

[handwritten: don't buy 100 units /shares = less than this is an odd-lot]

[handwritten margin: odd lot = small, retail investors buy/sell at the exact wrong times]

Typically, small investors engage in **odd-lot trading**. Followers of the **odd-lot theory** believe that these small investors invariably buy and sell at the wrong times. When odd-lot traders buy, odd-lot analysts are bearish. When odd-lot traders sell, odd-lot analysts are bullish.

This theory goes way back in time. Think of the 1930s when a house might cost $4,000. People took out mortgages for that kind of money. If a stock is priced at $40, and a round lot of that stock cost $4,000, most people didn't have that kind of money. So they bought one or two shares because that is what they could afford. They were not necessarily well-informed investors and often traded on emotion—buying when they should have sold, selling when they should have bought.

TEST TOPIC ALERT

The standard trading unit for equity securities is a round lot. A round lot is 100 shares. An odd lot is something less than 100 shares. If a trade is made for 550 shares of common stock, the trade was for five round lots (500 shares) and one odd lot (50 shares).

[handwritten: — odd lot = anything less than 100 shares / 1 round lot = 100 shares]

3. 6. 3. 3   Short-Interest Theory

Short interest refers to the number of shares that have been sold short. Because short positions must be repurchased eventually, some analysts believe that short interest reflects mandatory demand, which creates a support level for stock prices. High short interest is a bullish indicator, and low short interest is a bearish indicator.

[handwritten: high short interest = indicative of many people going to need to close out their short positions and purchase the stock = bullish]

QUICK QUIZ 3.F

Objective: Distinguish the characteristics of technical analysis

1. When a technical analyst says that the market is consolidating, the trendline is moving

    A. upward
    B. downward
    C. sideways
    D. unpredictably

C

2. From a chartist's (technical analyst's) viewpoint, which of the following statements is TRUE?

    A. Once a trendline is established, the price movement of a stock usually follows the trendline.
    B. More odd-lot buying than selling is bullish.
    C. Heavy volume in a declining market is bullish.
    D. Light volume in an advancing market is bullish.

A

3. Proponents of which of the following technical theories assume that small investors are usually wrong?

    A. Breadth-of-market theory
    B. Short-interest theory
    C. Volume-of-trading theory
    D. Odd-lot theory

D

4. Which of the following is the narrowest measure of the market?

    A. NYSE Composite Index
    B. Value Line Index
    C. DJIA
    D. Standard & Poor's 500

B

All Quick Quiz answers are found at the end of their units.

3. 7   EQUITY SECURITIES

Corporations issue equity (and debt) securities as a means of raising capital in order to implement ideas such as expanding operations or funding a merger or acquisition.

Investing in **equity securities** is perhaps the most visible and accessible means of creating wealth. Individual investors become owners of a publicly traded company by buying stock in that company. In doing so, they can participate in the company's success over time. They also share in the risk of operating a business; they can lose their investment.

Equity securities are more risky for investors compared with bonds because once you pay for a security, the issuer is under no obligation to ever give you any of your money back.

3. 7. 1   TYPES AND CHARACTERISTICS OF EQUITY SECURITIES

There are many different types of equity securities. The two primary types of equity securities most investors are familiar with are common and preferred stocks. These are considered ownership positions in a corporation. All corporations issue common stock. <u>Each share of common stock entitles its owner to a portion of the company's profits and dividends and an equal vote on directors and other important matters.</u> Most corporations are organized in such a way that their stockholders regularly vote for and elect candidates to a board of directors (BOD) to oversee the company's business. By electing a BOD, stockholders have some say in the company's management but are not involved with the day-to-day details of its operations.

TAKE NOTE

An individual's common stock ownership represents his proportionate interest in a company. If a company issues 100 shares of stock, each share represents an identical 1/100, or 1%, ownership position in the company. A person who owns 10 shares of stock owns 10% of the company; a person who owns 50 shares of stock owns 50% of the company.

Let's take a closer look at common stock.

3. 7. 1. 1 Common Stock

Corporations may issue two types of stock: common and preferred. When speaking of stocks, people generally refer to **common stock**. Preferred stock represents equity ownership in a corporation, but it usually does not have the same voting rights or appreciation potential as common stock. Preferred stock normally pays a fixed, semiannual dividend and has priority claims over common stock; that is, the preferred is paid first if a company declares bankruptcy.

Common stock can be classified as:

- authorized,
- issued,
- outstanding, and
- treasury.

3. 7. 1. 1. 1 Authorized Stock

Authorized stock refers to a specific number of shares the company has authorization to issue or sell. This is laid out in the company's original charter. Often, a company sells only a portion of the authorized shares to raise enough capital for its foreseeable needs. The company may sell the remaining authorized shares in the future or use them for other purposes. Should the company decide to sell more shares than are authorized, the charter must be amended through a stockholder vote.

3. 7. 1. 1. 2 Issued Stock

Issued stock has been authorized and distributed to investors. When a corporation issues, or sells, fewer shares than the total number authorized, it normally reserves the unissued shares for future needs, including:

- raising new capital for expansion;
- paying stock dividends;
- providing stock purchase plans for employees or stock options for corporate officers;

- exchanging common stock for outstanding convertible bonds or preferred stock; or
- satisfying the exercise of outstanding stock purchase warrants.

Authorized but unissued stock does not carry the rights and privileges of issued shares and is not considered in determining a company's total capitalization.

3. 7. 1. 1. 3   Outstanding Stock

Outstanding stock includes any shares that a company has issued but has not repurchased—that is, stock that is investor owned.

3. 7. 1. 1. 4   Treasury Stock

Treasury stock is stock a corporation has issued and subsequently repurchased from the public. The corporation can hold this stock indefinitely or can reissue or retire it. A corporation could reissue its treasury stock to fund employee bonus plans, distribute it to stockholders as a stock dividend, or under certain circumstances, redistribute it to the public in an additional offering. Treasury stock does not carry the rights of outstanding common shares, such as voting rights and the right to receive dividends.

By buying its own shares in the open market, the corporation reduces the number of shares outstanding. If fewer shares are outstanding and operating income remains the same, earnings per share increase. A corporation buys back its stock for a number of reasons, such as to:

- increase earnings per share;
- have an inventory of stock available to distribute as stock options, fund an employee pension plan, and so on; or
- use for future acquisitions.

TEST TOPIC ALERT

Expect to see a question on outstanding stock similar to the following:

ABC company has authorized 1 million shares of common stock. It issued 800,000 shares one year ago. It then purchased 200,000 shares for its treasury. How many shares of ABC stock are outstanding?

The solution requires that you know a basic formula:

issued stock – treasury stock = outstanding stock

In applying this formula to our sample question, the solution is as follows:

800,000 – 200,000 = 600,000

Alternatively, treasury stock equals issued shares minus outstanding shares.

TAKE NOTE

This question illustrates a point about FINRA exams. The question provided information about the number of shares of authorized stock, but that information was not necessary for you to solve the problem. Prepare for questions that give you more information than you need. The Series 7 exam expects you to know concepts so well that you can determine both what is and what is not essential to the solution of a problem.

3. 7. 2   RIGHTS OF COMMON STOCK OWNERSHIP

Stockholders are owners of a company and therefore have certain rights that protect their ownership interests.

3. 7. 2. 1   Voting Rights

Common stockholders use their voting rights to exercise control of a corporation by electing a board of directors and by voting on important corporate policy matters at annual meetings, such as:

- issuance of convertible securities (dilutive to current stockholders) or additional common stock;
- substantial changes in the corporation's business, such as mergers or acquisitions; and
- declarations of stock splits (forward and reverse).

Things common shareholder vote on

Stockholders have the right to vote on the issuance of convertible securities because they will dilute current stockholders' proportionate ownership when converted (changed into shares of common).

3. 7. 2. 1. 1   Calculating the Number of Votes

A stockholder can cast one vote for each share of stock owned. Depending on the company's bylaws and applicable state laws, a stockholder may have either a statutory or cumulative vote.

Statutory voting. Statutory voting allows a stockholder to cast one vote per share owned for each item on a ballot, such as candidates for the BOD. A board candidate needs a simple majority to be elected.

Cumulative voting. Cumulative voting allows stockholders to allocate their total votes in any manner they choose.

Statutory vs. Cumulative Voting

Example One: Mr. X owns 100 Shares

Statutory Voting	
Board of Directors Seat 1	100
Board of Directors Seat 2	100
Board of Directors Seat 3	100

Example Two: Mr. X owns 100 Shares

Cumulative Voting			Cumulative Voting	
Board of Directors Seat 1	175		Board of Directors Seat 1	300
Board of Directors Seat 2	50	OR	Board of Directors Seat 2	0
Board of Directors Seat 3	75		Board of Directors Seat 3	0

EXAMPLE

XYZ Corp. will be electing three directors at its annual meeting. Each XYZ shareholder has a number of votes equal to the number of shares owned times the number of directorships up for election. Assume a shareholder owns 100 shares. Under statutory voting, the shareholder may use a maximum of 100 votes for any one seat on the board.

Under cumulative voting, the shareholder may allocate all 300 votes to one director, giving the shareholder a greater impact.

cumulative benefit small investor : can have more impact

TAKE NOTE

Cumulative voting benefits the smaller investor, whereas statutory voting benefits larger shareholders.

TEST TOPIC ALERT

Do not vote on dividend related matters

Shareholders do not vote on dividend-related matters, such as when they are declared and how much they will be. They do vote on stock splits, board members, and issuance of additional equity-related securities such as common stock, preferred stock, and convertible securities.

3. 7. 3 PROXIES

- Slow up to a proxy meeting, the one you mailed in is cancelled

Stockholders often find it difficult to attend the annual stockholders' meeting, so most vote on company matters by means of a **proxy**, a form of absentee ballot. After it has been returned to the company, a proxy can be automatically canceled if the stockholder attends the meeting, authorizes a subsequent proxy, or dies. When a company sends proxies to shareholders, usually for a specific meeting, it is known as a proxy solicitation.

Companies that solicit proxies must supply detailed and accurate information to the shareholders about the proposals to be voted on. Before making a proxy solicitation, companies must submit the information to the Securities and Exchange Commission (SEC) for review.

If a proxy vote could change control of a company (a proxy contest), all persons involved in the contest must register with the SEC as participants or face criminal penalties. This registration requirement includes anyone providing unsolicited advice to stockholders about how to vote. However, brokers who advise customers who request advice are not considered to be participants. A stockholder may revoke a proxy at any time before the company tabulates the final vote at its annual meeting.

3. 7. 3. 1 Nonvoting Common Stock

Companies may issue both voting and nonvoting (or limited voting) common stock, normally differentiating the issues as Class A and Class B, respectively. Issuing nonvoting stock allows a company to raise additional capital while maintaining management control and continuity without diluting voting power.

3. 7. 4 PREEMPTIVE RIGHTS

When a corporation raises capital through the sale of additional common stock, it may be required by law or its corporate charter to offer the securities to its common stockholders before the general public. This is known as an antidilution provision. Stockholders then have a **preemptive right** to purchase enough newly issued shares to maintain their proportionate ownership in the corporation.

TAKE NOTE

Preemptive rights give investors the right to maintain a proportionate interest in a company's stock.

preserve ownership /. before a company sells to shares public

---

EXAMPLE

ABC has 1 million shares of common stock outstanding. Mr. X owns 100,000 shares of ABC common stock, or 10%. If ABC issues an additional 500,000 shares, Mr. X will have the opportunity to purchase 50,000 of those shares.

	Original		New		
ABC:	1,000,000 shares	+	500,000	=	1,500,000 shares
Mr. X:	100,000 shares	+	50,000	=	150,000 shares
	10%		10%		10%

3. 7. 5 LIMITED LIABILITY

Stockholders cannot lose more than the amount they have paid for a corporation's stock. **Limited liability** protects stockholders from having to pay a corporation's debts in bankruptcy.

3. 7. 6 INSPECTION OF CORPORATE BOOKS

Stockholders have the right to receive annual financial statements and obtain lists of stockholders. **Inspection rights** do not include the right to examine detailed financial records or the minutes of board of director's meetings.

3. 7. 7   RESIDUAL CLAIMS TO ASSETS

If a corporation is liquidated, the common stockholder (as owner) has a **residual right to claim** corporate assets after all debts and other security holders have been satisfied. The common stockholder is at the bottom of the liquidation priority list.

TAKE NOTE   Because common stock is last in line in a corporate liquidation, it is known as the most junior security.

3. 7. 8   STOCK SPLITS

Although investors and executives are generally delighted to see a company's stock price rise, a high market price may inhibit trading of the stock. To make the stock price attractive to a wider base of investors—that is, retail versus institutional investors—the company can declare a **stock split**.

A **forward stock** split increases the number of shares and reduces the price without affecting the total market value of shares outstanding; an investor will receive more shares, but the value of each share is reduced. The total market value of the ownership interest is the same before and after the split.

TAKE NOTE   For an investor that owns 100 shares valued at $20 per share:

■ A 2:1 stock split results in that investor owning 200 shares at $10 per share.

■ The value of the investment does not change, before and after the split the value is $2,000.

To determine the number of shares after a split, multiply the number of shares owned by the first number of the split and then divide by the second number (2:1).

A **reverse split** has the opposite effect on the number and price of shares. After a reverse split, investors own fewer shares worth more per share.

3. 7. 9   BENEFITS AND RISKS OF OWNING COMMON STOCK

Generally, and throughout this course, it is assumed an investor buys or owns shares of stock with the intent of selling them at a higher price in the future—buy low, sell high later.

An investor who buys shares is considered long the stock.

An investor may also sell shares before he owns them, with the intent of buying them back at a lower price in the future—sell high, buy low later. Such a transaction, known as a short sale, involves borrowing shares to sell that the investor must eventually replace. An investor who sells borrowed shares is considered short the stock until he buys and returns the shares to the lender.

People generally expect to receive financial growth, income, or both from common stock investments.

3. 7. 9. 1   Growth

An increase in the market price of shares is known as **capital appreciation**. Historically, owning common stock has provided investors with high real returns.

3. 7. 9. 2   Income

Many corporations pay regular quarterly cash dividends to stockholders, but dividends are not considered to be fixed like the dividend stated on preferred stock. A company's dividends may increase over time as profitability increases. Dividends, which can be a significant source of **income** for investors, are a major reason many people invest in stocks. Issuers may also pay stock dividends (additional shares in the issuing company) or property dividends (shares in a subsidiary company or a product sample).

TEST TOPIC ALERT

Stock dividends, rather than cash dividends, are more likely to be paid by companies that wish to reinvest earnings for research and development. Technology companies, aggressive growth companies, and new companies are examples of companies likely to pay stock a stock dividend. When a stock dividend is paid, the shareholder receives more common stock of the issuer. There is no economic benefit because the price of the security is reduced by the amount of the distribution on the morning of the ex-date.

QUICK QUIZ 3.G

Objective: Distinguish characteristics, risks and recommendations of common stock

1. Cumulative voting rights

    A.   benefit the large investor
    B.   aid the corporation's best customers
    C.   give preferred stockholders an advantage over common stockholders
    D.   benefit the small investor

2. ABC Company has authorized 1 million shares of common stock. It issued 800,000 shares 1 year ago. It then purchased 200,000 shares for its treasury. How many shares of ABC stock are outstanding?

    A.   200,000
    B.   600,000
    C.   800,000
    D.   1,000,000

3. All of the following are privileges or benefits of stock ownership EXCEPT

    A.   dividends
    B.   growth
    C.   guaranteed income
    D.   voting rights

All Quick Quiz answers are found at the end of their units.

3. 8   PREFERRED STOCK

Preferred stock is an equity security because it represents ownership in the corporation. However, it does not normally offer the appreciation potential associated with common stock. Not all corporations issue preferred stock.

Like a bond, a **preferred stock** is issued with a fixed (stated) rate of return. In the case of the preferred stock, it is a dividend rather than interest that is being paid. As such, these securities are generally purchased for income. Although the dividend of most preferred stocks is fixed, some are issued with a variable dividend payout known as adjustable-rate preferred stock. Like other fixed-income assets such as bonds, preferred stock prices tend to move inversely with interest rates. Most preferred stock is nonvoting.

Preferred stock does not typically have the same growth potential as common stock and therefore is subject to inflation risk. However, preferred stockholders generally have two advantages over common stockholders.

■ When the board of directors declares dividends, owners of preferred stock must receive their stated dividend in full before common stockholders may be paid a dividend.

■ If a corporation goes bankrupt, preferred stockholders have a priority claim over common stockholders on the assets remaining after creditors have been paid.

Because of these features, preferred stock appeals to investors seeking income and safety.

TAKE NOTE
Preferred stock has preference over common stock in payment of dividends and in claim to assets in the event the issuing corporation goes bankrupt. However, preferred stock does not get to vote.

3. 8. 1   FIXED RATE OF RETURN

Preferred stock's **fixed dividend** is a key attraction for income-oriented investors. Normally, a preferred stock is identified by its annual dividend payment stated as a percentage of its par value, which is usually $100 on the Series 7 exam. (A preferred stock's par value is meaningful to the investor, unlike that of common stock.) A preferred stock with a par value of $100 that pays $6 in annual dividends is known as a 6% preferred. The dividend of preferred stock with par value other than $100 is stated in a dollar amount, such as a $6 preferred.

The stated rate of dividend payment causes the price of preferred stock to act like the price of a bond: prices and interest rates have an inverse relationship.

Interest rate movements affect preferred stock prices

EXAMPLE
Consider a 6% preferred. If interest rates are at 8% and you want to sell your preferred, you will have to sell at a discounted price. Why would a buyer pay full value for an investment that is not paying a competitive market rate? But if interest rates fall to 5%, the 6% preferred will trade at a premium. Because it is offering a stream of income above the current market rate, it will command a higher price.

Preferred stock represents ownership in a company like common stock, but its price is sensitive to interest rates—just like the price of a bond.

No Maturity Date or Set Maturity Value. Although it is a fixed-income investment, preferred stock, unlike bonds, has no preset date at which it matures and no scheduled redemption date or maturity value.

3. 8. 2   CATEGORIES OF PREFERRED STOCK

Separate categories of preferred stock may differ in the dividend rate, profit participation privileges, or other ways. All, however, maintain a degree of preference over common stock. One or several of the features described next may characterize issues of preferred stock.

3. 8. 2. 1   Straight (Noncumulative)

Straight preferred has no special features beyond the stated dividend payment. Missed dividends are not paid to the holder. The year's stated dividend must be paid on straight preferred if any dividend is to be paid to common shareholders.

TAKE NOTE   Preferred stock with no special features is known as straight preferred.

3. 8. 2. 2   Cumulative Preferred

Buyers of preferred stock expect fixed dividend payments. The directors of a company in financial difficulty can reduce or suspend dividend payments to both common and preferred stockholders. With **cumulative preferred**, any dividends in arrears must be paid before paying a common dividend.

TAKE NOTE   Any special feature attached to preferred, such as a cumulative feature, has a price. The cost for such a benefit is less dividend income. Cumulative preferred typically has a lower stated dividend than straight preferred (less risk equals less reward).

All dividends due to cumulative preferred shareholders accumulate on the company's books until the corporation can pay them. When the company can resume full payment of dividends, cumulative preferred stockholders receive their current dividends plus the total accumulated dividends—dividends in arrears—before any dividends may be distributed to common or other straight preferred stockholders. Therefore, cumulative preferred stock is safer than straight preferred stock.

EXAMPLE

RST Corp. has both common stock and cumulative preferred stock outstanding.

Its preferred stock has a stated dividend rate of 5% (par value $100). Because of financial difficulties, no dividend was paid on the preferred stock last year or the year before. If RST wishes to declare a common stock dividend this year, RST is required to first pay how much in dividends to the cumulative preferred shareholders?

RST must pay missed dividends to cumulative preferred (as well as the current dividend) before dividends are paid on common stock. RST must pay $5 for the year before last, $5 for last year, and $5 for this year, for a total of $15.

For noncumulative preferred stock outstanding, the answer would have been $5. Only the current year dividend would need payment before common because noncumulative preferred is not entitled to dividends in arrears.

3. 8. 2. 3   Convertible Preferred

A preferred stock is convertible if the owner can exchange each preferred share for shares of common stock. The price at which the investor can convert is a preset amount and is noted on the stock certificate. Because the value of a **convertible preferred stock** is linked to the value of the issuer's common stock, the convertible preferred's price fluctuates in line with the common.

Convertible preferred is often issued with a lower stated dividend rate than nonconvertible preferred because the investor may have the opportunity to convert to common shares and enjoy capital gains. In addition, the conversion of preferred stock into shares of common increases the total number of common shares outstanding, which decreases earnings per common share and may decrease the common stock's market value. When the underlying common stock has the same value as the convertible preferred, it is said to be at its parity price.

EXAMPLE

XYZ Company's convertible preferred stock, with a par value of $100 and a conversion price of $20, can be exchanged for five shares of XYZ common stock ($100 ÷ $20 = 5). This is true, no matter what the current market value of either the preferred or the common stock. Thus, if an investor bought the preferred for $100 per share and the common stock rises in price eventually to more than $20 per share, the preferred stockholder could make a capital gain from converting.

3. 8. 2. 4   Participating Preferred

In addition to fixed dividends, **participating preferred** stock offers owners a share of corporate profits that remain after all dividends and interest due other securities are paid. The percentage to which participating preferred stock participates is noted on the stock certificate. Before the participating dividend can be paid, a common dividend must be declared.

↳ participating upto ...

EXAMPLE

If a preferred stock is described as "XYZ 6% preferred participating to 9%," the company could pay its holders up to 3% in additional dividends in profitable years, if the board so declares.

3. 8. 2. 5 Callable Preferred

Corporations often issue **callable, or redeemable, preferred**, which a company can buy back from investors at a stated price on the call date or any date thereafter. The right to call the stock allows the company to replace a relatively high fixed dividend obligation with a lower one should interest rates decline.

When a corporation calls a preferred stock, dividend payments and conversion rights cease on the call date. In return for the call privilege, the corporation usually pays a premium exceeding the stock's par value at the call, such as $103 for a $100 par value stock.

TAKE NOTE

Callable preferred stock is unique because of the risk that the issuer may buy it back and end dividend payments. Because of this risk, callable preferred has a higher stated rate of dividend payment than straight, noncallable preferred.

Issuers are likely to call securities when interest rates are falling. Like anyone, an issuer would prefer to pay a lower rate for money. Issuers call securities with high rates and replace them with securities that have lower fixed-rate obligations.

3. 8. 2. 6 Adjustable-Rate Preferred

Can be a hedge against inflation

Some preferred stocks are issued with **adjustable, or variable, dividend rates**. Such dividends are usually tied to the rates of other interest rate benchmarks, such as Treasury bill and money market rates, and can be adjusted as often as semiannually.

QUICK QUIZ 3.H

Objective: Distinguish characteristics, risks, and recommendations of preferred stock

1. If a preferred stock pays a stated dividend of 6% and the issuer calls the stock, which of the following is NOT related to the call?

   A. Interest rates are lower than when the stock was issued.
   B. The investor will be paid a little more than the par value.
   C. Dividends scheduled to be paid after the call date are not paid.
   D. If a preferred stock is going to be called, it must happen on the first available call date.

SUITABILITY

B

2. Which of the following choices would be a suitable recommendation for an investor that likes a fixed dividend but also would like to take advantage of capital appreciation if the company's common stock rises?

A. Cumulative preferred stock
B. Convertible preferred stock — *Can convert H stock @ a conversion rate*
C. Adjustable-rate preferred stock
D. Participating preferred stock

3. If your client wished to purchase a preferred stock that would offer him the highest likelihood of assured income plus the opportunity to take part in the growth of the company's common stock, which of these features might he consider?

I.   Callable
II. Convertible
III. Cumulative
IV. Straight

A. I and II
B. I and III
C. II and III
D. II and IV

All Quick Quiz answers are found at the end of their units.

3. 9   OTHER EQUITY SECURITIES

Here are other types of equity securities that you need to be familiar with.

3. 9. 1   PREEMPTIVE RIGHTS

So their percent ownership isn't diluted

Existing stockholders have **preemptive rights or stock rights** that entitle them to maintain their proportionate ownership in a company by buying newly issued shares before the company offers them to the general public. A **rights offering** allows stockholders to purchase common stock below the current market price. The rights are valued separately from the stock and trade in the secondary market during the subscription period.

A stockholder who receives rights may:

Exercise rights - buy stock @ below market price

Sell rights

■ exercise the rights to buy stock by sending the rights certificates and a check for the required amount to the rights agent;

■ sell the rights and profit from their market value (rights certificates are negotiable securities); or

■ let the rights expire and lose their value.

3. 9. 1. 1   Subscription Right Certificate

A **subscription right** is a certificate representing a short-term (typically 30 to 45 days) privilege to buy additional shares of a corporation. One right is issued for each common stock share outstanding.

Terms of the Offering

The **terms** of a rights offering are stipulated on the subscription right certificates mailed to stockholders. The terms describe how many new shares a stockholder may buy, the price, the date the new stock will be issued, and the final date for exercising the rights.

Rights offering

cum rights = investor buys stock w/ rights) until execution date

EXAMPLE

ABC Co. plans to raise capital by issuing additional stock and, on April 1, declares a rights offering. Common stockholders as of May 1, the record date, can subscribe to one new share, at a price of $30, for each 10 shares of stock they own. ABC stock trades in the open market for $41 per share. The rights will expire on June 18.

The corporation will issue rights to stockholders of record May 1. Stock is traded cum rights until the ex-date. An investor who buys stock **cum rights** receives the right. An investor who buys stock **ex-rights** does not.

The number of rights required to buy one new share is based on the number of shares outstanding and the number of new shares offered.

ex rights: investor does not receive (rights)

EXAMPLE

ABC has 10 million shares outstanding and will issue 1 million additional shares.

Because each existing share is entitled to one right, the company will issue 10 million rights. Because 10 million rights entitle stockholders to buy 1 million shares, it will require 10 rights to buy one new share.

TEST TOPIC ALERT

Rights have a theoretical value based on the savings to investors, who then purchase stock below the market price. Before the ex-date, when the stock is trading with rights, the value of a right is found using the cum rights formula. Consider the following: ABC's price per share is $41; the subscription per share is $30. Ten rights are needed to purchase one share of stock. The value of one right is found as follows:

$$\frac{\text{Market price} - \text{subscription price}}{\text{Number of rights to purchase 1 share} + 1}$$

$$\frac{41 - 30}{10 + 1} = \frac{11}{11} = \$1$$

On the morning of the ex-date, the market price typically drops by the value of the right. Use the ex-rights formula to determine the value of a right after the ex-date. The ex-rights formula is:

$$\frac{\text{Market price} - \text{subscription price}}{\text{Number of rights to purchase 1 share}}$$

TAKE NOTE

In dealing with any question on the value of a right, you will not have to adjust market price. The questions deal only with value, so your only decision is whether to divide MP-SP by N or N + 1. The easy way to remember is this: if you are asked the value of a right before the ex-date (cum rights), use the 1. If you are asked the value of a right on or after the ex-date, don't use the 1. Cum means "with," whereas ex means "without."

3. 9. 2 WARRANTS

A **warrant** is a certificate granting its owner the right to purchase securities from the issuer at a specified price (normally higher than the current market price) as of the date of issue of the warrant. Warrants represent the right to purchase shares but, in and of themselves, do not represent ownership. Therefore, warrant holders do not have voting rights like shareholders do until they exercise the warrants and become shareholders. Unlike a right, a warrant is usually a long-term instrument, giving the investor the choice of buying shares at a later date at the exercise price.

TAKE NOTE   Warrants typically have a life of five years, but in the past, perpetual warrants, which do not expire, have been issued.

3. 9. 2. 1 Origination of Warrants

Warrants are usually offered to the public as **sweeteners,** or inducements, in connection with other securities, such as bonds or preferred stock, to make those securities more attractive. The issuer is able to reduce the cost of debt or the fixed dividend of preferred stock because of the added benefit to investors that allows them to exercise the warrant. Such offerings are often bundled as **units**.

After issuance, the warrants are detachable and trade separately from the bond or preferred stock. When first issued, a warrant's exercise price is set well above the stock's market price. If the stock's price increases above the exercise price, the owner can exercise the warrant and buy the stock below the market price or sell the warrant in the market.

Rights	Warrants
Short term	Long term
On issuance, exercise price below market price	On issuance, exercise price higher than market price
May trade with or separate from the common stock	May trade with or separate from the units
Offered to existing shareholders with preemptive rights	Offered as a sweetener for another security

3. 9. 3 AMERICAN DEPOSITORY RECEIPTS (ADRs)

Foreign branches of large commercial U.S. banks issue ADRs. A custodian, typically a bank in the issuer's country, holds the shares of foreign stock that the ADRs represent. The stock must remain on deposit as long as the ADRs are outstanding because the ADRs are the depository bank's guarantee that it holds the stock.

3. 9. 3. 1   Rights of ADR Owners

ADR owners have most of the rights common stockholders normally hold. These include the right to receive dividends when declared. Generally, ADRs do not have voting rights, though some ADR issuers will pass on voting rights to the holders of ADRs. As for preemptive rights, the issuing bank sells off the rights and distributes the proceeds pro rata to holders.

3. 9. 3. 2   Delivery of Foreign Security

ADR owners have the right to exchange their ADR certificates for the foreign shares they represent. They can do this by returning the ADRs to the depository banks, which cancel the ADRs and deliver the underlying stock.

3. 9. 3. 3   Taxes on ADRs

In most countries, a withholding tax on dividends is taken at the source. In the case of investors holding ADRs this would be a foreign income tax. The foreign income tax may be taken as a credit against any U.S. income taxes owed by the investor.

3. 9. 3. 4   Currency Risk

In addition to the normal risks associated with stock ownership, ADR investors are subject to **currency risk**, the possibility that an investment denominated in one currency could decline if the value of that currency declines in its exchange rate with the U.S. dollar.

Currency exchange rates are an important consideration because ADRs represent shares of stock in companies located in foreign countries.

TAKE NOTE   Dividends are declared in the foreign currency but are payable in U.S. dollars, lending to currency risk.

3. 9. 3. 5   Registered Owner

ADRs are registered on the books of the U.S. banks responsible for them. The individual investors in the ADRs are not considered the stock's registered owners. ADRs are registered on the books of U.S. banks, so dividends are sent to the custodian banks as registered owners. The banks collect the payments and convert them into U.S. dollars.

3. 9. 3. 6   Sponsored ADRs

All exchange-listed ADRs are sponsored—that is, the foreign company sponsors the issue to increase its ownership base. Issuers that sponsor ADRs provide holders with financial statements in English. Sponsored ADRs are sometimes referred to as American depositary shares (ADSs). Nonsponsored ADRs are issued by banks without the assistance and participation of the issuer.

3. 9. 4   PENNY STOCKS

The SEC adopted the penny stock cold-calling rules to prevent certain abusive sales practices involving high-risk securities sold to unsophisticated investors. These rules involve the solicitation of non-Nasdaq equity securities traded in the over-the-counter (OTC) market for less than $5 per share. These equity securities are frequently called penny stocks and are considered highly speculative.

These rules state that when a broker-dealer's representative contacts a potential customer to purchase penny stocks, the representative must first determine suitability on the basis of information about the buyer's financial situation and objectives. The customer must sign and date this suitability statement before the penny stock trades can be affected. In addition, the broker-dealer must disclose:

- the name of the penny stock,
- the number of shares to be purchased,
- a current quotation, and
- the amount of commission that the firm and the representative received.

Regardless of activity, if the account holds penny stocks, broker-dealers must provide a monthly statement of account to the customer. This must indicate the market value and number of shares for each penny stock held in the account, as well as the issuer's name.

3. 9. 4. 1   Established Customers

Established customers are exempt from the suitability statement requirement but not from the disclosure requirements. An established customer is someone who:

- has held an account with the broker-dealer for at least one year (and has made a deposit of funds or securities), or
- has made at least three penny stock purchases of different issuers on different days.

TAKE NOTE

The provisions of the penny stock rules apply only to solicited transactions. Transactions not recommended by the broker-dealer are exempt.

QUICK QUIZ 3.1

Objective: Identify types and characteristics of other equity securities

1. An investor that seeks income from equity securities and has a conservative risk tolerance might be interested in all of the following EXCEPT

   A. utility stocks
   B. blue-chip stocks
   C. technology stocks
   D. preferred stock

2. An ADR represents
   A. a U.S. security in a foreign market
   B. a foreign security in a domestic market
   C. a U.S. security in both a domestic and a foreign market
   D. a foreign security in both a domestic and a foreign market

3. If a corporation attaches warrants to a new issue of debt securities, which of the following would be a resulting benefit?
   A. Dilution of shareholders' equity
   B. Reduction of the debt securities' interest rate
   C. Reduction of the number of shares outstanding
   D. Increase in earnings per share

4. Under SEC rules, a penny stock is defined as an unlisted, non-Nasdaq security trading at less than
   A. $1.00 per share only
   B. $2.00 per share only
   C. $2.50 per share only
   D. $5.00 per share only

5. Of the following S&P ratings shown here, below which one of them would all other S&P ratings be considered speculative?
   A. A
   B. B
   C. BB
   D. BBB

All Quick Quiz answers are found at the end of their units.

3. 10   TYPES AND CHARACTERISTICS OF DEBT SECURITIES

When investors purchase a company's debt, they lend money to the company and as a **creditor of the company**, the company is obligated to pay investors back. Therefore, when a corporation issues debt, it is considered risky for the issuer and conservative for investors.

Bonds have a fixed value—usually $1,000 per bond (par or face value). If a bond is held until maturity, the investor will get that amount back, plus the interest the bond earns, unless the issuer of the bond defaults, or fails to pay. In addition to the risk of default, investors also face potential market risk if bonds are sold before maturity.

For example, if the price of the bonds in the secondary market—or what other investors will pay to buy them—is less than par, and the bonds are sold at that point, the investor may realize a loss on the sale.

The market value of bonds may decrease if there's a rise in interest rates between the time the bonds were issued and their maturity dates. In that case, demand for older bonds paying lower rates decreases. If sold at that time, investors potentially take that loss. Market prices can also fall below par if the bonds are downgraded by an independent rating agency because of problems with the company's finances.

Bonds are risky for issuers to issue than issuing stock. Because when an investor purchases a bond, the issuer is obligated to pay interest as scheduled, and the principal at maturity.

TAKE NOTE

The par value (face/principal) of a bond is $1,000 unless otherwise stated

- Bonds are quoted as a percentage of par, 96 = 96% of par or $960

- 1 bond point is $10

- 100 basis points = 1%

- Most bonds pay interest, known as the coupon, nominal yield or stated yield. A 6% coupon will pay $60 interest annually, $30 every six months

- At maturity, the bond will pay the face amount plus the bond's last semiannual interest payment.

- When a bond is trading in the secondary market, it may trade at a premium (greater than par value) or a discount (less than par value).

- When interest rates rise, the price of bonds trading falls and when interest rates go down, the price of bonds trading goes up. This is known as inverse relationship.

- A bond's current yield (CY) is its annual interest divided by current market value

- A bonds yield to maturity (YTM) is the total return of the bond if held to maturity. If the bond is purchased at a discount, the YTM will be greater than the CY because the investor will make money at maturity (bought the bond at $950 and receives $1,000 at maturity). If the bond is purchased at a premium, the YTM will be less than the CY because the investor will lose money at maturity (bought the bond at $1,050 and receives $1,000 at maturity).

- For discount bonds the highest yield is the yield to call (YTC) because if the bond is called before maturity, the investor receives $1,000 and makes money sooner than the maturity.

- For premium bonds the lowest yield is the yield to call (YTC) because if the bond is called before maturity, the investor receives $1,000 and loses money sooner than the maturity.

The relationship of yields is diagrammed here:

Current Yield, Yield to Maturity, and Yield to Call

CY = Current Yield   YTM = Yield to Maturity   YTC = Yield to Call

1. What is the current yield of a 6% bond trading for $800?

    Current yield = annual income ÷ current market price

    Find the solution as follows: $60 ÷ $800 = 7.5%. This bond is trading at a discount. When prices fall, yields rise. The current yield is greater than the nominal yield when bonds are trading at a discount.

2. What is the current yield of a 6% bond trading for $1,200?

    Find the solution as follows: $60 ÷ $1,200 = 5%. This bond is trading at a premium. The price is up so the yield is down. The current yield is less than the nominal yield when bonds are trading at a premium.

    It is critical to understand the inverse relationship between price and yield. An effective way to visualize it is through the chart. When bonds are at par, coupon and current yield are equal. When bonds are at a premium, the CY is less than the coupon. When bonds are at a discount, the CY is greater than the coupon.

3. 10. 1 CORPORATE BONDS

Corporate bonds are issued to raise working capital or capital for expenditures such as plant construction and equipment purchases. The two primary types of corporate bonds are secured and unsecured.

Rating services, such as **Standard & Poor's (S&P)** and **Moody's**, evaluate the credit quality of bond issues and publish their ratings. Standard & Poor's and Moody's rate both corporate and municipal bonds. Both base their bond ratings primarily on an issuer's creditworthiness—that is, the issuer's ability to pay interest and principal as they come due.

A plus or minus sign in a Standard & Poor's rating indicates that the bond falls within the top (+) or bottom (–) of that particular category. Moody's uses A1 and Baa1 to indicate the highest-quality bonds within those two categories. Moody's provides ratings for short-term municipal notes, designating MIG 1–4 (best–adequate) and SG (speculative grade).

The rating organizations rate those issues that either pay to be rated or have enough bonds outstanding to generate constant investor interest. The fact that a bond is not rated does not indicate its quality; many issues are too small to justify the expense of a bond rating.

The SEC has recognized seven ratings firms under the Credit Rating Agency Reform Act of 2006 as being registered with the commission. They are A.M. Best Co., Inc. (historically associated with rating insurance companies' ability to pay claims and their debt issues); DBRS, Ltd.; Fitch, Inc.; Japan Credit Rating Agency, Ltd.; Moody's Investors Service, Inc.; Rating and Investment Information, Inc.; and Standard and Poor's Rating Service. Rating symbols used by Moody's and Standard & Poor's, are shown in the following chart. Note that Fitch uses rating symbols identical to those used by Standard & Poor's.

Bond Ratings

Standard & Poor's	Moody's	Interpretation
Bank-grade (investment-grade) bonds		
AAA	Aaa	Highest rating. Capacity to repay principal and interest judged high.
AA	Aa	Very strong. Only slightly less secure than the highest rating.
A	A	Judged to be slightly more susceptible to adverse economic conditions.
BBB	Baa	Adequate capacity to repay principal and interest. Slightly speculative.
Speculative (noninvestment-grade) bonds		
BB	Ba	Speculative. Significant chance that issuer could miss an interest payment.
B	B	Issuer has missed one or more interest or principal payments.
C	Caa	No interest is being paid on bond at this time.
D	D	Issuer is in default. Payment of interest or principal is in arrears.

The Comptroller of the Currency, the Federal Deposit Insurance Corporation (FDIC), the Federal Reserve, and state banking authorities have established policies determining which securities banks can purchase. A municipal bond must be investment grade (a rating of BBB/Baa or higher) to be suitable for purchase by banks. Investment-grade bonds are also known as bank-grade bonds.

A plus or minus sign in a Standard & Poor's rating indicates that the bond falls within the top or bottom of a particular category (e.g., AA+ or A–). Moody's, however, adds numerical qualifiers such as 1, 2, 3 to their categories (e.g., Aa1 or Baa2). The lower the number, the higher the rating within that category.

High-yield bonds that carry a speculative rating are suitable only for those with a high risk tolerance. They are characterized by greater returns coupled with greater credit risk.

TAKE NOTE   An easy way to distinguish between Moody's and S&P ratings is to remember that "Mood swings are Up and Down." This phrase reminds you that Moody's uses upper- and lowercase letters, while S&P uses only capital letters for its ratings. For Moody's, investment grade is Baa and above, whereas with S&P, investment grade is BBB and above.

3. 10. 1. 1 Secured Bonds

A bond is **secured** when the issuer has identified specific assets as collateral for interest and principal payments. A trustee holds the title to the assets that secure the bond. In a **default**, the bondholder can lay claim to the collateral.

3. 10. 1. 2 Mortgage Bonds

Mortgage bonds have the highest priority among all claims on assets pledged as collateral. Although mortgage bonds, in general, are considered relatively safe, individual bonds are only as secure as the assets that secure them and are rated accordingly. When multiple classes of a mortgage bond exist, the first claim on the pledged property goes to first-mortgage bonds, second claim to second-mortgage bonds, and so on.

3. 10. 1. 3 Collateral Trust Bonds

Collateral trust bonds are issued by corporations that own securities of other companies as investments. A corporation issues bonds secured by a pledge of those securities as collateral. The trust indenture usually contains a covenant requiring that a trustee hold the pledged securities. Collateral trust bonds may be backed by:

■ another company's stocks and bonds;

■ stocks and bonds of partially or wholly owned subsidiaries;

■ pledging company's prior lien long-term bonds that have been held in trust to secure

■ short-term bonds; or

■ installment payments or other obligations of the corporation's clients.

3. 10. 1. 4 Equipment Trust Certificates

Railroads, airlines, trucking companies, and oil companies use **equipment trust certificates (ETCs)**, or equipment notes and bonds, to finance the purchase of capital equipment. ETCs are issued serially so that the amount outstanding goes down year to year in line with the depreciating value of the collateral (e.g., aircraft or railroad cars).

Title to the newly acquired equipment is held in trust, usually by a bank, until all certificates have been paid in full. Because the certificates normally mature before the equipment wears out, the amount borrowed is generally less than the full value of the property securing the certificates.

3. 10. 2 UNSECURED BONDS

Unsecured bonds have no specific collateral backing and are classified as either debentures or subordinated debentures.

3. 10. 2. 1 Debentures

Debentures are backed by the general credit of the issuing corporation, and a debenture owner is considered a general creditor of the company. Debentures are below secured bonds and above subordinated debentures and preferred and common stock in the priority of claims on corporate assets.

3. 10. 2. 2 Subordinated Debentures

The claims of **subordinated debenture** owners are paid last of all debt obligations, including general creditors, in the case of liquidation. Subordinated debentures generally offer higher yields than either straight debentures or secured bonds because of their subordinate (thus riskier) status, and they often have conversion features.

3. 10. 2. 3 Liquidation

In the event a company goes bankrupt, the hierarchy of claims on the company's assets is:

■ secured debt (bonds and mortgages);

■ unsecured liabilities (debentures) and general creditors;

■ subordinated debt;

■ preferred stockholders; and

■ common stockholders.

TEST TOPIC ALERT   Be ready for a question on liquidation priority. Secured is safest, followed by unsecured or general creditors, then subordinated. Common stock is always last in line. Bonds are frequently called senior securities because of their priority in this hierarchy.

3. 10. 2. 4 Guaranteed Bonds

Guaranteed bonds are backed by a company other than the issuer, such as a parent company. This backing effectively increases the issue's safety.

3. 10. 2. 5 Income Bonds

Income bonds, also known as **adjustment bonds**, are used when a company is reorganizing and coming out of bankruptcy. Income bonds pay interest only if the corporation has enough income to meet the interest payment and if the BOD declares a payment. Because missed interest payments do not accumulate for future payment, these bonds are not suitable investments for customers seeking income.

3. 10. 2. 6 Zero-Coupon Bonds

Bonds are normally issued as interest-paying securities. **Zero-coupon bonds (zeroes)** are an issuer's debt obligations that do not make regular interest payments. Instead, zeroes are issued, or sold, at a deep discount to their face value and mature at par. The difference between the discounted purchase price and the full face value at maturity is the return, or accreted interest, the investor receives.

The price of a zero-coupon bond reflects the general interest rate climate for similar maturities. Zero-coupon bonds are issued by corporations, municipalities, and the U.S. Treasury and may be created by broker-dealers from other types of securities.

3. 10. 2. 6. 1   Advantages and Disadvantages

A zero-coupon bond requires a relatively small investment, perhaps $300 to $400 per bond, and matures at $1,000. Zero-coupon bonds offer investors a way to speculate on interest rate moves. Because they sell at deep discounts and offer no cash interest payments to the holder, zeroes are substantially more volatile than traditional bonds; their prices fluctuate wildly with changes in market rates. Moreover, the longer the time to maturity, the greater the volatility. When interest rates change, a zero's price changes much more as a percentage of its market value than an ordinary bond's price.

TEST TOPIC ALERT

Zero-coupon bonds, which are purchased at a discount and mature at face value, are a suitable investment for future anticipated expenses, such as college tuition.

3. 10. 2. 6. 2   Taxation of Zero-Coupon Bonds

Although zeroes pay no regular interest income, investors in zeroes owe income tax each year on the amount by which the bonds have accreted, just as if the investor had received it in cash. The income tax is due regardless of the direction of the market price.

EXAMPLE

A customer buys a 10-year zero at a cost of $400. At maturity, the customer will realize $600 of interest income. Each year, however, the customer must accrete the discount and pay income tax on this phantom income.

Here is how it works: The IRS requires the customer to accrete the discount annually on a straight-line basis. The total discount is $600. Because there are 10 years to maturity, the customer must accrete $60 annually ($600 ÷ 10 years). Each year, the customer pays income tax on $60 of interest income. The good news is that each year, the customer is permitted to adjust the cost basis of the zero upward by the amount of the annual accretion. After one year, the customer's cost basis is $460.

After two years, the cost basis is $520. After three years, it is $580, and so on. At maturity, the cost basis will be adjusted to par. Therefore, if held to maturity, there is no capital gain (cost basis is par; redeemed at par).

However, if the customer sells the zero before maturity, there may be a capital gain or a capital loss, depending on the difference between sales proceeds and the cost basis (accreted value) at time of sale.

If the same 10-year zero bought at $400 is sold five years later for $720, the customer will realize a $20 per bond gain. At that point, the customer's cost basis is $700 ($400 plus five years of annual accretion of $60 per year).

TEST TOPIC ALERT

If the exam asks you to choose the security that has no reinvestment risk, the answer to look for is a zero because, with no interest payments to reinvest, the investor has no reinvestment risk. Furthermore, because there is no reinvestment risk, buying a zero is the only way to lock in a rate of return.

3. 10. 2. 7   Convertible Bonds

Convertible bonds are corporate bonds that may be exchanged for a fixed number of shares of the issuing company's common stock. They are convertible into common stock, so convertible bonds pay lower interest rates than nonconvertible bonds and generally trade in line with the common stock. Convertible bonds have fixed interest payments and maturity dates, so they are less volatile than common stock.

3. 10. 2. 7. 1   Advantages of Convertible Securities to the Issuer

A corporation adds a conversion feature to its bonds or preferred stock to make it more marketable. Other reasons corporations issue convertible securities include the following:

- Convertibles can be sold with a lower coupon rate than nonconvertibles because of the conversion feature.
- A company can eliminate a fixed interest charge as conversion takes place, thus reducing debt.
- Because conversion normally occurs over time, it does not have an adverse effect on the stock price, which may occur after a subsequent primary offering.
- By issuing convertibles rather than common stock, a corporation avoids immediate dilution of primary earnings per share.
- At issuance, conversion price is higher than market price of the common stock.

3. 10. 2. 7. 2   Disadvantages of Convertible Securities to the Issuer

On the other hand, convertibles have potential disadvantages for a corporation and its stockholders.

- When bonds are converted, shareholders' equity is diluted; that is, more shares are outstanding, so each share now represents a smaller fraction of ownership in the company.
- Common stockholders have a voice in the company's management, so a substantial conversion could cause a shift in the control of the company.
- Reducing corporate debt through conversion means a loss of leverage.
- The resulting decrease in deductible interest costs raises the corporation's taxable income.

Therefore, the corporation pays increased taxes as conversion takes place.

3. 10. 2. 7. 3   The Market for Convertible Securities

Convertible bonds offer the safety of the fixed-income market and the potential appreciation of the equity market, providing investors with the following advantages:

- As a debt security, a **convertible debenture** pays interest at a fixed rate and is redeemable for its face value at maturity, provided the debenture is not converted. As a rule, interest income is higher and surer than dividend income on the underlying common stock. Similarly, convertible preferred stock usually pays a higher dividend than does common stock.
- If a corporation experiences financial difficulties, convertible bondholders have priority over common stockholders in the event of a corporate liquidation.
- In theory, a convertible debenture's market price tends to be more stable during market declines than the underlying common stock's price. Current yields of other competitive debt securities support the debenture's value in the marketplace.
- Because convertibles can be exchanged for common stock, their market price tends to move upward if the stock price moves up.

■ Conversion of a senior security into common stock is not considered a purchase and a sale for tax purposes. Thus, the investor incurs no tax liability on the conversion transaction.

■ Stable interest rates tend to result in a stable bond market. When rates are stable, the most volatile bonds tend to be those with a conversion feature because of their link to the underlying common stock. Therefore, in a stable rate environment, a convertible bond can be volatile if the underlying stock is volatile.

3. 10. 2. 7. 4   Conversion Price and Conversion Ratio

The **conversion price** is the stock price at which a convertible bond can be exchanged for shares of common stock. The **conversion ratio**, also called the **conversion rate**, expresses the number of shares of stock a bond may be converted into.

EXAMPLE

A bond with a conversion price of $40 has a conversion ratio of 25:1 ($1,000 ÷ $40 = 25).

Conversion terms are stated in the indenture agreement, either as a conversion ratio or as a conversion price.

TAKE NOTE

Although the conversion ratio of a bond is always stated on the bond certificate and the investor's confirmation, it is not stated directly in the number of shares, but in terms of the price at which a conversion can occur.

EXAMPLE

If a bond has a conversion price of $40 per share, you can determine that an investor is entitled to convert it into 25 shares. Always start with the par value of the instrument: par of $1,000 ÷ conversion price of $40 = conversion ratio of 25 shares.

The same concept applies to convertible preferred stock. An investor bought a share of preferred that converts at $20. By starting with an assumed par of $100, you can derive that the investor is entitled to five shares of common. $100 ÷ the conversion price of $20 = conversion ratio of 5 shares.

---

3. 10. 2. 7. 5   Calculating Conversion Parity

Parity means that two securities are of equal dollar value (in this case, a convertible bond and the common stock into which it can be converted).

Convertible parity / Arbitrage

EXAMPLE

If a corporation issues a bond convertible at $50, the conversion ratio is 20:1. If a bond selling for 104 ($1,040) is convertible into 20 shares of common, the common stock price would have to be $52 to be at parity with, or equal to, the convertible bond price ($1,040 ÷ 20 = 52). If the common stock is selling below 52, the convertible bond is worth more than the stock. If the stock is selling above 52, the investor can make more money by acquiring the bond, converting to common, and selling the shares.

The following formulas calculate the parity prices of convertible securities and their underlying common shares:

Market price of the bond

Conversion ratio (# of shares) = parity price of common stock

Market price of common × conversion ratio = parity price of convertible

---

TEST TOPIC ALERT

On the Series 7 exam, there will most likely be questions on parity. Here are two methods to help you solve the problem.

RST bond is convertible to common at $50. If RST bond is currently trading for $1,200, what is the parity price of the common?

Method One: Parity means equal. Solve for the conversion ratio as follows:

Par value: $1,000

Conversion price: $ 50

Conversion ratio: 20

[handwritten: Parity = price bonds and commons will have to be equal value at]

[handwritten: Par value of bond / conversion price = conversion ratio]

[handwritten: mkt price / conversion ratio = parity price of stock]

The parity stock price is found by dividing $1,200 by 20. The parity price of the common is $60.

Method Two: If you prefer to think in percentages, identify that the new bond price of $1,200 is 20% greater than the original $1,000 price. To be at equivalence, the stock price must also increase by 20%. So add 20% to 50 and the problem is solved. 20% of 50 is 10; 10 + 50 = parity price of $60.

Here is another style of parity question.

RST bond is convertible to common at $50. If the common is trading for $45, what is the parity price of the bond? Start by solving for the conversion ratio.

[handwritten: $\frac{x}{20} = \frac{45}{1}$ x = 20.45 = 900]

Par value: $1,000

Conversion price: $ 50

Conversion ratio: 20

The bond price is found by multiplying 20 × 45. The parity price of the bond is $900. Using the percentage method, you can determine that the market price of the common stock is 10% below that of the conversion price (5 ÷ 50 = 10%). Reducing the bond price of $1,000 by 10% results in a parity price of the bond of $900.

In a **rising** market, the convertible's value rises with the common stock's value.

In a **declining** market, the convertible's market price tends to level off when its yield becomes competitive with the yield on nonconvertible bonds, and it may not decline in price as much as the common stock. Convertible bonds normally sell at a premium above parity, which is why they are not constantly exchanged for common stock when the stock price is rising.

3. 10. 2. 8 Equity-Linked Notes (ELNs)

Equity-linked notes are debt instruments where the final payment at maturity is based on the return of a single stock, a basket of stocks, or an equity index. In the case where the note is based on the return of an index, the security would be known as an index-linked note (ILN).

In the instances where the securities are traded on an exchange (most still are not), they are generally referred to as exchange-traded notes (ETNs). ELNs, exchange traded or not, are considered nonconventional structured products with unique risks, and therefore, not suitable for most investors.

3. 10. 2. 9 Collateralized Mortgage Obligations (CMOs)

CMOs are a type of **asset-backed security**. Asset-backed securities are ones whose value and income payments are derived from or backed by a specific pool of underlying assets. These pools of assets can include expected payments from different types of loans such as mortgages, as is the case with CMOs, auto loans, or other types of loans. In some instances, asset-backed securities can pool expected cash flow from credit cards, leases, or even royalty payments.

Pooling the assets into financial instruments allows them to be sold to general investors more easily than selling them individually. This process is called securitization, and it allows the risk of investing in the underlying assets to be diversified because each security will now represent only a fraction of the total value of the diverse pool of underlying assets. CMOs pool a large number of mortgages, usually on single-family residences. A pool of mortgages is structured into maturity classes called **tranches**. CMOs are issued by private-sector financing corporations and are often backed by Ginnie Mae, Fannie Mae, and Freddie Mac pass-through securities. As a result, CMOs backed by government agency securities have historically been rated high.

A CMO pays principal and interest from the mortgage pool monthly; however, it repays principal to only one tranche at a time. In addition to interest payments, investors in a short-term tranche must receive all of their principal before the next tranche begins to receive principal repayments. Principal payments are made in $1,000 increments to randomly selected bonds within a tranche. Changes in interest rates affect the rate of mortgage prepayments, and this, in turn, affects the flow of interest payment and principal repayment to the CMO investor.

TAKE NOTE

This type of CMO, also called a plain vanilla CMO, pays interest on all tranches simultaneously. However, it pays principal to only one tranche at a time until it is retired. Subsequent principal payments are made to the next tranche in line until it is paid off, and so on.

A CMO's yield and maturity are estimates based on historical data or projections of mortgage prepayments from the **Public Securities Association (PSA)**. The particular tranche an investor owns determines the priority of his principal repayment. The time to maturity, amount of interest received, and amount of principal returned are not guaranteed. The model developed by the PSA compensates for the fact that prepayment assumptions will change during the life of an obligation and that this will affect the yield of the security.

Sample CMO Tranche Structure

Tranche	Interest Rate	Estimated Life in Years
1	5.125%	1.5
2	5.25%	3.5
3	5.5%	6.0
4	5.875%	8.5
5	6.125%	11.0

3. 10. 2. 10 Classes of CMOs

In addition to the standard CMOs discussed, some CMOs have been structured to suit specific needs of investors. Common CMO types include:

■ principal only,

■ interest only,

■ planned amortization class, and

■ targeted amortization class.

3. 10. 2. 10. 1   Principal-Only CMOs (POs)

The flow of income from underlying mortgages is divided into principal and interest streams and directed to the owners of **principal-only CMOs (POs)** and **interest-only CMOs (IOs)**, respectively. For a PO, the income stream comes from principal payments on the underlying mortgages—both scheduled mortgage principal payments and prepayments. Thus, the security ultimately repays its entire face value to the investor.

A PO sells at a discount from par; the difference between the discounted price and the principal value is the investor's return. Its market value, like all deeply discounted securities, tends to be volatile. POs, in particular, are affected by fluctuations in prepayment rates. The value of a PO rises as interest rates drop and prepayments accelerate, and its value falls when interest rates rise and prepayments decline.

3. 10. 2. 10. 2   Interest-Only CMOs (IOs)

IOs are by-products of POs. Whereas POs receive the principal stream from underlying mortgages, IOs receive the interest. An IO also sells at a discount, and its cash flow declines over time, just as the proportion of interest in a mortgage payment declines over time. Unlike POs, IOs increase in value when interest rates rise, and they decline in value when interest rates fall because the number of interest payments changes as prepayment rates change. Thus, they can be used to hedge a portfolio against interest rate risk.

When prepayment rates are high, the owner of an IO may receive fewer interest payments than anticipated. Because the entire CMO series receives more principal sooner, and therefore less overall interest, the IO owner does not know how long the stream of interest payments will last.

3. 10. 2. 10. 3   Planned Amortization Class CMOs (PACs)

PACs have targeted maturity dates; they are retired first and offer protection from **prepayment risk** and **extension risk** (the chance that principal payments will be slower than anticipated) because changes in prepayments are transferred to companion tranches, also called support tranches.

3. 10. 2. 10. 4   Targeted Amortization Class CMOs (TACs)

A TAC structure transfers prepayment risk only to a companion tranche and does not offer protection from extension risk. TAC investors accept the extension risk and the resulting greater price risk in exchange for a slightly higher interest rate.

3. 10. 2. 10. 5   Zero-Tranche CMO (Z-Tranche)

A Z-tranche receives no payment until all preceding CMO tranches are retired (the most volatile CMO tranches).

TEST TOPIC ALERT

SUITABILITY

Z-tranche CMOs would not be suitable for an investor needing funds in a specified amount of time, due to the unpredictable nature of when payment will be received.

3. 10. 3   CMO CHARACTERISTICS

Because mortgages back CMOs, they are considered relatively safe. However, their susceptibility to interest rate movements and the resulting changes in the mortgage repayment rate mean CMOs carry several risks.

- The rate of principal repayment varies.
- If interest rates fall and homeowner refinancing increases, principal is received sooner than anticipated (prepayment risk).
- If interest rates rise and refinancing declines, the CMO investor may have to hold his investment longer than anticipated (extended maturity risk).

3. 10. 3. 1   Yields

CMOs yield more than Treasury securities and normally pay investors interest and principal monthly. Principal repayments are made in $1,000 increments to investors in one tranche before any principal is repaid to the next tranche.

3. 10. 3. 2   Taxation

Interest from CMOs is subject to federal, state, and local taxes.

3. 10. 3. 3   Liquidity

There is an active secondary market for CMOs. However, the market for CMOs with more complex characteristics may be limited or nonexistent. Certain tranches of a given CMO may be riskier than others, and some CMOs in certain tranches carry the risk that repayment of principal may take longer than anticipated.

3. 10. 3. 4   Denominations

CMOs are issued in $1,000 denominations.

3. 10. 2. 10. 5   Zero-Tranche CMO (Z-Tranche)

A Z-tranche receives no payment until all preceding CMO tranches are retired (the most volatile CMO tranches).

TEST TOPIC ALERT

SUITABILITY

> Z-tranche CMOs would not be suitable for an investor needing funds in a specified amount of time, due to the unpredictable nature of when payment will be received.

3. 10. 3   CMO CHARACTERISTICS

Because mortgages back CMOs, they are considered relatively safe. However, their susceptibility to interest rate movements and the resulting changes in the mortgage repayment rate mean CMOs carry several risks.

- The rate of principal repayment varies.
- If interest rates fall and homeowner refinancing increases, principal is received sooner than anticipated (prepayment risk).
- If interest rates rise and refinancing declines, the CMO investor may have to hold his investment longer than anticipated (extended maturity risk).

3. 10. 3. 1   Yields

CMOs yield more than Treasury securities and normally pay investors interest and principal monthly. Principal repayments are made in $1,000 increments to investors in one tranche before any principal is repaid to the next tranche.

3. 10. 3. 2   Taxation

Interest from CMOs is subject to federal, state, and local taxes.

3. 10. 3. 3   Liquidity

There is an active secondary market for CMOs. However, the market for CMOs with more complex characteristics may be limited or nonexistent. Certain tranches of a given CMO may be riskier than others, and some CMOs in certain tranches carry the risk that repayment of principal may take longer than anticipated.

3. 10. 3. 4   Denominations

CMOs are issued in $1,000 denominations.

3. 10. 3. 5 Suitability

Some varieties of CMOs, such as PAC companion tranches, may be particularly unsuitable for small or unsophisticated investors because of their complexity and risks. The customer is required to sign a **suitability statement** before buying any CMO. Potential investors must understand that the rate of return on CMOs may vary because of early repayment. Also note that the performance of CMOs may not be compared with any other investment vehicle.

TEST TOPIC ALERT

It will be useful to know the following summary.

- CMOs are not backed by the U.S. government; they are corporate instruments.

- Interest paid is taxable at all levels.

- CMOs are backed by mortgage pools.

- CMOs yield more than U.S. Treasury securities.

- CMOs are subject to interest rate risk.

- CMOs are issued in $1,000 denominations and trade OTC.

- PACs have reduced prepayment and extension risk.

- TACs are protected against prepayment risk but not extension risk.

- PACs have lower yields than comparable TACs.

3. 10. 4 COLLATERALIZED DEBT OBLIGATIONS (CDOs)

CDOs are typically complex asset-backed securities. While CDOs do not specialize in any single type of debt, usually their portfolios consist of nonmortgage loans or bonds. The assets backing the CDOs can be a pool of bonds, auto loans, or other assets such as leases, credit card debt, a company's receivables, or even derivative products of any of the assets listed. While the individual assets may be small and not very liquid, pooling the assets facilitates them being sold to individual investors in the secondary markets. This pooling or repackaging of assets is sometimes called securitization. Securitization allows the risk of investing in the underlying assets to be diversified because each security will represent a fraction of the total value of the entire diverse pool of assets.

Similar in structure to collateralized mortgage obligations (CMOs), CDOs represent different types of debt and credit risk. Like CMOs, the different types of debt and risk categories are often called *tranches* or *slices*. Each tranche has a different maturity and risk associated with it. The higher the risk, the more the CDO pays. In practice, investors will choose a tranche with a risk-and-return combination that is suitable for them.

Cautions when investing with CDOs should include the following:

- Some CDOs are so complex that individual investors may not fully understand the product and, therefore, do not understand what they are purchasing. While the securitization of the assets easily enables their sale to individual investors, the product is recognized as being more suitable to institutional or sophisticated investors.

- The sale of the individual assets from the originators of the loans to those who are repackaging them allows the originators to avoid having to collect on them when they become due because they are now owned by someone else. In this case, the issuer of the CDO owns the assets. In turn, this may lead to originators of loans being less judicious and disciplined in adhering to sound lending practices when the loans are made.

3. 10. 5 TREASURY SECURITIES

The U.S. Treasury Department determines the quantity and types of government securities it must issue to meet federal budget needs. The marketplace determines the interest rates those securities will pay. In general, the interest that government securities pay is exempt from state and municipal taxation but subject to federal taxation.

The federal government is the nation's largest borrower, as well as the best credit risk. Interest and principal on securities issued by the U.S. government are backed by its full faith and credit, which is based on its power to tax.

Although there is no default risk to speak of with Treasury securities, that does not mean investors can't lose money. Government securities trade in the secondary market (over the counter) and are subject to interest rate risk just like other debt securities.

3. 10. 5. 1 Treasury Bills (T-Bills)

T-bills are short-term obligations issued at a discount from par. Rather than making regular cash interest payments, bills trade at a discount from par value; the return on a T-bill is the difference between the price the investor pays and the par value at which the bill matures.

3. 10. 5. 1. 1 Maturities and Denominations

Treasury bills are issued in denominations of $100 to $5 million, have original maturities of 4, 13, and 26 weeks and are auctioned weekly by the U.S. Treasury.

TAKE NOTE   Maximum T-bill maturities are subject to change.

---

3. 10. 5. 1. 2 Pricing for T-Bills

T-bills are quoted on a yield basis and sold at a discount from par. They are zero-coupon securities.

EXAMPLE

Issue	Bid	Ask
T-bills maturing 03/15/05	1.15	1.12

The bid reflects the yield buyers want to receive. The ask reflects the yield sellers are willing to accept.

TAKE NOTE   The exam will not require you to calculate the bid and ask prices of T-bills.

Because T-bills are quoted in yield, a T-bill quote has a bid higher than its asked, which is the reverse of bid-ask relationships for other instruments. Higher yield on the bid side translates into a lower dollar price.

3. 10. 5. 2 Treasury Notes (T-Notes)

Unlike Treasury bills, **T-notes** pay interest every six months. They are sold at auction every four weeks.

2 – 10
year)

3. 10. 5. 2. 1   Maturities and Denominations

Issued in denominations of $100 to $5 million, T-notes are intermediate-term bonds maturing in 2 to 10 years. T-notes mature at par, or they can be **refunded**. If a T-note is refunded, the government offers the investor a new security with a new interest rate and maturity date as an alternative to a cash payment for the maturing note.

3. 10. 5. 2. 2   Pricing for T-Notes

T-notes are issued, quoted, and traded as a percentage of par in $\frac{1}{32}$s.

EXAMPLE   A quote of 98.24, which can also be expressed as 98-24 or 98:24, on a $1,000 note means that the note is selling for $98\frac{24}{32}$% of its $1,000 par value. In this instance, .24 designates $\frac{24}{32}$ of 1%, not a decimal. A quote of 98.24 equals 98.75% of $1,000, or $987.50.

Pricing of T-Notes

A bid of:	Means:	Or:
98.01	$98\frac{1}{32}$% of $1,000	$980.3125
98.02	$98\frac{2}{32}$% of $1,000	$980.6250
98.03	$98\frac{3}{32}$% of $1,000	$980.9375
98.10	$98\frac{10}{32}$% of $1,000	$983.1250
98.11	$98\frac{11}{32}$% of $1,000	$983.4375
98.12	$98\frac{12}{32}$% of $1,000	$983.7500

3. 10. 5. 3 Treasury Bonds (T-Bonds)

T-bonds are long-term securities (10 to 30 years in original maturity) that pay interest every six months.

10 30 year)

3. 10. 5. 3. 1   Maturities and Denominations

Treasury bonds are issued in denominations of $100 to $5 million and mature in more than 10 years from the date of issue.

3. 10. 5. 3. 2   *Pricing for T-Bonds*

T-bonds are quoted exactly like T-notes.

Testable Features of Treasury Bills, Notes, and Bonds

Marketable Government Securities			
Type	**Maturity**	**Pricing**	**Form**
T-bills	Less than 1 year	Issued at a discount; priced on discount basis	Book entry
T-notes	2–10 years (intermediate-term)	Priced at percentage of par	Book entry
T-bonds	Greater than 10 years (long-term)	Priced at percentage of par	Book entry

TEST TOPIC ALERT   Testable Features of Treasury Bills, Notes, and Bonds

3. 10. 6   TREASURY RECEIPTS

Created by BDs, not backed by US govt

Brokerage firms can create a type of zero-coupon bond known as **Treasury receipts** from U.S. Treasury notes and bonds. Broker-dealers buy Treasury securities, place them in trust at a bank, and sell separate receipts against the principal and coupon payments. The Treasury securities held in trust collateralize the Treasury receipts. Unlike Treasury securities, Treasury receipts are not backed by the full faith and credit of the U.S. government.

EXAMPLE   To illustrate how Treasury receipts are created, think of a $1,000 10-year Treasury note with a 6% coupon as 21 separate payment obligations. The first 20 are the semiannual $30 interest payment obligations until maturity. The 21st is the obligation to repay the $1,000 principal at maturity. An investor may purchase a Treasury receipt for any of the 20 interest payments or the principal repayment.

Each Treasury receipt is priced at a discount from the payment amount, like a zero-coupon bond.

3. 10. 6. 1   STRIPS

Created by US govt

In 1984, the Treasury Department entered the zero-coupon bond market by designating certain Treasury issues as suitable for stripping into interest and principal components.

These securities became known as **Separate Trading of Registered Interest and Principal of Securities (STRIPS)**. Although the securities underlying Treasury STRIPS are the U.S. government's direct obligation, major banks and dealers perform the actual separation and trading.

TEST TOPIC ALERT STRIPS are backed in full by the U.S. government. Receipts are not. Treasury receipts are sold under names like Certificates of Accrual on Treasury Securities (CATS) and Treasury Income Growth Receipts (TIGRS). Both are quoted in yield.

3. 10. 7 TREASURY INFLATION PROTECTION SECURITIES (TIPS)

A type of Treasury issue, known as **Treasury Inflation Protection Securities (TIPS)**, helps protect investors against purchasing power risk. These notes are issued with a fixed interest rate, but the principal amount is adjusted semiannually by an amount equal to the change in the **Consumer Price Index (CPI)**, the standard measurement of inflation.

The interest payment the investor receives every six months is equal to the fixed interest rate times the newly adjusted principal. In times of inflation, the interest payments increase, while in times of deflation, the interest payments fall. These notes are sold at lower interest rates than conventional fixed-rate Treasury notes because of their adjustable nature.

Like other Treasury notes, TIPS are exempt from state and local income taxes on the interest income generated, but they are subject to federal taxation. However, in any year when the principal is adjusted for inflation, that increase is considered reportable income for that year even though the increase will not be received until the note matures.

3. 10. 8 AGENCY ISSUES

Congress authorizes the following agencies of the federal government to issue debt securities:

■ Farm Credit Administration
■ Government National Mortgage Association (GNMA or Ginnie Mae)

Other agency-like organizations operated by private corporations include the following:

■ Federal Home Loan Mortgage Corporation (FHLMC or Freddie Mac)
■ Federal National Mortgage Association (FNMA or Fannie Mae)
■ Student Loan Marketing Association (SLMA or Sallie Mae)

The term *agency* is sometimes used to refer to entities that are not technically government agencies but that do have ties to the government. Fannie Mae is privately owned but government sponsored.

TAKE NOTE Settlement of agency securities is regular way (two business days).

3. 10. 8. 1 Yields and Maturities

Agency issues have higher yields than direct obligations of the federal government but lower yields than corporate debt securities. Their maturities range from short to long term.

Agency issues are quoted as percentages of par and trade actively in the secondary market.

3. 10. 8. 2 Taxation for Agency Issues

Government agency issues that are backed by mortgages are taxed at the federal, state, and local levels. Other agency securities are generally taxed at the federal level only.

3. 10. 8. 3 Government National Mortgage Association (Ginnie Mae)

The **Government National Mortgage Association (GNMA)** is a government-owned corporation that supports the Department of Housing and Urban Development. Ginnie Maes are the only agency securities backed by the full faith and credit of the federal government.

3. 10. 8. 3. 1   Types of GNMA Issues

Ginnie Mae does not originate mortgage loans, nor does it purchase, sell, or issue securities. Instead, private lending institutions approved by GNMA originate eligible loans, pool them into securities, known as pass-through certificates, and sell the GNMA mortgage-backed securities (MBS) to investors. These lending institutions can include mortgage companies, commercial banks, and thrift institutions of all sizes, as well as state housing finance agencies. Ginnie Mae guarantees only mortgage-backed securities backed by single and multifamily home loans insured by government agencies, primarily the Federal Housing Association (FHA) and the Department of Veteran Affairs (VA) as well as others. Like the principal on a single mortgage, the principal represented by a GNMA certificate constantly decreases as the mortgages are paid down. GNMA pass-throughs pay higher interest rates than comparable Treasury securities, yet are guaranteed by the federal government.

GNMA also guarantees timely payment of interest and principal. GNMAs are backed directly by the government, so risk of default is nearly zero. Prices, yields, and maturities fluctuate in line with general interest rate trends. If interest rates fall, homeowners tend to pay off their mortgages early, which accelerates the certificates' maturities. If interest rates rise, certificates may mature more slowly.

GNMAs are issued in $25,000 face value certificates but can be purchased in minimum denominations as low as $1,000. Because few mortgages last the full term, yield quotes are based on a 12-year prepayment assumption; that is, a mortgage balance should be prepaid in full after 12 years of normally scheduled payments.

In addition to interest rate risk (the risk that rates rise, causing the value of the underlying mortgages to fall), there are two other types of risk associated with mortgage-backed securities.

The first is **prepayment risk**, the risk that the underlying mortgages will be paid off earlier than anticipated. This will occur if interest rates fall, causing homeowners to refinance their mortgages at lower rates.

The second is **extended maturity risk**, the risk that the underlying mortgages will remain outstanding longer than anticipated. This will occur if interest rates rise, virtually eliminating any refinancings.

3. 10. 8. 3. 2   Taxation for GNMA

Interest earned on GNMA certificates is taxable at the federal, state, and local levels.

TAKE NOTE

GNMAs are backed in full by the U.S. government. Other agency instruments discussed next are not; they are backed by their own issuing authority.

Know the following GNMA features:

- $1,000 minimums

- Monthly interest and principal payments

- Taxed at all levels

- Pass-through certificates

- Significant reinvestment risk

TEST TOPIC ALERT

The Series 7 exam expects you to know that mortgage-backed securities (MBS) are susceptible to reinvestment risk. The reasons are outlined below.

When interest rates fall, mortgage holders typically refinance at lower rates. This means that they pay off their mortgages early, which causes a prepayment of principal to holders of mortgage-backed securities. The early principal payments cannot be reinvested at a comparable return.

Sometimes the test asks which instruments are not subject to reinvestment risk.

Of the ones listed, the best answer is typically a zero-coupon bond. No interest is paid on a current basis, so the investor has no reinvestment risk.

3. 10. 8. 4 Farm Credit System

The **Farm Credit System (FCS)** is a national network of lending institutions that provides agricultural financing and credit. The system is a privately owned, government-sponsored enterprise that raises loanable funds through the sale of Farm Credit securities to investors.

These funds are made available to farmers through a nationwide network of eight banks and 225 Farm Credit lending institutions. The Farm Credit Administration (FCA), a government agency, oversees the system.

The federal Farm Credit System issues discount notes, bonds, and master notes. The maturities range from one day to 30 years. The proceeds from the sale of securities are used to provide farmers with real estate loans, rural home mortgage loans, and crop insurance. Interest paid on these securities is exempt from state and local taxation.

3. 10. 8. 5 Federal Home Loan Mortgage Corporation (Freddie Mac)

The **Federal Home Loan Mortgage Corporation (FHLMC)** is a public corporation. It was created to promote the development of a nationwide secondary market in mortgages by buying residential mortgages from financial institutions and packaging them into mortgage-backed securities for sale to investors.

3. 10. 8. 5. 1   Pass-Through Certificates

A pass-through security is created by pooling a group of mortgages and selling certificates representing interests in the pool. The term *pass-through* refers to the mechanism of passing homebuyers' interest and principal payments from the mortgage holder to the investors. Fannie Mae, Ginnie Mae, and Freddie Mac function this way.

FHLMC sells two types of pass-through securities: **mortgage participation certificates (PCs)** and **guaranteed mortgage certificates (GMCs)**. PCs make principal and interest payments once a month; GMCs make interest payments twice a year and principal payments once a year.

3. 10. 8. 5. 2   Taxation for Freddie Mac

Income from FHLMC securities is subject to federal, state, and local income taxes.

3. 10. 8. 6   Federal National Mortgage Association (Fannie Mae)

The **Federal National Mortgage Association (FNMA)** is a publicly held corporation that provides mortgage capital. FNMA purchases conventional and insured mortgages from agencies such as the FHA and the VA. The securities it creates are backed by FNMA's general credit.

3. 10. 8. 6. 1   Types of FNMA Issues

FNMA issues debentures, short-term discount notes, and mortgage-backed securities. The notes are issued in denominations of $5,000, $25,000, $100,000, $500,000, and $1 million. Debentures with maturities from 3 to 25 years are issued in minimum denominations of $10,000 in increments of $5,000. Interest is paid semiannually. They are issued in book-entry form only.

3. 10. 8. 6. 2   Taxation for FNMA

Interest from FNMA securities is taxed at the federal, state, and local levels.

3. 10. 8. 7   Sallie Mae

The **Student Loan Marketing Association (Sallie Mae)** issues discount notes and short-term floating rate notes. The floaters have six-month maturities. The proceeds from the securities sales are used to provide student loans for higher education. Interest paid on Sallie Mae securities is taxable at the federal level and is exempt from taxation in most states. SLM stock is listed for trading.

QUICK QUIZ 3.J

Objective: Describe the use of debt securities based on different investment objectives

1. A 27-year-old client is in a low tax bracket and wants an aggressive long-term growth investment. If his representative recommends a high-rated municipal bond fund, the representative has

   A. violated the suitability requirements of FINRA
   B. recommended a suitable investment because municipal bond funds are good long-term investments
   C. committed no violation because municipal bond funds weather the ups and downs of the markets well
   D. committed no violation if the customer agrees to the transaction

2. Your 45-year-old client is interested in obtaining the highest current income possible from his investment. He is willing to accept fluctuations in investment principal. Which of the following would best suit this client's investment objective?

   A. High-yield bond fund
   B. Aggressive growth fund
   C. Tax-free money market fund
   D. Balanced fund

3. An investor owns investment-grade corporate bonds that have an 8% coupon. They mature next year. Current interest rates are lower today than they were when the bonds were issued. What type of risk does the investor face when the bonds mature next year?

   A. Call risk
   B. Reinvestment risk
   C. Credit risk
   D. Interest rate risk

4. A customer wishes to buy a security providing periodic interest payments, safety of principal, and protection from purchasing power risk. The customer should purchase

   A. TIPS
   B. TIGRS
   C. CMOs
   D. STRIPS

5. Which of the following statements regarding U.S. government agency obligations are TRUE?

   A. They are all direct obligations of the U.S. government.
   B. They generally have higher yields than yields of Treasury securities.
   C. The FNMA interest is only taxed at the federal level.
   D. Securities issued by GNMA trade on the NYSE floor.

6. A registered representative may compare the performance of a CMO investment to the performance of a security issued by which of the following agencies?

A. GNMA
B. FDIC
C. SLMA
D. None of these

All Quick Quiz answers are found at the end of their units.

3. 11 MONEY MARKET INSTRUMENTS

Money market instruments are debt securities with short-term maturities, typically one year or less. Because they are short-term instruments, money market securities are highly liquid and they provide a relatively high degree of safety because most issuers have high credit ratings. For that reason, they are ideally suited for emergencies and to take advantage of investing opportunities.

Money market securities issued by the U.S. government and its agencies include the following:

■ Treasury bills that trade in the secondary market

■ Treasury and agency securities with remaining maturities of one year or less

■ Short-term discount notes issued by various smaller agencies

Money market portfolios that include municipal securities are considered tax-exempt money market instruments.

The primary risk that investors face with these types of investments, including U.S. Treasury bills and money market mutual funds, is losing ground to inflation, known as **inflation risk, constant dollar risk** or **purchasing power risk.** In addition, you should be aware that money in money market funds offered by investment companies usually is not insured. While such funds have rarely resulted in investor losses, the potential is always there.

3. 11. 1 THE MONEY MARKET AND INSTITUTIONS

Some money market securities are intended for retail investors, while other others are intended for institutional investors.

TAKE NOTE

Money market mutual funds for retail investors are designed to have a stable NAV of $1.00 per share. They are not guaranteed, nor are they protected by FDIC insurance. It is rare, but it is possible to lose money in a money market mutual fund as a retail investor.

An important distinction between institutional and retail money market funds lies in the pricing of the funds. Retail money market funds are allowed to keep a net asset value of $1 per share. Institutional funds, on the other hand, have a floating NAV. This means that the price can change from day to day, based on the actual conditions of the market.

The only other stable NAV are **institutional money market funds,** which are 99.5% government securities.

3. 11. 1. 1 Banker's Acceptance (BA)

Certain corporations in the import-export business will often use BAs as a short-term time draft with a specified payment date drawn on a bank—essentially a postdated check or line of credit. The payment date of a BA is normally between one and 270 days.

American corporations use bankers' acceptances extensively to finance international trade—that is, a BA typically pays for goods and services in a foreign country.

3. 11. 1. 2 Commercial Paper (Prime Paper)

Corporations issue short-term, unsecured **commercial paper**, or promissory notes, to raise cash to finance accounts receivable and seasonal inventory overages. Commercial paper interest rates are lower than bank loan rates. Commercial paper maturities range from one to 270 days, although most mature within 90 days. Commercial paper is issued at a discount from face value.

Typically, companies with excellent credit ratings issue commercial paper. The primary buyers of commercial paper are money market funds, commercial banks, pension funds, insurance companies, corporations, and nongovernmental agencies.

3. 11. 1. 3 Negotiable CDs (Jumbo CDs)

These represent time deposits that banks offer (issue). They have minimum face values of $100,000, but most are issued for $1 million or more. Any amount issued that is greater than FDIC insurance ($250,000) is an unsecured promissory note of the bank.

Most **negotiable CDs** mature in one year or less, with the maturity date often set to suit a buyer's needs. Because the CDs are negotiable, they can be traded in the secondary market.

QUICK QUIZ 3.K

Objective: Identify various money market securities and risks

1. What is the greatest risk associated with money market securities?
   A. Interest rate risk
   B. Default risk
   C. Call risk
   D. Constant dollar risk

2. All of the following are money market securities EXCEPT
   A. a 30 year treasury bond that matures in August
   B. a treasury bill
   C. a $150,000 CD that matures in 1½ years
   D. a banker's acceptances

3. All of the following are money market securities EXCEPT
   A. commercial paper that matures in 8 months
   B. a bankers acceptance that matures in 10 months
   C. a negotiable CD in the amount of $1 million
   D. a treasury note maturing in 2 years

All Quick Quiz answers are found at the end of their units.

3. 12   INVESTMENT COMPANIES

An **investment company** is a corporation or trust that pools investors' money and then invests that money in securities on their behalf. By investing these pooled funds as a single large account jointly owned by every investor in a company, the investment company management attempts to invest and manage funds for people more efficiently than the individual investors could themselves. Additionally, it is expected that a professional money manager should be able to outperform the average investor in the market.

3. 12. 1   INVESTMENT COMPANY PURPOSE

Investment companies allow investors to pool their money together and have a professional invest the money to a clearly defined investment objective.

Like corporate issuers, investment companies raise capital by selling shares to the public. Investment companies must abide by the same registration and prospectus requirements imposed by the **Securities Act of 1933** on other issuers. Investment companies are subject to regulations regarding how their shares are sold to the public, and they are regulated by the **Investment Company Act of 1940**.

The Investment Company Act of 1940 is the federal law that established the fact that there are three types of investment companies, only two of which are covered here because the third is not relevant for the exam.

3. 12. 2   UNIT INVESTMENT TRUSTS (UITs)

Unit investment trusts, or UITs, fall in the same category as mutual funds and closed-end funds. All three are investment companies, which means they pool money from many investors and invest it based on specific investment goals.

The key difference with UITs, however, is that once a UIT sets its portfolio, it remains the same for the life of the fund (barring any major corporate events, such as a merger or bankruptcy proceeding) and the term is fixed.

UITs raise money by selling shares known as "units" to investors, typically in a one-time public offering. Each unit represents an ownership slice of the trust and gives the investor a proportional right to income and capital gains generated by the fund's investments, typically either stocks or bonds.

The performance of a UIT's underlying investments, minus fund fees, determines the trust's investment return. Those investments are generally fixed, with a UIT generally holding the securities in which it invests for the life of the fund, which is determined at the time of the fund's initial offering.

UITs are designed to be held for the life of the fund, but many UITs are publicly traded, which might offer investors an opportunity to sell their shares early should their investment goals change.

3. 12. 3   EXCHANGE-TRADED FUNDS (ETFs)   — commissionable   transaction

Exchange-traded funds, or ETFs, are investment companies that are legally classified as open-end companies or unit investment trusts (UITs), but differ from traditional open-end companies and UITs. ETFs issue their shares in large blocks (blocks of 50,000 shares, for example) that are known as creation units. Those who purchase creation units are frequently large institutional traders or investors. The creation units can then be split up and sold as individual shares in the secondary markets. This permits individual investors to purchase individual shares (instead of creation units).

Investors who want to sell their ETF shares have two options: (1) they can sell individual shares to other investors in the secondary market, or (2) if they own creation units, they can sell the creation units back to the ETF. In addition, ETFs generally will redeem creation units by giving investors the securities that comprise the portfolio, instead of cash. It is important to remember that because of the limited redeemability of ETF shares, ETFs are not considered to be, nor may they call themselves, mutual funds.

For purposes of Series 7 testing, we will consider individual investors who own exchange-traded fund shares (not creation units) purchased in the secondary market. Understanding that exchange-traded fund shares are not mutual fund shares, it should be expected and is common that they are often compared to mutual fund shares. In that light, exchange-traded funds have some advantages and disadvantages to be considered when compared to open-end (mutual funds).

Following are some advantages of exchange-traded funds when compared to open-end (mutual funds).

- Pricing and ease of trading—because individual ETF shares are traded on exchanges, they can be bought or sold anytime during the trading day at the price they are currently trading at, as opposed to mutual funds, which use forward pricing and are generally priced once at the end of the trading day.

- Margin—ETFs can be bought and sold short on margin like other exchange-traded products. Mutual funds cannot be bought on margin nor can they be sold short.

- Operating costs—ETFs traditionally have operating costs and expenses that are lower than most mutual funds.

- Tax efficiency—ETFs can and sometimes do distribute capital gains to shareholders like mutual funds do but this is rare. Understanding that these capital gains distributions are not likely, there are no further tax consequences with ETF shares until investors sell their shares. This may be the single greatest advantage associated with ETFs.

Following are some disadvantages of exchange-traded funds when compared to open-end (mutual funds).

- Commissions—The purchase or sale of ETF shares is a commissionable transaction. The commissions paid can erode the low expense advantage of ETFs. This would have the greatest impact when trading in and out of ETF shares frequently or when investing smaller sums of money.

- Overtrading—Given the ability to trade in and out of ETFs easily, the temptation to do so is possible. Excessive trading can eliminate the advantages associated with investing in a diversified portfolio and add to overall commissions being paid by the investor, further eroding any of the other expense and operating advantages associated with ETFs

3. 12. 4 REAL ESTATE INVESTMENT TRUSTS (REITs)

REITs are not an investment company security but are extensively regulated in ways similar to the Investment Company Act of 1940. REITs allow investors to pool their money and form a trust to invest as it relates to real estate. REITs can be set up to have different portfolio structures. When the trusts own property, they are known as **equity REITs**. When the trusts own mortgages on property, they are known as **mortgage REITs**. Those that hold both are **hybrid REITs.**

Reasons that an investor might include REITs in their investment portfolio include the following:

■ REITs allow investors the opportunity to invest in real estate without incurring the degree of liquidity risk historically associated with real estate because REITs trade on exchanges and OTC.

■ REITs can provide some hedge to price movements in other equity markets. While it isn't always the case, real estate prices historically have had a negative correlation to stock prices.

■ REITs provide a reasonable expectation of income from dividends and capital appreciation due to the appreciation of the assets the trust holds.

Risks generally associated with REITs include the following:

■ The investor has no direct control over the portfolio and relies on professional management to make all purchase and sale decisions. While the expectation of having a professionally managed portfolio should be considered advantageous, the quality of the portfolio lies with the quality of the professional management.

■ Problematic loans within mortgage REIT portfolios can cause decreases in income flow and diminish capital returns.

■ Dividends paid by the trusts do not meet the requirements of qualified dividends and therefore are taxable at full ordinary income tax rates to the investor.

TEST TOPIC ALERT

REITs:

■ Not a limited partnership

■ Not an investment company

■ Pass-through income, not losses

■ 75% of total investment assets in real estate

■ 75% of gross income from rents or mortgage interest

■ Must distribute 90% or more of income to shareholders to avoid taxation as a corporation

■ Trade on exchanges or OTC

■ Dividends received from REITS are taxed as ordinary income

3. 12. 5 MANAGEMENT COMPANIES

The most familiar type of investment company is the **management investment company**, which actively manages a securities portfolio to achieve a stated investment objective. A management investment company is either **open-end** or **closed-end**. Both closed- and open-end companies sell shares to the public in an initial public offering; the primary difference between them is that a closed-end company's initial offering of shares is limited (it closes after its authorized number of shares number have been sold) and an open-end company is perpetually offering new shares to the public (it is continually open to new investors).

3. 12. 5. 1 Closed-End Management Companies

A closed-end management company will raise capital for its portfolio by conducting a common stock offering, much like any other publicly traded company that raises capital to invest in its business. In the initial offering, the company registers a fixed number of shares with the SEC and offers them all to the public with a prospectus for a limited time through underwriters.

Once all the shares have been sold, the fund is closed to new investors. Many times, a fund elects to be a closed-end company because the sector in which it intends to invest has a limited amount of securities available. Closed-end investment companies may also issue bonds and preferred stock.

Closed-end investment companies are often called publicly traded funds. After the stock is sold in the initial offering, anyone can buy or sell shares in the secondary market (i.e., on an exchange or OTC) in transactions between private investors. Supply and demand determine the bid price (price at which an investor can sell) and the ask price (price at which an investor can buy). Closed-end fund shares may trade above (at a premium to) or below (at a discount to) the shares' NAV. The bid price is also known as the NAV, and the ask price is also known as the POP (public offering price). When buying and selling closed-end investment companies in the secondary market, there will be a commission paid to execute the trade.

TEST TOPIC ALERT   Closed-end company shares, once issued, trade in the secondary market where price is determined by supply and demand. There is no prospectus delivery requirement once they trade in the secondary market.

3. 12. 5. 2 Open-End Management Companies

An open-end management company (**mutual fund**) only issues one class of security and that's a common share. It does not specify the exact number of shares it intends to issue but registers an open offering with the SEC. In other words, mutual funds conduct a continuous primary offering of common shares. You should understand that mutual funds can purchase common stock, preferred stock, and bonds for their investment portfolios, but as an investor that invests in the ABC Bond Fund, or any mutual fund, only purchases common shares of the fund. With this registration type, they can raise an unlimited amount of investment capital by continuously issuing new shares. Conversely, when investors want to sell their holdings in a mutual fund, the fund itself redeems those shares. Mutual fund shares do not trade in the secondary market.

Technically defined as an "**open-end management company**," a mutual fund is an investment company that pools money from many investors and invests it based on specific investment goals. The mutual fund raises money by selling its own shares to investors. The money is used to purchase a portfolio of stocks, bonds, short-term money market instruments, other securities or assets, or some combination of these investments. Each share represents an ownership slice of the fund and gives the investor a proportional right, based on the number of shares she owns, to income and capital gains that the fund generates from its investments.

The particular investments a fund makes are determined by its objectives and, in the case of an actively managed fund, by the investment style and skill of the fund's professional manager or managers. The holdings of the mutual fund are known as its underlying investments, and the performance of those investments, minus fund fees, determine the fund's investment return.

Comparison of Open-End and Closed-End Investment Companies

	Open-End	Closed-End – *ETF*
Capitalization	Unlimited; continuous offering of shares	Fixed; single offering of shares
Issues	Common stock only; no debt securities; permitted to borrow	May issue common and preferred stock and debt securities
Shares	Full or fractional	Full only
Offerings and Trading	Sold and redeemed by the fund only; continuous primary offering; must redeem shares	Initial primary offering; secondary trading OTC or on an exchange; does not redeem shares
Pricing	Selling price determined by formula in the prospectus	CMV + commission; price determined by supply and demand
Shareholder Rights	Dividends (when declared); voting	Dividends (when declared); voting; preemptive rights
Ex-Date	Set by BOD	Set by SRO

3. 12. 6 DIVERSIFIED AND NONDIVERSIFIED

Diversification provides risk management that makes mutual funds popular with many investors. However, not all investment companies feature diversified portfolios.

3. 12. 6. 1 Diversified

Under the Investment Company Act of 1940, a diversified investment company is one that meets the requirements of the 75-5-10 test:

- At least 75% of the fund's total assets must be invested in securities issued by companies other than the investment company itself or its affiliates.
- The 75% must be invested in such a way that

    — no more than 5% of the fund's total assets are invested in the securities of any one issuer, and

    — no more than 10% of the outstanding voting securities of any one issuer is owned (by the 75%).

TEST TOPIC ALERT   Remember, for testing purposes, the 5% and 10% limitations are part of the 75% invested. There are no conditions attached to the remaining 25%.

TEST TOPIC ALERT   If a security represents 5% or less of the fund's total assets at the time of purchase and thereafter exceeds 5% due to capital appreciation, no action is required in order to maintain a diversified status.

3. 12. 6. 2 Nondiversified — *Sector Stocks/funds perhaps*

A nondiversified investment company does not meet the 75-5-10 test. An investment company that specializes in one industry is not necessarily a nondiversified company. Some investment companies choose to concentrate their assets in an industry or a geographic area, such as health care stocks, technology stocks, or South American stocks; these are known as specialized funds or sector funds. Sector funds must have at least 25% of assets invested in a particular sector of the economy or geographic area. A sector fund can still be diversified, provided it meets the 75-5-10 test.

TEST TOPIC ALERT

Both open- and closed-end companies can be diversified or nondiversified.

QUICK QUIZ 3.L

Objective: Compare the different types of investment companies

1. A unit investment trust can best be described as

   I.   a managed investment company
   II. a nonmanaged investment company
   III. a company that issues redeemable securities
   IV. a company that issues securities that are actively traded in the secondary marketplace

   A. I and III
   B. I and IV
   C. II and III
   D. II and IV

2. Which of the following is NOT a management company?

   A. A mutual fund
   B. An open-end company
   C. A unit investment trust
   D. A closed-end company

3. How do closed-end investment companies differ from open-end investment companies?

   I.   Closed-end companies register their shares with the SEC; open-end companies do not.
   II. Closed-end company shares are sold with prospectus only in IPOs; open-end shares solicitations must always be accompanied by a prospectus.
   III. Closed-end companies issue a fixed number of shares; there is no limit on the number of shares issued by an open-end company.
   IV. Closed-end companies may only sell shares to institutional investors; open-end companies may sell to any investor.

   A. I and II
   B. I and III
   C. II and III
   D. III and IV

All Quick Quiz answers are found at the end of their units.

3. 13 MUTUAL FUND CHARACTERISTICS AND CATEGORIES

While there are literally thousands of individual mutual funds, there are only a handful of major fund categories:

■ Stock funds invest in stocks.

■ Bond funds invest in bonds.

■ Balanced funds invest in a combination of stocks and bonds.

■ Money market funds invest in very short-term investments and are sometimes described as cash equivalents.

Mutual funds are equity investments, as are individual stocks. When you buy shares of a fund, you become a part owner of the fund. This is true of bond funds, as well as stock funds, which means there is an important distinction between owning an individual bond and owning a fund that owns the bond. When you buy a bond, you are promised a specific rate of interest and return of your principal. That's not the case with a bond fund, which owns a number of different bonds with different rates and maturities. What your equity ownership of the fund provides is the right to a share of what the fund collects in interest, realizes in capital gains, and receives back if it holds a bond to maturity. In other words, with a mutual fund, you own a piece of what it is worth (its value), not a piece of the securities held in its portfolio.

When comparing mutual funds, investors should select funds that match their personal objectives. When comparing funds with similar objectives, the investor should review information regarding each of the following for each fund:

Performance

Securities law requires that each fund disclose the average annual total returns for 1-, 5-, and 10-year periods, or since inception if less than 10 years. Performance must reflect full sales loads with no discounts. The manager's track record in keeping with the fund's objectives in the prospectus is also important.

TEST TOPIC ALERT   Fund quotations of average annual return must be for 1-, 5-, and 10-year periods, or as long as the fund has operated.

Costs

Historically, mutual funds have charged front-end loads of up to 8.5% of the money invested. This percentage compensates a sales force. Many low-load funds charge between 2% and 5%. Other funds may charge a back-end load when funds are withdrawn. Some funds charge ongoing fees under Section 12b1 of the Investment Company Act of 1940. These funds deduct annual fees to pay for marketing and distribution costs.

Expense ratio

A fund's expense ratio relates the management fees and operating expenses to the fund's net assets. All mutual funds, load and no-load, have expense ratios. The expense ratio is calculated by dividing a fund's expenses by its average net assets. An expense ratio of 1% means that the fund charges $1 per year for every $100 invested. Typically, aggressive funds and international funds have higher expense ratios.

Sales loads and fund expenses are different

Stock funds generally have expense ratios between 1% and 1.5% of a fund's average net assets. For bond funds, the ratio is typically between .5% and 1%.

TEST TOPIC ALERT

You may be asked about the factors included in calculating a mutual fund's expense ratio. The BOD stipend, investment adviser fee, custodian fee, transfer agent fee, 12b-1 fee, and legal and accounting expenses are all included. The sales load is not. The formula for the computation of a mutual fund's expense ratio is:

fund expenses ÷ average net assets = expense ratio

EXAMPLE

$$\frac{\$1 \text{ million expenses}}{\$100 \text{ million average net assets}} = 1\% \text{ expense ratio}$$

TAKE NOTE

The fund's expense ratio is found in the prospectus and measures the efficiency of its management. The largest part of the expense ratio is the investment advisory fee.

Taxation

Mutual fund investors pay taxes on any dividends or capital gains the fund distributes. Even if the investor elects to reinvest some or all of the distribution, the total amount is taxable in the year earned by the fund.

Portfolio turnover

The costs of buying and selling securities, including commissions or markups and markdowns, are reflected in the portfolio turnover ratio. It is not uncommon for an aggressive growth fund to reflect an annual turnover rate of 100% or more. A 100% turnover rate means the fund replaces its portfolio annually. If the fund achieves superior returns, the strategy is working; if not, the strategy is subjecting investors to undue costs.

The portfolio turnover rate reflects a fund's holding period. If a fund has a turnover rate of 100%, it holds its securities, on average, for less than one year. Therefore, all gains are likely to be short term and subject to the maximum tax rate; a portfolio with a turnover rate of 25% has an average holding period of four years and gains are likely taxed at the long-term rate.

Services offered

The services mutual funds offer include:

■ retirement account custodianship,
■ investment plans,
■ check-writing privileges,
■ telephone transfers,
■ conversion privileges,

- combination investment privileges, and
- withdrawal plans.

Investors should always weigh the cost of services provided against the value of the services to the investor.

3. 13. 1 STOCK FUNDS

A mutual fund, which uses stock to meet its stated objectives, can generally be referred to as a stock fund. Common stock is normally found in the portfolio of any mutual fund that has growth as a primary or secondary objective. Equity funds have historically outpaced inflation over most 10-year time horizons.

3. 13. 2 GROWTH/VALUE FUNDS

Growth funds invest in stocks of companies whose businesses are growing rapidly. Growth companies tend to reinvest all or most of their profits for research and development rather than pay dividends. Growth funds are focused on generating capital gains rather than income.

Growth managers may consider stocks that many feel are overvalued because there may still be upside potential. As such, funds managed for growth tend to have elevated levels of risk.

Blue-chip or conservative growth funds invest in established and more recognized companies to achieve growth with less risk. Generally these funds own shares of companies with fairly large **market capitalization. Market cap,** as it is usually referred to, is the total number of shares of common stock outstanding multiplied by the current market value per share. So a listed company with 300 million shares outstanding where the share price is $50 would have a market cap of $15 billion and would be considered a large-cap stock. Funds investing in stocks like this are sometimes called **large-cap funds** (their portfolio consists of companies with a market capitalization of more than $10 billion). These types of funds can be more stable and less volatile in a turbulent market.

EXAMPLE   An investor who is willing to take moderate risk and is willing to invest for a minimum of 5–7 years may be interested in a blue-chip or large-cap growth fund.

3. 13. 3 AGGRESSIVE GROWTH FUNDS

Aggressive growth funds are sometimes called **performance funds.** These funds are willing to take greater risk to maximize capital appreciation. Some of these funds invest in newer companies with relatively small capitalization (less than $2 billion capitalization) and are called **small-cap funds.**

Mid-cap funds are somewhat less aggressive and have in their portfolios shares of companies with a market capitalization of between $2 billion and $10 billion.

Large-cap funds have market capitalization of greater than $10 billion. The lower the market cap, the greater the volatility.

EXAMPLE   An investor who is seeking high potential returns with the understanding that there can also be significant losses and is willing to invest for 10–15 years may be interested in an aggressive growth fund that focuses on small- or mid-cap companies.

3. 13. 4 VALUE FUNDS

Value funds (and, therefore, value managers) focus on companies whose stocks are currently undervalued (earnings potential is not reflected in the stock price). These undervalued companies are expected to perform better than the reports indicate, thus providing an opportunity to profit. Value stocks typically have dividend yields higher than growth stocks. Funds managed for value are considered more conservative than funds managed for growth.

EXAMPLE   An investor that is willing to take moderate risk when investing to purchase a vacation home in 7–10 years may be interested in a fund that is value oriented.

3. 13. 5 (EQUITY) INCOME FUNDS

An income fund, also known as an **equity income fund**, stresses current income over growth. The fund's objective may be accomplished by investing in the stocks of companies with long histories of dividend payments, such as utility company stocks, blue-chip stocks, and preferred stocks. These are managed for value, not growth.

EXAMPLE   An investor who is willing to take low to moderate risk and seeks income from equity investments in the form of dividends with some capital appreciation may be interested in an equity income fund, utility fund, or preferred stock fund.

3. 13. 6 OPTION INCOME FUNDS

Option income funds invest in securities on which call options can be sold (known as covered calls). They earn premium income from writing (selling) the options. They may also earn capital gains from trading options at a profit. These funds seek to increase total return by adding income generated by the options to appreciation on the securities held in the portfolio.

3. 13. 7 GROWTH AND INCOME FUNDS

A **growth and income fund** (combination fund) may attempt to combine the objectives of growth and current yield by diversifying its stock portfolio among companies showing long-term growth potential and companies paying high dividends. Often, both value and growth management styles are utilized.

EXAMPLE

An investor seeking dividends and capital appreciation with moderate risk may be interested in a growth and income fund.

3. 13. 8   SPECIALIZED (SECTOR) FUNDS

Many funds attempt to specialize in particular economic sectors or geographic areas. These funds must have a minimum of 25% of their assets invested in their specialties. **Sector funds** offer high appreciation potential, but may also pose higher risks to the investor as a result of the concentration of investments. These funds are speculative in nature. They include gold, technology, pharmaceutical, and biotechnology funds, but can also be geographic, such as investing in companies located in the Pacific Basin or Silicon Valley. Sector funds are often labeled as such in the newspaper listings of mutual fund companies that offer them.

EXAMPLE

An investor who believes the pharmaceutical industry is going to outperform the market over the next 5–10 years and is willing to speculate on the investment may be interested in a sector fund that focuses on the pharmaceutical industry.

3. 13. 9   SPECIAL SITUATION FUNDS

Special situation funds buy securities of companies that may benefit from a change within the companies or in the economy. Takeover candidates and turnaround situations are common investments. These funds are also speculative (high risk).

EXAMPLE

An investor believes the banking industry is going to be going through a phase of mergers and acquisitions. They are willing to take additional risk to possibly profit from the potential consolidation of the industry. They may be interested in a special situation fund that specializes in mergers and acquisitions.

3. 13. 10   BLEND/CORE FUNDS

Blend/core funds are stock funds with a portfolio comprising a number of different classes of stock. Such a fund might include both blue-chip stocks and high-risk/high-potential-return growth stocks. Both growth and value management styles are used. The purpose is to allow investors to diversify their investment via management and securities in a single fund.

TAKE NOTE

Value funds are considered more conservative than growth or blend/core funds.

3. 13. 11   INDEX FUNDS

Index funds invest in securities that mirror a market index, such as the S&P 500. An index fund buys and sells securities in a manner that mirrors the composition of the selected index.

The index may be broad, such as the S&P 500, or narrow, such as a transportation index. The fund's performance should closely track the underlying index performance. Turnover of securities in an index fund's portfolio is minimal, because the only trades that take place are triggered by a change in the index (one company is replaced by another company). As a result, an index fund generally has lower management costs than other types of funds.

EXAMPLE

An investor does not believe in paying for the professional stock selection of a managed fund. In other words, the belief is that it is difficult to outperform the market as a whole (or in part). Under these circumstances, recommending an index fund is appropriate.

3. 13. 12   FOREIGN STOCK FUNDS

Foreign stock funds and **international funds** invest only in the securities of foreign countries (companies that have their principal business activities outside the United States). Long-term capital appreciation is their primary objective, although some funds also seek current income.

3. 13. 13   GLOBAL FUNDS

Global and worldwide funds invest in the securities of both U.S. and foreign countries. The risks involved in a fund concentrating in foreign securities are somewhat different than those for a domestic fund. When a portfolio has a large percentage of foreign securities, currency risk and political risk becomes paramount. These risks are elevated when investing in frontier funds, which invest in pre-emerging economies, because accounting and regulatory schemes are often much less rigorous than what we are used to here in the United States.

Foreign and international stock funds are often purchased in order to diversify an investor's portfolio. After all, investing inside and outside the United States provides a more diversified portfolio than just investing within the United States.

EXAMPLE

An investor has a solid mix of securities, all based in the United States. It is conveyed that taking more risk and diversifying the portfolio at the same time is desired.

A foreign stock fund, international fund, or global or worldwide fund may be suggested with disclosure that the foreign and international funds provide greater diversification but have more risk than the global and worldwide funds.

TAKE NOTE   Foreign stock funds are often purchased in order to diversify an investor's portfolio.

3. 13. 14   BALANCED FUNDS

Invest in Stocks And Bonds

Balanced funds, also known as **hybrid funds,** invest in stocks for appreciation and bonds for income. In a balanced fund, different types of securities are purchased according to a formula the manager may adjust to reflect market conditions.

A balanced fund's portfolio might contain 60% stocks and 40% bonds.

EXAMPLE   A balanced fund may be appropriate for an investor that seeks a conservative balance between stocks and bonds.

3. 13. 15   ASSET ALLOCATION FUNDS

fund mngr switches asset allocation % as he sees fit

Asset allocation funds split investments between stocks for growth, bonds for income, and money market instruments or cash for stability. Fund advisers switch the percentage of holdings in each asset category according to the performance (or expected performance) of that group. These funds can also hold hard assets, such as precious metals like gold and silver, and real estate.

A fund may have 60% of its investments in stock, 20% in bonds, and the remaining 20% in cash. If the stock market is expected to do well, the adviser may switch from cash and bonds to stock. The result may be a portfolio of 80% in stock, 10% in bonds, and 10% in cash.

Conversely, if the stock market is expected to decline, the fund may invest heavily in cash and sell stocks.

Many asset allocation funds are target funds (see the following) that target a specific goal, such as retirement, in a 5-, 10-, 15-, or 20-year period. As the target year gets closer, the mix of investments becomes more conservative.

EXAMPLE   An investor seeks an investment for retirement in 20 years that performs well under most market conditions and is diversified by purchasing multiple types of securities. An asset allocation fund that targets the year of retirement may be appropriate.

3. 13. 16   TARGET-DATE FUNDS

reduce risk allocation as fund comes up on target date

One increasingly popular investment option is a **target-date fund,** sometimes called a **life-cycle fund** or **interval fund.** According to a report by a large retirement plan provider, target-date funds are offered by nearly 90% of employer-sponsored defined contribution plans, such as 401(k) plans.

Target-date funds are designed to help manage investment risk. With a target date in mind that is closest to the year an investor anticipates needing the money (i.e., retiring in 2030).

A *2030 fund* gradually reduces risk by changing the investments within the fund. That said, target-date funds are not risk free, even when the target date has been reached.

FINRA is concerned that many investors surveyed do not understand that target-date funds do not provide guaranteed income. Many investors also did not realize that similar-sounding funds may, in fact, have different investments and risk profiles.

Like all investments, target-date funds can lose money if the stocks and bonds owned by the fund drop in value. And even though funds with identical target dates may look the same, they may have very different investment strategies and asset allocations that can affect how risky they are and what they are worth, at any given point in time, including when and after retirement takes place.

3. 13. 17   BOND FUNDS – *INCOME*

Bond funds have income as their main investment objective. Some funds invest solely in investment-grade corporate bonds. Others, seeking enhanced safety, invest only in government issues. Still others pursue capital appreciation by investing in lower-rated bonds for higher yields.

TEST TOPIC ALERT

Remember:

- Bonds pay interest; bond funds pay dividends if declared by the fund's board of directors.

- Dividends are typically paid on a quarterly or semiannual basis, but there are income funds (both equity and debt oriented) that pay monthly dividends.

- When interest rates rise, the prices of bonds, and, therefore, bond funds, fall (and vice versa).

3. 13. 17. 1   Corporate Bond Funds

Corporate bond funds, in general, have higher credit risk than various government issues but can still be classified as investment-grade (safer) or non-investment-grade (riskier) portfolios.

The greater the risk, the greater the yield. **High-yield bond funds** provide the highest yields due to their increased credit risk and are considered speculative investments.

3. 13. 17. 2   Tax-Free (Tax-Exempt) Bond Funds – *MUNICIPAL BOND FUNDS*

Municipal bond funds invest in municipal bonds or notes that produce income (dividends) exempt from federal income tax. These funds are appropriate for investors in a high marginal tax bracket seeking income.

EXAMPLE

An investor is in a high marginal tax bracket and seeks income. A municipal bond fund may be appropriate.

3. 13. 17. 3 U.S. Government Funds

U.S. government funds purchase securities issued by the U.S. Treasury or an agency of the U.S. government, such as Ginnie Mae. Investors in these funds seek current income and maximum safety. **Agency security funds** are not considered quite as safe from default risk as U.S. government funds; therefore, the yields on agency security funds will be higher than U.S. government fund yields.

3. 13. 17. 4 Agency Funds

The word "agencies" is a generic term used to describe two types of bonds: (1) bonds issued or guaranteed by U.S. federal government agencies, and (2) bonds issued by **government-sponsored enterprises (GSEs)**—corporations created by Congress to foster a public purpose, such as affordable housing.

Bonds issued or guaranteed by federal agencies such as the **Government National Mortgage Association (Ginnie Mae)** are backed by the "full faith and credit of the U.S. government," just like Treasuries. This is an unconditional commitment to pay interest payments and to return the principal investment in full to you when a debt security reaches maturity.

Bonds issued by GSEs, such as the **Federal National Mortgage Association (Fannie Mae)** and the **Federal Home Loan Mortgage** (Freddie Mac), are not backed by the same guarantee as federal government agencies.

EXAMPLE

An investor is risk averse and seeks income, but the U.S. government bond fund yields are too low. An agency security fund may be appropriate.

3. 13. 18 PRINCIPAL-PROTECTED FUNDS

Principal-protected mutual funds offer investors a guarantee of principal, adjusted for fund dividends and distributions, on a set future date (maturity) while providing opportunities for higher returns through investment in higher risk and higher expected return asset classes such as equities. The basic guarantee is that the investor's return will never be less than the original investment, less any sales load.

The guarantees are sometimes provided by third-party insurers and at other times through investments in U.S. Treasury zero-coupon bonds. These appealing properties have led to considerable interest on the part of investors who have invested billions of dollars in such mutual funds in recent years. The usefulness and attractiveness of these principal-protected mutual funds is limited by three factors:

■ **Guarantee principal.** Most principal-protected funds guarantee the initial investment minus any front-end sales charge even if the stock markets fall. In many cases, the guarantee is backed by an insurance policy.

■ **Lock-up period.** If you sell any shares in the fund before the end of the "guarantee period"—a period of anywhere from 5 to 10 years—you lose the guarantee on those shares and could lose money if the share price has fallen since your initial investment.

■ **Hold a mixture of bonds and stocks.** Most principal-protected funds invest a portion of the fund in zero-coupon bonds and other debt securities, and a portion in stocks and other equity investments during the guarantee period. To ensure the fund can support the guarantee, many of these funds may be almost entirely invested in zero-coupon bonds or other debt securities when interest rates are low and equity markets are volatile. Because this allocation provides less exposure to the markets, it may eliminate or greatly reduce any potential gains the fund can achieve from subsequent gains in the stock market. It also may increase the risk to the fund of rising interest rates, which generally cause bond prices to fall.

Principal protected funds are typically front-end loaded, and their operating expense ratios tend to be higher than comparable funds.

EXAMPLE   An investor is very risk averse but wishes to invest without the possibility of losing the principal of the investment. A principal-protected fund may be appropriate.

3. 13. 19   FUNDS OF HEDGE FUNDS

Though hedge funds discussed later in this unit are generally available to and suitable for highly qualified or sophisticated (accredited) investors, there are registered mutual funds available to all investors that invest primarily in unregistered hedge funds known as **funds of hedge funds**. They can target and diversify among several hedge funds and, in this way, give nonaccredited investors access to hedge funds. These funds share some of the benefits and risks associated with hedge funds. One benefit could be that lower initial investments might be required than when investing directly in a hedge fund. In contrast, one risk to note is that like all mutual funds, the shares are not traded and that divesting of them can only occur if the mutual fund company redeems them. Because the underlying assets are not liquid, this fund is not as liquid as other mutual funds. Recommendations of funds of hedge funds would need to disclose the specific risks associated with hedge funds and the transfer of those risks that occurs when mutual funds invest in hedge funds.

3. 13. 20   INDEX TRACKING FUNDS

Some funds are designed to track the performance of an underlying investment portfolio or index.

These funds are known as index funds. While they are not investment company products, they do have characteristics similar to both open-end and closed-end funds.

Like closed-end funds, index fund shares trade and are priced like shares of stock. Like open-end funds, they can create (issue) additional shares.

TAKE NOTE   Index tracking funds have low portfolio turnover, which is a contributing factor to having low expense ratios.

Investors use index funds for:
- asset allocation,
- following industry trends,
- balancing a portfolio,

- speculative trading, and
- hedging.

Remember that index funds are different from mutual funds in the following ways:

- Intraday trading—Investors do not have to wait until the end of a trading day to purchase or sell shares. Shares trade and are priced continuously throughout the day, making it easier for investors to react to market changes.
- Margin eligibility—Index fund shares can be purchased on margin, subject to the same terms that apply to common stock.
- Short selling—Index funds can be sold short at any time during trading hours.

Popular index funds include one that tracks the S&P 500 Index. Spiders—There are also Spiders on various components of the S&P 500. There are nine Select Sector Index funds (e.g., consumer services, energy, and technology), and each of the 500 stocks in the S&P Index is allocated to only one Select Sector Index fund. These funds generally pay quarterly cash dividends that represent, after expenses, dividends accumulated on the underlying stock portfolio.

Finally, it should be noted that many index tracking funds are exchange-traded funds (ETFs) offered by a variety of different issuers. One popular exchange-traded index fund is the Q's (QQQQ), which tracks the price performance of the Nasdaq 100 Trust. This index tracking ETF trades on Nasdaq.

3. 13. 20. 1   Leveraged Funds

Use borrowing to juice returns

These funds attempt to deliver a multiple of the return of the benchmark index they are designated to track. For instance, a 2X leveraged fund would try to deliver two times the return of whatever index it is tracking. With leveraged funds, there are no limits by rule or regulation as to the amount of leverage that could be applied to a portfolio. Currently there are numerous 2X and 3X leveraged funds available to investors.

The risk associated with leverage is that it is always a "double-edged" sword. Therefore, the risk to be recognized regarding this fund strategy is that if the benchmark index is falling, then the fund's returns will be, in theory, the designated leverage amount (perhaps 2 or 3) times the loss. In addition, most of these funds use derivatives products such as options, futures, and swaps to enable them to achieve the stated goal. As these products are not suitable for all investors, so too can it be said of the leverage fund portfolio containing them. Ultimately, as always, suitability becomes an issue when recommending these products.

3. 13. 20. 2   Inverse (Reverse) Funds

Shorting funds

Inverse funds, sometimes called reverse or short funds, attempt to deliver returns that are the opposite of the benchmark index they are tracking. For example, if the benchmark is down 2%, the fund's goal is to be up 2%. In addition, inverse funds can also be leveraged funds, or said another way, two or three times the opposite of the indices return.

TAKE NOTE   Both leveraged and inverse index funds (leveraged or not) can be traded on an exchange. When they are, they are known as exchange-traded funds (ETFs). If the shares are exchange-traded, they are priced by supply and demand, can be purchased on margin, and bought and sold throughout the trading day, like all exchange-traded products. For those that are not exchange-traded, they would be priced, purchased, and redeemed like all investment company shares. Neither of these fund types carry any guarantee that they will achieve the stated goal or objective. — *Hedge funds def don't*

3. 13. 21   HEDGE FUNDS

— accredited investor
— invest in pretty much any securities
— can use leverage,
shorting
— private, unless
— highly regulated

Hedge funds are similar to mutual funds in that investments are pooled and professionally managed, but they differ in that the fund has more flexibility in the investment strategies employed and are unregulated by U.S. securities laws. They are aggressively managed portfolios of investments that use advanced investment strategies. Generally, these investment vehicles are considered suitable for sophisticated investors—those meeting the standard of accredited investors. While hedging is the practice of attempting to limit risk, most hedge funds specify generating high returns as their primary investment objective. Some of the more common strategies employed by hedge funds are:

■ highly leveraged portfolios,

■ the use of short positions,

■ utilizing derivative products such as options and futures,

■ currency speculation,

■ commodity speculation, and

■ investing in politically unstable international markets.

Because hedge funds, unlike mutual funds or investment companies, are unregulated, the very nature of the investment is almost always considered speculative. Most hedge funds are organized as private investment partnerships, allowing them to limit the number of investors or require large initial or minimum investments, if they so desire. Some also require that investors maintain the investment for a minimum length of time (e.g., one year) and to that extent they can be considered illiquid. These requirements are known as lock-up provisions.

TAKE NOTE

Can have 35 non-accredited investors?

While hedge funds are unregulated, U.S. laws do require that the majority of investors meet the test of a sophisticated investor. They should be considered "accredited" investors, having a minimum annual income and net worth, and have considerable investment knowledge.

3. 13. 21. 1   Hedge Fund Lock-Up Provisions

This provision provides that during a certain initial period, an investor may not make a withdrawal from the fund. The period when the investor cannot withdraw investment dollars is known as the actual lock-up period. Generally recognized as one way the manager of the hedge fund portfolio can have capital retained in the fund, it is also seen to be another factor adding to the unique risk of hedge funds—in this case, shares being illiquid for that specified length of time.

Lock-up periods are generally associated with new or start-up hedge funds and can differ in length from one fund to another. The length of the lock-up period will largely be dependent on what the investment strategy of the fund is and how long the portfolio manager anticipates it will take to implement the strategy and then see results of that implementation.

3. 13. 22   BLANK-CHECK OR BLIND-POOL HEDGE FUND

Some hedge funds target blank-check companies to invest in. Blank-check companies, sometimes known as special purpose acquisition companies (SPACS), carry their own unique risks. Blank-check companies are companies without business operations that raise money through IPOs in order to have their shares publicly traded for the sole purpose of seeking out a business or combination of businesses. When a business is located, they will present proposals to holders of their shares for approval.

Some hedge funds target blind-pool companies. Similar to blank-check companies, these issuers raise capital by selling securities to the public without telling investors what the specific use of the proceeds will be, but might target a particular industry or sector.

Some characterize blank-check companies as a type of blind pool, with one discernable difference. While the blind-pool company will usually provide at least some indication of what general industry the funds will be invested in, blank-check offerings do not identify any proposed investment intent.

While some hedge funds target these types of holdings for their portfolios, it should be noted that they might be included within any hedge fund portfolio and, in both cases, should be considered when assessing risk and determining suitability.

QUICK QUIZ 3.M

Objective: Compare the recommendations of mutual funds to investor objectives

1. Your customer is 26 years old and earns $45,000 a year as an advertising executive. He has already accumulated $5,000 in his savings account and is seeking a secure place to invest the amount and begin a periodic investment plan. He knows his long-term time frame means he should be willing to take some risk, but he is uncomfortable with the thought of losing money. He would prefer moderate overall returns rather than high returns accompanied by high volatility. Which of the following mutual funds is the most suitable for this customer?

   A. ATF Capital Appreciation Fund
   B. ATF Biotechnology Fund
   C. ABC Balanced Fund
   D. ATF Overseas Opportunities Fund

2. Your customer, age 29, makes $42,000 annually and has $10,000 to invest. Although he has never invested before, he wants to invest in something exciting. Which of the following should you suggest?

   A. An aggressive growth fund because the customer is young and has many investing years ahead
   B. A growth and income fund because the customer has never invested before
   C. A balanced fund because when the stock market is declining, the bond market will perform well
   D. Your customer should provide more information before you can make a suitable recommendation

3. Your 45-year-old client is interested in obtaining the highest current income possible from his investment. He is willing to accept fluctuations in investment principal. Which of the following would best suit this client's investment objective?

    A. High-yield bond fund
    B. Aggressive growth fund
    C. Tax-free money market fund
    D. Balanced fund

4. An investor would consider all the following advantages investing in a REIT EXCEPT

    A. liquidity
    B. tax deferral
    C. diversification
    D. professional management

All Quick Quiz answers are found at the end of their units.

3. 14   MUTUAL FUND DISTRIBUTIONS AND TAXATION

Before a mutual fund can pay a distribution, it must first realize a receipt of dividends from the stocks it owns or interest from interest-paying bonds. Then if it meets the objective of the fund and is approved by the fund's board of directors, the fund will make a distribution.

Most monies received by an individual are subject to income tax. This includes salaries, bonuses, commissions, gratuities, dividends, and interest. The current tax system includes brackets. The tax bracket is defined as the percentage of tax due on the next dollar the individual will receive. This is called your marginal income tax bracket.

Receipts from selling something for more (or less) than was originally paid for it fall under the capital gains tax. If there was a gain, tax must be paid on it. If there was a loss, it can be used to offset gains and income.

Mutual funds receive income in the form of dividends from the stocks in which they invest and interest from bonds. They may also realize capital gains from the sale of securities, which were held in the portfolio, that have appreciated in price. Funds may retain their gains and use them to buy other securities, or they may distribute them to their customers.

3. 14. 1 DIVIDEND DISTRIBUTIONS

A mutual fund may pay dividends to each shareholder in much the same way corporations pay dividends to stockholders. The Investment Company Act of 1940 requires a written statement to accompany dividend payments by management companies. Every written statement made by or on behalf of a management company must be made on a separate paper and clearly indicate what portion of the payment per share is made from. Mutual fund dividends are typically paid from the mutual fund's net investment income, usually on a quarterly basis.

Dividends may be identified as qualified or nonqualified. **Qualified dividends** are taxed at the lower long-term capital gains rate. **Nonqualified dividends** are distributed as short-term capital gains and are taxed as ordinary income.

3. 14. 2 NET INVESTMENT INCOME (NII)

NII includes gross investment income—dividend and interest income from securities held in the portfolio—minus operating expenses. Advertising and sales expenses are not included in a fund's operating expenses when calculating **net investment income**, but management fees, custodian bank charges, legal and accounting fees, and transfer agent costs are included. Dividends from net investment income are taxed as ordinary income to shareholders.

net investment income = dividends + interest – expenses of the fund

TEST TOPIC ALERT

You may see a question on the exam that asks for this calculation and gives a list of items to exclude or include in the calculation. Remember D + I – E and it will be easy to remember which items to include. Note that capital gains are NOT a part of NII.

TAKE NOTE

A bond fund does not pay interest to investors! Investors buy common stock of the bond fund and, therefore, will receive a dividend if declared. Interest paid in the form of a dividend is taxed as interest.

3. 14. 3 THE CONDUIT THEORY

Because an investment company is organized as a corporation or trust, you might correctly assume its earnings are subject to tax. Consider, however, how an additional level of taxation shrinks a dividend distribution value.

EXAMPLE

Triple taxation? GEM Fund owns shares of Mountain Brewing Co. First, Mountain Brewing is taxed on its earnings before it pays a dividend. Then, GEM Fund pays tax on the amount of the dividend it receives. Finally, the investor pays income tax on the distribution from the fund.

Triple taxation of investment income may be avoided if the mutual fund qualifies under **Subchapter M** of the Internal Revenue Code (IRC). If a mutual fund acts as a **conduit (pipeline)** for the distribution of net investment income, the fund may qualify as a **regulated investment company (RIC)** subject to tax only on the amount of investment income the fund retains. The investment income distributed to shareholders escapes taxation at the mutual fund level.

To avoid taxation under Subchapter M, a fund must distribute at least 90% of its net investment income to shareholders. The fund then pays taxes only on the undistributed amount.

EXAMPLE

If a fund distributes 89%, it must pay taxes on 100% of net investment income.

EXAMPLE
What are the tax consequences to a fund that distributes 98% of its net investment income? In this situation, the fund does not pay taxes on the 98% that is distributed; it pays taxes only on the 2% of retained earnings.

3. 14. 4 CAPITAL GAINS DISTRIBUTIONS

The appreciation or depreciation of portfolio securities is unrealized capital gain or loss if the fund does not sell the securities. Therefore, shareholders experience no tax consequences. When the fund sells the securities, the gain or loss is realized. A realized gain is an actual profit made.

Capital gains distributions are derived from realized gains. If the fund has held the securities for more than one year, the gain is a long-term capital gain, taxed at the long-term capital gains rate. The mutual fund may retain the gain or distribute it to shareholders. A long-term capital gains distribution may not be made more often than once per year.

TAKE NOTE
Long-term capital gain distributions may be made no more than once per year. A short-term capital gain is identified, distributed, but taxed as a dividend distribution, and taxed at ordinary income tax rates.

Long-term capital gain: Holding period of more than one year, taxed as a capital gain, which is (generally) lower than ordinary income tax rates for an investor.

Short-term capital gain: Holding period of one year or less, taxed at ordinary income tax rates for an investor.

TEST TOPIC ALERT
The exam is fond of asking a question like this: An investor purchases shares of a mutual fund. Three months later, the fund has a long-term capital gains distribution.

This would be taxed to the investor as _____.

And, the answer is long-term capital gain. Why? It makes no difference how long the investor held the fund shares, this is a distribution of the fund's long-term gains being passed through to the investor.

However, when the investor sells his shares, then the holding period of those shares is important for determining long-term or short-term status.

TAKE NOTE
The terms realized gains and unrealized gains can be confusing. Think of an **unrealized gain** as a paper profit and a **realized gain** as actual profit made.

EXAMPLE

If you had purchased a house for $150,000 and its value had appreciated to $200,000, you would experience an unrealized gain of $50,000. You would have no taxes to pay on these paper profits. If you had sold the house, the $50,000 would be taxable to you as a capital gain. The gain resulting from a sale is known as a realized gain. Unrealized profits are not taxable; realized profits are taxable as capital gains.

A mutual fund portfolio that has increased in value has unrealized profits; these are not taxable to investors. But when the fund sells appreciated portfolio securities, it has realized profits. These profits are distributed as capital gains to shareholders. Shareholders can take these capital gain distributions in cash or reinvest them to purchase additional shares. In either case, these distributions are taxable as capital gains to shareholders.

3. 14. 5 REINVESTMENT OF DISTRIBUTIONS

Dividends and capital gains are distributed in cash. However, a shareholder may elect to **reinvest distributions** in additional mutual fund shares. The automatic reinvestment of distributions is similar to compounding interest. The reinvested distributions purchase additional shares, which may earn dividends or gains distributions.

A mutual fund that is being formed today must offer the reinvestment of dividends and capital gains back into the fund without a sales charge (at NAV). This means that investors are able to buy new shares without a sales load—a significant advantage that results in faster growth to the investor.

3. 14. 6 TAXATION OF REINVESTED DISTRIBUTIONS

Distributions are taxable to shareholders whether the distributions are received in cash or reinvested. The fund must disclose whether each distribution is from income or capital gains. **Form 1099-DIV**, which is sent to shareholders after the close of the year, details tax information related to dividend distributions for the year. This enables the investor to enter the proper information on the investor's Form 1040.

TAKE NOTE

Just as with dividend distributions, whether capital gains are taken in cash or reinvested, they are currently taxable to the shareholder. Dividends will be reported as qualified (taxed at a lower rate) or nonqualified (taxed as ordinary income).

Any short-term capital gain is distributed as a nonqualified dividend. It is the shareholder's responsibility to report all dividends and long-term capital gains distributions to the IRS and state tax agency.

3. 14. 7 OTHER TAX CONSIDERATIONS

Mutual fund investors must consider many tax factors when buying and selling mutual fund shares.

3. 14. 7. 1 Cost Basis of Shares Inherited/Gifted

The **cost basis of inherited property** is either stepped up or stepped down to its fair market value (FMV) at the date of the decedent's death. In the case of open-end investment companies, this would be the net asset value per share (NAV). Shares inherited are always considered to have a holding period that is long term for tax purposes; therefore, the sale of inherited shares are subject to more favorable long-term tax rates, no matter how long (or short) they have been held.

If a gift of securities is made, under **federal gift tax rules**, the donor's cost basis becomes the donee's cost basis.

E X A M P L E

Grandpa bought $10,000 of stock 20 years ago; it is currently valued at $50,000.

If inherited, the cost basis of shares received equals the fair market value at Grandpa's death: $50,000.

If Grandpa instead gave it to Susie, who received the stock as a gift, the cost basis remains unchanged at $10,000.

3. 14. 7. 1. 1 Estate and Gift Taxes

Taxes can be levied upon the estate of a deceased person and upon those gifting securities to others. This section discusses these unique scenarios.

3. 14. 7. 1. 2 Donor Taxes

When a person dies, tax is due on the estate. This tax is payable by the estate, not by heirs who inherit the estate (although certain other taxes may apply to heirs). Likewise, if a person gives a gift, tax is due on the gift. Gift tax is payable by the donor, not the recipient. Estate and gift taxes are progressive taxes. For tax purposes, the valuation of the estate is the date of death; the valuation of a gift is the date it is given.

3. 14. 7. 1. 3 Gift Tax Exemption

Individuals may give gifts up to a maximum amount per year to any number of individuals without incurring gift tax. The amount of the exclusion is subject to change depending on current tax law. Interspousal gifts, no matter the size, are not subject to tax. If a gift tax is due, it is paid by the donor.

3. 14. 7. 1. 4 Estate Tax Exclusion

The estate of a deceased person is allowed to exclude some of that person's estate from taxation. The amount of the exclusion is subject to change depending on current tax law.

T A K E   N O T E

Estate and gift taxes are progressive taxes that increase with the size of the estate or the gift. Income taxes are another example of a progressive tax. Flat taxes are considered regressive taxes because they impact lower-income families and individuals to a greater degree.

3. 14. 7. 1. 5   Unlimited Marital Deduction

Married couples are allowed to transfer their entire estate to the surviving spouse at death. This unlimited marital deduction results in taxes being owed at the death of the survivor.

3. 14. 8   WASH SALES

Capital losses may not be used to offset gains or income if the investor sells a security at a loss and purchases the same or a substantially identical security within 30 days before or after the trade date. The sale at a loss and the repurchase within this period is a **wash sale**.

The rule disallows the loss or tax benefit from selling a security and repurchasing the security or one substantially identical to it in this manner. The term *substantially identical* refers to any other security with the same investment performance likelihood as the one being sold.

Examples are:

- securities convertible into the one being sold,
- warrants to purchase the security being sold,
- rights to purchase the security being sold, and
- call options to purchase the security being sold.

31st		SELL		31st
DAY <------------------------		@	------------------------>DAY	
OK	30 Days	LOSS	30 Days	OK

TAKE NOTE   The wash sale rule covers 30 days before and after the trade date. Including the trade date, this is a total time period of 61 days.

TEST TOPIC ALERT

- Funds that comply with Subchapter M (conduit theory) are known as regulated investment companies.

- Dividends and capital gains are taxable, whether reinvested or taken in cash.

- An investor's cost basis in mutual fund shares is what was paid to buy the share plus reinvested dividends and capital gains distributions.

- $3,000 of net capital loss may be used as a deduction against ordinary income each tax year. Unused capital loss may be carried forward indefinitely.

- Although an exchange from one fund to another within the same family is not subject to a sales charge, it is a taxable event. Any gain or loss on the shares sold is reportable at the time of the exchange.

- When a shareholder dies, his shares are assigned a cost basis equal to the value of the shares on the date of death.

3. 14. 9   FUND SHARE LIQUIDATIONS TO THE INVESTOR

When an investor sells mutual fund shares, he must establish his cost base, or basis, in the shares to calculate the tax liability. A simple definition of cost base is the amount of money invested. Upon liquidation, cost base represents a return of capital and is not taxed again.

3. 14. 9. 1   Valuing Fund Shares

The cost base of mutual fund shares includes the shares' total cost, including sales charges plus any reinvested dividend and capital gains distributions. For tax purposes, the investor compares cost base to the amount of money received from selling the shares. If the amount received is greater than the cost base, the investor reports a taxable gain. If the amount received is less than the cost base, the investor reports a loss.

3. 14. 9. 2   Accounting Methods — how to calculate cost basis of shares in order to get more favorable taxes on gains etc

If an investor decides to liquidate shares, he determines the cost base by electing one of three accounting methods: first in, first out (FIFO); share identification; or average basis. If the investor fails to choose, the IRS assumes the investor liquidates shares on a FIFO basis.

3. 14. 9. 2. 1   First In, First Out

When FIFO shares are sold, the cost of the shares held the longest is used to calculate the gain or loss. In a rising market, this method normally creates adverse tax consequences.

3. 14. 9. 2. 2   Share Identification

When using the share identification accounting method, the investor keeps track of the cost of each share purchased and uses this information when deciding which shares to liquidate. He then liquidates the shares that provide the desired tax benefits.

3. 14. 9. 2. 3   Average Basis

The shareholder may elect to use an average cost basis when redeeming fund shares. The shareholder calculates average basis by dividing the total cost of all shares owned by the total number of shares.

QUICK QUIZ 3.N

Objective: Identify different types of distributions and the taxation of those distributions from mutual funds

1. For how many days is the wash sale rule in effect?

    A. 30 days before the sale
    B. 30 days after the sale
    C. A total of 60 days
    D. A total of 61 days

2. The concept of a mutual fund passing distributions through to shareholders without first paying a tax is known as

A. the pass-through theory
B. the conduit theory
C. tax-free passage
D. free distribution

3. Which of the following factors would be used in calculating the tax due on a capital gains distribution by a mutual fund?

 I.   The length of time the fund held the securities
 II. The length of time the investor has held his shares
 III. The investor's tax bracket
 IV. The fund's tax bracket

A. I and III
B. I and IV
C. II and III
D. II and IV

4. A registered representative has recommended a growth and income fund to her client because the fund pays relatively high income and maintains strong capital appreciation. The client wishes to use the fund as the foundation of a long-term strategy for eventual retirement. The representative's recommendations and disclosures should state that

A. the client should reinvest any dividend and gain distributions to accelerate the growth process through a compounding effect
B. the client should take any dividend and gain distributions in cash and invest them in a growth fund of another fund family for diversification
C. all capital appreciation of securities within the fund are distributed on an annual basis
D. if dividends are reinvested, they are not currently taxable, which enhances growth within the fund

All Quick Quiz answers are found at the end of their units.

3. 15   PRICE OF MUTUAL FUND SHARES

Because mutual funds don't trade in the secondary market, the value of shares is not determined by supply and demand, but rather by a formula. Everything begins with net asset value (NAV) per share.

To calculate the NAV of a fund share, the fund starts with its total assets and subtracts out its liabilities (such as amounts due for securities purchased, but not yet paid for):

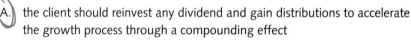

total assets − liabilities = net assets of the fund

The fund then divides the net assets by the number of shares outstanding. This gives the net asset value per share (NAV) of the fund:

Changes in NAV

Increases	Decreases	Does not change
Market value of securities increases	Market value of securities declines	Manager buys or sells securities
Fund receives dividends	Fund distributes dividends	Fund issues shares
Fund receives interest	Fund distributes capital gains	Fund redeems shares
Liabilities decline	Liabilities increase	

EXAMPLE

The ABC fund has total assets of $100 million and $5 million in liabilities. If it has 10 million shares outstanding, what is its NAV per share?

Net assets: $100 million − $5 million = $95 million

NAV: $95 million ÷ 10 million shares outstanding = $9.50 per share

The NAV of a fund share is the amount the investor receives upon redemption. It must be calculated at least once per business day. A typical fund calculates its NAV at 4:00 pm ET every business day, because that is when the New York Stock Exchange closes. The price the customer receives is the next NAV calculated after receipt of his redemption request. This practice is known as **forward pricing**; we always have to wait until the next available calculation to determine the value of shares redeemed or, for that matter, the number of shares purchased.

The purchase price of a fund share is called the public offering price, or POP. For the class of fund shares known as front-end loaded shares, it is simply the NAV plus the sales charge. The sales charge is paid as compensation for marketing the shares. As we will see, sales charges can be levied at the time of purchase (front-end load), at the time of redemption (back-end load), or there can simply be no sales charge (no-load), meaning that shares are purchased at NAV.

3. 15. 1 CLOSED-END FUNDS

After the initial public offering, **closed-end funds** do not have a sales charge embedded in the share price. In the secondary market, an investor pays a brokerage commission (in an agency transaction) or pays a markup or markdown (in a principal transaction). Closed-end funds may trade at a premium (above) or discount (below) relative to their NAV.

3. 15. 2 OPEN-END FUNDS

All sales commissions and expenses for an **open-end fund** are embedded in the POP or other fees. Sales expenses include commissions for the managing underwriter, dealers, brokers, and registered representatives, as well as all advertising and sales literature expenses. Mutual fund distributors use different methods to collect the fees for the sale of shares and one to compensate reps on an ongoing basis (trailer commissions):

■ Front-end loads (difference between POP and NAV)

■ Back-end loads (contingent deferred sales loads)
■ Level loads (asset-based fees—provide trail commissions to the registered representative servicing the account)

3. 15. 2. 1 Class A Shares

Shares sold with a front-end load are called **Class A shares**. Front-end sales loads are the charges included in a fund's public offering price. The charges are added to the NAV at the time an investor buys shares. Front-end loads are the most common way of paying for the distribution services a fund's underwriter and broker-dealers provide.

EXAMPLE

An investor deposits $10,000 with a mutual fund that has a 5% front-end load.

The 5% load amounts to $500, which is deducted from the invested amount. In this example, $9,500 is invested in the fund's portfolio on the investor's behalf.

3. 15. 2. 1. 1   Breakpoints

Breakpoints are available to any person. For a breakpoint qualification, person includes married couples, parents and their minor children, corporations, and certain other entities. Investment clubs or associations formed for the purpose of investing do not qualify for breakpoints.

The following are breakpoint considerations.

■ Breakpoint levels vary across mutual fund families. There is no industry standardized breakpoint schedule.

■ Mutual funds that offer breakpoints must disclose their breakpoint schedule in the prospectus and how an account is valued for breakpoint purposes.

■ The SEC further encourages that breakpoint discount availability information be accessible through various means of communication, including websites.

■ Discounts may be the result of a single large investment, a series of aggregated investments, or a promise to invest via a letter of intent (LOI).

■ Purchases made by the same investor in various accounts can be aggregated to qualify for a breakpoint discount. Eligible accounts include traditional brokerage, accounts held directly with a fund company, 401(k), IRA, and 529 college savings.

■ Shares purchased in the same fund family other than money market accounts are eligible to be aggregated together to qualify for a breakpoint discount, including those held at separate broker-dealers.

TEST TOPIC ALERT

You can expect a question on who is eligible for breakpoints. Married couples, parents with minor children, and corporations are eligible. Parents combined with adult children (even if they are legally considered dependents) and investment clubs are not eligible.

The discounts of sales charges are spelled out in a mutual fund's prospectus, but the table below illustrates a typical example.

Purchase Amount	Sales Charge
$0 to $24,999	6.00%
$25,000 to $49,999	5.50%
$50,000 to $99,999	5.00%
$100,000 to $249,999	4.00%
$250,000 to $499,999	3.00%
$500,000 to $999,999	2.00%
$1,000,000 +	0.00%

Breakpoint Sale. FINRA prohibits registered representatives from making or seeking higher commissions by selling investment company shares in a dollar amount just below the point at which the sales charge is reduced. This violation is known as a breakpoint sale, and is considered contrary to just and equitable principles of trade. It is the responsibility of all parties concerned, particularly the principal, to prevent deceptive practices.

TAKE NOTE

Breakpoints offer a significant advantage to mutual fund purchasers; however, breakpoint sales are prohibited.

3. 15. 2. 1. 2   Letter of Intent (LOI)

A person who plans to invest more money with the same mutual fund company may immediately decrease his overall sales charges by signing a letter of intent. In the LOI, the investor informs the investment company that he intends to invest the additional funds necessary to reach the breakpoint within 13 months.

The LOI is a one-sided contract binding on the fund only. However, the customer must complete the investment to qualify for the reduced sales charge. The fund holds some of the shares purchased in escrow. If the customer deposits the money to complete the LOI, he receives the escrowed shares. If not, he is given the choice to either pay the sales charge difference or have the underwriter liquidate enough of the escrowed shares to do so. Appreciation and reinvested dividends or capital gains do not count toward the LOI.

EXAMPLE

Refer back to the sample breakpoint schedule. A customer investing $24,000 is just short of the $25,000 breakpoint. In this situation, the customer might sign a letter of intent promising an amount that will qualify for the breakpoint within 13 months from the date of the letter. Investing an additional $1,000 within 13 months qualifies the customer for the reduced sales charge. The customer is charged the appropriate reduced sales charge at the time of the initial purchase.

A customer who has not completed the investment within 13 months will be given the choice of sending a check for the difference in sales charges or cashing in escrowed shares to pay the difference.

[handwritten margin notes: 13 month from investment date to put in more + to reach breakpoint — no matter when LOI is signed]

Backdating the letter. A fund often permits a customer to sign a letter of intent as late as the 90th day after an initial purchase. The LOI may be backdated by up to 90 days to include prior purchases but may not cover more than 13 months in total. A customer who signs the LOI 60 days after a purchase has 11 months to complete the letter.

EXAMPLE

$1–$24,999	5.00%
$25,000–$49,999	4.25%
$50,000–$99,999	3.75%
$100,000+	3.25%

If an investor wants to deposit $50,000 in a mutual fund over a 13-month period and puts in $25,000 when the account is opened, the investor is charged a sales charge of 3.75% on the initial and every subsequent investment if an LOI has been signed. If a letter was not signed, the sales charge on the initial amount of $25,000 would be 4.25%, based on this breakpoint schedule. The LOI allows for a discount on an installment plan purchase.

TEST TOPIC ALERT

■ Letters of intent are good for a maximum of 13 months and may be backdated 90 days.

■ If the letter of intent is not completed, the sales charge amount that applies is based on the total amount actually invested.

■ Share appreciation and income paid by the fund do not count toward completion of the letter.

3. 15. 2. 1. 3   *Rights of Accumulation*

Rights of accumulation, like breakpoints, allow an investor to qualify for reduced sales charges. The major differences are that rights of accumulation:

■ are available for subsequent investment and do not apply to initial transactions;

■ allow the investor to use prior share appreciation and reinvestment to qualify for breakpoints; and

■ do not impose time limits.

The customer may qualify for reduced charges when the total value of shares previously purchased and shares currently being purchased exceeds a certain dollar amount. For the purpose of qualifying customers for rights of accumulation, the mutual fund bases the quantity of securities owned on the higher of current NAV or the total of purchases made to date.

[handwritten margin notes: share value can appreciate and help you get into a breakpoint when you invest more money]

TAKE NOTE

Assume the following breakpoint schedule:

$1–$24,999	5.00%
$25,000–$49,999	4.25%
$50,000–$99,999	3.75%
$100,000+	3.25%

An investor deposits $5,000 (paying a 5% sales charge) in a mutual fund but does not sign an LOI. The $5,000 grows to $10,000 over time and the investor decides to invest another $15,000. If rights of accumulation exist, the new $15,000 is charged a sales charge of 4.25%, which is based on the new money plus the accumulated value in the account ($15,000 + $10,000 = $25,000). If rights of accumulation do not exist, the sales charge would have been 5%.

3. 15. 2. 1. 4   Combination Privilege

A mutual fund company frequently offers more than one fund and refers to these multiple offerings as its family of funds. An investor seeking a reduced sales charge may be allowed to combine separate investments in two or more funds within the same family to reach a breakpoint.

3. 15. 2. 1. 5   Exchanges Within a Family of Funds

Many sponsors offer exchange or conversion privileges within their families of funds. Exchange privileges allow an investor to convert an investment in one fund for an equal investment in another fund in the same family, often without incurring an additional sales charge.

Mutual funds may be purchased at NAV under a no-load exchange privilege. The following rules apply:

- Purchase may not exceed the proceeds generated by the redemption of the other fund.
- The redemption may not involve a refund of sales charges.
- The sales personnel and dealers must receive no compensation of any kind from the reinvestment.
- Any gain or loss from the redemption of shares must be reported for tax purposes.

3. 15. 2. 1. 6   Computing the Sales Charge Percentage

When the NAV and the POP are known, the sales charge percentage can be determined.

$$\text{POP } (\$10.50) - \text{NAV } (\$10) = \text{sales charge dollar amount } (\$.50)$$

$$\frac{\text{Sales charge dollar amount } (\$.50)}{\text{POP } (\$10.50)} = \text{sales charge percentage } (4.8\%)$$

If the dollar amounts for the NAV and sales charges are specified, the formula for determining the POP of mutual fund shares is:

$$\text{NAV } (\$10) + \text{sales charge dollar amount } (\$.50) = \text{POP dollar amount } (\$10.50)$$

A mutual fund prospectus must contain a formula that explains how the fund computes the NAV and how the sales charge is added. The sales charge is always based on the POP, not on the NAV.

If the dollar amount of the NAV and the sales charge percent are specified, the formula to determine POP is to divide the NAV by 100% minus the sales charge percentage.

$$\frac{\text{NAV (\$10)}}{100\% - \text{sales charge percentage (4.8\%)}} = \text{POP (\$10.50)}$$

Because of the sales charge, loaded funds should be recommended for long-term investing.

EXAMPLE

NAV = $20 and POP = $21.00. What is the sales charge percentage?

The sales charge percentage is calculated by finding the sales charge amount

($21.00 – $20.00) and dividing by the POP. Remember, sales charge is a percentage of the POP, not the NAV.

$1.00 ÷ $21.00 = 4.8% (when rounded)

Assume a NAV of $20 and a sales charge of 5%. What is the POP?

POP is found by dividing the NAV by 100% minus the sales charge percentage.

$20 ÷ .95 = $21.05

In determining the POP when provided with the NAV, the answer has to be more than the NAV. If such a question has only one choice with a higher POP than the NAV, the correct answer should be immediately apparent.

3. 15. 3   CLASS B SHARES

Class B shares do not charge a front-end sales charge, but they do impose an asset-based 12b-1 fee greater than those imposed on Class A shares.

EXAMPLE

The ABC Growth and Income Fund Class B shares have a 12b-1 fee of .75 (75 cents per $100). As such, a $10,000 investment in the fund would have an annual charge of $75 automatically deducted. If the value of the investor's account increases to $20,000, the 12b-1 fee would increase to $150 annually.

Class B shares also normally impose a contingent deferred sales charge (CDSC), also called a back-end load, which is paid when selling shares. Because of the back-end load and 12b-1 fee, Class B shares may not be referred to as noload shares. The CDSC normally declines and eventually is eliminated over time. Once the CDSC is eliminated, Class B shares often convert into Class A shares. When they convert, they will be charged the same (lower) asset-based 12b-1 fee as the Class A shares.

Class B shares do not impose a sales charge at the time of purchase, so unlike Class A share purchases, 100 cents of the invested dollar are invested.

The following table contains a typical CDSC Schedule for Class B shares:

Year	CDSC
1	5%
2	4%
3	3%
4	2%
5	1%
6+	0%

3. 15. 4 CLASS C SHARES (LEVEL LOAD)

Class C shares typically have a one year, 1% CDSC, a .75% 12b-1 fee (discussed shortly), and a .25% shareholder services fee. Because these fees are relatively high and never go away, C shares are commonly referred to as having a level load. Class C shares are appropriate for investors that have short time horizons because they become quite expensive to own if investing for more than four to five years.

3. 15. 5 12B-1 ASSET-BASED FEES

As an asset-based fee, **12b-1 fees** are often called asset-based distribution fees. Named after the SEC rule that allows them, 12b-1 fees are used to cover the costs of marketing and distributing the fund to investors. These 12b-1 fees are also used to compensate registered representatives for servicing an account (trailer commissions) but shouldn't be confused with sales charges. The fee is deducted quarterly as a percentage of the fund's average total NAV.

■ The maximum 12b-1 fee is .75% for distribution and promotion.

■ The fee must reflect the anticipated level of distribution services.

Board of directors. If the fund charges a 12b-1 fee, a simple majority of the board must be made up of noninterested persons, not just 40%.

Misuse of no-load terminology. A fund that has a deferred sales charge or an asset-based 12b-1 fee of more than .25% of average net assets may not be described as a no-load fund. To do so violates the Conduct Rules; the violation is not alleviated by disclosures in the fund's prospectus.

TEST TOPIC ALERT

Expect questions about 12b-1 fees and know the following points:

■ 12b-1 fee is expressed as an annual amount but is charged and reviewed quarterly.

■ Charges covered by 12b-1 fees include advertising, sales literature, and prospectuses delivered to potential customers, not fund management expenses.

12b-1 fee= charged for marketing and sales literature

■ In order for a fund to market itself to the public as a no-load fund, the fund may not charge more than .25% of average net assets for 12b-1 fees.

■ The maximum allowable 12b-1 charge under FINRA rules is .75% (75 basis points).

■ FINRA does permit an additional .25% charge for shareholder services (25 basis points), but that is treated separate from the 12b-1 fee for marketing and promotion.

3. 15. 6 NO-LOAD FUNDS

As the name implies, this means that the fund does not charge any type of sales load. However, not every type of shareholder fee is a sales load. No-loads may charge fees that are not sales loads. For example, a **no-load fund** is permitted to charge purchase fees, account fees, exchange fees, and redemption fees, none of which is considered to be a sales load. (Although a redemption fee is deducted from redemption proceeds just like a deferred sales load, it is not considered to be a sales load.) In addition, under FINRA rules, a fund is permitted to pay its annual operating expenses and still call itself no-load. However, the combined amount of the fund's 12b-1 fees or separate shareholder service fees cannot exceed 0.25% of the fund's average annual net assets.

QUICK QUIZ 3.0

Objective: Compare share classes, pricing, and expenses of mutual fund shares

1. Which of the following is NOT a management company?

A. A mutual fund
B. An open-end company
C. A unit investment trust
D. A closed-end company

2. Mutual fund redemption fees are

A. levied at the time of purchase
B. unlawful
C. levied when the shares are sold back to the fund
D. also known as 12b-1 fees

3. When a customer transfers the proceeds of a sale from one fund to another within the same family of funds, what are the tax consequences?

A. No gains or losses are recognized until the final redemption.
B. Gains are taxed at the time of the transfer, but losses are deferred until the final redemption.
C. Losses are deducted at the time of the transfer, but gains are deferred until the final redemption.
D. All gains and losses are recognized on the transfer date.

All Quick Quiz answers are found at the end of their units.

3. 16   ACCUMULATION AND WITHDRAWAL PLANS

Mutual funds have a number of arrangements to implement an investment program. A **voluntary accumulation plan** allows a customer to deposit regular periodic investments on a voluntary basis (minimum amounts found in the prospectus). The plan is designed to help the customer form regular investment habits while still offering some flexibility.

Voluntary accumulation plans may require a minimum initial purchase and minimum additional purchase amounts. Many funds offer automatic withdrawal from customer checking accounts to simplify contributions. If a customer misses a payment, the fund does not penalize him because the plan is voluntary. The customer may discontinue the plan at any time.

TAKE NOTE

In a voluntary accumulation plan, once the account has been opened, contribution and frequency are very flexible.

3. 16. 1   DOLLAR COST AVERAGING

One method of purchasing mutual fund shares is called **dollar cost averaging**, where a person invests identical amounts at regular intervals. This form of investing allows the individual to purchase more shares when prices are low and fewer shares when prices are high. In a fluctuating market and over a period of time, the average cost per share is lower than the average price of the shares. However, dollar cost averaging does not guarantee profits in a declining market because prices may continue to decline for some time. In this case, the investor buys more shares of a sinking investment.

EXAMPLE

The following illustrates how average price and average cost may vary with dollar cost averaging:

Month	Amount Invested	Price per Share	No. of Shares
January	$600	$20	30
February	$600	$24	25
March	$600	$30	20
April	$600	$40	15
Total	$2,400	$114	90

The average price per share is the sum of the prices paid divided by the number of investments: $114 / 4 = $28.50.

The average cost per share is total amount spent divided by the number of shares purchased: $2,400 / 90 = $26.67.

In this case, the average cost is $1.83 per share less than the average price.

TEST TOPIC ALERT

It is most important to understand the concept of dollar cost averaging. It involves investing a fixed amount of money every period, regardless of market price fluctuation.

If the market price of shares is up, fewer shares are purchased; if the market price of shares is down, more shares are purchased. Over time, if the market fluctuates, dollar cost averaging will achieve a lower average cost per share than average price per share.

TAKE NOTE

Dollar cost averaging neither guarantees profit nor protects from loss. It merely results in a lower cost per share than the average price per share.

3. 16. 2 WITHDRAWAL PLANS

In addition to lump-sum withdrawals, whereby customers sell all their shares, mutual funds offer systematic withdrawal plans. Withdrawal plans are normally a free service. Not all mutual funds offer withdrawal plans, but those that do may offer the plan alternatives described here.

3. 16. 2. 1 Fixed Dollar

A customer may request the periodic withdrawal of a **fixed dollar** amount. Thus, the fund liquidates enough shares each period to send that sum. The amount of money liquidated may be more or less than the account earnings during the period.

3. 16. 2. 2 Fixed Percentage or Fixed Share

Under a fixed-percentage or fixed-share withdrawal plan, either a fixed number of shares or a fixed percentage of the account is liquidated each period.

3. 16. 2. 3 Fixed Time

Under a fixed-time withdrawal plan, customers liquidate their holdings over a fixed period. Most mutual funds require a customer's account to be worth a minimum amount of money before a withdrawal plan may begin. Additionally, most funds discourage continued investment once withdrawals start.

3. 16. 2. 4 Withdrawal Plan Disclosures

Withdrawal plans are not guaranteed. With fixed-dollar plans, only the dollar amount to be received each period is fixed. All other factors, including the number of shares liquidated and a plan's length, are variable. For a fixed-time plan, only the time is fixed; the amount of money the investor receives varies each period.

Because withdrawal plans are not guaranteed, the registered representative must:

■ never promise an investor a guaranteed rate of return;

- stress to the investor that it is possible to exhaust the account by overwithdrawing;
- state that during a down market it is possible that the account will be exhausted if the investor withdraws even a small amount; and
- never use charts or tables unless the SEC specifically clears their use.

TAKE NOTE

Mutual fund withdrawal plans are not guaranteed in any way. All charts and tables regarding withdrawal plans must be cleared by the SEC before use.

QUICK QUIZ 3.P

Objective: Summarize voluntary accumulation and withdrawal plans

1. Which of the following statements regarding dollar cost averaging is TRUE?
   A. It is effective if smaller dollar purchases are made when the market prices rise.
   B. When the market fluctuates, it will result in a lower average cost per share.
   C. It will protect investors from losses in a falling market.
   D. It is most effective when the market remains constant.

2. Which of the following is a risk of a withdrawal plan?
   A. The sales charge for the service is high.
   B. The cost basis of the shares is high.
   C. The plan is illegal in many states.
   D. The investor may outlive his income.

3. An investor has requested a withdrawal plan from his mutual fund and currently receives $600 per month. This is an example of what type of plan?
   A. Contractual
   B. Fixed-share periodic withdrawal
   C. Fixed-dollar periodic withdrawal
   D. Fixed-percentage withdrawal

All Quick Quiz answers are found at the end of their units.

3. 17   ANNUITY PLANS

An **annuity** is an insurance contract designed to provide retirement income. The term *annuity* refers to a stream of payments guaranteed for some period of time—for the life of the annuitant, until the annuitant reaches a certain age, or for a specific number of years. The actual amount to be paid out may or may not be guaranteed, but the stream of payments itself is. Because an annuity can provide an income for the rest of someone's life, the contract has a mortality guarantee. When you think about a retiree's greatest fear, it is typically outliving her income. This product can take away that fear.

3. 17. 1   TYPES OF ANNUITY CONTRACTS

Insurance companies offer fixed and variable annuities. With both, the annuitant makes after-tax lump-sum or periodic payments to the insurance company, which invests the money in an account and grows tax deferred. At retirement, the funds become available for withdrawal, either as a lump sum or as periodic payments to the annuitant, typically for life.

Withdrawals before the age of 59½ result in a 10% penalty, in addition to full income tax on anything over cost basis taken out of the account. Exceptions to the 10% penalty include death and **annuitization** under Rule 72t. Annuitization is discussed later in this unit.

Usually 100% of the money goes into the annuity; however, surrender charges will be applied if the contract is canceled within a stated number of years such as 7 or 10 years from issue.

TAKE NOTE

Annuities discussed in this section are nonqualified; that is, they are funded with after-tax dollars, the money grows tax deferred, and only the earnings are taxed at distribution.

3. 17. 1. 1   Fixed Annuities

In a fixed annuity, investors pay premiums to the insurance company that are, in turn, invested in the company's general account. The insurance company is then obligated to pay a guaranteed amount of payout (typically monthly) to the annuitant based on how much was paid in.

Note that the insurer guarantees a rate of return and, therefore, bears the investment risk. Because the insurer is the one at risk, this product is not a security. An insurance license is required to sell fixed annuities, but a securities license is not.

Purchasing power risk (inflation risk) is a significant risk associated with fixed annuities. The fixed payment that the annuitant receives loses buying power over time due to inflation.

EXAMPLE

An individual who bought a fixed annuity in 1980 began to receive monthly income of $375 in 1990. Years later, this amount, which seemed sufficient monthly income at the time, may no longer be enough to live on.

3. 17. 1. 2   Index Annuity

In an effort to overcome the purchasing power risk of fixed annuities, but without the market risk of a variable annuity, the industry developed the **index annuity**.

Index annuities are currently popular among investors seeking market participation but with a guarantee against loss. Unlike a traditional fixed annuity, an index annuity credits interest to the owner's account, using a formula based on the performance of a particular stock index, such as the S&P 500. If the index does well, the annuitant is credited with a specified percentage of the growth of the index—typically 80% or 90% of the growth. This is known as the **participation rate**. If the index does poorly, the annuitant may receive a guaranteed minimum interest rate such as 1% or 2%.

To give you an idea of how an index annuity might work, consider a participation rate of 80% and a minimum guarantee of 1%. If the index shows growth of 9% during the measurement period, the annuitant would be credited with 7.2% growth (80% of 9%). If the index performed at –9%, the annuitant would receive the minimum guarantee of 1%.

In addition to the participation rate, there is usually a **cap rate**. A typical cap might be 12%. This means that if the index annuity was pegged to the S&P 500 and that index increased 30% during the year, your gain would be capped at 12%. One other negative characteristic of these products is that they tend to have longer surrender charge periods (as long as 15 years) than other annuities, especially if there is a front-end bonus.

TAKE NOTE   The only license required in order to sell index annuities is an insurance license.

3. 17. 2 VARIABLE ANNUITIES

Insurance companies introduced the **variable annuity** as an opportunity to keep pace with inflation. For this potential advantage, the investor assumes the investment risk rather than the insurance company. Because the investor takes on this risk, the product is considered a security. It must be sold with a prospectus by individuals who are both insurance licensed and securities licensed.

The premium payments for variable annuities are invested in the separate account of the insurer. The separate account is comprises various subaccounts that behave like mutual funds (we just can't call them mutual funds). These accounts will have a variety of investment objectives to choose from, such as growth, income, and growth and income. The returns in the separate account are not guaranteed, and therefore a loss of principal is possible.

As with all recommendations, suitability of any purchase is number one. However, in light of the large number of cases involving variable annuities where there was failure to supervise egregious unethical behavior, **FINRA Rule 2330** evolved. This rule applies to recommended purchases and 1035 exchanges of deferred variable annuities (NOT immediate) and recommended initial subaccount allocations.

Variable Annuity

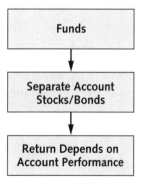

Fixed vs. Variable Annuity

Fixed Annuity	Variable Annuity
Payments made with after-tax dollars	Payments made with after-tax dollars
Payments are invested in the general account	Payments are invested in the separate account
Portfolio of fixed-income securities/real estate	Portfolio of equity, debt, or mutual funds
Insurer assumes investment risk	Annuitant assumes investment risk
Not a security	Is a security
Guaranteed rate of return	Return depends on separate account performance
Fixed administrative expenses	Fixed administrative expenses
Income guaranteed for life	Income guaranteed for life
Monthly payment never falls below guaranteed minimum	Monthly payments may fluctuate up or down
Purchasing power risk	Typically protects against purchasing power risk
Subject to insurance regulation	Subject to registration with the state insurance commission and the securities exchange commission (SEC)

Although annuitants of variable annuities can choose a guaranteed monthly income for life, the amount of monthly income received is dependent on the performance of the separate account. Monthly income either increases or decreases, as determined by the separate account performance.

Investors may purchase a **combination annuity** to receive the advantages of both the fixed and variable annuities. In a combination annuity, the investor contributes to both the general and separate accounts, which provides for guaranteed payments, as well as inflation protection.

TEST TOPIC ALERT   Whenever you see the term variable, as in variable annuity or variable life (discussed later), two licenses are required for the sale—an insurance license and a securities license. Suitability must be determined and a prospectus must be delivered prior to or with solicitation of the sale.

Investing Variable Annuity Premium Dollars

Fixed vs. Variable Annuity

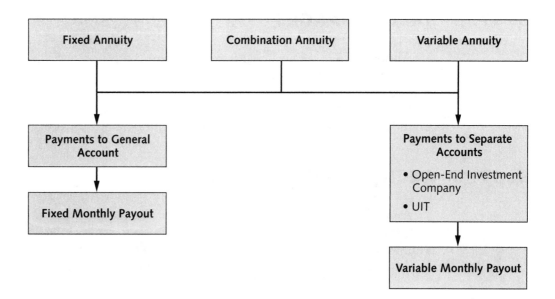

3. 17. 3 PURCHASING ANNUITIES

Insurance companies offer a number of purchase arrangements for annuities. The various purchasing plans are discussed next. Aggregate fees include not only sales charges on the front end, but also those levied upon surrender, commonly called conditional deferred sales loads, or CDSL. In many cases, there is no load to purchase, but if surrender, other than through annuitization, occurs during the early years of the contract, the charges can be significant.

An investor is offered a number of options when purchasing an annuity. Payments to the insurance company can be made either with a single **lump-sum payment** or periodically on a monthly, quarterly, or annual basis.

A single premium deferred annuity is purchased with a lump sum, but payment of benefits is delayed until a later date selected by the annuitant.

A **periodic payment deferred annuity** allows investments over time. Benefit payments for this type of annuity are always deferred until a later date selected by the annuitant.

An **immediate annuity** is purchased with a lump sum, and the payout of benefits usually commences within 60 days.

TEST TOPIC ALERT   There is no such thing as a **periodic payment immediate annuity**.

3. 17. 4 BONUS ANNUITIES

Direct financial benefits are sometimes offered with annuities, called **bonus annuities**. These benefits include enhancement of the buyer's premium, with the insurance company contributing an additional 3%–5% to the premium payment. This comes with a cost, of course, in the form of higher fees and expenses, and longer surrender periods than the typical

7–10 years of standard contracts. Recommendations to customers must include the additional costs, as well as the benefits of the bonuses and enhancements.

3. 17. 5 SALES CHARGES

Although there are no stated maximum sales charges on variable annuities, the SEC has charged FINRA with the responsibility of ensuring that they are fair and reasonable. As a practical matter, most annuities, both fixed and variable, are sold with little or no sales charge.

Instead, there is a surrender charge (think CDSC or CDSL) for early termination. This surrender period is longer for bonus annuities and generally the longest for index annuities.

3. 17. 6 ACCUMULATION PHASE

A variable annuity has two distinct phases. The growth phase is its **accumulation phase**, while the payout phase is its annuity phase. A contract owner's interest in the separate account is known as either accumulation units or annuity units depending on the contract phase.

Accumulation units vary in value based on the separate account's performance.

QUICK QUIZ 3.Q

Objective: Define annuities and their characteristics

1. Which of the following types of annuity contracts would your customer NOT be able to purchase?

   A. Periodic payment deferred annuity
   B. Periodic payment immediate life annuity
   C. Lump-sum payment immediate life annuity
   D. Lump-sum payment deferred annuity

2. A variable annuity contract guarantees

   I. a rate of return
   II. a fixed mortality expense
   III. a fixed administrative expense
   IV. a fixed investment risk

   A. I and III
   B. I and IV
   C. II and III
   D. II and IV

3. Which of the following annuities includes augmentation of the premium payments by the insurance company?

   A. Fixed annuity
   B. Combination annuity
   C. Equity index annuity
   D. Bonus annuity

All Quick Quiz answers are found at the end of their units.

3. 18   THE PAYOUT PHASE

When the annuitant decides to begin receiving payments from the annuity, they may choose to annuitize the contract and chose the desired settlement option. Although not required, if annuitized, the owner enters into a contractual obligation with the insurance company for the systematic distribution of the asset.

Once annuitized, the money will be distributed per the payout option chosen (discussed later). At that point, the accumulation units purchased over time will be converted into a fixed number of annuity units. This becomes one of the factors used to calculate the payout each month during retirement.

Annuitization

Accumulation phase	--------------->	Annuity phase
Accumulation units	--------------->	Annuity units

Annuity units vary in value based on the separate account performance.

TEST TOPIC ALERT   As mentioned earlier in our comparison chart with mutual funds, accumulation unit values are computed daily on a forward pricing basis. As you will soon see, annuity unit values are computed monthly based on actual performance versus the assumed interest rate.

3. 18. 1   RECEIVING DISTRIBUTIONS FROM ANNUITIES

An annuity offers several payment options for money accumulated in the account. The investor can withdraw the funds randomly, in a lump sum, or annuitize the contract (receive monthly income).

If the investor chooses annuitization, the amount of the monthly check is dependent on several factors:

- Amount of money in the contract (more money equals a bigger check)
- Age (the older one is, the larger the check will be)
- Sex (females live longer than males; therefore, the check would be less for a female)
- Payout option (reviewed in this segment)
- Investment return versus assumed interest rate for variable annuities (see the following)

3. 18. 2   ASSUMED INTEREST RATE

If the annuity is variable, the actuarial department of the insurance company determines the initial value for the annuity units and the amount of the first month's annuity payment. At this time, an **assumed interest rate (AIR)** is established. The AIR is a conservative projection of the performance of the separate account over the estimated life of the contract.

The value of an annuity unit and the annuitant's subsequent monthly income will vary, depending on separate account performance as compared to the AIR. To determine whether the monthly payment will increase, decrease, or stay the same as the previous month, the following rules apply.

- ■ If separate account performance is greater than the AIR, next month's payment is more than this month's.

- ■ If separate account performance is equal to the AIR, next month's payment stays the same as this month's.

- ■ If separate account performance is less than the AIR, next month's payment is less than this month's.

EXAMPLE

Assume an AIR of 4% and that the actuaries have determined the first payment to be $1,000.

Month 2's separate account performance is 6%, greater than AIR, so the next check goes up.

Month 3's separate account performance is 4%, right at AIR. The next check received equals the last check received.

Month 4's separate account performance is 3%, which is below AIR; therefore the next check received will be less than the last check received.

Month 5's separate account performance is 3% again, which, although the same as month 4's, is still below AIR. The next check is, therefore, less than that of the last.

Month 6's separate account performance is not shown, but if separate account performance is above the AIR of 4%, the next check will be more than $950; if it is below the AIR of 4%, the next check will be less than $950.

AIR = 4%	Month 1	Month 2	Month 3	Month 4	Month 5	Month 6
Separate Account Return		6%	4%	3%	3%	?
Monthly Payment	$1,000	$1,100	$1,100	$1,000	$950	?

TAKE NOTE

Consider this: If AIR is 4% and the separate account always returns 4%, the check would never change!

3. 18. 3 SURRENDER

If he wishes, the annuitant may simply cash in his annuity. In this case, his cost base is the total amount he has invested. He will be liable for income tax on the growth plus a 10% penalty on the growth if he is under the age of 59½.

3. 18. 4 DEATH OF ANNUITANT

If the annuitant dies during the accumulation period, the death benefit takes effect. His beneficiary is guaranteed either the total value of the annuity or the total amount invested, whichever is greater, and is liable for income tax on any growth.

3. 18. 5   ANNUITIZATION

If the annuitant wishes to receive scheduled payments for life, he may annuitize, in which case, he must select a payout option, such as:

- life annuity (also known as straight life or life only),
- life annuity with period certain,
- joint life with last survivor annuity, and
- unit refund option.

3. 18. 6   LIFE ANNUITY/STRAIGHT LIFE

If an annuitant selects the life income option, the insurance company will pay the annuitant for life. When the annuitant dies, there are no continuing payments to a beneficiary. Money remaining in the account reverts to the insurer. Because there is no beneficiary during the annuitization, this represents the largest monthly check an annuitant could receive for the rest of the annuitant's life. (The insurance company has no further obligation at death.)

TAKE NOTE   The life annuity probably would not have been a good choice if the annuitant died after receiving only one month's payment. With the life income option, all money accumulated that was not paid out at the time of the annuitant's death would belong to the insurer.

3. 18. 7   LIFE ANNUITY WITH PERIOD CERTAIN

The following options are a little less risky because they allow for payments to a beneficiary. To guarantee that a minimum number of payments are made even if the annuitant dies, the life with period certain option can be chosen. The contract will specifically allow the choice of a period of 10 or 20 years, for instance. The length of the period certain is a choice that is made when a payout option is selected. The annuitant is guaranteed monthly income for life with this option, but if death occurs within the period certain, a named beneficiary receives payments for the remainder of the period. Because there is a named beneficiary for the period certain, the size of this check will be smaller than a straight life option. (The insurance company is obligated to pay the named beneficiary an income if death occurs during the period certain.)

TAKE NOTE   To illustrate the life annuity with period certain option, assume a client selects a life annuity with a 10-year period certain. If the annuitant lives to be 150 years old, annuity payments are still made by the insurer. But, if the annuitant dies after receiving payments for two years, the beneficiary will receive payments for eight more years.

3. 18. 8 JOINT LIFE WITH LAST SURVIVOR ANNUITY

The joint life with last survivor option guarantees payments over two lives. It is often used for spouses. Because the insurance company is obligated to pay a check over two lifetimes, this check is considered to be smaller than a life with period certain option.

EXAMPLE

If the husband were to die first, the wife would continue to receive payments as long as she lives. If the wife were to die first, the husband would receive payments as long as he lives. Typically the payment amount is reduced for the survivor.

3. 18. 9 UNIT REFUND OPTION

If the annuitant chooses the unit refund option, a minimum number of payments are made upon retirement. If value remains in the account after the death of the annuitant, it is payable in a lump sum to the annuitant's beneficiary. This option may be added as a rider to one of the others.

TAKE NOTE

The unit refund option is the only lifetime annuitization option that guarantees all of the money in the contract will be distributed. If unit refund is chosen for a $100,000 contract, the insurance company guarantees that a minimum of $100,000 will be distributed and also guarantees a monthly check for life. Therefore, more than $100,000 may be distributed, but never less. Unit refund is sometimes offered as a rider.

For test purposes, this option represents the smallest check a person could receive for the rest of his life.

3. 18. 10 TAXATION OF ANNUITIES

All contributions to annuities are made with after-tax dollars, unless the annuity is part of an employer-sponsored (qualified) retirement plan or held in an IRA.

TEST TOPIC ALERT

Assume an annuity is nonqualified unless a question specifically states otherwise. When contributions are made with after-tax dollars, these already taxed dollars are considered the investor's cost basis and are not taxed when withdrawn. The earnings in excess of the cost basis are taxed as ordinary income when withdrawn.

EXAMPLE

An investor has contributed $100,000 to a variable annuity. The annuity is now worth $150,000. What is the investor's cost basis, and what amount is taxable upon withdrawal?

The cost basis is equal to the contributions, or $100,000. The taxable amount at withdrawal will be the earnings of $50,000.

Because annuities are designed to supplement retirement income and provide tax-deferred growth, withdrawals before age 59½ are subject to the 10% early withdrawal penalty and ordinary income tax on the earnings portion of the withdrawal.

When an investor chooses to annuitize and selects a monthly income payout option, each month's payment is considered partly a return of cost basis and partly earnings. Only the earnings portion is taxable.

Many contract owners choose random withdrawals over the annuity option. If this choice is made, last in, first out (LIFO) taxation applies. The IRS requires that all earnings are withdrawn first and are taxed at ordinary income rates. After earnings are completely withdrawn, there is no additional taxation because the cost basis has already been taxed.

TAKE NOTE

Assume the following:

$100,000	after-tax contributions (cost basis)
+ 50,000	earnings
$150,000	total account value

If the investor makes a random withdrawal of $60,000, what are the tax consequences?

Remember that LIFO applies—the IRS chooses tax revenue as early as possible.

Those earnings that accumulated tax deferred are now fully taxable. The investor must pay ordinary income taxes on the first $50,000 withdrawn because that is the amount of earnings. Furthermore, if the investor is under age 59½, an extra 10% early withdrawal tax applies. The remaining $10,000 is a return of the cost basis and is not taxed.

Any answer choice that mentions capital gains taxation on annuities or retirement plans is wrong. There is only ordinary income tax on distributions from annuities and retirement plans.

QUICK QUIZ 3.R

Objective: Compare the different ways to distribute money from an annuity

1. A customer invests in a variable annuity. At age 65, she chooses to annuitize. Under these circumstances, which of the following statements are TRUE?

   I.   She will receive the annuity's entire value in a lump-sum payment.
   II. She may choose to receive monthly payments for the rest of her life.
   III. The number and value of the accumulation units is used to calculate the total number of annuity units.
   IV. The accumulation unit's value is used to calculate the annuity unit's value.

   A. I and III
   B. I and IV
   C. II and III
   D. II and IV

2.   An investor is in the annuity period of a variable annuity purchased 15 years ago. During the present month, the annuitant receives a check for an amount that is less than the previous month's payment. The payment is smaller because the account's performance was

   A.   less than the previous month's performance
   B.   greater than the previous month's performance
   C.   less than the assumed interest rate
   D.   greater than the assumed interest rate

3.   An insurance company offering a variable annuity makes payments to annuitants on the 15th of each month. The contract has an AIR of 3%. In July of this year, the contract earned 4%. In August, the account earned 6%. If the contract earns 3% in September, the payments to annuitants in October will be

   A.   greater than the payments in September
   B.   less than the payments in September
   C.   the same as the payments in September
   D.   less than the payments in August

All Quick Quiz answers are found at the end of their units.

3. 19   VARIABLE ANNUITY SUITABILITY

A variable annuity can be a very important part of one's financial well-being if utilized correctly. However, there are suitability issues to consider. Variable annuities are meant to bring supplemental income into the household at a time in one's life when the income is needed.

Therefore, supplemental income for retirement, not preservation of capital, should be the catalyst to considering a VA. Here are some general rules of thumb regarding the suitability of variable annuities.

■   Variable contracts are considered most suitable for someone who can fund the contract with cash. In other words, enticements to cash out a life insurance policy or an existing annuity (either of which might come with high surrender charges) is considered abusive and not a suitable recommendation. Refinancing a home or withdrawing equity from a home to fund a purchase could never be considered suitable.

■   Variable contracts are not suitable for anyone who might need the lump sum of cash invested in the VA at a later time for any reason. Anticipating buying a home, needing cash for your children's college education, or any other upcoming expense would need to be considered outside the variable annuity investment.

■   Investing in a variable annuity within a tax-deferred account, such as an individual retirement account (IRA) may not be a good idea. Because IRAs are already tax-advantaged, a variable annuity will provide no additional tax savings. It will, however, increase the expense of the IRA compared with other funding choices, such as stocks, bonds or mutual funds.

   —   If the annuity is within a traditional (rather than a Roth) IRA, the government requires that you start withdrawing income no later than the April 1 that follows your 70½ birthday, regardless of any surrender charges the annuity might impose.

Variable annuity contracts are insurance company products that invest in a portfolio of securities via their separate account. If someone has a low risk tolerance or is wary of the stock market, a VA is not likely a very suitable recommendation for that individual.

■ Maximum contributions to all other retirement savings vehicles available to an individual should be made before a VA is considered a suitable recommendation. In other words, they are best considered supplements to retirement income one can already anticipate, such as pensions and IRA or 401(k) distributions.

3. 19. 1 1035 EXCHANGE

A **1035 exchange** is a tax-free exchange between like contracts. The IRS allows annuity and life policyholders to exchange their policies without tax liability. For example, if a life policyholder wanted to exchange his policy for one from another company, he could transfer all cash values from the old policy into the new policy without recognizing any tax consequences. This 1035 exchange provision applies to transfers of cash values from annuity to annuity, life to life and life to annuity. It cannot be used for transfers from an annuity to a life insurance policy.

TEST TOPIC ALERT   FINRA is concerned about Section 1035 exchange abuses where the registered representative emphasizes the tax-free nature of the exchange without pointing out possible disadvantages. Those include:

■ possible surrender charges on the old policy;

■ a new surrender charge period on the new policy; and

■ possible loss of a higher death benefit that existed on the old policy.

The representative and a principal of the firm must believe that the customer has been informed, in general terms, of various features of deferred variable annuities, such as:

■ the potential surrender period and surrender charge,

■ potential tax penalty if customers sell or redeem deferred variable annuities before reaching the age of 59½,

■ mortality and expense fees,

■ investment advisory fees,

■ potential charges for and features of riders,

■ the insurance and investment components of deferred variable annuities, and

■ market risk.

In addition, the firm must inquire as to whether the customer has had an exchange of a variable annuity at another broker-dealer within the last 36 months.

QUICK QUIZ 3.S   Objective: Recall suitability considerations of annuities

1. A 60-year-old male customer is interested in investing in a variable annuity. Which of the following would you consider to be the least important in the investment decision?

   A.   The customer's investment objective
   B.   The customer's sex
   C.   The performance history of the variable annuity
   D.   The investment choices available in the variable annuity

2.   If your customer wants a source of retirement income that is both stable and offering some protection against purchasing-power risk in times of inflation, you should recommend

   A.   a combination annuity
   B.   a variable annuity
   C.   a fixed annuity
   D.   a portfolio of common stocks and municipal bonds

3.   An 18-year-old, unmarried high school student sought a safe investment for a $30,000 bequest until after she graduated from college. Her intent was to use the funds for the down payment on a house after graduation. Her agent recommended she choose a variable annuity as a safe haven for the funds. This recommendation is unsuitable because

   A.   withdrawal of her cost basis is tax-free
   B.   the investment grows tax deferred
   C.   her situation exposes her to surrender charges and early withdrawal penalties
   D.   an 18-year-old can't own a variable annuity

4.   All of the following are true regarding variable annuities EXCEPT

   A.   variable annuities are best considered supplements to retirement income one can already anticipate, such as pensions and IRA or 401(k) distributions
   B.   recommendations to fund a variable annuity by liquidating other investments are generally not considered suitable
   C.   availability of funds in the future for life expenses such as college tuition or a home should be considered when recommending variable annuities
   D.   variable annuities are most suitable for those with low risk tolerance

All Quick Quiz answers are found at the end of their units.

3. 20   LIFE INSURANCE

Life insurance provides a death benefit to a named beneficiary in the event of an insured's premature death. There are many variations of whole life and term insurance, each serving different needs. We will review these policies and focus on one considered a security.

Permanent life insurance is designed to last until at least age 100 or the death of the insured, whichever occurs first. These policies also accrue cash value that may be borrowed for living needs. An insurance license is required to sell life insurance.

The premium for permanent life insurance is calculated according to the policyowner's health, age, and sex, as well as the policy's face amount at issue. Permanent life insurance is not a security and is not sold as an investment.

3. 20. 1   VARIABLE LIFE INSURANCE

Variable life (VL) insurance has a fixed, scheduled premium but differs from whole life insurance in that the premiums paid are split; part of the premium is placed in the general assets of the insurance company. These general assets are used to guarantee a minimum death benefit. The balance of the premium is placed in the **separate account** and represents the cash value of the policy. Because the cash value is invested in the separate account, which fluctuates in value, its cash value is not guaranteed. The policy's death benefit may increase above the minimum guaranteed amount as a result of investment results but may never fall below the minimum (as long as premiums are paid).

TAKE NOTE

Because a variable life insurance policy has a minimum death benefit, the premiums necessary to fund this part of the death benefit are held in the insurer's general account. Any policy benefit that is guaranteed is invested in the insurer's general account.

Any premium above what is necessary to pay for the minimum death benefit is invested in the separate account. This portion of the premium is subject to investment risk, and variable life insurance, therefore, is also defined as a security. As long as premiums are paid, the policy remains in force, even if the separate accounts lose money every year.

Once the premium has been determined and the expenses have been deducted, the net premium is invested in subaccounts (also called the separate account). There will be several subaccounts to choose from such as the following:

- Growth subaccount
- Income subaccount
- Balanced
- Index or indices
- Money market

3. 20. 2 VARIABLE LIFE PROSPECTUS DELIVERY

Because a variable life insurance policy is considered a security as well as an insurance product, a prospectus is required, just as with any new issue. The prospectus must be delivered before or at the time of solicitation and may not be altered in any way (no highlighting or writing in the prospectus).

TAKE NOTE

Both an insurance license and a securities license are needed in order to sell variable contracts.

3. 20. 3 ASSUMED INTEREST RATE AND VARIABLE DEATH BENEFIT

The death benefit payable under a variable life insurance policy is adjusted on an annual basis and can increase or decrease based on the performance of the separate account compared with an assumed interest rate (AIR). So one of the benefits of VL is that the death benefit may adjust upward and possibly keep pace with inflation.

If the separate account returns are greater than the AIR, these extra earnings are reflected in an increase in death benefit and cash value. If the separate account returns equal the AIR, actual earnings meet estimated expenses, resulting in no change in the death benefit. Should the separate account returns be less than the AIR, the contract's death benefit will decrease; however, it will never fall below the amount guaranteed at issue.

TAKE NOTE   The variable death benefit is adjusted annually. If there have been several months of negative performance, therefore, they must be offset by equivalent positive performance before the variable death benefit can be adjusted upward.

TAKE NOTE   The AIR has no effect on cash value accumulation in a variable life policy. The cash value will grow whenever the separate account has positive performance. The AIR, however, does affect the death benefit. Just remember the rules for variable annuities. The rules for the death benefits are analogous.

- If the separate account performance for the year is greater than the AIR, the death benefit will increase.

- If the separate account performance for the year is equal to the AIR, the death benefit will stay the same.

- If the separate account performance for the year is less than the AIR, the death benefit will decrease.

3. 20. 4 LOANS

Like traditional whole life (WL), a VL contract allows the insured to borrow against the cash value that has accumulated in the contract. **Loans** are not considered constructive receipt of income and therefore are received income tax free. However, certain restrictions exist. Usually, the insured may only borrow a percentage of the cash value. The minimum percentage that must be made available is 75% after the policy has been in force for three years. There is no scheduled repayment of a loan. However, if the death benefit becomes payable and a loan is outstanding, the loan amount is deducted from the death benefit before payment. The interest rate charged is stated in the policy. If an outstanding loan reduces cash value to a negative amount, the insured has 31 days to deposit enough into his account to make it positive. If he fails to do so, the insurance company will terminate the contract. If this happens, the loan, of course, need not be repaid.

3. 20. 5 CONTRACT EXCHANGE

During the early stage of ownership, a policyowner has the right to exchange a VL contract for a traditional fixed-benefit WL contract. The length of time this exchange privilege is in effect varies from company to company, but under no circumstances may the period be less than 24 months (federal law).

The exchange is allowed without evidence of insurability. If a contract is exchanged, the new WL policy has the same contract date and death benefit as the minimum guaranteed in the VL contract. The premiums equal the amounts guaranteed in the new WL contract (as if it were the original contract).

TEST TOPIC ALERT

Two testable facts about the contract exchange provision are as follows:

■ The contract exchange provision must be available for a minimum of two years.

■ No medical underwriting (evidence of insurability) is required for the exchange.

3. 20. 6   SALES CHARGES

The sales charges on a fixed-premium VL contract may not exceed 9% of the payments to be made over the life of the contract. The contract's life, for purposes of this charge, is a maximum of 20 years. For those of you familiar with life insurance compensation, the effect of this is that renewal commissions are earned up to the 20th anniversary of policy issue.

3. 20. 7   REFUND PROVISIONS

The insurer must extend a free-look period to the policyowner for 45 days from the execution of the application or for 10 days from the time the owner receives the policy, whichever is longer. During the free-look period, the policyowner may terminate the policy and receive all payments made.

The refund provisions extend for two years from issuance of the policy. If, within the two-year period, the policyowner terminates participation in the contract, the insurer must refund the contract's cash value (the value calculated after the insurer receives the redemption notice) plus a percentage of the sales charges deducted. After the two-year period has lapsed, only the cash value need be refunded; the insurer retains all sales charges.

TEST TOPIC ALERT

Several testable facts about sales charges and refunds are as follows:

■ The maximum sales charge over the life of the contract is 9%.

■ A policyowner who wants a refund within 45 days receives all money paid.

■ After a variable life policy has been in effect for two years, the surrender value of the policy is the cash value.

3. 20. 8 SUITABILITY OF VARIABLE LIFE INSURANCE

■ There must be a life insurance need.

■ The applicant must be comfortable with the separate account and the fact that the cash value is not guaranteed.

■ The applicant must understand the variable death benefit feature.

■ A prospectus must be delivered prior to or at the time of solicitation.

QUICK QUIZ 3.T

Objective: Distinguish the characteristics of variable life insurance and its suitability

1. An investor owns a variable life insurance policy on his wife. The policy names their daughter as the beneficiary. Presuming his wife dies, which of the following statements correctly describes the tax consequence associated with this policy?

    A. The death benefit will be taxable to the wife's estate upon distribution.
    B. The death benefit will not be taxable to the daughter upon distribution.
    C. The policyowner may deduct premiums paid into the policy in the year they are paid.
    D. There will be no federal income tax on any distribution, provided the variable life insurance separate account included only municipal bonds.

2. A registered representative presenting a variable life insurance policy proposal to a prospect must disclose which of the following about the insured's rights of exchange of the VLI policy?

    A. The insurance company will allow the insured to exchange the VLI policy for a traditional whole life policy within 45 days from the date of the application or 10 days from policy delivery, whichever is longer.
    B. Federal law requires the insurance company to allow the insured to exchange the VLI policy for a traditional whole life policy issued by the same company for 2 years with no additional evidence of insurability.
    C. Within the first 18 months, the insured may exchange the VLI policy for either a whole life or a universal variable policy issued by the same company with no additional evidence of insurability.
    D. The insured may request that the insurance company exchange the VLI policy for a traditional whole life policy issued by the same company within 2 years. The insurance company retains the right to have medical examinations for underwriting purposes.

3. A customer is considering the purchase of either a variable annuity or variable life insurance. In discussing the merits of the respective contracts, a registered representative may state that all of the following characteristics are common to both contracts EXCEPT

    A. all gains are tax deferred
    B. the AIR is a factor in determining certain values
    C. death benefits are received income tax free
    D. the representative must have a securities license and an insurance license

All Quick Quiz answers are found at the end of their units.

3. 21   EDUCATION PLANS

There are two education savings plans you should be familiar with for your Series 7 exam.

3. 21. 1   529 PLANS

Section 529 plans are state-sponsored, pre- and postsecondary education plans and, therefore, are defined as municipal fund securities.

There are two basic types of 529 plans: **prepaid tuition plans** and **college savings plans**. Both plans are funded with after-tax dollars and earnings grow tax deferred. Withdrawals taken for qualified education expenses are generally tax free. If the money is used for anything other than qualified education expenses, the earnings portion of the distribution will be taxable on your federal (and possibly state) income tax return in the year of the distribution. Also, you generally must pay a 10% federal penalty on the earnings portion of your distribution. (There are a couple of exceptions to the 10% penalty. The penalty is usually not charged if you terminate the account because your beneficiary has died or become disabled, or if you withdraw funds not needed for college because your beneficiary has received a scholarship.) Any person can open a 529 plan for a future college student; the donor does not have to be related to the student.

Prepaid tuition plans allow donors to lock in future tuition rates at today's prices, thus offering inflation protection.

The **college savings plan** allows the donor to invest a lump sum or make periodic payments. The money is typically invested into target-date funds. As the target date approaches (the date the money is needed) the portfolio gets more conservative. When the student is ready for college, the donor withdraws the amount needed to pay for qualified education expenses (e.g., tuition, room and board, and books). These plans do have investment risk, in other words, they can lose money.

Starting in 2018, up to $10,000 per year can be used for K–12 education purposes.

Other points to note include the following:

- College savings plans (but not prepaid tuition plans) may be set up in more than one state, though the allowable contribution amount varies from state to state.

- There are no age limitations for contributions or distributions.

- There are no income limitations on making contributions to a 529 plan.

- Contributions may be made in the form of periodic payments, but contributions follow the tax rules for gifts. Thus, unless willing to pay a gift tax, contributions are limited to an indexed maximum amount ($15,000 in 2018) per year per donor. Section 529 plans have a five-year election that allows a donor to contribute five times that amount in one year (a spouse can do the same to the same recipient), but then they may make no more contributions for five years.

- There are few restrictions on who may be the first beneficiary of a 529 plan. However, if the beneficiary is redesignated, the new beneficiary must be a close family member of the first.

The assets in the account remain the property of the donor, even after the beneficiary reaches legal age. However, if the account is not used for higher education, and the IRS concludes that the plan was not established in good faith, it may impose fines and other sanctions. This would generally mean the earnings in the account are taxed at ordinary income rates with an additional 10% penalty.

Plan assets remain outside the owner's estate for estate tax purposes.

TAKE NOTE

Because 529s are state-sponsored, individual states have their own version of the plan. The test does not expect you to have knowledge of specific state plans, only characteristics of the plan in general.

3. 21. 2 COVERDELL EDUCATION SAVINGS ACCOUNTS

After tax contributions
· distr tax free
· 2k max per year

Coverdell Education Savings Accounts are not municipal securities. They can be funded with traditional types of securities. These plans allow after-tax contributions of up to $2,000 per student per year for children until their 18th birthday.

Contributions may be made by any person, provided the total contribution per child does not exceed $2,000 in one year. Earnings grow tax deferred, and distributions are tax free as long as the funds are distributed prior to the beneficiary's 30th birthday and used for qualified education expenses.

TEST TOPIC ALERT

Coverdell Education Savings Accounts (CESAs)

- Contribution limit is $2,000 per year per child under age 18.

- Contributions may be made by persons other than parents; total for one child is still $2,000.

- Contributions must cease after the child's 18th birthday.

- Contributions are not tax deductible.

- Distributions are tax free if taken before age 30 and used for education expenses.

- Under most circumstances, if the money is not used for education or the money is distributed after age 30, earnings are subject to ordinary income tax plus a 10% penalty.

QUICK QUIZ 3.U

Objective: Define the general characteristics of education savings accounts

1. A 529 college savings plan offers all of the following to participants EXCEPT

 B

   A. tax-free withdrawals for qualified education expenses
   B. before-tax contributions to the plan — *after tax contributions*
   C. no time limit as to when the money must be withdrawn
   D. tax-deferred growth on the money invested

2. One type of municipal securities fund is titled a 529 A savings account or ABLE account. What is the main purpose of setting up an ABLE 529 A savings account?

D

   A. To save money for the education needs of children
   B. To provide for the well-being of foster children
   C. A type of retirement account funded with municipal securities
   D. Is set up for the care and needs of disabled individuals

All Quick Quiz answers are found at the end of their units.

Q U I C K   Q U I Z   A N S W E R S

Quick Quiz 3.A

1. **B.** Wanting to retire at age 65 is a goal and a nonfinancial consideration. Financial investment considerations can be expressed as a sum of money (total liabilities, for example) or as a numerical cash flow (gross income of $160,000 per year, for example).

2. **D.** When limited information is provided for the account, the representative will be limited to making recommendations that he believes are suitable based on the information he has.

3. **C.** Nonfinancial investment considerations are those that cannot be expressed as a concrete sum of money or as a specific monthly or yearly (or weekly) cash flow. Attitude toward risk cannot be expressed in numbers at all, and tax bracket is a percentage of income rather than a concrete sum of money.

Quick Quiz 3.B

1. **B.** The customer is facing a risk in that she only owns one security, and if something bad happens to the company, all her money is tied to it. It would make the most sense to consider an asset allocation model based on whatever her investment objectives are. There is no liquidity risk because the stock is listed on the NYSE and is, therefore, very liquid.

2. **A.** An international stock fund will diversify the portfolio and reduce overall risk. A portfolio that includes domestic securities and international securities is more diversified than a portfolio that just includes domestic securities.

3. **C.** These customers are preparing to make a major purchase within the next few months. They require a highly liquid investment to keep their money safe for a short time. The money market fund best matches this objective.

Quick Quiz 3.C

1. **D.** An investor cannot diversify away market risk. If the entire market is in a tailspin, all the investor's securities will likely decline.

2. **C.** Both stocks and bonds involve some degree of market risk—the risk that investors may lose some of their principal due to price volatility in the overall market (also known as systematic risk).

3. **C.** High-yield bond funds are below investment-grade bonds and are considered speculative in nature. They would not be appropriate for a risk averse investor.

4. **B.** Issuers want to call bonds that are costly to them at as low a price as possible. A high-interest bond with a no call premium is the best combination. The issuer would be least likely to call a low-interest bond with a high call premium.

Quick Quiz 3.D

1. **A.** It would be inappropriate to compare a growth fund with a bond fund with the intention of trying to sell the growth fund. These are two very different types of funds. Comparisons of investments should be done with similar types of securities.

2. **C.** Beta is a measurement tool that compares the volatility of a security versus the stock market as a whole. The lower the beta, the lower the returns (if the market goes up) and the lower the losses (if the market goes down) and vice versa.

3. **B.** When an investment has a negative alpha, it indicates the investment's return did not match the risk that it had. In other words, if the investment should have returned 10% return based on the risk of the investment, and only generated a 7% return, the investor took more risk than the return.

4. **B.** Market risk, sometimes referred to as systematic risk, cannot be diversified away. The risk of investing in a single industry or sector can be diversified away by investing in several industries with returns not correlated to one another. A general downturn in the market, however, cannot be eliminated through diversification.

Quick Quiz 3.E

1. **D.** The food industry is defensive in nature. During an economic downturn, people still eat! Therefore, the food industry would be fairly stable when the economy goes south.

2. **B.** Inventory is a part of current assets. Using the standard equation for a balance sheet: assets minus liabilities equals net worth; we can take assets [current assets plus fixed assets ($3,000,000)] minus liabilities ($2,000,000) equals net worth of $1,000,000.

3. **D.** The stocks trading range is not what a fundamental analyst looks at when evaluating a company. It is more interested in the company's fundamentals, such as how the current and future economy will impact the industry, quality of management, and market share.

4. **B.** Working capital (or net working capital) is, by definition, the difference between current assets and current liabilities.

5. **B.** The footnotes to the financial statements carry information such as potential legal actions, accounting methods used (e.g., FIFO or LIFO), and off-book debt.

Quick Quiz 3.F

1. **C.** If a market is staying within a narrow price range, it is said to be consolidating.

2. **A.** A trendline connects the lows in an uptrend and the highs in a downtrend. Once established, trendlines are not easily halted or reversed.

3. **D.** Odd-lot trading typically is done by small investors. Followers of the odd-lot theory act on the belief that small investors invariably buy and sell at the wrong times.

4. **C.** The narrowest measure of the market is the Dow Jones Industrial Average, which charts the performance of 30 industrial stocks.

Quick Quiz 3.G

1. **D.** The ability for small investors to lump their votes together and vote as one is a benefit to them.

2. **B.** The solution requires you to know a basic formula:

   issued stock – treasury stock = outstanding stock

   Thus, 800,000 – 200,000 = 600,000.

   ABC Company has 600,000 shares of common stock outstanding.

   This question illustrates another point about FINRA exams. The question gives the number of shares of authorized stock, but this information is unnecessary. Many questions give more information than you need. The Series 6 exam requires you to know concepts well enough that you can determine both what is and what is not essential to solving a problem.

3. **C.** Although stocks often pay regular dividends, they are not guaranteed. If the board decides the company cannot afford to pay a dividend this quarter, no dividend will be paid.

Quick Quiz 3.H

1. **D.** An issuer can exercise a call provision on the call date or any day after the call date.

2. **B.** Convertible preferred stock has a fixed stated dividend and can be converted to the company common stock if the price of the common stock appreciates.

3. **C.** The callable feature does nothing to ensure an investor income, whereas a cumulative preferred means that the common stockholder will never receive a dividend until the cumulative stockholder receives all current and prior dividends due the preferred. The only way to take part in the growth of the company's common stock would be to have an opportunity to obtain that common stock (the convertible feature).

Quick Quiz 3.I

1. **C.** Technology stocks are generally growth oriented, and therefore not suitable for investors looking for income.

2. **B.** ADR stands for American depositary receipt. ADRs are receipts issued by U.S. banks. They represent ownership of a foreign security and are traded in U.S. securities markets.

3. **B.** ADR stands for American depositary receipt. ADRs are receipts issued by U.S. banks. They represent ownership of a foreign security and are traded in U.S. securities markets.

4. **D.** SEC rules define penny stock as non-Nasdaq stock of less than $5 per share.

5. **D.** A rating of BBB is the lowest investment-grade rating assigned by Standard & Poor's. Any rating beneath this is considered speculative.

Quick Quiz 3.J

1. **A.** A. In recommending a conservative, tax-exempt investment to this customer, the representative has failed to make a suitable recommendation given the client's objectives. Municipal bond funds are better suited for individuals in high tax brackets. Further, these bonds offer little upside appreciation potential.

2. **A.** Because this investor's objective is income, a bond fund is suitable. Investors who are willing to accept risk and who are interested in high income should invest in corporate bond funds with some risk of principal. These bond funds are known as high-yield corporate bond funds.

3. **B.** The investor will not be able to reinvest the money he receives at maturity and get the same rate of return at the same level of risk and that is reinvestment risk. There is no interest rate risk if bonds are held to maturity because the investor will receive the principal amount at maturity.

4. **A.** TIPS offer inflation protection and safety of principal because they are backed by the U.S. government.

5. **B.** U.S. government agency debt is an obligation of the issuing agency. This causes agency debt to trade at higher yields reflecting this greater risk. FNMA was created as a government agency but was spun off in 1968 and is now an NYSE-listed corporation; interest is taxed at all levels. GNMA pass-through certificates trade OTC.

6. **D.** The performance of CMOs may not be compared with any other investment vehicle.

Quick Quiz 3.K

1. **D.** Money market investments have low yields; therefore, the greatest risk is that the money will not keep pace with inflation.

2. **C.** Negotiable CDs are considered money market securities but only if the amount is at least $100,000 and maturity occurs within 1 year or less. If the maturity is more than a year away, the security is not considered a money market security.

3. **B.** The treasury note that matures in 2 years is not a money market security until the maturing is 1 year or less. BAs and commercial paper are exempt from registration requirements if the maturity is no more than 270 days (9 months). But as long as they don't have a maturity that is, they are money market securities. In other words the BA listed here would have to register with the SEC.

Quick Quiz 3.L

1. **C.** A unit investment trust is a nonmanaged investment company that issues redeemable securities. There is no active investment manager, which means that once the securities for the trust have been selected, they are held. UIT units do not trade in the secondary marketplace.

2. **C.** The portfolio of a unit investment trust is not actively traded. Hence, it is not considered a management company.

3. **C.** Closed-end companies issue a fixed number of shares, whereas open-end companies do not specify the number of shares to be issued. Both types of companies register issues with the SEC, and any investor may invest in either type of company.

Quick Quiz 3.M — *SUITABILITY*

1. **C.** This customer is a young investor at the beginning of his earnings cycle. For other investors in his situation, an aggressive growth fund might help achieve maximum capital appreciation over a long-term time frame. However, he is risk averse and has not had any experience with investing in the securities markets. A balanced fund is a good place to begin investing for high total return and low volatility.

Balanced fund = stocks/bonds

2. **D.** It is necessary to get more information about this customer and his definitions of an exciting investment opportunity before making any recommendations. A thorough suitability and risk tolerance analysis should be performed before a recommendation is made.

3. **A.** Because this investor's objective is income, a bond fund is suitable. Investors who are willing to accept risk and who are interested in high income should invest in corporate bond funds with some risk of principal. These bond funds are known as high-yield corporate bond funds.

4. **B.** A REIT is a professionally managed company that invests in a diversified portfolio of real estate holdings. Many REITs are actively traded on exchanges and OTC, thereby providing liquidity. REITs must distribute at minimum of 90% of income to avoid taxation as a corporation.

Look up REIT taxation

Quick Quiz 3.N

1. **D.** The wash sale rule encompasses 61 days: 30 days before and 30 days after the sale, plus the day of the transaction.

2. **B.** Regulated companies under Subchapter M of the IRS Code are allowed to pass through income to beneficial owners without a tax at the fund level on the distributed income (known as conduit or flow-through of income and taxation).

3. **A.** The factors used to determine the tax due on a capital gains distribution are the length of time the fund held the securities before selling them, which would identify the gain as long or short term, and the investor's tax bracket, which would determine the actual percentage of tax due.

4. **A.** Because the client's goal is to use the fund as part of a long-term strategy for retirement, reinvestment of distributions should be encouraged. The compounding effect of reinvestment increases the number of shares upon which distributions are based during each period. The fact that distributions are taxable whether taken in cash or reinvested must be disclosed to the client. Net realized long-term capital gains of the portfolio are distributed annually.

Quick Quiz 3.O

1. **D.** Both open-end (mutual funds) and closed-end management companies are subclassifications of management investment companies.

2. **C.** Redemption fees are charged at the time of redemption (when the shares are sold back to the fund).

3. **D.** Although a transfer within a family of funds is generally not subject to a sales charge, there is liability for any taxes due. The IRS considers this transaction a sale and a purchase. Any losses or gains must be declared on that year's tax form.

Quick Quiz 3.P

1. **B.** Dollar cost averaging is effective when the market price of securities is fluctuating and investors continue to invest a fixed amount of money every period. Under these circumstances, the average cost per share will be lower than the average price that would have been paid for shares over the same period. Dollar cost averaging offers no advantage in a constant market and does not protect investors from loss in a falling market.

2. **D.** Mutual fund withdrawal plans are not guaranteed. Because principal values fluctuate, investors may not have sufficient income for their entire lives.

3. **C.** If the investor receives $600 a month, the dollar amount of the withdrawal is fixed; therefore, this must be a fixed-dollar plan.

Quick Quiz 3.Q

1. **B.** Periodic payment annuities may only be purchased on a deferred basis. Annuitization and regular payments into an annuity may not occur simultaneously.

2. **C.** A variable annuity does not guarantee an earnings rate. However, it does guarantee payments for life, though the payment amount may fluctuate, and normally guarantees that expenses will not increase above a specified level. Investment risk is assumed by the annuitant.

3. **D.** With a bonus annuity, the insurance company may contribute 3%–5% to the premium payments and may permit withdrawals of premiums or earnings with no penalty imposed by the company. Such annuities also have longer surrender periods and higher expenses.

Quick Quiz 3.R

1. **C.** When a variable contract is annuitized, the number and value of the accumulation units determine the number of annuity units in the annuitant's account, which does not change. This number is used with other factors to compute the annuitant's first monthly payment. Thereafter, the performance of the separate account compared with AIR determines the monthly payment.

2. **C.** In the annuity period of a variable annuity, the amount received depends on the account performance compared with the assumed interest rate. If actual performance is less than the AIR, the payout's value declines.

3. **C.** The contract earned 3% in September. The AIR for the contract is 3%. Payment size in October will not change from that of September's payment.

Quick Quiz 3.S

1. **B.** Because payouts for males and females are actuarially equal, gender is not a significant consideration in the purchase of a variable annuity. The customer's investment objective, past performance of the variable annuity, and available fund choices are critical considerations.

2. **A.**   Because the investor wants the advantages provided by both a fixed and variable annuity, a combination annuity would be suitable.

3. **C.**   The funds are not liquid due to the surrender fees, and there is also a 10% penalty on withdrawals before age 59½.

4. **D.**   Because of the investment component within the separate account, VAs are not suitable for those with low risk tolerances. These investments are best considered supplements to retirement income one can already anticipate, such as pensions and IRA or 401(k) distributions, and they should ideally be funded with available cash rather than by liquidating existing investments. Because of potentially high surrender charges, future needs for funds must always be considered before purchasing a VA contract.

Quick Quiz 3.T

1. **B.**   Death benefits under variable (and other) life insurance policies are generally not taxable to a beneficiary. Premiums are not deductible to the owner of the policy (payor). Presuming the insured is not the owner of the policy, the policy's death benefits are not included in the estate at death. Because of the tax-free buildup of life insurance cash values, variable life insurance products do not offer lower-yielding municipal bond subaccounts among their separate account choices.

2. **B.**   Federal law requires that issuers of variable life insurance policies allow exchange of these policies for traditional whole life policies issued by the same company for a period of no less than 2 years. The exchange must be made without additional evidence of insurability.

3. **C.**   Only variable life provides the beneficiary with a tax-free death benefit. The AIR affects the death benefit in variable life insurance and the payout in a variable annuity. All gains are deferred until withdrawn. When selling any variable contract, both a securities and an insurance license is required.

Quick Quiz 3.U

1. **B.**   529 college savings plans are funded with after-tax dollars; the money grows tax deferred and comes out tax free for qualified education expenses.

2. **D.**   The Achieving a Better Life Experience (ABLE) Act of 2014 provided Americans with disabilities the opportunity to save up to $15,000 per year in a tax-deferred account similar to a 529 college savings plan, as a supplement to their government benefits.

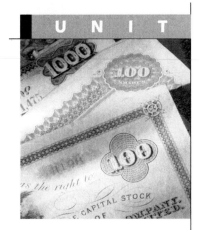

Options

For many Series 7 candidates, understanding option contracts is one of the more challenging concepts. Be sure to review each section of the Unit thoroughly.

The majority of questions will be on equity options (options on stock), but expect some to involve nonequity options, such as index, interest rate, and foreign currency contracts. As you review the Unit, remember that basic concepts have been covered in the Securities Industry Essentials (SIE) exam. If you are well-grounded in the basics, proficiency with the more complex concepts and strategies will follow.

The Series 7 exam will include 91 questions on the topics covered in units 3, 4, 5, and 6. (Function 3 of the FINRA exam). ■

In this Unit you will learn to:

- **list** the basic features of option contracts;

- **list** the basic features of long and short put contracts;

- **name** the components of call and put options premiums and calculate intrinsic values;

- **name** the components of an options premium and calculate intrinsic value;

- **calculate** breakeven, maximum gain, and maximum loss for put options;

- **calculate** profit and loss on options transactions involving exercise, expiration, or closing a position;

- **calculate** breakeven, maximum gain, and maximum loss for hedging strategies;

- **calculate** breakeven, maximum gain, and maximum loss for spreads;

- **identify** investor strategies for multiple option positions;

- **describe** the unique features and usage of nonequity options;

- **describe** the functions of the Options Clearing Corporation (OCC);

- **describe** the process of opening an options account; and

- **identify** tax consequences of exercise, expiration, or closing of a position.

4. 1   THE OPTIONS CONTRACT

General option definitions and basic option contracts, calls and puts, both long and short, are covered thoroughly in your Kaplan Securities Industry Essentials (SIE) material. While we recommend that all students review that content as needed, this section will give you a brief recap and summation of those concepts.

An **option** is a two-party contract that conveys a right to the buyer and an obligation to the seller. The **terms** of option contracts are standardized by the Options Clearing Corporation (OCC), which allows options to be traded easily on an exchange such as the Chicago Board Options Exchange (CBOE). The underlying security for which an option contract is created may be a stock, stock market index, foreign currency, interest rate, or government bond.

Options are called **derivative securities** because their value is derived from the value of the underlying instrument, such as stock, an index, or a foreign currency. The most common type of option contract is an equity option where each contract represents 100 shares of the underlying stock.

TAKE NOTE

The CBOE also offers option contracts known as mini-options. These contracts overlay only 10 shares of the underlying security instead of 100 shares, as is the case for standard options contracts.

With standard contracts the multiplier is 100 (Ex: 2 premium = $200). With mini-option contracts, the multiplier is only 10. Therefore, a mini-option contract premium of 2 represents only $20.

The following terminology and concepts should be associated with the two parties to each contract: buyer and seller.

Two Parties Are Involved in an Options Contract

Buyer = Long = Holder = Owner	Seller = Short = Writer
Pays premium (the cost of the contract) to seller. There is a debit (DR) to the account of the buyer when the premium is paid. The buyer *opens his position* with a debit to his account.	*Receives premium* from buyer. There is a credit (CR) to the account of the seller when the premium is received. The seller *opens his position* with a credit to his account.
Has *rights* to exercise (buy or sell stock)	Has *obligation* when contract is exercised. The writer will be assigned (must buy or sell as required by contract)

Every option contract has three specifications:

- **Underlying instrument:** anything with fluctuating value can be the underlying instrument of an option contract.

- **Price:** the contract specifies a strike or exercise price (SP) at which purchase or sale of the underlying security will occur.

- **Expiration:** all contracts have a specified life cycle and expire on a specified date. Once a contract is issued, it can be bought or sold any time during its life cycle.

— Standard contracts are issued with nine-month expirations and expire on the third Friday of the expiration month at 11:59 pm ET.

— Long-term equity anticipation securities (LEAPS) have maximum expirations of 39 months. Though the maximum is 39 months, most trade with a 30-month life cycle. The length of time until the contract expires is the one contract specification that can be customized between buyer and seller when the contract first trades.

— Weekly contracts are issued on a Thursday and expire on the Friday of the following week. They have much lower premiums as a result of the shorter time span between the day of issue and the day they expire. New weeklies are listed each week, except the week that standardized contracts expire.

4. 1. 1   CALLS AND PUTS

There are two types of options contracts: the **call** contract and the **put contract**.

4. 1. 1. 1   Calls

An investor may buy calls (go long) or sell calls (go short). The features of each side of a call contract are noted below.

- **Long call**: a call buyer owns the **right to buy** 100 shares of a specific stock at the SP before the expiration if he chooses to exercise.
- **Short call**: a call writer (seller) has the **obligation to sell** 100 shares of a specific stock at the SP if the buyer exercises the contract.

4. 1. 1. 2   Puts

An investor may buy puts (go long) or sell puts (go short). The features of each side of a put contract are noted below.

- **Long put**: a put buyer owns the **right to sell** 100 shares of a specific stock at the SP before the expiration if he chooses to exercise.
- **Short put:** a put writer (seller) has the **obligation to buy** 100 shares of a specific stock at the SP if the buyer exercises the contract.

TAKE NOTE

Buyers of options call the shots; they choose to exercise or not to exercise. That is why buyers pay premiums. The writer is at the mercy of the buyer's decision. Writers are only exercised against; they do not have the opportunity to choose to exercise.

- The buyer wants the contract to be **exercised**. He wins, and the seller loses at exercise.

- The seller wants the contract to **expire**. The seller wins at expiration because he gets to keep the premium. No purchase or sale of stock is required.

A significant number of test questions can be answered by knowing that buyers have **rights** and sellers have **obligations**.

4. 1. 2 SINGLE OPTION STRATEGIES

There are four basic strategies available to options investors:

■ Buying calls

■ Writing calls

■ Buying puts

■ Writing puts

The Four Basic Options Transactions

	Calls	
	Buy a Call	Write a Call
Buy		**Sell**
	Buy a Put	Write a Put
	Puts	

4. 1. 2. 1   Calls

Identified below are the key features of call contracts.

4. 1. 2. 1. 1   Features of a Long Call Contract

Long XYZ Jan 60 call at 3

Long	The investor has bought the call and has the right to exercise the contract.
XYZ	The contract includes 100 shares of XYZ stock.
Jan	The contract expires on the third Friday of January at 11:59 pm ET.
60	The SP of the contract is 60.
Call	The **type** of option is a call, and the investor has the right to buy the stock at 60 because he is long the call.
3	The premium of the contract is $3 per share. Contracts are issued with 100 shares, so the total premium is $300. The investor paid the premium to buy the call.

Buyers of calls want the market price of the underlying stock to rise. The investor who owns this call hopes that the market price will rise above 60. He then has the right to buy the stock at the SP of 60, even if the market price is higher (e.g., 80).

4. 1. 2. 1. 2   Features of a Short Call Contract

Short XYZ Jan 60 call at 3

Short   The investor has sold the call and has obligations to perform if the contract is exercised.

XYZ   The contract includes 100 shares of XYZ stock.

Jan   The contract expires on the third Friday of January at 11:59 pm ET. If expiration occurs, the writer keeps the premium without any obligation.

60   The SP of the contract is 60.

Call   The **type** of option is a call, and the investor is obligated to sell the stock at 60, if exercised, because he is short the call.

3   The premium of the contract is $3 per share. Options contracts are issued with 100 shares, so the total premium is $300.

Writers of calls want the market price of the underlying stock to fall or stay the same. The investor who owns this call hopes that the market price will rise above 60. The contract will not be exercised if the market price is at or below 60 at expiration, and the writer keeps the premium of $300 with no obligation.

4. 1. 2. 1. 3   Market Attitude

A call **buyer** is a bullish investor because he wants the market to rise. The call is exercised only if the market price rises.

A call **writer** is a bearish investor because he wants the market to fall. The contract is not exercised if the market price falls below the SP.

QUICK QUIZ 4.A

Objective: List the basic features of long and short call contracts

Consider the following contract:
Long XYZ Jan 60 call at 3
At expiration, the market price of XYZ is 70.

1.   Which of the following will occur?

   A.   Exercised by the buyer
   B.   Expires worthless

2.   Which of the following will the seller do if exercised?

   A.   Buy 100 shares of XYZ at 60
   B.   Sell 100 shares of XYZ at 60
   C.   Buy 100 shares of XYZ at 70
   D.   Sell 100 shares of XYZ at 70

3.   Which of the following will the buyer do if he elects to exercise?

   A.   Buy 100 shares of XYZ at 60
   B.   Sell 100 shares of XYZ at 60
   C.   Buy 100 shares of XYZ at 70
   D.   Sell 100 shares of XYZ at 70

Consider the following contract:
Short XYZ Oct 25 call at 4.50
At expiration the market price of XYZ is 20.

4. Which of the following will occur?

B

    A. Exercised by the buyer
    B. Expires worthless

5. Which of the following will the seller do at expiration?

D

    A. Buy 100 shares of XYZ at 25
    B. Sell 100 shares of XYZ at 25
    C. Pay $450 to the buyer
    D. Keep the $450 premium, no further obligation

6. Which of the following will the buyer do at expiration?

C

    A. Buy 100 shares of XYZ at 25
    B. Sell 100 shares of XYZ at 25
    C. Neither buy nor sell, but lose the $450 premium paid for the option
    D. Receive $450 premium from the seller

All Quick Quiz answers are found at the end of their units.

4. 1. 2. 2   Puts

Identified below are the key features of put contracts.

4. 1. 2. 2. 1   Features of a Long Put Contract

Long XYZ Jan 60 put at 3

Long   The investor has bought the put and has the right to exercise the contract.

XYZ   The contract includes 100 shares of XYZ stock.

Jan   The contract expires on the third Friday of January at 11:59 pm ET.

60   The SP of the contract is 60.

Put   The **type** of option is a put, and the investor has the right to sell the stock at 60 because he is long the put.

3   The premium of the contract is $3 per share. Contracts are issued with 100 shares, so the total premium is $300. The investor paid the premium to buy the put.

Buyers of puts want the market price of the underlying stock to fall. Having purchased this put, the owner hopes that the market price will fall below 60. He then has the right to sell the stock at the SP of 60, even if the market price is lower (e.g., 40).

4. 1. 2. 2. 2 Features of a Short Put Contract

Short XYZ Jan 60 put at 3

Short The investor has sold the put and has obligations to perform if the contract is exercised.

XYZ The contract includes 100 shares of XYZ stock.

Jan The contract expires on the third Friday of January at 11:59 pm ET. If expiration occurs, the writer keeps the premium without any obligation.

60 The SP of the contract is 60.

Put The **type** of option is a put, and the investor is obligated to buy the stock at 60, if exercised, because he is short the put.

3 The premium of the contract is $3 per share. Options contracts are issued with 100 shares, so the total premium is $300.

Writers of puts want the market price of the underlying stock to rise or stay the same. If the market price is at or above 60, the writer keeps the premium of $300 with no obligation because the contract will not be exercised.

4. 1. 2. 2. 3 Market Attitude

A put **buyer** is a bearish investor because he wants the market to fall. The put is exercised only if the market price falls below the SP.

A put **writer** is a bullish investor because he wants the market to rise or remain unchanged. The contract is not exercised if the market price rises above the SP.

QUICK QUIZ 4.B

Objective: list the basic features of a long and short put contracts

Consider the following contract:
Long XYZ Jan 60 put at 3
At expiration, the market price of XYZ is 70.

1. Which of the following will occur?

   A. Exercised by the buyer
   B. Expires worthless

2. Which of the following will the seller do at expiration?

   A. Buy 100 shares of XYZ at 60
   B. Sell 100 shares of XYZ at 60
   C. Do nothing; keep the premium of $300 already received
   D. Pay the premium of $300 to the buyer

3. Which of the following will the buyer do at expiration?

   A. Buy 100 shares of XYZ at 60
   B. Sell 100 shares of XYZ at 60
   C. Do nothing; the put expires and the buyer loses the $300 premium
   D. Pay the premium of $300 to the buyer

Consider the following contract:
Short XYZ Oct 25 put at 4.50
At expiration, the market price of XYZ is 20.

4   Which of the following will occur?

   A.   Exercised by the buyer
   B.   Expires worthless

5.   Which of the following will the seller do at expiration of the option?

   A.   Buy 100 shares of XYZ at 25
   B.   Sell 100 shares of XYZ at 25
   C.   Pay $450 to the buyer
   D.   Keep the $450 premium with no further obligation

6.   Which of the following will the buyer do at expiration?

   A.   Buy 100 shares of XYZ at 25
   B.   Sell 100 shares of XYZ at 25
   C.   Neither buy nor sell, but lose the $450 premium paid for the option
   D.   Receive $450 premium from the seller

All Quick Quiz answers are found at the end of their units.

4. 1. 3   BASIC OPTIONS DEFINITIONS

Options contracts are described with various terms unique to the options marketplace. These basic terms, which have been covered in the Securities Industry Essentials material in the discussion of options contracts, are:

- in the money,
- at the money,
- out of the money,
- intrinsic value, and
- breakeven.

In, at, and out of the money—An option is in the money by the amount of its intrinsic value.

Calls: In, At, and Out of the Money

Ex: Calls	Intrinsic Value	In, Out, At the Money
40 Call, stock @ 42	2 points	In the money 2 points
40 Call, stock @ 40	0 points (SP = stock)	At the money
40 Call, stock @ 38	0 points (SP > stock)	Out of the money

Puts: In, At, and Out of the Money

Ex: Puts	Intrinsic Value	In, Out, At the Money
40 Put, stock @ 37	3 points	In the money 3 points
40 Put, stock @ 40	0 points (SP = stock)	At the money
40 Put, stock @ 44	0 points (SP < stock)	Out of the money

Noting that these terms are defined differently for calls and puts, below is a Quick Quiz to test and refresh your competency.

QUICK QUIZ 4.C

Do not take into account premium paid for when calculating intrinsic value

Objective: Name the components of call and put options premiums and calculate intrinsic values

Consider the following contracts (CMV = current market value):

5 points . 100 shares

Long XYZ Jan 65 call at 7, CMV of XYZ is 70

_____ 1. Is this contract in, at, or out of the money?

_____ 2. What is the breakeven point?

_____ 3. How much intrinsic value does the contract have?

Short XYZ Jan 65 call at 7, CMV of XYZ is 70

_____ 4. Is this contract in, at, or out of the money?

_____ 5. What is the breakeven point?

_____ 6. How much intrinsic value does the contract have?

Short XYZ Sep 45 call at 4, CMV of XYZ is 39

_____ 7. Is this contract in, at, or out of the money?

_____ 8. What is the breakeven point?

_____ 9. How much intrinsic value does the contract have?

Consider the following contracts:

Long XYZ Sep 65 put at 2, CMV of XYZ is 70

_____ 10. Is this contract in, at, or out of the money?

_____ 11. What is the breakeven point?

_____ 12. How much intrinsic value does the contract have?

Short XYZ Jan 65 put at 2, CMV of XYZ is 70

_____ 13. Is this contract in, at, or out of the money?

_____ 14. What is the breakeven point?

_____ 15. How much intrinsic value does the contract have?

Short XYZ Sep 45 put at 8, CMV of XYZ is 39

_____ 16. Is this contract in, at, or out of the money?

───── 17. What is the breakeven point?

_____ 18. How much intrinsic value does the contract have?

All Quick Quiz answers are found at the end of their units.

4. 1. 3. 1   Quick Summary of Market Attitude

The following chart will help you remember the basics of options and an investor's market attitude (bullish or bearish). When you take the exam, consider drawing and referring to it when you encounter options questions. Each quadrant represents one of the four basic options positions.

■ Buyers are on the left side; sellers are on the right.

■ The arrow identifies the investor's market attitude. Up arrows represent bullish investors; down arrows represent bearish investors.

■ The information in the parentheses identifies what occurs at the exercise of the option.

■ The solid horizontal line represents the strike price (SP). The dashed horizontal lines represent the breakevens. For calls, the breakeven is SP plus premium, long or short, and for puts, the breakeven is SP minus premium, long or short.

■ Calls are above the horizontal line because they are in the money when the market price is above the SP, long or short (CALL UP).

■ Puts are below the horizontal line because they are in the money when the market price is below the SP, long or short (PUT DOWN).

Basic Options Chart

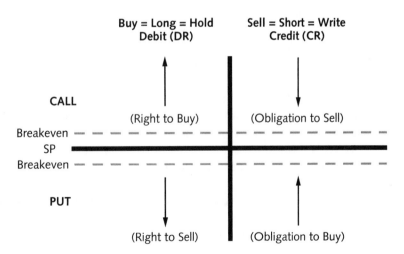

■ Buy = Long = Hold = Open the position with a debit (DR) to the account

■ Sell = Short = Write = Open the position with a credit (CR) to the account

4. 1. 4   OPTIONS PREMIUMS

As stated earlier, the price of an option contract is known as the **premium**. Both bid and ask prices are quoted in cents, with a minimum price interval of $.05. An option buyer will pay the **ask**, or **offer** price, and the option seller will receive the **bid** price. An option's premium reflects two types of values: **intrinsic value**, or the amount by which the option is in the money, and **time value,** which is the market's perceived worth of the time remaining to expiration.

4. 1. 4. 1   Options Quotes

Options premiums are quoted on a **per share** basis. Options contracts are issued to include 100 shares of stock, so the total premium is calculated by multiplying by 100. However, some contracts may be subject to stock splits and stock dividends and may include more than 100 shares. This is discussed later in this Unit.

4. 1. 4. 2   Factors Affecting Premium

The premium of an option is affected by many factors, including:
- volatility,
- amount of intrinsic value,
- time remaining until expiration, and
- interest rates.

The factor with the greatest influence is the **volatility** of the underlying stock. A stock that is highly volatile has the potential to experience greater price movement; it has the possibility of greater profit because of high volatility.

Premiums for options fluctuate constantly, like stock prices. If the underlying stock price fell from one day to the next, a call premium would fall and a put premium would rise. The amount of intrinsic value is affected by any change in the stock's price.

For AOL, note that the closing price on the previous day was $49.00. The SPs range from $42.50 to $60.00. The next column shows the expiration month followed by volume and premium on the AOL calls and by volume and premium on the AOL puts.

From the following chart, find the premium for the AOL July 45 call. The premium of $7.40 is made up of two components: intrinsic value and time value. Once you know intrinsic value, it is easy to back into time value:

intrinsic value + time value = premium

STOCK/ PRICE	OPTION/ STRIKE	EXP	-CALL- VOL	LAST	-PUT- VOL	LAST
AmOnline	4250	Apr	2431	650	49	010
49	4250	May	902	760	409	090
49	45	Apr	5790	420	3298	020
49	45	May	1376	530	1573	150
49	45	Jul	1371	740	94	150
49	4750	Apr	3169	205	1229	055
49	4750	May	3333	340	530	230
49	4750	Oct	294	820	2696	570
49	50	Apr	7618	050	1031	165
49	50	May	5307	220	1017	320
49	50	Jul	2436	450	197	520
49	55	May	3548	050	57	660
49	55	Jul	2574	230	18	8
49	55	Oct	86010	420	251	970
49	60	Jul	2869	110	22	12
ASM Litho	25	Apr	1060	165	...	...
ATT Wris	20	May	1752	130	3360	180
AT&T	20	Apr	1885	2	11	005
22	2250	Apr	1396	020	445	065

* This sample comprises formats, styles, and abbreviations from a variety of currently available sources and has been created for educational purposes.

A call option has intrinsic value if the market price of the underlying stock is higher than the SP. In the case of the July 45 call, the intrinsic value (in-the-money amount) is $4.00 ($49.00 – $45.00). The intrinsic value of $4.00 when added to the time value must equal $7.40. Therefore, the time value of the July 45 call is $3.40 ($7.40 – $4.00).

TAKE NOTE

If an option is at the money or out of the money, the intrinsic value is zero. There is no such thing as negative intrinsic value. Therefore, the premium on any out-of-the-money option is composed entirely of time value.

From the chart, compare the premium of the May 45 call ($5.30) to the premium of the July 45 call ($7.40). Both contracts are in the money by the same amount ($4.00), but the July contract has a higher premium because it has a greater time value. The further to expiration, the greater the time value.

The May 50 call is at 2.20, whereas the premium on the July 50 call is 4.50. Both of these contracts are out of the money by $1. Again, the further to expiration, the greater the time value.

The May 50 put is trading at 3.20, whereas the July 50 put is at 5.20. Both of these contracts are in the money by $1. The time value of these options is $2.20 and $4.20, respectively. Again, the further to expiration, the greater the time value.

TEST TOPIC ALERT

You are likely to see a question or two on option premiums. Be prepared to calculate the time value of an option premium and recognize the features that affect premiums. In calculating the premium, remember to determine intrinsic value by thinking CALL UP or PUT DOWN. What's left of the premium is the time value.

A likely test question might be: An XYZ Jan 50 put is trading for a premium of 5. The current market value of XYZ stock is 55. What is the time value and intrinsic value of the premium?

Think PUT DOWN. A put has intrinsic value when the market price of the stock is below the SP. In this example, that market price is up, so this option has no intrinsic value. The premium of 5 is all time value.

The solution is: intrinsic value = 0, time value = 5.

QUICK QUIZ 4.D

Objective: Name the components of an options premium and calculate intrinsic value

RST is trading for $54.

What are the intrinsic values and time values of the following options?

1. RST September 50 call for 6

2. RST October 55 call for 2.25

3. RST September 60 put for 7.25

4. RST October 50 put for 1.15

All Quick Quiz answers are found at the end of their units.

TEST TOPIC ALERT

Your customer buys 1 MCS Jul 70 call at 2.50 when the market is at 71. As time passes, the market price of MCS remains stable at 71. The premium, therefore, will probably

    A. stay the same
    B. go up
    C. go down
    D. exhibit extreme volatility

Answer: C. Remember that options are wasting assets. As the expiration date approaches, the option's time value diminishes. Time, therefore, is against the option owner. In this case, the intrinsic value stays the same because the stock price remains stable at 71. Intrinsic value for a call is the difference between the SP and the market price, if the market price is higher.

4. 2 BASIC OPTIONS TRANSACTIONS

Covered in the Securities Industry Essentials exam are the four basic options positions available to the options investor. Investors use these strategies to accomplish a variety of objectives. A brief overview of these strategies and their potential risks and rewards follows.

4. 2. 1   BUYING CALLS

Call buyers are **bullish** on the underlying stock. By purchasing calls, an investor can profit from an increase in a stock's price while investing a relatively small amount of money. There are many reasons why investors purchase calls.

4. 2. 1. 1   Speculation

Speculation is the most common reason for buying calls. Investors can speculate on the upward price movement of the stock by paying only the premium. Buying the actual stock would require a far greater investment.

4. 2. 1. 2   Deferring a Decision

An investor can buy a call on a stock and lock in a purchase price until the option expires. This allows him to postpone making a financial commitment other than the premium until the expiration date of the option.

4. 2. 1. 3   Diversifying Holdings

With limited funds, an investor can buy calls on a variety of stocks and possibly profit from any rise in the options premium.

4. 2. 1. 4   Protection of a Short Stock Position

Investors can use calls to protect a short stock position. The option acts as an insurance policy against the stock rising in price.

4. 2. 1. 5   Maximum Gain

Theoretically, the potential gains available to call owners are unlimited because there is no limit on the rise in a stock's price.

4. 2. 1. 6   Maximum Loss

The most the call buyer can lose is the premium paid; this happens if the market price is at or below the SP at the option's expiration.

4. 2. 2   WRITING CALLS

Call writers are **bearish** or **neutral** on the price of the underlying stock. An investor who believes a stock's price will decline or stay the same can write calls for any of the following reasons.

4. 2. 2. 1   Speculation

By writing calls, an investor can profit if the stock's price falls below or stays at the SP. The investor can earn the amount of the premium.

4. 2. 2. 2   Increasing Returns

Additional income can be earned for a portfolio by writing calls. Investors hope for expiration of the calls so they can keep the premiums.

4. 2. 2. 3   Locking in a Sale Price

If an investor has an unrealized profit in a stock and is interested in selling it, a call can be written at an SP that will attempt to lock in that profit.

4. 2. 2. 4   Protection of a Long Position

The premium collected Stock from writing a call provides limited downside protection to the extent of the premium received.

4. 2. 2. 5   Maximum Gain

An uncovered call (or naked call) writer's maximum gain is the premium received. If a call is uncovered, the investor does not own the underlying stock. The maximum gain is earned when the stock price is at or below the exercise price at expiration.

4. 2. 2. 6   Maximum Loss

An uncovered call (or naked call) writer's maximum loss is unlimited because the writer could be forced to buy the stock at a potentially unlimited price, if the option is exercised against him, for delivery at the SP.

Long Call/Short Call

Position	Maximum Gain	Maximum Loss
Long call	Unlimited	Premium
Short call	Premium	Unlimited

TAKE NOTE   Uncovered (naked) call writing strategies can be employed for equity-, index-, and yield-based options.

QUICK QUIZ 4.E   Objective: Calculate breakeven, maximum gain, and maximum loss for call options

1. An investor buys 1 DWQ May 60 call at 3.50. What is the investor's maximum potential gain?
    A. $350
    B. $5,650
    C. $6,350
    D. Unlimited

2. An investor buys 1 DWQ May 60 call at 3.50. What is the investor's maximum potential loss?
    A. $350
    B. $5,650
    C. $6,350
    D. Unlimited

3. An investor sells 1 KLP Dec 45 call at 3. What is the investor's maximum potential gain?
    A. $300
    B. $4,200
    C. $4,800
    D. Unlimited

4. An investor sells 1 KLP Dec 45 call at 3. What is the investor's maximum potential loss?
    A. $300
    B. $4,200
    C. $4,800
    D. Unlimited

5. A naked call position will usually result in a profit to the writer EXCEPT
    A. when the option contract expires without being exercised
    B. when the price of the underlying security falls below and remains below the exercise price of the option
    C. when the call is exercised and the price of the underlying security is greater than the exercise price plus the premium received
    D. when the price of the option contract declines

6. In buying listed call options, compared with buying the underlying stock, which of the following is NOT an advantage?
    A. Buying a call would require a smaller capital commitment.
    B. Buying a call has a lower dollar loss potential than buying the stock.
    C. The call has a time value beyond an intrinsic value that gradually dissipates.
    D. Buying a call allows greater leverage than buying the underlying stock.

7. All of the following are objectives of call buyers EXCEPT
    A. speculating for profit on the rise in price of stock
    B. delaying a decision to buy stock
    C. hedging a long stock position against falling prices
    D. diversifying holdings

All Quick Quiz answers are found at the end of their units.

4. 2. 3   BUYING PUTS

Put buyers are **bearish** on the underlying stock. By purchasing puts, an investor can profit from a decrease in a stock's price while investing a relatively small amount of money. Reasons that investors purchase puts are listed below.

4. 2. 3. 1   Speculation

Investors can speculate on the downward price movement of the stock that is not owned by paying only the premium.

4. 2. 3. 2   Deferring a Decision

An investor can buy a put on a stock and lock in a sale price until the option expires. This allows him to postpone a selling decision until the expiration date of the option. With this strategy, an investor not only locks in an acceptable sales price for stock that is owned but also protects its appreciation potential until the expiration date.

4. 2. 3. 3   Protection of a Long Stock Position

Investors can use puts to protect a long stock position. The option acts as an insurance policy against the stock declining in price.

4. 2. 3. 4   Maximum Gain

The maximum potential gain available to put owners is the option's SP less the amount of the premium paid (same as the breakeven). A stock's price can fall no lower than zero.

4. 2. 3. 5   Maximum Loss

The most the put buyer can lose is the premium paid. This happens if the market price is at or above the SP at the option's expiration.

4. 2. 4   WRITING PUTS

Put writers are **bullish** or neutral on the price of the underlying stock. An investor who believes a stock's price will increase or stay the same can write puts for the following reasons.

4. 2. 4. 1   Speculation

By writing puts, an investor can profit if the stock's price rises above or stays at the SP. The investor can earn the amount of the premium.

4. 2. 4. 2   Increasing Returns

Additional income can be earned for a portfolio by writing puts. Investors hope for expiration of the puts so that they can keep the premium.

4. 2. 4. 3   Buying Stock Below Its Current Price

The premium received from writing puts can be used to offset the cost of stock when the put is exercised against the writer. The writer buys his stock at a price that is reduced by the premium received.

4. 2. 4. 4   Maximum Gain

An uncovered put writer's maximum gain is the premium received. The maximum gain is earned when the stock price is at or above the exercise price at expiration.

4. 2. 4. 5   Maximum Loss

An uncovered put writer's maximum loss is the put's SP less the premium received (the same as the breakeven); it occurs when the stock price drops to zero. The investor is forced to buy the worthless stock at the option's SP. The investor's loss is reduced by the premium received.

Long Put/Short Put

Position	Maximum Gain	Maximum Loss
Long put	Strike price – premium	Premium
Short put	Premium	Strike price – premium

TAKE NOTE

Uncovered (naked) put writing strategies can be employed for equity-, index- and yield-based options.

QUICK QUIZ 4.F

Objective: Calculate breakeven, maximum gain, and maximum loss for put options

1. An investor buys 1 ABC Jan 50 put at 2. What is the investor's maximum potential gain?

    A. $200
    B. $4,800
    C. $5,200
    D. Unlimited

2. An investor buys 1 ABC Jan 50 put at 2. What is the investor's maximum potential loss?

    A. $100
    B. $200
    C. $4,800
    D. $5,200

3. An investor sells 1 DWQ Feb 30 put at 4.50. What is the investor's maximum potential gain?

    A. $450
    B. $2,550
    C. $3,450
    D. Unlimited

4. An investor sells 1 DWQ Feb 30 put at 4.50. What is the investor's maximum potential loss?

    A. $450
    B. $2,550
    C. $3,450
    D. Unlimited

All Quick Quiz answers are found at the end of their units.

TEST TOPIC ALERT

Options offer investors a great deal of flexibility. Maximum gain and loss are concepts that are normally heavily tested. When learning them, focus on the long positions. If you know the long position definitions, you can always remember the short position definitions because they are the opposite. The following chart summarizes this relationship.

Position	Maximum Gain	Maximum Loss
Long call	Unlimited	Premium
Short call	Premium	Unlimited
Long put	Strike price – premium	Premium
Short put	Premium	Strike price – premium

4. 2. 5   CHOICES AT EXPIRATION

The owner of a put or call option contract has three choices before the expiration of the contract. The investor can exercise the option, let the option expire, or sell the option contract before the expiration date.

4. 2. 5. 1   Exercise the Option

The holder of a call will buy the stock at the SP if exercising.
The holder of a put will sell the stock at the SP if exercising.

4. 2. 5. 2 Let the Option Expire

The holder of a call will allow the option to expire if the market price of the stock is equal to or less than the SP.

The holder of a put will allow the option to expire if the market price of the stock is equal to or greater than the SP.

4. 2. 5. 3 Sell the Option Contract Before the Expiration Date

The holder can sell the option for its current premium; there is no purchase or sale of underlying stock in this situation. The investor has profit or loss based on the increase or decrease of the option's premium from the time the option was purchased (**closing the position**).

TEST TOPIC ALERT

A significant number of your options questions will require determining the amount of profit or loss in an options transaction. Consider using the following T-chart to compare money paid out to money received in a transaction. Money paid out is identified as a **debit (DR)** to the investor's account. Money received is a **credit (CR)** to the investor's account.

DR	CR

If an investor pays a premium to buy an option, he opens his position with a debit to the account in the amount of the premium.

EXAMPLE

An investor buys one XYZ January 50 call for 3. The T-chart is filled out like this:

DR	CR
3	

If the investor had instead sold the XYZ January 50 call for 3, the T-chart would reflect that:

DR	CR
	3

Try using the T-chart on any option question that requires a calculation. It will keep your accounting organized, making it easy to determine profit and loss.

4. 2. 6   OPTION EXERCISE

Option contracts are **exercised** if they are in the money. Writers are required to fulfill their obligations as required. Exercises of listed equity options settle **regular way**: two business days from the exercise date.

4. 2. 7   OPTION EXPIRATION

Option contracts **expire** worthless if they are at the money or out of the money at expiration. At expiration, the buyer of the option loses the premium paid; the seller of the option profits by the amount of the premium received.

TEST TOPIC ALERT

Answer this question using the T-chart:

An investor with no other positions buys 1 DWQ May 75 call at 6.50. The investor exercises the call when the stock is trading at 77 and immediately sells the stock in the market. What is the investor's profit or loss?

The solution is a calculation, so draw a T-chart.

DR	CR
6.50	
75	77
81.50	77
4.50	

The position is opened by buying; a debit of the premium is made. The call is exercised. Exercise of a long call requires the investor to buy the stock at the SP. A debit of 75 must be made to the account.

When the stock is trading at 77, the investor sells. A credit of 77 must be made to the account. The resulting loss is $450 (4.50 × 100) because the investor paid out 81.50 and received only 77.

QUICK QUIZ 4.G

Objective: Calculate profit and loss on options transactions involving exercise, expiration, or closing a position

1. An investor with no other positions sells 1 KLP Jul 40 call at 3.50. The call is exercised when the stock is trading at 47. What is the investor's profit or loss?

    A. $350 profit
    B. $350 loss
    C. $450 profit
    D. $450 loss

[handwritten margin notes:]

out

m

Debit | Credit

350 | 6500 – sell at strike price

(6500)

buys   (350)

at   6700   6500

current

price   – 200

Debit out | credit in

9500 | 5.5

79

– 95 | 84.5

(-1050)

2. An investor with no other positions buys 1 COD May 65 put at 3.50. The investor buys the stock in the market and exercises the put when the stock is trading at 63.50. What is the investor's profit or loss?

   A. $200 profit
   B. $200 loss
   C. $350 profit
   D. $350 loss

3. An investor with no other positions sells 1 ALF 95 Jan put at 5.50. The put is exercised when the stock is trading at 79, and the investor immediately sells the stock in the market. What is the investor's profit or loss?

   A. $550 profit
   B. $550 loss
   C. $1,050 profit
   D. $1,050 loss

All Quick Quiz answers are found at the end of their units.

4. 2. 8   CLOSING TRANSACTIONS

If an investor has purchased an option before expiration, the investor can sell the option. A profit is made if the premium is greater than originally paid. In this situation, the sale of the option is known as the **closing transaction**.

If an investor initially sold an option, the investor can close the position by buying the option. This closing transaction is profitable if the investor is able to buy the option for a premium less than was received for its sale. Trading options accounts for a very large portion of activity in the options market.

TEST TOPIC ALERT

If an investor opens an option position by buying, he must close it by selling; if the position is opened by selling, he must close it by buying. Opening and closing transactions are always opposites of each other.

Opening and Closing Transactions

	Open	Close
Long	Buy contract	Sell contract
Short	Sell contract	Buy contract

The test may ask you to close transactions for their intrinsic value. Normally, a transaction is closed for its premium amount, but if an option is about to expire, it has no time value—intrinsic value is all that is left. Use a T-chart on questions that require you to close out options positions.

QUICK QUIZ 4.H   Objective: Calculate profit and loss on options transactions involving exercise, expiration, or closing a position

[handwritten margin notes: "premium the same; curls out. sold for a profit in regular stock"]

1. A customer with no other positions sells 1 MTN Jul 80 call for 10 and buys 100 shares of MTN stock for $85 per share. If the customer enters into a closing purchase for $10 for the MTN Jul call and sells 100 shares of MTN stock for $88 per share, he would realize

   A. a $300 loss
   B. a $300 profit
   C. a $800 loss
   D. a $800 profit

2. In April, a customer buys 1 MTN Oct 50 call for 9 and sells 1 MTN Jul 50 call for 4. What will the customer's pretax profit or loss be if he buys back the July call for $1 and sells the October call for $12?

   A. $100 loss
   B. $100 profit
   C. $600 loss
   D. $600 profit

[handwritten margin notes: "Use T charts to compare premiums received to calc PnL"]

3. In April, a customer purchases 1 TCB Jul 85 call for 5 and purchases 1 TCB Jul 90 put for 8. TCB stock is trading at 87. If TCB stays at 87 and both options are sold for their intrinsic value, the customer will realize

   A. a $500 profit
   B. an $800 loss
   C. a $1,000 profit
   D. an $1,100 profit

All Quick Quiz answers are found at the end of their units.

TEST TOPIC ALERT   Use a T-chart to simplify all questions that ask the investor's profit or loss.

If you feel comfortable with what you have done so far, advance to a different use of options—hedging. If not, go back and review before proceeding.

4. 3   USING OPTIONS TO PROTECT A POSITION—HEDGING

An investor with an established stock position can use options to help protect against the risk of the position. The option helps insure the investor against some of the possible loss from the stock position.

The investor who has a long stock position hopes for the market price of the stock to increase. The risk of the position, (i.e., a market price decline) can be offset by the purchase of a put or, to a limited degree, the sale of a call.

The investor who has a short stock position hopes for the market price of the stock to decline. The risk of the position (i.e., a market price increase) can be offset by the purchase of a call or, to a limited degree, the sale of a put.

TAKE NOTE

Here's an easy way to think about hedging strategy using the master options chart.

An investor has a long stock position that she wishes to protect. What is the risk of the long stock position?

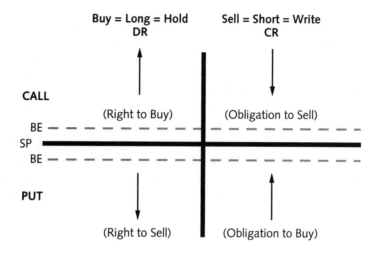

The risk is that the market price will fall (a downward arrow). To hedge the position, select an option position with a downward (bearish) arrow. The investor can protect a long stock position with a long put or short call.

Suppose an investor has a short stock position, it is profitable when the market price declines. Remember, in a short stock position, the investor has borrowed stock from the broker-dealer. She needs to buy back the shares to return to the broker-dealer. If she can buy them back at a price lower than the price at which she sold them, she makes a profit. What is the risk of the short stock position?

The risk is that the market price will rise (an upward arrow). To hedge the position, select an option position with an upward (bullish) arrow. The investor can protect a short stock position with a long call or short put.

Sometimes the hedging-strategy questions on the exam will ask you to determine which option will best or fully protect a stock position. The best protection is to buy an option (remember "Best Buy").

If the question asks for partial protection, or how the investor can improve his rate of return, select a short option position. The sale of the option generates premium income to improve the investor's rate of return. The risk of the stock position is reduced by the amount of the premium received, which is partial protection only.

The Use of Option Positions to Protect Stock Positions

Stock Position	Full Protection	Partial Protection
Long stock position	Long put	Short call
Short stock position	Long call	Short put

If an investor holds a long stock position, buying puts provides nearly total downside protection. The upside potential of the stock is reduced only by the amount of premiums paid.

Selling calls when holding a long stock position, also known as **covered call writing**, is partial protection that generates income and reduces the stock's upside potential.

The following examples explain the use of options to protect a long stock position.

4. 3. 1   LONG STOCK, LONG PUT (PROTECTIVE PUT)

An investor buys 100 shares of RST at 53 and buys an RST 50 put for 2. The maximum gain is unlimited. Should the stock price fall below the SP of 50, the investor will exercise the put to sell the stock for 50. The investor loses $3 per share on the stock and has spent $2 per share for the put. The total loss equals $500. The breakeven point is reached when the stock rises by the amount paid for the put; in this case, 53 + 2 = 55.

In this example, no matter how far the stock falls, the investor can get out at 50 by exercising the put. Therefore, the most the investor can lose on the stock position is $3 per share. The cost of this protection is $2 per share. Therefore, maximum potential loss is $5 per share or $500. On the other hand, maximum gain is unlimited because the stock price could rise infinitely. To break even, the stock must rise by the cost of the put option purchased. The breakeven point for long stock-long put is cost of stock purchased plus premium.

TAKE NOTE   Protective put strategies are most often employed with equity positions as in the example above or with index options to protect and entire portfolio.

4. 3. 2   LONG STOCK, SHORT CALL (COVERED CALL)

An investor buys 100 shares of RST at 53 and writes 1 RST 55 call for 2. The maximum gain equals $400. If the stock price rises above 55, the call will be exercised; thus, the investor will sell the stock for a gain of $200, in addition to the $200 premium received. The maximum loss is $5,100. Should the stock become worthless, the $200 premium reduces the loss on the stock. The breakeven point is reached when the stock falls by the amount of the premium received. Therefore, 53 – 2 = 51.

In this example, the customer is protected only on the downside by the amount of the premium received for writing the call. Thus, the stock could fall to $51, at which point the customer breaks even; the $2 loss on the stock is offset exactly by the premium received. Below $51, losses begin. If the stock becomes worthless, the customer could lose $5,100 (which is maximum loss). If the stock rises above $55, the option will be exercised and the customer will be assigned, forced to sell stock at $55 for a $2 per share gain. Combined with the $2 per share premium received, the maximum potential gain is $400. One of the drawbacks of writing calls against a long stock position is that it limits upside potential. Therefore, covered call writing is normally done in a stable market. The breakeven point for long stock-short call is cost of stock purchased minus premium.

TAKE NOTE   Covered call strategies are most often employed with equities as in the example above.

4. 3. 2. 1   Ratio Call Writing

Ratio call writing involves selling more calls than the long stock position covers. This strategy generates additional premium income for the investor, but also entails unlimited risk because of the short uncovered calls.

4. 3. 3   SHORT STOCK, LONG CALL

An investor sells short 100 shares of RST at 58 and buys an RST 60 call for 3. The investor's maximum gain is $5,500; if the stock becomes worthless, the investor gains $5,800 from the short sale minus the $300 paid for the call. The maximum loss is $500; if the stock price rises above $60, the investor will exercise the call to buy the stock for 60, incurring a $200 loss on the short sale, in addition to the $300 paid for the call. The breakeven point is the stock's sale price minus the premium paid in this case, 58 – 3, or 55.

In this example, no matter how high the stock rises, the investor can buy back his short position at 60 by exercising the call. Therefore, the most the investor can lose on the short stock position is $2 per share. The cost of this protection is $3 per share. Therefore, maximum potential loss is $5 per share or $500. On the other hand, maximum gain will occur if the stock becomes worthless. If the stock falls to zero, the customer will make $5,800 on the short stock position less the $300 paid to buy the call. Overall, maximum potential gain is $5,500. The breakeven point for short stock-long call is short sale price minus premium.

4. 3. 4   SHORT STOCK, SHORT PUT

A customer sells short 100 RST at 55 and writes an RST 55 put for 2.50 for partial protection. The maximum gain is $250. If the stock declines to zero and the put is exercised against him, the customer is obligated to pay $5,500 to buy the stock, losing $5,500. However, he receives a $5,500 gain from the short sale. Because he received the $250 premium, the stock can increase to 57.50, the breakeven point, before the short stock position generates a loss, which is potentially unlimited.

In this example, the customer is protected only on the upside by the amount of the premium received for writing the put. Thus, the stock could rise to $57.50, at which point the customer breaks even; the $2.50 per share loss on the short position is offset exactly by the premium received. Potentially unlimited losses could result if the stock rises above the breakeven point. If the stock falls below $55, the put will be in the money, at which point the customer will be exercised and forced to buy stock at $55 to close out his short position. Therefore, there is no gain or loss on the short stock position. The customer's gain is limited to $250, the premium received. The breakeven point for short stock-short put is the short sale price plus premium.

TAKE NOTE   Put writing strategies are most often employed with equities as in the example above.

4. 3. 5   COLLAR

Occasionally, an investor may hedge his downside risk on a long position of stock for no out-of-pocket cash.

EXAMPLE

An investor is long 100 shares of XYZ at 50 and buys a 45 put at 3 and sells a 55 call for 3. The net cost is zero. In return, if the stock falls to a very low price, the investor can put the stock to someone at 45. He knows that he can never lose more than $500. The downside is that he sacrifices any upside potential beyond $55. This is also known as a **cashless collar**.

TEST TOPIC ALERT

The following Quick Quiz questions require you to compute the breakeven, maximum gain, and maximum loss of hedged positions. To find breakeven, draw a T-chart and identify the debit or credit for both the stock position and the option position. The result is the breakeven point. To find maximum gain and maximum loss, focus on the stock position. What happens if the market goes up or down? Will the option be exercised?

QUICK QUIZ 4.1

Objective: Calculate breakeven, maximum gain, and maximum loss for hedging strategies

1. A customer holds the following positions:
    Long 100 XYZ shares at 62
    Long 1 XYZ 60 put at 3
    The customer breaks even if XYZ trades at
    A. 57
    B. 59
    C. 63
    D. 65

2. **Long 100 XYZ shares at 62**
    Long 1 XYZ 60 put at 3
    What is the maximum gain the customer can realize on these positions?
    A. $5,700
    B. $6,500
    C. $11,900
    D. Unlimited

3. **Long 100 XYZ shares at 62**
    Long 1 XYZ 60 put at 3
    What is the most the customer can lose on these positions?
    A. $300
    B. $500
    C. $1,000
    D. Unlimited

Debit	Credit
1	26

4. **Short 100 shares of XYZ at 26**
   Long XYZ 30 call at 1
   The customer breaks even if XYZ trades at

   A. 25   *SP - premium*
   B. 27
   C. 29
   D. 31

5. **Short 100 shares of XYZ at 26**
   Long XYZ 30 call at 1
   What is the maximum potential gain for the customer?

   A. $2,500
   B. $2,700
   C. $2,900
   D. $3,100

6. **Short 100 shares of XYZ at 26**
   Long XYZ 30 call at 1
   What is the maximum potential loss on the positions?

   - Short goes other way to 30

   A. $400
   B. $500
   C. $2,500
   D. Unlimited

   30 - 26 = 4 + premium =

   5

(out) | (in)
Debit	Credit
62	3
4

7. **Long 100 XYZ shares at 62**
   Short 1 XYZ 65 call at 3
   The customer breaks even if XYZ trades at

   A. 57
   B. 59
   C. 63
   D. 65

8. **Long 100 XYZ shares at 62**
   Short 1 XYZ 65 call at 3
   What is the maximum gain the customer can realize on these positions?

   = Call will be exercised on the seller @ 65 - gain 3 on prem and 3 on stock appreciation

   A. $300
   B. $600
   C. $5,900
   D. Unlimited

9. **Long 100 XYZ shares at 62**
   Short 1 XYZ 65 call at 3
   What is the most the customer can lose on these positions?

   A. $300
   B. $600
   C. $5,900
   D. Unlimited

   62 - 0

   minus premium received

10. **Short 100 shares of XYZ at 54**

Short XYZ 50 put at 2

What is the maximum potential loss to the customer?

A. $60

B. $200

C. $5,200

D. Unlimited

11. A customer is long 200 shares of XYZ at 90 and simultaneously writes 3 XYZ July 90 calls at 3. What is the maximum loss?

A. $900

B. $1,800

C. $18,000

D. Unlimited

All Quick Quiz answers are found at the end of their units.

4. 4   MULTIPLE OPTIONS TRANSACTIONS

Investors can simultaneously buy or sell more than one option contract on opposite sides of the market. These positions, known as **spreads**, **straddles**, and **combinations**, can be used to speculate on a security's price movement and limit position costs and risks.

4. 4. 1   SPREADS

A **spread** is the simultaneous purchase of one option and sale of another option of the same class.

■ A call spread is a long call and a short call.

■ A put spread is a long put and a short put.

TEST TOPIC ALERT

You may see questions on the exam that ask you to identify what position the investor has established. Again, the master options chart will give you the answer. The horizontal ovals shown in the following chart identify the two types of spreads: call spreads and put spreads.

As you solve questions, point at the investor's options positions on your chart. You will easily identify what type of position has been created.

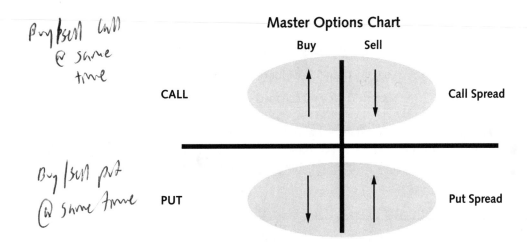

Master Options Chart

Buy / sell call @ same time

Buy / sell put @ same time

4. 4. 1. 1   Types of Spreads

Investors can buy or sell three types of spreads: a price or vertical spread, a time or calendar spread, or a diagonal spread.

A **price spread** or **vertical spread** is one that has different SPs but the same expiration date. It is called a vertical spread because SPs on options reports are reported vertically.

EXAMPLE

Example of a price or vertical spread:

Long RST Nov **50** call for 7

Short RST Nov **60** call for 3

TAKE NOTE

The most common spread, and the one most likely to occur on the Series 7 exam, is the price spread (vertical spread), in which the two options have the same expiration date but different SPs.

A **time spread** or **calendar spread,** also known as a **horizontal spread,** includes option contracts with different expiration dates but the same SPs. Investors who establish these do not expect great stock price volatility; instead they hope to profit from the different rates at which the time values of the two option premiums erode. Time spreads are called horizontal spreads because expiration months are arranged horizontally on options reports.

EXAMPLE

Example of a time or calendar spread:

Long RST **Nov** 60 call for 3

Short RST **Jan** 60 call for 5

A **diagonal spread** is one in which the options differ in both time and price. On an options report, a line connecting these two positions would appear as a diagonal.

EXAMPLE

Example of a diagonal spread:

Long RST **Jan 55** call for 6

Short RST **Nov 60** call for 3

 Spreads are categorized as either **debit spreads** or **credit spreads**. A spread is a debit spread if the long option has a higher premium than the short option; a spread is a credit spread if the short option has a higher premium than the long option.

EXAMPLE

more premium received than paid = debit spread

Long RST Jan 55 call for 6

Short RST Jan 65 call for 2

DR	CR
6	
	2
4	

This spread is a debit spread because more premium was paid than received.

EXAMPLE

Credit spread = more premium received than paid = benefit to your account

Long RST Jan 55 call for 2

Short RST Jan 45 call for 6

DR	CR
2	
	6
	4

This spread is a credit spread because more premium was received than paid.

4. 4. 1. 2   Debit Call Spread

Debit call spreads are used by investors to reduce the cost of a long option position. There is, however, a trade-off, because the potential reward of the investor is also reduced. The investor who establishes a debit call spread is bullish.

EXAMPLE

Buy 1 RST Nov 55 call for 6

Sell 1 RST Nov 60 call for 3

DR	CR
6	
	3
3	

Instead of paying $600 to buy the call, the investor reduced its cost to $300 by also selling a call. If the market price of the stock rises above 60, both calls will be exercised. The investor has the right to buy the stock for 55 but must then sell the stock for 60. The $500 profit on the stock is reduced by the $300 net premium paid, for a net profit of $200. This is the investor's maximum gain on the position.

If the stock price remains below 55, both options will expire, and the investor will lose the net premium paid. The investor's maximum loss is the $300 net premium.

The investor's breakeven point is always between the two SPs in a spread. For call spreads, breakeven is found by adding the net premium to the lower SP. Adding the net premium of 3 to the lower SP of 55 results in a breakeven point of 58.

Because this is a debit spread, the investor profits if exercise occurs. The difference in premiums on the two options widens as exercise becomes likely. Investors always want net debit spreads to widen.

[handwritten margin note: BE = add net premium to lower SP]

TEST TOPIC ALERT

The following tips may be helpful with spread questions:

debit = widen = exercise (When you begin to widen, you need to exercise.)

This reminds you that debit spreads are profitable if widening of premiums or exercise occurs. The test may ask you in which type of spread the investor wants the premiums to widen. Look for the debit spread.

credit = narrow = expire (When you become too narrow, you may expire.)

This reminds you that credit spreads are profitable if premiums narrow and expiration occurs. This is logical because sellers want expiration, and option premiums decline as expiration approaches. In which type of spread does the investor want premiums to narrow? Look for the credit spread.

In finding breakeven points on spreads, remember CAL and PSH:

■ For **C**all spreads: **A**dd the net premium to the **L**ower SP.

■ For **P**ut spreads: **S**ubtract the net premium from the **Hi**gher SP.

A final tip on finding maximum gain and maximum loss: Start by completing a T-chart. If the result is a net debit, the net debit equals maximum loss. Find the maximum gain by subtracting the net debit from the difference in the two SPs of the spread.

[handwritten margin notes: Buyers of options want to exercise = debit & premiums widen; Credit spreads = sellers = want expiration & premiums narrow; Debit call spreads — BE: Net premium + lower SP; ML = net debit; MG = (Diff in SP) − net debit]

EXAMPLE

Long XYZ 50 call at 9
Short XYZ 60 call at 5

[handwritten: paid / received premiums]

DR	CR
9	
	5

Net debit (4)

[handwritten margin notes: paid more premiums than received = bullish = want to be exercised; debit spread = want to widen]

The maximum loss is 4 because buyers of options lose premiums paid. The difference in SPs is 10 (60 − 50); 10 − 4 leaves 6 for the maximum gain.

Remember, the maximum loss plus the maximum gain must always total the difference in the SP.

Breakeven for the investor is found by CAL: 50 + 4 = 54.

If this had been a credit spread, the net premium would represent the maximum gain. The maximum loss would be found by subtracting the maximum gain from the difference in SPs.

4. 4. 1. 3   Credit Call Spread

Credit call spreads are created by investors to reduce the risk of a short option position. Again, there is a trade-off; the potential reward of the investor is reduced. The investor who establishes a credit call spread is bearish.

warrants struck to decline

EXAMPLE

Buy 1 RST Nov 55 call for 2 — *covering short call if stock rises*
Sell 1 RST Nov 45 call for 9 — *obliged to sell at 45 — wants stock to stay low*

net premium = max gain
(diff strike) - net premium = max loss
(premiums)

Net premium + = Breakeven
lower SP

DR	CR
2	
	9
	7

put together = bearish position

The investor reduced the unlimited risk of the short naked call by also purchasing a call. The long call gives the investor the right to purchase the stock at 55 if forced to sell at 45. The investor in this situation is bearish; if the stock price declines below the lower SP of 45, both options will expire worthless and the investor keeps the net premium. The net premium (in this case, $700) is the maximum gain for a credit spread.

If the market price of the stock rises above 45, the investor's loss is limited. The investor's long call can be exercised to buy the stock at 55. The loss on the stock is limited to 10, less the net premium of 7 collected. The maximum loss to the investor in a credit spread is the difference in the SPs minus the net premium (in this case $300).

The investor's breakeven point is always between the two SPs in a spread. For call spreads, breakeven is found by adding the net premium to the lower SP. Adding the net premium of 7 to the lower SP of 45 results in a breakeven point of 52.

Because this is a credit spread, the investor profits when the options expire. The difference in premiums on the two options narrows as the options are about to expire. Investors always want net credit spreads to narrow.

QUICK QUIZ 4.J

Objective: Calculate breakeven, maximum gain, and maximum loss for spreads

1. Buy 1 QRS Jan 40 call at 2.35; write 1 QRS Jan 45 call at .85. What is the breakeven point?

   A. 3.25
   B. 39.50
   C. 41.50
   D. 95.00

DR	CR
2.35	.85
1.50	

= debit call = bullish
BE = 41.50
nL = 1.50
mG = 5 - 1.50 = 3.50

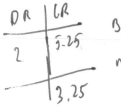

mb=3.25 Credit call
BE=53.25
mL=5-3.25
=
1.75

2. Write 1 MCS Dec 50 call at 5.25; buy 1 MCS Dec 55 call at 2. What is the break-even point?

   A. 7.25
   B. 50.00
   C. 53.25
   D. 57.00

BE = 33
mL= 7
3.00 = mb

3. Write 1 ABC Oct 30 call at 3.25; buy 1 ABC Oct 40 call at .25. What are the maximum gain and the maximum loss?

   I.   Maximum gain $300
   II.   Maximum gain $325
   III. Maximum loss $700
   IV.   Maximum loss $7,025

   A. I and III
   B. I and IV
   C. II and III
   D. II and IV

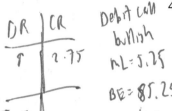

Debit call
bullish
mL=5.25
BE=85.25
mb=4.75

4. Buy 1 LMN Oct 80 call at 8; write 1 LMN Oct 90 call at 2.75. What is the maximum gain and the maximum loss?

   I.   Maximum gain $475
   II.   Maximum gain $525
   III. Maximum loss $475
   IV.   Maximum loss $525

   A. I and III
   B. I and IV   B
   C. II and III
   D. II and IV

Credit call
7.25=mb
mL 2.75
BE=137.25

5. Write 1 XYZ Jan 130 call at 26.75; buy 1 XYZ Jan 140 call at 19.50. What is the maximum gain and the maximum loss?

   I.   Maximum gain $275
   II.   Maximum gain $725
   III. Maximum loss $725
   IV.   Maximum loss $275

   A. I and III
   B. I and IV
   C. II and III
   D. II and IV

All Quick Quiz answers are found at the end of their units.

4. 4. 1. 4   Debit Put Spread

Debit put spreads are used by investors to reduce the cost of a long put position. The investor who establishes a debit put spread is bearish.

debit spreads= used to reduce
costs of long positions. Put/call spreads both used
to reduce costs

EXAMPLE

(handwritten: net)

(handwritten left margin:)
Maximum loss = premium paid
Breakeven = Higher SP - Net premium
Max gain = (Diff btwn SP) - Net premium paid

Buy 1 RST Nov 55 put for 6

Sell 1 RST Nov 50 put for 3

DR	CR
6	
	3
3	

Instead of paying $600 to buy the put, the investor reduced its cost to $300 by also selling a put. If the market price of the stock falls below 50, both puts will be exercised. The investor will sell the stock for 55 but will buy the stock for 50. The $500 profit on the stock is reduced by the $300 net premium paid for a net profit of $200. This is the investor's maximum gain on the position.

If the stock price remains above 55, both options will expire and the investor will lose the net premium paid. The investor's maximum loss is the $300 net premium.

The investor's breakeven point is always between the two SPs in a spread. For put spreads, breakeven is found by subtracting the net premium from the higher SP. Subtracting the net premium of 3 from 55 results in a breakeven point of 52.

This is a debit spread, so the investor profits if exercise occurs. The difference in premiums on the two options widens as exercise becomes likely. Investors always want net debit spreads to widen.

4. 4. 1. 5 Credit Put Spread

(handwritten: Credit = want options to expire worthless and collect premiums)

Credit put spreads are created by investors to reduce the risk of a short put position. Again, there is a trade-off: the potential reward of the investor is reduced. The investor who establishes a credit put spread is bullish. *(handwritten: need to memorize for spreads)*

EXAMPLE

(handwritten left margin:)
MG = net premium
ML = (Diff btwn SP) - Net Premium paid
Breakeven = Higher SP - Net premium paid

Buy 1 RST Nov 55 put for 2

Sell 1 RST Nov 65 put for 9

DR	CR
2	
	9
	7

The investor reduced the substantial risk of the short naked put by also purchasing a put. The long put gives the investor the right to sell stock if necessary to provide cash the investor needs to buy stock when the short put is exercised. The investor in this situation is bullish; if the stock price rises above the upper SP of 65, both options will expire worthless and the investor keeps the net premium. The net premium is the maximum gain for a credit spread.

If the market price of the stock falls below 55, the investor's loss is limited. The exercise of the investor's short put will require purchase of the stock at 65. The loss is limited to 10, less the net premium of 7 collected. The maximum loss to the investor in a credit spread is the difference in the SPs minus the net premium.

The investor's breakeven point is always between the two SPs in a spread. For put spreads, breakeven is found by subtracting the net premium from the higher SP. Subtracting the net premium of 7 from 65 results in a breakeven point of 58.

This is a credit spread, so the investor profits when the options expire. The difference in premiums on the two options narrows as the options are about to expire. Investors always want net credit spreads to narrow.

Maximum Gain and Maximum Loss for Debit and Credit Spreads

Calculation	Credit Spread	Debit Spread
Maximum gain	The net credit	The difference between the strike prices – the net debit
Maximum loss	The difference between the strike prices – the net credit	The net debit

---

QUICK QUIZ 4.K

Objective: Calculate breakeven, maximum gain, and maximum loss for spreads

1. Which of the following are spreads? = *same type of contract but short/long*

   I.   Long 1 ABC May 40 call; short 1 ABC May 50 call
   II. Long 1 ABC May 40 call; long 1 ABC May 50 call
   III. Long 1 ABC Aug 40 call; short 1 ABC May 40 call
   IV. Long 1 ABC Aug 40 call; short 1 ABC Aug 50 put

   A. I and II
   B. I and III
   C. ii and iii
   D. II and IV

2. Buy 1 XYZ Apr 30 put at 3.30; write 1 XYZ Apr 35 put at 5.80. What is the breakeven point?

   A. 21.00
   B. 26.00
   C. 27.50
   D. 32.50

   Credit put spread
   mG = 2.5
   mL = 2.5
   BE = 32.5

   DR | CR
   3.3 | 5.8
   2.5

3. Buy 1 LMN Jan 40 put at 6.50; write 1 LMN Jan 30 put at 2.25. What is the maximum gain and the maximum loss?

   I.   Maximum gain $425
   II. Maximum gain $575
   III. Maximum loss $425
   IV. Maximum loss $575

   A. I and III
   B. I and IV
   C. II and III
   D. II and IV

   DR | CR
   6.50 | 2.25
   4.25

   Debit put spread bearish
   mL = 4.25
   mG = 5.75
   BE = 45.75

4. An investor who has entered into a debit spread will profit if
    A. the spread widens
    B. the spread narrows
    C. the spread remains unchanged
    D. both contracts expire unexercised

5. In March, a customer sells 1 CW Oct 50 put for 3 and buys 1 CW Oct 60 put for 11. The customer will experience a pretax profit from these positions if
    I.   the difference between the premiums narrows to less than $8 per share
    II. the difference between the premiums widens to more than $8 per share
    III. both puts are exercised at the same time
    IV. both puts expire unexercised

    A. I and III
    B. I and IV
    C. II and III
    D. II and IV

All Quick Quiz answers are found at the end of their units.

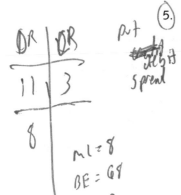

handwritten: DR | DR ; 11 | 3 ; 8 ; ML=8 ; BE=68 ; mb=2 ; put ; spread ; debit = what to widen

4. 4. 1. 6   Determining a Spread Investor's Market Attitude (Bull or Bear)

The **market attitude** of a spread investor is determined by the option that is the more costly of the two.

For **call** spreads, the option contract with the *lower strike price* has the *higher premium*. Whether the spread is a debit or credit spread will depend on if the investor purchased the option with the lower SP or sold it.

It is a *debit* if the investor purchased the one with the lower SP (higher premium).

It is a *credit* if the investor sold the one with the lower SP (higher premium).

Examples:
Long 1 July 40 call
Short 1 July 45 call
Purchasing the one with the lower SP (higher premium) is a *debit*, and debit call spreads are *bullish*.

Long 1 Aug. 40 call
Short 1 Aug. 30 call
Selling the one with the lower SP (higher premium) is a *credit*, and credit call spreads are *bearish*.

For **put** spreads, it is just the opposite. The option with the *higher strike price* has the *higher premium*. Whether the spread is a debit or credit spread depends on if the investor purchased the option with the higher SP or sold it.

It is a *debit* if the investor purchased the one with the higher SP (higher premium).

It is a *credit* if the investor sold the one with the higher SP (higher premium).

handwritten left margin: If you buy the option w/ the lower strike price you are Bullish. No matter what type of Spread

handwritten bottom: buy higher strike price = BEARISH

Examples:
Long 1 Sept. 40 put
Short 1 Sept. 30 put
Purchasing the one with the higher SP (higher premium) is a *debit*, and debit put spreads are *bearish*.

Long 1 Dec. 20 put
Short 1 Dec. 25 put
Selling the one with the higher SP (higher premium) is a *credit*, and credit put spreads are *bullish*.

TEST TOPIC ALERT

You may be asked to determine whether a spread is bullish or bearish. With premiums shown, use a T-chart to determine debit or credit. If no premiums are shown, it is up to you to determine which of the options is more valuable. Expect to see one or two questions on this concept.

A quick way to determine whether a spread is bullish or bearish is the following: in any spread, put or call, if you are buying the lower SP, you are a bull.

Buy XYZ Jan 20 call at 7; sell XYZ Jan 30 call at 3: bull call spread – debit spread

Buy ABC Aug 35 call at 1; sell ABC Aug 25 call at 8; bear call spread – credit spread

Buy DEF Mar 70 put at 6; sell DEF Mar 90 put at 17; bull put spread – credit spread

Buy LRK Sep 30 put at 9; sell LRK Sep 20 put at 3; bear put spread – debit spread

---

QUICK QUIZ 4.L

Objective: Identify investor strategies for multiple option positions

1. A customer buys 1 DOH Nov 70 put and sells 1 DOH Nov 60 put when DOH is selling for 65. This position is

    spread = same type of contract but buy/sell
    = buying higher strike price: bear

    A. a bull spread
    B. a bear spread
    C. a combination
    D. a straddle

2. All of the following are credit spreads EXCEPT

    A. write 1 Nov 35 put and buy 1 Nov 30 put
    B. buy 1 Apr 40 call and write 1 Apr 30 call
    C. buy 1 Jul 50 call and write 1 Jul 60 call
    D. buy 1 Jan 50 put and write 1 Jan 60 put

In Questions 3–10, answer A to identify a bear spread and B for a bull spread.

____ 3. Write 1 Nov 35 put; buy 1 Nov 30 put

____ 4. Buy 1 Jan 70 call; write 1 Jan 75 call

____ 5. Write 1 Apr 30 call; buy 1 Apr 40 call

_____ 6.   Write 1 Dec 45 put; buy 1 Dec 60 put

_____ 7.   Buy 1 Jul 50 call; write 1 Jul 60 call

_____ 8.   Buy 1 Dec 45 put; write 1 Dec 40 put

_____ 9.   Write 1 Jan 60 put; buy 1 Jan 50 put

_____10.   Buy 1 May 25 put; write 1 May 20 put

11.   In which of the following cases would the investor want the spread to widen?
  I.   Write 1 May 25 put; buy 1 May 30 put
  II.   Write 1 Apr 45 put; buy 1 Apr 55 put
  III.   Buy 1 Nov 65 put; write 1 Nov 75 put
  IV.   Write 1 Jan 30 call; buy 1 Jan 40 call

  A.   I and II
  B.   I and IV
  C.   II and III
  D.   II and IV

All Quick Quiz answers are found at the end of their units.

4. 4. 2   STRADDLES — Buying 2 different option types = buy buy a call and a put

A **straddle** is composed of a call and a put with the same SP and expiration month. Straddles can be long or short and are used by investors to speculate on the price movement of stock.

TAKE NOTE

Like spreads, straddles can also be identified easily with the master options chart. Straddles are identified by vertical ovals rather than horizontal ovals on the chart.

Straddles Chart

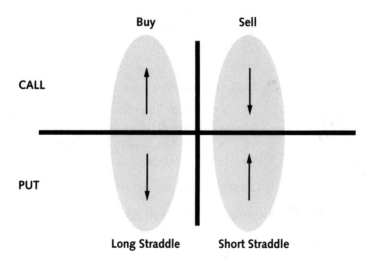

Long straddle:
wants vol and price movement

The chart also provides a tip about the strategy behind straddles. Notice the market attitude arrows pushing away from each other on the long straddle. This reminds you that the investor who buys a straddle expects a large amount of movement in the price of the stock.

The arrows on the short side are pointing toward each other and signify little or no market price movement: the objective of the seller of the straddle.

4. 4. 2. 1   Long Straddles — buys call/put

short straddle: wants low vol/price movement

An investor who uses a **long straddle** expects substantial volatility in the stock's price but is uncertain of the direction the price will move. To be ready for either occurrence, the investor purchases both a call and a put.

EXAMPLE

BE for call = added premiums + sp of call

BE for put = added premiums + sp of put

Buy 1 ABC Jan 50 call at 3

Buy 1 ABC Jan 50 put at 4

maximum gain = unlimited — because you buy a call

maximum loss = $700 = premium paid

breakevens = 57, 43   profit at above or below these prices - not between

The investor has created a long straddle by purchasing a call and a put with the same SP and expiration. If the market price of the stock rises sufficiently, the call will be profitable and the put will expire. The investor's gain on the call will be reduced by the premiums paid on both the call and the put.

If the market price of the stock falls substantially instead, the put will be profitable and the call will expire. The investor's gain on the put will be reduced by the premiums paid on both the call and the put.

The maximum gain of the long straddle is unlimited because the potential gain on a long call is unlimited. The maximum loss of the long straddle is both premiums paid. There are two breakeven points because there are two options. The breakeven for the call is the SP plus both premiums paid; the breakeven for the put is the SP minus both premiums paid. The investor does not experience profit unless the market price is above the breakeven of the call or below the breakeven of the put.

4. 4. 2. 2   Short Straddles — sells call/put

An investor who writes a short straddle expects that the stock's price will not change or will change very little. The investor collects two premiums for selling a straddle.

expects low vol and is an income play

EXAMPLE

Sell 1 ABC Jan 45 call at 4

Sell 1 ABC Jan 45 put at 5 = 900 premiums

maximum gain = $900

maximum loss = unlimited - selling a call - would have to purchase stock at market unlimited

breakevens = 54, 36

The investor has created a short straddle by selling a call and a put with the same SP and expiration. If the market price of the stock changes little or not at all, the call and put will expire. The investor's maximum profit is the two premiums collected.

If the market price of the stock rises or falls substantially, either the put or call will be exercised against the investor. The investor's maximum loss in this position is unlimited because of the short naked call.

The breakeven points for the short straddle are found the same way as for the long straddle. The call breakeven is the SP plus both premiums paid; the breakeven for the put is the SP minus both premiums paid. The investor does not experience profit unless the market price stays within the breakeven points at expiration.

Straddle Calculations

Calculation	Long Straddle	Short Straddle
Maximum gain	Unlimited	Total premiums received
Maximum loss	Total premiums paid	Unlimited
Breakevens	Call: strike price + both premiums Put: strike price – both premiums	Call: strike price + both premiums Put: strike price – both premiums

4. 4. 2. 3   Combinations

A **combination** is composed of a call and a put with different SPs, expiration months, or both. Combinations are similar to straddles in strategy. Investors typically use combinations because they are cheaper to establish than long straddles if both options are out of the money.

EXAMPLE

An investor could establish a long combination by buying an XYZ Jan 40 call and buying an XYZ Jan 45 put. If the investor were to write both options, a short combination would result. Breakeven points are computed in the same manner as straddles. Add the combined premiums to the SP of the call and subtract combined premiums from the SP of the put. As with straddles, the holder of a long combination makes money if the underlying stock trades outside the breakeven points. The writer of a short combination makes money if the stock stays inside the breakeven points.

EXAMPLE

With XYZ trading at 25, a customer writes 1 XYZ Jan 20 call at 6 and writes 1 XYZ Jan 30 put at 7. This is an example of a short combination where both contracts are in the money. Both the call and the put are in the money by 5 points. The Series 7 exam could ask you the following question: Just before expiration, with XYZ now trading at 27, the customer closes his positions at intrinsic value. How much did the customer make or lose?

In this example, closing means buying back the two options that were originally sold. What will be the cost of buying back both options? The answer is their intrinsic value. With XYZ now at 27, the call is in the money by 7 points and the put is in the money by 3 points. Now it is just a simple computation. The call was sold for 6 and bought back for 7, a loss of $100. The put was sold for 7 and bought back for 3, a gain of $400. Overall, the gain is $300.

QUICK QUIZ 4.M

Objective: Identify investor strategies for multiple option positions

1. Your customer sells a DOH Mar 35 call. To establish a straddle, he would

   A. sell a DOH Mar 40 call   *same ex/sp*
   B. buy a DOH Mar 35 put
   C. sell a DOH Mar 35 put
   D. buy a DOH Mar 40 call

2. ACM issues a news release that your customer believes will strongly affect the market price of ACM stock. However, your customer is not sure whether the effect will be positive or negative. In this situation, which of the following strategies would be best?

   A. Buy a call
   B. Write a call
   C. Write a straddle
   D. Buy a straddle = *Buy call @ same Exp/sr = vol play*
                       Buy put

3. Your customer buys 2 QRS Jul 30 calls at 2 and 2 QRS Jul 30 puts at 2.50. The customer will break even when the price of the underlying stock is

   I. 25.50
   II. 27.50
   III. 32
   IV. 34.50

   A. I and IV
   B. II and III
   C. III only
   D. IV only

Identify the positions described by indicating one of the following terms.

   A. Price spread
   B. Long straddle
   C. Time spread
   D. Short straddle
   E. Diagonal spread
   F. Combination

___ 4. Buy 1 QRS May 40 call; sell 1 QRS May 50 call

___ 5. Buy 1 QRS May 40 call; buy 1 QRS May 40 put

___ 6. Buy 1 QRS Aug 40 call; sell 1 QRS Dec 40 call

___ 7. Buy 1 DOH May 30 call; buy 1 DOH Jul 40 put

___ 8. Write 1 DOH Jan 30 call; write 1 DOH Jan 40 put

___ 9. Buy 1 DOH Mar 35 call; write 1 DOH Jun 45 call

All Quick Quiz answers are found at the end of their units.

4. 5   NONEQUITY OPTIONS

Nonequity options function nearly the same as equity options. However, because the underlying instruments are not shares of stock, nonequity options have different contract sizes and delivery and exercise standards.

4. 5. 1   INDEX OPTIONS

Options on indexes allow investors to profit from the movements of markets or market segments and hedge against these market swings. They may be based on broad-based, narrow-based, or other indexes with a particular focus.

Broad-based indexes reflect movement of the entire market and include the S&P 100 (OEX), S&P 500, and the Major Market Index (MMI).

Narrow-based indexes track the movement of market segments in a specific industry, such as technology or pharmaceuticals.

Some indexes have a very particular focus, such as the VIX (volatility market index). This index is a measure of the implied volatility of the S&P 500 Index options traded on the CBOE. VIX index options, also traded on the CBOE, are designed to reflect investor expectations of market volatility over the next 30 days. It is often referred to as the "fear" gauge or index. High readings are not bullish, nor are they bearish, but instead are a measure of the expectation (fear) that the market will be volatile. The expectation of greater volatility generally translates into higher premiums for options contracts.

4. 5. 1. 1   Index Option Features

4. 5. 1. 1. 1   Multiplier

Index options typically use a multiplier of $100. The premium amount is multiplied by $100 to calculate the option's cost, and the SP is multiplied by $100 to determine the total dollar value of the index.

4. 5. 1. 1. 2   Trading

Purchases and sales of index options, like equity options, settle on the next business day. Index options stop trading at 4:15 pm ET if they are broad-based. Narrow-based index options stop trading at 4:00 pm ET.

4. 5. 1. 1. 3   Exercise

The exercise of an index option settles in cash rather than in delivery of a security, and the cash must be delivered on the next business day. If the option is exercised, the writer of the option delivers cash equal to the intrinsic value of the option to the buyer.

4. 5. 1. 1. 4   Settlement Price

When index options are exercised, their settlement price is based on the closing value of the index on the day of exercise, not the value at the time of exercise.

4. 5. 1. 1. 5 Expiration Dates

Index options expire on the third Friday of the expiration month.

TAKE NOTE

[handwritten: equity options settle T+2 -regularly]

With regard to settlement, there is one major difference between index options and equity options. The exercise of an index option settles next business day, whereas the exercise of an equity option settles regular way (two business days). With regard to trading (i.e., buying or selling), settlement is the next business day for both.

4. 5. 1. 1. 6 Index Option Exercise

EXAMPLE

[handwritten: Premium - Intrinsic Value = Time Value]

A customer buys 1 OEX Jan 460 call at 3.20 when the OEX index is trading at 461.

What is the premium?	$320 (3.20 x $100)
What is the breakeven point?	463.20 (SP + premium)
What is the intrinsic value?	$100 (461 – 460)
What is the time value?	$220 ($320 – $100)

One month later, with the index at 472 and the Jan 460 call trading at 13.70, the customer elects to exercise.

How much cash will the customer receive from the writer?	$1,200, the intrinsic value of the option (472 – 460)
How much profit did the customer make?	$880, which is the cash received from the writer less the premium paid ($1,200 – $320)

Now, instead of exercising, assume the customer closes the position.

[handwritten: Close v. exercise the position]

How much profit would the customer make?	$1,050, which is the difference between the premium received on selling ($1,370) and the premium paid to open the position ($320)

[handwritten: closing position: Selling in market to receive options premium where it trades at in market. If option in $: premium goes up and y it can sell in market]

Note that instead of making $880 by exercising, the customer would have made $1,050 by closing the position. Why the $170 difference? As long as there is time value in the option, the customer will always make more by closing an index option rather than by exercising. The time value of the 460 call trading at 13.70 is $170 when the index is at 472.

4. 5. 1. 2 Index Options Strategy

Index options may be used to speculate on movement of the market overall. If an investor believes the market will rise, he can purchase index calls or write index puts. If an investor believes the market will fall, he can purchase index puts or write index calls.

Hedging a portfolio is an important use of index options. If a portfolio manager holds a diverse portfolio of equity, he can buy a put on the index to offset loss if the market value of the stocks fall. This use of index puts is known as **portfolio insurance**. Index options protect against the risk of a decline in the overall market, which is **systematic** or **systemic risk**.

E X A M P L E

A customer has a broad-based stock portfolio worth $920,000 and is concerned about a possible market downturn. In order to hedge, the customer could buy broad-based index puts (e.g., the OEX). If the market does turn downward, the loss on the portfolio would be offset by a gain on the puts. Remember, a put increases in value as the underlying security or portfolio goes down in value. If the OEX is trading at 460, each contract has a value of $46,000 (460 × $100). Therefore, to hedge a $920,000 stock portfolio, the customer would buy 20 OEX 460 puts (20 × $46,000).

TAKE NOTE

Weekly index options contracts provide an efficient way to trade options around certain news or events, such as economic data or earnings announcements. New options series are listed on Thursday and expire the Friday of the following week. Other than the expiration date and time to expiry, weeklies have the same contract specifications as standard options.

4. 5. 1. 3   Beta

Beta is a measure of the volatility of a stock or a portfolio related to the volatility of the market in general. If a portfolio has a beta of 1.0, it has the same volatility characteristics as the market in general. In other words, if the market rises by 5%, the portfolio should rise by the same amount. If a portfolio has a beta of 1.2, it is 20% more volatile than the market in general. For example, if the market rises by 10%, a portfolio with a beta of 1.2 should rise by 20% more, or 12%. Conversely, should the market decline, a portfolio with a beta of more than 1.0 will fall more than the overall market.

E X A M P L E

Back to our original example: if the $920,000 portfolio has a beta of 1.2, instead of purchasing 20 OEX 460 puts to hedge, the customer must purchase 24 OEX 460 puts. Because the portfolio is 20% more volatile, the customer needs 20% more protection (1.2 × 20 puts = 24).

Portfolio managers may also choose to write index options to generate income.

QUICK QUIZ 4.N

Objective: Describe the unique features and usage of nonequity options

1. Your customer is bullish on the market. If he buys 1 Jul 490 call on the XMI, which of the following options might he write to create a debit spread?

   I.   Jul 485 call
   II. Jul 480 call
   III. Jul 500 call
   IV. Jul 505 call

   — debit Spread : bullish = purchase
   4 I

   A. I only
   B. I and II
   C. II, III and IV
   D. III and IV

2. Your client owns a portfolio of blue-chip stocks. He tells you that he believes the securities will provide good, long-term appreciation but also believes that the market will decline over the short term. Which index options strategy should you recommend that will protect against the expected decline and still allow for long-term capital appreciation?

   A. Buy puts
   B. Buy calls
   C. Sell covered puts
   D. Sell covered calls

3. When an investor exercises an OEX option, he receives

   A. common stock
   B. cash equal to the strike price
   C. cash equal to the intrinsic value
   D. nothing because index options cannot be exercised.

4. Which of the following statements regarding stock index options are TRUE?

   I.   Trades are settled the next business day.
   II. Trades are settled on the second business day.
   III. Exercise settlement involves the delivery of stock.
   IV. Exercise settlement involves the delivery of cash.

   A. I and III
   B. I and IV
   C. II and III
   D. II and IV

All Quick Quiz answers are found at the end of their units.

4. 5. 2   INTEREST RATE OPTIONS

Interest rate options are yield based (i.e., they have a direct relationship to movements in interest rates). These options are based on yields of T-bills, T-notes, and T-bonds. A yield-based option with an SP of 35 reflects a yield of 3.5%. Assume an investor believes that rates on T-notes, currently at 3.5%, will rise in the near term. The investor could purchase a call option with a 35 SP (at the money). If rates rise to 4.5%, the investor could exercise and receive cash equal to the intrinsic value of the option.

Rates have gone up by 10 points—35 to 45—so the investor would receive $1,000 because each point is worth $100. Profit would be the $1,000 received on exercise less the premium paid. On the other hand, the investor could have closed his position, profiting from the difference between the premium paid and the premium received on closing.

The strategy is straightforward. If a portfolio manager believes rates will fall, the manager will buy puts or write calls. If the manager believes rates will rise, buying calls and writing puts would be appropriate.

4. 5. 3   FOREIGN CURRENCY OPTIONS

Currency options allow investors to speculate on the performance of currencies other than the U.S. dollar or to protect against fluctuating currency exchange rates against the U.S. dollar. Currency options are available for trading on U.S. listed exchanges on the Australian dollar, British pound, Canadian dollar, Swiss francs, Japanese yen, and Euro. Importers and exporters frequently use currency options to hedge currency risk.

4. 5. 3. 1   Features of Foreign Currency Options

When purchased, sold or exercised foreign currency options contracts are cash settled in U.S. dollars with no physical delivery of foreign currency.

4. 5. 3. 1. 1   Contract Sizes

Currency options contracts sizes are now smaller to accommodate retail investors. A British pound contract, for instance, covers 10,000 pounds. Each currency has its own contract size as follows:

Foreign Currency Contracts

Currency		Options Contract Size
Australian $	(XDA)	10,000
British £	(XDB)	10,000
Canadian $	(XDC)	10,000
Euro €	(XDE)	10,000
New Zealand $	(XDZ)	10,000
Swiss Fr	(XDS)	10,000
Japanese ¥	(XDN)	1,000,000

4. 5. 3. 1. 2   Strike Prices

SPs of most foreign currency options are quoted in U.S. cents. The Japanese yen is an exception and is quoted in 1/100th of a cent.

EXAMPLE

SP of .85 = 85 U.S. cents except for Japanese yen where a SP denoted as 121 = 1.21 U.S. cents (121 × 1/100).

4. 5. 3. 1. 3   Premiums

Currency options are quoted in cents per unit. Just as with equity options, one point of premium = $100. The total premium of the contract is found by multiplying the premium by the number of units. If a Swiss franc contract (10,000 units) is quoted with a premium of 1.5, the cost of the contract is 10,000 × .015, or $150.

4. 5. 3. 1. 4   Trading

Listed currency options are primarily traded on the Nasdaq OMX PHLX (formerly the Philadelphia Stock Exchange). Trading hours are 9:30 am–4:00 pm ET.

4. 5. 3. 1. 5   Expiration Date

Currency options expire on the third Friday of the expiration month just as equity options do.

4. 5. 3. 1. 6   Settlement

Currency options settle, like ~~equity~~ options, on the next business day. When a foreign currency option is exercised, settlement occurs on the next business day as well.

4. 5. 3. 1. 7   Strategies

If an investor believes the value of a currency is going to rise, he will buy calls or sell puts on the currency. If an investor expects the value of a currency to fall, he will buy puts or sell calls on the currency. Currency options are measured relative to the U.S. dollar, and an inverse relationship exists between their exchange rates. Therefore, if the U.S. dollar is rising, relative to other currencies, then those currencies are falling. Conversely, if the U.S. dollar is falling against other currencies, then those currencies are rising.

EXAMPLE

A U.S. importer must pay for Swiss chocolates in Swiss francs within three months. The importer is fearful that the value of the dollar will fall. Using foreign currency options, what should this investor do?

If the importer believes the U.S. dollar will fall, then foreign currency values will rise. The investor should buy calls on the Swiss franc to lock in the purchase price for the francs needed in three months.

TAKE NOTE

As a rule, importers buy calls on the foreign currency to hedge; exporters buy puts to hedge. However, keep in mind that there are no options available on the U.S. dollar. As an example, consider a Japanese company that exports stereos to the United States. The company will be paid in dollars upon delivery. The risk to the

[Handwritten margin note: Buy calls or puts on US dollar if you think it will decline and your company's rate will be risky]

Japanese company is that the dollar will decline between now and the delivery, which means $1 will be worth fewer yen. How should this company hedge this risk?

The rule of thumb is that exporters should buy puts on the foreign currency. However, because there are no options on the U.S. dollar, the Japanese company should buy calls on its own currency, the yen.

EXAMPLE

A British company is exporting sweaters to the United States. How should the company hedge its foreign exchange risk?
- A. Buy BP calls
- B. Sell BP calls
- C. Buy BP puts
- D. Sell BP puts

Answer: A. Because options on the U.S. dollar are not available, exporters to the United States should buy calls on their own currency.

QUICK QUIZ 4.0

Objective: Describe the unique features and usage of nonequity options

1. Which of the following currency options is NOT listed for trading on U.S. exchanges?
   - A. British pound
   - B. Japanese yen
   - C. Canadian dollar
   - D. U.S. dollar

2. An investor is long 5 PHLX Dec puts on the Canadian dollar. These options will expire in December on
   - A. the 3rd Friday of the month
   - B. the Saturday after the 3rd Friday
   - C. the Wednesday after the 3rd Saturday
   - D. the Friday preceding the 3rd Wednesday

3. A U.S. company expects to receive British pounds upon delivery of manufactured goods to a British distributor. How can the company best hedge against the risk of a strengthened U.S. dollar?
   - A. Buy puts on the pound
   - B. Buy calls on the pound
   - C. Sell puts on the pound
   - D. Sell calls on the pound

4. An investor who believes the U.S. dollar will soon strengthen in relation to the Canadian dollar might profit from which of the following strategies?

   I. Buying puts on the Canadian dollar
   II. Writing puts on the Canadian dollar
   III. Writing a straddle on the Canadian dollar
   IV. Establishing a call credit spread on the Canadian dollar

   A. I and III
   B. I and IV
   C. II and IV
   D. I, II, III and IV

5. An investor purchases 2 Dec .56 Swiss franc calls at 2.5. One SF contract includes 10,000 units. How much does the investor pay for this position?

   A. $56
   B. $250
   C. $500
   D. $560

6. A customer opens a spread on Canadian dollars (10,000 units) by purchasing 1 Dec .74 call for 1.30 and selling 1 Dec .77 call for .50. What is the total cost of this debit spread?

   A. $80
   B. $125
   C. $135
   D. $400

All Quick Quiz answers are found at the end of their units.

4. 6   HOW THE OPTIONS MARKET FUNCTIONS

Options trade on the major U.S. exchanges and OTC. Exchange-traded options are known as **listed options** and have standardized SPs and expiration dates. OTC options are not standardized; as a result, little secondary-market activity exists. Contract terms are individually negotiated between buyer and seller.

TAKE NOTE   If a security is subject to a trading halt, options on that security stop trading as well.

4. 6. 1   STANDARD FEATURES OF OPTIONS TRADING AND SETTLEMENT

4. 6. 1. 1   Trading Times

Listed stock options trade from 9:30 am–4:00 pm ET (3:00 pm CT). Note that broad-based index options trade until 4:15 pm ET (3:15 pm CT).

4. 6. 1. 2   Expiration

Listed stock options expire on the third Friday of the month at 11:59 pm. Final trades may be made until 4:00 pm on the final day of trading (expiration).

4. 6. 1. 3   Settlement

Listed options transactions settle on the next business day. Stock delivered as a result of exercise is settled on a **regular way basis** (two business days).

4. 6. 1. 4   Automatic Exercise

Contracts that are in the money by at least .01 at expiration are automatically exercised as a service to the customer unless other instructions have been given. Automatic exercise applies to both customer and institutional accounts. Customers may give "do not exercise" instructions for any contract in the money if they do not want to have their contract exercised. All instructions must be received by OCC no later than 5:30 pm ET on the third Friday of the expiration month (last day of trading).

Exercise, Trading, or Expiration of Options

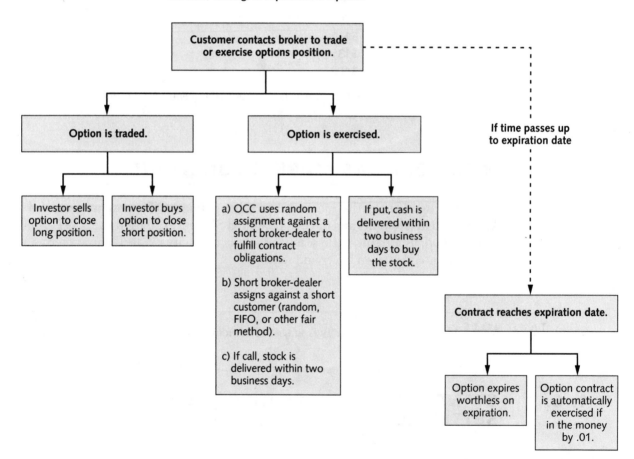

4. 6. 1. 5   Position Limits

For the most heavily traded equity options contracts, position limits are 250,000 contracts on the same side of the market. This limit is subject to frequent adjustment. No more than 250,000 contracts on the same side of the market may be exercised within a five-business-day period.

Position limits apply to individuals, registered representatives acting for discretionary accounts, and individuals acting in concert (acting together as one person). LEAPS are added to traditional options to determine whether a violation of the position limit rules has occurred.

Position limits are measured by the number of contracts on the same side of the market. There are two sides: the bull side and the bear side. Long calls and short puts represent the former; long puts and short calls, the latter.

Take a company subject to a 250,000 contract limit. If a customer were long 140,000 calls and 140,000 puts, there would be no violation. However, if the same customer were long 140,000 calls and short 140,000 puts, the customer would have 280,000 contracts on the bull side of the market, a violation. In determining whether a violation has occurred, long calls are aggregated with short puts and long puts are aggregated with short calls.

Handwritten margin notes: 250 K / option annual limit 7 for same side of market / you can have 150 bought calls and 150 written puts / - 150 k short - 150 k long

4. 6. 1. 6   Exercise Limits

OCC exercise limits are the maximum number of contracts that can be exercised on the same side of the market within a specified time frame. Currently, the time frame is five consecutive business days. As with position limits, the maximum number applicable to exercise limits can vary from one underlying security to another, and to determine if a violation has occurred, long calls and short puts (bullish contracts) are aggregated, and short calls and long puts (bearish contract) are aggregated.

Like position limits, exercise limits apply to individuals, individuals acting in concert, and registered representatives acting for discretionary accounts, among others.

4. 6. 1. 7   American- or European-Style Contracts

Call or put buyers can exercise a contract anytime before expiration if the contract is an American-style option. European-style options can be exercised on expiration day (last day of trading) only. Nearly all equity options are American style. Foreign currency options may be either American style or European style, and most index options are European-style contracts, including weekly index contracts. Yield-based options are European style contracts.

4. 6. 2   OPTIONS TRADING PERSONNEL

Options are traded most heavily on the **Chicago Board Options Exchange (CBOE)** in a double-auction market. Following are the key trading roles.

4. 6. 2. 1   Designated Primary Market Maker

A **designated primary market maker (DPM)** is a floor trader responsible for maintaining a two-sided market for a specific product on the CBOE and is the trading firm designated by the exchange to ensure a fair and orderly market—the CBOE's equivalent to a specialist on the NYSE Amex options exchange. A DPM can perform the roles of a market maker and/or a floor broker, if the conditions warrant. All equity options on the CBOE have a DPM.

Also note that an electronic designated market maker (eDPM) functions with the same responsibilities as a DPM, except that they are permitted to conduct business electronically from off-floor locations.

4. 6. 2. 2   Market Makers

Options market makers are registered with the exchange to trade for their own accounts. They must stand ready to buy or sell options in which they make markets. Not only does this provide liquidity but it helps to maintain an orderly market.

4. 6. 2. 3   Floor Brokers

Floor brokers are a firm's representatives on the floor of the exchange. They execute orders on behalf of the firm and its customers.

4. 6. 2. 4   Order Routing Systems

Computerized order routing systems are often used to route customer orders directly to the trading post and back to the firm. Notice of execution is sent directly to the broker-dealer.

4. 6. 3   OPTIONS CLEARING CORPORATION (OCC)

While the basic functions of the Options Clearing Corporation are covered in the Securities Industry Essentials exam, following is a more in-depth discussion applicable to Series 7 licensing testing.

The **Options Clearing Corporation (OCC)** is the clearing agent for listed options contracts and is owned by the exchanges that trade options. Its primary functions are to standardize, guarantee the performance of, and issue option contracts. The OCC determines when new option contracts should be offered to the market. It designates the SPs and expiration months for new contracts within market standards to maintain uniformity and liquidity. The market determines the premium for the contracts.

The exercise of options contracts is guaranteed by the OCC. If a holder of an option wishes to exercise, her broker-dealer notifies the OCC. The OCC then assigns exercise notice against a short broker-dealer, who assigns to a short customer.

The OCC assigns exercise notices on a **random** basis. Broker-dealers may then assign exercise notices to customers on a random basis, on a first in, first out (FIFO) method, or any other method that is fair and reasonable.

Options contracts are traded without a certificate. An investor's proof of ownership is the trade confirmation.

4. 6. 3. 1   Documentation of Customer Accounts

Can do
options
trade
before
returning and
signing ODD

The OCC requires that certain documents be provided to customers that open options accounts. The **OCC Options Disclosure Document** must be provided at or before the account approval. This document explains options strategies, risks, and rewards and is designed to provide full and fair disclosure to customers before they begin options trading.

Before any trading can take place, an options account must be approved by the branch manager. Then, not later than 15 days after the account approval, the customer must return the signed **options agreement**. This document states that the customer has read the disclosure document, understands the risks of options trading, and will honor position limit rules. By signing, the customer also agrees to advise the firm if any changes occur in his financial situation, investment objectives, and so forth.

If the signed options agreement is not returned within 15 days of account approval, the investor cannot open new options positions. Only closing transactions are allowed if the options agreement is not returned as required.

4. 6. 3. 2   Supervision and Compliance

Member firms are required to integrate the responsibility for supervision and compliance of their public customer options business into their overall supervisory and compliance programs. A registered option principal (ROP) must be designated by a firm to handle compliance and supervisory issues regarding customer options business. An ROP is Series 4 licensed.

Any options literature (advertising or sales) intended to communicate with the public must be approved by the ROP before distribution. Options worksheets, which identify the risks, rewards, and costs of various option strategies, or any material considered educational in nature regarding options, is considered communications. While OCC distinguishes between advertising and sales literature, how any communications piece will be regulated depends on if it is considered retail, institutional, or correspondence.

EXAMPLE

In accordance with the distinction that OCC makes between options advertising and sales literature recommendations, past performance and projected performance are not permitted in options advertising, but they are permitted in sales literature. In general, sales literature must be preceded or accompanied by a copy of the Options Disclosure Document (ODD) if it includes past or projected performance figures or it constitutes a recommendation pertaining to options. Communications that are educational in nature but do not contain projected performance figures or make recommendations pertaining to options need not be preceded by the ODD but instead must be accompanied by a notice providing the name and address where an ODD can be obtained.

Options Account Diagram

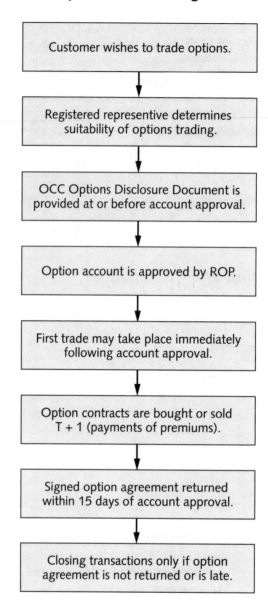

Customer wishes to trade options.

Registered representive determines suitability of options trading.

OCC Options Disclosure Document is provided at or before account approval.

Option account is approved by ROP.

First trade may take place immediately following account approval.

Option contracts are bought or sold T + 1 (payments of premiums).

Signed option agreement returned within 15 days of account approval.

Closing transactions only if option agreement is not returned or is late.

4. 6. 3. 3   Options Contract Adjustments

Options contracts are adjusted for stock splits, reverse stock splits, stock dividends, and rights offerings. They are not adjusted for ordinary cash dividends or for cash distributions of less than $12.50 per option contract. Adjustments to the number of shares are rounded down to the next whole share.

When **even** stock splits occur, additional options contracts are created. An even split ends in 1—such as a 2:1, 3:1, or 4:1 split.

EXAMPLE

After a 2:1 split, 1 ALF 60 call becomes 2 ALF 30 calls. A 2:1 creates 200 shares instead of 100, so the owner has twice as many contracts as before, at half the exercise price.

The total exercise value remains the same:

Original contract: 100 × 60 = $6,000

New contracts: 200 × 30 = $6,000

An **uneven split,** also known as a **fractional split,** such as a 3:2 or 5:4, does not create additional options contracts. Contracts adjusted for uneven splits include a larger number of shares and will receive a new option contract symbol.

EXAMPLE

After a 3:2 split, 1 ALF 60 call will effectively be represented by 1 ALF 40 call with 150 shares in the contract.

The total exercise value effectively remains the same as before:

Original contract: 100 × 60 = $6,000

New contract when closed or exercised: 150 × 40 = $6,000

EXAMPLE

Expect to see five to seven questions on the information presented in the previous section. Be familiar with documentation of options accounts, the contract adjustments, and the times and dates discussed. Note that stock dividends are treated as uneven splits; the number of contracts remains the same, the SP is adjusted, and the contract now covers more shares.

4. 6. 3. 4   Opening vs. Closing

When filling out an order ticket for an option transaction, the representative must indicate whether the trade is an opening or closing transaction. An opening transaction establishes a position, whereas a closing transaction eliminates a position. Furthermore, if an opening transaction involves the sale of an option, the representative must indicate whether it is covered or uncovered.

EXAMPLE

If you enter an order to sell 1 XYZ Jan 30 call at the market, are you establishing a short position or closing out an existing long position in that contract? If you are establishing a short position, the order ticket must be marked as an opening sale. If you are closing out an existing long position, the ticket must be marked as a closing sale.

EXAMPLE   If you are writing a call against an existing long position in the stock, the ticket must be marked as an opening sale covered.

4. 6. 3. 5   Open Interest

The open interest in an option is the number of contracts outstanding. The higher the open interest, the more liquid the option. As an option approaches expiration, open interest begins to decline as investors close out or exercise existing positions.

4. 6. 3. 5. 1   Put-Call Ratio

The put-call ratio reflects the current open interest in the trading of put options to call options. The ratio can be used as a gauge of investor sentiment (bullish or bearish) and can be calculated to measure broad sectors of the market across many underlying securities or indexes, or it can be used to gauge investor sentiment for just one underlying security.

The ratio is calculated by dividing the number of traded put options by the number of traded call options. The higher the ratio, the more bearish investors have been up to that point in time. For instance, as the ratio increases, it can be interpreted as an indication that investors felt the market sector or underlying security would move lower and were buying more puts, or investors were purchasing puts to hedge existing long portfolios in anticipation of a downward move.

However, it should also be noted that the ratio can be used as a contrarian indicator by traders. For example, the higher the ratio becomes, it is likely that traders may feel it is time to close or cover short positions in favor of long positions. In other words, the ratio may have become so high that the continued bearish sentiment begins to diminish indicating that a reversal may be near.

QUICK QUIZ 4.P   Objectives: Describe the functions of the Options Clearing Corporation (OCC) describe the process of opening an options account

1. An investor buys 1 DWQ Apr 70 call at 5, giving him the right to buy 100 shares of DWQ at $70 per share. Which aspect of the transaction is NOT set or standardized by the OCC?

    A. Contract size of 100 shares
    B. Premium of 5
    C. Exercise price of 70
    D. Expiration date in April

2. A customer first discusses options trading with a registered representative on July 3. On July 7, the customer is approved for trading listed options, and on July 12, he enters the first trade. The investor must receive an options disclosure document no later than

    A. July 3
    B. July 7
    C. July 12
    D. July 13

3. When applying the exercise limit rules, which of the following could be considered as acting in concert?

   A. Registered representative who has discretionary control over 10 customer accounts
   B. Many options customers of the same brokerage firm acting independently on a recent recommendation published by the firm
   C. Registered representatives making recommendations to nondiscretionary customers
   D. All of the above

4. MES is a stock subject to a 25,000 options position limit. Which of the following positions violate the rules governing position limits?

   I. Long 14,000 SSS Aug 40 calls; short 12,000 SSS Aug 40 puts
   II. Long 14,000 SSS Aug 40 calls; short 12,000 SSS Jan 40 puts
   III. Long 14,000 SSS Aug 40 calls; short 12,000 SSS Aug 40 calls

   A. I and II
   B. I and III
   C. II and III
   D. I, II, and III

5. If a 50% stock dividend is declared, the owner of 1 XYZ Jul 30 call now owns

   A. 1 contract for 100 shares with an exercise price of 20
   B. 1 contract for 150 shares with an exercise price of 20
   C. 2 contracts for 100 shares with an exercise price of 20
   D. 2 contracts for 150 shares with an exercise price of 30

6. When must a new options customer who has not yet traded options receive the Options Clearing Corporation's current disclosure document?

   A. At or before the time the registered representative signs the customer approval form
   B. Within 15 days after the registered representative has approved the customer's account for options trading
   C. At or before the time the account receives the registered options principal's final approval for options trading
   D. No later than 15 days after the registered options principal signs the options customer approval form

7. Equity options cease trading at

   A. 11:00 am ET on the business day before the expiration date
   B. 4:00 pm ET on the last day of trading (expiration)
   C. 1:00 am ET on the expiration date
   D. 4:10 pm ET on the expiration date

8.   The Options Clearing Corporation uses which of the following methods in assigning exercise notices?

I.   Random selection
II. First in, first out
III. To the member firm holding a long position that first requests an exercise
IV. On the basis of the largest position

A.   I only
B.   I, II, and III
C.   I and III
D.   II and IV

All Quick Quiz answers are found at the end of their units.

4. 7 TAX RULES FOR OPTIONS

Because options are capital assets, capital gains tax rules apply. The tax consequences will vary depending on how an existing position is handled.

4. 7. 1 EXPIRATION, CLOSE, OR EXERCISE

There are three ways to handle an existing (open) option position. An open positon can expire, be closed in the open market, or be exercised by the party who is long (owner).

4. 7. 1. 1 Expiration

At the expiration of an options contract, the buyer loses the premium; the seller profits from the premium. The buyer reports a capital loss equal to the premium amount; the seller reports a capital gain equal to the premium amount.

The tax treatment for LEAPS writers at expiration is unique. Although investors may have held the contract for more than 12 months, LEAPS writers must report **short-term capital gains** at expiration. LEAPS buyers will report long-term losses and gains if the contact is held for more than 12 months. Essentially, LEAP contracts for buyers are handled like most other securities regarding long- and short-term gains and losses.

4. 7. 1. 2 Closing Out

Closing sales or purchases generate a capital gain or loss equal to any price difference. This gain or loss must be reported on the basis of the date of the closing transaction.

4. 7. 1. 3 Exercise

The exercise of options does not generate a capital gain or loss until a subsequent purchase or sale of the stock occurs. If a long call is exercised, the option holder buys the stock. Because the investor paid a premium for the stock, the total cost basis for the stock includes the premium and SP. The chart identifies the tax consequences of these options strategies.

Possible Tax Consequences of Options Strategies

Strategy	Option Expires	Option Exercised	Position Closed
Buy a call	Capital loss	Strike price + premium = cost basis	Capital gain or loss
Sell a call	Capital gain	Strike price + premium = sale proceeds	Capital gain or loss
Buy a put	Capital loss	Strike price − premium = sale proceeds	Capital gain or loss
Sell a put	Capital gain	Strike price − premium = cost basis	Capital gain or loss

4. 7. 2   STOCK HOLDING PERIODS

The IRS does not allow the use of options to postpone the sale of stock for the purpose of generating long-term capital gains treatment. Options that allow an investor to lock in a sale price are long puts. If stock has been held 12 months or less before the purchase of a put, the gain will be classified as short term.

EXAMPLE

An investor bought XYZ 11 months ago at 50. It now trades for 70. If the investor were to sell it now, the gain would be classified as short term.

Assume the investor buys a 70 put that will expire in nine months. Even though the sale of the stock is postponed until up to 20 months have elapsed, the IRS still requires the holding period to be classified as short term for tax purposes. If the stock had already been held for more than 12 months, its holding period will not be affected by the purchase of a put.

4. 7. 2. 1   Married Put

If, on the same day, a customer buys stock and buys a put option on that stock as a hedge, the put is said to be **married** to the stock. For tax purposes, irrespective of what happens to the put, the cost basis of the stock must be adjusted upward by the premium paid. Even if the put expires worthless, there is no capital loss on the put. Rather, the premium paid is reflected in the cost basis of the stock, which is the breakeven point for long stock/long put (cost of stock purchased plus premium).

EXAMPLE

If, on the same day, a customer buys 100 XYZ at 52 and buys 1 XYZ Jan 50 put at 2, the customer's cost basis in the stock is 54.

TEST TOPIC ALERT

Expect to see about five to seven questions on options taxation. Many of these questions are a matter of finding the profit or loss, so use a T-chart. Remember that option exercise alone does not create a taxable event.

QUICK QUIZ 4.Q   Objective: Identify tax consequences of exercise, expiration, or closing of a position

1. In September, an investor sells 2 AMF Jan 60 puts at 3. If the investor buys the 2 puts back at 4.50, the result for tax purposes is

    A. a $150 capital gain
    B. a $150 capital loss
    C. a $300 capital gain
    D. a $300 capital loss

2. In September, an investor sells 2 AMF Jan 60 puts at 3. If the 2 AMF Jan 60 puts expire in January, what are the tax consequences for the seller?

    A. $600 gain realized in September
    B. $600 loss realized in September
    C. $600 gain realized in January
    D. $600 loss realized in January

3. Your customer buys 1 FLB Oct 50 call at 3. He exercises the option to buy 100 shares when the market is at 60. What is the cost basis of the 100 shares?

    A. $5,000
    B. $5,300
    C. $6,000
    D. $6,300

4. A customer writes 1 Jul 50 put at 7. The put is exercised when the market price is 40. For tax purposes, what is the effective cost basis of the stock put to the seller?

    A. $40
    B. $43
    C. $50
    D. $57

5. Your customer buys 100 shares of TIP stock at 59 and sells a TIP 60 call at 4. The stock's price rises to 70 and the option is exercised. For tax purposes, the customer must report sales proceeds of

    A. $6,400 and cost basis of $5,900
    B. $6,000 and cost basis of $5,500
    C. $7,000 and cost basis of $5,900
    D. $7,000 and cost basis of $6,500

6. An investor buys a LEAPS contract at issuance and allows it to expire unexercised. What is the investor's tax consequence at expiration?

    A. Short-term capital gain
    B. Short-term capital loss
    C. Long-term capital gain
    D. Long-term capital loss

7. A customer buys 100 shares of stock at 67 and sells a 70 call for 4. The stock rises to 75, and the option is exercised. For tax purposes, this investor reports sales proceeds of
    A. $7,000 and cost basis of $6,300
    B. $7,400 and cost basis of $6,700
    C. $7,500 and cost basis of $6,700
    D. $7,500 and cost basis of $7,400

All Quick Quiz answers are found at the end of their units.

QUICK QUIZ ANSWERS

Quick Quiz 4.A

1. **A.** A call is exercised when the market price is higher than the SP.

2. **B.** The seller of a call is required to sell 100 shares of stock at the SP when the call is exercised. Exercise occurs in this situation because the market price of the stock is greater than the SP.

3. **A.** The buyer of the call has the right to buy 100 shares of stock at the SP if he elects to exercise.

4. **B.** Expiration occurs in this situation because the market price of the stock is lower than the SP. There is no value for the holder in exercising a call with a SP that is more than the market price.

5. **D.** The seller has no obligation to perform at expiration because the market price of the stock is lower than the SP. The option will expire, and the seller will keep the premium received without obligation.

6. **C.** Because the market price of the stock is lower than the SP, the buyer will not exercise the call. The buyer will lose the premium of $450 paid.

Quick Quiz 4.B

1. **B.** A put is exercised when the market price is lower than the SP. In this situation, the put is not exercised. The buyer will lose the premium; the seller will keep the premium with no obligation.

2. **C.** The put will expire because the market price is greater than the SP. The seller has no obligation to perform and keeps the premium received.

3. **C.** The buyer of the put will not exercise this put because the market price is higher than the SP. The buyer will lose the premium of $300.

4. **A.** A put is exercised by the owner of the put when the market price is lower than the SP. The writer of the put (the premise in this question "short") is obligated to buy 100 shares of XYZ at the SP of $25 per share when the owner of the put exercises the right to sell the stock at $25 per share.

5. **A.** The put will be exercised because the market price is lower than the SP. The seller of the put is obligated to buy 100 shares of XYZ at a price of $25.

6. **B.** Because the market price of the stock is lower than the SP of the put, the buyer will exercise the put. The buyer of the put has the right to sell 100 shares of XYZ at the SP of $25. The buyer of the put can buy the stock in the marketplace at 20 and exercise his right to sell the stock at 25.

Quick Quiz 4.C

1. **In** Market price is higher than the SP.

2. **72** SP + premium

3. **500** Market price is higher than SP by $5; $5 × 100=$500.

4. **In** Market price is higher than the SP.

5. **72** SP + premium

6. **500** With the stock price at 70, a Jan 65 call with a market value of 70 has 5 points of intrinsic value.

7. **Out** Market price is lower than the SP.

8. **49** SP + premium

9. **0** Intrinsic value is never negative.

10. **Out** Market price is higher than the strike price.

11. **63** SP − premium

12. **0** Intrinsic value is never negative.

13. **Out** Market price is higher than the SP.

14. **63** SP – premium

15. **0** Intrinsic value is never negative.

16. **In** Market price is lower than the SP.

17. **37** SP – premium

18. **600** Market price is lower than the SP by $6; $6 × 100 shares = $600.

Quick Quiz 4.D

1. $4 intrinsic; $2 time

2. No intrinsic; $2.25 time

3. $6 intrinsic; $1.25 time

4. No intrinsic; $1.15 time

Quick Quiz 4.E

1. **D.** The maximum gain on a long call is unlimited because, theoretically, there is no limit on a rise in stock price.

2. **A.** The maximum loss on a long call is equal to the premium paid for the option. One contract represents 100 shares, and the buyer paid a $3.50 per share premium, which equals $350.

3. **A.** The maximum gain on a short call is equal to the premium received by the seller. One contract represents 100 shares, and the seller received a $3 per share premium, which equals $300.

4. **D.** The maximum loss on a short call is unlimited because, theoretically, there is no limit on a rise in stock price.

5. **C.** If the option expires out of the money, the naked call writer keeps the premium. This occurs when the market price stays below the SP. Breakeven is the SP plus the premium. If the price rises above this, the naked call writer, when exercised, will lose.

6. **C.** Call options allow greater leverage than buying the underlying stock, and the capital requirements are smaller, allowing for a smaller loss potential. The fact that options expire (i.e., have a time value that erodes as the option nears expiration) is a disadvantage of options. Stock purchases have no time value component—there is no expiration and therefore no value erosion due to this factor.

7. **C.** The right to purchase more shares of stock does not provide a hedge against falling prices.

Quick Quiz 4.F

1. **B.** The maximum gain on a long put is calculated by subtracting the premium from the SP. Subtract the premium paid of 2 from the SP of 50 and multiply by the number of shares to determine the maximum potential gain. One contract represents 100 shares, so the buyer's maximum gain is $4,800.

2. **B.** The maximum loss on a long put is equal to the premium paid for the option. One contract represents 100 shares, and the buyer paid a $2 per share premium, which equals $200.

3. **A.** The maximum gain on a short put is equal to the premium received by the seller. One contract represents 100 shares, and the seller received a $4.50 per share premium, which equals $450.

4. **B.** The maximum loss on a short put occurs when the stock drops to $0 and is calculated by subtracting the premium from the SP. Subtract the premium received by the seller of 4.50 from the SP of 30 to determine the maximum loss of 25.50 per share. One contract represents 100 shares, so the seller's maximum loss is $2,550.

Quick Quiz 4.G

1. **B.** The solution is a calculation, so draw a T-chart.

DR	CR
	3.50
47	40
47	43.50
3.50	

   1. The position is opened by selling; a credit of the premium is made.

   2. The call is exercised. Exercise of a short call requires the investor to sell the stock at the SP. A credit of 40 must be made to the account.

   3. The investor must buy the stock at the current price to have it to sell. A debit of 47 must be made.

2. **B.** The solution is a calculation, so draw a T-chart.

DR	CR
3.50	
63.50	
	65
67	65
2	

   1. The position is opened by buying; a debit of the premium of 3.50 is made.

   2. The investor buys the stock at the current price; a debit of 63.50 must be made.

   3. The put is exercised. Exercise of a long put enables the investor to sell the stock at the SP. A credit of 65 must be made to the account.

3. **D.** The position is a calculation, so draw a T-chart.

DR	CR
	5.50
95	79
95	84.50
10.50	

   1. The position is opened by selling; a credit of the premium is made.

   2. The put is exercised. Exercise of a short put requires the investor to buy the stock at the SP. A debit of 95 must be made to the account.

   3. The investor sells the stock at the current price. A credit of 79 must be made.

Quick Quiz 4.H

1. **B.** The customer bought and sold the call for 10, experiencing no gain or loss. Because the stock purchased for $85 was sold for $88, the gain is $300.

DR	CR
	10
85	88
10	
95	98
	3

2. **D.** $600 profit.

DR	CR
9	4
1	
	12
10	16
	6

3. **B.** The opening purchase of the Jul 85 call was made at 5, and the closing sale of that call was made at 2; the difference of 3 represents a $300 loss. The opening purchase of the Jul 90 put was made at 8, and the closing sale of that put was made at 3; the difference of 5 represents a $500 loss. The total loss for the account was $800.

DR	CR
5	
8	
	2 (87 – 85)
	3 (90 – 87)
13	5
8	

With the stock at 87, the intrinsic value of the 85 call is 2 and the intrinsic value of the 90 put is 3.

Quick Quiz 4.1

1. **D.** The customer must recover the cost of the premium paid to be at the breakeven. Because this is a long stock position, the market must advance 3 points for this to occur. Therefore, the breakeven of this hedged position is found by adding the premium of the option to the price of the stock (62 + 3 = 65).

DR	CR
62	
3	
65	

2. **D.** The customer has protected his stock position from downside loss by purchasing the put. If the market rises, the put is not exercised and the unlimited upside potential of the stock is not affected. If the market falls, the put will be exercised, allowing the customer to sell his stock at the option SP.

3. **B.** The customer has protected his stock position from downside loss by purchasing the put. If the market falls, the put will be exercised, allowing the customer to sell his stock at the option SP of 60. Therefore, the most the customer can lose is $200 on the stock position (62 – 60), plus the premium paid for the option ($200 + $300 = $500).

DR	CR
62	60
3	
65	60
5	

4. **A.** The customer must recover the cost of the premium paid to be at the breakeven. Because this is a short stock position, the price of the stock must decline 1 point for this to occur. Therefore, the breakeven of this hedged position is found by subtracting the premium of the option from the price of the stock (26 – 1 = 25).

DR	CR
	26
1	
	25

5. **A.** The customer has protected his short stock position from a market advance by buying the call. If the market rises, the call will be exercised, allowing the customer to buy the stock and cover his short position at the option SP. But because a premium was paid to buy the option, the premium reduces the gain. The maximum gain is the stock price minus the option premium (26 – 1 = 25). On 100 shares, this translates into a $2,500 maximum potential gain, which occurs if the stock becomes worthless.

6. **B.** The customer has protected his short stock position from loss by purchasing a call. If the market rises, the call would be exercised, allowing the customer to buy the stock at the option SP of 30 to cover the short position. Therefore, the most the customer can lose is $400 on the stock position (the difference between the option SP and the short sale price), plus the premium paid for the option ($400 + $100 = $500).

DR	CR
	26
30	
1	
31	26
5	

7. **B.** Even if the market falls by 3, the investor has not lost money on his overall position. Therefore, the breakeven of this hedged position is found by subtracting the premium of the option from the price of the stock (62 − 3 = 59).

DR	CR
62	
	3
59	

8. **B.** The customer makes money on the long stock position if the market price of the stock increases. If the stock rises above the SP of the call, the call will be exercised, requiring the customer to sell his stock at the option SP and capping the upside potential of the stock position. The premium received adds to the amount of investor profit.

DR	CR
62	
	3
	65
62	68
	6

9. **C.** The customer has protected his stock position from downside loss only by the amount of the premium received from the short call. The investor can lose $5,900 (62 − 3 = 59).

10. **D.** The customer has protected his short stock position from loss by the amount of the premium received from writing the put. The premium does little to offset the unlimited risk of the short stock position. The maximum loss is unlimited in this situation.

11. **D.** This is a ratio write. There are three short calls to only 200 shares. Two of the calls are covered; one is uncovered (naked). This is an inappropriate recommendation for a risk-averse customer.

Quick Quiz 4.J

1. **C.** This is a call spread, so the breakeven point is found by adding the net debit of 1.50 to the lower SP: 40 + 1.50 = 41.50.

2. **C.** To find the breakeven point on this call credit spread, add the net credit of 3.25 to the lower SP of 50.

3. **A.** The maximum gain is $300. The maximum potential gain on a credit spread is the net credit. The maximum loss is $700. The maximum potential loss on a credit spread is the difference between the SPs minus the net credit: 10 − 3 = 7; 7 × 100 shares = $700.

4. **B.** The maximum loss is $525. In a debit spread, the net debit represents maximum loss. To find maximum gain, subtract the maximum loss from the difference between the SPs.

5. **D.** The maximum gain is $725. The maximum gain on a credit spread is the net credit received. The maximum loss is $275. The maximum loss on a credit spread is the difference between the SPs minus the net credit: 10 − 7.25 = 2.75; 2.75 × 100 shares = $275.

Quick Quiz 4.K

1. **B.** Choices I and III fit the definition of a call spread because each includes one long and one short option of the same type with either different SPs or different expiration dates. Choice II involves options of the same type, but both are long. Choice IV involves options of different types.

2. **D.** This is a put spread established at a credit of 2.50. To find the breakeven point on a put spread, subtract the net credit or debit from the higher SP. (PSH: Puts Subtract from Higher). In this case, subtract the credit of 2.50 from the higher SP of 35.

3. **C.** The maximum loss on a debit spread is the net debit. The maximum gain on a debit spread is the difference between the SPs minus the net debit: $10 - 4.25 = 5.75$; 5.75×100 shares = \$575. The maximum loss is \$425.

4. **A.** Debit spreads are profitable if the spread between the premiums widens.

5. **C.** This is a debit spread that will be profitable if the spread between the premiums widens. If both puts are exercised, the spread is profitable. If the short 50 put is exercised, the customer buys the stock that is then sold for 60 by exercising the long 60 put. The \$1,000 profit less \$800 paid in premiums equals a net \$200 profit.

Quick Quiz 4.L

1. **B.** This put spread is established at a debit because the investor pays more for the 70 put than he receives for the 60 put. Bears buy puts and put spreads. Another easy way to think of this: long the lower SP is bullish so the investor is short the lower SP; the position is bearish.

2. **C.** The lower the SP, the more expensive the call option. The higher the SP, the more expensive the put option. In answer choice C., the investor has bought the call option with the lower SP which is the more expensive, so this is a debit spread.

3. **B.** This is a credit put spread. The investor receives more for the Nov 35 put than he paid for the Nov 30 put. Bulls sell put spreads. The put with the higher SP is more likely to be in the money as the market falls.

4. **B.** This is a debit call spread. Bulls buy calls. A lower SP call is more likely to be in the money as the market rises.

5. **A.** This is a credit call spread. Bears sell calls.

6. **A.** This is a debit put spread. Bears buy puts. The 60 put is worth more because it has a higher SP.

7. **B.** This is a debit call spread. Bulls buy calls.

8. **A.** This a debit put spread. Bears buy puts.

9. **B.** This is a credit put spread. Bulls sell puts.

10. **A.** This is a debit put spread. Bears buy puts.

11. **A.** Choices I and II are debit spreads: an investor wants a debit spread to widen. As the distance between the premiums increases, the investor's potential profit also increases.

Quick Quiz 4.M

1. **C.** Straddles involve options of different types, but both options must be long or both must be short. They must have the same expiration date and SP.

2. **D.** Investors who are unsure of market attitude but expect substantial volatility may profit from buying straddles.

3. **A.** The customer buys calls and puts with the same SP and expiration date, so the position is a straddle. Straddles have two breakeven points: the SP plus and minus the sum of the two premiums.

4. **A.** The most common spread, and the one most likely to occur on the Series 7 exam, is the price spread (vertical spread), in which the two options have the same expiration date but different exercise prices.

5. **B.** The investor is long a call and long a put with the same SP and expiration date; this is a long straddle.

6. **C.** Also called a horizontal or calendar spread, a time spread involves two options with different expiration dates.

7. **F.** A combination is similar to a straddle in that the investor buys or sells a call and a put. With a combination, however, the SPs, expiration dates, or both are different. This is a long combination.

8. **F.** The investor is selling a call and a put with different SPs. This is a short combination.

9. **E.** A diagonal spread involves the purchase and sale of two options of the same type with different expiration dates and SPs.

Quick Quiz 4.N

1. **D.** If the customer sold either a 500 call or a 505 call, he would have a debit spread because he has purchased the more expensive call—the one with a lower SP. The customer would create a credit spread by selling the 480 call or the 485 call. Because they have lower SPs, they would be more expensive than the 490 call.

2. **A.** Because your client is long stock, his position would be hurt by a drop in the market. To hedge against that risk, he must take an option position that appreciates in value as the market declines: long puts or short calls. Because your client also wishes to benefit from any appreciation, the long put is the better hedging vehicle. If the market averages increase, the put position will lose only the premium, and your client could still gain on the portfolio.

3. **C.** Exercise settlement on index options is in cash, not stock. When the owner of an option exercises, the person who has a short position must deliver cash equal to the intrinsic value (the in-the-money amount). This is computed on the basis of the closing value of the index on the day the option is exercised.

4. **B.** Index option trades settle on the next business day, and cash is delivered upon exercise of the option. Exercise of index options is also on the next business day.

Quick Quiz 4.O

1. **D.** Option contracts exist on foreign currencies, not on the U.S. dollar.

2. **A.** Foreign currency options expire on the third Friday of the expiration month.

3. **A.** The long puts guarantee that the British pounds, when received, can be exercised for a number of U.S. dollars at the SP.

4. **B.** The investor is bearish on the Canadian dollar. Bears buy puts and write calls and call spreads. Short straddles pay off when the market does not move either way.

5. **C.** Swiss franc options are quoted in cents per unit. One call at 2.5 cents × 10,000 units (.025 × 10,000) = $250. The investor has purchased two contracts, so the total premium is $500.

6. **A.** The customer pays a premium of 1.30 and receives a premium of .50, for a net payment of .80. Multiply the net premium by the number of units in the contract for the answer: 10,000 × .008 (.8 cents) = $80.

Quick Quiz 4.P

1. **B.** The OCC sets standard exercise prices and expiration dates for all listed options, but the premiums that buyers pay for options are determined by the market.

2. **B.** The OCC disclosure document must be given to the customer no later than at the time the account is approved for options trading.

3. **A.** Acting in concert, rules apply to position limits and exercise limits. Acting in concert means acting together with knowledge of each other's activities or having one person control a number of accounts.

4. **A.** The expiration dates and SPs may be different or the same. However, the total number of contracts on the same side of the market on this stock is limited to 25,000. The OCC considers long calls and short puts to be on the same side of the market.

5. **B.** When a company pays a stock dividend or effects a fractional stock split, the number of contracts will remain the same but the number of shares the contract represents increases. The effective SP will be adjusted accordingly, in this case downward.

6. **C.** Customers must be furnished with options disclosure documents before or at the time their accounts receive a registered options principal's approval.

7. **B.** Equity options cease trading at 4:00 pm ET on the last day of trading (expiration).

8. **A.** The OCC assigns exercise notices to member firms on a random basis. The members may choose the customers to be exercised on either a random or FIFO basis.

Quick Quiz 4.Q

1. **D.** The closing cost of $900 minus $600 opening sale proceeds equals a $300 loss.

2. **C.** Expiration of a short option generates a gain at the time the option expires.

3. **B.** The cost basis of the 100 shares is the total amount the investor spent to acquire them. He paid $300 to buy the call option. When he exercised the call, he purchased 100 shares of FLB at $50 per share, for a total price of $5,000. The cost basis, therefore, is $5,300.

4. **B.** The cost basis is 50 (the price at which the writer must buy) minus 7 (the premium the writer was paid), or $43 per share.

5. **A.** When a call option is exercised, the writer's sale proceeds are equal to the sum of the SP plus the call premium ($6,000 + $400 = $6,400). The cost basis of the stock is the original purchase price, which equals $5,900. The investor's total gain is $500.

6. **D.** A LEAPS contract has an expiration of more than one year. Upon expiration, the buyer incurs a long-term capital loss equal to the amount of the premium paid.

7. **B.** When the call is exercised, the investor must sell the stock at $70 per share. The investor reports sales proceeds of $7,400 ($7,000 from the sale of stock + $400 premium) and cost basis of $6,700 (the original cost to purchase the stock).

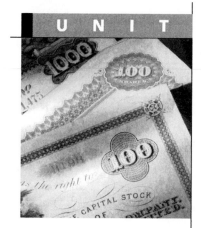

5

Direct Participation Programs

Direct participation programs (DPPs) are illiquid investments that pass income, gains, losses, and tax benefits (such as depreciation, depletion, and tax credits) directly to the limited partners. There are some unique tax concepts and suitability issues associated with DPPs. Limited partnerships (LPs) are one of the most common types of direct participation programs. As you review the Unit, remember that basic DPP concepts have been covered in the Securities Industry Essentials (SIE) exam. If you are well-grounded in the basics, proficiency with the more complex concepts will follow.

The Series 7 exam will include 91 questions on the topics covered in units 3, 4, 5, and 6. (Function 3 of the FINRA exam). ■

In this Unit you will learn to:

■ **outline** the structure of DPPs as flow-through vehicles;

■ **list** the rights and responsibilities of DPP participants;

■ **name** and define the critical documents in the administration of LPs;

■ **list** the payment order priority at dissolution;

■ **identify** the unique tax concepts related to DPP interests;

■ **compare** and contrast the features of various real estate programs, as well as oil and gas programs; and

■ **describe** methods of analysis of DPP performance.

5. 1   CHARACTERISTICS OF LIMITED PARTNERSHIPS

The basis for the content included in the following sections is found in the Securities Industry Essentials Exam (SIE) study material. Please review as needed. Here that content is expanded and built upon for Series 7 testing proficiency.

Limited partnerships are unique investment opportunities that permit the economic consequences of a business to flow through to investors. These programs offer investors a share in the income, gains, losses, deductions, and tax credits of the business entity.

Limited partners (LPs) in DPPs enjoy several advantages:

- An investment managed by others
- Limited liability
- Flow-through of income and certain expenses

The greatest disadvantage to LPs is their lack of liquidity. The secondary market for LP interests is extremely limited; investors who wish to sell their interests frequently cannot locate buyers (i.e., the shareholder's interest is not freely transferable).

Lack of liquidity at an L.P disadvantage

TAKE NOTE

A small number of LP interests are negotiable and trade on the OTC and exchanges. These partnerships are known as **master limited partnerships (MLPs)**.

5. 1. 1   TAX REPORTING FOR PARTNERSHIPS

DPPs are generally structured as **limited partnerships** or **Subchapter S corporations**. These business forms are not tax-paying entities like corporations; instead, they only report income and losses to the IRS, and then the **partners** (in an LP) or **shareholders** (in a Subchapter S corporation) have the responsibility to report income and losses individually and pay the taxes due.

By contrast, in a typical corporation, taxes must be paid on the earnings of the corporation before a dividend is distributed. Then the shareholder is taxed again on the dividend received.

Because an investment in a DPP is not taxed first at the level of the business, double taxation is avoided. The term *flow-through* (or pass-through) means that all the income and losses and corresponding tax responsibilities go directly to the investors with no taxation to the business entity.

Features of Corporations and DPPs

Corporation	Direct Participation Program
Tax-paying entity	Tax-reporting entity (entity does not pay taxes)
Shareholders receive dividend distributions	Investors receive a share of all income and losses of the business reported on Form K-1
Dividend distributions are subject to double taxation	No double taxation on distributions

B/c entity is not taxed

DPPs (LPs) are the only investment opportunity that you will study that offer a pass-through of losses to the investor. Also, DPP passive losses shelter passive income, not ordinary income.

- Income can be either active or passive. Income derived exclusively from holding or trading securities is known as portfolio income.
- **Earned income** includes salary, bonuses, and income derived from active participation in a trade or business. Earned income is sometimes known as **active income**.
- **Passive income** and losses come from rental property, limited partnerships, and enterprises (regardless of business structure) in which an individual is not actively involved. For the general partner, income from a limited partnership is earned income; for the limited partner, such income is passive. Passive income is netted against passive losses to determine net taxable income. Passive losses may be used to offset passive income only.
- **Portfolio income** includes dividends, interest, and net capital gains derived from the sale of securities. No matter what the source of the income, it is taxed during the year in which it is received.

5. 1. 1. 1   Profit Motive

Any DPP established without a profit motive or with the intention of only generating tax losses for investors may be determined abusive. Investors in abusive DPPs may be subject to:

- back taxes,
- recapture of tax credits,
- interest penalties, or
- prosecution for fraud.

5. 1. 1. 2   Organizations Classified as Partnerships

An unincorporated organization with two or more members is generally classified as a partnership for federal tax purposes if its members engage in a trade, business, financial operation, or venture and divide its profits. However, a joint undertaking merely to share expenses is not a partnership. For example, co-ownership of property maintained and rented or leased is not a partnership unless the co-owners provide services to the tenants.

An organization is classified as a **partnership** for federal tax purposes if it has two or more members and is none of the following:

- An organization formed under a federal or state law that refers to itself as incorporated or as a corporation, body corporate, or body politic
- An organization formed under a state law that refers to itself as a joint-stock company or joint-stock association
- An insurance company
- Certain banks
- An organization wholly owned by a state or local government
- An organization specifically required to be taxed as a corporation by the Internal Revenue Code (e.g., certain publicly traded partnerships)
- Certain foreign organizations

- A tax-exempt organization
- A real estate investment trust
- An organization classified as a trust or otherwise subject to special treatment under the Internal Revenue Code
- Any other organization that elects to be classified as a corporation by filing Form 8832

To qualify as a partnership, the business entity must avoid corporate characteristics such as continuity of life. This is the easiest of the corporate characteristics to avoid because partnerships have a predetermined date of dissolution when they are established, whereas corporations are expected to exist in perpetuity.

TEST TOPIC ALERT
Exam questions may test avoidance of corporate characteristics. For example:

1. Which of these characteristics is the most difficult to avoid?

    Centralized management—no business can function without it.

2. Which of these characteristics is the easiest to avoid?

    Continuity of life—there is a predetermined time at which the partnership interest must be dissolved.

3. Which two corporate characteristics are most likely to be avoided by a DPP?

    Continuity of life and *freely transferable interests*—interests cannot be freely transferred; GP approval is required to transfer shares.

Important tax concepts associated with DPPs include the following.

- DPPs were formerly known as tax shelters because investors used losses to reduce or shelter ordinary income (by writing off passive losses against ordinary income).
- Tax law revisions now classify income and loss from these investments as passive income and loss. Current law allows passive losses to shelter only passive income, not all ordinary income as before. Many programs lost their appeal because of this critical change in tax law.

TAKE NOTE
Investors should not purchase DPPs primarily for tax shelter; the partnership program should be economically viable and offer investors the potential of cash distributions and capital gains.

TEST TOPIC ALERT
1. When considering the purchase of an LP interest, an investor should be most concerned with

    A.   loss pass-through
    B.   potential tax shelter
    C.   economic viability
    D.   short-term trading opportunities

Answer: C. Economic viability is the number one reason for the purchase of an interest in a limited partnership. Tax sheltering and loss pass-through are also considerations but should not be the primary motive to invest. Short-term trading opportunities do not exist. The investor should expect to hold the interest until the partnership is dissolved or liquidated.

5. 1. 2   FORMING A LIMITED PARTNERSHIP

LPs may be sold through private placements or public offerings. If sold privately, investors receive a **private placement memorandum** for disclosure. Generally, such private placements involve a small group of LPs, each contributing a large sum of money. These investors must be **accredited investors**—that is, they must have substantial investment experience. The general public does not meet this description.

In a public offering, partnerships are sold with a prospectus to a larger number of LPs, each making a relatively small capital contribution, such as $1,000 to $5,000.

The **syndicator** oversees the selling and promotion of the partnership. The syndicator is responsible for the preparation of any paperwork necessary for the registration of the partnership. Syndication or "finders" fees are limited to 10% of the gross dollar amount of securities sold.

5. 1. 2. 1   Required Documentation

Three important documents are required for a limited partnership to exist:

- The certificate of limited partnership
- The partnership agreement
- The subscription agreement

5. 1. 2. 1. 1   Certificate of Limited Partnership

For legal recognition, this document must be filed in the home state of the partnership. It includes:

- the partnership's name;
- the partnership's business;
- the principal place of business;
- the amount of time the partnership expects to be in business;
- the size of each LP's current and future expected investments;
- the contribution return date, if set;
- the share of profits or other compensation to each LP;
- the conditions for LP assignment of ownership interests;
- the whether LPs may admit other LPs; and
- whether business can be continued by remaining GPs at death or incapacity of a GP.

If any material information on the certificate has changed, an update must be made within 30 days of the event.

5. 1. 2. 1. 2   Partnership Agreement

Each partner receives a copy of this agreement. It describes the roles of the general and limited partners and guidelines for the partnership's operation.

TAKE NOTE

Rights of the GP as defined in the partnership agreement include:

■ the right to charge a management fee for making business decisions for the partnership;

■ the authority to bind the partnership into contracts;

■ the right to determine which partners should be included in the partnership; and

■ the right to determine whether cash distributions will be made.

5. 1. 2. 1. 3   Subscription Agreement

All investors interested in becoming LPs (passive investors) must complete a subscription agreement. The agreement appoints one or more GPs to act on behalf of the LPs and is only effective when the GPs sign it. Along with the subscriber's money, the subscription agreement must include:

■ the investor's net worth;

■ the investor's annual income;

■ a statement attesting that the investor understands the risk involved; and

■ a power of attorney appointing the GP as the agent of the partnership.

In addition to a cash contribution, subscribers may assume responsibility for the repayment of a portion of a loan made to the partnership. This type of loan is called a **recourse loan**. Frequently, partnerships borrow money through **nonrecourse loans**; the GPs have responsibility for repayment of nonrecourse loans (not the LPs).

TEST TOPIC ALERT

LPs are liable for a proportionate share of recourse loans assumed by partnerships. LPs have no liability for nonrecourse loans, except in real estate partnerships.

5. 1. 3   DISSOLVING A LIMITED PARTNERSHIP

Generally, the partnerships are liquidated on the date specified in the partnership agreement. Early shutdown may occur if the partnership sells or disposes of its assets or if a decision is made to dissolve the partnership by the LPs holding a majority interest. When **dissolution** occurs, the GP must cancel the certificate of limited partnership and settle accounts in the following order:

■ Secured lenders

■ Other creditors

- LPs

  — First, for their claims to shares of profits

  — Second, for their claims to a return of contributed capital

- GPs

  — First, for fees and other claims not involving profits

  — Second, for a share of profits

  — Third, for capital return

DPP Life Cycle Diagram

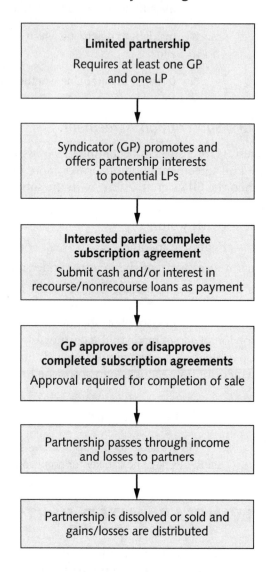

Limited partnership

Requires at least one GP and one LP

↓

Syndicator (GP) promotes and offers partnership interests to potential LPs

↓

Interested parties complete subscription agreement

Submit cash and/or interest in recourse/nonrecourse loans as payment

↓

GP approves or disapproves completed subscription agreements

Approval required for completion of sale

↓

Partnership passes through income and losses to partners

↓

Partnership is dissolved or sold and gains/losses are distributed

5. 1. 4   INVESTORS IN A LIMITED PARTNERSHIP

The limited partnership form of DPP involves two types of partners: the GP(s) and the LP(s). A limited partnership must have at least one of each.

General Partners vs. Limited Partners

General Partners	Limited Partners
Unlimited liability: personal liability for all partnership business losses and debts	Limited liability: can lose no more than their investment and proportionate interest in recourse notes
Management responsibility: assumes responsibility for all aspects of the partnership's operation	No management responsibility: provides capital for the business but may not participate in its management; known as a passive investor
	Attempting to take part in a management role jeopardizes limited liability status
Fiduciary responsibility: morally and legally bound to use invested capital in the best interest of the investors	May sue the GP: lawsuits may recover damages if the GP does not act in the best interest of the investors or uses assets improperly

The following tables compare other activities of GPs and LPs.

General Partners and Limited Partners: Allowed Activities

General partners can:	Limited partners can:
make decisions that legally bind the partnership	vote on changes to partnership investment objectives or the admission of a new GP
buy and sell property for the partnership	vote on sale or refinancing of partnership property
maintain a financial interest in the partnership (must be a minimum of 1%)	receive cash distributions, capital gains, and tax deductions from partnership activities
receive compensation as specified in the partnership agreement	inspect books and records of the partnership
	exercise the partnership democracy (vote under special circumstances, such as permitting the GP to act contrary to the agreement, to contest a judgment against the partnership, or admit a new GP)

General Partners and Limited Partners Cannot: Prohibited Activities

General partners cannot:	Limited partners cannot:
compete against the partnership for personal gain	act on behalf of the partnership or participate in its management
borrow from the partnership	knowingly sign a certificate containing false information
commingle partnership funds with personal assets or assets of other partnerships	have their names appear as part of the partnership's name
admit new GPs or LPs or continue the partnership after the loss of a GP unless specified in the partnership agreement	

QUICK QUIZ 5.A

Objectives:

■ Outline the structure of DPPs as flow-through vehicles
■ List the rights and responsibilities of DPP participants
■ Name and define the critical documents in the administration of LPs
■ List the payment order priority at dissolution

1. DPP stands for

    A. direct placement program
    B. directed profits program
    C. direct participation program
    D. directors' and principals' program

2. The person who organizes and registers a partnership is known as

    A. a syndicator
    B. a property manager
    C. a program manager
    D. an underwriter

3. A limited partnership becomes effective when

    A. the certificate is filed with the proper authorities
    B. all LP interests are sold
    C. all LPs are notified that all units are sold
    D. the partnership registration is filed

4. When a certificate of limited partnership must be rerecorded, it must be filed

    A. before the change
    B. within 5 business days of the change
    C. within 30 days of the change
    D. within 60 days of the change

5. The rights and liabilities of GPs and LPs are listed in

    A. the certificate of partnership
    B. the Uniform Limited Partnership Act
    C. the partnership agreement
    D. the partnership title

6. Which of the following corporate characteristics do most limited partnerships avoid?

    I.   Continuity of life
    II. Limited liability
    III. Centralized management
    IV. Free transferability of interest

    A. I and II
    B. I and IV
    C. II and III
    D. II and IV

7. A subscription for a limited partnership is accepted when

    A. the proposed LP signs the partnership agreement
    B. the LP's check is cashed
    C. the GP signs the subscription agreement
    D. the certificate of limited partnership is filed

8. All of the following statements are true with respect to a limited partnership subscription agreement EXCEPT

    A. the investor's registered representative must verify that the investor has provided accurate information
    B. the general partner endorses the subscription agreement, signifying that a limited partner is suitable
    C. the investor's signature indicates that he has read the prospectus
    D. the general partner's signature grants the limited partners power of attorney to conduct the partnership's affairs

All Quick Quiz answers are found at the end of their units.

5. 2   TYPES OF LIMITED PARTNERSHIP PROGRAMS

Limited partnerships can be formed to run any type of business. The most common types are real estate, oil and gas, and equipment leasing businesses.

5. 2. 1   REAL ESTATE PARTNERSHIPS

Real estate limited partnerships provide investors with the following benefits:

■ **Capital growth potential**—achieved through appreciation of property

■ **Cash flow (income)**—collected from rents

■ **Tax deductions**—from mortgage interest expense and depreciation allowances for "wearing out the building" and capital improvements

■ **Tax credits**—for government-assisted housing and historic rehabilitation (reduce tax liability dollar for dollar but are subject to recapture)

Five types of real estate programs and their features follow.

Raw Land	
Partnership Objective	Purchase undeveloped land for its appreciation potential
Advantages	Appreciation potential of the property
Disadvantages	Offers no income distributions or tax deductions
Tax Features	No income or depreciation deductions
	Not considered a tax shelter
Degree of Risk	Most speculative real estate partnership

New Construction	
Partnership Objective	Build new property for potential appreciation
Advantages	Appreciation potential of the property and structure; minimal maintenance costs in the early years
Disadvantages	Potential cost overruns; no established track record; difficulty of finding permanent financing; inability to deduct current expenses during construction period
Tax Features	Depreciation and expense deductions after construction is completed and income is generated
Degree of Risk	Less risky than new land; more risky than existing property

Existing Property	
Partnership Objective	Generate an income stream from existing structures
Advantages	Immediate cash flow; known history of income and expenses
Disadvantages	Greater maintenance or repair expenses than for new construction; expiring leases that may not be renewed; less than favorable rental arrangements
Tax Features	Deductions for mortgage interest and depreciation
Degree of Risk	Relatively low risk

Government-Assisted Housing Programs	
Partnership Objective	Develop low-income and retirement housing
Advantages	Tax credits and rent subsidies
Disadvantages	Low appreciation potential; risk of changing government programs; high maintenance costs
Tax Features	Tax credits and losses
Degree of Risk	Relatively low risk

Historic Rehabilitation	
Partnership Objective	Develop historic sites for commercial use
Advantages	Tax credits for preserving historic structure
Disadvantages	Potential cost overruns; no established track record; difficulty of finding permanent financing; inability to deduct current expenses during construction period
Tax Features	Tax credit and deductions for expenses and depreciation
Degree of Risk	Similar to risk of new construction

5. 2. 2   OIL AND GAS PARTNERSHIPS

Oil and gas programs include speculative drilling programs and income programs that invest in producing wells. Unique tax advantages associated with these programs include intangible drilling costs and depletion allowances.

5. 2. 2. 1   Intangible Drilling Costs (IDCs)

Write-offs for the expenses of drilling are usually 100% deductible in the first year of operation. These include costs associated with drilling such as wages, supplies, fuel costs, and insurance. **An intangible drilling cost** can be defined as any cost that, after being incurred, has no salvage value.

5. 2. 2. 2   Tangible Drilling Costs (TDCs)

Tangible drilling costs are those costs incurred that have salvage value (e.g., storage tanks and wellhead equipment). These costs are not immediately deductible; rather, they are deducted (depreciated) over several years.

5. 2. 2. 3   Depletion Allowances

The IRS allows allowances in the form of tax deductions that compensate the partnership for the decreasing supply of oil or gas (or any other resource or mineral).

TAKE NOTE   Depletion allowances may be taken only once the oil or gas is sold.

Three types of oil and gas programs are exploratory, developmental, and income.

5. 2. 2. 4   Exploratory (Wildcatting)

Partnership Objective	Locate undiscovered reserves of oil and gas
Advantages	High rewards for discovery of new reserves
Disadvantages	Few new wells actually produce
Tax Features	High IDCs for immediate tax sheltering
Degree of Risk	High; most risky oil and gas program

5. 2. 2. 5   Developmental

Partnership Objective	Drill near existing fields to discover new reserves (called step out wells)
Advantages	Less discovery risk than exploratory
Disadvantages	Few new wells actually produce
Tax Features	Medium IDCs, immediate tax sheltering
Degree of Risk	Medium to high risk

5. 2. 2. 6   Income

Partnership Objective	Provide immediate income from sale of existing oil
Advantages	Immediate cash flow
Disadvantages	Oil prices; well stops producing
Tax Features	Income sheltering from depletion allowances
Degree of Risk	Low

TAKE NOTE

There is a fourth type of oil and gas partner: combination. In this program, the partnership allocates dollars between income and exploratory drilling.

5. 2. 2. 7   Sharing Arrangements

The costs and revenues associated with oil and gas programs are shared in a variety of ways. A description of these arrangements follows.

Overriding Royalty Interest. The holder of this interest receives royalties but has no partnership risk. An example of this arrangement is a landowner that sells mineral rights to a partnership.

Reversionary Working Interest. The GP bears no costs of the program and receives no revenue until LPs have recovered their capital. LPs bear all deductible and nondeductible costs.

Net Operating Profits Interest. The GP bears none of the program's costs but is entitled to a percentage of net profits. The LP bears all deductible and nondeductible costs. This arrangement is available only in private placements.

Disproportionate Sharing. The GP bears a relatively small percentage of expenses but receives a relatively large percentage of the revenues.

Carried Interest. The GP shares tangible drilling costs with the LPs but receives no IDCs. The LP receives the immediate deductions, whereas the GP receives write-offs from depreciation over the life of the property.

Functional Allocation. Under this most common sharing arrangement, the LP receives the IDCs, which allow immediate deductions. The GP receives the tangible drilling costs, which are depreciated over several years. Revenues are shared.

5. 2. 3 EQUIPMENT LEASING PROGRAMS

Equipment leasing programs are created when DPPs purchase equipment leased to other businesses. Investors receive income from lease payments and also a proportional share of write-offs from operating expenses, interest expense, and depreciation. Tax credits were once available through these programs but were discontinued by tax law changes. The primary investment objective of these programs is tax-sheltered income.

5. 2. 4 ANALYSIS OF LIMITED PARTNERSHIPS

In selecting a limited partnership interest to participate in, an investor should first consider whether the partnership matches his investment objectives and has economic viability. **Economic viability** means that there is potential for returns from cash distributions and capital gains. Although tax benefits may be attractive, they should not be the first consideration in the purchase of an LP interest.

5. 2. 4. 1 Measuring Economic Viability

How is economic viability measured? Two methods applied to the analysis of DPPs are cash flow analysis and internal rate of return.

- **Cash flow analysis** compares income (revenues) to expenses.
- **Internal rate of return (IRR)** determines the present value of estimated future revenues and sales proceeds to allow comparison to other programs.

5. 2. 4. 2   Tax Features to Consider

As described, a partnership distributes income, losses, and gains to the LPs because of their pass-through nature. LPs are able to apply certain deductions and tax credits to income as described here.

5. 2. 4. 2. 1   Deductions

Expenses of the partnership, such as salaries, interest payments, and management fees, result in deductions in the current year to the LPs. Principal payments on property are not deductible expenses.

Cost recovery systems offer write-offs over a period of years as defined by IRS schedules. **Depreciation write-offs** apply to cost recovery of expenditures for equipment and real estate (land cannot be depreciated). **Depletion allowances** apply to the using up of natural resources, such as oil and gas. Depreciation and depletion allowances may be claimed only when income is being produced by the partnership. Also recognize that some assets are not depreciable nor can they be depleted. For example, farm crops fall into this category and are generally known to be renewable assets.

TAKE NOTE

Depreciation may be taken on a straight line (i.e., the same amount each year) or accelerated basis. Accelerated depreciation, known as a modified accelerated cost recovery system (MACRS), increases deductions during the early years and decreases them during the later years.

5. 2. 4. 2. 2   Tax Credits

Tax credits are dollar-for-dollar reductions of taxes due and are the greatest tax benefit available to taxpayers. Currently, there are few available. The partnership programs that offer them currently are government-assisted housing programs and historic rehabilitation programs. Formerly, tax credits were available through equipment leasing programs, but tax law changes discontinued this credit. The partnership reports its income and losses to the IRS and then reports to each partner their individual share of income, gains, losses, deductions, and credits.

TAKE NOTE

The **crossover point** is the point at which the program begins to generate taxable income instead of losses. This generally occurs in later years when income increases and deductions decrease.

LPs must keep track of their **tax basis**, or amount at risk, to determine their gain or loss upon the sale of their partnership interest. An investor's basis is subject to adjustment periodically for occurrences such as cash distributions and additional investments.

The tax benefits offered by the partnership should be of secondary importance to the economic viability it offers.

TAKE NOTE

An LP's basis consists of:

■ cash contributions to the partnership,

■ property contributions to the partnership,

■ recourse debt of the partnership, and

■ nonrecourse debt for real estate partnerships only.

Partners must adjust their basis at year-end. Any distributions of cash or property and repayments of recourse debt (also nonrecourse debt for real estate only) are reductions to a partner's basis. Partners are allowed deductions up to the amount of their adjusted cost basis.

EXAMPLE

If a partner's basis is $25,000 at year-end and the investor has losses of $35,000, only $25,000 of the losses may be used to deduct against passive income. The remaining $10,000 may be carried forward.

5. 2. 4. 3   Other Features to Analyze

Other important factors that investors should consider in their overall analysis of these partnerships include the following:

■ Management ability and experience of the GP in running other similar programs

■ **Blind pool** or nonspecific program—in a blind pool, less than 75% of the assets are specified as to use; however, in a specified program, more than 75% have been identified

■ Time frame of the partnership

■ Similarity of start-up costs and revenue projections to those of comparable ventures

■ Lack of liquidity of the interest

Partnership interests are not for all investors. Careful consideration must be given to the overall safety and lack of liquidity of these programs before investing.

5. 2. 5   CASH FLOW

Cash flow is defined as net income or loss plus noncash changes (such as depreciation).

EXAMPLE

Revenue	$300,000
– Costs	
Selling	$50,000
Interest	$70,000
Operating	$160,000
Depreciation	$50,000
	$330,000
Net loss	($30,000)

The above shows a loss of $30,000. However, when we add back in depreciation, the cash flow is a positive $20,000.

Net income or loss	($30,000)
+ Depreciation	$50,000
Cash flow	+$20,000

5. 2. 6   BASIS

In a partnership, the term *basis* defines the liability assumed by the LP. An LP can lose no more than his basis, and his basis puts a limit on how much he may deduct on his tax return. This ensures that an LP cannot deduct losses in excess of his basis.

Basis is computed using the following formula:

investment in partnership + share of recourse debt – cash distribution

It is important to note that any up-front costs incurred by the LP will not affect beginning basis. Assume that an LP invests $50,000 in a partnership unit, and the broker-dealer selling the unit takes a commission of $3,000. Therefore, only $47,000 of the LP's investment goes into the partnership. However, the LP's beginning basis is $50,000, not $47,000.

TEST TOPIC ALERT

1. A customer invests $10,000 in a DPP and signs a recourse note for $40,000. During the first year, the investor receives a cash distribution from the partnership in the amount of $5,000. At year-end, he receives a statement showing that his share of partnership losses is $60,000. How much of that $60,000 can he deduct on his tax return?

    Answer: The investor cannot deduct losses in excess of his year-end basis, $45,000, computed as follows:

Investment	$10,000
+ Recourse debt	$40,000
	$50,000
– Cash distributions	$5,000
Year-end basis	$45,000

    Therefore, the customer can deduct $45,000 on her tax return. The remaining $15,000 is carried forward.

TAKE NOTE

If a partnership interest is sold, the gain or loss is the difference between sales proceeds and adjusted basis at the time of sale. If, at the time of sale, the customer has unused losses, these losses may be added to the cost basis. If a customer has an adjusted cost basis of $22,000 and unused losses of $10,000 and sells his partnership interest for $20,000, his loss on the sale would be $12,000.

5. 2. 6. 1   Depreciation Recapture

When a partnership unit is sold, recapture may apply if the partnership has been depreciating its fixed assets using accelerated depreciation. If, at the time of sale, the LP had taken depreciation deductions in excess of what would have been taken had the partnership been using the straight-line method, that difference is subject to ordinary income tax. Clearly, depreciation recapture is not a tax advantage.

QUICK QUIZ 5.B

Objectives:

- Identify the unique tax concepts related to DPP interests
- Compare and contrast the features of various real estate programs, as well as oil and gas programs
- Describe methods of analysis of DPP performance

1. All of the following would generally be associated with an existing real estate DPP EXCEPT

   A. immediate income stream
   B. appreciation potential
   C. known history of income and expenses
   D. lower risk than other types of real estate programs

2. Which of the following limited partnership programs provide potential tax credits to partners?

   A. New construction real estate
   B. Equipment leasing
   C. Developmental oil and gas
   D. Government-assisted housing

3. Which of the following sharing arrangements is the most common?

   A. Net operating profits interest
   B. Carried interest
   C. Functional allocation
   D. Overriding royalty interest

4. Cost basis for an LP is best defined as

   A. cash contributions + recourse debt – distributions
   B. noncash contribution + nonrecourse debt – recourse debt
   C. cash contributions – distributions
   D. recourse debt – cash contributions

All Quick Quiz answers are found at the end of their units.

QUICK QUIZ ANSWERS

Quick Quiz 5.A

1. **C.** DPP stands for direct participation program.

2. **A.** The individual who organizes and registers the partnership is the syndicator.

3. **A.** The certificate creates the partnership's limited nature; until the document is properly filed, the partnership is a general partnership.

4. **C.** Refiling must occur within 30 days.

5. **C.** The agreement is the contract between the partners and contains each entity's rights and duties.

6. **B.** The 2 corporate characteristics that most limited partnerships avoid are continuity of life and free transferability of interest.

7. **C.** Acceptance of an investor as an LP occurs when the GP signs the subscription agreement. The LP receives confirmation of acceptance when the subscription agreement is returned.

8. **D.** The LP's signature on the subscription agreement grants the general partner power of attorney to conduct the partnership's affairs. The subscription agreement for an LP is deemed accepted when the GP signs the subscription agreement.

Quick Quiz 5.B

1. **B.** Appreciation potential is generally not associated with existing real estate programs because most appreciation occurs in the earliest years for real estate assets.

2. **D.** Historic rehabilitation and government-assisted housing are the two programs offering credits to partners. Developmental oil and gas programs offer high IDCs, not ITCs (investment tax credits).

3. **C.** Functional allocation is most commonly used because it gives the best benefits to both parties. The LPs receive the immediate tax write-offs from the IDCs, whereas the GPs receive continued write-offs from the tangible costs over the course of several years. Both share equally in the revenues.

4. **A.** Cost basis for an LP is best defined as cash contributions + recourse debt (debt the LP is responsible for) – distributions. Nonrecourse debt would only be included for real estate programs. These are the only programs where LPs can be responsible for both recourse and nonrecourse debt.

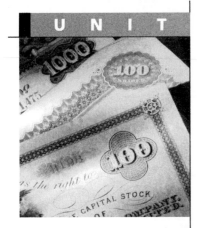

6

Municipal Securities

T he municipal securities Unit is a critical section for success on the Series 7 exam. Learn the language of the municipal industry and pay attention to definitions and industry rules. There are very few calculations in this Unit—the primary emphasis is on knowing the industry. As you review the Unit, remember that basic concepts have been covered in the Securities Industry Essentials (SIE) exam. If you are well-grounded in the basics, proficiency with the more complex concepts will follow.

Municipal securities offer investors a relatively safe means of investing for tax-free income. Because the interest municipal securities pay is not taxable by the federal government, the yield is lower than that of taxable corporate or government bonds. The two primary types of municipal securities are general obligation bonds and revenue bonds.

The Series 7 exam will include 91 questions on the topics covered in units 3, 4, 5, and 6. (Function 3 of the FINRA exam). ∎

In this Unit you will learn to:

■ **differentiate** municipal bonds from government and corporate bonds;

■ **define** the underwriting process and the participants' roles in municipal securities underwriting;

■ **describe** the role of the syndicate and specific rules that apply to the syndicate manager;

■ **identify** documentation associated with a new issue of municipals;

■ **compare** and contrast general obligation (GO) and revenue bonds;

■ **identify** unique features of municipal securities trading;

■ **identify** the role of the MSRB and list significant rules that affect the municipal securities industry;

■ **describe** the tax treatment of municipal securities; and

■ **describe** the tax treatment of municipal securities.

6. 1   MUNICIPAL DEBT CHARACTERISTICS

Municipal bonds are securities issued either by state or local government or by U.S. territories, authorities, and special districts. Investors that buy such bonds are loaning money to the issuers for the purpose of public works and construction projects (e.g., roads, hospitals, civic centers, sewer systems, and airports). Municipal securities are considered second in safety of principal only to U.S. government and U.S. government agency securities. The safety of a particular issue is based on the issuing municipality's financial stability.

Municipal securities are exempt from the filing requirements of the Act of 1933. However, like all other securities, they are subject to the anti-fraud provisions of the **Securities Exchange Act of 1934**.

6. 1. 1   UNIQUE CHARACTERISTICS

We'll begin our discussion of municipal securities with an overview of the characteristics that make them unique among other debt securities.

6. 1. 1. 1   Tax Benefits — *munis) are federally tax exempt*

Purchasers of municipal debt often benefit from favorable tax treatment on the interest payments. The federal government does not generally tax the interest payments. This tax treatment originated from the **doctrine of reciprocal immunity** (**doctrine of mutual reciprocity**), established by a Supreme Court decision in 1895.

The doctrine specifies that a level of government can tax only the interest of its own issues. Interest on municipal securities may be taxed by the municipal level (state and local governments) but not by the federal government. Interest on issues of the federal government (Treasury bills, notes, and bonds) is taxed by the federal government but is exempt from taxation at the state and local levels. Interest on issues of U.S. territories is subject to a triple exemption (federal, state, and local).

TAKE NOTE

Two important municipal tax issues must be clarified.

- The interest on municipal debt is largely exempt from taxation, but not capital gains. Municipal bond investors who buy low and sell high will have capital gains to report.

- Investors who purchase municipal bonds issued by the state in which they live often receive a special tax exemption; they may not be required to pay taxes on interest to the federal *or* state government. For instance, if you live in Los Angeles, California, and buy a State of California municipal bond, the interest will not be subject to taxation on your federal or State of California return. However, if you live in Tempe, Arizona, and buy a California municipal bond, the interest will be exempt from taxation by the federal government but will be taxed by the State of Arizona.

As a result of the tax-advantaged status of municipal bond interest, municipalities generally pay lower interest rates than do corporate issuers. The amount of tax savings experienced by an investor will determine whether a municipal bond is a better investment choice than a corporate bond. Investors should be aware of the tax-equivalent yield when assessing the merits of a municipal bond investment. In general, tax-free municipal securities are more appropriate for investors in high tax brackets and are not suitable for investors in low tax brackets.

6. 1. 1. 2   Issuers

The following three entities are legally entitled to issue municipal debt securities:

■ Territorial possessions of the United States (U.S. Virgin Islands, Puerto Rico, and Guam)
■ State governments
■ Legally constituted taxing authorities (county and city governments, agencies created by these governments, and authorities that supervise ports and mass transit systems, such as port authorities and special districts)

6. 1. 1. 3   Maturity Structures

Municipal notes and bonds are issued with maturities that range from less than 1 year to more than 30 years. There are three types of maturity schedules common to municipal and corporate debt issues.

6. 1. 1. 3. 1   Term Maturity

All principal matures at a single date in the future.

EXAMPLE

Consider the following municipal bond issue:
$200 million Illinois GO 5% debentures due November 1, 2016.

Some issuers establish a **sinking fund account** to accumulate funds to pay off term bonds at or before the established maturity date. Term bonds are quoted by price (like corporate bonds) and are called **dollar bonds**.

6. 1. 1. 3. 2   Serial Maturity

Bonds within an issue mature on different dates according to a predetermined schedule. The sample serial maturity structure table below shows an example of a $100 million State of Illinois GO serial issue.

Sample Serial Maturity Structure

Amount	Coupon	Maturity	Price/Yield
$10,000,000	6%	11-1-14	5.80%
$10,000,000	6%	11-1-15	5.90%
$10,000,000	6%	11-1-16	100%
$10,000,000	6%	11-1-17	6.10%
$20,000,000	6%	11-1-18	6.20%
$20,000,000	6%	11-1-19	6.30%
$20,000,000	6%	11-1-20	6.40%

Serial bonds are quoted on the basis of their yield to maturity, called basis, to reflect the difference of maturity dates within one issue. A price/yield of 100% indicates the yield to maturity is equal to the coupon rate, which means the bond is being offered at par.

6. 1. 1. 3. 3   Balloon Maturity

An issuer pays part of a bond's maturity before the final maturity date, but the largest portion is paid off at maturity. The sample balloon maturity table below shows an example of a $100 million State of Illinois GO balloon maturity issue due November 1, 2017.

Sample Balloon Maturity

Amount	Coupon	Maturity	Price/Yield
$10,000,000	6%	11-1-14	5.80%
$10,000,000	6%	11-1-15	5.90%
$10,000,000	6%	11-1-16	100%
$70,000,000	6%	11-1-17	6.10%

TAKE NOTE   A balloon maturity is a type of serial maturity. Also note that most municipal bonds are issued serially.

6. 1. 2   TYPES OF MUNICIPAL ISSUES

The basis of the content included in the following sections is found in the Securities Industry Essentials Exam (SIE). That content is expanded and built upon here. Please review the Kaplan SIE content as needed.

Two categories of municipal securities exist: general obligation bonds (GOs), which are backed by the full faith, credit, and taxing powers of the municipality, and revenue bonds, which are backed by the revenues generated by the municipal facility the bond issue finances.

6. 1. 2. 1   General Obligation Issues (GOs)

General obligation bonds (GOs) are municipal bonds issued for capital improvements that benefit the entire community. Typically, these projects do not produce revenues, so principal and interest must be paid by taxes collected by the municipal issuer. Because of this backing, GOs are known as **full faith and credit issues**.

6. 1. 2. 1. 1   Sources of Funds

GOs are backed by the issuing municipality's taxing power. Bonds issued by states are backed by income taxes, license fees, and sales taxes. Bonds issued by towns, cities, and counties are backed by property (**ad valorem**) taxes, license fees, fines, and all other sources of revenue to the municipality. School, road, and park districts may also issue municipal bonds backed by property taxes.

6. 1. 2. 1. 2 *Statutory Debt Limits*

The amount of debt that a municipal government may incur can be limited by state or local statutes to protect taxpayers from excessive taxes. Debt limits can also make a bond safer for investors. The lower the debt limit, the less risk of excessive borrowing and default by the municipality.

If a municipality wishes to issue GO bonds that would put it above its statutory limit, a public referendum is required. Voter approval on the referendum must follow.

Tax Limits. Some states limit property taxes to a certain percentage of the assessed property value or to a certain percentage increase in any single year. The tax rate is expressed in mills; one mill equals $1 per $1,000, or $.001.

Limited Tax GO. A limited tax GO is a bond secured by a specific tax (e.g., income tax). In other words, the issuer is limited as to what tax or taxes can be used to service the debt. As a result, there is more risk with a limited tax GO than with a comparable GO backed by the full taxing authority of the issuer.

Overlapping Debt. Several taxing authorities that draw from the same taxpayers can issue debt. Bonds issued by different municipal authorities that tap the same taxpayer wallets are known as **coterminous debt**.

TEST TOPIC ALERT

In the context of municipal securities, the term coterminous refers to two or more taxing agencies that share the same geographic boundaries and are able to issue debt separately. Overlapping debt occurs when two or more issuers are taxing the same property to service their respective debt.

EXAMPLE

Take the town of Smithville, located in Jones County. If Smithville issues GO debt, it will tax property in Smithville to service that debt. If Jones County issues GO debt, it will tax property in the county, which includes Smithville, to service its debt. As a result, there are two issuers taxing the same property.

TAKE NOTE

Coterminous debt only occurs in property taxing situations. Because states do not generally tax real estate, state debt never overlaps.

Double-Barreled Bonds. **Double-barreled bonds** are revenue bonds that have characteristics of GO bonds. Interest and principal are paid from a specified facility's earnings. However, the bonds are also backed by the taxing power of the state or municipality and therefore have the backing of two sources of revenue. Although they are backed primarily by revenues from the facility, double-barreled bonds are rated and traded as GOs.

TEST TOPIC ALERT

You might see questions on GOs similar to the following.

1. Which of the following is NOT included in the definition of coterminous debt?
   A. County
   B. City
   C. School district
   D. State

Answer: D. Coterminous, or overlapping, debt occurs when property taxes from one property are used in support of debt issued by various municipal issuers. For instance, property taxes on a home might support county, city, and school district debt obligations. Property taxes are not assessed by states, so states are not included in the definition of coterminous or overlapping debt.

2. All of the following are used to pay debt service on GOs EXCEPT
   A. sales taxes
   B. license fees
   C. tolls
   D. ad valorem taxes

Answer: C. Generally, associate GOs with taxes. There will be some exceptions, but GOs are predominately backed by tax collections.

6. 1. 2. 2   Revenue Bonds

Revenue bonds can be used to finance any municipal facility that generates sufficient income. Revenue bonds are not subject to statutory debt limits and do not require voter approval. A particular revenue bond issue, however, may be subject to an additional bonds test before subsequent bond issues with equal liens on the project's revenue may be issued. The additional bonds test ensures the adequacy of the revenue stream to pay both the old and new debt.

6. 1. 2. 2. 1   Feasibility Study

Before issuing a revenue bond, an issuer will engage various consultants to prepare a report detailing the economic feasibility and the need for a particular project (e.g., a new bridge or airport). The study will include estimates of revenues that will be generated and details of the operating, economic, and engineering aspects of the proposed project.

6. 1. 2. 2. 2   Sources of Revenue

Revenue bonds' interest and principal payments are payable to bondholders only from the specific earnings and net lease payments of revenue-producing facilities, such as:

- utilities (water, sewer, and electric);
- housing;
- transportation (airports and toll roads);
- education (college dorms and student loans);
- health (hospitals and retirement centers);

■ industrial (industrial development and pollution control); and

■ sports.

Debt service payments do not come from general or real estate taxes and are not backed by the municipality's full faith and credit. Revenue bonds are considered self-supporting debt because principal and interest payments are made exclusively from revenues generated by the project for which the debt was issued.

6. 1. 2. 2. 3   Protective Covenants

The face of a revenue bond certificate may refer to a **trust indenture** (or **bond resolution**). This empowers the trustee to act on behalf of the bondholders.

In the trust indenture, the municipality agrees to abide by certain protective covenants, or promises, meant to protect bondholders. A trustee appointed in the indenture supervises the issuer's compliance with the bond covenants.

6. 1. 2. 2. 4   Bond Covenants

The trust indenture's provisions may vary, but a number of standard provisions are common to most bond issues, including the following:

■ **Rate covenant**—a promise to maintain rates sufficient to pay expenses and debt service

■ **Maintenance covenant**—a promise to maintain the equipment and facility(ies)

■ **Insurance covenant**—a promise to insure any facility built so bondholders can be paid off if the facility is destroyed or becomes inoperable

■ **Additional bonds test**—whether the indenture is **open-ended** (allowing further issuance of bonds with the same status and equal claims on assets or revenues if permitted under the provisions of the bond indenture) or **closed-ended** (allowing no further issuance of bonds with an equivalent lien on assets or revenues); with a closed-end provision, any additional bonds issued will be subordinated to the original issue unless the funds are specifically required to complete construction of the facility

■ **Sinking fund**—money to pay off interest and principal obligations

■ **Catastrophe clause**—a promise to use insurance proceeds to call bonds and repay bondholders if a facility is destroyed; a catastrophe call is also called a calamity call or an extraordinary mandatory call

■ **Flow of funds**—the priority of disbursing the revenues collected

■ **Books and records covenant**—requires outside audit of records and financial reports

■ **Call features**

[handwritten margin note: make bond issue more marketable and attractive to investors]

TAKE NOTE   Trust indentures are not required for municipal bonds by the Trust Indenture Act of 1939. Municipal issues are exempt from this act. The use of trust indentures is optional, but it greatly enhances the marketability of revenue issues. Revenue bonds have either a trust resolution or trust indentures, whereas GOs commonly have a bond resolution.

6. 1. 2. 2. 5 *Types of Revenue Bonds*

There are a number of categories of revenue bonds, depending on the type of facility the bond issue finances.

Industrial Development Revenue Bonds. A municipal development authority issues **industrial development revenue bonds** (**IDRs** or **IDBs**) to construct facilities or purchase equipment, which is then leased to a corporation. The municipality uses the money from lease payments to pay the principal and interest on the bonds. The ultimate responsibility for the payment of principal and interest rests with the corporation leasing the facility; therefore, the bonds carry the corporation's debt rating.

Technically, industrial revenue bonds are issued for a corporation's benefit. Under the **Tax Reform Act of 1986**, the interest on these nonpublic purpose bonds (or **private purpose** bonds) may be taxable because the act reserves tax exemption for public purposes. Because these bonds are used for a nonpublic purpose, the interest income may be subject to the **alternative minimum tax (AMT)**.

Congress enacted the alternative minimum tax (AMT) to make certain that high-income taxpayers do not escape paying taxes. Certain items receive favorable tax treatment. These items must be added back into taxable income for the AMT. These **tax preference items** include:

- accelerated depreciation on investment property;
- certain costs associated with DPPs, such as research and development costs and intangible drilling costs;
- local tax and interest on investments that do not generate income;
- tax-exempt interest on private purpose, nonessential government service municipal bonds; and
- incentive stock options exceeding their fair market value.

TAKE NOTE   The Internal Revenue Code (IRC) language says that taxpayers are required to add the excess of the AMT over the regular tax to their regular tax to determine their total tax liability.

Lease-Rental Bonds. Under a typical lease-rental (or lease-back) bond arrangement, a municipality issues bonds to finance office construction for itself or its state or community.

EXAMPLE   An example of a lease-back arrangement follows.

A municipality might issue bonds to raise money to construct a school and lease the finished building to the school district. The lease payments provide backing for the bonds.

Lease payments come from funds raised through special taxes or appropriations, from the lessor's revenues, such as the school's tuition or fees, or from the municipality's general fund.

Certificates of Participation (COPs). These are a form of lease revenue bond that permits the investor to participate in a stream of revenue from lease, installment, or loan payments related to the acquisition of land or the acquisition or construction of specific equipment or facilities by the municipality. Like other revenue issues, they require no voter approval. COPs are not viewed legally as debt of a municipality because payment is tied to an annual appropriation that is made by the government body. One unique feature with these certificates, though this would be a rare occurrence, is that in theory the certificate holders themselves can foreclose on the equipment or the facility that the certificates financed in the event of default.

Special Tax Bonds. These are bonds secured by one or more designated taxes other than ad valorem (property) taxes. For example, bonds for a particular purpose might be supported by sales, tobacco, fuel, or business license taxes. However, the designated tax does not have to be directly related to the project purpose. Such bonds are not considered self-supporting debt.

Special Assessment Bonds (or Special District Bonds). Special assessment bonds are issued to finance the construction of public improvements such as streets, sidewalks, or sewers. The issuer assesses a tax only on the property that benefits from the improvement and uses the funds to pay principal and interest.

New Housing Authority Bonds. Local housing authorities issue **New Housing Authority bonds (NHAs)** to develop and improve low-income housing. NHAs are backed by the full faith and credit of the U.S. government. NHAs are sometimes called **Public Housing Authority bonds (PHAs)**. Because of their federal backing, they are considered the most secure of all municipal bonds. PHAs are backed by the rental income from the housing. If the rental income is not sufficient to service the debt, the federal government makes up any shortfall. Note that these bonds are not considered to be double-barreled. To be **double-barreled**, a bond must be backed by more than one municipal revenue source. In this case, the second backing is the federal government.

TEST TOPIC ALERT   PHAs (or NHAs) are the only municipal issues backed in full by the U.S. government. They are also called **Section 8** bonds.

Moral Obligation Bonds. A **moral obligation** bond is a state- or local-issued, or state- or local agency–issued, bond. If revenues or tax collections backing the bond are not sufficient to pay the debt service, the state legislature has the authority to appropriate funds to make payments. The potential backing by state revenues tends to make the bond more marketable, but the state's obligation is not established by law; it is a moral obligation only.

TAKE NOTE   Moral obligation bonds are revenue bonds only. For instance, a state may take on the moral obligation to service debt on city-issued GO bonds when the city has surpassed its statutory debt limit. This situation occurred in New York City's financial crisis of 1975. Typically, moral obligation bonds are issued in times of financial distress and have increased credit risk.

6. 1. 2. 2. 6   *Issuer Default*

If a GO bond goes into default, bondholders have the right to sue to compel a tax levy to pay off the bonds. If a moral obligation bond goes into default, the only way bondholders can be repaid is through **legislative apportionment**. The issuer's legislature would have to apportion money to satisfy the debt but is not legally obligated to do so. Remember, the issuer has a moral but not legal obligation to service the debt.

TEST TOPIC ALERT

Be ready for five to seven questions that require you to differentiate between the features of GOs and revenue bonds. If you are not confident about the basic features of these instruments, review before continuing. It is important to be extremely familiar with these basics.

Following are typical questions on revenue bonds.

1. Which of the following is backed by the full faith and credit of the U.S. government?

   A. Moral obligation bonds
   B. PHAs
   C. IDRs
   D. Special tax bonds

   Answer: B. PHAs or NHAs are issued to construct, maintain, and improve low-income housing. The U.S. government guarantees the rent on these properties, and they are considered the most secure of all municipal revenue bonds.

2. All of the following are used to provide debt service for revenue bonds EXCEPT

   A. excise taxes
   B. business license taxes
   C. ad valorem taxes
   D. alcohol taxes

   Answer: C. Property taxes, or ad valorem taxes, are associated with GOs. Special taxes are used to back revenue bonds. Examples include hotel, tobacco, liquor, and gasoline taxes. These are the exceptions to the rule that taxes should be associated with GO issues.

6. 1. 2. 3   Municipal Notes

Municipal anticipation notes are short-term securities that generate funds for a municipality that expects other revenues soon. Usually, municipal notes have less than 12-month maturities, although maturities may range from three months to three years. They are repaid when the municipality receives the anticipated funds. Municipal notes fall into several categories.

■ Municipalities issue **tax anticipation notes (TANs)** to finance current operations in anticipation of future tax receipts. This helps municipalities to even out cash flow between tax collection periods.

■ **Revenue anticipation notes (RANs)** are offered periodically to finance current operations in anticipation of future revenues from revenue-producing projects or facilities.

■ **Tax and revenue anticipation notes (TRANs)** are a combination of the characteristics of both TANs and RANs.

- **Bond anticipation notes (BANs)** are sold as interim financing that will eventually be converted to long-term funding through a sale of bonds.
- **Tax-exempt commercial paper** is often used in place of BANs and TANs for up to 270 days, though maturities are most often 30, 60, and 90 days.
- **Construction loan notes (CLNs)** are issued to provide interim financing for the construction of housing projects.
- **Variable-rate demand notes** have a fluctuating interest rate and are usually issued with a put option.
- **Grant anticipation notes (GANs)** are issued with the expectation of receiving grant money from the federal government.

6. 1. 2. 4   Variable-Rate Municipals (Variable-Rate Demand Obligations, VRDOs)

Some municipal bonds and notes are issued with **variable**, or **floating**, rates of interest. A **variable-rate municipal bond** offers interest payments tied to the movements of another specified interest rate, much like an adjustable-rate mortgage. Because the coupon rate of the bond changes with the market, the price of these bonds remains relatively stable.

TAKE NOTE   Variable-rate municipal bonds are sometimes called **reset bonds**. Their price remains near par at all times because their coupon is usually reset to the market rate of interest every six months.

6. 1. 2. 4. 1   Auction Rate Securities (ARS)

Typically issued by municipalities, nonprofit hospitals, utilities, housing finance agencies and universities, auction rate securities (ARS) are long-term, variable-rate bonds tied to short-term interest rates. With long-term maturities of 20 to 30 years, the interest rates are determined using a Dutch auction method at predetermined short-term intervals, typically 7, 28, or 35 days. This type of auction uses a competitive bid process where the lowest bid rate at which all of the bonds can be sold at par is used to establish the new or "reset" rate. This reset rate is referred to as the "clearing rate." Any customers that bid above the clearing rate receive no bonds and those that bid at or below the clearing rate receive the bonds at that rate. Interest paid in the current period is based on the interest rate reset in the prior auction.

Failed auctions are a hazard associated with ARSs. A failed auction can result from a lack of demand which means that there are no bids received to reset the rate. To help ensure the success of an auction, underwriting broker-dealers can submit a clearing rate bid but are not required to do so. This may change in the future as a result of numerous litigations. The failed auctions usually result in downgrades in the credit ratings of the securities and their issuers.

These securities trade at par and are callable at par on any interest payment date at the discretion of the issuer. They do not carry put features.

TAKE NOTE   Dealers for ARS or variable-rate demand obligations (VRDOs) are required to submit basic information to the MSRB through its Short-term Obligation Rate Transparency (SHORT) System about each auction remarketing, including the interest rate set for the next period.

6. 1. 2. 5   State and Local Government Securities Series (SLGS)

Bonds are often prefunded well before a call date if interest rates have fallen. With regard to municipal bonds, in order to comply with the complex arbitrage restrictions imposed by the IRS, the proceeds of a municipal prefunding are placed in an escrow account that immediately invests in **state and local government securities series** (SLGS). These are U.S. government securities issued directly by the Treasury to municipal issuers only in connection with prefundings.

6. 1. 2. 6   Build America Bonds (BABs)

Build America Bonds (BABs) were created under the Economic Recovery and Reinvestment Act of 2009 to assist in reducing costs to issuing municipalities and stimulating the economy. While bonds to fund municipal projects have traditionally been sold in the tax-exempt arena, BABs are taxable obligations. Bondholders pay tax on interest received from BABs, but tax credits are provided in lieu of the tax-exempt status usually afforded the interest on municipal securities. These bonds attracted investors who would normally not buy tax-exempt municipal bonds and expanded the pool of investors to include those in lower income tax brackets, investors funding retirement accounts where tax-free securities would normally not be suitable, public pension funds, and foreign investors. There are two types of Build America Bonds issued: tax credit BABs and direct payment BABs.

6. 1. 2. 6. 1   Tax Credit BABs

These types of BABs provide the bondholder with a federal income tax credit equal to 35% of the interest paid on the bond in each tax year. If the bondholder lacks sufficient tax liability to fully use that year's credit, the excess credit may be carried forward.

6. 1. 2. 6. 2   Direct Payment BABs

Direct payment BABs provide no credit to the bondholder but instead provide the municipal issuer with payments from the U.S. Treasury equal to 35% of the interest paid by the issuer.

TAKE NOTE   The BABs program expired on December 31, 2010, without being renewed. However, in the short time that municipalities were permitted to issue BABs, billions of dollars of capital had been raised to fund municipal projects throughout the United States, and many of these issues will remain outstanding for a number of years. Finally, it should be noted that the program could be reinstated at some time in the future, and the types of BABs offered and the credits they provide could be amended as well.

6. 1. 2. 7   Local Government Investment Pools (LGIPs)

States establish local government investment pools (LGIPs) to provide other government entities, such as cities, counties, school districts, or other state agencies, with a short-term investment vehicle to invest funds. The LGIPs are generally formed as a trust in which municipalities can purchase shares or units in the LGIP's investment portfolio.

While not a money market fund, most LGIPs operate similar to one. For instance, an LGIP may be permitted to maintain a fixed $1.00 net asset value (NAV). Maintaining a stable NAV, similar to a money market mutual fund, facilitates liquidity and minimum price volatility.

LGIPs are not required to register with the SEC and are not subject to the SEC's regulatory requirements, given that LGIPs fall within the governmental exemption, just as municipal securities do. Therefore, investment guidelines and oversight for LGIPs can vary from state to state.

With no SEC registration required, there is no prospectus. However, LGIP programs do have disclosure documents, which generally include information statements, and investment policy and operating procedures. The information statement typically details the management fees associated with participation in the LGIP.

6. 1. 2. 8   Achieving a Better Life Experience (ABLE) Accounts

ABLE accounts are tax-advantaged savings accounts for individuals with disabilities and their families. They were created as a result of the passage of the Achieving a Better Life Experience Act of 2014. The beneficiary of the account is the account owner, and income earned by the accounts is not taxed.

The ABLE Act limits eligibility to individuals with significant disabilities where the age of onset of the disability occurred before turning age 26. In this light, remember that one need not be under the age of 26 to be eligible to establish an ABLE account. One could be over the age of 26, but as long as the onset of the disability occurred before age 26, they are eligible to establish an ABLE account.

If an individual meets the age/onset criteria and is also receiving benefits either through Social Security insurance (SSI) and/or Social Security disability insurance (SSDI), they are automatically eligible to establish an ABLE account. Only one ABLE account per person is allowed.

Contributions to these accounts, which can be made by any person including the account beneficiary themselves, as well as family and friends, must be made using after-tax dollars and is not tax deductible for purposes of federal income taxes. Some states, however, do allow income tax deductions for contributions made to an ABLE account. Contributions by all participating individuals are limited to a specified dollar amount per year, which may be adjusted periodically to account for inflation.

6. 1. 3   MUNICIPAL SECURITY DOCUMENTS

6. 1. 3. 1   Bond Contract

A municipal issuer enters into a **bond contract** with the underwriters of, and prospective investors in, its securities. The bond contract is a collection of legal documents that includes the bond resolution or trust indenture, any applicable state and federal law documents, and other legal documents pertaining to that particular issue and issuer. By issuing its securities, the issuer has agreed to abide by the terms and covenants in the documents that compose the bond contract.

6. 1. 3. 2   Authorizing Resolution

The municipality authorizes the issue and sale of its securities through the **bond resolution**. The authorizing resolution contains a description of the issue.

6. 1. 3. 3   Bond Resolution Indenture

On the face of most municipal revenue bond certificates is a reference to the bonds' **underlying trust indenture**, also known as a **protective covenant**. Although it is not required by law, most municipal issuers use indentures to make the issue more marketable. The indenture serves as a contract between the bond's issuer and a trustee appointed on behalf of the bond's investors.

Normally, the indenture includes a **flow of funds statement** establishing the priority of payments made from a facility's revenues. The indenture is too long to supply to all bondholders, although the issuer must make a complete copy available upon request. The official statement outlines the indenture's covenants.

6. 1. 3. 4   Official Statement (OS)

The **official statement**, which must be signed by an officer of the issuer, is the municipal securities industry's equivalent of the corporate prospectus. The OS serves as a disclosure document and contains any material information an investor might need about an issue. Prepared by the issuer, the OS identifies the issue's purpose, the source from which the interest and principal will be repaid, and the issuer's and community's financial and economic backgrounds. The OS also has information relating to the issue's creditworthiness.

A typical OS includes:

- the offering terms;
- the summary statement;
- the purpose of issue;
- the authorization of bonds;
- the security of bonds;
- a description of bonds;
- a description of issuer, including organization and management, area economy, and a financial summary;
- the construction program;
- the project feasibility statement;
- any regulatory matters;
- any specific provisions of the indenture or resolution, including funds and accounts, investment of funds, additional bonds, insurance, and events of default;
- any accompanying legal proceedings;
- the tax status;

■   any appropriate appendices, including consultant reports, the legal opinion, and financial statements; and

■   any credit enhancements.

6. 1. 3. 4. 1   Preliminary Official Statement

Municipal issuers may also prepare preliminary OS. The **preliminary official statement** discloses most of the same material information as the OS, with the exception of the issue's interest rate(s) and offering price(s). Underwriters use a preliminary OS to determine investors' and dealers' interest in the issue.

Any municipal securities dealer involved in the sale of a new issue must deliver a final OS to every customer who has purchased the issue, at or before settlement date (T + 2).

6. 1. 3. 5   Legal Opinion

Printed on the face of every bond certificate (unless the bond is specifically stamped *Ex-Legal*) is a legal opinion written and signed by the **bond counsel**, an attorney specializing in tax-exempt bond offerings. The legal opinion states that the issue is legally binding on the issuer and conforms to applicable laws. If interest from the bond is tax exempt, that too is stated in the legal opinion.

The legal opinion is issued either as a **qualified opinion** (there may be a legal uncertainty of which purchasers should be informed) or as an **unqualified opinion** (issued by the bond counsel unconditionally).

Some issuers, normally smaller municipalities, choose not to obtain a legal opinion. In such a case, the bond certificate must clearly state that the bonds are **ex-legal**. The ex-legal designation allows a bond to meet good delivery requirements without an attached legal opinion.

6. 1. 3. 5. 1   The Underwriter's Counsel

The managing underwriter may choose to employ another law firm as underwriter's counsel. This firm is not responsible for the legal opinion and is employed to represent the underwriter's interests.

TAKE NOTE

Issuers desire an unqualified legal opinion.

QUICK QUIZ 6.A

Objective: Differentiate municipal bonds from government and corporate bonds

1.   The main advantage of a variable-rate municipal bond investment is that

   A.   the bond is likely to increase in value
   B.   the bond's price should remain relatively stable
   C.   the bond is noncallable
   D.   the bond's interest is exempt from all taxes

2. If a municipality wants to even out its cash flow, it is most likely to issue which of the following securities?

    A. TANs
    B. BANs
    C. RANs
    D. CLNs

3. All of the following are true of a municipality's debt limit EXCEPT

    A. the purpose of debt restriction is to protect taxpayers from excessive taxes
    B. revenue bonds are not affected by statutory limitations
    C. the debt limit is the maximum amount a municipality can redeem in a year
    D. a public referendum is required if an issuer wishes to issue GO debt that would put the issuer above its statutory debt limit

4. All of the following are TRUE of auction rate securities EXCEPT

    A. maturities can vary but are generally long term
    B. they are tied to long-term interest rates
    C. interest rates are reset at predetermined intervals
    D. if no bids are received to reset rates, the auction is considered "failed"

5. Your customer, a resident of Minnesota, is in the 28% federal tax bracket and the 14% state tax bracket. She must pay both federal and state taxes on which of the following investments?

    A. Minneapolis Housing Authority bonds
    B. Series HH bonds
    C. Ginnie Mae pass-throughs
    D. Treasury bills

6. Which of the following is an accurate statement regarding Build America Bonds?

    A. All Build America Bonds pay tax credits to the issuer.
    B. Build America Bonds are issued by both corporate and municipal issuers.
    C. All Build America Bonds offer tax credits to the bondholder.
    D. Interest payments received from Build America Bonds are taxable to bondholders.

All Quick Quiz answers are found at the end of their units.

6. 2   ISSUING MUNICIPAL SECURITIES

A uniform sequence of events leads to a new municipal issue. The issuer must first obtain a **legal opinion**, which determines whether and how the bonds may be offered. Then, the terms of the municipal bond offering may be set by either **negotiation** or **competitive bidding**.

6. 2. 1   NEGOTIATED UNDERWRITING

In a **negotiated underwriting**, the municipality appoints an investment banker to underwrite the offering. The underwriter works with the issuer to establish the interest rate and the offering price in light of the issuer's financial needs and market conditions.

Negotiated underwritten issues can be distributed as either a public offering or via a private placement.

Investment banks or bankers are financial institutions that assist corporations and municipal governments in raising capital by underwriting new securities and/or acting as the issuer's agent in the issuance of securities. Unlike traditional banks, investment banks do not take deposits or issue loans.

6. 2. 2   COMPETITIVE BIDDING

With competitive bid underwritings, a municipality publishes an invitation to bid. Investment bankers respond in writing to the issuer's attorney or other designated official requesting information on the offering. The bid representing the lowest net interest cost to the issuer is the winner in a competitive bid.

6. 2. 2. 1   Official Notice of Sale

The notice of bond sale to solicit bids for the bonds is usually published in *The Bond Buyer* and local newspapers and includes:

- date, time, and place of sale;
- name and description of issuer;
- type of bond;
- bidding restrictions (usually requiring a sealed bid);
- interest payment dates;
- dated date (interest accrual date) and first coupon payment date;
- maturity structure;
- call provisions (if any);
- denominations and registration provisions;
- expenses to be borne by purchaser or issuer;
- amount of good-faith deposit that must accompany bid;
- paying agent or trustee;
- name of the firm (the **bond counsel**) providing the legal opinion;
- details of delivery;
- issuer's right of rejection of all bids;
- criteria for awarding the issue; and
- issuer's obligation to prepare the final OS and deliver copies to the successful bidder.

The bond's rating and the underwriter's name are not included in a notice of sale because they have yet to be determined.

Investment bankers prepare bids for the securities based on information in the notice of sale, comparable new issue supply and demand, and general market conditions.

All new municipal debt is issued in fully registered form or in book-entry form.

6. 2. 3   SOURCES OF MUNICIPAL SECURITIES INFORMATION

A number of publications and services offer information on proposed new issues and secondary-market activity for municipal issues. These include *The Bond Buyer* and *Thomson Muni News*, which publish the *Thomson Muni Market Monitor* (formerly known as *Munifacts*).

6. 2. 3. 1   The Bond Buyer

The Bond Buyer is published every business day and serves as an authoritative source of information on primary market municipal bonds. The Bond Buyer publishes the **30-day visible supply** (the total dollar volume of municipal offering, not including short-term notes, expected to reach the market in the next 30 days) and the **placement, or acceptance, ratio indexes** (the percentage of the total dollar value of new issues sold versus the total dollar value of new issues offered for sale the prior week).

If the visible supply is exceptionally large, interest rates are likely to rise to attract investors to the larger number of bonds available. A small visible supply is an indication that interest rates are likely to fall.

If the placement ratio is high, the market for municipal bonds is strong. If it is low, dealers will be likely to exhibit concern about bidding on new issues. A placement ratio of 90% means that market has absorbed 90% of the dollar volume of bonds issued for the week, with 10% left in the dealer's inventory.

The Bond Buyer also compiles the 40 Bond Index, 20 Bond Index, 11 Bond Index, and the Revdex 25.

Bond Buyer Compiled Indexes

40 Bond Index

Daily price index of 40 GO and revenue bonds with an average maturity of 20 years. A rise in the index indicates bond prices are rising and yields are falling.

20 Bond Index

Weekly index of 20 GO bonds with 20 years to maturity, rated A or better.

11 Bond Index

Weekly index of 11 of the 20 bonds from the 20 Bond Index, rated AA or better.

Revdex 25

Weekly index of 25 revenue bonds with 30 years to maturity, rated A or better.

The yields on the Revdex are always higher than the yields on the GO 20 Bond Index because revenue bonds have higher risk. The yields on the 11 Bond Index are lower than the yields on the 20 Bond Index because the 11 Bond Index is more highly rated.

6. 2. 3. 2 *Thomson Muni Market Monitor* (Formerly *Munifacts*)

Thomson has been offering wire services, such as *Thomson Muni News* and the *Thomson Muni Market Monitor* (formerly *Munifacts*), used by numerous municipal dealers for many years. Current news items pertaining to the secondary municipals market appear in these wire services throughout the day along with current municipal offerings. Comparatively, these wire services should be considered a source for bonds already trading in the municipal secondary markets, while the *Daily Bond Buyer* is a source for new issue municipal bonds (primary market).

Test your knowledge of information sources on the municipal bond market.

1. Which municipal publication includes the 30-day visible supply index?

2. Which municipal publication provides the most up-to-the-minute information relevant to the secondary municipal bond market?

Answers: 1. *The Bond Buyer*; 2. *Thomson Muni Market Monitor*

6. 2. 3. 3 Real-Time Transaction Reporting System (RTRS)

Up-to-the-minute pricing information regarding eligible municipal bond transactions is made available through an approved portal such as the National Securities Clearing Corporation (NSCC). The data is captured and made available to the marketplace within 15 minutes of a trade by the MSRB's Real-Time Transaction Reporting System (RTRS).

6. 2. 4 FORMATION OF THE UNDERWRITING SYNDICATE

Once an issuer's notice of sale has circulated, those investment bankers interested in placing competitive bids for an issue form **syndicates**. A syndicate is an account that helps spread the risk of underwriting an issue among a number of underwriters. Although the bidding process is competitive, successive offerings of a particular municipality are often handled by the same syndicate, which is composed of the same members.

To acquire relevant details about a new issue, the syndicate manager typically orders the New Issue Worksheet from *The Bond Buyer*. This worksheet provides, in an organized format, all information presented in the official notice of sale. It shows a schedule of year-by-year maturities and their corresponding dollar amounts and a computation of bond years. Bond years are the number of $1,000 bonds of a maturity multiplied by the number of years the bonds are outstanding. This computation is used to calculate the average life of an issue and its total interest cost.

**Sample Computation of Bond Years and Average Life
of a $3.5 Million Issue Dated 9/1/00**

Maturity	Years to Maturity	Number of Bonds	Bond Years
9/1/10	10	1,000	10,000
9/1/11	11	1,000	11,000
9/1/12	12	1,000	12,000
9/1/13	13	500	6,500
		Total 3,500	Total 39,500

$$\text{average life} = \frac{\text{total bond years}}{\text{total number of bonds}} = \frac{39,500}{3,500} = 11.286 \text{ years}$$

A firm makes the decision to participate as a syndicate member after it considers the:

- potential demand for the security;
- existence of presale orders;
- determination and extent of liability;
- scale and spread; and
- ability to sell the issue.

Participants formalize their relationship by signing a **syndicate letter.** or **syndicate agreement,** in a competitive bid or a **syndicate contract,** or **agreement among underwriters,** in a negotiated underwriting. About two weeks before the issue is awarded, the syndicate manager sends the syndicate letter or contract to each participating firm for an authorized signature. The member's signature indicates that the member agrees with the offering terms. Syndicate letters include:

- each member firm's level of participation or commitment;
- priority of order allocation;
- duration of the syndicate account;
- appointment of the manager(s) as agent(s) for the account;
- fee for the managing underwriter and breakdown of the spread; and
- other obligations, such as member expenses, good-faith deposits, observance of offering terms, and liability for unsold bonds.

TAKE NOTE   Syndicate letters are not legally binding until the syndicate's submission of the bid. Firms may drop from the group until this point.

6. 2. 4. 1   Types of Syndicate Accounts

The financial liability to which each underwriter is exposed depends on the type of syndicate account. Underwriting syndicates use two arrangements: accounts and Eastern accounts.

6. 2. 4. 1. 1   Western Account

The **Western account** is a divided account. Each underwriter is responsible only for its own underwriting allocation.

6. 2. 4. 1. 2   Eastern Account

An **Eastern account** is an **undivided** account. Each underwriter is allocated a portion of the issue. After the issue has been substantially distributed, each underwriter is allocated additional bonds representing its proportionate share of any unsold bonds. Thus, an underwriter's financial liability might not end when it has distributed its initial allocation.

TAKE NOTE

When remembering the difference between Western and Eastern, divided and undivided accounts, try this phrase: "The continental *divide* is in the *West*." It helps remind you that Western accounts and divided accounts are the same, as are Eastern and undivided.

EXAMPLE

A syndicate is underwriting a $5 million municipal bond issue. There are five syndicate members, each with equal participation, including your firm. Your firm sells its entire allocation, but bonds worth $1 million remain unsold by the other syndicate members.

If this is a Western account, what is your firm's liability?

In a Western account, your firm would have no remaining liability because its entire share was sold. However, if your firm had sold only $700,000 of its $1 million allocation, it would have to purchase the remaining $300,000 for its own inventory.

If this is an Eastern account, what is your firm's liability?

In an Eastern account, the unsold amount is divided among all syndicate members based on their initial participation. In this example, your firm would be allocated 20% of the remaining amount, or $200,000. The responsibility for any unsold bonds continues until the entire bond issue is sold.

6. 2. 4. 2   Due Diligence

Municipal underwriters must investigate an issuer's financing proposals thoroughly. With revenue bonds, this due diligence investigation is conducted through a feasibility study, which focuses on the projected revenues and costs associated with the project and an analysis of competing facilities.

6. 2. 5   THE SYNDICATE BID

A syndicate will present a bid to the issuer in order to win the right to represent the new issue in the primary market. If a syndicate wins the bid they will be selling the bonds to the public in the initial primary offering (IPO).

6. 2. 5. 1   Establishing the Bid

The syndicate arrives at its competitive bid over a series of meetings during which member dealers discuss the proposed reoffering scale and spread for the underwriters. Their goal is to arrive at the best price to the issuer while still making a profit. At a preliminary meeting, the manager seeks tentative agreement from members on the prices or yields of all maturities in the issue as well as the gross profit or underwriting spread.

A final bid price for the bond is set at a meeting conducted just before the bid is due. If the member dealers cannot all agree on a final bid, the syndicate can go ahead with its bid as long as the syndicate members agree to abide by the majority's decision.

T A K E   N O T E   To win the bid, the syndicate must resolve this question: What is the lowest interest rate that can win the bid and provide a competitive investment to public buyers as well as provide a profit for the underwriter?

The process of establishing the reoffering yield (or price) for each maturity is called **writing the scale**. A scale is the list of the bond issue's different maturities. If the coupon rate has already been determined, each maturity listed is assigned a yield. If the rate has not been set, each maturity is assigned a coupon. A normal scale has higher yields for long-term bonds.

Once the underwriters have written a scale that allows them to resell the bonds, they prepare the final bid. Put another way, writing the scale involves first determining what prices (yields) are necessary in order to be able to sell the various serial maturities and then backing off a little to arrive at a bid. Before they submit the bid, the underwriters must ensure that they have met any unique specifications the issuer has set.

Competitive bids are submitted as firm commitments. This means that the underwriters are committing to sell all the bonds. If any are left unsold, the underwriters must take them for their own accounts Therefore, bids must be carefully written to be competitive yet profitable. Underwriters receive no profit guarantee. Note that syndicates bidding on the proposed issue must bid on the entire amount being offered for sale.

6. 2. 5. 2   Disclosure of Fees

Fees to be paid to a clearing agency and the syndicate manager must be disclosed to syndicate members in advance. Normally, this disclosure is part of the syndicate letter or the agreement among underwriters. Management fees include any amount in the gross spread that is paid to the manager alone and not shared with syndicate members.

6. 2. 5. 3   Awarding the Issue

After the issuing municipality meets with the municipality's attorneys and accountants to analyze each bid, it awards the municipal bond issue to the syndicate that offers to underwrite the bonds at the lowest net interest cost or true interest cost to the issuer.

Net interest cost (NIC) is a common calculation used for comparing bids and awarding the bond issue. It combines the amount of proceeds the issuer receives with the total coupon interest it pays. **True interest cost** (TIC) provides the same type of cost comparison adjusted for the time value of money.

In **split-rate bids** (bids with more than one interest rate), interest is determined by the lowest average interest cost to the issuer. If each bid calls for one rate for the whole issue, the award goes to the syndicate with the lowest rate.

TAKE NOTE   NIC is a straight mathematical interest rate calculation. The lowest NIC is the winner. TIC weights early interest payments more heavily to give greater value to dollars of today over dollars to be paid in the future, consistent with present value calculations.

When the issuer makes its choice, it announces the successful bidder and returns the good-faith deposits to the remaining syndicates.

The successful syndicate has a firm commitment to purchase the bonds from the issuer and reoffer them to the public at the offering price the members agreed on. The issuer keeps the successful bidder's good-faith deposit to ensure that the syndicate carries out its commitment.

TAKE NOTE   While the amount of the good-faith deposit can differ from one issue to another, it is usually 1%–2% of the total par value of the offering.

6. 2. 5. 4   Syndicate Account

The **syndicate account** is created when the issue is awarded. The **syndicate manager** is responsible for keeping the books and managing the account. All sale proceeds are deposited to the syndicate account, and all expenses are paid out of the account. Settlement of syndicate accounts is 30 calendar days after the issuer delivers the securities to the syndicate. Therefore, the maximum length of time for the syndicate to exist is 30 calendar days from the time the issuer delivers the securities to the syndicate.

6. 2. 6   BREAKDOWN OF THE SPREAD

The price at which the bonds are sold to the public is known as the **reoffering price** (or **reoffering yield**). The syndicate's compensation for underwriting the new issue is the **spread**, or the difference between the price the syndicate pays the issuer and the reoffering price. Each participant in the syndicate is entitled to a portion of the spread, depending on the role each member plays in the underwriting.

TAKE NOTE   The term *production* refers to the total dollar sales earned from a municipal issue. The production less the amount bid for the issue results in the spread.

6. 2. 6. 1   Syndicate Management Fee

Syndicate managers receive a per bond fee for their work in bringing the new issue to market.

↳ only managers get the fee

EXAMPLE
The manager might receive 1/8 point ($1.25) as a management fee from a total spread of 1 point ($10).

6. 2. 6. 2 Total Takedown

Spread-mgmt fee = Total Takedown = spread syndicate members buy bonds from syndicate @.

The portion of the spread that remains after subtracting the management fee is called the **total takedown**. Members buy the bonds from the syndicate manager at the takedown.

In the example, for a 1-point spread with a management fee of 1/8 point, the takedown is 7/8 point ($8.75). A syndicate member that has purchased bonds at the takedown can sell its bonds either to customers at the offering price or to a dealer in the selling group below the offering price.

Unlike syndicate members, firms that are part of the selling group do not assume financial risk. They are engaged to help the syndicate members sell the new issue. Their compensation for each bond sold is termed the **concession.**

- selling group = do not take financial risk and receive concession

6. 2. 6. 3 Selling Concession and Additional Takedown

A syndicate member can buy bonds from the manager for $991.25, sell them to the public for $1,000, and earn the takedown of 7/8 point ($8.75). If the firm chooses instead to sell bonds to a member of the selling group, it does so at a price less than $1,000, in this case $995.00. The discount the selling group receives from the syndicate member is called the concession—1/2 point ($5.00).

Selling group members buy bonds from syndicate members at the concession. The syndicate member keeps the remainder of the total takedown, called the **additional takedown**. The additional takedown in this example is 3/8 point ($3.75).

remainder of spread after selling to selling group at a concession; addl takedown = spread that syndicate member keeps

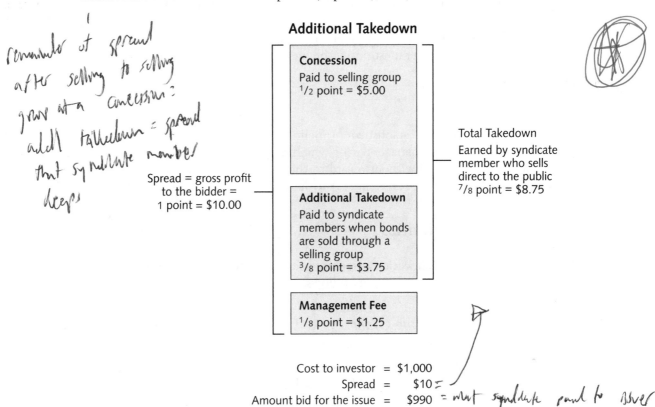

Additional Takedown

Concession
Paid to selling group
1/2 point = $5.00

Additional Takedown
Paid to syndicate members when bonds are sold through a selling group
3/8 point = $3.75

Management Fee
1/8 point = $1.25

Spread = gross profit to the bidder = 1 point = $10.00

Total Takedown
Earned by syndicate member who sells direct to the public
7/8 point = $8.75

Cost to investor = $1,000
Spread = $10
Amount bid for the issue = $990 *= what syndicate paid to issuer*

The syndicate manager may notify other firms that are not syndicate or selling group members of the new issue through *The Bond Buyer*. Interested firms may buy the bonds from the syndicate at a small discount from the reoffer price. This discount is termed a **reallowance,** which is generally one-half of the concession amount.

Municipal spread questions are generally asked in terms of points, not dollars. One bond point equals $10.

Be ready for a question that asks you to rank parts of the spread in order of their size. Remember that the manager's fee is typically the smallest, and the total takedown is the largest. The additional takedown is actually a part of the total takedown amount, even though the name is a bit misleading.

You may see a question that asks under what circumstances a syndicate member can receive the full spread when a bond is sold. The answer is that the syndicate member receives the full spread if the member is also the syndicate manager. Also, be ready to define total takedown as the concession plus the additional takedown.

6. 2. 7   ORDER ALLOCATION

Municipal bond orders are allocated according to priorities the syndicate sets in advance. The **Municipal Securities Rulemaking Board (MSRB)** requires syndicates to establish **priority allocation provisions** for orders. The managing underwriter must submit these provisions to all syndicate members in writing. Normally, the manager includes allocation priorities and confirmation procedures in the syndicate agreement.

The syndicate must establish a definite sequence in which orders will be accepted and cannot simply state that the order priority will be left to the manager's discretion.

Syndicate members must signify in writing their acceptance of the allocation priorities. In addition, the manager must notify the members in writing of any change to the set priorities.

6. 2. 7. 1   Order Period

The MSRB has established a timeline for municipal underwritings. The **order period** is the time set by the manager during which the syndicate solicits customers for the issue and all orders are allocated without regard to the sequence in which they were received. The order period usually runs for an hour on the day following the award of the bid.

6. 2. 7. 2   Allocation Priorities

A syndicate's **allocation priorities** become especially important when a bond issue is oversubscribed. The normal priority follows.

6. 2. 7. 2. 1   Presale Order

A **presale order** is entered before the date that the syndicate wins the bid, which means that a customer is willing to place an order without knowing the final price or whether the syndicate will even win the bid. A presale order takes priority over other types of orders, and individual syndicate members are not credited with any takedown on presale orders. The takedown is split among all syndicate members according to participation.

6. 2. 7. 2. 2   Group Net Order

priority order by syndicate member for a customer

A group order is placed after the bid is awarded. A syndicate member that wants a customer's order to receive priority enters the order as a **group net order**. The takedown on a group net order is deposited in the syndicate account, and upon completion of the underwriting, it is split among all syndicate members according to participation.

6. 2. 7. 2. 3   Designated Order

The next highest priority for orders received during the order period is assigned to **designated orders**. These orders are usually from institutions that wish to allocate the takedown to certain syndicate members.

6. 2. 7. 2. 4   Member Order and Member-Related Order

The lowest priority for orders goes to member and member-related orders. A member firm enters such an order for its own inventory or related accounts, such as for a dealer-sponsored **unit investment trust (UIT)**. The easiest way to remember the priority of the various types of orders is that the highest priority is given to those orders that benefit the most members. The lowest priority is given to orders that benefit a single member.

Under MSRB rules, a syndicate member placing an order for a related account must disclose this fact to the syndicate manager when the order is placed. Therefore, the manager knows to accord these orders the lowest priority.

Within two business days of the sale date, the syndicate manager must send a written summary of how orders were allocated to the other syndicate members.

TAKE NOTE   A simple way to remember the normal order allocation priority found in the syndicate letter is: "**P**ro **G**olfers **D**on't **M**iss." PGDM stands for **P**resale, **G**roup, **D**esignated, and **M**ember.

6. 2. 8   PAYMENT AND DELIVERY

New municipal bond issues are usually sold on a **when-issued** basis, meaning the securities are authorized but not yet issued. After awarding an issue to a syndicate, the issuer has the bond certificates printed and finalizes any other legal matters. If the bonds are to be eligible for automated comparison and clearing, the managing underwriter must register the securities with a registered clearing agency, providing the agency with notice of the securities' coupon rate and settlement date as soon as they are known.

When the bonds are ready, the syndicate manager gives notice of the **settlement date**. The syndicate members, in turn, give notice of the settlement date to the purchasers. On the settlement date, the newly issued bonds are delivered to the underwriters with a final legal opinion, and the underwriters pay for the bonds on delivery.

6. 2. 8. 1   Confirmations of Sales to Customers

On or before the completion of the transaction (settlement date), final confirmations must be sent to investors who purchased bonds from the underwriters. The investors' confirmations disclose the purchase price and settlement date for the transaction. The underwriters then deliver the bonds, accompanied by the legal opinion, to the investors.

The settlement date should not be confused with the **dated date** the issuer assigns to the bond issue. The dated date is the date on which interest begins to accrue. An investor must pay any interest that has accrued from the dated date up to, but not including, the settlement date. The investor starts receiving interest on the settlement date.

TAKE NOTE

When a bond is first issued, the first interest payment date may represent a **long coupon**. For example, assume a bond is issued on March 1 and the first interest payment date is the following January 1, with subsequent payments every six months (a J&J bond). The first payment date will include 10 months of interest—March 1 through January 1.

QUICK QUIZ 6.B

Objectives:

- Define the underwriting process and the participants roles in municipal securities underwriting
- Describe the role of the syndicate and specific rules that apply to the syndicate manager
- Identify documentation associated with a new issue of municipals

1. Your manager notifies you that a new municipal bond issue that you have been working on has been oversubscribed. How is the priority for acceptance of orders for this issue determined?

    A.   On a first-come, first-served basis
    B.   As outlined in the official statement (OS)
    C.   As outlined in the official notice of sale
    D.   As outlined in the syndicate agreement

2. Who signs the syndicate agreement for a municipal bond issue?

    A.   Managing underwriter and the issuer
    B.   Managing underwriter and the trustee
    C.   Managing underwriter and the bond counsel
    D.   All members of the underwriting syndicate

3. In a municipal underwriting, the scale is

    A.   the first thing determined by the underwriting syndicate in calculating its bid
    B.   the yield at which the syndicate plans to reoffer the bonds to the public
    C.   both A and B
    D.   neither A nor B

4. Your firm is bidding on a new municipal bond issue. As the issuer weighs and evaluates the competitive bids, what will be the most important factor in deciding who will be awarded the winning bid?

    A.   Net interest cost
    B.   Scale
    C.   Takedown
    D.   Concession

5. An order confirmed for the benefit of the entire underwriting syndicate placed after the bid is awarded is called

    A.   a group net order
    B.   a net designated order
    C.   a presale order
    D.   a member at the takedown order

6. A dealer should consider all of the following factors when determining the spread on a new issue EXCEPT

    A.   the prevailing interest rates in the marketplace
    B.   the amount bid on the issue
    C.   the type and size of the issue
    D.   the amount of the good-faith check

7. An unqualified legal opinion means that

    A.   the issue is legal, but certain contingencies may limit the flow of funds in the future
    B.   the interest is not exempt from state or local taxes
    C.   the bond counsel has rendered an opinion without any qualifying limitations
    D.   the underwriter has failed to disclose sufficient information to qualify the issue

8. The reoffering yield on a new municipal bond issue is

    A.   the coupon rate on the new issue
    B.   the tax-equivalent yield of the new issue
    C.   the interest rate less any premiums that underwriters are willing to pay
    D.   the yield at which the bonds are offered to the public

All Quick Quiz answers are found at the end of their units.

6. 3   ANALYSIS OF MUNICIPAL SECURITIES

Different criteria are used to evaluate the merits of general obligation and revenue bonds. When analyzing GOs, investors assess the municipality's ability to raise enough tax revenue to pay its debt. Revenue bond debt service depends on the income generated from a specific facility to cover its operating costs and pay its debt.

6. 3. 1 GENERAL OBLIGATION BOND ANALYSIS

6. 3. 1. 1 General Wealth of the Community

Because GOs are backed primarily by tax revenues, their safety is determined by the community's general wealth, which includes the following demographic data:

■ Property values
■ Retail sales per capita
■ Local bank deposits and bank clearings
■ Diversity of industry in its tax base
■ Population growth or decline

A GO issuer's taxing power enables it to make principal and interest payments through all but the most unusual economic circumstances.

6. 3. 1. 2 Characteristics of the Issuer

A **quantitative analysis** focuses on objective information regarding a municipality's population, property values, and per capita income. A **qualitative analysis** focuses on subjective factors that affect a municipality's securities. The community's attitude toward debt and taxation, population trends, property value trends, and plans and projects being undertaken in the area are all relevant considerations.

6. 3. 1. 3 Debt Limits

To protect taxpayers from excessive taxes, statutory limits may be placed on the overall amount of debt a municipality can have. Suppose a city's total debt is limited to 5% of the estimated market value of all taxable property within the city's boundary. The total value of those properties multiplied by 5% would be city's statutory debt limit. A bond's OS discloses how close total outstanding debt, including newly issued debt, comes to its statutory debt limit.

A state constitution or city charter can also limit the purposes for which a city may issue bonds. Often, a city may issue bonds to finance capital improvements only if those bonds mature within the expected lifetimes of the improvements. This provision ensures that the city will not owe money on a facility when it becomes obsolete.

6. 3. 1. 4 Income of the Municipality

The primary sources of municipal income are discussed below.

■ Income and sales taxes are major sources of state income.

AD VALOREM TAXES

■ Real property taxes are the principal income source of counties and school districts are the largest source of city income.

■ City income can include fines, license fees, assessments, sales taxes, hotel taxes, city income taxes, utility taxes, and any city personal property tax.

6. 3. 1. 5   Ad Valorem Taxes

Property taxes are based on a property's assessed valuation. Assessed valuation is a percentage of the estimated market value. That percentage is established by each state or county and varies substantially. The market value of each piece of property in a county is determined by the county assessor, who relies on recent sale prices of similar properties, income streams, replacement costs, and other information.

Because the real property tax is based on the property's value, it is said to be an **ad valorem**, or per value, tax. The tax is a lien on the property, which means the property can be seized if the tax is not paid. GOs, backed by the power to tax and seize property, are considered safer than revenue bonds of the same issuer and therefore can be issued with a lower interest rate.

6. 3. 1. 6   Analyzing the Official Statement

Analysts study the documents included in the OS to determine the issuer's financial condition at the present and in the foreseeable future.

6. 3. 1. 6. 1   Future Financial Needs

The municipality's financial statements should be scrutinized for signs of future debt requirements. The municipality might need to issue more debt if:

- its annual income is not sufficient to make the payments on its short-term (or floating) debt;
- principal repayments are scheduled too close together;
- sinking funds for outstanding term bonds are inadequate;
- pension liabilities are unfunded; or
- it plans to make more capital improvements soon.

Issuing more debt in the near future could damage an issuer's credit rating, which would cause the current issue to trade at a lower price.

6. 3. 1. 6. 2   The Debt Statement

The **debt statement** is used in the analysis of GO debt. It includes the estimated full valuation of taxable property, the estimated assessed value of property, and the assessment percentage.

To evaluate the municipality's debt structure, an analyst calculates **total debt**, the sum of all bonds issued by the municipality, and subtracts **self-supporting debt** from this figure. Although revenue bond debt is included in total debt, it is backed by revenues from the facility it financed and is not a burden on the municipality's taxpayers.

The result is the municipality's **net direct debt**, which includes GOs and short-term notes issued in anticipation of taxes or for interim financing.

Overlapping debt disclosed on the debt statement is the city's proportionate share of the debts of the county, school district, park district, and sanitary district. The city's **net total debt**, also called **net overall debt**, is the sum of the overlapping debt and the net direct debt.

6. 3. 1. 6. 3   *Calculating a Municipality's Net Total Debt*

A municipality's net total debt can be calculated as follows:

	total debt
−	self-supporting debt
−	sinking fund accumulations
=	net direct debt
+	overlapping debt
=	net total debt

TEST TOPIC ALERT   A question might ask about what is or is not included in the various categories on the debt statement. A good rule: for any category that uses the word *net*, self-supporting debt and sinking fund accumulations are not included. For instance, net total debt includes all GOs and overlapping debt but does not include the self-supporting and sinking fund accumulations.

Do not expect a calculation question on this topic. The exam will test your understanding of the concept.

6. 3. 2   REVENUE BOND ANALYSIS

Revenue bonds are rated according to a facility's potential to generate sufficient money to cover operating expenses and principal and interest payments. Revenue bonds are not repaid from taxes, so they are not subject to statutory debt limits. Revenue bonds are meant to be self-supporting, and if the facility they finance does not make enough money to repay the debts, the bondholders, not the taxpayers, bear the risk. When assessing the quality of revenue bonds, an investor should consider the following factors.

- **Economic justification:** the facility being built should be able to generate revenues.
- **Competing facilities:** a facility should not be placed where better alternatives are easily available.
- **Sources of revenue: the sources** should be dependable.
- **Call provisions:** with callable bonds, the higher the call premium, the more attractive a bond is to an investor.
- **Flow of funds:** revenues generated must be sufficient to pay all of the facility's operating expenses and to meet debt service obligation.

6. 3. 2. 1   Applications of Revenues

Principal and interest on revenue bonds are paid exclusively from money generated by the facility the issue finances. The issuer pledges to pay expenses in a specific order, called the **flow of funds**.

In most cases, a **net revenue pledge** is used, meaning that operating and maintenance expenses are paid first. The remaining funds (or net revenues) are used to pay debt service and meet other obligations.

6. 3. 2. 1. 1   Flow of Funds in a Net Revenue Pledge

In a **net revenue pledge**, total receipts from operating the facility are usually deposited in the **revenue fund**, and funds are disbursed as follows:

- **Operations and maintenance**—used to pay current operating and maintenance expenses; remaining funds are called **net revenues**
- **Debt service account**—used to pay the interest and principal maturing in the current year and serves as a sinking fund for term issues
- **Debt service reserve fund**—used to hold enough money to pay one year's debt service
- **Reserve maintenance fund**—used to supplement the general maintenance fund
- **Renewal and replacement fund**—used to create reserve funds for major renewal projects and equipment replacements
- **Surplus (sinking) fund**—used for a variety of purposes, such as redeeming bonds or paying for improvements

If the issuer has not pledged to pay operating and maintenance expenses first, debt service is the priority expense. When debt service is paid first, the flow of funds is called a **gross revenue pledge**.

The debt service includes current principal and interest due, plus any sinking fund obligations. If revenues exceed operating and other obligations, the money is usually placed in a surplus fund.

Gross and Net Revenue Pledges

Gross Revenue Pledge	Net Revenue Pledge
Issuer pays debt service first from gross revenues.	Issuer pays operations and maintenance expenses first from gross revenues.
Issuer pays operations and maintenance expenses.	Issuer pays debt service second from net revenues.

TEST TOPIC ALERT   If you see questions that require differentiating gross revenue and net revenue pledges, maybe this will help: the name of the pledge tells you how debt service is paid. In a gross revenue pledge, debt service is paid first, from gross revenues. Operations and maintenance expenses are paid after debt service. In a net revenue pledge, debt service is paid from the net revenues, meaning operations and maintenance costs are paid first. This is the more common of the two pledges.

6. 3. 3   MUNICIPAL DEBT RATIOS

A community's ability to meet its debt service is reflected in the following mathematical ratios based on information in the debt statement and other documents.

- **Net debt to assessed valuation:** a ratio of 5% ($5,000 of debt per $100,000 of assessed property value) is considered reasonable for a municipality.
- **Net debt to estimated valuation:** assessed valuation varies among municipalities, so most analysts prefer to use **estimated valuation** of property.

- **Taxes per person or per capita:** this ratio equals the city's tax income divided by the city population; it is used to evaluate the population's tax burden.
- **Debt per capita:** larger cities can assume more debt per capita because their tax bases are more diversified.
- **Debt trend:** this number indicates whether the ratios are rising or falling. Bonds can be long-term investments, so it is important to anticipate the community's future financial position.
- **Collection ratio:** this ratio equals the taxes collected divided by the taxes assessed; it can help detect deteriorating credit conditions.
- **Coverage ratio:** this ratio shows how many times annual revenues will cover debt service. A coverage of 2:1 is considered adequate for a typical municipal revenue bond. For utility revenue bonds (i.e., sewer, water, and electricity), a coverage of 5:4 (125%) of fixed charges is considered adequate.

Basic demographic information (e.g., average age, average income, or number of children in or expected to be in public schools) for a population living in a particular area is also used to evaluate GO bonds.

TEST TOPIC ALERT

Memorizing the ratios is less important than understanding them. A question might ask if a ratio is used to analyze GOs or revenues. Associate all ratios with GOs, except for debt service coverage ratio, which analyzes revenues.

1. A municipal revenue bond indenture contains a net revenue pledge. The following are reported for the year: $30 million of gross revenues, $18 million of operating expenses, $4 million of interest expense, and $2 million of principal repayment. What is the debt service coverage ratio?

   A. 2:1
   B. 3:1
   C. 5:1
   D. 9:1

   Answer: A. Under a net revenue pledge, bondholders are paid from net revenue, which equals gross revenue minus operating expenses. Net revenue is $12 million ($30 million – $18 million). Debt service is the combination of interest and principal repayment. The debt service is $6 million ($4 million + $2 million). To compute the debt service ratio, divide net revenue by debt service: $12 million ÷ $6 million = a ratio of 2:1.

6. 3. 4   OTHER SOURCES OF INFORMATION FOR MUNICIPAL BOND ANALYSIS

6. 3. 4. 1   Interest Rate Comparisons

In addition to issuer-specific information, the value of any bond is affected by trends in the overall bond market. Municipal bond prices tend to fluctuate more than government and corporate bond prices because each issue is unique and may have few regular market makers. Because fewer market makers exist in the municipal bond market than exist in the OTC equity market, the market for any specific municipal bond is typically thinner than the market for comparable corporate or government bonds.

6. 3. 4. 2 Municipal Bond Insurance

Municipal bond issuers can insure their securities' principal and interest payments by buying insurance from a number of insurers. Among those specializing in insuring municipal issues are National Public Finance Guarantee Corp. (formerly the Municipal Bond Investors Assurance Corporation—MBIA), Financial Guaranty Insurance Company (FGIC), Assured Guaranty Corporation (AGC), and AMBAC Indemnity Corporation (AMBAC). While AMBAC is not currently insuring new municipal issues, there are many AMBAC insured municipal bonds still outstanding.

Insured bonds are generally issued with lower coupon rates because investors will accept lower rates of return for the added safety insurance affords. In addition, the cost of insurance may also lessen the yield a municipal issuer is willing to pay. If not rated, insured bonds are typically implied to be rated AAA.

6. 3. 4. 3 Bond Ratings

Rating services, such as Standard & Poor's, Moody's, and Fitch, evaluate the credit quality of municipal bonds and publish their ratings. They also provide ratings for short-term municipal notes.

Moody's Investment Grade (MIG) short-term note ratings are from MIG 1 (best quality) through MIG 4 (adequate quality). If a note is speculative, it is listed as SG. S&P's rates notes as SP-1, SP-2, and SP-3, and Fitch rates notes as F-1, F-2, and F-3.

EXAMPLE   All municipalities have **pension liabilities**, which are their legal obligation to pay retirement benefits to future retirees. An **unfunded pension liability** is one where adequate reserves have not been set aside to meet this future obligation. Poor investment performance of the monies set aside today can lead to an unfunded liability later. This type of liability will be noted by municipal bond credit rating agencies and ultimately have an adverse effect on the municipalities credit rating.

QUICK QUIZ 6.C   Objective: Compare and contrast general obligation (GO) and revenue bonds

1. If an insured municipal bond defaults, the insurance company must pay

    A. interest only
    B. principal only
    C. both A and B
    D. neither A nor B

2. Which of the following are considered sources of debt service for GO bonds?

   I. Personal property taxes
   II. Real estate taxes
   III. Fees from delinquent property taxes
   IV. Liquor license fees

   A. I and IV
   B. II and III
   C. II, III and IV
   D. I, II, III and IV

3. In rating a general obligation bond, an analyst must consider

   I. debt per capita
   II. total outstanding debt
   III. tax collection ratio
   IV. political attitude

   A. I and II
   B. I and III
   C. II, III and IV
   D. I, II, III and IV

4. Which of the following is NOT considered when evaluating municipal revenue bond credit risk?

   A. Competing facilities
   B. Quality of management
   C. Coverage ratios
   D. Interest rate movements

5. A municipal bond issue would be nonrated when

   A. the municipality's credit is not good
   B. the municipality's debt is too small to be rated
   C. the issue is a term bond
   D. the municipality has an outstanding bond in default

6. A qualitative analysis of a general obligation bond that is to be issued would take into consideration all the following factors EXCEPT

   A. the tax base of the community
   B. the economic character of the community
   C. the dollar denominations of the bonds to be issued
   D. the makeup of the community's population

7. Which of the following would a customer examine to evaluate the credit quality of a new municipal security?

   A. Official statement
   B. Legal opinion
   C. Prospectus
   D. Trust indenture

8. An increase in any of the following would indicate deteriorating credit conditions EXCEPT

   A. bankruptcies
   B. consumer debt
   C. bond defaults
   D. assessed valuations

9. Which of the following could insure payment of principal and interest on a municipality's outstanding debt?

   I. FGIC
   II. AGC
   III. SIPC
   IV. FDIC

   A. I and II
   B. I, II and III
   C. III and IV
   D. I, II, III and IV

All Quick Quiz answers are found at the end of their units.

6. 4   MUNICIPAL TRADING AND TAXATION

The following sections will cover some of the trading terminology and concepts associated with municipals as well as their unique tax consequences.

6. 4. 1   QUOTATIONS

Municipal bonds are bought and sold in the over-the-counter (OTC) market. Most large brokerages maintain trading departments that deal exclusively in municipal bonds. Many of the rules governing the trading of other OTC securities also apply to municipal bond transactions.

Municipal dealers are called upon regularly to provide current quotations for municipal securities. The term **quotation** means any bid for or offer of municipal securities. Any indication of interest or solicitation by a municipal dealer (such as **bid wanted** or **offer wanted**) would be considered a quotation request.

Municipal bonds are usually priced and offered for sale on a **yield-to-maturity (YTM)** basis rather than a dollar price. This is called a **basis quote**. Municipal bonds with serial maturities are quoted in basis (YTM).

The following sections will cover trading terminology and concepts associated with municipals as well as their unique tax consequences.

TEST TOPIC ALERT

If a question mentions a 6% bond quoted on a 6.5 basis, you should be able to determine that the coupon of the bond is 6% and its YTM is 6.5%. Because the YTM is higher than the coupon, the bond is trading at a discount.

YTM/YTC and Premium and Discount

Are the following bonds trading at premium or a discount?

1. 7% bond, 6.25% basis
2. 7% bond, 7.64% basis
3. 5% bond, 4.85% basis
4. 6% bond, 6.45% basis

(handwritten: YTM)

Answers: 1. Premium; 2. Discount; 3. Premium; 4. Discount

6.4.1.1 Dollar Bonds

Some municipal revenue bonds are quoted on a percentage of par dollar basis rather than on a yield basis. Such bonds are commonly called dollar bonds. Dollar bonds are usually term bonds callable before maturity.

Be sure to recognize that a bond quoted at 104 for example is a dollar bond, and that the "104" actually represents its price expressed as a percentage of par value. Therefore, a quote of 104 = 104% of par value or 104% × $1,000 = $1,040.

6.4.1.2 Bona Fide Quotes

If a municipal dealer gives, distributes, or publishes a quotation for a security, that quote must be **bona fide**. For a quote to be considered bona fide, or **firm**, the dealer must be prepared to trade the security at the price specified in the quote and under the conditions and restrictions (if any) accompanying the quote. A bona fide quote:

■ must reflect the dealer's best judgment and have a reasonable relationship to the fair market value for that security, and

■ may reflect the firm's inventory and expectations of market direction.

In other words, a quotation need not represent the best price, but it must have a reasonable relationship to fair market value. A quotation may take into consideration such other factors as the dealer's inventory position and any anticipated market movement.

If the dealer distributes or publishes the quotation on behalf of another dealer, it must have reason to believe that the quote is bona fide and based on the other dealer's best judgment of fair market value. Dealers cannot knowingly misrepresent a quote made by another municipal securities dealer.

Quotations are always subject to prior sale or change in price. Any means of communication, including print, voice, and electronic media, can be used to disseminate, distribute, or publish quotations.

TAKE NOTE Municipal dealers can make offers to sell securities by providing quotes without owning the bonds. The dealer, however, must know where to obtain the bonds if such offers are accepted.

6.4.1.3   Types of Quotations

A municipal securities dealer can give several types of quotations. The most common are bona fide and nominal. Bona fide is a firm quote, meaning that the dealer is prepared to act.

■ **A workable indication** reflects a bid price at which a dealer will purchase securities from another dealer. A dealer giving a workable indication is always free to revise its bid for the securities as market conditions change.

■ A **nominal, or subject, quotation** indicates a dealer's estimate of a security's market value. Nominal quotations are provided for informational purposes only and are permitted if the quotes are clearly labeled as such. The rules on nominal quotes apply to all municipal bond quotes distributed or published by any dealer.

6.4.1.4   Holding a Quote

A municipal securities dealer may quote a bond price that is firm for a certain time. This is called an **out-firm with recall** quote. Generally, these quotes are firm for an hour (or half hour) with a five-minute recall period. This provides time for the dealer that requested the quote to search for a better quote before selling the bonds. If, during this period, the firm that made the quote has another buyer interested in the same bonds, that firm can contact the dealer and give her five minutes to act on the quote. If no action is taken and a transaction does not take place within the five-minute recall period, she loses the right to buy the bonds at the quoted price.

TAKE NOTE Receiving an out-firm quote allows a dealer to try to sell bonds that it does not own, knowing that if it finds a buyer within the allotted time, it can buy the bonds at a fixed price from the firm providing the out-firm quote.

6.4.1.5   Secondary-Market Joint or Trading Accounts

A secondary-market joint or trading account is often formed by a group of investment bankers to purchase large blocks of bonds from institutions and resell them. As with underwritings, the size of the financial commitment requires more than one firm to handle such an undertaking. Agreements are signed by the participating firms outlining the terms and conditions under which the joint account will operate. In short, the secondary joint account agreement formalizes the creation of the account; identifies the dealers involved; and specifies the lead manager, the securities to be purchased, and all other terms and conditions of the account.

A key provision of these agreements is that the joint account, when reselling the bonds, can only give one quote for the bonds. In other words, all participants must sell the bonds at the same price.

Like syndicate accounts for new underwritings, settlement of secondary-market joint or trading accounts is 30 calendar days after the securities purchased are delivered to the secondary joint account members.

6. 4. 2   REPORTS OF SALES

MSRB rules prohibit dealers from distributing or publishing any report of a municipal security's purchase or sale unless they know or have reason to believe that the transaction took place. BDs reporting the sale must believe that the reported trade is real and not fictitious, fraudulent, or deceitful.

Municipal securities dealers must report trades with other dealers to the **National Securities Clearing Corporation (NSCC)**. The report must include the two executing firms' names and the amount of accrued interest, if known.

TAKE NOTE   A round lot for municipal bonds is usually $100,000 face amount.

6. 4. 2. 1   Broker's Broker

Some municipal brokers specialize in trading only with institutional customers, such as banks and other municipal brokers, not with the retail public. These firms are called **broker's brokers** because their business focuses on helping other municipal dealers place unsold portions of new bond issues. They do not disclose the identity of the customers they represent. Furthermore, they act solely as agents and do not maintain an inventory of bonds.

TEST TOPIC ALERT   Broker's brokers protect the identity of their customers.

6. 4. 3   BROKER-DEALER REGULATION

6. 4. 3. 1   Reciprocal Dealings (Anti-Reciprocal Rule)

A dealer cannot solicit trades in municipal securities from an investment company in return for sales by the dealer of shares or units in the investment company (**anti-reciprocal rule**).

EXAMPLE   If a municipal bond fund makes a large number of trades every month in its portfolio, a municipal dealer cannot be selected to execute the fund's portfolio trades only on the basis of the firm's promise that its account executives will increase sales of the bond fund's shares. The firm can be selected to execute those trades on the basis of the services the dealer offers to the fund, such as prompt execution and research.

6. 4. 3. 2   Customer Recommendations and Suitability

MSRB rules require municipal securities broker-dealers to make suitable recommendations to customers. Before making a recommendation, a municipal securities firm must make a reasonable effort to learn the customer's financial status, tax status, investment objectives, and other holdings. The **suitability test** applies to discretionary accounts and all other accounts.

Regarding suitability, one should always remember that the tax-free interest paid by municipal bonds makes them better suited to those in higher tax brackets. In addition, the ability to receive tax-free interest payments means that these bonds have no place in an investor's tax-advantaged accounts, such as individual retirement accounts (IRAs) or 401(k) plans. Of course, because they are bonds, and bonds pay interest income, they are best suited for those who list income as an investment objective.

Any recommendations beyond these parameters would be unusual and the practice of increasing commissions through excessive trading, known as **churning**, is specifically prohibited. Before an account is opened, it must be approved in writing by a principal, and if investment objectives noted when the account was approved do not align with transactions in the account later, this would present a red flag to be addressed.

TAKE NOTE   If a customer refuses to disclose net worth, income, or both, the account can still be opened. However, in this situation, recommendations cannot be made.

6. 4. 3. 2. 1   Protecting Customer Accounts

Municipal securities dealers cannot misuse securities or funds held for another person. Dealers also may not guarantee customers against loss (put options and repurchase agreements are not considered guarantees against loss) or share in the profits or losses of a customer's account. An exception to this rule applies in the case of an associated person who establishes a personal joint account with a customer and obtains written permission from the firm. In this situation, the associated person may share in the account's profits and losses only in proportion to the amount of capital contributed to the account.

6. 4. 3. 2. 2   Disclosure of Control

A municipal securities firm that has a control relationship with respect to a municipal security is subject to additional disclosure requirements. A **control relationship** exists if the dealer controls, is controlled by, or is under common control with that security's issuer.

EXAMPLE   An officer of a municipal dealer sits on the BODs of an issuer.

The dealer must disclose the control relationship to the customer before it can affect any transaction in that security for that customer. Although, initially, this disclosure can be verbal, the dealer must make a written disclosure at or before the transaction's completion. The disclosure is normally made on the confirmation. If the transaction is for a discretionary account, the customer must give express permission before the transaction can be executed.

6. 4. 4   MARKUPS AND COMMISSIONS

A dealer acts as an agent when it arranges trades for customers and charges **commissions**. A dealer acts as a principal when it buys for or sells securities from its own inventory. The dealer charges a **markup** for principal transactions when it sells securities to customers and a **markdown** when it buys securities from customers.

6. 4. 4. 1   Principal Transactions

Each **principal transaction** is executed at a net price, which includes the markup or markdown. Some of the factors taken into consideration include:

- the dealer's best judgment of fair market value;
- the expense of affecting the transaction;
- the fact that the dealer is entitled to a markup or markdown (profit);
- the total dollar amount of the transaction; and
- the value of any security exchanged or traded.

TAKE NOTE   Markups or markdowns are not disclosed separately on a customer's confirmation.

6. 4. 4. 2   Agency Transactions

Each agency transaction is executed for a commission that is not in excess of a fair and reasonable amount, considering all relevant factors. For an agency commission calculation, a dealer takes into consideration:

- the security's availability;
- the expense of executing the order;
- the value of services the dealer renders; and
- the amount of any other compensation received or to be received in connection with the transaction.

6. 4. 4. 2. 1   Best Execution

When executing an order as an agent, a dealer must make a reasonable effort to obtain a fair and reasonable price.

TAKE NOTE   Commissions are disclosed on customer confirmations.

6. 4. 5   CONFIRMATIONS

Customers must receive a written **confirmation** of each municipal secu̶
they have entered. The confirmation must describe the security; list the trade date, settlement
date (T+2), and amount of accrued interest; state the firm's name, address, and phone number;
and indicate whether the firm acted as agent or principal in the trade. A confirmation that
does not include the time of execution must indicate that this information will be provided if
the customer requests it.

6. 4. 5. 1   Disclosing Yield

In disclosing yield on a customer confirmation, there are rules that will apply. For instance,
if the bond is noncallable, the actual life of the bond is known with certainty. Therefore, the
yield shown is the yield to maturity.

If the bond is callable, there will always be the uncertainty surrounding a possible call. If
interest rates have risen since the bond's issuance, causing the price to fall and trade at a discount, the issuer is not likely to call the bonds because any refunding bonds would have to be
sold at higher yields. If rates have fallen since the bond's issuance, causing the price to rise and
trade at a premium, the issuer is more likely to call the bonds because any refunding bonds can
be sold at lower yields. Therefore, discount bonds are not likely to be called, whereas premium
bonds are likely to be called.

To deal with all the uncertainty noted above, the MSRB requires that the yield shown on
a customer confirmation be the lower of YTM or YTC. For discount bonds, the lower is YTM.
For premium bonds, the lower is YTC. If a premium bond has a number of call dates and prices,
rather than computing yield to all of the possible call dates and prices to determine which is
the lowest, the MSRB permits firms to show yield to the nearest in-whole call.

Furthermore, if the issuer has announced an in-whole call, there is no longer any uncertainty. Therefore, the confirmation should show yield computed to the announced call date
and price, which is the new maturity of the bond. If an issue is subject to a partial call, there
is uncertainty as to whether the bond being sold to the customer will be one of the bonds
selected for the call. In this situation, the basic rule applies: show the lower of YTM or YTC.

There are three cases where no separate yield disclosure is required.

- **Variable-rate bonds (reset bonds)**: As the coupon is adjusted periodically, a yield computation is impossible.

- **Bonds in default**: If a bond is no longer paying interest, a yield computation is impossible.

- **Bonds sold at par**: For bonds sold at par, no separate yield disclosure is required because
  the yield cannot be anything other than the coupon rate. Remember: at par, all yields are
  the same.

6. 4. 5. 1. 1   Zero-Coupon Municipal Securities

A zero-coupon bond is issued at a deep discount from par and pays no current interest.
The confirmation must indicate an interest rate of 0% and state that accrued interest is not
calculated.

6. 4. 5. 1. 2   Required Information on Confirmations

Each confirmation must also include the following information:

- In an agency transaction, the name of the party on the other side of the transaction and the source and amount of any commission (the name of the other party must be disclosed on request if it is not listed on the confirmation)
- The dated date if it affects the interest calculation
- Whether the securities are fully registered, registered as to principal only, in book-entry form, or in bearer form
- Whether the securities are called or prerefunded, as well as the date of maturity fixed by the call notice and the amount of the call price
- Any special qualification or factor that might affect payment of principal or interest
- Whether the bond interest is taxable or subject to the alternative minimum tax (AMT)

6. 4. 6   ADVERTISING

Any material designed for use in the public media is considered **advertising**. This includes abstracts and summaries of the OS; offering circulars; reports; market letters; and form letters, including professional, product, and new issue advertisements.

A municipal securities principal or general securities principal of the dealer must approve all advertising before use, and a copy of each advertisement must be kept on file for three years.

TAKE NOTE   Preliminary and final OSs are not considered advertising because they are prepared by or on behalf of an issuer. Also note that copies of advertising are never filed with the MSRB.

---

6. 4. 7   THE BROKER-DEALER AS FINANCIAL ADVISER

6. 4. 7. 1   Financial Advisers

The MSRB has established ethical standards and disclosure requirements for municipal securities dealers that act as **financial advisers** to municipal securities' issuers. A financial advisory relationship exists when a municipal dealer provides financial advisory or consulting services to an issuer with respect to a new issue for a fee or other compensation. This includes advice regarding the structure, timing, and terms of, as well as other matters concerning, the issue or issuer.

6. 4. 7. 1. 1   Basis of Compensation

Each financial advisory relationship must be documented in writing before, upon, or promptly after its inception. This document establishes the basis of compensation for the advisory services to be rendered.

6. 4. 7. 2   Conflicts of Interest

Potential **conflicts of interest** arise if a firm acts as both underwriter and financial adviser for the same issue. The MSRB has the following requirements.

The MSRB simply prohibits a broker-dealer that serves as a financial advisor to a municipal issuer for any issue sold on either a negotiated or competitive bid basis from switching roles and underwriting the same issue. In other words, if a broker-dealer is acting as a financial advisor to the issuer, generally the broker-dealer may not participate in underwriting the bonds of the issuing municipality.

However, there are some allowable exceptions. For example, a broker-dealer that has a financial advisory relationship with an issuer regarding the issuance of municipal securities, will still be permitted to assist with preparing the official statement and other similar duties normally associated with underwriting. They can also purchase the bonds from an underwriter either for their own trading account or for the accounts of their customers. But in all cases, if performing such functions or acting in such a capacity as described above, the broker-dealer may not receive any compensation other than for financial advisory services to the issuer. In other words, no underwriting compensation can be received by the broker-dealer who is acting in an advisory capacity.

Customers who are purchasing new securities from a broker-dealer that is acting in an advisory capacity to a municipality must be informed that the advisory relationship exists at or before confirmation of the sale.

6. 4. 7. 2. 1   Assistance With Official Statement

As part of its financial advisory services to an issuer, a municipal securities dealer may help prepare the final OS for a new issue. If it prepares the OS, the adviser must make a copy of that statement available to the managing underwriter promptly after the award is made and at least two days before the syndicate manager delivers the securities to the syndicate members.

6. 4. 7. 2. 2   Use of Ownership Information

While acting in a fiduciary capacity for an issuer, a municipal securities dealer often obtains confidential information about its bondholders. The dealer cannot use this information to solicit purchases or sales of municipal securities or to pursue other financial gain without the issuer's consent.

Examples of fiduciary capacities include but are not limited to acting as paying agent, transfer agent, registrar, or indenture trustee for an issuer.

6. 4. 8   TAXATION OF MUNICIPAL ISSUES

6. 4. 8. 1   Tax-Exempt Interest Payments

The **Tax Reform Act of 1986** restricted the federal income tax exemption of interest for municipal bonds to public purpose bonds, which are bonds issued to finance projects that benefit citizens in general rather than particular private interests. If a bond channels more than 10% of its proceeds to private parties, it is considered a private activity bond and is not automatically granted tax exemption.

6. 4. 8. 1. 1 Calculating Tax Benefits

An investor considering the purchase of a tax-exempt bond should compare its yield carefully with that of taxable securities. The tax savings of the tax-free bond may be more attractive than a taxable bond with a higher interest rate. This depends, in part, on the investor's tax bracket: the higher the tax bracket, the greater the tax exemption's value.

To determine a municipal bond investment's tax benefit, an investor must calculate the tax-equivalent yield. To do so, divide the tax-free yield by 100% less the investor's tax rate.

TEST TOPIC ALERT

When answering a tax-equivalent yield question, keep in mind that the municipal yield will always be less than the corporate yield.

An investor is in the 30% tax bracket. A municipal bond currently yields 7%. To offer an equivalent yield, what must a corporate bond yield?

Divide the municipal yield by 100% minus the investor's tax bracket. This is known as the tax-equivalent yield formula.

$$7\% \div (100\% - 30\%) = 10\%$$

Assume the same investor is in the 30% tax bracket. If a corporate bond currently yields 11%, what would be the equivalent municipal yield?

To find the answer, multiply the corporate yield by 100% minus the investor's tax bracket. This is known as the tax-free equivalent yield formula.

$$11\% \times (100\% - 30\%) = 7.7\%$$

6. 4. 8. 2 No Interest Deductions

The expenses associated with purchasing or holding municipal bonds are not deductible. This includes interest on loans to acquire bonds, such as margin loans, and safe deposit box rental. These rules apply because of the tax-free nature of the interest income at the federal government level.

6. 4. 8. 2. 1 Exception for Banks

When banks purchase certain issues of GO bonds (limited to a maximum face amount of $10 million), they are allowed to deduct 80% of the interest carrying cost of the deposits funding the purchase of the bonds.

EXAMPLE

A bank buys municipal bonds with $1 million of deposits paying 3% interest. Because these bonds are bank qualified, the bank can deduct 80% of the interest paid (1 million × .03 × .8 = $24,000). The bank also receives interest on the newly purchased municipal bonds free of federal income tax.

6. 4. 9   TRACKING MUNICIPAL SECURITIES

Tax-exempt bonds are listed in financial publications such as *The Bond Buyer* and *The Wall Street Journal*.

Tax-Exempt Bond Transactions

Tax-Exempt Bonds

Representative prices for tax-exempt revenue and GO bonds based on institutional trades. Changes rounded to nearest 1/8. Yield is YTM.

Issue	Coupon	Maturity	Price	Chg	Bid Yld
Alaska Hsg Fin Corp	6.600	12-01-23	97 1/2	- 1/4	6.79
Cal Dept of Wtr Res	6.125	12-01-13	95 3/4	- 1/2	6.50
Charlotte Hosp Auth	6.250	01-01-20	95 3/8	+ 1/2	6.62
Farmington NM Util Sys	5.750	05-15-13	91 1/4	- 1/8	6.53
Ill State Toll Hwy Auth	6.375	01-01-15	96	+ 3/8	6.72
Kenton Co KY Airport	6.300	03-01-15	95 1/4	- 1/2	6.71

* This sample comprises formats, styles, and abbreviations from a variety of currently available sources and has been created for educational purposes.

EXAMPLE

Examine the Kenton County, Kentucky, Airport bond. The name of the bond appears in the left column under the "Issue" column. The entries in the "Coupon" and "Maturity" columns indicate that the bond pays 6.300% interest and matures on March 1, 2015. The bond was traded at 95¼, or $952.50 per $1,000 bond.

The price represents a half-point ($5) decrease from the last trade, as reported under the "Chg" (change) column. The 6.71 yield is the bid yield and the yield to maturity. Because the bond is selling at a discount, the yield to maturity is higher than the coupon yield.

6. 4. 9. 1   Electronic Municipal Market Access (EMMA)

EMMA is a centralized online site used to locate key information about municipal securities. The information on EMMA is presented for retail, nonprofessional investors. EMMA makes available OSs for most new municipal bond offerings, 529 college savings plans, and other municipal securities. EMMA also provides real-time access to prices, as well as prices and rates from remarketing agents regarding auction rate securities.

QUICK QUIZ 6.D

Objective: Identify unique features of municipal securities trading

1. Municipal advertising material includes

    A. a preliminary official statement
    B. a final official statement
    C. both preliminary and final official statements
    D. neither a preliminary or final official statement

2. A broker-dealer who acts as a financial advisor to a municipality wants to participate in the underwriting of that municipality's new issue bonds. This activity is

   A. allowed for negotiated underwritings only
   B. allowed for competitive bid underwritings only
   C. allowed for either a completive bid or negotiated underwritng
   D. prohibited for either a completive bid or negotiated underwritng

3. If an investor in the 27% federal marginal income tax bracket invests in municipal general obligation public purpose bonds nominally yielding 4.5%, what is the tax-equivalent yield?

   A. .0616
   B. .0436
   C. .0270
   D. .0045

4. Certain municipal bond investors would be allowed to deduct some margin interest paid to borrow funds used to purchase specific municipal bond issues. Those investors would be

   A. banks purchasing revenue bonds only
   B. banks purchasing bank qualified general obligation (GO) issues
   C. individuals purchasing revenue notes
   D. individuals purchasing either revenue or general obligations bonds.

5. Churning, a prohibited activity refers to

   A. entering more transactions than necessary, solely for the purpose of generating commissions.
   B. purchasing municipal bonds for your own account before entering a large customer order for the stock.
   C. selling municipal bonds at a discount to institutional buyers
   D. selling short municipal bonds

6. A municipal securities dealer informed a municipal bond fund that it was the leading retailer of that funds shares hoping that the fund would use the dealers trading department to do more trades for the fund's portfolio. If the fund were to oblige, which of the following statements regarding this scenario is TRUE?

   A. It is permissible because MSRB rules do not cover municipal bond issuers or funds.
   B. It is permissible because MSRB rules suggest that coordination on all levels between the two should occur.
   C. It is not permissible because municipal securities dealers are not allowed to execute trades for the portfolios they underwrite.
   D. It is not permissible because it violates the MSRB anti-reciprocal rule.

7. One of the functions of a broker's broker in the municipal bond business is to do which of the following?

   A. Offer bonds at a discount to the investing public
   B. Assist in preparing bids for an underwriting syndicate
   C. Help sell new municipal bonds that a syndicate has been unable to sell
   D. Maintain a current bid and offer price in the secondary market

8. An online site intended for use by retail, nonprofessional investors to locate key information about municipal securities, including current prices is known as:

    A. electronic municipal market access (EMMA)
    B. Municipal Securities Rulemaking Board (MSRB)
    C. Moody's
    D. broker check

All Quick Quiz answers are found at the end of their units.

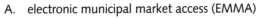

6. 5 MUNICIPAL SECURITIES RULES AND REGULATIONS

Rules and regulations applicable to all firms and individuals having to do with muniipal securities are written by the Muncipal securities rule making board (MSRB).

6. 5. 1 MUNICIPAL SECURITIES RULEMAKING BOARD (MSRB)

The Securities Acts Amendments of 1975 established the **Municipal Securities Rulemaking Board** as an independent SRO. The MSRB governs the issue and trade of municipal securities. The rules require municipal securities underwriters and dealers to protect investors' interests, be ethical in offering advice, and be responsive to complaints and disputes. The MSRB rules apply to all firms and individuals engaged in the conduct of municipal securities business. The MSRB does not regulate issuers.

6. 5. 1. 1 Rule Enforcement

The MSRB has no authority to enforce the rules it makes. While the SEC oversees all securities-related rule enforcement, the MSRB rules concerning municipal securities dealers (e.g., NYSE member firms) are specifically enforced by FINRA; the Office of the Comptroller of the Currency enforces those rules that apply to national banks.

The **Federal Reserve Board (FRB)** enforces MSRB rules governing any non-national banks that are members of the Federal Reserve System. The **Federal Deposit Insurance Corporation (FDIC)** enforces MSRB rules for non-national banks that are not members of the Federal Reserve System.

6. 5. 1. 2 Municipal Finance Professional

As defined by the MSRB, a municipal finance professional (MFP) is an associated person of a broker-dealer who is primarily engaged in municipal securities activities other than retail sales to individuals. The MFP designation also includes anyone who solicits municipal securities business for the broker-dealer, or is in the supervisory chain above another person with the MFP designation. This can include senior officials of the broker-dealer, or executives, or management committee members of the broker-dealer.

Of note, the MSRB is clear that anyone designated as an MFP is subject to the rules regarding political contributions (as stated in Rule G-37 later in this unit) and required to report those contributions to the MSRB, as well as any other payments made to a state or local political party. There are exceptions for de minimis contributions.

6. 5. 1. 3   General Regulations

This section addresses the rules of the MSRB that can conceptually be Series 7 testable. Each rule is identified with a G-number, such as G-1, G-2 and so on. It is unnecessary to memorize these rules by their numbers; instead, be comfortable with the concepts they convey.

The three categories of MSRB rules include (1) rules that provide consistent legal definitions of terms used in the business of trading municipal securities, (2) administrative rules that cover the organization and functions of the MSRB, and (3) general rules and regulations that describe MSRB policies. The following sections highlight the important MSRB rules.

Rule G-1. A bank that has a separately identifiable department or division engaged in any activity related to the municipal securities business is classified as a municipal securities dealer and must comply with MSRB regulations. A separately identifiable division is one under the direct supervision of an officer of the bank responsible for the day-to-day conduct of municipal securities business.

Municipal securities-related activity includes underwriting, trading, or selling municipal securities, or serving as an issuer's financial adviser. In addition, a firm that provides research or advisory services for municipal securities investors or that communicates with the public in any way about investing in municipal securities is considered a municipal securities dealer and must register with the MSRB.

Rules G-2 and G-3. Those who must qualify by examination under MSRB rules include municipal securities principals, financial and operations principals, and municipal securities representatives. A municipal securities representative is any person who gives financial advice to municipal securities issuers or investment advice to investors. Anyone who communicates with the public about municipal securities acts as a representative.

A person must pass the Municipal Securities Representative Qualification Exam (Series 52) or the General Securities Representative Exam (Series 7) to be qualified as a municipal securities representative. To qualify as a municipal securities principal, a person must pass the Municipal Securities Principal Qualification Exam (Series 53).

TAKE NOTE
Excluded from the licensing requirements are persons acting in a clerical or ministerial capacity who:

■ read approved quotes,

■ provide trade reports, or

■ record or enter orders.

Persons who take a qualification exam and fail cannot retake the exam for 30 days. After failing the exam three or more times, a six-month wait is imposed before another attempt is allowed. FINRA has adopted this rule.

If a new municipal representative has not passed the appropriate exam within 180 days, he must stop performing all functions of a municipal representative.

Rule G-6. The MSRB requires municipal broker-dealers to maintain blanket fidelity bonds as mandated by the SRO to which a broker-dealer belongs. The dollar amount of coverage required varies according to the firm's size. Banks are not affected by this rule.

Rule G-7. A municipal securities dealer must obtain and keep on file specific information about its associated persons. Most of the required information (e.g., employment history, disciplinary actions, residence, and personal data) is contained on the U-4 and U-5 forms.

Rule G-10. Anytime a municipal securities firm receives a written complaint from a customer, the firm must enter the complaint in a complaint file, indicating what action, if any, the firm has taken. It must also deliver a copy of the MSRB's *Investor Brochure* to that customer.

Rule G-11. During the underwriting period, a syndicate must establish a priority for allocating orders and identify conditions that might alter the priority.

Rule G-12. This rule outlines the procedures, or **uniform practices**, for settling transactions between municipal securities firms. The MSRB uniform practices include regulations regarding settlement dates, which are the same for municipal securities firms as they are for the rest of the securities industry.

- **Cash trades** settle on the trade date.
- **Regular way** trades settle on the second business day after the trade date (T+2).

Rule G-12 also discusses **good delivery requirements**. Securities that are not in good delivery form are rejected (buyer does not accept delivery) or reclaimed (buyer accepts delivery only to find the bonds are not good delivery). This does not invalidate the trade; the seller is still obligated to sell the securities.

Delivery is made in denominations of $1,000 or $5,000 for bearer bonds. Registered bonds are delivered in multiples of $1,000 par value, with a maximum par value on any one certificate of $100,000.

Mutilated certificates are not good delivery unless the transfer agent or some other acceptable official of the issuer validates the security. The issuer or a commercial bank must endorse mutilated coupons for them to be considered good delivery. Coupon bonds must have all unpaid coupons attached in proper order.

In the case of an issue's **partial call**, the called securities are not good delivery unless they are identified as called when traded. Municipal securities without legal opinions attached are not good delivery unless it is specified on the trade date that the transaction is ex-legal.

Rule G-13. Dealers can publish quotations only for bona fide bids or offers. Nominal quotes (informational only) are permissible if identified as such. No dealer participating in a joint account may distribute a quotation indicating more than one market for that security.

Rule G-15. Confirmations of trades must be sent or given to customers at or before a transaction's completion. Each confirmation must include:

- broker-dealer's name, address, and telephone number;
- customer's name;
- detailed description of the security, including issuer, interest rate and maturity, whether it is callable, and so forth;
- trade date and time of execution;
- settlement date;
- CUSIP number, if any;
- yield and dollar price;

- amount of accrued interest;
- extended principal amount (the total principal of all securities the information covers);
- total dollar amount (the extended principal plus any accrued interest);
- whether the firm acted as broker or dealer (if it acted as broker, the name of the person on the other side of the trade must be given, if requested, and the dollar amount of commission earned from both parties must be disclosed);
- dated date, if it affects the interest calculation and the first interest payment date;
- level of registration of the security (fully registered, registered as to principal only, or book-entry);
- whether the bonds are called or prerefunded; and
- any other special fact about the security traded (e.g., escrowed to maturity, ex-legal trade, federally taxable, or odd denominations).

Rule G-16. Each municipal broker-dealer must be examined at least once every two calendar years to ensure that the firm is in compliance with MSRB regulations, SEC rules, and the Securities Exchange Act of 1934. Because the MSRB does not enforce its own rules, it does not examine municipal securities firms. The appropriate enforcement agency (e.g., FINRA, FDIC, Comptroller of the Currency, or FRB) administers the examinations.

Rule G-17. Municipal securities dealers must deal fairly with everyone in transacting municipal securities business and must not engage in deceptive, dishonest, unfair, or manipulative practices.

Rule G-18. Dealers must try to obtain prices for customers that are reasonable and fairly related to the market. This rule also applies to broker's brokers, which regularly effect trades for the accounts of other municipal brokers and dealers.

Rule G-19. A municipal securities firm, through its representatives, must obtain extensive financial, personal, and investment information about a client to ensure suitable recommendations and transactions. A representative must obtain and use as much information as possible when making recommendations and must have reasonable grounds for recommending any particular security or transaction.

The MSRB prohibits broker-dealers from recommending municipal securities to a customer if a broker-dealer has not obtained the customer's financial information, tax status, and investment objectives, even if the broker-dealer has reasonable grounds to believe that the recommendation is suitable for the customer.

Rule G-20. Municipal securities dealers cannot give gifts valued at more than $100 to any person in one year other than their employees. Payments for services rendered are allowed. Gifts of occasional meals or tickets to sporting events or concerts (not season passes) are permitted. Sponsorship of legitimate business functions is also permissible.

Rule G-21. Municipal securities firms must be truthful in their advertising. They must not publish advertisements that are false or misleading in regard to their services, skills, or products. An advertisement for a new issue can show the original reoffering price, even though it may have changed, if the advertisement contains the sale date. A firm's municipal or general securities principal must approve each advertisement in writing before first use.

Rule G-22. Clients must be informed if a **control relationship** exists between a municipal firm and an issuer. A control relationship means the dealer or one of its officers is in a position to influence the issuer or is in a position to be influenced by the issuer. The phrase "controls, is controlled by, or is under common control with" allows the broadest interpretation of *control*. Verbal disclosure is required before the trade is effected, with written disclosure following no later than at the time of the confirmation.

TAKE NOTE   Particular care must be taken in a discretionary account. If a control relationship exists, no transaction is permitted without prior authorization from the customer.

Rule G-23. Prohibits a broker-dealer or municipal securities dealer that serves as financial advisor to a municipal issuer from underwriting the issuer's bonds in either a negotiated or competitive bid underwriting except in the instance of certain defined allowable functions (i.e., assisting with the preparation of the official statement).

Rule G-24. In the normal course of business, dealers gain access to confidential, nonpublic information about their customers. Municipal securities firms may not use this confidential information to solicit trades of municipal securities except with an issuer's express consent.

Rule G-25. Like other types of broker-dealers, municipal securities firms and their representatives may not misuse securities or money held for other people. They must not guarantee a customer against loss or share in the profits or losses of a customer's account, although joint accounts in a private capacity are allowed. Bona fide put options and repurchase agreements are not considered guarantees against loss.

Rule G-27. Each municipal securities firm must designate a principal to supervise the firm's representatives and must create and maintain a written supervisory procedures manual. The designated principal for the firm must approve in writing:

- the opening of new customer accounts;
- every municipal securities transaction;
- actions taken on customer complaints; and
- correspondence regarding municipal securities trades.

Every broker-dealer, but not bank dealers, must have a **financial and operations principal (FinOp)** who maintains the financial books and records.

Rule G-28. If a municipal securities dealer employee opens an account with another municipal securities firm, MSRB rules require the firm opening the account to notify the employer in writing and to send duplicate confirmations to the employer. The firm opening the account must comply with any other requests the employer makes.

Rule G-29. Every municipal securities dealer's office must keep a copy of MSRB regulations so that it may provide a copy of these rules for review to any customer upon request.

Rule G-30. The markups or markdowns that municipal securities dealers charge must be fair and reasonable, taking into account all characteristics of a trade, such as:

- fair market value of the securities at trade time;

■ total dollar amount of the transaction;
■ any special difficulty in doing the trade; and
■ the fact that the dealer is entitled to a profit.

Rule G-31. A municipal securities broker-dealer may not solicit business from an investment company on the basis of the broker-dealer's record of sales of the investment company's shares.

Rule G-32. When a new issue of municipal securities is delivered to a customer, a copy of the OS must accompany or precede the delivery.

If the issue is a negotiated underwriting, the municipal firm must disclose in writing to the customer the amount of the spread, the amount of any fee received if the firm acted as an agent in the sale, and the initial offering price for each maturity in the issue. There is no requirement to disclose the spread in competitive underwritings.

Rule G-33. Municipal dealers must calculate accrued interest when a municipal security transaction occurs and is designated "and interest," meaning it is trading with accrued interest. Municipal bonds, like corporates, use a 360-day year with 30-day months.

Rule G-37. Rule G-37 prohibits municipal firms from engaging in municipal securities business with an issuer for two years after any political contribution is made to an official of that issuer. In this context, municipal securities business refers to negotiated underwritings, not to competitive underwritings. The idea is to prevent firms from making large political contributions in return for being selected as underwriter for that issuer.

The rule applies to contributions by the firm, its MFPs, and by political action committees controlled by the firm or its representatives. Contributions of up to $250 per election are permitted by municipal finance professionals, as long as these individuals are eligible to vote for the issuer official. This exemption does not apply to firms.

Rule G-39. Telemarketers calling on behalf of a firm may not call a person before 8:00 am or after 9:00 pm in the called person's time zone. The caller must disclose his name and the firm's name, the firm's telephone number or address, and the fact that he is calling to solicit the purchase of municipal bonds or investment services.

The requirements do not apply if the person called is an established customer. Calls made to other brokers or dealers are also exempt.

Rule G-41. Every broker, dealer, or municipal securities dealer must establish and implement an anti-money laundering compliance program reasonably designed to achieve and monitor ongoing compliance with the requirements of the Bank Secrecy Act.

Rule G-42. This rule specifically limits political contributions by advisors.

QUICK QUIZ 6.E

Objective: Identify the role of the MSRB and list significant rules that affect the municipal securities industry

1. A municipal finance professional is

   A. an officer of the MSRB engaged in writing municipal securities rules and regulations

   B. any individual engaged in the sale of municipal securities to both retail and institutional clients

   C. an associate of a broker-dealer engaged in municipal securities representative activities, other than retail sales

   D. a municipal official elected to oversee the issuance of new municipal bonds

2. The Municipal Securities Rulemaking Board rules for NYSE broker-dealer member firms are enforced by

   A. FINRA

   B. MSRB

   C. NYSE

   D. SEC

3. Municipal securities transactions settling regular way will settle on

   A. the trade date plus 1 business day

   B. the trade date plus 2 business days

   C. the trade date plus 3 business days

   D. the same day as the transaction

4. An investor purchases a new issue municipal bond. A copy of the official statement (OS)

   A. must precede the delivery of the bonds

   B. need only be delivered if requested in writing by the investor

   C. need not be delivered because an OS is not a prospectus

   D. must accompany or precede the delivery of the bonds

All Quick Quiz answers are found at the end of their units.

6. 6   ACCRUED INTEREST CALCULATIONS

Most bonds trade and interest, meaning a buyer pays a seller a bond's market price, plus any accrued interest since the last interest payment. The buyer receives the full amount of the next interest payment, including interest that accrued while the seller owned the bond.

Most bonds pay interest every six months on either the 1st or the 15th of the specified months. The payment dates are known as coupon dates. Accrued interest affects bond transactions when settlement occurs between coupon dates. Some examples of coupon dates follow.

If the interest dates are:	The bonds are known as:
January 1 and July 1	J&J bonds
February 15 and August 15	F&A 15 bonds
March 1 and September 1	M&S bonds
April 1 and October 1	A&O bonds
May 15 and November 15	M&N 15 bonds
June 15 and December 15	J&D 15 bonds

TAKE NOTE When payment dates within the month are not specified, always assume the first of the month (e.g., J & J, assume January 1 and July 1).

6. 6. 1 ACCRUED INTEREST AND THE DATED DATE

For a new bond issue, the date from which interest accrual begins is called the **dated date**. Even if a bond is issued at a later date, the bond starts accruing interest on the date designated as the dated date.

TAKE NOTE The accrued interest amount is calculated to add to the price that the buyer pays and the seller receives when the bond trades between its coupon payment dates. Consider a bond with interest payments on January 1 and July 1. If a trade is made in April, the seller is entitled to some of the July interest payment. Specifically, the seller will receive interest up to, but not including, the settlement date of the transaction.

6. 6. 2 MUNICIPAL BOND ACCRUED INTEREST CALCULATION

Rules for calculating municipal bond accrued interest are the same as they are for corporate bonds.

Unless a bond is trading flat (discussed later), the bond cost to the buyer and the proceeds to the seller include accrued interest. Accrued interest increases the bond cost to the buyer and the proceeds to the seller.

Accrued interest is calculated from the last interest payment date up to but not including the settlement date. The buyer owns the bond on the settlement date, which means that the interest for that day belongs to the buyer.

6. 6. 2. 1   The Calculation

This calculation requires assuming that all months have 30 days. The 30-day-month method is used on all corporate and municipal bonds. Therefore, for purposes of this calculation, the year contains 360 days.

TAKE NOTE

A method using actual-calendar-days (365-day-year) is used on all U.S. government bonds (not corporates or municipals).

EXAMPLE

If an F&A municipal bond is traded regular way on Monday, March 5, the number of days of accrued interest is calculated as follows:

February	30 days
March 5 trade	6 days (settles T+2 regular way March 7)
Days of accrued interest	36 days

Because the trade settles on March 7, six days of interest accrue for March. Remember: up to <u>but not including the settlement date</u>.

If the municipal bond transaction was a cash settled one (not regular way), settlement in cash would be on the same day as the trade date (same-day settlement). Therefore, calculating up to but not including the settlement date, the days of accrued interest for March would be 4, making the total days of accrued interest 34.

TEST TOPIC ALERT

Recap for calculating accrued interest as follows.

- Corporate and municipals: use 30-day months (360-day year)

- Government securities: use actual day months (365-day year)

When counting days:

- Go back and include the last interest payment date

- Go up to but not including the settlement date.

QUICK QUIZ 6.F

Objective: Describe the tax treatment of municipal securities

1. To calculate accrued interest for a municipal bond, which of the following is used?

   A. 30-day months and a 360-day year
   B. 31-day months and a 360-day year
   C. actual day months and a 360-day year
   D. actual day months and a 365-day year

2. At settlement, accrued interest

    A. increases the amount the buyer must pay and decreases the amount the seller will receive

    B. decreases the amount the buyer must pay and increases the amount the seller will receive

    C. decreases the amount the buyer must pay and decreases the amount the seller will receive

    D. increases the amount the buyer must pay and increases the amount the seller will receive

All Quick Quiz answers are found at the end of their units.

6. 7   ADJUSTING THE COST BASIS OF MUNICIPAL BONDS

If and how cost basis is adjusted for municipal bonds depends first on if the bond was purchased at a premium or a discount.

6. 7. 1   MUNICIPAL BONDS PURCHASED AT A PREMIUM

The investor who buys a municipal bond at a premium, whether as a new issue or in the secondary market, must amortize the premium (straight line) over the remaining life of the bond. Straight-line amortization means that an equal amount of the premium will be amortized each year the bond is held.

EXAMPLE

A customer buys an 8% municipal bond with eight years to maturity at a dollar price of 108. The premium of eight points ($80) must be amortized over the remaining eight years to maturity. The annual amortization amount is one point, or $10 per bond. After one year, the cost basis is 107; after two years, 106; and so on. If held to maturity, there is no capital loss because the cost basis at that time has been reduced to par.

Amortization:

■ reduces cost basis, and

■ reduces reported interest income.

In the example, cost basis is reduced each year by $10 per bond. In addition, interest income of $80 per bond is reduced to $70 per bond (the amount of the annual amortization). Because interest income on municipal bonds is not taxed, its annual amortization has no tax effect.

If the bond is sold before maturity, gain or loss is the difference between sales price and adjusted cost basis. Take the following example. A customer buys a five-year municipal bond at 105. Two years later, the bond is sold at 104. What is the customer's gain or loss?

The premium of five points must be amortized over a five-year period, so the annual amortization is one point, or $10 per bond. After two years, the bond's cost basis is 103. Therefore, a sale at 104 creates a one-point capital gain per bond.

6. 7. 2   MUNICIPAL BONDS PURCHASED AT A DISCOUNT

If a municipal bond is bought at a discount, the discount is accreted. Accretion is the process of adjusting the cost basis back up to par. The actual tax effect of accretion depends on whether the bond was purchased as an original issue discount (OID) (i.e., a new issue being offered at a discount) or an issue purchased at a discount in the secondary market.

Accretion:

■ increases cost basis, and

■ increases reported interest income.

EXAMPLE

A customer buys a 5% municipal bond with 10 years to maturity at 90. The amount of the annual accretion is $10 per bond (10-point discount ÷ 10 years to maturity). Each year, the cost basis is adjusted upward by one point. At maturity, there is no reported capital gain.

If the bond was purchased as an OID, the reported interest income would be $60 per bond ($50 plus the annual accretion of $10). Because interest income on municipal bonds is tax free, the accretion has no tax effect. If, however, the bond was purchased at a discount in the secondary market, the annual accretion would be taxed as ordinary income.

OIDs in this case are zero-coupon Bonds

EXAMPLE

Assume a customer buys a 5% municipal bond with a 10-year maturity at 90 in the secondary market. Five years later, the customer sells the bond at 97. What are the tax consequences? The annual accretion of $10 per bond is taxable each year as ordinary income. The customer's cost basis at the time of sale is 95. When sold at 97, the customer has a capital gain of $20 per bond.

Had the bond been purchased as an OID, the only tax consequence would be a capital gain of $20 per bond. The annual accretion for an OID is considered municipal interest income and is therefore not taxable.

Disc =10   +1 point each year
10 years to mat
5 years later   cost= 95
sold @ 97 = +2
Gain = $20/bond

= OID accretion = muni interest income - NOT capital gain tax

---

QUICK QUIZ 6.G

Objective: Describe the tax treatment of municipal securities

1. An investor purchases a 5% municipal bond in the secondary market at 90. With 10 years left to maturity, the annual accretion and capital gain at maturity is

    A.   zero with no capital gain at maturity
    B.   zero with a $100 capital gain at maturity
    C. $10 per bond with no capital gain at maturity
    D. $10 per bond with a $100 capital gain at maturity

is not taxable

2.   Your customer purchases a 6% municipal bond at 106 having 6 years left to maturity. If the bond is held until it matures, reportable cost basis and gain or loss at that time will be

A.   a cost basis of par ($1,000) with no gain or loss
B.   a cost basis of par with $60 capital loss
C.   a cost basis of 106 ($1,060) with no gain or loss
D.   a cost basis of 106 ($1,060) with $60 capital loss

All Quick Quiz answers are found at the end of their units.

QUICK QUIZ ANSWERS

Quick Quiz 6.A

1. **B.** A variable-rate bond has no fixed coupon rate. The interest rate is tied to a market rate (for example, T-bill yields) and is subject to change at regular intervals. Because the interest paid reflects changes in overall interest rates, the price of the bond remains relatively close to its par value.

2. **A.** Property taxes are a primary source of cash flow for most municipalities, but property taxes are collected at established intervals. Issuing tax anticipation notes (TANs) backed by future tax revenues can help a municipality maintain an even cash flow throughout its fiscal year.

3. **C.** The debt limit is the maximum amount of debt a municipality can incur. Such restrictions have made revenue bonds increasingly popular because they are normally not subject to statutory debt limitations.

4. **B.** Auction rate securities (ARS) are long-term bonds tied to short-term interest rates. Dutch auctions are used to reset the rates at predetermined intervals, but if no bids are received at the time of the auction, it is considered failed. In essence, a lack of demand for the bonds culminating in no interested bidders is one of the risks associated with owning an ARS.

5. **C.** The interest income from most U.S. government and agency securities is exempt from state and local taxes, but not federal taxes. The interest on municipal issues (like the Minneapolis Housing Authority bonds) is exempt from both federal taxes and, because this investor is a Minnesota resident, state taxes. Ginnie Maes are subject to taxation on all levels.

6. **D.** Under the Economic Recovery and Reinvestment Act of 2009, Build America Bonds, issued by municipalities, make interest payments that are taxable to bondholders. While some types of BABs offer tax credits to the issuer and others offer tax credits to the bondholder, neither of these characteristics are applicable to all BABs.

Quick Quiz 6.B

1. **D.** The priority of filling municipal orders is established by the managing underwriter in the release terms letter sent to the syndicate once the bid is won. This letter is an amendment to the syndicate agreement.

2. **D.** The syndicate agreement is signed by all members of the syndicate, including the managing underwriter. It is not signed by the issuer, the bond counsel, or the trustee.

3. **C.** The scale, or reoffering scale, is the yield(s) to maturity at which the syndicate will reoffer the bonds to the public. Syndicate participants consider the market for bonds of similar quality in deciding at what yield to market the issue on which they are bidding.

4. **A.** Net interest cost (NIC) measures an issuer's overall cost of borrowing for a particular bond issue. It is therefore the most important item considered by an issuer when evaluating competing bids. Coupon rate, par value, and maturity length are elements of the net interest cost calculation. The reoffering scale is the arrangement of yields at which the bonds will be sold to the public and is unrelated to the issuer's cost of borrowing. Takedown and concession refer to the arrangements for allocating bonds and assigning underwriting profit to the various underwriters once the winning bid has been awarded. These do not affect the net interest cost.

5. **A.** A municipal group net order is credited to syndicate members according to their percentage participation in the account. This order type is given priority over designated or member takedown orders, but not over presale orders. By placing this type of order, syndicate members are stipulating that they want those bond orders to have the highest priority still available. Note that presale orders are also confirmed for the benefit of the entire syndicate, but these are placed before the time the winning bid is awarded.

6. **D.** The spread is the difference between the reoffering price and the amount bid on an issue in competitive bidding. MSRB rules state that a dealer is entitled to make a profit in an underwriting. Therefore, the dealer can take into account such factors as market conditions, the type and size of the issue, the dollar volume of the transaction, and any extraordinary costs incurred by the syndicate. The amount of the good-faith check deposited before bidding on the issue has no relevance to the bid or to the reoffering price.

7. **C.** An unqualified legal opinion means that the bond counsel found no problems with the issue. A qualified opinion means that the issue is legal, but some qualification is necessary because certain contingencies exist. For example, the bond counsel might render a qualified opinion because competing facilities may restrict the flow of funds in the future. If the issuer does not have clear title to the property, the legal opinion may be qualified. The legal opinion has nothing to do with broker-dealer disclosure.

8. **D.** In a competitive bidding situation, each syndicate submits a sealed written bid. The price at which the bonds are sold is called the reoffering yield.

Quick Quiz 6.C

1. **C.** Municipal bond insurance is purchased to insure the payments of principal and interest in the event the issuer defaults.

2. **D.** All the fees and taxes listed are payments received by the municipality that are not the result of a revenue-producing facility. General revenues of the municipality may be used to pay the debt service on a general obligation bond.

3. **D.** General obligation bonds are backed by the full faith and credit of an issuer, which is based on its ability to levy and collect taxes. Although these quantitative factors, are important to an analyst, qualitative factors such as a community's attitude toward borrowing and repaying debt, are also important considerations.

4. **D.** Interest rate movements have no bearing on determining the quality of revenue bond issues.

5. **B.** The size of the municipality does not count, but the size of the debt outstanding for a municipality does. A municipality with a small amount of debt will not have enough activity in those debt instruments to warrant a rating by a rating agency.

6. **C.** The dollar denomination of bonds to be issued has no bearing on a GO bond analysis. The tax base, economic character, and population makeup would all be considered.

7. **A.** The official statement is an offering document that discloses material information on a new issue of municipal securities. Because it commonly includes information concerning the purpose of the issue, how the securities will be repaid, and the financial, economic, and social characteristics of the issuer, it is an appropriate place to review the creditworthiness of an issue. The legal opinion reviews the legality of the issue, including certain legal exemptions. A prospectus is the document that provides material information about a nonexempt security being publicly distributed. The trust indenture is the basic bond contract between the issuer and the trustee.

8. **D.** When credit conditions deteriorate, bankruptcies rise, bond defaults increase, and consumer debt increases. An increase in assessed valuation, or property value, would indicate a strengthening economy.

9. **A.** FGIC and AGC insure municipal bonds.

Quick Quiz 6.D

1. **D.** Neither a preliminary or final OS is considered municipal advertising because they are prepared by or on behalf of an issuer rather than for the purpose of enhancing sales for dealers.

2. **D.** The MSRB prohibits broker-dealers acting as financial advisers to a municipality to participate in underwriting that municipality's new issue bonds, whether being done in a competitive bid or negotiated underwriting.

3. **A.** The formula for computing tax-equivalent yield is: nominal yield divided by (1 − federal marginal income tax rate) .045 / (1 − .27) = 6.16%.

4. **B.** Margin interest charged for loans to purchase municipal bonds is generally not deductible on a tax return. However, for certain GO municipal issues (known as bank qualified municipal issues) the IRS allows a bank to deduct up to 80% of the margin interest charged for funds borrowed to purchase the bonds.

5. **A.** Unnecessary transactions entered into for the purpose of generating commissions constitute churning. A charge of churning can result from both excessive number and excessive size of transactions.

6. **D.** An investment company must select a broker-dealer to execute trades based on the quality of services provided. It is a violation of the anti-reciprocal rule for an investment company to choose a broker-dealer based on how much of the fund the BD sells to the public.

7. **C.** A broker's broker helps sell any bonds a syndicate has left in a new municipal bond offering. These are bonds that the syndicate was unable to sell during the IPO.

8. **A.** EMMA is a centralized online site used to locate key information about municipal securities presented for retail, nonprofessional investors. Available on the site are OSs for most new municipal bond offerings, 529 education savings plans, and other municipal securities. Additionally it offers real-time access to prices for municipal bonds trading in the secondary market.

Quick Quiz 6.E

1. **C.** A municipal finance professional (MFP) is an associate of a broker-dealer engaged in municipal securities representative activities, other than retail sales.

2. **A.** For NYSE member firms, MSRB rules are enforced by FINRA. While the board has the authority to create rules, it has no authority to enforce them.

3. **B.** Regular way municipal transaction settlement is the same as it is for corporate securities; trade date plus 2 business days; (T+2).

4. **D.** While not a prospectus, the OS is the municipal industry's disclosure document. When municipal bonds are purchased, a copy of the official statement must accompany or precede the delivery of the bonds.

Quick Quiz 6.F

1. **A.** To calculate accrued interest for a municipal bond or a corporate bond, a 30-day month is assumed for all months, which totals to a 360-day year.

2. **D.** Remember, at settlement, buyers pay any accrued interest due and sellers receive the accrued interest. Therefore, any accrued interest will increase the amount the buyer must pay and increase the amount the seller will receive.

Quick Quiz 6.G

1. **C.** $10 per bond with no capital gain at maturity. One bond point equals $10. A 10-point discount represents a $100 discount. $100 divided by 10 years to maturity equals $10 accretion each year. With the accretion taxed each year, there is no capital gain reported at maturity.

2. **A.** Original cost basis is 106 ($1,060). Premium bonds must always be amortized. $60 amortized over 6 years represents $10 per year. $10 × 6 years equals $60 total amortization. Therefore, at maturity the entire $60 premium will have been amortized down to zero leaving only par ($1,000) as the new adjusted cost basis. With cost basis amortized (reduced) to $1,000 and par ($1,000) returned at maturity, there is no reportable gain or loss.

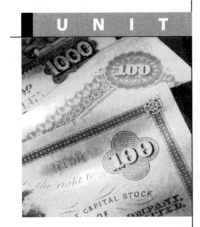

7

Margin Accounts

Margin accounts allow investors to leverage their investment dollars. Through margin accounts, investors can borrow money through brokerage firms by pledging collateral. The Federal Reserve Board regulates margin transactions.

Broker-dealers are required to impose initial and maintenance requirements on all margin accounts. They must mark to market all positions daily to ensure account equity meets the minimum requirements. As you review the Unit, remember that basic concepts have been covered in the Securities Industry Essentials (SIE) exam. If you are well-grounded in the basics, proficiency with the more complex concepts and margin accounting will follow.

Although this Unit involves substantial calculation and accounting scenarios, students should expect that only about one-third to one-half of the margin test questions will involve computations.

The Series 7 exam will include 14 questions on the topics covered in Units 7 and 8 (function 4). ■

In this Unit you will learn to:

- **identify** documentation required when extending credit to customers;

- **identify** regulations and regulatory bodies that affect margin account transactions;

- **define** Regulation T and its importance to margin accounts;

- **calculate** initial and maintenance requirements for long and short margin accounts;

- **calculate** equity in long, short, and combined margin accounts; and

- **compute** SMA.

7. 1   EXTENSION OF CREDIT IN THE SECURITIES INDUSTRY

Buying **on margin** is a common practice in the securities industry. It allows customers to increase their trading capital by borrowing from broker-dealers.

7. 1. 1   TYPES OF MARGIN ACCOUNTS

There are two types of margin accounts: **long** and **short**. In a **long margin account**, customers purchase securities and pay interest on the money borrowed until the loan is repaid. In a **short margin account**, stock is borrowed and then sold short, enabling the customer to profit if its value declines. All short sales must be executed through and accounted for in a margin account.

In long margin accounts, customers borrow money; in short margin accounts, customers borrow securities.

Advantages of margin accounts for customers are that the customer can:

■ purchase more securities with a lower initial cash outlay; and

■ **leverage** the investment by borrowing a portion of the purchase price.

Leveraging magnifies the customer's rate of return, or rate of loss in adverse market conditions.

Cash/Margin Purchase

	Cash Purchase	Margin Purchase
Purchase of 1,000 shares of ABC for $20	Customer pays $20,000 for purchase	Customer borrows 50% ($10,000) from broker-dealer, deposits equity of $10,000
Return after increase from $20 to $30 per share	Customer experiences 50% return (gain/initial investment: $10,000 ÷ $20,000 = 50%)	Customer experiences 100% return (gain/initial investment: $10,000 ÷ $10,000 = 100%)
Return after decrease from $20 to $15 per share	Customer experiences 25% loss (loss/initial investment: –$5,000 ÷ $20,000 = –25%)	Customer experiences 50% loss (loss/initial investment: –$5,000 ÷ $10,000 = –50%)

The advantages of margin accounts for broker-dealers are:

■ margin account loans generate interest income for the firm; and

■ margin customers typically trade larger positions because of increased trading capital, generating higher commissions for the firm.

7. 1. 2   MARGIN AGREEMENT

Customers who open margin accounts must sign a **margin agreement** before trading can begin. The agreement consists of three parts: the credit agreement, the hypothecation agreement, and the loan consent form.

7. 1. 2. 1   Credit Agreement

The **credit agreement** discloses the terms of the credit extended by the broker-dealer, including the method of interest computation and situations under which interest rates may change.

TAKE NOTE

Margin interest is a tax-deductible expense. The one exception is interest expenses incurred in the purchase of municipal securities. Because municipal interest income is federally tax exempt, the IRS does not allow taxpayers to claim deductions for the margin interest expense on municipal securities. Investors can deduct interest expenses for other securities to the extent that they do not exceed their net investment income, which includes interest income, dividends, and all capital gains.

7. 1. 2. 2   Hypothecation Agreement

The **hypothecation agreement** gives permission to the broker-dealer to pledge customer margin securities as collateral. The firm hypothecates customer securities to the bank, and the bank loans money to the broker-dealer on the basis of the loan value of these securities. All customer securities must be held in **street name** (registered in the name of the firm) to facilitate this process. When customer securities are held in street name, the broker-dealer is known as the **nominal**, or **named, owner**. The customer is the **beneficial owner**, because he retains all rights of ownership.

After customers pledge their securities to the broker-dealer by signing the hypothecation agreement, the broker-dealer **rehypothecates** (repledges) them as collateral for a loan from the bank. Regulation U oversees the process when a bank lends money to a broker-dealer based on customer securities that have been pledged as collateral.

Broker-dealers are limited to **pledging** 140% of a customer's debit balance as collateral. Any customer securities in excess of this amount must be physically segregated. The firm cannot commingle customer securities with securities owned by the firm.

Firms can only commingle one customer's securities with another customer's securities for hypothecation if customers have given specific permission by signing the hypothecation agreement.

Rehypothecation of Customer Securities

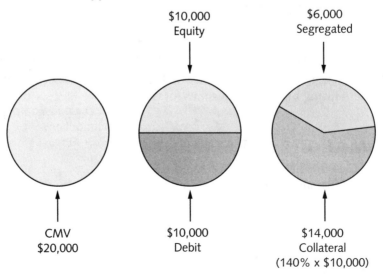

| CMV $20,000 | $10,000 Equity / $10,000 Debit | $6,000 Segregated / $14,000 Collateral (140% x $10,000) |

7.1.2.3   Loan Consent Form

If signed, the loan consent form gives permission to the firm to loan customer margin securities to other customers or broker-dealers, usually for short sales.

TAKE NOTE   It is mandatory that the customer sign the credit agreement and hypothecation agreement. The loan consent form is optional.

TEST TOPIC ALERT   The interest paid by margin customers on money borrowed is a variable rate based on the **broker call rate**.

7.1.2.4   Risk Disclosure

Before opening a margin account, a broker-dealer must provide customers with a risk disclosure document. This information must also be provided to margin customers on an annual basis. The document discusses the risks associated with margin trading, some of which are shown in the following:

- Customers are not entitled to choose which securities can be sold if a maintenance call is not met.
- Customers can lose more money than initially deposited.
- Customers are not entitled to an extension of time to meet a margin call.
- Firms can increase their in-house margin requirements without advance notice.

7.1.3   REGULATION T

The Securities Act of 1934 gives the Federal Reserve Board (FRB) the authority to regulate the extension of credit in the securities industry. For margin accounts, Regulation T states that customers must deposit a minimum of 50% of the market value of the transaction within two additional business days of regular way settlement; T+2. Therefore, within four business days of the transaction. The minimum required is 50%; a customer can choose to pay a larger percentage of the purchase price.

TAKE NOTE   Regulation T applies to both cash and margin accounts; customers have four business days to pay for the purchase regardless of the account type. Firms, however, expect payment the regular way: within two business days of trade date.

7.1.3.1   Marginable Securities

Regulation T also identifies which securities are eligible for purchase on margin and which may be used as collateral for loans for other purchases.

TAKE NOTE

Differentiate between use of the terms *margin* and *marginable*.

■ **Margin** is the amount of equity that must be deposited to buy securities in a margin account.

■ **Marginable** refers to securities that can be used as collateral in a margin account.

May be purchased on margin and used as collateral:
• Exchange-listed stocks, bonds
• Nasdaq stocks
• Non-Nasdaq OTC issues approved by the FRB
• Warrants

Cannot be purchased on margin and *cannot* be used as collateral:
• Put and call options
• Rights
• Non-Nasdaq OTC issues *not* approved by the FRB
• Insurance contracts

Cannot be bought on margin but *can* be used as collateral after 30 days:
• Mutual funds
• New issues

TEST TOPIC ALERT

With the exception of LEAPS options, options cannot be purchased on margin. When buying options, customers must deposit 100% of the premium. When writing a covered call, there is no Regulation T requirement for the call. All the customer must do is have 50% of the purchase price of the stock in the account. If you see a margin question on covered call writing, be sure to focus on what is being asked: Is it the Regulation T requirement, or is it the margin deposit? Consider the following examples.

If a customer buys stock and receives a premium by writing a call, the premium received for the call reduces the margin deposit that would be required.

Question: A customer purchases 100 ABC at 62 and also writes an ABC 65 call at 3. What is the margin deposit?

Answer: The Regulation T requirement for establishing both positions is $3,100 (50% × $6,200). The margin deposit is $2,800, which is the Regulation T requirement reduced by the premium received.

Question: A customer in a cash account purchases 100 ABC at 62 and also writes an ABC 65 call at 3. What is the required deposit?

Answer: In a cash account, the Regulation T requirement is 100% of the purchase price of the stock—that is, $6,200. The required deposit, however, is $5,900.

If, in a margin account, a customer buys stock and simultaneously buys an option, the customer must deposit 50% of the purchase price of the stock and 100% of the premium.

Question: A customer purchases 100 ABC at 62 and at the same time buys an ABC 60 put at 3. What is the margin deposit?

Answer: The margin deposit is $3,400. The 50% requirement on the stock is $3,100. Because options cannot generally be purchased on margin, the customer must pay the entire premium of $300.

TAKE NOTE

LEAPS options with more than nine months to expiration can be purchased on margin. The initial (and maintenance) requirement is 75%.

EXAMPLE

A customer buys 10 XYZ LEAPS at $4.50 each. The LEAPS expire in 24 months. What must the customer deposit?

The customer must deposit $3,375, which is 75% of the total cost of $4,500. When the time remaining to expiration reaches nine months, the maintenance requirement is 100% of the current market value.

With regard to option spreads, Regulation T requires customers to deposit the maximum loss. In debit spreads, the net debit represents maximum loss. In credit spreads, subtract the net credit from the difference between the strike prices to determine maximum loss.

Question: A customer buys 1 XYZ Jan 60 put at 8.50 and writes 1 XYZ Jan 50 put at 2.25. What must the customer deposit?

Answer: This is a bear put spread established at a net debit of 6.25. Because the net debit represents maximum loss, the customer must deposit $625.

7. 1. 3. 2   Exempt Securities

Certain securities are exempt from Regulation T margin requirements. If they are bought or sold in a margin account, they are subject to the firm's determination of an initial requirement, and firms must follow maintenance requirements established by FINRA or their SRO rules.

Securities exempt from Regulation T include:

■ U.S. Treasury bills, notes, and bonds;

■ government agency issues; and

■ municipal securities.

TAKE NOTE

The FRB can change Regulation T, but the current requirement has been in place for more than 20 years. Assume Regulation T equals 50% in test questions.

7. 1. 4   INITIAL REQUIREMENTS

Customers are required to deposit a minimum amount of equity for their **first purchase** in a margin account. Although Regulation T states that a deposit of 50% of the market value of the purchase is required, FINRA rules require that this initial deposit cannot be less than $2,000.

Initial Requirements Example

Customer Purchase	Regulation T Requirement	FINRA Minimum Rule	Customer Deposit Required
100 shares at $50/share	$2,500	$2,000	$2,500
100 shares at $30/share	$1,500	$2,000	$2,000
100 shares at $15/share	$750	$1,500	$1,500

The customer is required to deposit the greater of the Regulation T requirement or the FINRA minimum. The exception occurs when the customer's initial purchase is less than $2,000; the customer is not required to deposit $2,000, only the full purchase price.

There is another way to look at this: if the customer's first purchase in a margin account is less than $2,000, deposit 100% of the purchase price. If the first purchase is between $2,000 and $4,000, deposit $2,000. If the first purchase is greater than $4,000, deposit 50%.

TAKE NOTE   The FINRA minimum rule also applies to short margin accounts. However, because short transactions are more speculative, the minimum of $2,000 is never waived. If a short sale margin requirement is less than $2,000, the required deposit is still $2,000.

7. 1. 5   DEADLINES FOR MEETING MARGIN CALLS

As previously discussed, Regulation T requires margin account customers to meet initial margin deposit requirements no more than four business days after the trade date. The deposit may be made in cash or in fully paid marginable securities valued at twice (200%) the amount of the Regulation T cash call.

If payment is late, the broker-dealer may apply to the designated examining authority (DEA) for an extension, as it may do on behalf of cash account customers. The DEA for a broker-dealer can be either FINRA, an exchange or the Federal Reserve Bank in some cases. For introducing broker-dealers, those who do not clear their own trades, the request is made by the clearing firm. For an amount less than $1,000, the broker-dealer can choose to take no action.

If no extension is requested on the morning of the fifth business day (one day after the deposit is required to be made), the firm must sell out the securities purchased and freeze the account for 90 days. If the customer wants to purchase securities in a frozen account, the customer must have good funds in the account before order entry.

TAKE NOTE

"Freeriding" is a term used when securities are purchased and then sold before making payment for the purchase. Freeriding is generally prohibited in both cash and margin accounts. As a penalty, the account will be frozen for 90 days and no new transactions can occur unless there is cash or marginable securities in the account before the purchase is made.

QUICK QUIZ 7.A

Objectives:

- Identify documentation required when extending credit to customers
- Identify regulations and regulatory bodies that affect margin account transactions
- Define Regulation T and its importance to margin accounts

1. An investor opens a new margin account and buys 200 shares of DWQ at 50, with Regulation T at 50%. What is the investor's initial margin requirement?

   A. $2,500
   B. $3,000
   C. $5,000
   D. $10,000

2. In order to open a margin account, it is mandatory that the customer sign

   A. the credit agreement and the loan consent agreement
   B. the credit agreement and hypothecation agreement
   C. the hypothecation agreement and the loan consent agreement
   D. the credit agreement only

3. A customer wishes to deposit fully paid-for securities as collateral for securities purchased on margin. The value of the securities deposited must equal

   A. 200% of the amount of the Regulation T cash call
   B. 100% of the amount of the Regulation T cash call
   C. 50% of the amount of the Regulation T cash call
   D. 25% of the amount of the Regulation T cash call

4. For both cash and margin accounts the initial Regulation T deposit for an equity transaction settling regular way must be made

   A. on the same day as the transaction
   B. by the settlement date
   C. within one day of settlement
   D. no more than four business days after the trade date

5. A customer has failed to make the required Reg. T deposit for a transaction. An extension for payment could be first requested by and then granted by

   A. the customer and the broker-dealer
   B. the customer and a principal at the broker-dealer
   C. the clearing firm and the broker-dealer's designated examining authority
   D. the clearing firm and the Securities Exchange Commission

All Quick Quiz answers are found at the end of their units.

RGIN ACCOUNTING

After margin accounts have been opened, broker-dealers must verify that equity in the account still meets minimum requirements following fluctuations in market value.

The practice of recalculation to check the status of the equity in the account is called **marking to the market**. It is typically done every business day on the basis of the closing price of the stock. This concept applies to both long and short margin accounts, which will be discussed separately.

7. 2. 1   LONG MARGIN ACCOUNTING

The Series 7 exam uses the following terms to describe activity in long margin accounts:

- **Long market value (LMV)**—the current market value of the stock position the investor purchased
- **Debit register (DR)**—the amount of money borrowed by the customer
- **Equity (EQ)**—the customer's net worth in the margin account; it represents the portion of the securities the customer fully owns

The amount of equity in the account is determined by this equation:

$$LMV - DR = EQ$$

To simplify long margin accounts, think of them as a house with a mortgage. If the market value of a house goes up or down, the mortgage amount does not change, but the equity goes up or down. The same is true in a margin account; when market value of securities goes up, the debit balance (what the customer owes the broker-dealer) stays the same, while the equity increases. When market value of securities goes down, the debit balance stays the same and the equity decreases.

Continuing the analogy, consider a house payment. The payment does not affect the market value of the house but reduces the debit balance and consequently increases the equity. When money is paid into a margin account, the debit balance is decreased, and the equity is increased.

7. 2. 1. 1   Analyzing Long Margin Accounts

To analyze long margin account activity, a simplified balance sheet will be used, as shown below.

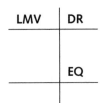

TAKE ✓ NOTE   Draw a chart whenever you are asked to compute equity in a margin account. Remember the master margin account equation: **LMV – DR = EQ**. Be sure that your account is balanced before going to the next step.

EXAMPLE

A customer purchases 1,000 shares of XYZ at 60 on margin and borrows the maximum 50% from the broker-dealer.

The margin chart is set up as follows:

LMV	DR
60,000	30,000
	EQ
	30,000

In this instance, the customer must deposit $30,000. The customer may deposit cash or fully paid securities. Meeting the margin requirement in securities requires double the necessary cash margin when Regulation T is 50%. For a margin requirement of $30,000, the customer may pay $30,000 in cash or deposit $60,000 of fully paid securities to meet the Regulation T requirement.

When the market value of securities changes, the broker-dealer must **mark to market the positions** to ensure that enough equity remains in the account. The customer's account must always meet the **maintenance requirement** of FINRA. In a long margin account, minimum maintenance is 25% of the LMV.

Marking to the market identifies the status of the customer's account. The determination of the status requires the computation of two **benchmarks**:

- **Regulation T** (50% of LMV)
- **Minimum maintenance** (25% of LMV)

If XYZ declines to 50, both of these benchmarks are computed on the basis of the new market value of the account, as shown below:

LMV	DR
	30,000
~~60,000~~	
50,000	
	EQ
	~~30,000~~
	20,000

Regulation T = 25,000 (50% × 50,000)

minimum maintenance = 12,500 (25% × 50,000)

[handwritten annotations: "if equity falls below 50% of LMV = becomes a restricted security"; "minimum amt of equity you need"]

TAKE NOTE

Here are some helpful tips in long margin accounting.

- When the market value of securities goes up or down, the DR does not change.

- When marking to the market, the calculation of Regulation T and minimum maintenance is based on the new LMV.

7. 2. 1. 2   Restricted Accounts

If the equity in the account is less than the Regulation T requirement but greater than or equal to the minimum maintenance requirement, the account is **restricted**.

TAKE NOTE

If an account becomes restricted, there is no requirement for the customer to take any action to remove the account from the restricted status. A maintenance call will be sent only if the account falls below the minimum maintenance requirement.

7. 2. 1. 2. 1   Restricted Account Rules

If an account is restricted, the following rules apply:

■ To purchase additional securities, put up 50%.

■ To withdraw securities from the account, the customer must deposit cash equal to 50% of the value of the securities to be withdrawn.

■ If securities are sold in a restricted account, at least half the proceeds must be retained in the account to reduce the debit balance. This is called the **retention requirement**. Also, 50% of the proceeds are credited to SMA.

EXAMPLE

LMV $50,000; DR $30,000; EQ $20,000

This account is restricted by $5,000; if the equity was $5,000 higher, the account would be at 50% and not restricted. The customer wants to sell $10,000 worth of stock.

Initially, all the proceeds are applied against the debit balance, and a credit of $5,000 is made to SMA. The account now looks as follows:

LMV $40,000; DR $20,000; EQ $20,000; SMA $5,000

If the customer wants to withdraw half the proceeds (remember, at least 50% must be retained in the account to reduce the debit balance, and the customer can remove the other half), he does so by using SMA and borrowing from the account. After the customer withdraws $5,000, the account looks like this:

LMV $40,000; DR $25,000; EQ $15,000; SMA 0

The reason all the proceeds of the sale are initially applied against the debit balance is this: what if the customer does not want any of the proceeds to be sent to him? In this case, the firm has the obligation to reduce the debit and thus his interest charges. If, however, the customer changes his mind and wants half the proceeds, he can always take out the $5,000 by using SMA.

TEST TOPIC ALERT

For the Series 7 exam, watch for the following: if securities are sold in a restricted account, which of the following are affected? LMV, DR, EQ, SMA?

All but equity are affected: LMV, DR, and SMA. Equity is affected only if the customer elects to remove half the proceeds.

7. 2. 1. 3   Maintenance Requirements

When the equity in the account falls below the minimum maintenance requirement, the customer receives a **maintenance margin call**. **Maintenance calls** are a demand that the customer make a payment to bring the account back to minimum. If payment is not made, the broker-dealer will liquidate enough of the securities in the account to bring the account back to minimum. The customer can meet a maintenance call by depositing cash or fully paid marginable securities.

TAKE NOTE

A firm can impose a maintenance level higher than the FINRA minimum maintenance rule levels. This is a **house minimum**. Many firms today impose 30%–35% minimum maintenance requirements.

Consider the previous example. By evaluating the amount of equity in the account relative to the Regulation T and minimum maintenance benchmarks, it can be determined that the account is in **restricted status**.

The new equity of $20,000 is less than the Regulation T requirement of $25,000, but more than the minimum maintenance of $12,500.

LMV	DR
	30,000
~~60,000~~ 50,000	
	EQ
	~~30,000~~ 20,000

Regulation T = 25,000 (50% × 50,000)

minimum maintenance = 12,500 (25% × 50,000)

TAKE NOTE

When calculating equity in the margin account using a T-chart, be sure to follow the steps below:

- Calculate the equity after a market value change: LMV − DR = EQ.

- Calculate the new Regulation T: 50% of the new LMV.

- Calculate the new minimum maintenance: 25% of the new LMV.

7. 2. 1. 4   Maintenance Call

Assume that the market value of the securities falls from $50,000 to $36,000. To find the status of the account, the chart would be adjusted as follows:

LMV	DR
	30,000
~~50,000~~	
36,000	
	EQ
	~~20,000~~
	6,000

Regulation T = 18,000 (50% × 36.000)

minimum maintenance = 9,000 (25% × 36,000)

Note the adjustment to the LMV. The LMV has fallen to $36,000, so the EQ must be changed to $6,000 ($36,000 − $30,000 = $6,000). After adjusting EQ in the account, the new Regulation T and minimum maintenance levels are calculated. (Regulation T = 50% of $36,000, or $18,000; minimum maintenance = 25% of $36,000, or $9,000).

This account is subject to a **maintenance call** because the equity is below the minimum requirement by $3,000. If the call is not met promptly, the broker-dealer will liquidate the customer's securities as needed.

A formula can be applied to calculate the market value to which securities can fall before there is a maintenance call. This formula is known as the **market value at maintenance formula** and is calculated as follows:

$$DR \div .75$$

EXAMPLE

A customer buys $90,000 worth of stock on margin and meets the initial Regulation T requirement by depositing $45,000. The debit balance is $45,000. To what level would the market value have to fall in order for the account to be at minimum maintenance?

Divide the debit balance of $45,000 by .75, which results in a maintenance market value of $60,000. If the market value does fall to $60,000, the account will look like this: LMV $60,000; DR $45,000; EQ $15,000. At this point, the account is exactly at 25% equity.

TAKE NOTE

If an account falls below minimum, a maintenance call will be sent in an amount sufficient to bring the account back to minimum.

TAKE NOTE

[handwritten: With maintenance Call – Payment, you pay down DR]

A customer has a long margin account with a market value of $12,000 and a debit balance of $10,000. The equity in the account is $2,000, which is approximately 16% of the market value. To bring the account back to minimum, which is $3,000 (25% × $12,000), the customer will receive a maintenance call for $1,000. Once the call is met, the account will look like this: LMV $12,000; DR $9,000; EQ $3,000.

7. 2. 1. 5   Excess Equity and the Special Memorandum Account (SMA)

Excess equity (EE) in a margin account = "is the amount of equity exceeding the Regulation T requirement.

To illustrate, return to the example account:

LMV	DR
60,000	30,000
	EQ
	30,000

Assume that the market value of the securities increases to $80,000. After marking to the market, the account appears as shown below:

LMV	DR	
	30,000	(2) SMA = 10,000
~~60,000~~ 80,000		
	EQ	
	~~30,000~~ 50,000	(1) EE = 10,000

[handwritten: increased by 20,000 = creates 10,000 SMA; 1/2 of value goes into SMA; increased market goes into SMA]

[handwritten: 1/2 above $40,000 Reg T = 10,000 EE]

Regulation T = 40,000 (50% × 80,000)

minimum maintenance = 20,000 (25% × 80,000)

The increase in market value creates equity of $50,000 because the DR does not change. The new Regulation T requirement is $40,000 (50% of $80,000), and the new minimum maintenance is $20,000 (25% of $80,000). Because the equity exceeds Regulation T, this account has EE of $10,000 ($50,000 – $40,000 = $10,000).

Item 1 in the example shows the EE. Item 2 shows the SMA, discussed in the following.

TAKE NOTE

A rule to determine SMA is as follows: for every $1 increase in market value, $.50 of SMA is created. In the previous example, market value increased by $20,000, which created SMA of $10,000.

EE creates **SMA**, or **buying power**, in the account.

Item 1 shows the EE. Item 2 shows the SMA.

SMA stands for **special memorandum account**, a line of credit that a customer can borrow from or use to purchase securities.

SMA is perhaps the most complicated margin concept. The house analogy can also help simplify SMA. Assume that a house has increased substantially in value. Homeowners with large amounts of equity sometimes borrow against their equity through home equity loans. When they take a loan, the amount they owe on their house is more than before and the equity falls. SMA is like a home equity loan. It is created because of increased equity in the account and is an additional line of credit. When the SMA line of credit is used, the debit balance in the customer's account is increased and the equity falls.

TAKE NOTE
The amount of SMA in the account is equal to the greater of the EE or the amount already in SMA.

Until this transaction, our example account had no EE. The EE of $10,000 generated SMA of $10,000.

What happens to SMA if the market value of the securities falls? The example below depicts the market value falling to $70,000:

LMV	DR	
~~80,000~~	30,000	(2) SMA = 10,000
70,000		
	EQ	
	~~50,000~~	(1) EE = 5,000
	40,000	~~10,000~~

Regulation T = 35,000 (50% × 70,000)

minimum maintenance = 17,500 (25% × 70,000)

The decrease in market value creates equity of $40,000. The new Regulation T requirement is $35,000 (50% of $70,000), and the new minimum maintenance is $17,500 (25% of $70,000). Because the equity exceeds Regulation T, this account has EE of $5,000 ($40,000 − $35,000 = $5,000).

What is the new SMA amount? Regulation T states that the SMA amount is equal to the greater of the EE or the SMA already in the account. Because the SMA of $10,000 is greater than the EE of $5,000, the SMA remains at $10,000. In summary, remember that although SMA increases when market value in the account increases, it does not decrease as a result of a market value decline.

TAKE NOTE
SMA may be more than EE and may exist even if there is no EE in the account.

TAKE NOTE

Although the SMA is not reduced by a decline in market value, its use may be restricted under certain conditions.

SMA can always be used, even in a restricted account, as long as its use does not bring the account below minimum.

The following is one last example in calculating the SMA balance. Assuming the market value of securities rises to $100,000, what is the new SMA balance?

LMV	DR	
~~70,000~~	30,000	(2) SMA = ~~10,000~~
100,000	20,000	20,000
	EQ	
	~~40,000~~	(1) EE = ~~5,000~~
	70,000	20,000

Regulation T = 50,000 (50% × 100,000)

minimum maintenance = 25,000 (25% × 100,000)

The increase in market value creates equity of $70,000. The new Regulation T requirement is $50,000 (50% of $100,000), and the new minimum maintenance is $25,000 (25% of $100,000). Because the equity exceeds Regulation T, this account has EE of $20,000 ($70,000 − $50,000 = $20,000). This impacts the amount of SMA. The SMA rule explains that the SMA amount is equal to the greater of the EE or the SMA already in the account. Because the EE of $20,000 is greater than the existing SMA of $10,000, the SMA balance becomes $20,000.

It has now been illustrated that SMA is increased by EE from market value increases. Any of the following also generate SMA.

- **Nonrequired cash deposits:** If a customer deposits cash that is not required to meet a margin call, the full amount reduces the debit and is also credited to SMA.

- **Dividends:** Dividends received on securities in the margin account are added to SMA. The customer can withdraw these income distributions, even if the account is restricted.

TAKE NOTE

If a customer wants to remove cash dividends coming into his margin account, he must do so within 30 days of receipt. Otherwise, the cash dividend will be applied against the debit balance, thereby increasing the equity in the account.

- **Loan value:** If a customer makes a nonrequired deposit of marginable stock, the stock's loan value is credited to SMA. The credit is equal to half the value of a cash deposit.

- **Sale of stock:** When stock is sold, 50% of the sales proceeds is credited to SMA.

7. 2. 1. 6   Using SMA

SMA is a line of credit; therefore, the investor can use it to withdraw cash or meet the margin requirement on stock purchases.

Assume a margin account appears as follows:

LMV	DR	
70,000	30,000	SMA = 20,000
	EQ	
	40,000	

Regulation T = 35,000 (50% × 70,000)

minimum maintenance = 17,500 (25% × 70,000)

The customer can withdraw cash by borrowing against the credit line of $20,000, which will increase the debit balance by $20,000. If the full $20,000 is withdrawn, the account will appear as follows:

LMV	DR	
70,000	~~30,000~~	SMA = ~~20,000~~
	50,000	0
	EQ	
	~~40,000~~	
	20,000	

Regulation T = 35,000 (50% × 70,000)

minimum maintenance = 17,500 (25% × 70,000)

The use of $20,000 of SMA reduces the SMA balance to zero. The debit balance is increased to $50,000, because SMA is a loan. The equity balance falls to $20,000, and the account is in restricted status. The customer can use SMA as long as it does not cause a maintenance call.

SMA can be used when the account has EE or is in restricted status. SMA can also be used to meet the initial margin requirements on stock purchases. SMA gives the investor buying power. Assume a margin account appears as follows:

LMV	DR	
70,000	30,000	SMA = 20,000
	EQ	
	40,000	

Regulation T = 35,000 (50% × 70,000)

minimum maintenance = 17,500 (25% × 70,000)

The SMA of $20,000, when used as the margin requirement, allows the custo chase $40,000 of stock. In other words, for every $1 of SMA, the customer can purchase $2 of stock. SMA has a buying power of 2 to 1. After the purchase of $40,000, the account appears as follows:

LMV	DR	
~~70,000~~	~~30,000~~	SMA = ~~20,000~~
110,000	70,000	0
	EQ	
	40,000	

Regulation T = 55,000 (50% × 110,000)

minimum maintenance = 27,500 (25% × 110,000)

The $40,000 purchase was paid for by a debit balance increase of $40,000. Anytime SMA is used to buy stock, the debit balance increases by the full amount of the purchase.

The use of SMA to meet the purchase price is like borrowing on a credit card. The customer owes more money. This account is in restricted status after the purchase of $40,000 of stock.

TEST TOPIC ALERT

Here is a quick review of critical long margin account concepts.

■ The first transaction in a margin account requires a deposit of the greater of 50% of the LMV or $2,000. The $2,000 minimum is waived if 100% of the transaction is less than $2,000.

■ The basic margin equation is: LMV – DR = EQ.

■ Regulation T = 50% of the LMV.

■ Minimum maintenance = 25% of the LMV (50% of Regulation T requirement).

■ SMA can be borrowed from the account, dollar for dollar.

■ Utilizing SMA increases the debit balance.

■ The buying power of SMA is 2 to 1.

■ EE and SMA are not necessarily equal.

■ SMA cannot be used to meet a maintenance margin call.

■ The market value at maintenance equation for long margin accounts is DR ÷ .75. This calculates what the market value can fall to before a maintenance call is sent.

■ Exempt securities are not subject to Regulation T but are subject to the maintenance requirements of FINRA.

7. 2. 1. 6. 1   *Special Memorandum Account Review*

The following table reviews how SMA is impacted by various account activities in a long margin account.

Activity	Effect on SMA	Remarks
Rise in market value	Increase	SMA increases only if the new EE is higher than the old SMA.
Sale of securities	Increase	The client is entitled to EE in the account after the sale, or to 50% of the sale proceeds, whichever is greater.
Deposit of cash	Increase	The full amount of the deposit is credited to SMA.
Deposit of marginable securities	Increase	SMA is increased by the loan value of the securities deposited, as prescribed by Regulation T at the time of the deposit (50%).
Dividends or interest	Increase	100% of a cash dividend or interest (a nonrequired deposit) is credited to SMA.
Purchase of securities	Decrease	The margin requirement on new purchases is deducted from SMA. If SMA is insufficient to meet the charge, a Regulation T call is issued for the balance.
Withdrawal of cash	Decrease	The full amount of the cash withdrawal is deducted from SMA. Remaining equity may not fall below FINRA rules or house equity requirement.
Fall in long account market value	No effect	After the SMA balance is established, it is not affected by a fall in market value in a long account.
Interest charges to account	No effect	SMA remains the same.
Stock dividend or split	No effect	SMA remains the same.

7. 2. 2   PATTERN DAY TRADERS

A **day trader** is someone who buys and sells the same security on the same day to try to take advantage of intraday price movements. A **pattern day trader** is someone who executes four or more day trades in a five-business-day period.

The minimum equity requirement for pattern day traders is $25,000; they must have on deposit in the account equity of at least $25,000 on any day on which day trading occurs. The d minimum maintenance margin requirement for pattern day traders is 25%, the same as for regular customers.

Pattern day traders are also treated differently when it comes to **buying power**. Buying power for day traders is four times the maintenance margin excess. **Maintenance margin excess** is defined as the equity in the account above the 25% minimum requirement. For regular customers, buying power is two times SMA.

Margin rules also prohibit day trading accounts from using **account guarantees,** which are otherwise permitted. A **cross guarantee** is one for which another customer, in writing, agrees to the use of money or securities in his account to carry the guaranteed accounts (i.e., to meet any margin calls).

7. 2. 2. 1   Approval for Day Trading Accounts

Member firms who promote day trading strategies must now implement procedures to approve day trading accounts.

Before opening an account, the member must:

■ provide the customer with a **risk disclosure** statement that outlines all the risks associated with day trading (the statement can be furnished in writing or electronically); and

■ approve the account for a day trading strategy or receive from the customer a written statement that the customer does not intend to engage in day trading.

7. 2. 3   SHORT SALES AND MARGIN REQUIREMENTS

Selling short is a strategy an investor uses to profit from a decline in a stock's price. Selling short must always be done through a margin account. The investor then sells the borrowed stock at the market price with the hope of buying back the shares at a lower price. The short seller profits when the loan of stock can be repaid with shares purchased at a lower price.

In a short sale, there is a **short seller**, a **stock lender** (from whom the shares are borrowed), and a **buyer** who purchases the shares being sold short. One of the basic requirements of short selling is that the short seller, on the dividend payment date, must make good to the stock lender for the dividends the lender is no longer receiving from the issuer. The buyer of the shares is receiving the dividends directly from the issuer. Therefore, on the dividend payment date, the short seller's account is debited the amount of the cash dividend for remittance to the stock lender.

7. 2. 3. 1   Margin Deposits

To borrow shares for short sales, an investor must make **margin deposits**. Regulation T specifies that the initial margin for short sales can be met with either cash or marginable securities, just as in long margin transactions.

7. 2. 3. 2   Terminology

The Series 7 exam uses the following terms to describe activity in short margin accounts:

■ **Short market value (SMV)**—the current market value of the stock position the investor sells short

■ **Credit register (CR)**—the amount of money in the customer's account; equal to the sales proceeds plus the margin deposit requirement

■ **Equity (EQ)**—the customer's net worth in the margin account; the amount by which the credit balance exceeds the current SMV of the securities in the account

The amount of equity in the account is determined by this equation:

$$CR - SMV = EQ$$

7. 2. 3. 3 Analyzing Short Margin Account Activity

To analyze short margin account activity, a simplified balance sheet will be used, as shown here:

CR	SMV
	EQ

When establishing a short margin account, there is a minimum deposit of $2,000. This minimum must be met even if the customer sells short less than $2,000 worth of securities. The Regulation T requirement for short sales is the same as it is for long purchases: 50%.

Customer Sells Short

Customer Sells Short	Regulation T Requirement	FINRA Minimum Rule	Customer Deposit Required
100 shares at $50 per share	$2,500	$2,000	$2,500
100 shares at $30 per share	$1,500	$2,000	$2,000
100 shares at $15 per share	$750	$2,000	$2,000

TAKE NOTE

Shorting stock that is below $5 per share requires an initial deposit of $2,000 or $2.50 per share, whichever is greater.

7. 2. 3. 4 Minimum Maintenance

FINRA **minimum maintenance requirement** rules on short positions are 30%, compared with 25% on long positions. As with long margin accounts, the firm may impose a higher house minimum.

TEST TOPIC ALERT

Before you continue, answer the questions below.

1. What is the minimum initial dollar requirement in a short margin account?

2. What is the Regulation T requirement in a short margin account?

3. What is the minimum maintenance requirement in a short margin account?

Answers: 1. $2,000; 2. 50%; 3. 30%

7. 3. 3. 1   Short Margin Account

To illustrate how a short margin account works, assume the following:

A client sells short 1,000 shares of ABC at $70,000 and meets the Regulation T requirement. The market value of securities falls to $60,000. What is the new equity in the account? The accounting in the short margin chart should appear as follows:

(handwritten marginal notes: "add approved from to EU" "SMV + EU ?" "CR")

(handwritten note near chart: "sold securities at 70,000 and put up half that $ for margin deposit requirement")

CR	SMV
105,000 (3)	70,000 (1)
	EQ
	35,000 (2)

- The market value of the securities sold short is entered as the SMV.
- The Regulation T requirement of 50% of the SMV is entered as equity.
- The credit balance (CR) is the stock sales proceeds plus the equity deposited (SMV + EQ).

The **credit balance (CR)** provides assurance to the broker-dealer that there will be cash available for the customer to purchase the securities if the market value of the securities rises. The risk of a short account is a stock price increase; a short seller profits only if the market value of the securities declines.

TEST TOPIC ALERT   For short margin accounting questions: once you get the credit balance by adding the SMV and EQ together, do not change it. Use it to compute equity after a market value change with the basic equation: CR – SMV = EQ.

The following illustrates the accounting for the market value decline and the resulting new equity:

CR	SMV
105,000	~~70,000~~ 60,000 (1)
	EQ
	~~35,000~~ 45,000 (2)

- The market value of the securities sold short declines to $60,000.
- The equity increases to $45,000 as a result of the decline. This is determined as follows: CR – SMV = EQ ($105,000 – $60,000 = $45,000).

TAKE NOTE   Short positions, like long positions, are marked to market daily to reflect any change in position value.

What is the status of this investor's account? Just as in long margin accounts, the short margin account statuses are as follows:

- **Excess equity**—equity in excess of Regulation T (50% of the current SMV)
- **Restricted**—equity less than Regulation T, and greater than or equal to minimum maintenance
- **Maintenance call**—equity less than minimum maintenance (30% of the SMV)

By calculating the Regulation T benchmark, we can see that this account has EE and has created SMA of $15,000, as shown:

CR	SMV	
105,000	~~70,000~~	SMA = 15,000
	60,000	
	(1)	
	EQ	
	~~35,000~~	EE = 15,000
	45,000	
	(2)	

Regulation T = 30,000 (50% × 60,000)

minimum maintenance = 18,000 (30% × 60,000)

TAKE NOTE   Multiply the decrease in SMV by 1.5 to arrive at the EE and the amount that would be credited to the SMA.

The EE and SMA of $15,000 are available because the equity in the account ($45,000) exceeds the Regulation T requirement ($30,000) by $15,000. Now assume that the market value of the securities in this account rises to $80,000. How much cash must the customer deposit?

CR	SMV	
	~~60,000~~	The increase of short market
	80,000	value to $80,000 causes the equity to fall to $25,000 (CR – SMV = EQ).
		The new Regulation T requirement is $40,000 (50% of $80,000); the new minimum maintenance is $24,000 (30% of $80,000).
105,000	**EQ**	
	~~45,000~~	Because the equity of $25,000
	25,000	exceeds the minimum maintenance of $24,000, there is no cash deposit required.

Regulation T = 40,000 (50% × 80,000)

minimum maintenance = 24,000 (30% × 80,000)

To find the maximum market value to which a short sale position can increase before a maintenance call is issued, apply the following formula:

$$\text{total credit balance} \div 130\% \ (1.3)$$

This is known as the **short market value at maintenance**.

7. 3. 3. 2   Minimum Maintenance in a Short Account

The minimum maintenance margin requirement for short accounts is 30%. However, there are exceptions based on price per share.

- For stock trading under $5 per share, a customer must maintain 100% of SMV or $2.50 per share, whichever is greater.
- For stock trading at $5 per share and above, the minimum requirement is $5 per share or 30%, whichever is greater.

EXAMPLE   A customer sells short 1,000 shares of stock at $4 per share. The margin deposit would be $4,000, not $2,000.

A customer sells short 1,000 shares at $2 per share. The margin deposit would be $2,500.

In both cases, the minimum maintenance margin requirement exceeds the initial requirement. Therefore, each customer must deposit the higher amount.

EXAMPLE   A customer has a short margin account. In it, there is one stock currently trading at $10 per share. The minimum maintenance requirement for this account is

A.   100%
B.   30%
C. $5 per share
D. $2.50 per share

Answer: C. With the stock at $10, $5 per share is greater than 30%.

7. 3. 1   COMBINED ACCOUNTS

A client who has a margin account with both long and short positions in different securities has a **combined account**. In combined accounts, equity and margin requirements are determined by calculating the long and short positions separately and combining the results.

The following example shows the use of the long and short margin charts in calculating combined equity.

An investor has the following margin account positions:

LMV = $50,000; SMV = $40,000; CR = $60,000; DR = $20,000
SMA = $5,000 (The combined equity in this example is $50,000.)

LMV	DR		CR	SMV
	20,000			40,000
50,000	EQ		60,000	EQ
	30,000			20,000

The basic equation for the calculation of combined equity is:

$$LMV + CR - DR - SMV = EQ$$

The formula above shows combined equity, but questions may ask for combined Regulation T requirement or combined minimum maintenance requirements. As with combined equity questions, to calculate combined Regulation T or minimum maintenance requirements, first calculate the long, then the short, and add the two together.

7. 3. 2 CUSTOMER PORTFOLIO MARGINING (CPM)

Customer portfolio margining (CPM) is a different way to calculate margin requirements for an account based on the net risk of an entire portfolio of securities rather than a standardized percentage applied to each individual position. Margin requirements calculated this way are generally lower than those calculated conventionally. Certain rules must be met in order to offer portfolio margining to customers.

QUICK QUIZ 7.B

Objectives:

- Calculate initial and maintenance requirements for long and short margin accounts
- Calculate equity in long, short, and combined margin accounts
- Compute SMA

1. Combined net equity for an investor having both a long and short account is calculated as
   A. SMV + LMV − DR − CR = EQ
   B. SMV − LMV − DR − CR = EQ
   C. LMV − CR + DR + SMV = EQ
   D. LMV + CR − DR − SMV = EQ

2. An investor has an established margin account with a current market value of $4,000 and a debit balance of $2,250, with Regulation T at 50%. How much equity does the investor have in the account?
   A. $1,750
   B. $2,000
   C. $2,250
   D. $4,000

3. An investor has an established margin account with a current market value of $6,000 and a debit balance of $2,500. With Regulation T at 50%, how much EE does the investor have in the account?

    A. $6,000
    B. $2,500
    C. $500
    D. $250

4. In a new margin account, a customer buys 100 shares of GGG, Inc., at $30 per share and meets the initial margin requirement. If the stock falls to $25 per share, the equity in the account is equal to

    A. $1,000
    B. $1,500
    C. $2,000
    D. $2,500

5. A margin account has LMV of $6,000 and a debit of $5,000. How much money must the investor deposit to satisfy the maintenance requirement?

    A. $500
    B. $1,000
    C. $2,000
    D. $5,000

6. A margin account is restricted by $2,000. Which of the following actions may the customer take to bring the account to the Regulation T requirement?

    I.   Cancel $2,000 of SMA
    II. Deposit $2,000 cash
    III. Deposit $4,000 of fully paid marginable stock

    A. I only
    B. I and II
    C. II and III
    D. I, II, and III

7. When stock held in a long margin account appreciates, which of the following increase(s)?

    I.   Current market value
    II. Debit balance
    III. Equity

    A. I only
    B. I and III
    C. II only
    D. I, II, and III

8. A client has a margin account with $23,000 in securities and a debit of $12,000. If Regulation T is 50%,

    I.   the account is restricted
    II. the client will receive a margin call for $500
    III. the client may withdraw securities if he deposits 50% of the securities' value
    IV. the account has EE of $5,250

    A. I and II
    B. I and III
    C. II, III, and IV
    D. I, II, III, and IV

9. A client has a margin account with $23,000 in securities and a debit of $12,000. The stock increases in value to $26,000. How much money may the client withdraw from the account?

    A. $1,000
    B. $2,000
    C. $3,000
    D. $4,000

10. Which of the following can change the SMA balance in a long account?

    I.   Sale of securities in the account
    II. Market appreciation of securities in the account
    III. Interest and cash dividends deposited in the account
    IV. Decrease in value of securities in the account

    A. I only
    B. I and II
    C. I, II, and III
    D. I, II, III, and IV

11. An investor opens a new margin account, sells short 100 shares of KLP at $45 per share, and meets the Regulation T requirement of 50%. How much equity does the investor have in the account?

    A. $2,000
    B. $2,250
    C. $4,500
    D. $6,750

12. An investor has an established margin account with a SMV of $4,000 and a credit balance of $6,750, with Regulation T at 50%. How much EE does the investor have in the account?

    A. $750
    B. $1,500
    C. $2,000
    D. $2,750

13. An investor opens a new margin account and sells short 100 shares of COD at 32.50, with Regulation T at 50%. What is the investor's required deposit?

    A. $812.50
    B. $1,625
    C. $2,000
    D. $3,250

14. A customer sells short 100 shares of ABC at $80 per share and meets the minimum Regulation T requirement. Two months later, he covers the short position by buying ABC at $70 per share. This was the only transaction in the account. What is the maximum amount he can withdraw from the account after closing the short position (Regulation T is 50%)?

    A. $1,000
    B. $4,000
    C. $5,000
    D. $12,000

15. A broker-dealer is using portfolio margining as opposed to having margin calculated conventionally for one of its customer's accounts. Which of the following is TRUE?

    A. The calculated margin will be based on the net value of the securities in the account portfolio and will be higher than the requirement if calculated conventionally.
    B. The calculated margin will be based on the net value of the securities in the account portfolio and will be lower than the requirement if calculated conventionally.
    C. The calculated margin will be based on the net risks associated with all the securities in the account portfolio and will be higher than the requirement if calculated conventionally.
    D. The calculated margin will be based on the net risks associated with all the securities in the account portfolio and will be lower than the requirement if calculated conventionally.

All Quick Quiz answers are found at the end of their units.

QUICK QUIZ ANSWERS

Quick Quiz 7.A

1. **C.** The initial margin requirement is calculated by multiplying the market value of $10,000 by the Regulation T requirement of 50%, which equals $5,000.

2. **B.** In order to open a margin account, it is mandatory that the customer sign both the credit and the hypothecation agreements. The loan consent agreement is optional.

3. **A.** When depositing fully paid-for securities as collateral for securities purchased on margin, the value of the securities deposited must equal twice the amount (200%) of the amount of the Regulation T cash call.

4. **D.** Regulation T allows deposits to be made within two additional business days of settlement for both cash and margin accounts. Therefore, the initial Regulation T deposit for a regular-way (T+2) equity transaction is required to be made no more than four business days after the trade date.

5. **C.** When a customer has not made the required Regulation T deposit for a transaction on time, an extension for payment can be requested. The request must always be made by a clearing firm. For self-clearing BDs, that would be the BD themselves. In the case of introducing BDs, the request must be made by the BD's clearing firm. Requests for extensions can only be granted by the broker-dealer's designated examining authority.

Quick Quiz 7.B

1. **D.** For a long account (LMV – DB) and short account (CR – SMV), the combined equity formula equals the two formulas together. This is generally written LMV + CR – DR – SMV.

2. **A.** Equity is calculated by subtracting the debit balance of $2,250 from the current market value of $4,000, which equals $1,750.

3. **C.** The Regulation T requirement is 50% of the current market value of $6,000, which equals $3,000. Equity is equal to the current market value of $6,000 minus the debit balance of $2,500, which equals $3,500. EE is then calculated by subtracting the Regulation T requirement of $3,000 from the equity of $3,500, which equals $500.

4. **B.** FINRA rules require a minimum equity deposit of $2,000 on the first transaction in a new margin account. After the customer sends in the required deposit, the equity is $2,000 (LMV of $3,000 – DR of $1,000 = EQ of $2,000). When the market value falls to $2,500 (a decrease of $500), the equity also declines by $500, leaving $1,500 of equity in the account.

5. **A.** The maintenance requirement in a long margin account is 25% of the market value of the stock. The equity in the account is $1,000, and the required maintenance margin is $1,500 (25% of the $6,000 LMV). Therefore, the account will receive a margin call for $500.

6. **C.** Equity may be increased by depositing cash or fully paid securities. SMA represents a line of credit, but there is no such thing as cancellation of an SMA balance.

7. **B.** The debit balance changes only when money is borrowed or deposited. A withdrawal of cash is borrowed against the loan value of the securities in the account, increasing the debit balance. A deposit of cash into the account reduces the debit balance.

8. **B.** The account is restricted by $500. The client will not, however, receive a margin call for the $500 because Regulation T applies only to the initial purchase. Because the account is restricted, withdrawal of securities requires a cash deposit of 50% or a deposit of securities with a loan value of 50% of the value of the securities withdrawn. The account is $5,250 above the required minimum, but this amount is not considered EE.

9. **A.** The account now has equity of $14,000. The Regulation T requirement is $13,000. This leaves $1,000 in EE that may be withdrawn.

$26,000	CMV
− 12,000	DR
$14,000	EQ
− 13,000	Regulation T
$1,000	EE

10. **C.** The sale of securities in the account results in an automatic release of funds to SMA. Nonrequired cash deposits, such as interest and dividends, are also automatically credited to SMA. An increase in the value of the securities will increase SMA if the EE becomes greater than existing SMA. A decrease in the market value of the securities will not increase or decrease SMA.

11. **B.** Equity in a short margin account is calculated by subtracting the SMV of $4,500 from the credit balance of $6,750 ($4,500 stock sales proceeds + $2,250 initial margin deposit of 50% = $6,750 credit balance). The initial deposit of $2,250 is the equity.

12. **A.** The Regulation T requirement and equity must be calculated before EE can be determined. The Regulation T requirement is 50% of the SMV of $4,000, which equals $2,000. Equity is calculated by subtracting the SMV of $4,000 from the credit balance of $6,750, which equals $2,750. EE is then calculated by subtracting the Regulation T requirement of $2,000 from the equity of $2,750, which equals $750.

13. **C.** When selling stock short in a new account, an investor must meet the FINRA initial minimum requirement rules of $2,000. This is required although the Regulation T requirement is $1,625 ($3,250 × 50%).

14. **C.** The customer originally sold the stock at $80 per share and deposited $4,000 per the Regulation T requirement ($8,000 × 50%). He now has an SMV of $8,000 and a credit balance of $12,000 ($8,000 sale proceeds + $4,000 deposit). The market value of the stock is now down to $7,000. The customer may withdraw the equity of $5,000 when the position is closed.

15. **D.** When using customer portfolio margining (CPM) to calculate margin, the requirements are based on the net risks associated with all of the securities in a portfolio and will be lower than the margin requirements calculated conventionally.

8

Customers' Purchase and Sales Instructions, Processing Transactions and Complaint and Dispute Resolutions

S ince the Great Depression, the securities industry has been closely regulated in the interest of protecting the investor. To that end, the processes of issuing securities and trading them once issued are subject to careful regulatory procedures. It is also recognized that investing money is inherently risky, so laws cannot require that risk be eliminated; rather, the laws require that the investor receive enough information to be able to assess the risk accurately and be able to make sound investment decisions. In order to apply an understanding of the requirements the registered representative must follow, the rep must recognize regulatory standards. Therefore, this Unit can be generally considered a view of the "back office" directives; the mechanics of what happens when the customer decides to implement a decision to buy or sell securities.

The Series 7 exam will include 14 questions on the topics covered in Units 7 and 8 (function 4). ∎

In this Unit you will learn to:

■ **define** the function and procedures of securities trading in the secondary market;

■ **differentiate** the characteristics of the types of orders that can be placed when trading listed securities;

■ **apply** the characteristics of time sensitive orders to market conditions;

■ **summarize** short sales and the rules regarding short sales;

■ **define** the characteristics of the over-the-counter market;

■ **summarize** the process from when orders are placed to the confirmation of a trade;

■ **identify** transaction settlement dates and terms;

■ **define** the various components that make up good delivery of securities; and

■ **recognize** the formal resolution methods and disputes-reporting requirements.

8. 1   ROLE OF THE BROKER-DEALER

Firms engaged in buying and selling securities for the public must register as broker-dealers. Most firms act both as brokers and dealers, but not in the same transaction.

A broker:	**A dealer:**
■ acts as an agent, transacting orders on the client's behalf;	■ acts as a principal, dealing in securities for its own account and at its own risk;
■ charges a commission;	■ charges a markup or markdown;
■ is not a market maker; and	■ may make markets and take positions (long or short) in securities; and
■ must disclose its role to the client and the amount of its commission.	■ must disclose its role to the client and the markup or markdown if a Nasdaq security.

8. 1. 1   BROKERS

Brokers are agents that arrange trades for clients and charge commissions. Brokers do not effect trades as principal but arrange trades between buyers and sellers.

8. 1. 2   DEALERS

Dealers, or **principals**, buy and sell securities for their own accounts, often called **position trading**. When selling from their inventories, dealers charge their clients markups rather than commissions. A **markup** is the difference between the current interdealer offering price and the actual price charged to the client. When a price to a client includes a dealer's markup, it is called a **net price**.

TAKE NOTE
To clarify the role of dealers in the securities marketplace, try thinking of dealers as a car dealer. If you were a car dealer, you would maintain an inventory, or lot, of cars. If someone bought a car from you, you would not sell it at the wholesale price. Instead, you mark up the price to make a profit.

If someone wanted to sell you his used car, you would not offer him top dollar. Instead, you would mark down the price to make a profit. Securities dealers hold inventories of securities and buy and sell from inventory. They profit on transactions by charging markups and markdowns.

8. 1. 3   QUOTES

The market in which securities are bought and sold is also known as the secondary market, as opposed to the primary market for new issues. All securities transactions take place in secondary markets.

Quotes for securities trading in the secondary market are done in terms of bid and ask. The ask price is the price at which dealers are willing to sell. The bid price is the price at which dealers are willing to buy. To make a profit, the ask is always higher than the bid. The difference between bid and ask is called the spread.

EXAMPLE   A dealer is quoting a stock at 21.50 bid–21.55 ask. The dealer is offering stock to any buyer at 21.55. The dealer is willing to buy stock from any seller at 21.50. The spread, the dealer's gross profit, is $.05 per share. The size of the market is expressed by two numbers: If the quote is 21.50–21.55 19 × 7, it means that the dealer is willing to buy up to 1,900 shares at 21.50 and is willing to sell up to 700 shares at 21.55.

8. 1. 4   TRADE REPORTING FACILITY (TRF)

The FINRA Trade Reporting Facility (TRF) is an automated trade reporting and reconciliation service that is operated on the Automated Confirmation Transaction (ACT) service platform. TRF electronically facilitates all the data reporting, such as price and volume, after a trade has taken place, as well as trade comparison and clearing functions. It is used to report data for trades in Nasdaq-listed securities, as well as trades that take place in NYSE listed and other exchange-listed securities that occur off of the exchange trading floors. In this light, the system handles trades that are negotiated between brokers.

8. 1. 5   FILLING AN ORDER

A broker-dealer may fill a customer's order to buy securities in any of the following ways:
- A firm may act as the client's agent by finding a seller of the securities and arranging a trade.
- A firm may buy the securities from a market maker, mark up the price, and resell them to the client.
- If it has the securities in its own inventory, the firm may sell the shares to the client from that inventory.

8. 1. 6   NYSE EURONEXT

The **NYSE** is the most widely known stock exchange. Although exchanges are called stock markets, other securities may trade there as well. Often called the **Big Board**, the NYSE is the largest of all U.S. listed exchanges. Stocks listed on the NYSE can also be listed on regional exchanges, such as the Chicago Stock Exchange. It should be noted that the exchange does not influence or determine price.

8. 1. 6. 1   Exchange Listing Requirements

Securities traded on the NYSE, known as **listed securities**, must satisfy the exchange's listing requirements. Generally, a corporation that wants its securities listed must have a minimum number of publicly held shares and a minimum number of shareholders, each holding

100 shares or more. Although the minimum numerical criteria are not tested, it is important that you recognize that only companies of significant size and public ownership qualify for listing on the NYSE.

Only NYSE members (individual seat owners) can trade on the floor.

The NYSE is not the only exchange; regional exchanges tend to focus on the securities of companies within their regions, although they also offer trading in many securities listed on the NYSE. This is known as dual listing. Listing requirements on regional exchanges are often less stringent than those of the national exchanges, and the companies they list are usually among the smallest and newest in their industries.

8. 1. 6. 2   Designated Market Maker (DMM)

DMMs facilitate trading in specific stocks, and their chief function is to maintain a fair and orderly market in those stocks. In fulfilling this function, they act as both brokers and dealers; they act as dealers when they execute trades for their own accounts and as brokers when they execute orders other members leave with them. The specialist (DMM) acts as an auctioneer. In return for providing this service to the exchange, DMMs receive rebates on fees charged by the exchange whenever their quotes result in trades.

TAKE NOTE

The New York Stock Exchange now allows floor traders to handle non-NYSE listed stocks. NYSE floor traders can now transmit orders to and access liquidity from other exchanges without leaving the NYSE trading floor.

8. 1. 6. 3   Auction Market

Exchange securities are bought and sold in an **auction market**. Exchange markets are also sometimes called **double auction markets** because both buyers and sellers call out their best bids and offers in an attempt to transact business at the best possible price.

To establish the best bid, a buying broker-dealer must initiate a bid at least $.01 higher than the current best bid. The best offer by a selling broker-dealer must be at least $.01 lower than the current best offer.

EXAMPLE

A quote might look like this:

Last	Bid	Ask	Size
$46.71	$46.66	$46.74	30 × 14

Several bids at the same price and several offers at the same price may occur. To provide for the orderly transaction of business on the floor, the highest bids and lowest offers always receive first consideration.

8. 1. 6. 4   Volatile Market Conditions

Rules known as the market-wide circuit breaker rules (MWCB) protect against rapid, uncontrolled drops in the market. Based on the S&P 500 index (recalculated daily), the circuit breakers work as follows:

Level 1 halt = 7% decline in S&P 500
Before 3:25 pm—15 minutes;
At or after 3:25 pm—trading may continue, unless there is a Level 3 halt.

Level 2 halt = 13% decline in S&P 500
Before 3:25 pm—15 minutes;
At or after 3:25 pm—trading may continue, unless there is a Level 3 halt.

Level 3 halt = 20% decline in S&P 500
At any time—trading will halt and not resume for the rest of the day.

A Level 1 or 2 halt cannot occur more than one time per day. In other words, if a Level 1 halt has already occurred, it would take a Level 2 halt to stop trading again.

Finally, trading halts for listed securities trading on an exchange will generally be initiated by the exchange itself or by the SEC. For OTC stocks, either the specific trading venue such as Nasdaq or FINRA can initiate a trading halt.

TAKE NOTE   During a market halt, while no trading can occur, investors can still cancel existing (open) orders that had been entered previously.

8. 1. 6. 5   Arbitrage

Arbitrage is a trading strategy that specialized traders, called **arbitrageurs**, use to profit from temporary price differences between markets or securities. In general, arbitrageurs look for ways to profit from temporary price disparities in the same or equivalent securities.

8. 1. 6. 5. 1   Market Arbitrage

Some securities trade in more than one market—on two exchanges, for instance—creating the possibility that one security may sell for two different prices at the same time. When that happens, arbitrageurs buy at the lower price in one market and sell at the higher price in the other.

8. 1. 7   FLOOR STRUCTURE AND ORDER TYPES

NYSE Euronext has adopted a multi-dealer structure for the NYSE. Following is a discussion of that market maker structure and the different order types commonly entered.

8. 1. 7. 1   Role of the Designated Market Maker (DMM)

In addition to maintaining an orderly market, a secondary function of the designated market maker (DMM) is to minimize price disparities that may occur at the opening of daily trading. He does this by buying or selling (as a dealer) stock from his own inventory only when a need for such intervention exists. Otherwise, the specialist (DMM) lets public supply and demand set the market's course. Maintaining a market in a stock requires considerable financial resources. Therefore, the specialist (DMM) must have enough capital to maintain a substantial position in the security.

8. 1. 7. 1. 1   Responsibilities of the Designated Market Maker

A specialist (DMM) must abide by certain NYSE floor rules in the daily conduct of his business. The specialist:

- must maintain a fair and orderly market;
- must stand ready to buy and sell for his own account, if necessary, to maintain a fair and orderly market;
- is expected to transact business for his own account in such a way as to maintain price continuity and minimize temporary price disparities attributable to supply and demand differences;
- must avoid transacting business for his own account at the opening or reopening of trading in a stock if this would upset the public balance of supply and demand;
- must file the reports and keep the books and records the Exchange requires; and
- may trade for his own account in between the current bid and ask quotes in his book.

8. 1. 8   AGENT AND PRINCIPAL

The specialist (DMM) is both agent and principal. On the Exchange floor, they can act in the following ways.

As **agents**, or brokers' brokers, they execute all orders other brokers leave with them. They accept certain kinds of orders from members, such as limit and stop orders, and execute these as conditions permit. As **principals**, or dealers, they buy and sell in their own accounts to make markets in assigned stocks. They are expected to maintain continuous, fair, and orderly markets—that is, markets with reasonable price variations. A specialist, however, may not buy stock for his own account at a price that would compete with the current market. In other words, a specialist cannot buy, as principal, at a price that would satisfy a customer order to buy.

QUICK QUIZ 8. A   Objective: Describe roles and activities involved when trading listed securities

1. During a trading halt, an investor can
    A. cancel an order that was placed before the halt
    B. execute a market order
    C. execute a limit order
    D. close an existing position

2. Which of the following activities is NOT a function of a specialist (designated market maker) on the NYSE?

   A. Setting strike prices for options on the securities he works
   B. Keeping a book of public orders
   C. Maintaining a bid and offer at all times
   D. Buying and selling stock for his own account

3. An immediate-or-cancel (IOC) order

   I.   must be executed in its entirety
   II. may be executed in part or in full
   III. must be executed in one attempt
   IV. may be executed after several attempts

   A. I and III
   B. I and IV
   C. II and III
   D. II and IV

4. If the S&P 500 is down 13% by 11 a.m. at the NYSE, what happens?

   A. This is a Level 1 halt and the market will halt trading for 15 minutes
   B. This is a Level 2 halt and the market will halt trading for 15 minutes
   C. This is a Level 3 halt and the market will halt trading for 30 minutes
   D. Nothing happens until the S&P 500 drops 15%, then trading will halt for 30 minutes

All Quick Quiz answers are found at the end of their units.

8. 2   TYPES OF ORDERS

Customers have the ability to place different types of orders depending on what they anticipate regarding the price movement of a security.

8. 2. 1   PRICE-RESTRICTED ORDERS

Some orders, such as limit and stop limit, restrict the price of the transaction. Typical orders include the following:

- Market—executed immediately at the market price
- Limit—limits the amount paid or received for securities
- Stop—becomes a market order if the stock reaches or goes through the stop (trigger or election) price
- Stop limit—entered as a stop order and changed to a limit order if the stock hits or goes through the stop (trigger or election) price.

8. 2. 2   MARKET ORDERS

A **market order** is sent immediately to the floor for execution without restrictions or limits. It is executed immediately at the current market price and has priority over all other types of orders. A market order to buy is executed at the lowest offering price available; a market order to sell is executed at the highest bid price available. As long as the security is trading, a market order guarantees execution.

8. 2. 3   LIMIT ORDERS

In a **limit order**, a customer limits the acceptable purchase or selling price. A limit order can be executed only at the specified price or better. If the order cannot be executed at the market, it is placed on the book and executed if and when the market price meets the order limit price. Buy limit orders are placed below the current market, whereas sell limit orders are placed above the current market.

8. 2. 3. 1   Risks of Limit Orders

A customer who enters a limit order risks missing the chance to buy or sell, especially if the market moves away from the limit price. The market may never go as low as the buy limit price or as high as the sell limit price. Sometimes limit orders are not executed, even if the stock trades at the limit price.

Stock Ahead. Limit orders on the DMM's book for the same price are arranged according to when they were received. If a limit order at a specific price was not filled, chances are another order at the same price took precedence; that is, there was stock ahead.

TAKE NOTE   Limit orders stand in time priority. There may be multiple orders to buy stock at a particular price. Once the stock begins trading at that price, those limit orders that were entered first will be filled first.

8. 2. 4   STOP ORDERS

A **stop order**, also known as a **stop loss order**, is designed to protect a profit or prevent a loss if the stock begins to move in the wrong direction.

The stop order becomes a market order once the stock trades at or moves through a certain price, known as the stop price. Stop orders are left with and executed by the DMM. No guarantee exists that the executed price will be the stop price, unlike the price on a limit order. Buy stop orders are entered above the current market, whereas sell stop orders are entered below the current market.

A trade at the stop price triggers the order, which then becomes a market order. A stop order takes two trades to execute, which are:

- **trigger**—the trigger transaction at or through the stop price activates the trade; and then
- **execution**—the stop order becomes a market order and is executed at the next price, completing the trade.

8. 2. 4. 1 Buy Stop Order

[handwritten: = entered above mkt value]

[handwritten left margin: Buy stop = placed when you have a short]

A buy stop order protects a profit or limits a loss in a short stock position. The buy stop is entered at a price above the current market and is triggered when the market price touches or goes through the buy stop price.

EXAMPLE

A customer has shorted 1,000 shares of XYZ stock at $55, and the stock is now at $48. The customer would like to hang on for more gain but is concerned the stock will reverse itself and begin to rise, eroding some of the unrealized profit. To deal with this, the customer could place the following order: buy 1,000 XYZ 49 stop. If the stock does start to head north, once it trades at or through the stop price of 49, the order becomes a market order to buy 1,000 XYZ.

Buy stop orders are also used by technical traders who track support and resistance levels for stocks. For instance, COD stock trades between 38 and 42. It never seems to go above 42 or below 38. Technicians believe that if the stock breaks through resistance, it will continue to move upward at a rapid pace. Therefore, they will not buy at 40 because there is little upside potential. However, they may place a buy stop order above the resistance level knowing that if the stock breaks resistance and begins to move up, they will buy the stock before it develops upward momentum.

An investor might place a stop order to buy 100 COD at 42.25 stop when the market is at 40 if he believes 42 represents a technical resistance point, above which the stock price will continue to rise.

COD Buy Stop Order

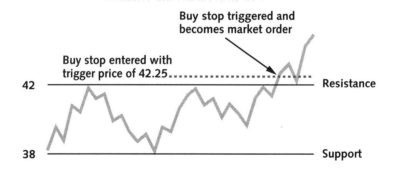

8. 2. 4. 2 Sell Stop Order

[handwritten: = entered below market value]

[handwritten left margin: protects a long position]

A **sell stop order** protects a profit or limits a loss in a long stock position and is entered at a price below the current market.

EXAMPLE

A customer is long 1,000 shares of XYZ at $32, and the stock is now at $41. The customer would like to hang on for more gain but is concerned the stock will reverse itself and begin to fall, eroding some of the unrealized profit. To deal with this, the customer could place the following order: sell 1,000 XYZ 40 stop. If the stock does start to head south, once it trades at or through the stop price of 40, the order becomes a market order to sell 1,000 XYZ.

Sell stop orders are also used by technical traders. Technicians believe that if a stock breaks through support, it will fall like a rock. Therefore, they will not short the stock at 40 because there is little downside potential. Historically, the stock has not traded below 38.

However, they may place a sell stop order just below the support level knowing that if the stock breaks through support and begins to move down, they will short the stock before it develops downward momentum.

An investor who is long stock might place a stop order to sell 100 COD at 37.75 stop when the market is at 40 if he believes 38 represents a technical support point below which the stock will continue to fall.

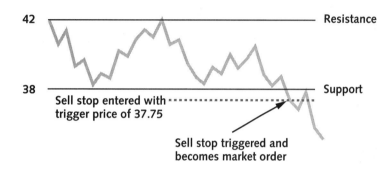

COD Sell Stop Order

If a large number of stop orders are triggered at the same price, a flurry of trading activity takes place as they become market orders. This activity will accelerate the advance or decline of the stock price.

8. 2. 4. 3   Stop Limit Order

A **stop limit order** is a stop order that, once triggered, becomes a limit order instead of a market order.

EXAMPLE

A customer calls you and says, "I want to sell my ABC stock if it falls to $30, but I don't want less than $29.95 for my shares." So you enter the following order: sell 1,000 ABC 30 stop 29.95. Once ABC trades at or below 30, the order becomes a limit order to sell at 29.95 or better. The problem here is that the market could leapfrog between the stop price and the limit price. As a result, the customer will not get an execution.

Assume once the order is entered, the stock trades as follows: 30.01, 29.97, 29.94, 29.92, and so on. The trade at 29.97 triggers the order, at which point the order becomes a limit order to sell at 29.95 or better (higher). In the above scenario, the customer does not sell. The moral of this example is if you are concerned that a stock is heading south, place a market order to sell or a stop order. A stop limit may leave you without an execution.

8. 2. 4. 4   Stop and Limit Orders

Stop and Limit Orders

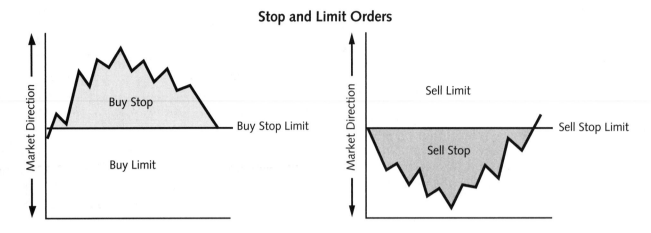

Be prepared for two to four questions regarding limit and stop orders. Use the chart to solve some problems, starting with limit orders.

XYZ is currently trading at 52. Where would a customer enter a buy limit order?

Refer to the chart. Think of the horizontal middle line as the current price. The buy limit would be entered somewhere below 52. The investor wants to buy at a better price—a lower price for a buyer. The order would be filled at or below the order price.

A sell limit order for XYZ would be entered above the market price. The seller is waiting for a price that is better than 52. The order would be filled at a price equal to or higher (better for a seller) than the order price.

Stop orders are a little trickier because they have two parts: trigger (election) and execution. Consider a buy stop at 52 entered when the market is 51. Based on the ticks below, at what price would this order be executed?

51.88   51.99   52.13   52.13   51.88

Look at the chart. The chart shows you that a buy stop is entered above the market price. This reminds you that it is only elected or triggered at the first price where the market is at or above the order price. Stops become market orders when triggered, so it executes at the price immediately following the trigger. Based on this example, this buy stop triggers at 52.13 and could execute at 52.13.

If this had been a buy stop limit at 52, the trigger would still be 52.13. Just as before, it triggers at or above the order price. When a stop limit is triggered, it becomes a limit order, which means it will execute only at a price at or below the stated price (lower is better for a buyer).

Based on this example, this buy stop limit triggers at 52.13 and could execute at 51.88.

Consider a sell stop at 52 entered when the market is 53. Based on the ticks shown below, at what price could this order be executed?

52.50   51.88   51.50   51.75   52.25

The chart shows you that a sell stop is entered below the market price. This reminds you that it is only elected or triggered when the market is at or below the order price. Stops become market orders when triggered, so it executes at the next available price immediately following the trigger. Based on this example, this sell stop triggers at 51.88 and executes at 51.50.

If this had been a sell stop limit at 52, the trigger would still be 51.88. Just as before, it triggers at or below the order price. When a stop limit is triggered, it becomes a limit order, which means it will execute only at a price at or above the stated price (higher is better for a seller). This sell stop limit triggers at 51.88 and could execute at 52.25.

When drawing your order reference chart, think of the word BLISS. It stands for "buy limits and sell stops." These are the orders that are placed below the market price. ("B" in BLISS reminds you of "B" in below.)

Why use stop orders?

Buy stop orders:
- protect against loss in a short stock position;
- protect a gain from a short stock position; and
- establish a long position when a breakout occurs above the line of resistance.

Sell stop orders:
- protect against loss in a long stock position;
- protect a gain from a long stock position; and
- establish a short position when a breakout occurs below the line of support.

TAKE NOTE

There is no guarantee that if a stop order is elected (triggered), the investor will pay or receive the stop price.

Comparison of Order Characteristics

Order Type	Description	Exchange Orders	OTC Orders
Market	Buy or sell at the best available market price	Most common order type on all exchanges	Most common OTC order type
Limit	Minimum price for sell orders; maximum price for buy orders	Can be handled by a specialist (DMM) or floor broker as a day order. GTCs may not be acceptable depending on the exchange.	Acceptable on either a day or GTC basis if GTCs are accepted
Stop	Buy orders entered above the market; sell orders entered below the market	May or may not be acceptable depending on the exchange	Acceptable by some dealers
Stop Limit	Stop order that becomes a limit order once the stop price has been reached or exceeded	May or may not be acceptable depending on the exchange	Acceptable by some dealers

8. 2. 5   REDUCING ORDERS

Certain orders on the order book are reduced when a stock goes ex-dividend. All orders entered below the market are reduced on the ex-dividend date (or ex-date), the first date on which the new owner of stock does not qualify for the current dividend. On the ex-date, the stock price opens lower by the amount of the distribution. Orders reduced include buy limits, sell stops, and sell stop limits. These orders are reduced by the dividend amount. Without this reduction, trading at the lower price on the ex-dividend date could cause an inadvertent execution.

EXAMPLE

ABC closes at 35.00. The following day is the ex-date for a $.31 cash dividend. ABC stock should open at 34.69.

8. 2. 5. 1   Do Not Reduce (DNR)

A DNR order is not reduced by an ordinary cash dividend. In this case, the customer does not care if there is an execution due solely to the ex-date reduction.

TEST TOPIC ALERT

You are likely to be asked which orders are reduced for cash dividends. Only those placed below the market price are automatically reduced. Remember that BLISS (buy limits and sell stops) orders are placed below the market price and are reduced for cash dividend distributions. All orders are adjusted for stock dividends and stock splits, whether placed above or below the market.

8. 2. 5. 2   Reductions for Stock Splits

If there is a stock dividend or stock split, the DMM will adjust all open orders.

EXAMPLE   There is an open order to sell 100 XYZ at 50 stop. If there is a 2-for-1 split, the order becomes sell 200 XYZ at 25 stop.

Stock dividends/splits: treat like normal - increase share amount and reduce share etc.

EXAMPLE   There is an open order to buy 500 XYZ at 30. If there is a 20% stock dividend, the order becomes buy 600 XYZ at 25.

EXAMPLE   There is an open order to buy 100 XYZ at 30. If there is a 20% stock dividend, the order becomes buy 100 XYZ at 25. Common sense says the order size should be 120 shares. However, only round lots are allowed on the order book. The additional 20 shares are in the customer's account but cannot be part of an open order. For reverse splits, all open orders are canceled.

Only round lots allowed on the order book

8. 2. 6   COMPUTERIZED ORDER ROUTING

A large percentage of the orders the NYSE receives each day are processed through a computerized trading and execution system called super display book (SDBK).

8. 2. 6. 1   Super Display Book (SDBK)

Broker-dealers use this computerized order routing system to route an order directly to the appropriate equity post on the trading floor.

Orders can be sent through the system either preopening or post-opening. The computer automatically pairs preopening orders received before the opening of trading with other orders and executes them at the opening price. Any order that cannot be matched before the opening is left on the display book for the designated market maker to handle. If an order is received post-opening, it is sent directly to the display book and presented to the crowd. All NYSE-listed stocks are eligible for order entry over the super display book (SDBK).

QUICK QUIZ 8.B   Objective: Differentiate the characteristics of the types of orders that can be placed when trading listed securities

1.   An order that instructs the specialist (DMM) not to adjust the limit (or stop) price when a stock goes ex-dividend is designated

   A.   DNA
   B.   DNR
   C.   FOK
   D.   EX

2. An order to sell at 38.63 stop, 38.63 limit is entered before the opening. The subsequent trades are 38.88, 38.50, 38.38. The order

   A. was executed at 38.50
   B. was executed at 38.63
   C. was executed at 38.88
   D. has not yet been executed

3. A sell stop order is entered

   A. above the current market price
   B. below the current market price
   C. either above or below the current market price
   D. at the current market price

4. All of the following are true of stop orders EXCEPT

   A. they can limit a loss in a declining stock
   B. they become market orders when there is a trade at, or the market passes through, a specific price
   C. they are the same as limit orders
   D. they can affect the price of the stock when the specific stop price is reached

5. A client bought 100 shares of MCS at 20. The stock rose to 30, and the client wants to protect his gain. Which of the following orders should be entered?

   A. Sell stop at 29
   B. Sell limit at 30
   C. Sell limit at 30.13
   D. Sell stop at 30.13

6. A customer sold 100 shares of QRS short when the stock was trading at 19. QRS is now trading at 14, and the customer wants to protect his gain. Which of the following orders should he place?

   A. Sell stop at 13.88
   B. Sell limit at 14
   C. Buy limit at 14
   D. Buy stop at 14.38

7. ZOO is trading at 50.63. Your customer, who owns 100 shares of the stock, places an order to sell ZOO at 50.25 stop limit. The tape subsequently reports the following trades:

   ZOO 50.63 50.75 50.13 50.13 50.25

   Your customer's order could first be executed at

   A. 50.13
   B. 50.25
   C. 50.63
   D. 50.75

8. Which of the following orders would be reduced by the specialist (DMM) on the ex-dividend date?

   I.   Buy limit order

   II. Sell stop order

  III. Buy stop order

  IV. Sell limit order

   A. I and II

   B. I and IV

   C. II, III, and IV

   D. III and IV

9. A company is about to pay a dividend of $.70. On the ex-dividend date, an open order to sell at 46 stop would

   A. be automatically adjusted to 45.30 stop

   B. be automatically adjusted to 45.38 stop

   C. be automatically adjusted to 45.50 stop

   D. remain 46 stop

All Quick Quiz answers are found at the end of their units.

8. 3 TIME-SENSITIVE ORDERS

Orders based on time considerations include the following:

- Day
- Good til canceled
- At the open and market on close
- Not held
- Fill or kill
- Immediate or cancel
- All or none
- Alternative, which provides two alternatives, such as sell a stock at a limit or sell it on stop

8. 3. 1 DAY ORDERS

Unless marked to the contrary, an open order (stop or limit) is assumed to be a day order, valid only until the close of trading on the day it is entered. If the order has not been filled, it is canceled at the close of the day's trading.

8. 3. 2 GOOD TIL CANCELED (GTC) ORDERS

GTC orders are valid until executed or canceled. However, all GTC orders are automatically canceled if unexecuted on the last business day of April and the last business day of October. If the customer wishes to have the order remain working beyond those specific days, the customer must reentered the order.

8. 3. 3 AT-THE-OPEN AND MARKET-ON-CLOSE ORDERS

At-the-open orders are executed at the opening of the market. Partial executions are allowable. They must reach the post by the open of trading in that security or else they are canceled. Market-on-close orders are executed at or as near as possible to the closing price in the OTC market. On the NYSE, however, a market-on-close order must be entered before 3:40 pm and will be executed at the closing price.

8. 3. 4 NOT HELD (NH) ORDERS

= market maker decides time and price

A **market order** coded NH indicates that the customer agrees not to hold the floor broker or broker-dealer to a particular time and price of execution. This provides the floor broker with authority to decide the best time and price at which to execute the trade. Market not held orders may not be placed with the specialist (DMM).

TAKE NOTE Market not held orders in which a retail customer gives you authority over price or timing are limited to the day the order is given. In other words, they are day orders. An exception is granted if the customer, in writing, states that the order is GTC.

---

8. 3. 5 FILL-OR-KILL (FOK) ORDERS

The commission house broker is instructed to fill an entire FOK order immediately at the limit price or better. A broker that cannot fill the entire order immediately cancels it and notifies the originating branch office.

8. 3. 6 IMMEDIATE-OR-CANCEL (IOC) ORDERS *= partial OK*

IOC orders are like FOK orders except that a partial execution is acceptable. The portion not executed is canceled.

8. 3. 7 ALL-OR-NONE (AON) ORDERS

AON orders must be executed in their entirety or not at all. AON orders can be day or GTC orders. They differ from the FOKs in that they do not have to be filled immediately.

8. 3. 8 ALTERNATIVE ORDERS (OCO)

Assume a customer is long stock at $50 that was purchased six months earlier at $30. To protect his unrealized gain, the customer might enter a sell stop at $48. Alternatively, if the stock continues to rise, he wants out at $53. What he might do is enter both orders with the notation "one cancels the other" (OCO). If one of the orders is executed, the other is immediately canceled.

TAKE NOTE

[handwritten margin note: NYSE does not accept Good till Cancelled, stop orders, all-or-none, or fill or Kill]

Exchanges can limit the order types they will accept. For instance, the NYSE does not accept GTC or stop orders (stop loss or stop limit) or all-or-none (AON) or fill-or-kill (FOK) orders to be entered in its equity market. Because these different order types are also used in the bond market and Nasdaq, students should still be familiar with them and be able to distinguish them from other order types. Additionally, though an exchange might not accept them, broker-dealers are still able to do so if they wish to, but would need to manually monitor the status of the order if entered on an exchange that does not accept them.

QUICK QUIZ 8.C

Objective: Apply the characteristics of time sensitive orders to market conditions

1. An immediate-or-cancel (IOC) order

    I.   must be executed in its entirety
    II. may be executed in part or in full
    III. must be executed in one attempt
    IV. may be executed after several attempts

    A. I and III
    B. I and IV
    C. II and III
    D. II and IV

2. A fill-or-kill (FOK) order

    I.   must be executed in its entirety
    II. may be executed in part or in full
    III. must be executed in one attempt
    IV. may be executed after several attempts

    A. I and III
    B. I and IV
    C. II and III
    D. II and IV

3. A customer wants to purchase 100,000 shares of a stock at the current market value. The stock is trading at $51. They would like to buy all the shares at one time, but if they can't buy the entire 100,000 shares, they will take what is available. What kind of order should be placed?

    A. A market order AON
    B. A market order IOC
    C. A buy limit @ $51 FOK
    D. A buy stop market-on-close

All Quick Quiz answers are found at the end of their units.

8. 4   SHORT SALE RULES

The SEC has rescinded rules previously in place to limit how and when short sales could be done. This process to eliminate what were previously known as the "up-tick" rules began in

2004 with Regulation SHO and was completed in 2008. Short sales may now occur anytime during the trading day including at the opening and closing of the day.

A **short sale** involves the sale of a security that the customer does not own. Essentially, a short sale is the sale of borrowed stock from the customer's broker-dealer. The customer sells the stock and puts the proceeds in the account.

The short seller profits if the stock declines in value BUT has potentially unlimited loss if the stock appreciates and the seller must buy the stock for more than what it sold for.

EXAMPLE

- Customer Sells 100 shares of ABC stock at $40 = $4,000.

  In order to profit, the stock must decline in value. The short seller buys the stock in order to replace the borrowed shares he sold.

- Buy 100 shares of ABC stock at $20 = $2,000.

  The investor profits ($2,000) because he bought it for less than he sold it for.

If the price goes up, there is no limit how high the price can go and, therefore, there is unlimited loss potential.

All sort sales must be done in a short margin account, and the broker-dealer must make sure the customer that sells short understands the risk and that opening the account is suitable.

8. 4. 1   REGULATION SHO

Regulation SHO also mandates a locate requirement, which means that before the short sale of any equity security, firms must locate the securities for borrowing to ensure that delivery will be made on settlement date. Not doing so is known as naked short selling and is not permitted.

8. 4. 2   INSIDER SHORT SALE REGULATIONS

The Securities Exchange Act of 1934 prohibits directors, officers, and principal stockholders (insiders) from selling short stock in their own companies.

8. 4. 3   SELL ORDER TICKETS

The SEC requires that all sell orders be identified as either long or short. No sale can be marked long unless the security to be delivered is in the customer's account or is owned by the customer and will be delivered to the broker by the settlement date.

A person is long a security if he:

- has title to it;
- has purchased the security or has entered into an unconditional contract to purchase the security but has not yet received it;
- owns a security convertible into or exchangeable for the security and has tendered such security for conversion or exchange; or
- has an option to purchase the security and has exercised that option.

Unless one or more of these conditions are met, the SEC considers any sale of securities a short sale.

TAKE NOTE   When a customer is both long and short shares of the same stock simultaneously, the positions must be netted out to determine if the customer is net long or net short.

For example, if a customer is long 500 shares of XYZ and short 200 shares of XYZ, the net position is long 300 shares. In this case, if the customer wished to sell 400 shares of XYZ, the sell order ticket must read: SELL 300 shares long and 100 shares short because the customer is only long 300 shares (net).

8. 4. 4   SHORTING BONDS

Securities, such as listed stocks, have many equivalent securities trading at any time. For instance, it is easy to short 100 shares of GM because an equivalent 100 shares of GM can be purchased on the NYSE at any time. It is not easy to cover shorts for most municipal bonds because the limited number of bonds available in each issue could make it difficult to buy in the short position. In other words, the municipal market is too thin.

QUICK QUIZ 8.D   Objective: Summarize short sales and the rules regarding short sales

1. All the following statements regarding the short sale of a listed security are true EXCEPT

    A.   the order ticket must indicate that the sale is short
    B.   short sales may take place at the opening
    C.   the buyer must be advised that he is purchasing borrowed shares
    D.   short sales may take place at the closing

2. A customer is interested in selling securities short. The most important disclosure to the customer is that

    A.   the customer has unlimited financial risk
    B.   the customer profits when the price of the stock goes up
    C.   the safest securities to short are municipal securities
    D.   the best time to sell short is in a bull market

All Quick Quiz answers are found at the end of their units.

8. 5   THE OVER-THE-COUNTER MARKET

The largest securities market (in terms of number of issues) is the **over-the-counter (OTC) market**, in which broker-dealers negotiate trades directly with one another. When we say that the OTC market is a negotiated market, we mean that it is one in which market makers may bargain during a trade. A negotiated market is competitive: a firm competes against other brokerage firms, each trading for its own inventory.

The OTC market is a highly sophisticated telecommunications and computer network connecting brokers/dealers across the country. Securities that can be traded in the OTC market include, but are not limited to:

- American depositary receipts (ADRs);
- common stocks, especially of banks and insurance and technology companies;
- most corporate bonds (typically convertibles);
- municipal bonds;
- U.S. government securities;
- preferred stock;
- equipment trust certificates;
- closed-end investment companies; and
- warrants.

The OTC market is historically associated with unlisted securities—those not listed on U.S. exchanges. However, in recent years some traditional OTC market participants such as Nasdaq have purchased U.S. exchanges (for example, the Philadelphia Stock Exchange was purchased by and is now a part of the Nasdaq OMX Group).

OTC Versus NYSE Markets

OTC	NYSE
Securities' prices determined through negotiation	Securities' prices determined through auction bidding
Regulated by FINRA	Regulated by FINRA
Market Makers must register with both the SEC and FINRA	Designated Market Makers must be registered with the SEC and must be Exchange members
Traded at many locations across the country	Traded only on the NYSE floor

TAKE NOTE   OTC trading is regulated by both the SEC and FINRA, the self-regulatory organization (SRO) for the OTC market.

8. 5. 1   NASDAQ

The computerized information system that tracks OTC equities trading is called the National Association of Securities Dealers Automated Quotation service (Nasdaq).

TAKE NOTE   Not all OTC securities are listed on Nasdaq. For instance, government securities, while traded OTC, are not listed on Nasdaq.

govt security = not traded/listed on nasdaq

8. 5. 1. 1   Order Audit Trail System (OATS)

The **order audit trail system (OATS)** is an automated computer system created to record information relating to orders, quotes, and other trade information from all equities that are traded on Nasdaq. OATS helps to ensure that all the time-sensitive information relating to the sequence of events throughout the order execution process is recorded accurately. OATS tracks orders from the time of order entry until execution or cancellation, and in doing so provides an accurate audit trail. For example, one detail required by the system is that all computer clocks and time stamps be coordinated and capable of providing time to the hour, minute, and second. OATS reports are made on an order-by-order basis to FINRA.

8. 5. 1. 1. 1   Dark Pools of Liquidity

Dark pools, sometimes called dark pools of liquidity or simply dark liquidity, is trading volume that occurs or liquidity that is not openly available to the public. The bulk of this volume represents trades engaged in by institutional traders and trading desks away from the exchange markets. Generally, these are large volume transactions that occur on crossing networks or alternative trading systems (ATS) that match buy and sell orders electronically for execution without routing the order to an exchange or other market where quote, last sale price, and volume information is displayed.

Institutional trading desks that choose to utilize dark pools are able to execute large block orders without impacting public quotes or price, or revealing their investment strategy regarding any of their holding accumulations or divestitures. Additionally, orders can be placed anonymously so that the identity of the entity placing the order is unknown to the general investing public, along with the volume and price for the transaction. The concern with dark pools is that some market participants are left disadvantaged because they cannot see the trades, volume, or prices agreed upon within the pools, and thus market transparency is darkened.

8. 5. 1. 2   Trade Reporting and Compliance Engine (TRACE)

The **Trade Reporting and Compliance Engine (TRACE)** is the FINRA-approved trade reporting system for corporate and government agency bonds trading in the OTC secondary market. Reporting to TRACE enables better market transparency as trade details are disseminated immediately to the investing public.

TRACE is a trade-reporting system only. It is not an execution system. It does not accept quotations, nor does it provide settlement and clearance functions. Following are the reporting rules for TRACE:

- Both sides of the transaction must report.
- Trades must be reported as soon as practicable and no later than 15 minutes of execution.
- Execution date, time of trade, quantity, price, yield, and if price reflects a commission charged are all reportable and displayed.

While most corporate debt securities, asset-backed securities (ABS), Treasury securities, and collateralized mortgage obligations (CMOs) are TRACE eligible, there are exclusions. The following is a list of exclusions to know:

- Debt of foreign governments
- Money market instruments
- Debt securities that are not depository trust eligible

8. 5. 1. 3 OTC Market Makers

Designated market makers on an exchange stand ready to trade in specified securities. The OTC market has no specialists. Rather, firms wishing to make a market in a particular security must register with, and receive approval from, FINRA. They buy and sell for their own inventories, for their own profit, and at their own risk. A broker-dealer acting as a market maker, buying and selling for its own account rather than arranging trades, acts as a principal, not an agent.

8. 5. 2 BIDS, OFFERS, AND QUOTES

A full quote consists of a bid price and an offer (ask) price.

The current bid is the highest price at which the dealer will buy, and the current offer is the lowest price at which the dealer will sell. The difference between the bid and ask is known as the spread. A typical quote might be expressed as bid 63–offered 63.07. The highest price the dealer will pay is 63, and the lowest price the dealer will accept is 63.07. The spread is .07 of a point between the bid and ask. The broker could also say 63 bid–63.07 ask or 63 to .07.

The Customer's and the Market Maker's Relationship to the Quote

	Bid-63	Ask/Offer-63.07
Quoting dealer	Buys	Sells
Customer	Sells	Buys

When a customer buys a stock from a firm acting as principal, the broker marks up the ask price to reach the net price to the customer. Likewise, when a customer sells stock to a firm acting as principal, the dealer marks down from the bid price to reach the net proceeds to the customer.

EXAMPLE

If WXYZ is quoted as 43.25 to .50, (short hand for 43.25 bid / 43.50 ask or offer), and the dealer wants a half-point for the trade, a customer buying would pay 44 net, and a customer selling would receive 42.75 net. The additional half point (added to the ask or offer, or subtracted from the bid) is the dealer's markup and markdown, respectively.

8. 5. 2. 1 Quotes

As a negotiated market where broker-dealers are trading with other broker-dealers, many different types of quotes have been defined and are reviewed here.

8. 5. 2. 1. 1 Firm Quote

A firm quotation is the price at which a market maker stands ready to buy or sell at least one trading unit—100 shares of stock or five bonds—at the quoted price with other member firms. When an OTC firm makes a market in a security, the broker-dealer must be willing to buy or sell at least one trading unit of the security at its firm quote. All quotes are firm quotes unless otherwise indicated.

As is true of market order executions on an exchange floor, an OTC trader may attempt to negotiate a better price with a market maker by making a counteroffer or a counterbid, especially if the spread between the market maker's bid and ask is fairly wide. However, the only way to guarantee an immediate execution is to buy stock at the market maker's ask price or sell at the bid price.

In a typical bond transaction, a trader at one broker-dealer calls a trader at another broker-dealer (a market maker) to buy a specific bond. A market maker might give another broker-dealer a quote that is firm for an hour with five-minute recall. This is a firm quote that remains good for an hour. If, within that hour, the market maker receives another order for the same security, the trader calls the broker-dealer back and gives it five minutes to confirm its order or lose its right to buy that security at the price quoted.

8. 5. 2. 1. 2   Backing Away

A market maker can revise a firm quote in response to market conditions and trading activity, but a market maker that refuses to do business at the price(s) quoted is backing away from the quote. Backing away is a violation of trading rules.

8. 5. 3   RECOGNIZED QUOTATION

A recognized quotation under FINRA rules is any public bid or offer for one or more round lots or other normal trading units. Any bid for less than a round lot must state the amount of the security for which it is good. If the bid or offer is made for multiple round lots, it must also be good for a smaller number of units.

EXAMPLE   If the bid is for 1,000 shares of stock, the bidder must buy any round lots offered of 100 or more at the same price.

8. 5. 3. 1   Subject Quote

A **subject quote** is one in which the price is tentative, subject to confirmation by the market maker. When a market maker knows the transaction size, the broker-dealer firms up the subject quote or gives a replacement quote. Some typical expressions used to denote subject and firm quotes are shown in the following. Firm quotes are absolute statements, but subject quotes are hedged.

8. 5. 3. 2   Qualified Quotes

A quote will often be given with qualifiers intended to allow the broker-dealer to back away if market conditions change.

8. 5. 3. 2. 1 Workout Quote

This term is usually reserved for situations in which a market maker knows that special handling will be required to accommodate a particular trade. Either the order size is too big for the market to absorb without disruption or the market is too thin or temporarily unstable. A **workout quote** is an approximate figure used to provide the buyer or the seller with an indication of price, not a firm quote. Block positioners use workout quotes frequently.

Subject or Workout Market	Firm Market
"It is around 40–41."	"The market is 40–41."
"Last I saw, it was 40–41."	"It is currently 40–41."
"It is 40–41 subject."	
"40–42.50 workout."	

8. 5. 3. 2. 2 Nominal Quote

A **nominal quote** is someone's assessment of where a stock might trade in an active market. Nominal quotes may be used to give customers an idea of the market value of an inactively traded security, but they are not firm quotes. Nominal quotes in print must be clearly labeled as such.

8. 5. 4 QUOTATION SPREAD AND SIZE

The difference between a security's bid and offer (ask) price is known as the spread. The size of the quote tells you how many shares are bid for or offered.

8. 5. 4. 1 Spread

Many factors influence a spread's size, including:

■ the issue's size;
■ the issuer's financial condition;
■ the amount of market activity in the issue; and
■ the market conditions.

8. 5. 4. 2 Size

Unless otherwise specified, a firm quote is always good for one round lot (100 shares).

EXAMPLE

A firm quote of 8.25–.50 means the market maker stands ready to buy 100 shares of stock from another broker-dealer at the 8.25 bid price or sell 100 shares at the 8.50 ask price.

8. 5. 5   NON-NASDAQ

For securities quoted on either the OTC Pink or the over-the-counter .... board (OTCBB), the three-quote rule often applies. Unless there are at least two market makers displaying quotes, broker-dealers receiving orders to buy or sell non-Nasdaq securities must contact a minimum of three dealers to determine the prevailing price.

If not traded in exchange but

---

traded in
nasdaq OTC pink -
need 3 quotes to
determine price

TAKE NOTE

Quotes disseminated in this fashion are not considered to be firm quotes because they are generally updated on a basis too infrequent to be considered current. Therefore, in order to obtain a current and firm quote, the dealers listed as making quotes for a particular security must be contacted. Once a firm quote is gotten, a transaction can occur if both parties agree to a price.

TEST TOPIC ALERT

Following is a list of important test points about OTC quotes.

- Markups and markdowns are charged when a market maker is acting as a principal (dealing from inventory with financial risk).

- Firm quotes are good for a round lot only, unless otherwise stated. A quote of 11–11.50 3 × 5 is firm between dealers for 300 shares at the bid of 11 and 500 shares at the asked of 11.50.

- Nominal quotes can be given for informational purposes and can be printed only if clearly labeled as such.

- A relatively wide spread indicates a thin trading market for the security.

8. 5. 6   THE 5% MARKUP POLICY

The 5% markup policy was adopted to ensure that the investing public receives fair treatment and pays reasonable rates for brokerage services in both exchange and OTC markets. It is considered a guideline only and is not a firm rule for markups and markdowns. A firm charging a customer more or less than a 5% markup may or may not be in violation of fair and equitable trade practices. The markup may be considered excessive once all the relevant factors are taken into account.

A broker-dealer can fill a customer order in the following three ways:

- If the broker-dealer is a market maker in the security, it will (as principal) buy from or sell to the customer, charging a markup or markdown.

- If the firm is not a market maker in the security, it can fill the order as agent, without taking a position in the security, and charge a commission for its execution services.

- An order can be filled as a riskless and simultaneous transaction.

8. 5. 6. 1   Markup Based on Representative Market Prices

The 5% markup is based on the price representative of prevailing (inside) market prices at the time of a customer transaction. The 5% markup policy applies to all transactions in nonexempt listed or unlisted securities traded on an exchange or OTC, regardless of whether the transactions are executed as agency or principal trades.

TAKE NOTE   The 5% policy applies to markups, markdowns, and commissions.

---

8. 5. 6. 2   Fixed Public Offering Price Securities

The 5% markup policy does not apply to mutual funds, variable annuity contracts, or securities sold in public offerings, all of which are sold by a prospectus, nor does it apply to municipal securities.

8. 5. 6. 3   Dealer's Inventory Costs

If a customer's buy order is filled from a broker-dealer's inventory, the net price to the customer is based on the prevailing market price, regardless of whether the broker-dealer selling to the customer is also making a market in the stock and what the firm's quote might be.

The price at which the broker-dealer acquired the stock being sold to the customer has no bearing on the net price to the customer; the price to the customer must be reasonably related to the current market.

8. 5. 6. 4   Riskless and Simultaneous Transactions

A riskless and simultaneous transaction is an order to buy or sell stock in which the firm receiving the order is not a market maker. The dealer has the following two options for filling the order:

■ As agent for the customer, it could buy or sell on the customer's behalf and charge a commission, subject to the 5% policy.

■ It could buy or sell for its riskless principal account, then buy or sell to the customer as principal, charging a markup or markdown subject to the 5% policy.

When the order is filled as a principal transaction, the broker-dealer must disclose the markup to the customer.

8. 5. 6. 5   Proceeds Transactions

When a customer sells securities and uses the proceeds to purchase other securities in a proceeds transaction, the broker-dealer's combined commissions and markups must be consistent with the 5% markup policy. In other words, member firms must treat proceeds transactions as one transaction for markup and markdown purposes.

8. 5. 6. 6 Markup Policy Considerations

While the policy is applicable to all account types, in assessing the fairness of a broker-dealer's commission and markup practices, the following factors are considered:

Type of Security. In general, more market risk is associated with making markets and trading common stocks than is associated with dealing in bonds. The policy gives guidance to markups specific to both stock and bond transactions, including government securities. The more risk a broker-dealer assumes, the greater the justification for higher markups.

Inactively Traded Stocks. The thinner the market for a security, the more volatile the stock and the greater the market risk to anyone dealing in the stock. Thus, a broker-dealer is justified in charging higher markups on inactively traded stocks.

Selling Price of Security. Commission and markup rates should decrease as a stock's price increases.

Dollar Amount of Transaction. Transactions of relatively small dollar amounts generally warrant higher percentage markups than large-dollar transactions.

Nature of the Broker-Dealer's Business. This standard pertains to full-service brokers versus discount brokers. In most cases, a general securities firm has higher operating costs than does a discount broker and thus may justify higher commissions and markups.

Pattern of Markups. Although the regulators are concerned primarily with detecting cases where broker-dealers have established patterns of excessive markups, a single incident could still be considered an unfair markup.

Markups on Inactive Stocks (Contemporaneous Cost). For inactive stocks and situations where no prevailing market quotes are available, a broker-dealer may base a markup on its cost in the stock.

TEST TOPIC ALERT

The 5% markup policy is peculiarly named for two reasons:
1. It applies to markups, markdowns, and commissions, meaning it is applicable to principal and agency transactions.
2. Five percent is not the limit. A transaction charge of more than 5% might be fine if it is reasonably based on the circumstances of the trade.

Examples of subject transactions are REITS, closed-end company shares, ADRs, third-market trades, listed and unlisted stocks, bonds, and government securities.

New issues sold by prospectus and municipal securities are not subject to this policy.

Remember that all computations must be based on the inside quote (the best available from all the market makers), not the firm's quote.

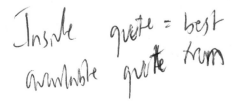

QUIZ **QUIZ 8.E**   Objective: Define the characteristics of the over-the-counter market

1. A member firm is selling stock to a customer from inventory. The broker-dealer has held the shares sold for several months. What price should the dealer use as a basis for a markup?

    A. Price at which it purchased the securities
    B. Offer price shown on the OTC Pink on the day of the current sale
    C. Broker-dealer's own current offer price
    D. Best offering price quoted in the interdealer market

2. A broker-dealer is looking for a Nasdaq security for a customer and calls a market maker for a quote and is told that the quote is 20,000 shares at $20.22 for the 10 minutes. What kind of quote would this be defined as?

    A. Nominal
    B. Firm
    C. Workout
    D. Subject

3. The 5% markup policy applies to

    I.   commissions charged when executing customer agency (broker) transactions
    II. markups and markdowns on principal (dealer) transactions filled for customers from a firm's trading inventory
    III. markups on stocks or bonds bought for inventory, then immediately resold to customers
    IV. markdowns on stocks or bonds bought from customers for inventory, then immediately resold to another broker-dealer

    A. I and II
    B. II only
    C. III and IV
    D. I, II, III, and IV

All Quick Quiz answers are found at the end of their units.

8.6 AUTOMATED QUOTATION SYSTEM

Nasdaq provides a computer link between broker-dealers that trade OTC.

8.6.1 NASDAQ QUOTATION SERVICE

The system provides three levels of stock quotation service to the securities industry.

■ **Nasdaq Level 1** is available to registered representatives through a variety of public vendors. Level 1 displays the inside market only, the highest bids and the lowest asks for securities included in the system, and other basic information such as last sale and volume. Normal market price fluctuations prevent a registered representative from guaranteeing a Level 1 price to a client.

■ **Nasdaq Level 2** is available to approved subscribers only. Level 2 provides the current quote and quote size available from each market maker in a security in the system. To list a quote on Level 2, a market maker must guarantee that the quote is firm for at least 100 shares.

■ **Nasdaq Level 3** provides subscribers with all the services of Levels 1 and 2 and allows registered market makers to input and update their quotes on any securities in which they make a market.

Levels of Nasdaq Service

DWAQ 35 – 35.13

Level 1: The inside quote

DWAQ 35 – 35.13		
DWAQ	Bid	Ask
Serendip	35	35.25
Tippec	34.88	35.13
Cheath	35	35.13

Level 2: The inside quote plus quotes from all market makers

DWAQ 35 – 35.13		
DWAQ	Bid	Ask
Serendip	35	35.25
Tippec	34.88	35.13
Cheath	35	35.13
Enter	BID:	ASK:

Level 3: The inside quote, all other quotes, plus ability to enter or change your own quote

8. 6. 2   TRANSACTIONS AND TRADE SETTLEMENT

Processes must be in place in order to accept an order from a customer, report the execution back to the customer, and ultimately have the transaction settle.

8. 6. 3   RECEIPT AND DELIVERY OF SECURITIES

When a representative accepts a buy or sell order from a customer, the representative must be assured that the customer can pay for or deliver the securities. If the customer claims the securities are being held in street name at another firm, the representative must verify this before executing a sale for the customer.

8. 6. 4   ORDER MEMORANDUM

To enter a customer order, the registered representative traditionally has filled out an order ticket. Increasingly, representatives are entering orders electronically.

After the representative prepares the order ticket, it is sent to the wire room or desk, where the order is routed to the proper market for execution. A registered principal must approve the order promptly after execution. Promptly after execution is interpreted as meaning no later than the end of the trading day.

A customer order is most susceptible to error at two points: communication of the order between customer and broker and transmission of the order from broker to wire operator.

Breakdowns in communication in the ordering process most often occur because of inaccurate information on a ticket.

The information required on the order ticket includes:

■ customer account number;

- registered representative identification number;
- whether the order is solicited or unsolicited;
- whether the order is subject to discretionary authority;
- description of the security (symbol);
- number of shares or bonds to be traded;
- action (buy, sell long, or sell short);
- options (buy, write, covered, uncovered, opening, or closing);
- order restrictions and price qualifications (e.g., market, GTC, or day order);
- type of account (cash or margin); and
- the time the order was received, the time of entry, and the price at which it was executed.

TAKE NOTE   The account name or number must be on an order ticket before order execution.

If a mistake is made (e.g., a wrong account number), no change to the order can be made without the approval of a principal or the branch manager. All the facts surrounding the change must be put in writing and retained for three years.

8. 6. 5   REPORT OF EXECUTION

The registered representative receives a report after a trade is executed. He first checks the **execution report** against the order ticket to make sure that everything was done as the customer requested. If everything is in order, he reports the execution to the customer. If an error exists, the representative must report it to the branch office manager (BOM) or principal immediately. Changing an account number on an order ticket (cancel and rebill) requires manager approval.

8. 6. 5. 1   Incorrect Trade Reports

Sometimes the details of a trade are reported to a customer incorrectly. Despite the mistaken report, the actual trade is binding on the customer. However, if an order is executed outside the customer's instructions, the trade is not binding.

8. 6. 5. 2   Reporting an Error

FINRA rules require that a record of any errors made be reported to the person designated to receive such error reports by the firm. At a broker-dealer, that individual would always be a manager or someone who holds a principal's license. All such reports should be made immediately in writing and retained for three years under the general record retention rules.

These reports may be referred to as error reports, error records, trade correction reports, or any number of generic names a firm might assign to such records.

8. 6. 6   TRADE CONFIRMATIONS

A **trade confirmation** is a printed document that confirms a trade, its settlement date, and the amount of money due from or owed to the customer. For each transaction, a customer must be sent or given a written confirmation of the trade at or before the completion of the transaction, the settlement date.

The trade confirmation includes the following information:

- Trade date—day on which the transaction is executed (the settlement date is usually the second business day after the trade date)
- Account number—branch office number followed by an account number
- Registered representative internal ID number (or AE number)—account executive's identification number
- BOT (bought) or SLD (sold)—indicates a customer's role in a trade
- Number (or quantity)—number of shares of stock or the par value of bonds bought or sold for the customer
- Description—specific security bought or sold for the customer
- Yield—indicates that the yield for callable bonds may be affected by the exercise of a call provision
- CUSIP number—applicable Committee on Uniform Securities Identification Procedures (CUSIP) number, if any
- Price—price per share for stock or bonds before a charge or deduction
- Amount—price paid or received before commissions and other charges, also referred to as extended principal for municipal securities transactions
- Commission—added to buy transactions; subtracted from sell transactions completed on an agency basis; a commission will not appear on the confirmation if a markup has been charged in a principal transaction
- Net amount—obtained on purchases by adding expenses (commissions and postage) to the principal amount (whether the transaction is a purchase or sale, interest is always added whenever bonds are traded with accrued interest)

8. 6. 6. 1   Disclosure of Capacity

The confirmation must also show the capacity in which the broker-dealer acts (agency or principal) and the commission in cases where the broker-dealer acts as an agent. Markups or markdowns are disclosed for Nasdaq securities.

TAKE NOTE

All firms can act in one of two capacities in a customer transaction. If the firm acts as an agent, it is the broker between the buying and selling parties. Agents receive commissions for transactions they perform, and commissions must be disclosed on confirmations.

If the firm acts as a dealer and transacts business for or from its inventory, it acts in a principal capacity and is compensated by a markup or markdown.

Additionally, confirmations must disclose markups or markdowns for Nasdaq securities, and a firm can never act as both agent and principal in the same transaction.

8. 6. 6. 2   Timely Mailing of Confirmations

Customer confirmations must be sent no later than at or before the completion of the transaction.

8. 6. 7   CUSTOMER ACCOUNT STATEMENTS

At a minimum, firms must send each customer a quarterly statement, but most firms send customers monthly statements. A statement shows:

■ all activity in the account since the previous statement;

■ securities positions, long or short; and

■ account balances, debit or credit.

If a customer's account has a cash balance, the firm may hold it in the account. However, the statement must advise the customer that these funds are available on request.

TAKE NOTE   If there is activity in an account or if penny stocks are held in the account, statements are sent monthly. If neither of these conditions exists, there is no activity, and penny stocks are not being held, then statements may be sent quarterly.

TEST TOPIC ALERT

Order Process Diagram

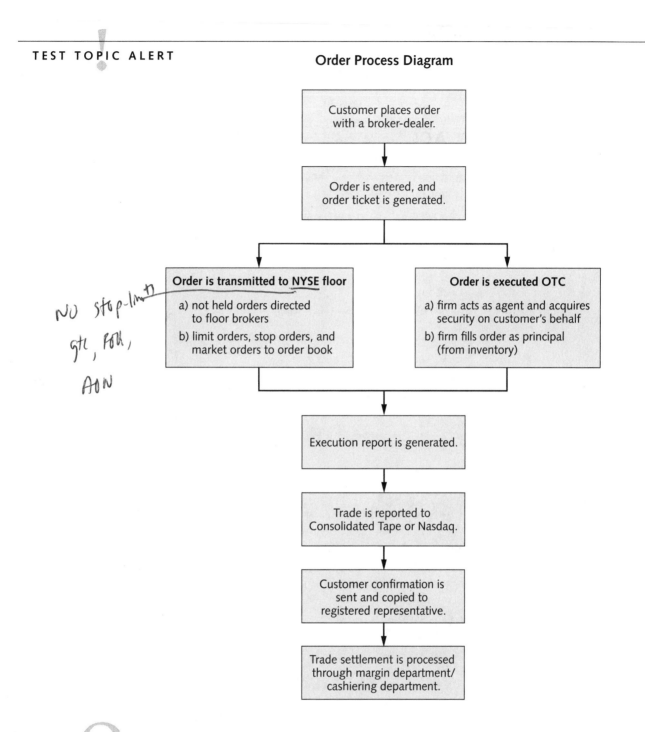

NO stop-limit

gtc, FOK,

AON

QUICK QUIZ 8.F

Objective: Summarize the process from when orders are placed to the confirmation of a trade

1. Which department in a brokerage firm handles all credit transactions for a customer?

   A. Margin
   B. Cashiering
   C. Purchases and sales
   D. Reorganization

2. Once orders are received, in which sequence do they flow through a brokerage firm?

    I.   Order or wire room
    II. Purchases and sales department
    III. Margin department
    IV. Cashiering department

    A. I, II, III, IV
    B. I, IV, II, III
    C. II, I, IV, III
    D. III, IV, II, I

3. Rules require that a statement for an inactive account should be sent to each customer

    A. weekly
    B. monthly
    C. quarterly
    D. immediately after each trade

4. A confirmation of each customer trade must be given or sent

    A. on the trade date
    B. before the trade date
    C. on or before the settlement date
    D. before the settlement date

All Quick Quiz answers are found at the end of their units.

8. 7   TRANSACTION SETTLEMENT DATES AND TERMS

Settlement date is the date on which ownership changes between buyer and seller. It is the date on which broker-dealers are required to exchange the securities and funds involved in a transaction and customers are requested to pay for securities bought and to deliver securities sold.

The Uniform Practice Code (UPC) standardizes the dates and times for each type of settlement.

8. 7. 1   REGULAR WAY SETTLEMENT

Regular way settlement for most securities transactions is the second business day following the trade date, known as T+2.

EXAMPLE

If a trade occurs on a Tuesday (trade date), it will settle regular way on Thursday.

If a trade takes place on a Thursday, it will settle the following Monday.

Knowing that not all securities settle T+2 is equally important, and a summary of settlement rules is included later in this section. Briefly, corporate securities, municipals, and government agency securities settle T+2. U.S. government T-bills, T-notes, T-bonds, and options settle next business day, T+1. Money market securities transactions settle the same day. In trades between dealers, if the seller delivers before the settlement date, the buyer may either accept the security or refuse it without prejudice.

TAKE NOTE   Interdealer trades in government securities settle in federal funds. Interdealer trades in all other securities settle in clearinghouse funds.

8. 7. 2   CASH SETTLEMENT

Cash settlement, or same day settlement, requires delivery of securities from the seller and payment from the buyer on the same day a trade is executed. Stocks or bonds sold for cash settlement must be available on the spot for delivery to the buyer.

Cash trade settlement occurs no later than 2:30 pm ET if the trade is executed before 2:00 pm. If the trade occurs after 2:00 pm, settlement is due within 30 minutes.

8. 7. 3   SELLER'S OPTION CONTRACTS

This form of settlement is available to customers who want to sell securities but cannot deliver the physical securities in time for regular way settlement. A seller's option contract lets a customer lock in a selling price for securities without having to make delivery on the second business day. Instead, the seller can settle the trade as specified in the contract. Or, if the seller elects to settle earlier than originally specified, the trade can be settled on any date from the third business day through the contract date, provided the buyer is given a one-day written notice.

A buyer's option contract works the same way, with the buyer specifying when settlement will take place.

8. 7. 4   WHEN-, AS-, AND IF-ISSUED CONTRACTS (WHEN-ISSUED TRADES)

Typically, new municipal bond issues are sold to investors before the bonds are issued. An investor receives a when-issued confirmation describing the bonds. The confirmation does not include a total dollar amount or settlement date because, until the settlement date is known, the accrued interest cannot be calculated to determine the total dollar amount. Once the bonds are issued, the investor receives a new confirmation stating the purchase price and settlement date.

A when-issued transaction confirmation must include:

■ a description of the security, with the contract price (yield); and
■ the trade date.

Because the settlement date is unknown, a when-issued confirmation for municipal bonds cannot include accrued interest.

8. 7. 5   REGULATION T PAYMENT

1 + 4

Regulation T specifies the date customers are required to pay for purchase transactions. The settlement date, however, is the date customers are requested to deliver cash or securities involved in transactions. Under Regulation T, payment is due two business days after regular way settlement.

8. 7. 5. 1   Extensions

If a buyer cannot pay for a trade within four business days from the trade date as allowed under Regulation T, the broker-dealer may request an extension from its designated examining authority (DEA) before the fourth business day. In the case of introducing broker-dealers, those that do not clear their own trades, the extension request is made by the clearing firm.

The broker-dealer has the option of ignoring amounts of $1,000 or less without violating Regulation T requirements. If the customer cannot pay by the end of the extension, the broker-dealer has the option to either request an additional extension from its DEA or sell the securities in a closeout transaction.

Broker-dealers are not likely to request too many extensions as a firm and are generally reluctant to request many for the same customer repeatedly unless severe circumstances warrant the request.

If the option to close out the position is chosen, the account is frozen for 90 days. A frozen account must have sufficient cash in it before a buy transaction can be executed.

Can only close transactions in a frozen acct

TAKE NOTE   Regulation T deals with the extension of credit for regular security trades. If a broker-dealer must close out a transaction and freeze the account, the customer may not be extended credit.

8. 7. 5. 2   Frozen Accounts

If a customer buys securities in a cash account and sells them before paying for the buy side by the fourth business day, the account is frozen. Any additional buy transactions require full payment in the account, and sell transactions need securities on deposit. Frozen account status continues for 90 calendar days. Frozen account status is lifted if the customer pays by the fourth business day.

TEST TOPIC ALERT   The following table gives a summary of the trade settlements and delivery times for different securities and different types of settlement choices.

[Handwritten margin notes: Regular way (T+2) · Equities, Corp. bonds, Agency securities]

[Handwritten margin notes: T+1 · Govt Treasury, notes, bonds · Equity & index options]

[Handwritten margin notes: Cash settle · Same day]

[Handwritten margin notes: sellers option · T+3]

Summary of Settlement Rules

Regular way—Equity	2 business days
Regular way—Corporate and municipal bonds	2 business days
Regular way—Equity options	Next business day *[T+1]*
Regular way—Index options	Next business day *[T+1]*
Regular way—T-bills, T-notes, and T-bonds	Next business day *[T+1]*
Regular way—U.S. government agency	2 business days
Seller's option	No sooner than T+3
Cash settlement	Same day
Regulation T	2 days after regular way *[T+4]*

Assume a question is asking about the normal customer settlement terms, regular way, unless the question specifically mentions Regulation T.

Also, here's a hint on municipal when-issued settlements. A probable question will ask either what is not included or what is included on a when-issued confirmation. To discern the correct answer, remember SAT, which identifies what is not included:

- Settlement date

- Accrued interest

- Total dollar amount due at settlement

If a question asks when customer confirmations must be sent, the answer is no later than the settlement date. But if the question asks when broker-to-broker confirmations must be sent, the answer is no later than the business day following the trade date (T+1).

8. 7. 6   DON'T KNOW (DK)

In an interdealer trade, each side electronically submits its version of the transaction to ACT (Automated Confirmation Transaction System). If one side does not recognize the other side's details of the transaction (e.g., the number of shares is wrong or the price is wrong), it will electronically DK (don't know) the trade.

TAKE NOTE

DKs are used in interdealer trades for which one party to the transaction does not recognize the trade or, if it does, disagrees with the terms of the trade as submitted by the other party.

The term can also be used within a broker-dealer when an order or wire room does not recognize the account number or other information on an order ticket.

8. 7. 6. 1   Due Bills

If one of your customers buys stock before the ex-date, your customer is entitled to the dividend. However, if the trade is somehow mishandled and does not settle until after the record date, the seller will receive the dividend in error. In this case, your firm will send a due bill to the seller's firm stating, "Our customer is due the dividend—kindly remit."

TAKE NOTE   Due bills are sent when the wrong party receives a dividend from the issuer.

QUICK QUIZ 8.G   Objective: Identify transaction settlement dates and terms

1. To be considered in good delivery form, certificates must be

    A.   accompanied by a preliminary prospectus
    B.   called for redemption by the issuing body
    C.   accompanied by an assignment or a stock power
    D.   in the name of the deceased person if the person died after the trade date

2.   If a broker-dealer chooses to close out a customer's position rather than request an extension, the account will be frozen for

    A.   20 days
    B.   30 days
    C.   90 days
    D.   120 days

3. Broker-to-broker confirmations are sent no later than

    A.   the regular way settlement date
    B.   the next business day
    C.   the same day as the transaction
    D.   the trade date plus three business days

4. When a client's cash account is frozen, the client

    A.   must deposit the full purchase price no later than the settlement date for a purchase
    B.   must deposit the full purchase price before a purchase order may be executed
    C.   may make sales with the firm's permission
    D.   may not trade under any circumstances

All Quick Quiz answers are found at the end of their units.

8. 8   RULES OF GOOD DELIVERY

A security must be in good delivery form before it can be delivered to a buyer. It is the registered representative's responsibility to ensure that a security is in good deliverable form when a customer sells it.

8. 8. 1   PHYSICAL REQUIREMENTS

Good delivery describes the physical condition of, signatures on, attachments to, and denomination of the certificates involved in a securities transaction. Good delivery is normally a back-office consideration between buying and selling brokers. In any broker-to-broker transaction, the delivered securities must be accompanied by a properly executed uniform delivery ticket. The transfer agent is the final arbiter of whether a security meets the requirements of good delivery.

8. 8. 1. 1   Overdelivery and Underdelivery

In settling customer sell transactions in which the securities delivery matches the exact number of shares or bonds sold, the first rule of good delivery is met. But if the customer overdelivers or underdelivers, the transaction is not good delivery.

EXAMPLE

Overdelivery:
A customer sells 300 shares and brings in one certificate for 325 shares.

Underdelivery:
A customer sells 100 shares and brings in one certificate for 80 shares.

8. 8. 1. 2   Partial Delivery

A broker-to-broker partial delivery must be accepted if the remainder of the delivery constitutes a round lot or multiple thereof.

8. 8. 1. 3   Good Delivery Clearing Rule (100-Share Uniform Units)

When one broker-dealer delivers stock to another broker-dealer, single round lots and odd lots are cleared separately. However, odd-lot certificates can be used to clear round-lot trades provided the odd lot certificates add up to single round lots (100 shares).

EXAMPLE

For a 300-share sale, the seller could deliver:

- one 300-share certificate;
- three 100-share certificates;
- six 50-share certificates;
- two 100-share certificates, one 60 share certificate, and one 40 share certificate; or
- three 60-share certificates and three 40-share certificates.

Each of the above deliveries meets the requirements of the rule. However, delivering four 75-share certificates would not be good delivery. Think of it this way: can you take the certificates and make piles of 100 shares? If the answer is yes, it is good delivery.

8. 8. 1. 4   Good Delivery for Bonds

Delivery of bonds in coupon or bearer form should be made in denominations of $1,000 or $5,000. Fully registered bonds are delivered in denominations of $1,000 or multiples of $1,000, but in no case larger than $100,000. Municipal bonds may settle in bearer or registered form and be delivered in the denominations stated above.

8. 8. 1. 5   Missing Coupons

If coupons are missing from a bond, it is not good delivery. If an issuer is in default on a coupon bond, all of the unpaid coupons must be attached for it to be good delivery.

8. 8. 2   CERTIFICATE NEGOTIABILITY

In order for ownership to change hands, the certificate representing ownership must be negotiable. Following are the criteria that determine negotiability.

8. 8. 3   ASSIGNMENT

Each stock and bond certificate must be assigned (endorsed by signature) by the owner(s) whose name is registered on the certificate's face. Certificates registered in a joint name require all owners' signatures.

Endorsement by a customer may be made on the back of a certificate on the signature line or on a separate stock or bond power of substitution. One stock or bond power can be used with any number of certificates for one security, but a separate power is required for each security.

8. 8. 3. 1   Alteration

If an alteration or a correction has been made to an assignment, a full explanation of the change signed by the person or firm who executed the correction must be attached.

8. 8. 4   SIGNATURE GUARANTEE

All customer signatures must be guaranteed by a party acceptable to the transfer agent (e.g., an exchange member or a national bank).

8. 8. 5   SIGNATURE REQUIREMENTS

A customer's signature must match exactly the name registered on the face of a security.

TAKE NOTE   Regarding signature requirements for purposes of good delivery the only two acceptable abbreviations within a signature are "Co." for the word company and "&" for the word and. No other abbreviations, such as Inc. or Corp., are permitted.

8. 8. 6   LEGAL TRANSFER ITEMS

Any form of registration other than individual or joint ownership may require supporting guarantees or documentation to render a certificate negotiable.

For business registrations involving sole proprietorships or partnerships, a simple guarantee by a broker-dealer is usually sufficient. For corporate registrations and certificates in the names of fiduciaries, a transfer agent may require a corporate resolution naming the person signing a certificate as authorized to do so. Fiduciaries must supply either a certified copy of a trust agreement or a copy of a court appointment, depending on the type of fiduciary involved.

8. 8. 7   INVALID SIGNATURES

If a broker-dealer guarantees a forged signature, such as that of a deceased person, the firm becomes liable. The executor or administrator of the estate must endorse the certificate or furnish a stock power and transfer the securities to the name of the estate before they can be sold. Minors' signatures are invalid for securities registration purposes.

8. 8. 7. 1   Stock or Bond Power

A **stock power** or **bond power**, often called a "security power," is a legal document—separate from a securities certificate—that investors can use to transfer or assign ownership to another person. Securities powers typically are used either: (1) as a matter of convenience when an owner cannot sign the actual certificates, or (2) for safety (such as sending unsigned certificates in one envelope and signed powers in another). Physically, a securities power looks like the backside of a securities certificate, and it can be completed in the same manner. Market professionals typically attach a customer's signed powers to the related unsigned certificates for processing purposes.

8. 8. 8   GOOD CONDITION OF SECURITY

If a certificate is mutilated or appears to be counterfeit, appropriate authentication must be obtained before a transfer agent can accept the security for replacement. If the damage is so extensive that the transfer agent doubts the certificate's authenticity, it will require a surety bond.

8. 8. 9   CUSIP REGULATIONS

Committee on Uniform Securities Identification Procedures (CUSIP) numbers are used in all trade confirmations and correspondence regarding specific securities. A separate CUSIP number is assigned to each issue of securities; if an issue is subdivided into classes with differing characteristics, each class is assigned a separate CUSIP number. In general, a CUSIP number will aid in identifying and tracking a security throughout its life.

8. 8. 10 LEGAL OPINION: MUNICIPAL SECURITIES

Unless a municipal bond is traded and stamped ex-legal (without a legal opinion), the legal opinion must be printed on or attached to the bond as evidence of the bond's validity. Securities traded ex-legal are in good delivery condition without the legal opinion.

8. 8. 11 FAIL TO DELIVER

A fail to deliver situation occurs when the broker-dealer on the sell side of a contract does not deliver the securities in good delivery form to the broker-dealer on the buy side on settlement.

As long as a fail to deliver exists, the seller will not receive payment.

In a fail to deliver situation, the buying broker-dealer may buy in the securities to close the contract and may charge the seller for any loss caused by changes in the market. If a customer fails to deliver securities to satisfy a sale, the firm representing the seller must buy in the securities after 10 business days from settlement date.

8. 8. 12 RECLAMATION

Reclamation occurs when a buying broker-dealer, after accepting securities as good delivery, later discovers that the certificates were not in good deliverable form (e.g., certificates are mutilated). The securities can be sent back to the selling broker-dealer with a Uniform Reclamation Form attached within specific time frames, depending on the reason reclamation is being made.

- If the certificates delivered have minor irregularities, the time frame for reclamation is 15 days from the delivery date.
- If the certificates delivered are refused by the transfer agent (for whatever reason) or if the certificates are stolen or counterfeit, the time frame is 30 months from the delivery date.
- If the certificates (bonds) are subject to partial call, there is no time limit for reclamation.

There are two types of bond deliveries that are never subject to reclamation: (1) bond certificates subject to an in-whole call and (2) bonds where the issuer goes into default after trade date.

QUICK QUIZ 8.H

Objective: Define the various components that make up good delivery of securities

1. All of the following would be good delivery for 470 shares EXCEPT

    A. 2 100-share certificates and 3 90-share certificates
    B. 4 100-share certificates and 1 70-share certificate
    C. 8 50-share certificates, 1 40-share certificate, and 1 30-share certificate
    D. 47 10-share certificates

2. Instead of signing on the back of a security sold, the registered owner could sign on a separate paper called

    A. an endorsement
    B. a stock (or bond) power
    C. a proxy
    D. a stock split

3. As long as a fail-to-deliver situation exists, the seller

    A. will have all accounts frozen
    B. must conduct all transactions on a cash basis
    C. will not receive payment
    D. will not receive accrued interest on bonds

All Quick Quiz answers are found at the end of their units.

8. 9   HANDLING OF COMPLAINTS AND DISPUTES

For trade practice violations FINRA follows the Code of Procedure and for monetary disputes FINRA follows the Code of Arbitration.

8. 9. 1   CODE OF PROCEDURE

The Code of Procedure deals with alleged violations of FINRA rules, MSRB rules, and federal securities laws. If, after an investigation or audit, FINRA believes a member and/or its associated persons has violated one or more rules or laws, the Department of Enforcement will issue a formal complaint. With the filing of a complaint, the department will name a hearing officer to preside over the disciplinary proceeding (hearing) and will appoint panelists to serve as a jury. All panelists in Code of Procedure hearings are from the industry.

The respondent has 25 days after receiving the complaint to file an answer with the hearing officer. Answers must specifically admit, deny, or state that the respondent does not have sufficient information to admit or deny.

FINRA requires that records of customer complaints be kept on file by a broker-dealer for four years.

TAKE NOTE   If a complaint is filed against a registered representative, it is not all that unusual for that person's designated supervisor (e.g., branch manager) to be charged as well for failure to supervise.

8. 9. 1. 1   Hearing

At the hearing, which resembles a courtroom proceeding, the prosecution (Department of Enforcement) proceeds first. Cross-examination of witnesses is permitted. At the conclusion, panelists convene and, within 60 days, render a written decision reflecting the majority view.

8. 9. 1. 2   Sanctions

Sanctions against a member or associated person, if found guilty, are included with the written decision. Under Code of Procedure, sanctions could include:

- censure;
- fine;
- suspension of the membership of a member or suspension of the registration of an associated person for a definite period;
- expulsion of the member, canceling the membership of the member;
- barring an associated person from association with all members; and
- imposition of any other fitting sanction.

Suspension. If an associated person is suspended, that person may not remain associated with the member in any capacity, including a clerical or administrative capacity (during the suspension period, that person may not remain on the member's premises). Also, the member is prohibited from paying a salary, commission, or remuneration that the person might have earned during the suspension period.

8. 9. 1. 3   Appeals

If either side is displeased with the decision, an appeal may be made to the NAC. Any appeal must be made within 25 days of the decision date; otherwise, the decision is final. If no satisfaction is received from the NAC, the appealing party may take the case to the SEC. Again, if turned down, the appealing party has the right to continue the appeal process by taking its case to the federal court system. Appealing a decision stays the effective date of any sanctions other than a bar or expulsion.

8. 9. 2   CODE OF ARBITRATION

The Code of Arbitration was originally established to mediate unresolved industry disputes. It was mandatory in controversies involving:

- a member against another member or registered clearing agency;
- a member against an associated person; and
- an associated person against another associated person.

Over time, customer complaints became subject to mandatory arbitration resulting in two codes: the "Customer Code" and the "Industry Code."

Today, virtually all new account forms contain a predispute arbitration clause that must be signed by customers before account opening. Thus, assuming the customer has signed the arbitration agreement or the new account form containing the predispute arbitration agreement, unresolved customer complaints must be mediated under the Code of Arbitration.

TAKE NOTE   In the absence of a signed arbitration agreement, a customer can still force a member to arbitration, but a member cannot force a customer to arbitration.

Class action claims are not subject to arbitration. In addition, claims alleging employment discrimination brought against a member firm by its own employees, including sexual harassment claims, are not required to be arbitrated unless the parties agree.

The advantages of arbitration over suits in state or federal courts are savings of time, money, and the fact that all decisions are final and binding; no appeals are allowed. One party may not like the result, but the dispute is settled.

TAKE NOTE   If a customer requests to see the predispute arbitration agreement she has signed, a member firm must supply her with a copy within 10 business days of the request.

8. 9. 2. 1   Initiation of Proceedings

Any party to an unresolved dispute may initiate proceedings by filing a claim with the director of arbitration of FINRA. The statement of claim must describe in detail the controversy in dispute, include documentation in support of the claim, and state the remedy being sought (dollar amount). The claimant must also include a check for the required claim filing fee. The director will then send a copy of the claim to the other party (respondent).

The respondent then has 45 calendar days to respond to both the director and the claimant. The answer must specify all available defenses and any related counterclaim the respondent may have against the claimant. A respondent who fails to answer within 45 days may, at the sole discretion of the director, be barred from presenting any matter, arguments, or defenses at the hearing.

If the dispute involves irreparable injury to one of the parties, that party may seek an interim injunction or a permanent injunction. The party seeking relief must make a clear showing that its case is likely to succeed on its merits and that it will suffer permanent harm unless immediate relief is granted.

8. 9. 2. 2   Mediation

An alternate dispute resolution process and a reasonable, inexpensive first step is mediation.

If both parties agree, prior to the opening of hearings, a meeting may be held in an attempt to work out a settlement. A mediator is selected to preside over the discussions and to assist the parties, if possible, in reaching their own solution. If mediation is unsuccessful, a hearing is conducted. A mediator is prohibited from serving on an arbitration panel regarding any matter in which that person served as mediator. Sometimes, parts of a dispute settle in mediation, leaving fewer differences to be settled in arbitration, which can translate into savings of time and money. The issue is settled when the memo of understanding (MOU) is signed.

TAKE NOTE   Once mediation begins, either party may withdraw at any time without the consent of the mediator or the other party.

8. 9. 2. 3   Selection of Arbitrators

FINRA maintains a list of arbitrators divided into two categories: nonpublic and public.

Nonpublic arbitrators are as follows:

- Any persons who worked in the financial industry for any duration during their careers, including persons associated with a mutual fund or a hedge fund, and persons associated with an investment adviser, will always be classified as nonpublic arbitrators.

- Any financial industry professional who regularly represents or provides services to investor parties in disputes concerning investment accounts or transactions including attorneys, accountants, or other professionals whose firms earned significant revenue from representing individual and/or institutional investors relating to securities matters are classified as nonpublic arbitrators. However, for these individuals, waiting five years (cooling-off period) after ending the affiliation based on their own activities, or two years after ending an affiliation based on someone else's activities reclassifies and allows them to serve as public arbitrators.

Public arbitrators are as follows:

- Any persons who do not meet the definition of nonpublic arbitrator may serve as a public arbitrator.

8. 9. 2. 4   Arbitration Thresholds and Simplified Arbitration

For both the customer and the industry codes, the following threshold rules apply:

- $50,000 or less—one arbitrator
- Greater than $50,000 and up to and including $100,000—one arbitrator unless both parties agree to three
- Greater than $100,000—three arbitrators unless both parties agree to one

Any dispute involving a dollar amount of $50,000 or less is eligible for simplified arbitration. In this instance, a single arbitrator reviews all of the evidence and renders a binding decision within 30 business days.

8. 9. 2. 4. 1   Awards

All monetary awards must be paid within 30 days of the decision date. Any award not paid within this time will begin to accrue interest as of the decision date. In addition, all awards and details on the underlying arbitration claim are made publicly available by FINRA.

8. 9. 2. 5   Statute of Limitations

No claim is eligible for submission to arbitration if six years or more have elapsed from the time of the event giving rise to the claim.

8. 9. 3   AVAILABILITY OF MANUAL TO CUSTOMERS

Members must make available a current copy of the FINRA procedures manual for examination by customers upon request. Members may comply with this rule by maintaining electronic access to the FINRA Manual and providing customers with such access upon request.

8. 9. 4   REPORTING REQUIREMENTS

If the firm or an associated person has violated any securities, insurance, commodities, financial or investment-related laws, rules, regulations or standards of conduct of any domestic or foreign regulatory body or self-regulatory organization, it must be reported. FINRA requires firms to report those specified events to FINRA no later than 30 calendar days after the firm knows or should have known of their existence.

8. 9. 5   FORM U4

To register with FINRA, the member files Form U-4. The information required on Form U-4 is extensive and includes:

- name, address, and any aliases used;
- five-year residency history;
- 10-year employment history (verify the past three years); and
- information on any charges, arrests, or convictions relating to the investment business. A yes answer to any of these questions requires a detailed explanation on a DRP (disclosure reporting form).

Any changes to this information require filing an amended form with the CRD (central registration depository) no later than 30 days after the member becomes aware of these changes.

Qualifications Investigated. Before submitting an application to enroll a person with FINRA as a registered representative, a member firm must certify that it has investigated the person's business reputation, character, education, qualifications, and experience, and that the candidate's credentials are in order.

If, during its routine review of the U-4, FINRA discovers that any portion of the U-4 information submitted, especially relating to personal history and past disciplinary or law enforcement encounters, is misleading or omits material information, disciplinary action may be taken resulting in a bar to the individual. In addition, the principal signing the application may be liable as well.

TAKE NOTE   Education achievements or changes to marital status are not required to be updated in the U-4.

QUICK QUIZ 8.1   Objective: Recognize the formal resolution methods and disputes-reporting requirements

1. When addressing customer complaints, FINRA may require the firm or rep to do all the following EXCEPT to

    A. provide information orally
    B. give testimony under oath
    C. provide access to any books
    D. record any response in an easily transferable medium

2. Assuming the customer has signed the proper agreements, unresolved customer complaints must be

    A. aligned with the firm's directives of resolving issues
    B. mediated under the Code of Arbitration
    C. taken to FINRA's Code of Conduct
    D. brought before the proper panel via legal representation

3. Nonpublic arbitrators meet which of the following criteria?

    A. Any person who worked in the financial industry for any duration
    B. Private persons who were not associated with a mutual fund
    C. A person who only worked for a hedge fund for less than three years
    D. A person associated with an investment adviser for more than five years

4. A dispute involving a dollar amount of $50,000 or less is eligible for

    A. shortened remediation
    B. a stay of the decision
    C. an appeal
    D. simplified arbitration.

5. The Uniform Application for Securities Industry Registration or Transfer is filed with

    A. the SEC
    B. FINRA
    C. the CRD
    D. the member

All Quick Quiz answers are found at the end of their units.

Q U I C K   Q U I Z   A N S W E R S

Quick Quiz 8.A

1. **A.** If trading is halted in a security, investors cannot buy or sell the security. An open order can be canceled during a trading halt.

2. **A.** A specialist (designated market maker) keeps a book of public orders, must maintain a bid and offer at all times, and will buy or sell stock for his own account. He may not set option strike prices. That is the prerogative of the Options Clearing Corporation (OCC).

3. **C.** An immediate-or-cancel order is one in which the firm handling the order has one attempt to fill the order but a partial execution is binding on the customer.

4. **B.** A Level 2 halt occurs when the S&P 500 drops 13% from the opening. Trading will halt for 15 minutes.

Quick Quiz 8.B

1. **B.** The qualifying price on a do-not-reduce (DNR) order will not be reduced by ordinary cash dividends on the ex-dividend date.

2. **D.** A stop limit order is a stop order that becomes a limit order once the stop price has been triggered. When the limit price is the same as the stop price on a stop limit order, the order can be executed only at or better than the limit price. In this case, the order has not yet been executed because no transaction has occurred at or above 38.63 since the stop was triggered at 38.50.

3. **B.** Sell stop orders are always entered below the market price. A sell stop order is triggered when a transaction occurs at or below the price specified on the order. A buy stop order is always entered at a price above the current offering price. Once elected, stop orders become market orders.

4. **C.** A stop order becomes a market order once the market price reaches or passes the specific stop price. An investor in a long position can use the sell stop order for protection against a market decline. When a large number of stop orders are triggered at a particular price, the advance or decline of the market at that point can be magnified. Stop orders are not the same as limit orders because there is no guarantee of a specific execution price for a stop order.

5. **A.** A sell limit order is used to sell out a long position at a higher price (when the market moves up). A sell stop order is used to sell out a long position at a lower price (when the market moves down). To protect against erosion of the gain, a sell stop order would be placed just below where the stock is currently trading.

6. **D.** A buy limit order is used to buy in a short position at a lower price (when the market moves down). A buy stop order is used to buy in a short position at a higher price (when the market moves up). To protect against a loss of the gain, a buy stop order would be placed just above where the stock is currently trading.

7. **B.** The sell stop limit order is elected (triggered) at the first trade of 50.13, when the stock trades at or below the stop price of 50.25. The order becomes a sell limit order at 50.25. The order can be executed at that price or higher (the limit placed by the customer). The next trade reported after the trigger is reached is below the limit price. The order could be executed at the next trade of 50.25.

8. **A.** When a stock goes ex-dividend, the specialist (designated market maker) will reduce open buy limit orders and open sell stop orders because they are placed below the market price and could be triggered when the market price is reduced for the loss of dividend. The specialist will not reduce open sell limit orders and open buy stop orders.

9. **A.** When a stock goes ex-dividend, the price of the stock falls by the amount of the dividend. A dividend of $.70 would reduce the stop price by that amount.

Quick Quiz 8.C

1. **C.** An immediate-or-cancel order is one in which the firm handling the order has one attempt to fill the order but a partial execution is binding on the customer.

2. **A.** A fill-or-kill order is one in which the firm handling the order can make one attempt to fill the order in its entirety. If unable to do so, the order is canceled.

3. **B.** The customer should place a market order immediate-or-cancel. The customer is willing to buy at the current market value and a market order does that. If only 50,000 shares are available then the IOC order will buy 50,000 shares and cancel the rest.

Quick Quiz 8.D

1. **C.** A buyer need not be advised that shares purchased were sold short, but the order ticket prepared by the brokerage firm representing the seller must indicate that the sale is short. Short sales may be executed at any time during the trading day including the opening and closing.

2. **A.** The most important disclosure when selling short is that if the stock goes up instead of down, the customer is losing money and, theoretically, there is no limit how high the price can go before the position is closed. Therefore, the customer is exposed to unlimited financial risk.

Quick Quiz 8.E

1. **D.** Rules require that a dealer's markup to a customer be based on the current market rather than the dealer's cost. The dealer's potential loss on inventory is considered to be the risk of making a market.

2. **B.** This quote is firm; the market maker has extended the quote with a given size and price and a time for how long the quote is good for. If the broker making the call decides to purchase the security in the next 10 minutes, they can buy 20,000 shares at the designated price of $20.22.

3. **D.** The 5% policy applies both to commission charges on agency transactions and to markups and markdowns on principal transactions with customers.

Quick Quiz 8.F

1. **A.** The credit that a broker-dealer extends to its customers is handled by its margin department.

2. **A.** Orders are received by the wire room and then are sent to the appropriate market. When the wire room gets the transaction report back, it sends it to the purchases and sales department. The P&S department sends a confirmation to the customer and then sends notice of the trade to the margin department. Margin then notifies the cashier of any balance due to or from the customer.

3. **C.** Broker-dealers must send quarterly statements to customers with inactive accounts.

4. **C.** A confirmation must be given or sent to a customer at or before the completion of the transaction (the settlement date).

Quick Quiz 8.G

1. **C.** To be considered in good delivery form, certificates must be accompanied by an assignment or a stock power.

2. **C.** When a broker-dealer chooses to close out a customer's position rather than request an extension, the customer's account will be frozen for 90 days.

3. **B.** Confirmations between brokers (broker-to-broker confirmations) are sent no later than the next business day (T+1).

4. **B.** When an account is frozen, the client must deposit the full purchase price before any subsequent orders.

Quick Quiz 8.H

1. **A.** Shares must add up to 100 or be in multiples of 100, with the exception of odd lots.

2. **B.** If the client were to assign the back of the certificate, that security would now be completely negotiable. If lost, it would be the same as losing an endorsed check. To minimize problems, make the assignment on a stock power, which is a separate piece of paper, and when it is put together with the actual certificate, it is treated as if the certificate itself had been signed.

3. **C.** Until the seller delivers the securities sold, he will not receive payment for them.

Quick Quiz 8.I

1. **D.** In connection with any investigation, customer complaint, or examination by FINRA, the association may require a member firm or any person associated with a member to provide information orally, in writing, or electronically; give testimony under oath; and provide access to or copies of any books, records, or accounts.

2. **B.** The customer will either sign a separate arbitration agreement or the account opening documentation and in so doing agree that any unresolved complaint to be processed through arbitration.

3. **A.** Any persons who worked in the financial industry for any duration during their careers, including persons associated with a mutual fund or a hedge fund, and persons associated with an investment adviser, will always be classified as nonpublic arbitrators.

4. **D.** Any dispute involving a dollar amount of $50,000 or less is eligible for simplified arbitration. In this instance, a single arbitrator reviews all the evidence and renders a binding decision within 30 business days.

5. **C.** The filing of Form U-4 is accomplished and filed electronically with the Central Registration Depository (CRD) or the Investment Adviser Registration Depository.

5/16/19

- Suitability
- margin, DPP, and Customer
purchase/sale instructions practice
problems

Mutual Fund Customer Suitability Quiz

Joe Smith is a registered representative with ABC Investments, Inc. Last week, Joe opened accounts for 10 new customers. Each customer wants Joe to recommend the best mutual fund that he can find.

Joe knows that the best mutual fund for one customer is not necessarily the best choice for every customer. Before he makes a recommendation, he collects important information about the customer's needs, goals, and financial status. For example, Joe asks each customer:

- What is your income?
- How stable is your income?
- What plans do you have for the money you invest?
- What kinds of risks are you comfortable taking?
- How liquid must your investments be?
- How important are tax considerations?
- Are you seeking long-term or short-term investments?
- What is your investment experience?

After Joe has noted a customer's financial status and investment objectives, he can begin to search for the most appropriate mutual fund. Joe has prepared a brief description of each of his 10 new customers, and this is followed by a list of top-performing mutual funds in 10 categories.

Which mutual fund would you recommend to each of Joe's customers? After you have read the descriptions of the customers and the funds, answer each question based on which fund best meets the customer's objectives. Fund descriptions are listed after the questions.

The Customers

1. Andy Jones, 52, and Patty Jones, 56, have a large investment portfolio concentrated in stocks and stock mutual funds, including an international fund. They maintain their cash reserves in a money market account at their local bank. Andy is employed as a consultant, where he earns a $400,000/year salary. The Joneses are seeking a safe investment because they will need to liquidate a portion of their portfolio when Andy retires in about 5 years. They also recognize the need for additional diversification of their portfolio.

   A. Spencer Cash Reserve Fund
   B. MacDonald Balanced Fund
   C. Spencer Tax-Free Municipal Bond Fund — best choice 1/2 high tax bracket
   D. MacDonald Stock Index Fund

2. Sarah Davis, 30, and Jim Davis, 32, have been married for 4 years. Both work and they have no children, so their disposable income is relatively high. They live in the suburbs and plan to buy a condominium downtown so they can enjoy some of their favorite activities on the weekends. They need a safe place to invest the amount they have saved for their down payment for about 6 months while they shop for the perfect unit.

   A. ATF Biotechnology Fund
   B. ATF Capital Appreciation Fund
   C. Spencer Cash Reserve Fund
   D. Laramie Equity Income Fund

3. Adam Garcia is 26 and earns $45,000/year as an advertising executive. He already has accumulated $5,000 in a savings account and is seeking a secure place to invest the amount and begin a periodic investment plan. He knows his long-term time-frame means he should be willing to take some risk, but he is uncomfortable with the thought of losing money. Adam would prefer moderate overall returns rather than high returns accompanied by high volatility.

   A. Spencer Tax-Free Municipal Bond Fund
   B. MacDonald Balanced Fund
   C. XYZ Government Income Fund
   D. MacDonald Stock Index Fund

4. Mark Blair is a retired widower, 72, seeking a moderate level of current income to supplement his Social Security benefits and his company pension plan. Mark is a Depression-era grandfather of 6 with a conservative attitude toward investments. An equally important goal for him is capital preservation.

   A. MacDonald Stock Index Fund
   B. Spencer Tax-Free Municipal Bond Fund
   C. XYZ Government Income Fund
   D. ATF Overseas Opportunities Fund

5. Helen Wong is 29 and is seeking a long-term growth investment. She is concerned about the loss of purchasing power as a result of inflation and often complains about high commissions and charges that reduce her investment returns. When she was in college, she took a few economics courses and firmly believes that securities analysts cannot consistently outperform the overall market.

   A. MacDonald Balanced Fund
   B. MacDonald Stock Index Fund
   C. Spencer Cash Reserve Fund
   D. ATF Biotechnology Fund

6. Gina and Peter Stout, both 42, have two children, ages 14 and 12. The Stouts have spent the past 10 years accumulating money to provide for their children's education. Their oldest child will enter college in 4 years and they are not willing to take risks with the money they worked hard to accumulate. They need a safe investment that provides regular income to help them meet tuition payments.

   A. Laramie Equity Income Fund
   B. ATF Capital Appreciation Fund
   C. Spencer Cash Reserve Fund
   D. MacDonald Investment-Grade Bond Fund

7. Pat Long, 60, and Sadie Long, 58, are married and have raised 3 children. Both have decided to retire this year and are looking forward to an active retirement. They have accumulated a nest egg of about $1 million, which they plan to use to travel the world, pursue their hobbies, and care for their health. Both are concerned about rising inflation and are comfortable with a reasonable level of risk.

   A. Spencer Tax-Free Municipal Bond Fund
   B. XYZ Government Income Fund
   C. Laramie Equity Income Fund = income and growth potential
   D. MacDonald Stock Index Fund

8. Amy Cain, 50, and Eric Cain, 48, have a combined annual income of more than $200,000. Their portfolio consists of common stocks and bonds that offer a wide range of safety and return potential. The Cains are becoming even more concerned about the effects of rising inflation in the U.S. economy. They are seeking to invest a small percentage of their portfolio in a fund that will provide additional diversification.

   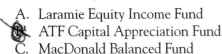

   A. ATF Biotechnology Fund = too risky
   B. XYZ Government Income Fund
   C. MacDonald Stock Index Fund
   D. ATF Overseas Opportunities Fund

9. Mike and Mary Cole are both 34 and employed in their computer software business. They have one daughter, age 4. The Coles want to begin accumulating the money required to send their daughter to one of the nation's top universities in 14 years. In addition, they have not yet begun to accumulate money for their retirement.

   A. MacDonald Balanced Fund
   B. Laramie Equity Income Fund
   C. ATF Capital Appreciation Fund
   D. Spencer Tax-Free Municipal Bond Fund

10. Liz Scott, 45, is single and in search of maximum capital appreciation. She inherited a substantial amount of money a few years ago and has taken an active interest in managing her investments. Her portfolio is diversified among common stocks, tax-exempt bonds, international investments, and limited partnerships. She has a long-term time frame and is not averse to risk.

   A. Laramie Equity Income Fund
   B. ATF Capital Appreciation Fund
   C. MacDonald Balanced Fund
   D. ATF Biotechnology Fund - long-term

The Mutual Funds (listed alphabetically)

ATF Biotechnology Fund.   The fund seeks maximum capital appreciation through investment in stocks of companies providing innovative products in the biotechnology sector, including pharmaceutical developers and medical equipment suppliers. Fund management seeks to evaluate emerging economic and political trends and to select individual companies that may benefit from technological advances.

ATF Capital Appreciation Fund.   The fund seeks to achieve maximum capital appreciation with little or no pursuit of current income. The fund invests in stocks of small and medium-size companies that demonstrate significant long-term growth potential. The fund's management believes that despite year-to-year fluctuations, the strategy of investing in companies that show strong earnings growth can result in superior investment returns.

ATF Overseas Opportunities Fund.   The fund seeks maximum capital appreciation by investing in common stocks of companies located outside the United States. The management selects well-established companies that are listed on their native stock exchanges and that have demonstrated high earnings potential. Although the fund may be affected by fluctuations in currency exchange rates, over the long term it may provide protection against downturns in U.S. markets.

Laramie Equity Income Fund.   The fund seeks primarily current income, with secondary objectives of capital growth and growth of income. Its portfolio consists of common stock, preferred stock, and convertible securities of large, well-established companies with a history of paying high dividends. Its equity concentration can help protect against the loss of purchasing power owing to inflation.

MacDonald Balanced Fund.   The fund seeks to preserve capital, to generate current income, and to provide long-term capital growth. Its strategy is to invest 60% of its portfolio in common stocks and 40% in bonds and fixed-income securities. Through diversification, the fund intends to provide protection against downturns in the market. In its endeavors to produce positive returns during market decline, the fund may not participate fully in rising stock markets.

MacDonald Investment-Grade Bond Fund.   The fund seeks high current yield accompanied by reasonable risk. It invests most of its portfolio in corporate bonds having one of the top three ratings according to Moody's and Standard & Poor's. It seeks to reduce the risk associated with interest rate fluctuations by investing a portion of its assets in short-term corporate debt.

MacDonald Stock Index Fund.   The fund seeks to duplicate the price and yield performance of Standard & Poor's Composite Index of 500 stocks. The fund invests in each of the index's 500 stocks in approximately the same composition as the index. The portfolio is not actively traded and therefore features a low turnover ratio.

Spencer Cash Reserve Fund.   The fund's objectives are to maintain a stable net asset value and to provide current income. The fund invests in high-quality, short-term obligations, including U.S. Treasury bills, commercial paper certificates of deposit, and repurchase agreements. Check-writing privileges are available.

Spencer Tax-Free Municipal Bond Fund.   The fund seeks to maximize tax-exempt current yield. It invests in a portfolio of high-quality municipal debt obligations. The portfolio is diversified among securities issued by many different state and municipal taxing authorities. Income distributions provided by the fund are exempt from federal income tax.

XYZ Government Income Fund.   The fund seeks to maximize safety of invested principal while providing current income. By investing in a broad range of debt securities issued by the U.S. Treasury, as well as by government agencies such as the Government National Mortgage Association, the fund provides reduced risk. It aims for a current yield higher than the yield of short-term debt instruments and money market instruments.

MUTUAL FUND CUSTOMER SUITABILITY QUIZ ANSWERS

1. **C.** **Spencer Tax-Free Municipal Bond Fund** The Joneses are almost entirely invested in the stock market. As they approach retirement, they should shift some of their portfolio to bonds. Because they are in a high tax bracket, a municipal bond fund best meets their objectives of diversification and safety.

2. **C.** **Spencer Cash Reserve Fund** Jim and Sarah Davis are preparing to make a major purchase within the next 6 months. They require a highly liquid investment to keep their money safe for a short time. The money market fund best matches this objective.

3. **B.** **MacDonald Balanced Fund** Adam Garcia is a young investor who is at the beginning of his investment cycle. For other investors in his situation, an aggressive growth fund might help achieve maximum capital appreciation over a long-term timeframe. However, Adam is risk averse and has not had any experience investing in the securities markets. A balanced fund is a good place to begin investing for moderate return and low volatility.

4. **C.** **XYZ Government Income Fund** Mark Blair requires maximum safety and current income. While all fixed-income funds aim to provide current income, the U.S. government bond fund offers the best combination of safety and a higher yield than a money market fund.

5. **B.** **MacDonald Stock Index Fund** Helen Wong requires a mutual fund that offers the potential for long-term capital growth. She believes money managers cannot consistently outperform the overall market; this indicates that an index fund that attempts to match the performance of the stock market is the most appropriate investment for her.

6. **D.** **MacDonald Investment-Grade Bond Fund** The Stouts' investment goal of providing for their children's education is about 4 years away. They cannot afford to take a risk that a downturn in the stock market will occur within that time. A safe alternative that also provides additional returns is the high-quality corporate bond fund.

7. **C.** **Laramie Equity Income Fund** The Longs are preparing for retirement. They want to maintain a comfortable standard of living, which means staying ahead of inflation. A combined fund that offers both current income and growth potential is the best choice for this couple.

8. **D.** **ATF Overseas Opportunities Fund** The Cains' substantial portfolio is diversified between equity and debt investments. However, to counteract the effects of the U.S. economy on their portfolio returns, they should invest a portion of their assets in the international stock fund.

9. **C.** **ATF Capital Appreciation Fund** The Coles require maximum capital appreciation. Their long-term time frame enables them to ride out the fluctuations of the stock market. The best investment for them is the stock market fund that concentrates solely on achieving long-term growth rather than on generating current income.

10. **D.** **ATF Biotechnology Fund** Liz Scott has a high net worth and substantial investment experience. She is capable of assuming the higher risk and return potential of a speculative investment such as the biotechnology sector fund.

Common Abbreviations

ABS asset-backed security
ADR/ADS American depositary receipt (share)
AGC Assured Guaranty Corporation
AIR assumed interest rate
AMBAC AMBAC Indemnity Corporation
ARS auction rate security
BA banker's acceptance
BD broker-dealer
BDC business development (growth) company
CAPM capital asset pricing model
CD certificate of deposit
CDO collateralized debt obligation
CEO chief executive officer
CMO collateralized mortgage obligation
CMV current market value
COA code of arbitration
COP Code of Procedure
CPI Consumer Price Index
CQS Consolidated Quotation System
CY current yield
DBCC District Business Conduct Committee
DEA designated examining authority
DJIA Dow Jones Industrial Average
DMM designated market maker
EE Series EE savings bonds
ELN equity-linked note
EPS earnings per share
ERISA Employee Retirement Income Security Act of 1974
ETF exchange-traded fund
FAC face-amount certificate
Fed Federal Reserve System
FDIC Federal Deposit Insurance Corporation
FGIC Financial Guaranty Insurance Company
FIFO first in, first out
FINRA Financial Industry Regulatory Authority
FMV fair market value
FNMA Federal National Mortgage Association
FOMC Federal Open Market Committee
FRB Federal Reserve Board
GDP gross domestic product
GNMA Government National Mortgage Association
GO general obligation bond
HH Series HH savings bond
HSA health savings account
IDR/IDB industrial development revenue bond
IPO initial public offering
IRA individual retirement account
IRC Internal Revenue Code

IRS Internal Revenue Service
JTIC joint tenants in common
JTWROS joint tenants with right of survivorship
LIFO last in, first out
LOI letter of intent
MIG Moody's Investment Grade
MPT modern portfolio theory
MSRB Municipal Securities Rulemaking Board
NASAA North American Securities Administrators' Association
Nasdaq National Association of Securities Dealers Automated Quotation system
NAV net asset value
NHA New Housing Authority
NL no load
NMS National Market System
NYSE New York Stock Exchange
OSJ office of supervisory jurisdiction
OTC over the counter
PAC planned (programed) amortization class
PE price-to-earnings ratio
PHA Public Housing Authority
POP public offering price
PPN principal protected note
REIT real estate investment trust
RR registered representative
SAI statement of additional information
SEC Securities and Exchange Commission
SEP simplified employee pension plan
SIPC Securities Investor Protection Corporation
SLMA Student Loan Marketing Association
SRO self-regulatory organization
STRIPS Separate Trading of Registered Interest and Principal of Securities
T+3 trade date plus three business days settlement
TAC targeted amortization class
TCPA Telephone Consumer Protection Act
TSA tax-sheltered annuity
UGMA/UTMA Uniform Gift (Transfers) to Minors Act
UIT unit investment trust
UPC Uniform Practice Code
VIX volatility market index
VL variable life insurance
VRDOS variable rate demand obligations
YLD yield
YTC yield to call
YTM yield to maturity
ZR zero-coupon

Calculations

To Calculate...	Use Formula...
Dividend yield	$\dfrac{\text{Annual dividend}}{\text{Current market price}}$
Current yield	$\dfrac{\text{Annual interest}}{\text{Current market price}}$
Number of shares for conversion	$\dfrac{\text{Par value}}{\text{Conversion price}}$
Parity	$\dfrac{\text{Bond market value}}{\text{Number of shares}}$
Tax-free equivalent yield	Corporate rate × (100% − tax bracket)
Tax-equivalent yield	$\dfrac{\text{Municipal rate}}{(100\% - \text{tax bracket})}$
NAV of mutual fund share	$\dfrac{\text{Fund NAV}}{\text{Number of shares outstanding}}$
Sales charge percentage	$\dfrac{\text{POP} - \text{NAV}}{\text{POP}}$
Public offering price (POP)	$\dfrac{\text{NAV per share}}{(100\% - \text{sales charge percentage})}$
Dollar cost average	$\dfrac{\text{Total dollars invested}}{\text{Number of shares purchased}}$
Average market price	$\dfrac{\text{Share price total}}{\text{Number of investments}}$
Number of outstanding shares	Issued shares − treasury shares
Shareholders' equity	Assets − liabilities

Glossary

A

acceptance ratio *See* placement ratio.

acceptance, waiver, and consent A process for settling a charge or complaint that is quicker and less formal than the regular complaint procedure. *Related item(s):* Code of Procedure.

account executive (AE) *See* registered representative.

accredited investor As defined in Rule 502 of Regulation D, any institution or individual meeting minimum net worth requirements for the purchase of securities qualifying under the Regulation D registration exemption.

An accredited investor is generally accepted to be one who:

■ has a net worth of $1 million or more, not including net equity in a primary residence; or

■ has had an annual income of $200,000 or more during each of the two most recent years (or $300,000 jointly with a spouse) and who has a reasonable expectation of reaching the same income level during the current year.

accretion of bond discount An accounting process whereby the initial cost of a bond purchased at a discount is increased annually to reflect the basis of the bond as it approaches maturity.

accrual accounting A method of reporting income when earned and expenses when incurred, as opposed to reporting income when received and expenses when paid.

accrued interest The interest that has accumulated since the last interest payment up to, but not including, the settlement date and is added to a bond transaction's contract price.

There are two methods for calculating accrued interest: the 30-day-month (360-day-year) method for corporate and municipal bonds and the actual-calendar-days (365-day-year) method for government bonds. Income bonds, bonds in default, and zero-coupon bonds trade without accrued interest (flat). *Related item(s):* flat.

accumulation account An account established to hold securities pending their deposit into a municipal securities unit investment trust.

accumulation stage The period during which contributions are made to an annuity account. *Related item(s):* accumulation unit; distribution stage.

accumulation unit An accounting measure used to determine an annuitant's proportionate interest in the insurer's separate account during an annuity's accumulation (deposit) stage. *Related item(s):* accumulation stage; annuity unit; separate account.

acid-test ratio A measure of a corporation's liquidity, calculated by adding cash, cash equivalents, and accounts and notes receivable, and dividing the result by total current liabilities. It is a more stringent test of liquidity than current ratio. *Syn.* quick ratio. *Related item(s):* cash assets ratio; current ratio.

ACT *See* Automated Confirmation Transaction service.

Act of 1933 *See* Securities Act of 1933.

Act of 1934 *See* Securities Exchange Act of 1934.

adjacent acreage Producing or nonproducing oil or gas leases located within the area of an existing well site. Adjacent acreage may prove valuable for continued development of the original oil or gas prospect.

adjusted basis The value attributed to an asset or security that reflects any deductions taken on, or capital improvements to, the asset or security. Adjusted basis is used to compute the gain or loss on the sale or other disposition of the asset or security.

adjusted gross income (AGI) Earned income plus net passive income, portfolio income, and capital gains. *Related item(s):* tax liability.

administrator (1) A person authorized by a court of law to liquidate an intestate decedent's estate. (2) An official or agency that administers a state's securities laws.

ADR *See* American depositary receipt.

ad valorem tax A tax based on the value of real or personal property. Property taxes are the major source of revenues for local governing units. *Related item(s):* assessed value.

advance/decline line A technical analysis tool representing the total of differences between advances and declines of security prices. The advance/decline line is considered the best indicator of market movement as a whole. *Related item(s):* breadth-of-market theory.

advance refunding Refinancing an existing municipal bond issue before its maturity or call date by using money from the sale of a new bond issue. The proceeds of the new bond issue are used to purchase government securities, and the municipality puts the principal and interest received from these securities into an escrow account; it then uses these funds to pay off the original bond issue at the first call date. *Syn.* prerefunding. *Related item(s):* defeasance; refunding.

advertisement Any promotional material designed for use by newspapers, magazines, billboards, radio, television, telephone recording, or other public media where the firm has little control over the type of individuals exposed to the material. *Related item(s):* sales literature.

advisory board Under the Investment Company Act of 1940, a board that advises an investment company on matters concerning its investments in securities, but does not have the power to make investment decisions or take action itself. An advisory board must be composed of persons who have no other connection with, and serve no other function for, the investment company.

AE *See* registered representative.

affiliate (1) A person who directly or indirectly owns, controls, or holds with power to vote 10% or more of the outstanding voting securities of a company. (2) With respect to a direct participation program, any person who controls, is controlled by, or is under common control with the program's sponsor and includes any person who beneficially owns 50% or more of the equity interest in the sponsor. (3) Under the Investment Company Act of 1940, a person who has any type of control over an investment company's operations, which includes anyone with 5% or more of the outstanding voting securities of the investment company or any corporation of which the investment company holds 5% or more of outstanding securities. *Related item(s):* control person; insider.

agency basis *See* agency transaction.

agency issue A debt security issued by an authorized agency of the federal government. Such an issue is backed by the issuing agency itself, not by the full faith and credit of the U.S. government (except GNMA and Federal Import Export Bank issues). *Related item(s):* government security.

agency transaction A transaction in which a broker-dealer acts for the accounts of others by buying or selling securities on behalf of customers. *Syn.* agency basis. *Related item(s):* agent; broker; principal transaction.

agent (1) An individual or a firm that effects securities transactions for the accounts of others. (2) A person licensed by a state as a life insurance agent. (3) A securities salesperson who represents a broker-dealer or an issuer when selling or trying to sell securities to the investing public; this individual is considered an agent whether he actually receives or simply solicits orders. *Related item(s):* broker; broker-dealer; dealer; principal.

aggressive investment strategy A method of portfolio allocation and management aimed at achieving maximum return. Aggressive investors place a high percentage of their investable assets in equity securities and a far lower percentage in safer debt securities and cash equivalents, and they pursue aggressive policies, including margin trading, arbitrage, and option trading. *Related item(s):* balanced investment strategy; defensive investment strategy.

AGI *See* adjusted gross income.

agreement among underwriters The agreement that sets forth the terms under which each member of an underwriting syndicate will participate in a new issue offering and states the duties and responsibilities of the underwriting manager. *Related item(s):* syndicate; underwriting manager.

agreement of limited partnership The contract that establishes guidelines for the operation of a direct participation program, including the roles of the general and limited partners.

AIR *See* assumed interest rate.

allied member A general partner of an NYSE member firm who is not an NYSE member, an owner of 5% or more of the outstanding voting stock of an NYSE member corporation, or a principal executive director or officer of a member corporation. Allied members do not own seats on the NYSE.

all-or-none order (AON) An order that instructs the firm to execute the entire order. Firm does not have to execute immediately.

all-or-none underwriting (AON) A form of best efforts underwriting in which the underwriter agrees that if it is unable to sell all the shares (or a prescribed minimum), the issuer will cancel the offering. This type of agreement may be used when the issuer requires a minimum amount of capital to be raised; if the minimum is not reached, the securities sold and the money raised are returned. Commissions are not paid unless the offering is completed. *Related item(s):* underwriting.

alpha Alpha measures the effectiveness of investment management by looking at the actual return and comparing it with the expected return based on the amount of risk taken.

alternative minimum tax (AMT) An alternative tax computation that adds certain tax preference items back into adjusted gross income. If the AMT is higher than the regular tax liability for the year, the regular tax and the amount by which the AMT exceeds the regular tax are paid. *Related item(s):* tax preference item.

alternative order An order to execute either of two transactions—for example, placing a sell limit (above the market) and a sell stop (below the market) on the same stock. *Syn.* either/or order; one cancels other order.

AMBAC Indemnity Corporation (AMBAC) A corporation that offers insurance on the timely payment of interest and principal obligations of municipal securities. Nonrated insured bonds typically have a AAA-implied rating.

American depositary receipt (ADR) A negotiable U.S. security certificate representing a given number of shares of stock in a foreign corporation. It is bought and sold in the American securities markets, just as stock is traded. *Syn.* American depositary share.

amortization (1) The paying off of debt in regular installments over a period of time. (2) The ratable deduction of certain capitalized expenditures over a specified period of time.

amortization of bond premium An accounting process whereby the initial cost of a bond purchased at a premium is decreased to reflect the basis of the bond as it approaches maturity. *Related item(s):* accretion of bond discount.

annual compliance review The annual meeting that all registered representatives and principals must attend, the purpose of which is to review compliance issues.

annual ROI The annual return on a bond investment, which equals the annual interest and either plus the prorated discount or minus the prorated premium.

annuitant A person who receives an annuity contract's distribution.

annuitize To change an annuity contract from the accumulation (pay-in) stage to the distribution (pay-out) stage.

annuity A contract between an insurance company and an individual, generally guaranteeing lifetime income to the individual on whose life the contract is based in return for either a lump-sum or a periodic payment to the insurance company. The contract holder's objective is usually retirement income. *Related item(s):* deferred annuity; fixed annuity; immediate annuity; variable annuity.

annuity unit An accounting measure used to determine the amount of each payment during an annuity's distribution stage. The calculation takes into account the value of each accumulation unit and such other factors as assumed interest rate and mortality risk. *Related item(s):* accumulation unit; annuity; distribution stage.

anti-money laundering Programs developed under the Bank Secrecy Act to prevent and detect the act of "clean" money or money that has been laundered through legitimate businesses later being used for "dirty" purposes such as terrorist activities.

AON *See* all-or-none order; all-or-none underwriting.

AP *See* associated person of a member.

appreciation The increase in an asset's value.

approved plan *See* qualified retirement plan.

arbitrage The simultaneous purchase and sale of the same or related securities to take advantage of a market inefficiency.

arbitrageur One who engages in arbitrage.

arbitration The arrangement whereby FINRA or a designated arbitration association hears and settles disagreements between members, member organizations, their employees, and customers.

ascending triangle On a technical analyst's trading activity chart, a pattern indicating that the market has started to move back up; considered to be a bullish indicator. *Related item(s):* descending triangle.

ask An indication by a trader or a dealer of a willingness to sell a security or a commodity; the price at which an investor may buy from a broker-dealer. *Syn.* offer. *Related item(s):* bid; public offering price; quotation.

assessed value The value of a property as appraised by a taxing authority for the purpose of levying taxes. Assessed value may equal market value or a stipulated percentage of market value. *Related item(s):* ad valorem tax.

assessment An additional amount of capital that a participant in a direct participation program may be called upon to furnish beyond the subscription amount. Assessments may be mandatory or optional and must be called within 12 months.

asset (1) Anything that an individual or a corporation owns. (2) A balance sheet item expressing what a corporation owns.

asset allocation fund A mutual fund that splits its investment assets among stocks, bonds, and other vehicles in an attempt to provide a consistent return for the investor. *Related item(s):* mutual fund.

asset-backed security One whose value and income payments are backed by the expected cash flow from a specific pool of underlying assets. Pooling the assets into financial instruments allows them to be sold to investors more easily than selling them individually. This process is called securitization.

assignee A person who has acquired a beneficial interest in a limited partnership from a third party, but who is neither a substitute limited partner nor an assignee of record.

assignee of record A person who has acquired a beneficial interest in a limited partnership and whose interest has been recorded on the books of the partnership and is the subject of a written instrument of assignment.

assignment (1) A document accompanying or part of a stock certificate that is signed by the person named on the certificate for the purpose of transferring the certificate's title to another person's name. (2) The act of identifying and notifying an account holder that the option owner has exercised an option held short in that account. *Related item(s):* stock power.

associated person of a member (AP) Any employee, manager, director, officer, or partner of a member broker-dealer or another entity (e.g., issuer or bank) or any person controlling, controlled by, or in common control with that member. *Related item(s):* registered representative.

assumed interest rate (AIR) The net rate of investment return that must be credited to a variable life insurance policy to ensure that at all times the variable death benefit equals the amount of the death benefit. The AIR forms the basis for projecting payments, but it is not guaranteed.

at-the-close order *See* market-on-close order.

at the money The term used to describe an option when the underlying stock is trading precisely at the exercise price of the option. *Related item(s):* in the money; out of the money.

at-the-opening order An order that specifies it is to be executed at the opening of the market of trading in that security or else it is to be canceled. The order will be executed at the opening price. *Related item(s):* market-on-close order.

auction market A market in which buyers enter competitive bids and sellers enter competitive offers simultaneously. The NYSE is an auction market. *Syn.* double auction market.

auction rate securities (ARS) Issued by municipalities, nonprofit hospitals, utilities, housing finance agencies, and universities, auction rate securities are long-term variable rate bonds tied to short-term interest rates.

audited financial statement A financial statement of a program, a corporation, or an issuer (including the profit and loss statement, cash flow and source and application of revenues statement, and balance sheet) that has been examined and verified by an independent certified public accountant.

authorized stock The number of shares of stock that a corporation can issue. This number of shares is stipulated in the corporation's state-approved charter and may be changed by a vote of the corporation's stockholders.

authorizing resolution The document enabling a municipal or state government to issue securities. The resolution provides for the establishment of a revenue fund in which receipts or income is deposited.

Automated Confirmation Transaction (ACT) Service The post-execution, online transaction reporting and comparison system.

automatic exercise Unless other instructions have been given, contracts that are in the money by a specified amount at expiration will automatically be exercised. The amount, determined by OCC, applies to both customer and institutional accounts.

average A price at a midpoint among a number of prices. Technical analysts frequently use averages as market indicators. *Related item(s):* index.

average basis An accounting method used when an investor has made multiple purchases at different prices of the same security; the method averages the purchase prices to calculate an investor's cost basis in shares being liquidated. The difference between the average cost basis and the selling price determines the investor's tax liability. *Related item(s):* first in, first out; last in, first out; share identification.

average price A step in determining a bond's yield to maturity. A bond's average price is calculated by adding its face value to the price paid for it and dividing the result by two.

B

B Consolidated Tape market identifier for the Boston Stock Exchange.

BA *See* banker's acceptance.

BABs See Build America Bonds.

back away The failure of a market maker to honor a firm bid and asked price. This violates the Conduct Rules.

back-end load A commission or sales fee that is charged when mutual fund shares or variable annuity contracts are redeemed. It declines annually, decreasing to zero over an extended holding period—up to eight years—as described in the prospectus. *Syn.* contingent-deferred sales load. *Related item(s):* front-end load.

balanced fund A mutual fund whose stated investment policy is to have at all times some portion of its investment assets in bonds and preferred stock, as well as in common stock, in an attempt to provide both growth and income. *Related item(s):* mutual fund.

balanced investment strategy A method of portfolio allocation and management aimed at balancing risk and return. A balanced portfolio may combine stocks, bonds, packaged products, and cash equivalents.

balance of payments (BOP) An international accounting record of all transactions made by one particular country with others during a certain time period; it compares the amount of foreign currency the country has taken in with the amount of its own currency it has paid out. *Related item(s):* balance of trade.

balance of trade The largest component of a country's balance of payments; it concerns the export and import of merchandise (not services). Debit items include imports, foreign aid, domestic spending abroad, and domestic investments abroad. Credit items include exports, foreign spending in the domestic economy, and foreign investments in the domestic economy. *Related item(s):* balance of payments.

balance sheet A report of a corporation's financial condition at a specific time.

balance sheet equation A formula stating that a corporation's assets equal the sum of its liabilities plus shareholders' equity.

balloon maturity A repayment schedule for an issue of bonds wherein a large number of the bonds come due at a prescribed time (normally at the final maturity date); a type of serial maturity. *Related item(s):* maturity date.

BAN *See* bond anticipation note.

banker's acceptance (BA) A money market instrument used to finance international and domestic trade. A banker's acceptance is a check drawn on a bank by an importer or exporter of goods and represents the bank's conditional promise to pay the face amount of the note at maturity (normally less than three months).

bank guarantee letter The document supplied by a commercial bank in which the bank certifies that a put writer has sufficient funds on deposit at the bank to equal the aggregate exercise price of the put; this releases the option writer from the option margin requirement.

banking act *See* Glass-Steagall Act of 1933.

Bank Secrecy Act The act establishing the U.S. Treasury Department as the lead agency for developing regulation in connection with anti-money laundering programs, which require broker-dealers to establish internal compliance procedures to detect abuses.

bar chart A tool used by technical analysts to track the price movements of a commodity over several consecutive time periods. *Related item(s):* moving average chart; point-and-figure chart.

basis point A measure of a bond's yield, equal to 1/100 of 1% of yield. A bond whose yield increases from 5.0 to 5.5% is said to increase by 50 basis points. *Related item(s):* point.

basis quote The price of a security quoted in terms of the yield that the purchaser may expect to receive.

BD *See* broker-dealer.

bear An investor who acts on the belief that a security or the market is falling or will fall. *Related item(s):* bull.

bearer bond *See* coupon bond.

bear market A market in which prices of a certain group of securities are falling or are expected to fall. *See* bull market.

best efforts underwriting A new issue securities underwriting in which the underwriter acts as an agent for the issuer and puts forth its best efforts to sell as many shares as possible. The underwriter has no liability for unsold shares, unlike in a firm commitment underwriting. *Related item(s):* underwriting.

beta coefficient A means of measuring the volatility of a security or a portfolio of securities in comparison to the market as a whole. A beta of 1 indicates that the security's price will move with the market. A beta greater than 1 indicates that the security's price will be more volatile than the market. A beta less than 1 means that the security's price will be less volatile than the market.

bid An indication by an investor, a trader, or a dealer of a willingness to buy a security; the price at which an investor may sell to a broker-dealer. *Related item(s):* offer; public offering price; quotation.

bid form The form submitted by underwriters in a competitive bid on a new issue of municipal securities. The underwriter states the interest rate, price bid, and net interest cost to the issuer.

blind pool A direct participation program that does not state in advance all of the specific properties in which the general partners will invest the partnership's money. At least 25% of the proceeds of the offering are kept in reserve for the purchase of nonspecified properties. *Syn.* nonspecified property program.

block trade In general, 10,000 shares of stock would be considered a block trade.

blue-chip stock The equity issues of financially stable, well-established companies that have demonstrated their ability to pay dividends in both good and bad times.

blue sky To register a securities offering in a particular state. *Related item(s):* blue-sky laws; registration by coordination; registration by filing; registration by qualification.

blue-sky laws The nickname for state regulations governing the securities industry. The term was coined in the early 1900s by a Kansas Supreme Court justice who wanted regulation to protect against "speculative schemes that have no more basis than so many feet of blue sky." *Related item(s):* Series 63; Uniform Securities Act.

board of directors (1) Individuals elected by stockholders to establish corporate management policies. A board of directors decides, among other issues, if and when dividends will be paid to stockholders. (2) The body that governs the NYSE. It is composed of 20 members elected by the NYSE general membership for a term of two years.

bona fide quote An offer from a broker-dealer to buy or sell securities. It indicates a willingness to execute a trade under the terms and conditions accompanying the quote. *Related item(s):* firm quote; nominal quote.

bond An issuing company's or government's legal obligation to repay the principal of a loan to bond investors at a specified future date. Bonds are usually issued with par, or face, values of $1,000, representing the amount of money borrowed. The issuer promises to pay a percentage of the par value as interest on the borrowed funds. The interest payment is stated on the face of the bond at issue.

bond anticipation note (BAN) A short-term municipal debt security to be paid from the proceeds of long-term debt when it is issued.

bond attorney *See* bond counsel.

Bond Buyer indexes Indexes of yield levels of municipal bonds published daily by *The Bond Buyer*. The indexes are indicators of yields that would be offered on AA- and A-rated general obligation bonds with 20-year maturities and revenue bonds with 30-year maturities.

bond counsel An attorney retained by a municipal issuer to give an opinion concerning the legality and tax-exempt status of a municipal issue. *Syn.* bond attorney. *Related item(s):* legal opinion of counsel.

bond fund A mutual fund whose investment objective is to provide stable income with minimal capital risk. It invests in income-producing instruments, which may include corporate, government, or municipal bonds. *Related item(s):* mutual fund.

bond interest coverage ratio An indication of the safety of a corporate bond. It measures the number of times by which earnings before interest and taxes exceeds annual interest on outstanding bonds. *Syn.* fixed charge coverage ratio; times fixed charges earned ratio; times interest earned ratio.

bond laddering A fixed income investment strategy that involves purchasing several smaller bonds, each with a different maturity date spread over months or years rather than one larger bond maturing on a single date.

bond quote One of a number of quotations listed in the financial press and most daily newspapers that provide representative bid prices from the previous day's bond market. Quotes for corporate and government bonds are percentages of the bonds' face values (usually $1,000). Corporate bonds are quoted in increments of 1/8, where a quote of 991/8 represents 99.125% of par ($1,000), or $991.25. Government bonds are quoted in 32nds. Municipal bonds may be quoted on a dollar basis or on a yield-to-maturity basis. *Related item(s):* quotation; stock quote.

bond rating An evaluation of the possibility of a bond issuer's default, based on an analysis of the issuer's financial condition and profit potential. Standard & Poor's, Moody's Investors Service, and Fitch Investors Service, among others, provide bond rating services.

bond ratio One of several tools used by bond analysts to assess the degree of safety offered by a corporation's bonds. It measures the percentage of the corporation's capitalization that is provided by long-term debt financing, calculated by dividing the total face value of the outstanding bonds by the total capitalization. *Syn.* debt ratio.

bond swap The sale of a bond and the simultaneous purchase of a different bond in a like amount. The technique is used to control tax liability, extend maturity, or update investment objectives. *Syn.* tax swap. *Related item(s):* wash sale.

bond yield The annual rate of return on a bond investment. Types of yield include nominal yield, current yield, yield to maturity, and yield to call. Their relationships vary according to whether the bond in question is at a discount, a premium, or at par. *Related item(s):* current yield; nominal yield.

book-entry security A security sold without delivery of a certificate. Evidence of ownership is maintained on records kept by a central agency; for example, the Treasury keeps records of Treasury bill purchasers. Transfer of ownership is recorded by entering the change on the books or electronic files. *Related item(s):* coupon bond; registered; registered as to principal only.

book value per share A measure of the net worth of each share of common stock. It is calculated by subtracting intangible assets and preferred stock from total net worth, then dividing the result by the number of shares of common outstanding. *Syn.* net tangible assets per share.

branch office Any location identified by any means to the public as a place where a registered broker-dealer conducts business.

breadth-of-market theory A technical analysis theory that predicts the strength of the market according to the number of issues that advance or decline in a particular trading day. *Related item(s):* advance/decline line.

breakeven point The point at which gains equal losses.

breakout In technical analysis, the movement of a security's price through an established support or resistance level. *Related item(s):* resistance level; support level.

breakpoint The schedule of sales charge discounts a mutual fund offers for lump-sum or cumulative investments.

breakpoint sale The sale of mutual fund shares in an amount just below the level at which the purchaser would qualify for reduced sales charges. This violates the Conduct Rules.

broad-based index An index designed to reflect the movement of the market as a whole. Examples include the S&P 100, the S&P 500, the Major Market Index, and the *Value Line* Composite Index. *Related item(s):* index.

broker (1) An individual or a firm that charges a fee or commission for executing buy and sell orders submitted by another individual or firm. (2) The role of a firm when it acts as an agent for a customer and charges the customer a commission for its services. *Related item(s):* agent; broker-dealer; dealer.

broker-dealer (BD) A person or firm in the business of buying and selling securities. A firm may act as both broker (agent) and dealer (principal), but not in the same transaction. Broker-dealers normally must register with the SEC, the appropriate SROs, and any state in which they do business. *Related item(s):* agent; broker; dealer; principal.

broker fail *See* fail to deliver.

broker's broker (1) A specialist (DMM) executing orders for a commission house broker or another brokerage firm. (2) A floor broker on an exchange or a broker-dealer in the over-the-counter market executing a trade as an agent for another broker.

broker's loan Money loaned to a brokerage firm by a commercial bank or other lending institution for financing customers' margin account debit balances. *Related item(s):* call loan; rehypothecation.

bucketing Accepting customer orders without executing them immediately.

Build America Bonds Issued by municipalities under the Economic Recovery and Reinvestment Act of 2009, Build America Bonds (BABs) make interest payments that are taxable to bondholders. Some types of BABs offer tax credits to the issuer (Tax Credit or Issuer BABs), and others offer tax credits to the bondholder (Direct Payment BABs).

bull An investor who acts on the belief that a security or the market is rising or will rise. *Related item(s):* bear.

bulletin board *See* OTC Bulletin Board.

bull market A market in which prices of a certain group of securities are rising or will rise. *Related item(s):* bear market.

business cycle A predictable long-term pattern of alternating periods of economic growth and decline. The cycle passes through four stages: expansion, peak, contraction, and trough.

business day A day on which financial markets are open for trading. Saturdays, Sundays, and legal holidays are not considered business days.

business development company A business development company (BDC) is one that is created to help grow small companies while still in the initial stages of their development. Also referred to as growth development companies, these allow smaller nonaccredited investors the opportunity to invest in startup companies.

buyer's option A settlement contract that calls for delivery and payment according to a number of days specified by the buyer. *Related item(s):* regular way; seller's option.

buy-in The procedure that the buyer of a security follows when the seller fails to complete the contract by delivering the security. The buyer closes the contract by buying the security in the open market and charging the account of the seller for transaction fees and any loss caused by changes in the markets. *Related item(s):* sell-out.

buying power The amount of fully margined securities that a margin client may purchase using only the cash, securities, and special memorandum account balance and without depositing additional equity.

buy stop order An order to buy a security that is entered at a price above the current offering price and that is triggered when the market price touches or goes through the buy stop price.

C

C Consolidated Tape market identifier for the Cincinnati Stock Exchange.

calendar spread *See* horizontal spread.

call (1) An option contract giving the owner the right to buy a specified amount of an underlying security at a specified price within a specified time. (2) The act of exercising a call option. *Related item(s):* put.

callable bond A type of bond issued with a provision allowing the issuer to redeem the bond before maturity at a predetermined price. *Related item(s):* call price.

callable preferred stock A type of preferred stock issued with a provision allowing the corporation to call in the stock at a certain price and retire it. *Related item(s):* call price; preferred stock.

call buyer An investor who pays a premium for an option contract and receives, for a specified time, the right to buy the underlying security at a specified price. *Related item(s):* call writer; put buyer; put writer.

call date The date, specified in the prospectus of every callable security, after which the security's issuer has the option to redeem the issue at par or at par plus a premium.

call feature *See* call provision.

call loan A collateralized loan of a brokerage firm having no maturity date that may be called (terminated) at any time. The loan has a fluctuating interest rate that is recomputed daily. Generally, the loan is payable on demand the day after it is contracted. If not called, the loan is automatically renewed for another day. *Related item(s):* broker's loan.

call loan rate The rate of interest a brokerage firm charges its margin account clients on their debit balances.

call price The price, usually a premium over the issue's par value, at which preferred stocks or bonds may be redeemed before an issue's maturity.

call protection A provision in a bond indenture stating that the issue is noncallable for a certain period of time (e.g., 5 years or 10 years) after the original issue date. *Related item(s):* call provision.

call provision The written agreement between an issuing corporation and its bondholders or preferred stockholders giving the corporation the option to redeem its senior securities at a specified price before maturity and under certain conditions. *Syn.* call feature.

call risk The potential for a bond to be called before maturity, leaving the investor without the bond's current income. Because this is more likely to occur during times of falling interest rates, the investor may not be able to reinvest the principal at a comparable rate of return.

call spread An option investor's position in which the investor buys a call on a security and writes a call on the same security but with a different expiration date, exercise price, or both.

call writer An investor who receives a premium and takes on, for a specified time, the obligation to sell the underlying security at a specified price at the call buyer's discretion. *Related item(s):* call buyer; put buyer; put writer.

capital Accumulated money or goods available for use in producing more money or goods.

capital appreciation A rise in an asset's market price.

capital asset All tangible property, including securities, real estate, and other property, held for the long term.

capital asset pricing model CAPM states that the only risk that can be defined is systematic risk because that cannot be eliminated by diversification.

capital contribution The amount of a participant's investment in a direct participation program, not including units purchased by the sponsors.

capital gain The profit realized when a capital asset is sold for a higher price than the purchase price. *Related item(s):* capital loss; long-term gain.

capitalization The sum of a corporation's long-term debt, stock, and surpluses. *Syn.* invested capital. *Related item(s):* capital structure.

capitalization ratio A measure of an issuer's financial status that calculates the value of its bonds, preferred stock, or common stock as a percentage of its total capitalization.

capital loss The loss incurred when a capital asset is sold for a lower price than the purchase price. *Related item(s):* capital gain; long-term loss.

capital market The segment of the securities market that deals in instruments with more than one year to maturity—that is, long-term debt and equity securities.

capital risk The potential for an investor to lose all money invested owing to circumstances unrelated to an issuer's financial strength. For example, derivative instruments such as options carry risk independent of the underlying securities' changing value. *Related item(s):* derivative.

capital stock All of a corporation's outstanding preferred stock and common stock listed at par value.

capital structure The composition of long-term funds (equity and debt) a corporation has as a source for financing. *Related item(s):* capitalization.

capital surplus The money a corporation receives in excess of the stated value of stock at the time of first sale. *Syn.* paid-in capital; paid-in surplus. *Related item(s):* par.

capped index option A type of index option issued with a capped price at a set interval above the strike price (for a call) or below the strike price (for a put). The option is automatically exercised once the underlying index reaches the capped price. *Related item(s):* index option.

capping Placing selling pressure on a stock in an attempt to keep its price low or to move its price lower; this violates the Conduct Rules.

carried interest A sharing arrangement in an oil and gas direct participation program whereby the general partner shares the tangible drilling costs with the limited partners but pays no part of the intangible drilling costs. *Related item(s):* sharing arrangement.

cash account An account in which the customer is required by the SEC's Regulation T to pay in full for securities purchased not later than two days after the standard payment period set by the Uniform Practice Code. *Syn.* special cash account.

cash assets ratio The most stringent test of liquidity, calculated by dividing the sum of cash and cash equivalents by total current liabilities. *Related item(s):* acid-test ratio; current ratio.

cash dividend Money paid to a corporation's stockholders out of the corporation's current earnings or accumulated profits. The board of directors must declare all dividends.

cash equivalent A security that may be readily converted into cash. Examples include Treasury bills, certificates of deposit, and money market instruments and funds.

cash flow The money received by a business minus the money paid out. Cash flow is also equal to net income plus depreciation or depletion.

cashiering department The department within a brokerage firm that delivers securities and money to and receives securities and money from other firms and clients of the brokerage firm. *Syn.* security cage.

cash market Transactions between buyers and sellers of commodities that entail immediate delivery of and payment for a physical commodity. *Syn.* cash-and-carry market; spot market.

cash trade *See* cash transaction.

cash transaction A settlement contract that calls for delivery and payment on the same day the trade is executed. Payment is due by 2:30 pm ET or within 30 minutes of the trade if it occurs after 2:00 pm ET. *Syn.* cash trade. *Related item(s):* regular way; settlement date.

catastrophe call The redemption of a bond by an issuer owing to disaster (e.g., a power plant that has been built with proceeds from an issue burns to the ground).

CATS *See* certificate of accrual on Treasury securities.

CBOE *See* Chicago Board Options Exchange.

CD *See* negotiable certificate of deposit.

certificates of accrual on Treasury securities (CATS) One of several types of zero-coupon bonds issued by brokerage firms and collateralized by Treasury securities. *Related item(s):* Treasury receipt.

certificate of deposit (CD) *See* negotiable certificate of deposit.

change (1) For an index or average, the difference between the current value and the previous day's market close. (2) For a stock or bond quote, the difference between the current price and the last trade of the previous day.

chartist A securities analyst who uses charts and graphs of the past price movements of a security to predict its future movements. *Syn.* technician. *Related item(s):* technical analysis.

CHB *See* commission house broker.

Chicago Board Options Exchange (CBOE) The self-regulatory organization with jurisdiction over all writing and trading of standardized options and related contracts listed on that exchange. Also, the first national securities exchange for the trading of listed options.

Chicago Stock Exchange (CHX) Regional exchange that provides a listed market for smaller businesses and new enterprises. In 1949, the exchange merged with the St. Louis, Cleveland, and Minneapolis-St. Paul exchanges to form the Midwest Stock Exchange, but in 1993, the original name was reinstated. *Related item(s):* regional exchange.

churning Excessive trading in a customer's account by a registered representative who ignores the customer's interests and seeks only to increase commissions. This violates the Conduct Rules. *Syn.* overtrading.

class Options of the same type (i.e., all calls or all puts) on the same underlying security. *Related item(s):* series; type.

Class A share A class of mutual fund share issued with a front-end sales load. A mutual fund offers different classes of shares to allow investors to choose the type of sales charge they will pay. *Related item(s):* Class B share; Class C share; Class D share; front-end load.

Class B share A class of mutual fund share issued with a back-end load. A mutual fund offers different classes of shares to allow investors to choose the type of sales charge they will pay. *Related item(s):* back-end load; Class A share; Class C share; Class D share.

Class C share A class of mutual fund share issued with a level load. A mutual fund offers different classes of shares to allow investors to choose the type of sales charge they will pay. *Related item(s):* Class A share; Class B share; Class D share; level load.

Class D share A class of mutual fund share issued with both a level load and a back-end load. A mutual fund offers different classes of shares to allow investors to choose the type of sales charge they will pay. *Related item(s):* back-end load; Class A share; Class B share; Class C share; level load.

classical economics The theory that maximum economic benefit will be achieved if government does not attempt to influence the economy (i.e., if businesses are allowed to seek profitable opportunities as they see fit).

clearing agency An intermediary between the buy and sell sides in a securities transaction that receives and delivers payments and securities. Any organization that fills this function, including a securities depository but not including a Federal Reserve Bank, is considered a clearing agency.

clearing broker-dealer A broker-dealer that clears its own trades, as well as those of introducing brokers. A clearing broker-dealer may hold customers' securities and cash. *Syn.* carrying broker.

CLN *See* construction loan note.

close The price of the last transaction for a particular security on a particular day.

closed-end covenant A provision of a bond issue's trust indenture stating that any additional bonds secured by the same assets must have a subordinated claim to those assets. *Related item(s):* junior lien debt; open-end covenant.

closed-end investment company An investment company that issues a fixed number of shares in an actively managed portfolio of securities. The shares may be of several classes; they are traded in the secondary marketplace, either on an exchange or over the counter. The market price of the shares is determined by supply and demand and not by net asset value. *Syn.* publicly traded fund. *Related item(s):* dual-purpose fund; mutual fund.

closed-end management company An investment company that issues a fixed number of shares in an actively managed portfolio of securities. The shares may be of several classes; they are traded in the secondary marketplace, either on an exchange or over the counter. The shares' market price is determined by supply and demand, not by net asset value. *Syn.* publicly traded fund. *Related item(s):* dual-purpose fund.

closing date The date designated by the general partners in a direct participation program as the date when sales of units in the program cease; typically the offering period extends for one year.

closing purchase An options transaction in which the seller buys back an option in the same series; the two transactions effectively cancel each other out, and the position is liquidated. *Related item(s):* closing sale; opening purchase.

closing range The relatively narrow range of prices at which transactions take place during the final minutes of the trading day. *Related item(s):* close.

closing sale An options transaction in which the buyer sells an option in the same series; the two transactions effectively cancel each other out, and the position is liquidated. *Related item(s):* closing purchase; opening sale.

CMO *See* collateralized mortgage obligation.

CMV *See* current market value.

COD *See* delivery vs. payment.

Code of Arbitration Procedure The formal method of handling securities-related disputes or clearing controversies between members, public customers, clearing corporations, or clearing banks. Any claim, dispute, or controversy between member firms or associated persons must be submitted to arbitration.

Code of Procedure (COP) The formal procedure for handling trade practice complaints involving violations of the Conduct Rules. The Department of Enforcement (DOE) is the first body to hear and judge complaints. The National Adjudicatory Council handles appeals and review of DOE decisions.

coincident indicator A measurable economic factor that varies directly and simultaneously with the business cycle, thus indicating the current state of the economy. Examples include nonagricultural employment, personal income, and industrial production. *Related item(s):* lagging indicator; leading indicator.

collateral Certain assets set aside and pledged to a lender for the duration of a loan. If the borrower fails to meet obligations to pay principal or interest, the lender has claim to the assets.

collateralized mortgage obligation (CMO) A mortgage-backed corporate security. Unlike pass-through obligations issued by FNMA and GNMA, its yield is not guaranteed, and it does not have the federal government's backing. These issues attempt to return interest and principal at a predetermined rate.

collateral trust bond A secured bond backed by stocks or bonds of another issuer. The collateral is held by a trustee for safekeeping. *Syn.* collateral trust certificate.

collateral trust certificate *See* collateral trust bond.

collection ratio (1) For corporations, a rough measure of the length of time accounts receivable have been outstanding. It is calculated by multiplying the receivables by 360 and dividing the result by net sales. (2) For municipal bonds, a means of detecting deteriorating credit conditions; it is calculated by dividing taxes collected by taxes assessed.

collect on delivery (COD) *See* delivery vs. payment.

combination An option position that represents a put and a call on the same stock at different strike prices, expirations, or both.

combination fund An equity mutual fund that attempts to combine the objectives of growth and current yield by dividing its portfolio between companies that show long-term growth potential and companies that pay high dividends. *Related item(s):* mutual fund.

combination privilege A benefit offered by a mutual fund whereby the investor may qualify for a sales charge breakpoint by combining separate investments in two or more mutual funds under the same management.

combined account A customer account that has cash and long and short margin positions in different securities. *Syn.* mixed account.

combined distribution *See* split offering.

commercial bank An institution that is in the business of accepting deposits and making business loans. Commercial banks may not underwrite corporate securities or most municipal bonds. *Related item(s):* investment banker.

commercial paper An unsecured, short-term promissory note issued by a corporation for financing accounts receivable and inventories. It is usually issued at a discount reflecting prevailing market interest rates. Maturities range up to 270 days.

commingling (1) The combining by a brokerage firm of one customer's securities with another customer's securities and pledging them as joint collateral for a bank

loan; unless authorized by the customers, this violates SEC Rule 15c2-1. (2) The combining by a brokerage firm of customer securities with firm securities and pledging them as joint collateral for a bank loan; this practice is prohibited.

commission A service charge an agent assesses in return for arranging a security's purchase or sale. A commission must be fair and reasonable, considering all the relevant factors of the transaction. *Syn.* sales charge. *Related item(s):* markup.

commissioner The state official with jurisdiction over insurance transactions.

commission house broker (CHB) A member of an exchange who is eligible to execute orders for customers of a member firm on the floor of the exchange. *Syn.* floor broker.

Committee on Uniform Securities Identification Procedures (CUSIP) A committee that assigns identification numbers and codes to all securities, to be used when recording all buy and sell orders.

common stock A security that represents ownership in a corporation. Holders of common stock exercise control by electing a board of directors and voting on corporate policy. *Related item(s):* equity; preferred stock.

common stock ratio One of several tools used by bond analysts to assess the degree of safety offered by a corporation's bonds. It measures the percentage of the corporation's total capitalization that is contributed by the common stockholders and is calculated by adding the par value, the capital in excess of par, and the retained earnings and then dividing the result by the total capitalization. *Related item(s):* bond ratio.

communications with the public FINRA categorizes public communications into three categories: retail, institutional, and correspondence. See retail communications, institutional communications and correspondence.

competitive bid underwriting A form of firm commitment underwriting in which rival syndicates submit sealed bids for underwriting the issue. *Related item(s):* negotiated underwriting.

compliance department The department within a brokerage firm that oversees the firm's trading and market-making activities. It ensures that the firm's employees and officers abide by the rules and regulations of the SEC, exchanges, and SROs.

Composite Average *See* Dow Jones Composite Average.

concession The profit per bond or share that an underwriter allows the seller of new issue securities. The selling group broker-dealer purchases the securities from the syndicate member at the public offering price minus the concession. *Syn.* reallowance.

Conduct Rules Regulations designed to ensure that FINRA member firms and their representatives follow fair and ethical trade practices when dealing with the public. The rules complement and broaden the Securities Act of 1933, the Securities Exchange Act of 1934, and the Investment Company Act of 1940.

conduit theory A means for an investment company to avoid taxation on net investment income distributed to shareholders. If a mutual fund acts as a conduit for the distribution of net investment income, it may qualify as a regulated investment company and be taxed only on the income the fund retains. *Syn.* pipeline theory.

confidence theory A technical analysis theory that measures the willingness of investors to take risks by comparing the yields on high-grade bonds to the yields on lower-rated bonds.

confirmation A printed document that states the trade date, settlement date, and money due from or owed to a customer. It is sent or given to the customer on or before the settlement date. *Related item(s):* duplicate confirmation.

congestion A technical analysis term used to indicate that the range within which a commodity's price trades for an extended period of time is narrow.

Consolidated Quotation System (CQS) A quotation and last-sale reporting service for members that are active market makers of listed securities in the third market. It is used by market makers willing to stand ready to buy and sell securities for their own accounts on a continuous basis but that do not wish to do so through an exchange.

Consolidated Tape (CT) A New York Stock Exchange service that delivers real-time reports of securities transactions to subscribers as they occur on the various exchanges.

The Tape distributes reports to subscribers over two different networks that the subscribers can tap into through either the high-speed electronic lines or the low-speed ticker lines. Network A reports transactions in NYSE-listed securities. Network B reports regional exchange transactions.

consolidation The technical analysis term for a narrowing of the trading range for a commodity or security, considered an indication that a strong price move is imminent.

constant dollar plan A defensive investment strategy in which the total sum of money invested is kept constant, regardless of any price fluctuation in the portfolio. As a result, the investor sells when the market is high and buys when it is low.

constant ratio plan An investment strategy in which the investor maintains an appropriate ratio of debt to equity securities by making purchases and sales to maintain the desired balance.

construction loan note (CLN) A short-term municipal debt security that provides interim financing for new projects.

constructive receipt The date on which the Internal Revenue Service considers that a taxpayer receives dividends or other income.

Consumer Price Index (CPI) A measure of price changes in consumer goods and services used to identify periods of inflation or deflation.

consumption A term used by Keynesian economists to refer to the purchase by household units of newly produced goods and services.

contemporaneous trader A person who enters a trade at or near the same time and in the same security as a person who has inside information. The contemporaneous trader may bring suit against the inside trader. *Related item(s):* Insider Trading and Securities Fraud Enforcement Act of 1988.

contingent deferred sales load *See* back-end load.

contingent order An order that is conditional upon the execution of a previous order and that will be executed only after the first order is filled.

contra broker The broker on the buy side of a sell order or on the sell side of a buy order.

contraction A period of general economic decline, one of the business cycle's four stages. *Related item(s):* business cycle.

contractionary policy A monetary policy that decreases the money supply, usually with the intention of raising interest rates and combating inflation.

control (controlling, controlled by, under common control with) The power to direct or affect the direction of a company's management and policies, whether through the ownership of voting securities, by contract or otherwise. Control is presumed to exist if a person, directly or indirectly, owns, controls, holds with the power to vote, or holds proxies representing at least 10% of a company's voting securities.

control person (1) A director, an officer, or another affiliate of an issuer. (2) A stockholder who owns at least 10% of any class of a corporation's outstanding securities. *Related item(s):* affiliate; insider.

control security Any security owned by a director, an officer, or another affiliate of the issuer or by a stockholder who owns at least 10% of any class of a corporation's outstanding securities. Who owns a security, not the security itself, determines whether it is a control security.

conversion parity Two securities, one of which may be converted into the other, of equal dollar value. A convertible security holder can calculate parity to help decide whether converting would lead to gain or loss.

conversion price The dollar amount of a convertible security's par value that is exchangeable for one share of common stock.

conversion privilege A feature the issuer adds to a security that allows the holder to change the security into shares of common stock. This makes the security attractive to investors and, therefore, more marketable.

Related item(s): convertible bond; convertible preferred stock.

conversion rate *See* conversion ratio.

conversion ratio The number of shares of common stock per par value amount that the holder would receive for converting a convertible bond or preferred share. *Syn.* conversion rate.

conversion value The total market value of common stock into which a senior security is convertible.

convertible bond A debt security, usually in the form of a debenture, that may be exchanged for equity securities of the issuing corporation at specified prices or rates. *Related item(s):* debenture.

convertible preferred stock An equity security that may be exchanged for common stock at specified prices or rates. Dividends may be cumulative or noncumulative. *Related item(s):* cumulative preferred stock; noncumulative preferred stock; preferred stock.

cooling-off period The period (a minimum of 20 days) between a registration statement's filing date and the registration's effective date. In practice, the period varies in length.

COP *See* Code of Procedure.

corporate account An account held in a corporation's name. The corporate agreement, signed when the account is opened, specifies which officers are authorized to trade in the account. In addition to standard margin account documents, a corporation must provide a copy of its charter and bylaws authorizing a margin account.

corporate bond A debt security issued by a corporation. A corporate bond typically has a par value of $1,000, is taxable, has a term maturity, and is traded on a major exchange.

corporation The most common form of business organization, in which the organization's total worth is divided into shares of stock, each share representing a unit of ownership. A corporation is characterized by a continuous life span and its owners' limited liability.

correspondence FINRA defines this category of communications with the public as any written (including electronic) communication that is distributed or made available to 25 or fewer retail investors within any 30 calendar-day period.

cost basis The price paid for an asset, including any commissions or fees, used to calculate capital gains or losses when the asset is sold.

cost depletion A method of calculating tax deductions for investments in mineral, oil, or gas resources. The cost of the mineral-, oil- or gas-producing property is returned to the investor over the property's life by an annual deduction, which takes into account the number of known recoverable units of mineral, oil, or gas to arrive at a cost-per-unit figure. The tax deduction is determined by multiplying the cost-per-unit figure by the number of units sold each year.

coterminous A term used to describe municipal entities that share the same boundaries. For example, a municipality's school district and fire district may issue debt separately although the debt is backed by revenues from the same taxpayers. *Related item(s):* overlapping debt.

coupon bond A debt obligation with attached coupons representing semiannual interest payments. The holder submits the coupons to the trustee to receive the interest payments. The issuer keeps no record of the purchaser, and the purchaser's name is not printed on the certificate. *Syn.* bearer bond. *Related item(s):* book-entry security; registered; registered as to principal only.

coupon yield *See* nominal yield.

covenant A component of a debt issue's trust indenture that identifies bondholders' rights and other provisions. Examples include rate covenants that establish a minimum revenue coverage for a bond; insurance covenants that require insurance on a project; and maintenance covenants that require maintenance on a facility constructed by the proceeds of a bond issue.

coverage ratio A measure of the safety of a bond issue, based on how many times earnings will cover debt service plus operating and maintenance expenses for a specific time period.

covered call writer An investor who sells a call option while owning the underlying security or some other asset that guarantees the ability to deliver if the call is exercised.

covered put writer An investor who sells a put option while owning an asset that guarantees the ability to pay if the put is exercised (e.g., cash in the account).

CPI *See* Consumer Price Index.

CQS *See* Consolidated Quotation System.

CR *See* credit balance.

credit agreement A component of a customer's margin account agreement, outlining the conditions of the credit arrangement between broker and customer.

credit balance (CR) The amount of money remaining in a customer's account after all commitments have been paid in full. *Syn.* credit record; credit register. *Related item(s):* debit balance.

credit department *See* margin department.

creditor Any broker or dealer, member of a national securities exchange, or person associated with a broker-dealer involved in extending credit to customers.

credit risk The degree of probability that a bond's issuer will default in the payment of either principal or interest. *Syn.* default risk; financial risk.

credit spread A position established when the premium received for the option sold exceeds the premium paid for the option bought. *Related item(s):* debit spread.

crossed market The situation created when one market maker bids for a stock at a price higher than another market maker is asking for the same stock, or when one market maker enters an ask price to sell a stock at a price lower than another market maker's bid price to buy the same stock. This violates the Conduct Rules. *Related item(s)*: locked market.

crossover point The point at which a limited partnership begins to show a negative cash flow with a taxable income. *Related item(s)*: phantom income.

CTR See currency transaction report.

cum rights A term describing stock trading with rights. *Related item(s)*: ex-rights.

cumulative preferred stock An equity security that offers the holder any unpaid dividends in arrears. These dividends accumulate and must be paid to the cumulative preferred stockholder before any dividends may be paid to the common stockholders. *Related item(s)*: convertible preferred stock; noncumulative preferred stock; preferred stock.

cumulative voting A voting procedure that permits stockholders either to cast all of their votes for any one candidate or to cast their total number of votes in any proportion they choose. This results in greater representation for minority stockholders. *Related item(s)*: statutory voting.

currency transaction report (CTR) A report filed by financial institutions to the IRS for deposits of any currency on a single day of more than $10,000.

current assets Cash and other assets that are expected to be converted into cash within the next 12 months. Examples include such liquid items as cash and equivalents, accounts receivable, inventory, and prepaid expenses.

current liabilities A corporation's debt obligations due for payment within the next 12 months. Examples include accounts payable, accrued wages payable, and current long-term debt.

current market value (CMV) The worth of the securities in an account. The market value of listed securities is based on the closing prices on the previous business day. *Syn.* long market value. *Related item(s)*: market value.

current price See public offering price.

current ratio A measure of a corporation's liquidity; that is, its ability to transfer assets into cash to meet current short-term obligations. It is calculated by dividing total current assets by total current liabilities. *Syn.* working capital ratio.

current yield The annual rate of return on a security, calculated by dividing the interest or dividends paid by the security's current market price. *Related item(s)*: bond yield.

CUSIP See Committee on Uniform Securities Identification Procedures.

custodial account An account in which a custodian enters trades on behalf of the beneficial owner, often a minor. *Related item(s)*: custodian.

custodian An institution or a person responsible for making all investment, management, and distribution decisions in an account maintained in the best interests of another. Mutual funds have custodians responsible for safeguarding certificates and performing clerical duties. *Related item(s)*: mutual fund custodian.

customer Any person who opens a trading account with a broker-dealer. A customer may be classified in terms of account ownership, trading authorization, payment method, or types of securities traded.

customer agreement A document that a customer must sign when opening a margin account with a broker-dealer; it allows the firm to liquidate all or a portion of the account if the customer fails to meet a margin call.

customer ledger The accounting record that lists separately all customer cash and margin accounts carried by a firm.

customer statement A document showing a customer's trading activity, positions, and account balance. The SEC requires that customer statements be sent quarterly, but customers generally receive them monthly.

cyclical industry A fundamental analysis term for an industry that is sensitive to the business cycle and price changes. Most cyclical industries produce durable goods, such as raw materials and heavy equipment.

D

dated date The date on which interest on a new bond issue begins to accrue.

day order An order that is valid only until the close of trading on the day it is entered; if it is not executed by the close of trading, it is canceled.

day trader A trader in securities who opens all positions after the opening of the market and offsets or closes out all positions before the close of the market on the same day.

dealer (1) An individual or a firm engaged in the business of buying and selling securities for its own account, either directly or through a broker. (2) The role of a firm when it acts as a principal and charges the customer a markup or markdown. *Syn.* principal. *Related item(s)*: broker; broker-dealer.

dealer paper Short-term, unsecured promissory notes that the issuer sells through a dealer rather than directly to the public.

debenture A debt obligation backed by the issuing corporation's general credit. *Syn.* unsecured bond.

debit balance (DR) The amount of money a customer owes a brokerage firm. *Syn.* debit record; debit register. *Related item(s)*: credit balance.

debit register See debit balance.

debit spread A hedge position established when the premium paid for the option bought exceeds the premium received for the option sold. *Related item(s)*: credit spread.

debt financing Raising money for working capital or for capital expenditures by selling bonds, bills, or notes to individual or institutional investors. In return for the money lent, the investors become creditors and receive the issuer's promise to repay principal and interest on the debt. *Related item(s):* equity financing.

debt per capita *See* net debt per capita.

debt ratio *See* bond ratio.

debt security A security representing an investor's loan to an issuer such as a corporation, a municipality, the federal government, or a federal agency. In return for the loan, the issuer promises to repay the debt on a specified date and to pay interest. *Related item(s):* equity security.

debt service The schedule for repayment of interest and principal (or the scheduled sinking fund contribution) on an outstanding debt. *Related item(s):* sinking fund.

debt service ratio An indication of the ability of an issuer to meet principal and interest payments on bonds.

debt service reserve fund The account that holds enough money to pay one year's debt service on a municipal revenue bond. *Related item(s):* flow of funds.

debt-to-equity ratio The ratio of total long-term debt to total stockholders' equity; it is used to measure leverage.

declaration date The date on which a corporation announces an upcoming dividend's amount, payment date, and record date.

decreasing debt service A schedule for debt repayment whereby the issuer repays principal in installments of equal size over the life of the issue. The amount of interest due therefore decreases, and the amount of each payment becomes smaller over time. *Related item(s):* level debt service.

deduction An item or expenditure subtracted from adjusted gross income to reduce the amount of income subject to tax.

default The failure to pay interest or principal promptly when due.

default risk *See* credit risk.

defeasance The termination of a debt obligation. A corporation or municipality removes debt from its balance sheet by issuing a new debt issue or creating a trust that generates enough cash flow to provide for the payment of interest and principal. *Related item(s):* advance refunding.

defensive industry A fundamental analysis term for an industry that is relatively unaffected by the business cycle. Most defensive industries produce nondurable goods for which demand remains steady throughout the business cycle; examples include the food industry and utilities.

defensive investment strategy A method of portfolio allocation and management aimed at minimizing the risk of losing principal. Defensive investors place a high percentage of their investable assets in bonds, cash

equivalents, and stocks that are less volatile than average.

deferred annuity An annuity contract that delays payment of income, installments, or a lump sum until the investor elects to receive it. *Related item(s):* annuity.

deferred compensation plan A nonqualified retirement plan whereby the employee defers receiving current compensation in favor of a larger payout at retirement (or in the case of disability or death).

deficiency letter The SEC's notification of additions or corrections that a prospective issuer must make to a registration statement before the SEC will clear the offering for distribution. *Syn.* bedbug letter.

defined benefit plan A qualified retirement plan that specifies the total amount of money that the employee will receive at retirement.

defined contribution plan A qualified retirement plan that specifies the amount of money that the employer will contribute annually to the plan.

deflation A persistent and measurable fall in the general level of prices. *Related item(s):* inflation.

delivery The change in ownership or in control of a security in exchange for cash. Delivery takes place on the settlement date.

delivery vs. payment (DVP) A transaction settlement procedure in which securities are delivered to the buying institution's bank in exchange for payment of the amount due. *Syn.* collect on delivery (COD).

demand A consumer's desire and willingness to pay for a good or service. *Related item(s):* supply.

demand deposit A sum of money left with a bank (or borrowed from a bank and left on deposit) that the depositing customer has the right to withdraw immediately. *Related item(s):* time deposit.

demand-pull An excessive money supply that increases the demand for a limited supply of goods that is believed to result in inflation.

depletion A tax deduction that compensates a business for the decreasing supply of the natural resource that provides its income (oil, gas, coal, gold, or other nonrenewable resource). There are two ways to calculate depletion: cost depletion and percentage depletion. *Related item(s):* cost depletion; percentage depletion.

depreciation (1) A tax deduction that compensates a business for the cost of certain tangible assets. (2) A decrease in the value of a particular currency relative to other currencies.

depreciation expense A bookkeeping entry of a noncash expense charged against earnings to recover the cost of an asset over its useful life.

depression A prolonged period of general economic decline.

derivative An investment vehicle, the value of which is based on another security's value. Futures contracts, forward contracts, and options are among the most common types of derivatives. Institutional investors generally use derivatives to increase overall portfolio return or to hedge portfolio risk.

descending triangle On a technical analyst's trading activity chart, a pattern indicating that the market has started to fall; considered to be a bearish indicator. *Related item(s):* ascending triangle.

designated market maker (DMM) Previously known as specialists, they are exchange members who are assigned to securities on the trading floor and are charged with keeping a fair and orderly market in those securities while providing liquidity to the market place.

designated order In a municipal bond underwriting, a customer order that is submitted by one syndicate member but that specifies more than one member to receive a percentage of the takedown. The size of the order establishes its priority for subscription to an issue. *Related item(s):* group net order; member-at-the-takedown order; presale order.

devaluation A substantial fall in a currency's value, compared with the value of gold or to the value of another country's currency.

developmental drilling program A limited partnership that drills for oil, gas, or minerals in areas of proven reserves or near existing fields. *Related item(s):* exploratory drilling program; income program; step-out well.

diagonal spread An option position established by the simultaneous purchase and sale of options of the same class but with different exercise prices and expiration dates. *Related item(s):* spread.

dilution A reduction in earnings per share of common stock. Dilution occurs through the issuance of additional shares of common stock and the conversion of convertible securities.

direct debt The total of a municipality's general obligation bonds, short-term notes, and revenue debt.

direct paper Commercial paper sold directly to the public without the use of a dealer.

direct participation program (DPP) A business organized so as to pass all income, gains, losses, and tax benefits to its owners, the investors; the business is usually structured as a limited partnership. Examples include oil and gas programs, real estate programs, agricultural programs, cattle programs, condominium securities, and Subchapter S corporate offerings. *Syn.* program.

discount The difference between the lower price paid for a security and the security's face amount at issue.

discount bond A bond that sells at a lower price than its face value. *Related item(s):* par.

discount rate The interest rate charged by the 12 Federal Reserve Banks for short-term loans made to member banks.

discretion The authority given to someone other than an account's beneficial owner to make investment decisions for the account concerning the security, the number of shares or units, and whether to buy or sell. The authority to decide only timing or price does not constitute discretion. *Related item(s):* limited power of attorney.

discretionary account An account in which the customer has given the registered representative authority to enter transactions at the representative's discretion.

disintermediation The flow of money from low-yielding accounts in traditional savings institutions to higher-yielding investments. Typically, this occurs when the Fed tightens the money supply and interest rates rise.

disposable income (DI) The sum that people divide between spending and personal savings. *Related item(s):* personal income.

disproportionate sharing A sharing arrangement whereby the sponsor in an oil and gas direct participation program pays a portion of the program's costs but receives a disproportionately higher percentage of its revenues. *Related item(s):* sharing arrangement.

distribution Any cash or other property distributed to shareholders or general partners that arises from their interests in the business, investment company, or partnership.

distribution stage The period during which an individual receives distributions from an annuity account. *Syn.* payout stage. *Related item(s):* accumulation stage; accumulation unit.

diversification A risk management technique that mixes a wide variety of investments within a portfolio, thus minimizing the impact of any one security on overall portfolio performance.

diversified common stock fund A mutual fund that invests its assets in a wide range of common stocks. The fund's objectives may be growth, income, or a combination of both. *Related item(s):* growth fund; mutual fund.

diversified investment company As defined by the Investment Company Act of 1940, an investment company that meets certain standards as to the percentage of assets invested. These companies use diversification to manage risk. *Related item(s):* management company; nondiversified investment company; 75-5-10 test.

diversified management company As defined by the Investment Company Act of 1940, a management company that meets certain standards for percentage of assets invested. These companies use diversification to manage risk. *Related item(s):* management company; 75-5-10 test.

divided account *See* Western account.

dividend A distribution of a corporation's earnings. Dividends may be in the form of cash, stock, or property. The board of directors must declare all dividends. *Syn.* stock dividend. *Related item(s):* cash dividend; dividend yield; property dividend.

dividend department The department within a brokerage firm that is responsible for crediting client accounts with dividends and interest payments on client securities held in the firm's name.

dividend disbursing agent (DDA) The person responsible for making the required dividend distributions to the broker-dealer's dividend department.

dividend exclusion rule An IRS provision that permits a corporation to exclude from its taxable income 50% of dividends received from domestic preferred and common stocks. The Tax Reform Act of 1986 repealed the dividend exclusion for individual investors.

dividend payout ratio A measure of a corporation's policy of paying cash dividends, calculated by dividing the dividends paid on common stock by the net income available for common stockholders. The ratio is the complement of the retained earnings ratio.

dividends per share The dollar amount of cash dividends paid on each common share during one year.

dividend yield The annual rate of return on a common or preferred stock investment. The yield is calculated by dividing the annual dividend by the stock's purchase price. *Related item(s):* current yield; dividend.

DJIA *See* Dow Jones Industrial Average.

DK *See* don't know.

DNR *See* do not reduce order.

doctrine of mutual reciprocity The agreement that established the federal tax exemption for municipal bond interest. States and municipalities do not tax federal securities or properties, and the federal government reciprocates by exempting local government securities and properties from federal taxation. *Syn.* mutual exclusion doctrine; reciprocal immunity.

dollar bonds Municipal revenue bonds that are quoted and traded on a basis of dollars rather than yield to maturity. Term bonds, tax-exempt notes, and New Housing Authority bonds are dollar bonds.

dollar cost averaging A system of buying mutual fund shares in fixed dollar amounts at regular fixed intervals, regardless of the share's price. The investor purchases more shares when prices are low and fewer shares when prices are high, thus lowering the average cost per share over time.

donor A person who makes a gift of money or securities to another. Once the gift is donated, the donor gives up all rights to it. Gifts of securities to minors under the Uniform Gifts to Minors Act provide tax advantages to the donor. *Related item(s):* Uniform Gifts to Minors Act.

do not reduce order (DNR) An order that stipulates that the limit or stop price should not be reduced in response to the declaration of a cash dividend.

don't know (DK) A response to a confirmation received from a broker-dealer indicating a lack of information about, or record of, the transaction.

double-barreled bond A municipal security backed by the full faith and credit of the issuing municipality as well as by pledged revenues. *Related item(s):* general obligation bond; revenue bond.

Dow Jones averages The most widely quoted and oldest measures of change in stock prices. Each of the four averages is based on the prices of a limited number of stocks in a particular category. *Related item(s):* average; Dow Jones Industrial Average.

Dow Jones Composite Average (DJCA) A market indicator composed of the 65 stocks that make up the Dow Jones Industrial, Transportation, and Utilities Averages. *Related item(s):* average; Dow Jones Industrial Average; Dow Jones Transportation Average; Dow Jones Utilities Average.

Dow Jones Industrial Average (DJIA) The most widely used market indicator, composed of 30 large, actively traded issues of industrial stocks. *Related item(s):* average.

Dow Jones Transportation Average (DJTA) A market indicator composed of 20 transportation stocks. *Related item(s):* average; Dow Jones Composite Average; Dow Jones Industrial Average; Dow Jones Utilities Average.

Dow Jones Utilities Average (DJUA) A market indicator composed of 15 utilities stocks. *Related item(s):* average; Dow Jones Composite Average; Dow Jones Industrial Average; Dow Jones Transportation Average.

Dow theory A technical market theory that long-term trends in the stock market may be confirmed by analyzing the movements of the Dow Jones Industrial Average and the Dow Jones Transportation Average.

down tick *See* minus tick.

DPP *See* direct participation program.

DR *See* debit balance.

dry hole A well that is plugged and abandoned without being completed or that is abandoned for any reason without having produced commercially for 60 days. *Related item(s):* productive well.

dual-purpose fund A closed-end investment company that offers two classes of stock: income shares and capital shares. Income shares entitle the holder to share in the net dividends and interest paid to the fund. Capital shares entitle the holder to profit from the capital appreciation of all securities the fund holds. *Related item(s):* closed-end management company.

due bill A printed statement showing the obligation of a seller to deliver securities or rights to the purchaser. A due bill is also used as a pledge to deliver dividends when the transaction occurs after the record date.

due diligence The careful investigation by the underwriters that is necessary to ensure that all material information pertinent to an issue has been disclosed to prospective investors.

due diligence meeting A meeting at which an issuing corporation's officials and representatives of the underwriting group present information on and answer questions about a pending issue of securities. The meeting is held for the benefit of brokers, securities analysts, and institutional investors.

duplicate confirmation A copy of a customer's confirmation that a brokerage firm sends to an agent or an attorney if the customer requests it in writing. In addition, if the customer is an employee of another broker-dealer, SRO regulations may require a duplicate confirmation to be sent to the employing broker-dealer. *Related item(s):* confirmation.

DVP *See* delivery vs. payment.

E

earned income Income derived from active participation in a trade or business, including wages, salary, tips, commissions, and bonuses. *Related item(s):* portfolio income; unearned income.

earned surplus *See* retained earnings.

earnings per share (EPS) A corporation's net income available for common stock divided by its number of shares of common stock outstanding. *Syn.* primary earnings per share.

earnings per share fully diluted A corporation's earnings per share calculated by assuming that all convertible securities have been converted. *Related item(s):* earnings per share.

Eastern account A securities underwriting in which the agreement among underwriters states that each syndicate member will be responsible for its own allocation as well as for a proportionate share of any securities remaining unsold. *Syn.* undivided account. *Related item(s):* syndicate; Western account.

economic risk The potential for international developments and domestic events to trigger losses in securities investments.

EE savings bond *See* Series EE bond.

effective date The date the registration of an issue of securities becomes effective, allowing the underwriters to sell the newly issued securities to the public and confirm sales to investors who have given indications of interest.

efficient market theory A theory based on the premise that the stock market processes information efficiently. The theory postulates that, as new information becomes known, it is reflected immediately in the price of stock and, therefore, stock prices represent fair prices.

Employee Retirement Income Security Act of 1974 (ERISA) The law that governs the operation of most corporate pension and benefit plans. The law eased pension eligibility rules, set up the Pension Benefit Guaranty Corporation, and established guidelines for the management of pension funds. Corporate retirement plans established under ERISA qualify for favorable tax treatment for employers and participants. *Syn.* Pension Reform Act.

endorsement The signature on the back of a stock or bond certificate by the person named on the certificate as the owner. An owner must endorse certificates when transferring them to another person. *Related item(s):* assignment.

EPS *See* earnings per share.

EQ *See* equity.

equipment bond *See* equipment trust certificate.

equipment-leasing limited partnership A direct participation program that purchases equipment for leasing to other businesses on a long-term basis. Tax-sheltered income is the primary objective of such a partnership.

equipment trust certificate A debt obligation backed by equipment. The title to the equipment is held by an independent trustee (usually a bank), not the issuing company. Equipment trust certificates are generally issued by transportation companies such as railroads. *Syn.* equipment bond; equipment note.

equity (EQ) Common and preferred stockholders' ownership interests in a corporation. *Related item(s):* common stock; preferred stock.

equity financing Raising money for working capital or for capital expenditures by selling common or preferred stock to individual or institutional investors. In return for the money paid, the investors receive ownership interests in the corporation. *Related item(s):* debt financing.

equity option A security representing the right to buy or sell common stock at a specified price within a specified time. *Related item(s):* option.

equity security A security representing ownership in a corporation or another enterprise. Examples of equity securities include common and preferred stock, and put and call options on equity securities.

ERISA *See* Employee Retirement Income Security Act of 1974.

escrow agreement The certificate provided by an approved bank that guarantees that the indicated securities are on deposit at that bank. An investor who writes a call option and can present an escrow agreement is considered covered and does not need to meet margin requirements.

eurobond A long-term debt instrument of a government or corporation that is denominated in the currency of the issuer's country but is issued and sold in a different country.

eurodollar U.S. currency held in banks outside the United States.

excess equity (EE) The value of money or securities in a margin account that is in excess of the federal requirement. *Syn.* margin excess; Regulation T excess.

excess margin securities The securities in a margin account that are in excess of 140% of the account's debit balance. Such securities are available to the broker-dealer for debit balance financing purposes, but they must be segregated and earmarked as the customer's property.

exchange Any organization, association, or group of persons that maintains or provides a marketplace in which securities may be bought and sold. An exchange need not be a physical place, and several strictly electronic exchanges do business around the world.

Exchange Act *See* Securities Exchange Act of 1934.

exchange-listed security A security that has met certain requirements and has been admitted to full trading privileges on an exchange. The NYSE and regional exchanges set listing requirements for volume of shares outstanding, corporate earnings, and other characteristics. Exchange-listed securities may also be traded in the third market, the market for institutional investors.

exchange market All of the exchanges on which listed securities are traded.

exchange privilege A feature offered by a mutual fund allowing an individual to transfer an investment in one fund to another fund under the same sponsor without incurring an additional sales charge.

exchange rate *See* foreign exchange rate.

exchange-traded fund (ETF) An investment company legally classified as an open-end company or unit investment trust (UIT), but differing from traditional open-end companies (mutual funds) and UITs. An ETF issues shares in large blocks that are known as creation units. Those who purchase creation units are frequently large institutional traders or investors. The creation units can then be split up and sold as individual shares in the secondary markets, allowing individual investors to purchase shares.

ex-date The first date on which a security is traded that the buyer is not entitled to receive distributions previously declared. *Syn.* ex-dividend date.

ex-dividend date *See* ex-date.

executor A person given fiduciary authorization to manage the affairs of a decedent's estate. An executor's authority is established by the decedent's last will.

exempt security A security exempt from the registration requirements (although not from the antifraud requirements) of the Securities Act of 1933. Examples include U.S. government securities and municipal securities.

exempt transaction A transaction that does not trigger a state's registration and advertising requirements under the Uniform Securities Act. Examples of exempt transactions include:

- nonissuer transactions in outstanding securities (normal market trading),

- transactions with financial institutions,

- unsolicited transactions, and

- private placement transactions.

No transaction is exempt from the Uniform Securities Act's antifraud provisions.

exercise To effect the transaction offered by an option, a right, or a warrant. For example, an equity call holder exercises a call by buying 100 shares of the underlying stock at the agreed-upon price within the agreed-upon time period.

exercise price The cost per share at which an option or a warrant holder may buy or sell the underlying security. *Syn.* strike price.

ex-legal A municipal issue that trades without a written legal opinion of counsel from a bond attorney. An ex-legal issue must be designated as such at the time of the trade. *Related item(s):* legal opinion of counsel.

expansion A period of increased business activity throughout an economy; one of the four stages of the business cycle. *Syn.* recovery. *Related item(s):* business cycle.

expansionary policy A monetary policy that increases the money supply, usually with the intention of lowering interest rates and combating deflation.

expense ratio A ratio for comparing a mutual fund's efficiency by dividing the fund's expenses by its net assets.

expiration cycle A set of four expiration months for a class of listed options. An option may have expiration dates of January, April, July, and October (JAJO); February, May, August, and November (FMAN); or March, June, September, and December (MJSD).

expiration date The specified date on which an option buyer no longer has the rights specified in the option contract.

exploratory drilling program A limited partnership that aims to locate and recover undiscovered reserves of oil, gas, or minerals. These programs are considered highly risky investments. *Syn.* wildcatting. *Related item(s):* developmental drilling program; income program.

exploratory well A well drilled either in search of an undiscovered pool of oil or gas or with the hope of substantially extending the limits of an existing pool of oil or gas.

ex-rights Stock trading without rights. *Related item(s):* cum rights.

ex-rights date The date on or after which stocks will be traded without subscription rights previously declared.

F

FAC *See* face-amount certificate company.

face-amount certificate company (FAC) An investment company that issues certificates obligating it to pay an investor a stated amount of money (the face amount) on a specific future date. The investor pays into the certificate in periodic payments or in a lump sum.

face value *See* par.

fail to deliver A situation where the broker-dealer on the sell side of a transaction or contract does not deliver the specified securities to the broker-dealer on the buy side. *Syn.* broker fail; fails; fails to deliver; failure to deliver.

fail to receive A situation where the broker-dealer on the buy side of a transaction or contract does not receive the specified securities from the broker-dealer on the sell side. *Syn.* fails; fails to receive; failure to receive.

Fannie Mae *See* Federal National Mortgage Association.

Farm Credit Administration (FCA) The government agency that coordinates the activities of the banks in the Farm Credit System. *Related item(s):* Farm Credit System.

Farm Credit System (FCS) An organization of 37 privately owned banks that provide credit services to farmers and mortgages on farm property. Included in the system are the Federal Land Banks, Federal Intermediate Credit Banks, and Banks for Cooperatives. *Related item(s):* Federal Intermediate Credit Bank.

FCA *See* Farm Credit Administration.

FCO *See* foreign currency option.

FCS *See* Farm Credit System.

FDIC *See* Federal Deposit Insurance Corporation.

Fed *See* Federal Reserve System.

Fed call *See* margin call.

federal call *See* margin call.

Federal Deposit Insurance Corporation (FDIC) The government agency that provides deposit insurance for member banks and prevents bank and thrift failures.

federal funds The reserves of banks and certain other institutions greater than the reserve requirements or excess reserves. These funds are available immediately.

federal funds rate The interest rate charged by one institution lending federal funds to another.

Federal Home Loan Bank (FHLB) A government-regulated organization that operates a credit reserve system for the nation's savings and loan associations.

Federal Home Loan Mortgage Corporation (FHLMC) A publicly traded corporation that promotes the nationwide secondary market in mortgages by issuing mortgage-backed pass-through debt certificates. *Syn.* Freddie Mac.

Federal Intermediate Credit Bank (FICB) One of 12 banks that provide short-term financing to farmers as part of the Farm Credit System.

Federal National Mortgage Association (FNMA) A publicly held corporation that purchases conventional mortgages and mortgages from government agencies, including the Federal Housing Administration, Department of Veterans Affairs, and Farmers Home Administration. *Syn.* Fannie Mae.

Federal Open Market Committee (FOMC) A committee that makes decisions concerning the Fed's operations to control the money supply.

Federal Reserve Board (FRB) A seven-member group that directs the operations of the Federal Reserve System. The president appoints board members, subject to Congressional approval.

Federal Reserve System The central bank system of the United States. Its primary responsibility is to regulate the flow of money and credit.

FHLB *See* Federal Home Loan Bank.

FHLMC *See* Federal Home Loan Mortgage Corporation.

FICB *See* Federal Intermediate Credit Bank.

fictitious quotation A bid or an offer published before being identified by source and verified as legitimate. A fictitious quote may create the appearance of trading activity where none exists; this violates the Conduct Rules.

fidelity bond Insurance coverage required by the self-regulatory organizations for all employees, officers, and partners of member firms to protect clients against acts of lost securities, fraudulent trading, and check forgery. *Syn.* surety bond.

fiduciary A person legally appointed and authorized to hold assets in trust for another person and manage those assets for that person's benefit.

filing *See* registration by filing.

filing date The day on which an issuer submits to the SEC the registration statement for a new securities issue.

fill-or-kill order (FOK) An order that instructs the floor broker to fill the entire order immediately; if the entire order cannot be executed immediately, it is canceled.

final prospectus The legal document that states a new issue security's price, delivery date, and underwriting spread as well as other material information. It must be given to every investor who purchases a new issue of registered securities. *Syn.* prospectus.

Financial Guaranty Insurance Corporation (FGIC) An insurance company that offers insurance on the timely payment of interest and principal on municipal issues and unit investment trusts.

financial risk *See* credit risk.

firewall A descriptive name also referred to as an information barrier for the division within a brokerage firm that prevents insider information from passing from corporate advisers to investment traders, who could make use of the information to reap illicit profits. Related item(s): Insider Trading and Securities Fraud Enforcement Act of 1988.

firm commitment underwriting A type of underwriting commitment in which the underwriter agrees to sell an entire new issue of securities. The underwriter acts as a dealer, pays the issuer a lump sum for the securities, and assumes all financial responsibility for any unsold shares. *Related item(s):* underwriting.

firm quote The actual price at which a trading unit of a security (such as 100 shares of stock or five bonds) may be bought or sold. All quotes are firm quotes unless otherwise indicated. *Related item(s):* bona fide quote; nominal quote.

first in, first out (FIFO) An accounting method used to assess a company's inventory, in which it is assumed that the first goods acquired are the first to be sold. The same method is used by the IRS to determine cost basis for tax purposes. *Related item(s):* average basis; last in, first out; share identification.

fiscal policy The federal tax and spending policies set by Congress or the President. These policies affect tax rates, interest rates, and government spending in an effort to control the economy. *Related item(s):* monetary policy.

5% markup policy The guideline for the percentage markups, markdowns, and commissions on securities transactions. The policy is intended to ensure fair and reasonable treatment of the investing public.

fixed annuity An insurance contract in which the insurance company makes fixed dollar payments to the annuitant for the term of the contract, usually until the annuitant dies. The insurance company guarantees both earnings and principal. *Syn.* fixed dollar annuity; guaranteed dollar annuity. *Related item(s):* annuity; variable annuity.

fixed asset A tangible, physical property used in the course of a corporation's everyday operations; it includes buildings, equipment, and land.

fixed charge coverage ratio *See* bond interest coverage ratio.

fixed dollar annuity *See* fixed annuity.

fixed unit investment trust An investment company that invests in a portfolio of securities in which no changes are permissible.

flat A term used to describe bonds traded without accrued interest. They are traded at the agreed-upon market price only. *Related item(s):* accrued interest.

flat yield curve A chart showing the yields of bonds with short maturities as equal to the yields of bonds with long maturities. *Syn.* even yield curve. *Related item(s):* inverted yield curve; normal yield curve; yield curve.

floor broker *See* commission house broker.

floor trader An exchange member who executes transactions from the floor of the exchange only for his own account. *Syn.* local.

flow of funds The schedule of payments disbursed from the proceeds of a facility financed by a revenue bond. The flow of funds determines the order in which the operating expenses, debt service, and other expenses are paid. Typically, the priority is (1) operations and maintenance, (2) debt service, (3) debt service reserve, (4) reserve maintenance, (5) renewal and replacement, (6) surplus. *Related item(s):* debt service reserve fund.

flow-through A term that describes the way income, deductions, and credits resulting from the activities of a business are applied to individual taxes and expenses as though each incurred the income and deductions directly. *Related item(s):* limited partnership.

FNMA *See* Federal National Mortgage Association.

FOK *See* fill-or-kill order.

FOMC *See* Federal Open Market Committee.

forced conversion Market conditions created by a corporation to encourage convertible bondholders to exercise their conversion options. Often conversion is forced by calling the bonds when the market value of the stock is higher than the redemption price offered by the corporation. *Related item(s):* redemption.

forced sell-out The action taken when a customer fails to meet the deadline for paying for securities and no extension has been granted: the broker-dealer must liquidate enough securities to pay for the transaction.

foreign currency Money issued by a country other than the one in which the investor resides. Options and futures contracts on numerous foreign currencies are traded on U.S. exchanges.

foreign currency option (FCO) A security representing the right to buy or sell a specified amount of a foreign currency. *Related item(s):* option.

foreign exchange rate The price of one country's currency in terms of another currency. *Syn.* exchange rate.

foreign fund *See* specialized fund.

Form 10K An annual audited report that covers essentially all the information contained in an issuing company's original registration statement. A Form 10K is due within 90 days of year end.

Form 10Q A quarterly report containing a corporation's unaudited financial data. Certain nonrecurring events that arise during the quarterly period, such as significant litigation, must be reported. A Form 10Q is due 45 days after the end of each of the first three fiscal quarters.

forward pricing The valuation process for mutual fund shares, whereby an order to purchase or redeem shares is executed at the price determined by the portfolio valuation calculated after the order is received. Portfolio valuations occur at least once per business day.

401(k) plan A tax-deferred defined contribution retirement plan offered by an employer.

403(b) plan A tax-deferred annuity retirement plan available to employees of public schools and certain nonprofit organizations.

fourth market The exchange where securities are traded directly from one institutional investor to another without a brokerage firm's services, primarily through ECNs.

fractional share A portion of a whole share of stock. Mutual fund shares are frequently issued in fractional amounts. Fractional shares used to be generated when corporations declared stock dividends, merged, or voted to split stock, but today it is more common for corporations to issue the cash equivalent of fractional shares.

fraud The deliberate concealment, misrepresentation, or omission of material information or the truth to deceive or manipulate another party for unlawful or unfair gain.

FRB *See* Federal Reserve Board.

Freddie Mac *See* Federal Home Loan Mortgage Corporation.

free credit balance The cash funds in customer accounts. Broker-dealers must notify customers of their free credit balances at least quarterly.

freeriding Buying and immediately selling securities without making payment. This practice violates the SEC's Regulation T.

freeriding and withholding The failure of a member participating in the distribution of a hot issue to make a bona fide public offering at the public offering price. This practice violates the Conduct Rules. *Related item(s):* hot issue.

front-end fee The expenses paid for services rendered during a direct participation program's organization or acquisition phase, including front-end organization and offering expenses, acquisition fees and expenses, and any other similar fees designated by the sponsor.

front-end load (1) A mutual fund commission or sales fee that is charged at the time shares are purchased. The load is added to the share's net asset value when calculating the public offering price. *Related item(s):* back-end load.

frozen account An account requiring cash in advance before a buy order is executed and securities in hand before a sell order is executed. An account holder under such restrictions has violated the SEC's Regulation T.

Full Disclosure Act *See* Securities Act of 1933.

full power of attorney A written authorization for someone other than an account's beneficial owner to make deposits and withdrawals and to execute trades in the account. *Related item(s):* limited power of attorney.

full trading authorization An authorization, usually provided by a full power of attorney, for someone other than the customer to have full trading privileges in an account. *Related item(s):* limited trading authorization.

fully registered bond A debt issue that prints the bondholder's name on the certificate. The issuer's transfer agent maintains the records and sends principal and interest payments directly to the investor. *Related item(s):* registered; registered as to principal only.

functional allocation A sharing arrangement whereby the investors in an oil and gas direct participation program are responsible for intangible costs and the sponsor is responsible for tangible costs; revenues are shared. *Related item(s):* sharing arrangement.

fundamental analysis A method of evaluating securities by attempting to measure the intrinsic value of a particular stock. Fundamental analysts study the overall economy, industry conditions, and the financial condition and management of particular companies. *Related item(s):* technical analysis.

funded debt All long-term debt financing of a corporation.

funding An ERISA guideline stipulating that retirement plan assets must be segregated from other corporate assets.

fund manager *See* portfolio manager.

funds statement The part of a corporation's annual report that analyzes why working capital increased or decreased.

fungible Interchangeable, owing to identical characteristics or value. A security is fungible if it can be substituted or exchanged for another security.

G

GAN See grant anticipation note.

GDP *See* gross domestic product.

general account The account that holds all of an insurer's assets other than those in separate accounts. The general account holds the contributions paid for traditional life insurance contracts. *Related item(s):* separate account.

general obligation bond (GO) A municipal debt issue backed by the full faith, credit, and taxing power of the issuer for payment of interest and principal. *Syn.* full faith and credit bond. *Related item(s):* double-barreled bond; revenue bond.

general partner (GP) An active investor in a direct participation program who is personally liable for all debts of the program and who manages the business of the program. The GP's duties include making decisions that bind the partnership; buying and selling property; managing property and money; supervising all aspects of the business; and maintaining a 1% financial interest in the partnership. *Related item(s):* limited partner.

general partnership (GP) An association of two or more entities formed to conduct a business jointly. The partnership does not require documents for formation, and the general partners are jointly and severally liable for the partnership's liabilities. *Related item(s):* limited partnership.

General Securities Principal *See* Series 24.

General Securities Representative *See* Series 7.

generic advertising Communications with the public that promote securities as investments but that do not refer to particular securities. *Syn.* institutional advertising.

Ginnie Mae *See* Government National Mortgage Association.

Glass-Steagall Act of 1933 Federal legislation that forbids commercial banks to underwrite securities and forbids investment bankers to open deposit accounts or make commercial loans. *Syn.* banking act.

GNMA *See* Government National Mortgage Association.

GNP *See* gross domestic product.

GO *See* general obligation bond.

good delivery A term describing a security that is negotiable, in compliance with the contract of the sale, and ready to be transferred from seller to purchaser.

good-faith deposit A deposit contributed by each syndicate involved in a competitive bid underwriting for a municipal issue. The deposit ensures performance by the low bidder. The amount required to be deposited is stipulated in the official notice of sale sent to prospective underwriters; it is usually 2% of the par value.

good til canceled order (GTC) An order that is left on the order book until it is either executed or canceled. *Syn.* open order.

goodwill An intangible asset that represents the value that a firm's business reputation adds to its book value.

Government National Mortgage Association (GNMA) A wholly government-owned corporation that issues pass-through mortgage debt certificates backed by the full faith and credit of the U.S. government. *Syn.* Ginnie Mae.

government security A debt obligation of the U.S. government, backed by its full faith, credit, and taxing power, and regarded as having no risk of default. The government issues short-term Treasury bills, medium-term Treasury notes, and long-term Treasury bonds. *Related item(s):* agency issue.

GP *See* general partner; general partnership.

grant anticipation notes (GANs) Short-term municipal revenue notes issued with the expectation of receiving grant money from the federal government.

Green Shoe option A provision of an issue's registration statement that allows an underwriter to buy extra shares from the issuer (thus increasing the size of the offering) if public demand proves exceptionally strong. The term derives from the Green Shoe Manufacturing Company, which first used the technique.

gross domestic product (GDP) The total value of goods and services produced in a country during one year. It includes consumption, government purchases, investments, and exports minus imports.

gross income All income of a taxpayer, from whatever source derived.

gross proceeds The total of the initial invested capital in a direct participation program contributed by all the original and additional limited partners.

gross revenue pledge The flow of funds arrangement in a municipal revenue bond issue indicating that debt service is the first payment to be made from revenues received. The pledge is contained in the trust indenture. *Related item(s):* net revenue pledge.

gross revenues All money received by a business from its operations. The term typically does not include interest income or income from the sale, refinancing, or other disposition of properties.

group net order In a municipal bond underwriting, an order received by a syndicate member that is credited to the entire syndicate. Takedowns on these orders are paid to members according to their participation in the syndicate. *Related item(s):* designated order; member-at-the-takedown order; presale order.

growth development company *See* business development company (BDC).

growth fund A diversified common stock fund that has capital appreciation as its primary goal. It invests in companies that reinvest most of their earnings for expansion, research, or development. *Related item(s):* diversified common stock fund; mutual fund.

growth industry An industry that is growing faster than the economy as a whole as a result of technological changes, new products, or changing consumer tastes.

growth stock A relatively speculative issue that is believed to offer significant potential for capital gains. It often pays low dividends and sells at a high price/earnings ratio.

GTC *See* good til canceled order.

guaranteed bond A debt obligation issued with a promise from a corporation other than the issuing corporation to maintain payments of principal and interest.

guaranteed dollar annuity *See* fixed annuity.

guaranteed stock An equity security, generally a preferred stock, issued with a promise from a corporation other than the issuing corporation to maintain dividend payments. The stock still represents ownership in the issuing corporation, but it is considered a dual security.

guardian A fiduciary who manages the assets of a minor or an incompetent for that person's benefit. *Related item(s):* fiduciary.

H

HALT A message on the Consolidated Tape indicating that trading in a particular security has been stopped. *Related item(s):* trading halt.

head and shoulders On a technical analyst's trading chart, a pattern that has three peaks resembling a head and two shoulders. The stock price moves up to its first peak (the left shoulder), drops back, then moves to a higher peak (the top of the head), drops again, but recovers to another, lower peak (the right shoulder). A head and shoulders top typically forms after a substantial rise and indicates a market reversal. A head and shoulders bottom (an inverted head and shoulders) indicates a market advance.

hedge An investment made to reduce the risk of adverse price movements in a security. Normally, a hedge consists of a protecting position in a related security. *Related item(s):* long hedge.

HH savings bond *See* Series HH bond.

high The highest price a security reaches during a specified period of time. *Related item(s):* low.

holder The owner of a security. *Related item(s):* long.

holding company A company organized to invest in and manage other corporations.

holding period A time period signifying how long the owner possesses a security. It starts the day after a purchase and ends on the day of the sale.

hold in street name A securities transaction settlement and delivery procedure whereby a customer's securities are transferred into the broker-dealer's name and held by the broker-dealer. Although the broker-dealer is the nominal owner, the customer is the beneficial owner. *Related item(s):* transfer and hold in safekeeping; transfer and ship.

horizontal spread The purchase and sale of two options on the same underlying security and with the same exercise price but different expiration dates. *Syn.* calendar spread; time spread. *Related item(s):* spread.

hot issue A new issue that sells or is anticipated to sell at a premium over the public offering price. *Related item(s):* freeriding and withholding.

house maintenance call *See* margin maintenance call.

house maintenance requirement *See* margin maintenance requirement.

Housing Authority bond *See* New Housing Authority bond.

HR-10 plan *See* Keogh plan.

hypothecation Pledging to a broker-dealer securities bought on margin as collateral for the margin loan. *Related item(s):* rehypothecation.

I

IDB *See* industrial development bond.

IDC *See* intangible drilling cost.

identified security The particular security designated for sale by an investor holding identical securities with different acquisition dates and cost bases. This allows the investor to control the amount of capital gain or loss incurred through the sale.

IDR *See* industrial development bond.

immediate annuity An insurance contract purchased for a single premium that starts to pay the annuitant immediately following its purchase. *Related item(s):* annuity.

immediate family A parent, mother- or father-in-law, husband or wife, child, sibling, or other relative supported financially by a person associated with the securities industry.

immediate-or-cancel order (IOC) An order that instructs the floor broker to execute it immediately, in full or in part. Any portion of the order that remains unexecuted is canceled.

income bond A debt obligation that promises to repay principal in full at maturity. Interest is paid only if the corporation's earnings are sufficient to meet the interest payment and if the board of directors declares the interest payment. Income bonds are usually traded flat. *Syn.* adjustment bond. *Related item(s):* flat.

income fund A mutual fund that seeks to provide stable current income by investing in securities that pay interest or dividends. *Related item(s):* mutual fund.

income program A limited partnership that buys and markets proven reserves of oil and gas: it buys the value of the oil in the ground. *Related item(s):* developmental drilling program; exploratory drilling program.

income statement The summary of a corporation's revenues and expenses for a specific fiscal period.

index A comparison of current prices to some baseline, such as prices on a particular date. Indexes are frequently used in technical analysis. *Related item(s):* average.

index option A security representing the right to receive in cash the difference between the underlying value of a market index and the strike price of the option. The investor speculates on the direction, degree, and timing of the change in the numerical value of the index. *Related item(s):* capped index option.

indication of interest (IOI) An investor's expression of conditional interest in buying an upcoming securities issue after the investor has reviewed a preliminary prospectus. An indication of interest is not a commitment to buy.

individual retirement account (IRA) A retirement investing tool for employed individuals that allows an annual contribution of 100% of earned income up to a maximum annual allowable limit. Some or all of the contribution may be deductible from current taxes, depending on the individual's adjusted gross income and coverage by employer-sponsored qualified retirement plans. *Related item(s):* Keogh plan; nonqualified retirement plan; qualified retirement plan; simplified employee pension plan.

industrial development bond (IDB) A debt security issued by a municipal authority, which uses the proceeds to finance the construction or purchase of facilities to be leased or purchased by a private company. The bonds are backed by the credit of the private company, which is ultimately responsible for principal and interest payments. *Syn.* industrial revenue bond.

industrial revenue bond (IRB) *See* industrial development bond.

industry fund *See* sector fund.

inflation A persistent and measurable rise in the general level of prices. *Related item(s):* deflation.

inflation risk *See* purchasing power risk.

information barrier A descriptive name also referred to as a "firewall" for the division within a brokerage firm that prevents insider information from passing from corporate advisers to investment traders, who could make use of the information to reap illicit profits. Related item(s): Insider Trading and Securities Fraud Enforcement Act of 1988.

informer bounty (award) An award paid in connection for original information concerning any violation of securities law. Under Dodd-Frank legislation, awards may range from 10% to 30% of amounts recovered.

initial margin requirement The amount of equity a customer must deposit when making a new purchase in a margin account. The SEC's Regulation T requirement for equity securities is currently 50% of the purchase price. The initial minimum requirement is a deposit of $2,000 but not more than 100% of the purchase price. *Related item(s)*: margin; margin call.

initial public offering (IPO) A corporation's first sale of common stock to the public. *Related item(s)*: new issue market; public offering.

in-part call The redemption of a certain portion of a bond issue at the request of the issuer. *Related item(s)*: in-whole call.

inside information Material information that has not been disseminated to, or is not readily available to, the general public.

inside market The best (highest) bid price at which an OTC stock may be sold, and the best (lowest) ask price at which the same stock may be bought in the interdealer market. *Related item(s)*: affiliate; control person.

insider Any person who possesses or has access to material nonpublic information about a corporation. Insiders include directors, officers, and stockholders who own at least 10% of any class of equity security of a corporation.

Insider Trading Act *See* Insider Trading and Securities Fraud Enforcement Act of 1988.

Insider Trading and Securities Fraud Enforcement Act of 1988 Legislation that defines what constitutes the illicit use of nonpublic information in making securities trades and the liabilities and penalties that apply. *Syn.* Insider Trading Act. *Related item(s)*: Chinese wall; insider.

institutional account An account held for the benefit of others. Examples of institutional accounts include banks, trusts, pension and profit-sharing plans, mutual funds, and insurance companies.

institutional communication FINRA defines this category of communications with the public as any written (including electronic) communication that is distributed or made available only to institutional investors, but does not include a member's internal communications (i.e., internal memos).

institutional investor A person or organization that trades securities in large enough share quantities or dollar amounts that it qualifies for preferential treatment such as lower commissions. Institutional investors are covered by fewer protective regulations because it is assumed that they are more knowledgeable and better able to protect themselves. Examples would include another member firm, bank or savings and loan, insurance company, registered investment company, government entity, or any entity with $50 million or more in total assets.

insurance covenant A provision of a municipal revenue bond's trust indenture that helps ensure the safety of the issue by promising to insure the facilities built. *Related item(s)*: maintenance covenant; rate covenant.

intangible asset A property owned that is not physical, such as a formula, a copyright, or goodwill. *Related item(s)*: goodwill.

intangible drilling cost (IDC) In an oil and gas limited partnership, a tax-deductible cost; usually this is for a nonphysical asset, such as labor or fuel, which does not depreciate. The cost may be expensed in the year incurred, or deductions may be amortized over the life of the well. *Syn.* intangible drilling development expense.

intangible drilling development expense *See* intangible drilling cost.

interbank market An unregulated, decentralized, international market in which the various major currencies of the world are traded.

interest The charge for the privilege of borrowing money, usually expressed as an annual percentage rate.

interest coverage ratio *See* bond interest coverage ratio.

interest rate option A security representing the right to buy or sell government debt securities. The federal deficit has created a large market in securities that are sensitive to changes in interest rates; the investor can profit from fluctuations in interest rates and can hedge the risks created by the fluctuations.

interest rate risk The risk associated with investments relating to the sensitivity of price or value to fluctuation in the current level of interest rates; also, the risk that involves the competitive cost of money. This term is generally associated with bond prices, but it applies to all investments. In bonds, prices carry interest risk because, if bond prices rise, outstanding bonds will not remain competitive unless their yields and prices adjust to reflect the current market.

Internal Revenue Code (IRC) The legislation that defines tax liabilities and deductions for U.S. taxpayers.

Internal Revenue Service (IRS) The U.S. government agency responsible for collecting most federal taxes and for administering tax rules and regulations.

interstate offering An issue of securities registered with the SEC sold to residents of states other than the state in which the issuer does business.

in the money The term used to describe an option that has intrinsic value, such as a call option when the stock is selling above the exercise price or a put option when the stock is selling below the exercise price. *Related item(s)*: at the money; intrinsic value; out of the money.

intrastate offering An issue of securities exempt from SEC registration, available to companies that do business in one state and sell their securities only to residents of that same state. *Related item(s)*: Rule 147.

intrinsic value The potential profit to be made from exercising an option. A call option is said to have intrinsic value when the underlying stock is trading above the exercise price. *Related item(s):* time value.

inverted yield curve A chart showing long-term debt instruments having lower yields than short-term debt instruments. *Syn.* negative yield curve. *Related item(s):* flat yield curve; normal yield curve.

invested capital *See* capitalization.

investment adviser (1) Any person who makes investment recommendations in return for a flat fee or a percentage of assets managed. (2) For an investment company, the individual who bears the day-to-day responsibility of investing the cash and securities held in the fund's portfolio in accordance with objectives stated in the fund's prospectus.

Investment Advisers Act of 1940 Legislation governing who must register with the SEC as an investment adviser. *Related item(s):* investment adviser.

investment banker An institution in the business of raising capital for corporations and municipalities. An investment banker may not accept deposits or make commercial loans. *Syn.* investment bank.

investment banking business A broker, dealer, or municipal or government securities dealer that underwrites or distributes new issues of securities as a dealer or that buys and sells securities for the accounts of others as a broker. *Syn.* investment securities business.

investment company A company engaged in the business of pooling investors' money and trading in securities for them. Examples include face-amount certificate companies, unit investment trusts, and management companies.

Investment Company Act of 1940 Congressional legislation regulating companies that invest and reinvest in securities. The act requires an investment company engaged in interstate commerce to register with the SEC.

investment grade security A security to which the rating services (e.g., Standard & Poor's and Moody's) have assigned a rating of BBB/Baa or above.

investment objective Any goal a client hopes to achieve through investing. Examples include current income, capital growth, and preservation of capital.

investment pyramid A portfolio strategy that allocates investable assets according to an investment's relative safety. The pyramid base is composed of low-risk investments, the middle portion is composed of growth investments, and the pyramid top is composed of speculative investments.

investment value The market price at which a convertible security (usually a debenture) would sell if it were not converted into common stock. *Related item(s):* conversion value; convertible bond; debenture.

investor The purchaser of an asset or security with the intent of profiting from the transaction.

invitation for bids A notice to securities underwriters soliciting bids for the issuing of a bond issue. These notices are published in The Bond Buyer, newspapers, and journals.

in-whole call The redemption of a bond issue in its entirety at the option of the issuer, as opposed to its redemption based on a lottery held by an independent trustee. *Related item(s):* in-part call.

IOC *See* immediate-or-cancel order.

IOI *See* indication of interest.

IPO *See* initial public offering.

IRA *See* individual retirement account.

IRA rollover The reinvestment of assets that an individual receives as a distribution from a qualified tax-deferred retirement plan into an individual retirement account within 60 days of receiving the distribution. The individual may reinvest either the entire sum or a portion of the sum, although any portion not reinvested is taxed as ordinary income. *Related item(s):* individual retirement account; IRA transfer.

IRA transfer The direct reinvestment of retirement assets from one qualified tax-deferred retirement plan to an individual retirement account. The account owner never takes possession of the assets, but directs that they be transferred directly from the existing plan custodian to the new plan custodian. *Related item(s):* individual retirement account; IRA rollover.

IRC *See* Internal Revenue Code.

irrevocable stock power *See* stock power.

issued stock Equity securities authorized by the issuer's registration statement and distributed to the public. *Related item(s):* outstanding stock; treasury stock.

issuer The entity, such as a corporation or municipality, that offers or proposes to offer its securities for sale.

J

joint account An account in which two or more individuals possess some form of control over the account and may transact business in the account. The account must be designated as either tenants in common or joint tenants with right of survivorship. *Related item(s):* tenants in common; joint tenants with right of survivorship.

joint life with last survivor An annuity payout option that covers two or more people, with annuity payments continuing as long as one of the annuitants remains alive.

joint tenants with right of survivorship (JTWROS) A form of joint ownership of an account whereby a deceased tenant's fractional interest in the account passes to the surviving tenant(s). It is used almost exclusively by husbands and wives. *Related item(s):* tenants in common.

joint venture The cooperation of two or more individuals or enterprises in a specific business enterprise rather than in a continuing relationship—as in a partnership.

JTWROS *See* joint tenants with right of survivorship.

junior lien debt A bond backed by the same collateral backing a previous issue and having a subordinate claim to the collateral in the event of default. *Related item(s):* closed-end covenant; open-end covenant.

K

Keogh plan A qualified tax-deferred retirement plan for persons who are self-employed and unincorporated or who earn extra income through personal services aside from their regular employment. *Syn.* HR-10 plan. *Related item(s):* individual retirement account; nonqualified retirement plan; qualified retirement plan.

Keynesian economics The theory that active government intervention in the marketplace is the best method of ensuring economic growth and stability.

know your customer rule *See* Rule 405.

L

lagging indicator A measurable economic factor that changes after the economy has started to follow a particular pattern or trend. Lagging indicators are believed to confirm long-term trends. Examples include average duration of unemployment, corporate profits, and labor cost per unit of output. *Related item(s):* coincident indicator; leading indicator.

last in, first out (LIFO) An accounting method used to assess a corporation's inventory in which it is assumed that the last goods acquired are the first to be sold. The method is used to determine cost basis for tax purposes; the IRS designates last in, first out as the order in which sales or withdrawals from an investment are made. *Related item(s):* average basis; first in, first out; share identification.

leading indicator A measurable economic factor that changes before the economy starts to follow a particular pattern or trend. Leading indicators are believed to predict changes in the economy. Examples include new orders for durable goods, slowdowns in deliveries by vendors, and numbers of building permits issued. *Related item(s):* coincident indicator; lagging indicator.

LEAPS *See* long-term equity option.

lease rental bond A debt security issued by a municipal authority to raise funds for new construction with the understanding that the finished structure will be rented to the authority and that the rental payments will finance the bond payments.

legal list The selection of securities that a state agency (usually a state banking or insurance commission) determines to be appropriate investments for fiduciary accounts, such as mutual savings banks, pension funds, and insurance companies.

legal opinion of counsel The statement of a bond attorney affirming that an issue is a municipal issue and that interest is exempt from federal taxation. Each municipal bond certificate must be accompanied by a legal opinion of counsel. *Related item(s):* ex-legal; qualified legal opinion; unqualified legal opinion.

legislative risk The potential for an investor to be adversely affected by changes in investment or tax laws.

letter of intent (LOI) A signed agreement allowing an investor to buy mutual fund shares at a lower overall sales charge, based on the total dollar amount of the intended investment. A letter of intent is valid only if the investor completes the terms of the agreement within 13 months of signing the agreement. A letter of intent may be backdated 90 days. *Syn.* statement of intention.

Level 1 The basic level of Nasdaq service; through a desktop quotation machine, it provides registered representatives with up-to-the-minute inside bid and ask quotations on hundreds of over-the-counter stocks. *Related item(s):* National Association of Securities Dealers Automated Quotation System.

Level 2 The second level of Nasdaq service; through a desktop quotation machine, it provides up-to-the-minute inside bid and ask quotations and the bids and askeds of each market maker for a security. *Related item(s):* National Association of Securities Dealers Automated Quotation System.

Level 3 The highest level of Nasdaq service; through a desktop quotation machine, it provides up-to-the-minute inside bid and ask quotations, supplies the bids and askeds of each market maker for a security, and allows each market maker to enter changes in those quotations. *Related item(s):* National Association of Securities Dealers Automated Quotation System.

level debt service A schedule for debt repayment whereby principal and interest payments remain essentially constant from year to year over the life of the issue. *Related item(s):* decreasing debt service.

level load A mutual fund sales fee charged annually based on the net asset value of a share. A 12b-1 asset-based fee is an example of a level load. *Related item(s):* back-end load; Class C share; Class D share; front-end load.

leverage Using borrowed capital to increase investment return. *Syn.* trading on the equity.

liability A legal obligation to pay a debt owed. Current liabilities are debts payable within 12 months. Long-term liabilities are debts payable over a period of more than 12 months.

LIBOR *See* London Interbank Offered Rate.

life annuity/straight life An annuity payout option that pays a monthly check over the annuitant's lifetime.

life annuity with period certain An annuity payout option that guarantees the annuitant a monthly check for a certain period and thereafter until the annuitant's death. If the annuitant dies before the period expires, the payments go to the annuitant's named beneficiary.

life contingency An annuity payout option that provides a death benefit during the accumulation stage. If the annuitant dies during this period, a full contribution is made to the account, which is paid to the annuitant's named beneficiary.

LIFO *See* last in, first out.

limited liability An investor's right to limit potential losses to no more than the amount invested. Equity shareholders, such as corporate stockholders and limited partners, have limited liability.

limited partner (LP) An investor in a direct participation program who does not participate in the management or control of the program and whose liability for partnership debts is limited to the amount invested in the program. *Related item(s):* general partner; participant; passive investor.

limited partnership (LP) An association of two or more partners formed to conduct a business jointly and in which one or more of the partners is liable only to the extent of the amount of money invested. Limited partners do not receive dividends but enjoy direct flow-through of income and expenses. *Related item(s):* flow-through; general partnership.

limited partnership agreement The contract between a partnership's limited and general partners that provides the guidelines for partnership operation and states the rights and responsibilities of each partner.

limited power of attorney A written authorization for someone other than an account's beneficial owner to make certain investment decisions regarding transactions in the account. *Related item(s):* discretion; full power of attorney.

limited tax bond A general obligation municipal debt security issued by a municipality whose taxing power is limited to a specified maximum rate.

limited trading authorization An authorization, usually provided by a limited power of attorney, for someone other than the customer to have trading privileges in an account. These privileges are limited to purchases and sales; withdrawal of assets is not authorized. *Related item(s):* full trading authorization.

limit order An order that instructs the floor broker to buy a specified security below a certain price or to sell a specified security above a certain price. *Syn.* or better order. *Related item(s):* stop limit order; stop order.

limit order book *See* specialist's book.

liquidation priority In the case of a corporation's liquidation, the order that is strictly followed for paying off creditors and stockholders:

1. Secured claims (mortgages)
2. Secured liabilities (bonds)
3. Unsecured liabilities (debentures) and general creditors
4. Subordinated debt
5. Preferred stockholders
6. Common stockholders

liquidity The ease with which an asset may be converted to cash in the marketplace. A large number of buyers and sellers and a high volume of trading activity provide high liquidity.

liquidity ratio A measure of a corporation's ability to meet its current obligations. The ratio compares current assets to current liabilities. *Related item(s):* acid-test ratio; current ratio.

liquidity risk The potential that an investor might not be able to sell an investment as and when desired. *Syn.* marketability risk.

listed option An option contract that may be bought and sold on a national securities exchange in a continuous secondary market. Listed options carry standardized strike prices and expiration dates. *Syn.* standardized option. *Related item(s):* OTC option.

listed security A stock, a bond, or another security that satisfies certain minimum requirements and is traded on a regional or national securities exchange such as the New York Stock Exchange.

LMV *See* current market value.

loan consent agreement An optional contract between a brokerage firm and a margin customer that permits the firm to lend the margined securities to other brokers; the contract is part of the margin agreement. *Syn.* consent to lend agreement.

locked market The situation created when there is no spread between the bid and the ask on the same security; that is, one market maker bids for a stock at the same price that another market maker quotes its ask price. This violates the Conduct Rules. *Related item(s):* crossed market.

LOI *See* letter of intent.

London Interbank Offered Rate (LIBOR) The average of the interbank-offered interest rates for dollar deposits in the London market, based on the quotations at five major banks.

long The term used to describe the owning of a security, contract, or commodity. For example, a common stock owner is said to have a long position in the stock. *Related item(s):* short.

long hedge Buying puts as protection against a decline in the value of a long securities or actuals position. *Related item(s):* hedge.

long market value (LMV) *See* current market value.

long straddle An option investor's position that results from buying a call and a put on the same stock with the same exercise price and expiration month. *Related item(s):* short straddle; spread; straddle.

long-term equity option An option contract that has a longer expiration than traditional equity option contracts. The most common long-term equity option is the CBOE's long-term equity anticipation security (LEAPS).

long-term gain The profit earned on the sale of a capital asset that has been owned for more than 12 months. *Related item(s):* capital gain; capital loss; long-term loss.

long-term loss The loss realized on the sale of a capital asset that has been owned for more than 12 months. *Related item(s):* capital gain; capital loss; long-term gain.

loss carryover A capital loss incurred during one tax year that is carried over to the next year or later years for use as a capital loss deduction. *Related item(s):* capital loss.

low The lowest price a security or commodity reaches during a specified period. *Related item(s):* high.

LP *See* limited partner; limited partnership.

M

M1 A category of the money supply that includes all coins, currency, and demand deposits (i.e., checking accounts and NOW accounts). *Related item(s):* M2; M3; money supply.

M2 A category of the money supply that includes M1 in addition to all time deposits, savings deposits, and non-institutional money market funds. *Related item(s):* M1; M3; money supply.

M3 A category of the money supply that includes M2 in addition to all large time deposits, institutional money market funds, short-term repurchase agreements, and certain other large liquid assets. *Related item(s):* M1; M2; money supply.

maintenance call *See* margin maintenance call.

maintenance covenant A provision of a municipal revenue bond's trust indenture that helps ensure the safety of the issue by promising to keep the facility and equipment in good working order. *Related item(s):* insurance covenant; rate covenant.

maintenance requirement *See* margin maintenance requirement.

Major Market Index (MMI) A market indicator designed to track the Dow Jones industrials. It is composed of 15 of the 30 Dow Jones industrials and five other large NYSE-listed stocks. *Related item(s):* index.

make a market To stand ready to buy or sell a particular security as a dealer for its own account. A market maker accepts the risk of holding the position in the security. *Related item(s):* market maker.

managed underwriting An arrangement between the issuer of a security and an investment banker in which the banker agrees to form an underwriting syndicate to bring the security to the public. The syndicate manager then directs the entire underwriting process.

management company An investment company that trades various types of securities in a portfolio in accordance with specific objectives stated in the prospectus. *Related item(s):* closed-end management company; diversified management company; mutual fund; nondiversified management company.

management fee The payment to the sponsor of a direct participation program for managing and administering the program. The fee is capped at about 5% of the program's gross revenues.

manager of the syndicate *See* underwriting manager.

managing partner The general partner of a direct participation program that selects the investments and operates the partnership.

managing underwriter *See* underwriting manager.

mandatory call The redemption of a bond by an issuer authorized in the trust indenture and based on a predetermined schedule or event. *Related item(s):* catastrophe call; partial call.

margin The amount of equity contributed by a customer as a percentage of the current market value of the securities held in a margin account. *Related item(s):* equity; initial margin requirement; margin call; Regulation T.

margin account A customer account in which a brokerage firm lends the customer part of the purchase price of securities. *Related item(s):* cash account; Regulation T.

margin call The Federal Reserve Board's demand that a customer deposit a specified amount of money or securities when a purchase is made in a margin account; the amount is expressed as a percentage of the market value of the securities at the time of purchase. The deposit must be made within one payment period. *Syn.* Fed call; federal call; federal margin; Reg T call; T call. *Related item(s):* initial margin requirement; margin.

margin deficiency *See* margin maintenance requirement.

margin department The department within a brokerage firm that computes the amount of money clients must deposit in margin and cash accounts. *Syn.* credit department.

margin excess *See* excess equity.

margin maintenance call A demand that a margin customer deposit money or securities when the customer's equity falls below the margin maintenance requirement set by the broker-dealer or the SRO the broker dealer reports to. *Syn.* house maintenance call; maintenance call; FINRA maintenance call.

margin maintenance requirement The minimum equity that must be held in a margin account, determined by the broker-dealer and by the SRO the broker-dealer reports to. The amount of equity required varies with the type of security bought on margin, and the broker-dealer's house requirement is usually higher than that set by the SRO. *Syn.* house maintenance requirement; maintenance requirement; FINRA maintenance requirement.

margin risk The potential that a margin customer will be required to deposit additional cash if his security positions are subject to adverse price movements.

margin security A security that is eligible for purchase on margin, including any registered security, OTC margin stock or bond, or Nasdaq Global Select or Global Market security. A firm is permitted to lend money to help customers purchase these securities and may accept these securities as collateral for margin purchases. *Syn.* eligible security. *Related item(s):* nonmargin security; OTC margin security.

markdown The difference between the highest current bid price among dealers and the lower price that a dealer pays to a customer.

marketability The ease with which a security may be bought or sold; having a readily available market for trading.

market letter A publication that comments on securities, investing, the economy, or other related topics and is distributed to an organization's clients or to the public. *Related item(s):* sales literature.

market maker A dealer willing to accept the risk of holding a particular security in its own account to facilitate trading in that security. *Related item(s):* make a market.

market NH *See* not held order.

market not held order *See* not held order.

market-on-close order An order that specifies it is to be executed at the close. The order will be executed at the closing price. *Syn.* at-the-close order. *Related item(s):* at-the-opening order.

market order An order to be executed immediately at the best available price. A market order is the only order that guarantees execution. *Syn.* unrestricted order.

market-out clause The standard provision of a firm commitment underwriting agreement that relieves the underwriter of its obligation to underwrite the issue under circumstances that impair the investment quality of the securities.

market risk The potential for an investor to experience losses owing to day-to-day fluctuations in the prices at which securities may be bought or sold. *Related item(s):* systemic risk.

market value The price at which investors buy or sell a share of common stock or a bond at a given time. Market value is determined by buyers' and sellers' interaction. *Related item(s):* current market value.

mark to market To adjust the value of the securities in an account to the current market value of those securities; used to calculate the market value and equity in a margin account.

markup The difference between the lowest current offering price among dealers and the higher price a dealer charges a customer.

markup policy A guideline for reasonable markups, markdowns, and commissions for secondary transactions.

According to the policy, all commissions on broker transactions and all markups or markdowns on principal transactions should be fair and reasonable for a particular transaction.

married put The simultaneous purchase of a stock and a put on that stock specifically identified as a hedge.

material information Any fact that could affect an investor's decision to trade a security.

maturity date The date on which a bond's principal is repaid to the investor and interest payments cease. *Related item(s):* par; principal.

maximum loan value The percentage of market value a broker-dealer is permitted to lend a margin customer for the purchase of securities. Loan value is equal to the complement of the Regulation T requirement: if Reg T were 65%, the maximum loan value would be 35%. *Syn.* loan value.

maximum market value The market value to which a short sale position may advance before a margin maintenance call is issued. Maximum market value is set by the SRO the broker-dealer reports to and currently equals the credit balance divided by 130%. *Syn.* maximum short market value.

member-at-the-takedown order In a municipal bond underwriting, a customer order submitted by one syndicate member who will receive the entire takedown. Member-at-the-takedown orders receive the lowest priority when the securities of the issue are allocated. *Syn.* member order. *Related item(s):* designated order; group net order; presale order.

member firm A broker-dealer in which at least one of the principal officers is a member of an exchange, a self-regulatory organization or a clearing corporation.

member order *See* member-at-the-takedown order.

mini-max underwriting A form of best efforts underwriting in which the issuer sets a floor and a ceiling on the amount of securities to be sold. *Related item(s):* underwriting.

minimum increment price rule Under SEC Regulation NMS, this rule sets the minimum price increments for stocks depending on their current price. *Related item(s):* sub-penny price.

minimum margin requirement *See* margin maintenance requirement.

mini-options Option contracts that overlay only 10 shares of the underlying security instead of 100 shares as is the case for standard options contracts.

minor rule violation (MRV) In instances where the Department of Enforcement considers a violation minor and the respondent does not dispute the allegation, the Department of Enforcement may prepare and request that the respondent sign an MRV letter, accepting a finding of violation. Once the respondent signs an MRV letter, the settlement is final.

minus tick A security transaction's execution price that is below the previous execution price, by a minimum amount. *Syn.* down tick. *Related item(s):* plus tick; tick; zero-minus tick.

modern portfolio theory (MPT) A mathematical approach that is designed to reduce risk and increase performance of an investment portfolio by using different classes of securities that don't always move in the same direction at the same time.

monetarist theory An economic theory holding that the money supply is the major determinant of price levels and that, therefore, a well-controlled money supply will have the most beneficial impact on the economy.

monetary policy The Federal Reserve Board's actions that determine the size and rate of the money supply's growth, which, in turn, affect interest rates. *Related item(s):* fiscal policy.

money laundering The act of cleaning money gotten from illegitimate businesses through three stages known as placement, layering, and integration for the purpose of hiding its origin in anticipation of its later use for both legitimate and illegitimate purposes.

money market The securities market that deals in short-term debt. Money market instruments are liquid forms of debt that mature in less than one year. Treasury bills make up the bulk of money market instruments.

money market fund A mutual fund that invests in short-term debt instruments. The fund's objective is to earn interest while maintaining a stable net asset value of $1 per share. Generally sold with no load, the fund may also offer draft-writing privileges and low opening investments. *Related item(s):* mutual fund.

money supply The total stock of bills, coins, loans, credit, and other liquid instruments in the economy. It is divided into four categories—L, M1, M2, and M3—according to the type of account in which the instrument is kept. *Related item(s):* M1; M2; M3.

Moody's Investors Service One of the best known investment rating agencies in the United States. A subsidiary of Dun & Bradstreet, Moody's rates bonds, commercial paper, preferred and common stocks, and municipal short-term issues. *Related item(s):* bond rating; Standard & Poor's Corporation.

moral obligation bond A municipal revenue bond for which a state legislature has the authority, but no legal obligation, to appropriate money in the event the issuer defaults.

mortgage bond A debt obligation secured by a property pledge. It represents a lien or mortgage against the issuing corporation's properties and real estate assets.

moving average chart A tool used by technical analysts to track the price movements of a commodity. It plots average daily settlement prices over a defined period (e.g., over three days for a three-day moving average). *Related item(s):* bar chart; point-and-figure chart.

MSRB *See* Municipal Securities Rulemaking Board.

multiplier effect The expansion of the money supply that results from a Federal Reserve System member bank's being able to lend more money than it takes in. A small increase in bank deposits generates a far larger increase in available credit.

municipal bond A debt security issued by a state, a municipality, or another subdivision (such as a school, a park, or a sanitation or other local taxing district) to finance its capital expenditures. Such expenditures might include the construction of highways, public works, or school buildings. *Syn.* municipal security.

municipal bond fund A mutual fund that invests in municipal bonds and operates either as a unit investment trust or as an open-end fund. The fund's objective is to maximize federally tax-exempt income. *Related item(s):* mutual fund; unit investment trust.

municipal note A short-term municipal security issued in anticipation of funds from another source. *Related item(s):* municipal security.

Municipal Securities Rulemaking Board (MSRB) A self-regulatory organization that regulates the issuance and trading of municipal securities. The Board functions under the Securities and Exchange Commission's supervision; it has no enforcement powers. *Related item(s):* Securities Acts Amendments of 1975.

municipal security *See* municipal bond.

mutual fund An investment company that continuously offers new equity shares in an actively managed portfolio of securities. All shareholders participate in the fund's gains or losses. The shares are redeemable on any business day at the net asset value. Each mutual fund's portfolio is invested to match the objective stated in the prospectus. *Syn.* open-end investment company; open-end management company. *Related item(s):* asset allocation fund; balanced fund; net asset value.

mutual fund custodian A national bank, a stock exchange member firm, a trust company, or another qualified institution that physically safeguards the securities a mutual fund holds. It does not manage the fund's investments; its function is solely clerical.

N

naked The position of an option investor who writes a call or a put on a security he does not own. *Syn.* uncovered.

naked call writer An investor who writes a call option without owning the underlying stock or other related assets that would enable the investor to deliver the stock should the option be exercised. *Syn.* uncovered call writer. *Related item(s):* naked put writer.

naked put writer An investor who writes a put option without owning the underlying stock or other related assets that would enable the investor to purchase the stock should the option be exercised. *Syn.* uncovered put writer. *Related item(s):* naked call writer.

narrow-based index An index that is designed to reflect the movement of a market segment, such as a group of stocks in one industry or a specific type of investment. Examples include the Technology Index and the Gold/ Silver Index. *Related item(s):* broad-based index; index.

Nasdaq *See* National Association of Securities Dealers Automated Quotation system.

Nasdaq Capital Market (formerly the Nasdaq SmallCap Market) The new name better reflects the capitalization of the issuers included in this market tier. Of the three Nasdaq market tiers, this market has the least stringent listing requirements.

Nasdaq Global Market (formerly the Nasdaq National Market) The largest of the three Nasdaq market tiers was renamed to better reflect the global nature of the securities included. These OTC stocks have high interest and appeal.

Nasdaq Global Select Market This market tier, the newest for Nasdaq, has initial listing standards, both financial and with regard to liquidity, that are among the highest of any other market.

Nasdaq 100 An index of the largest 100 nonfinancial stocks on Nasdaq, weighted according to capitalization.

National Association of Securities Dealers Automated Quotation system (Nasdaq) The nationwide electronic quotation system for up-to-the-minute bid and asked quotations on approximately 5,500 over-the-counter stocks.

National Market System (Regulation NMS) A broad sweeping SEC regulation designed to bring trading and reporting uniformity to U.S. securities markets. *Related item(s):* order protection rule; minimum increment price rule.

National Public Finance Guarantee A public corporation offering insurance as to the timely payment of principal and interest on qualified municipal issues (formerly Municipal Bond Investors Assurance Corp.—MBIA). Nonrated issues with insurance are implied to be rated AAA.

National Securities Clearing Corporation (NSCC) An organization that acts as a medium through which member brokerage firms and exchanges reconcile accounts with each other.

NAV *See* net asset value.

NAV of fund The net total of a mutual fund's assets and liabilities; used to calculate the price of new fund shares.

NAV per share The value of a mutual fund share, calculated by dividing the fund's total net asset value by the number of shares outstanding.

negotiability A characteristic of a security that permits the owner to assign, give, transfer, or sell it to another person without a third party's permission.

negotiable certificate of deposit (CD) An unsecured promissory note issued with a minimum face value of $100,000. It evidences a time deposit of funds with the issuing bank and is guaranteed by the bank.

negotiated underwriting A form of underwriting agreement in which a brokerage firm consults with the issuer to determine the most suitable price and timing of a forthcoming securities offering. *Related item(s):* competitive bid underwriting.

net asset value (NAV) A mutual fund share's value, calculated once a day, based on the closing market price for each security in the fund's portfolio. It is computed by deducting the fund's liabilities from the portfolio's total assets and dividing this amount by the number of shares outstanding. *Related item(s):* mutual fund.

net change The difference between a security's closing price on the trading day reported and the previous day's closing price. In over-the-counter transactions, the term refers to the difference between the closing bids.

net current asset value per share The calculation of book value per share that excludes all fixed assets. *Related item(s):* book value per share.

net debt per capita A measure of the ability of a municipality to meet its debt obligations; it compares the debt issued by the municipality to its property values.

net debt to assessed valuation A measure of the financial condition of a municipality; it compares the municipality's debt obligations to the assessed value of its property. *Related item(s):* net debt to estimated valuation.

net debt to estimated valuation A measure of the financial condition of a municipality; it compares the municipality's debt obligations to the estimated value of its property. *Related item(s):* net debt to assessed valuation.

net direct debt The amount of debt obligations of a municipality, including general obligation bonds and notes and short-term notes. Self-supported debt from revenue bond issues is not included in the calculation.

net domestic product A measure of the annual economic output of a nation adjusted to account for depreciation. It is calculated by subtracting the amount of depreciation from the gross domestic product. *Related item(s):* gross domestic product.

net fixed assets per bond A measure of a bond's safety; it is a conservative measure because it excludes intangible assets, working capital, and accumulated depreciation.

net income to net sales *See* net profit ratio.

net interest cost (NIC) A means of evaluating the competitive bids of prospective bond underwriting syndicates. It calculates the coupon interest to be paid by the issuer over the life of the bond. *Related item(s):* true interest cost.

net investment income The source of an investment company's dividend payments. It is calculated by subtracting the company's operating expenses from the total dividends and interest the company receives from the securities in its portfolio.

net investment return The rate of return from a variable life insurance separate account. The cumulative return for all years is applied to the benefit base when calculating the death benefit.

net operating profits interest A sharing arrangement in an oil and gas direct participation program whereby the general partner bears none of the program's costs but is entitled to a percentage of profits after all royalties and operating expenses have been paid. *Related item(s):* sharing arrangement.

net proceeds The amount of money received from a direct participation program offering less expenses incurred, such as selling commissions, syndicate fees, and organizational costs.

net profit margin *See* net profit ratio.

net profit ratio A measure of a corporation's relative profitability. It is calculated by dividing after-tax income by net sales. *Syn.* net income to net sales; net profit margin; net profits to sales; profit after taxes; profit ratio.

net profits to sales *See* net profit ratio.

net revenue pledge The flow of funds arrangement in a municipal revenue bond issue pledging that operating and maintenance expenses will be paid before debt service. The pledge is contained in the trust indenture. *Related item(s):* gross revenue pledge.

net tangible assets per share *See* book value per share.

net total debt The sum of the debt obligations of a municipality, calculated by adding the municipality's net direct debt to its overlapping debt. *Related item(s):* net direct debt; overlapping debt.

Network A A Consolidated Tape reporting system that provides subscribers with information on transactions in NYSE-listed securities. *Related item(s):* Consolidated Tape.

Network B A Consolidated Tape reporting system that provides subscribers with information on transactions in regional exchange-listed securities. *Related item(s):* Consolidated Tape.

net worth The amount by which assets exceed liabilities. *Syn.* owners' equity; shareholders' equity; stockholders' equity.

new account form The form that must be filled out for each new account opened with a brokerage firm. The form specifies, at a minimum, the account owner, trading authorization, payment method, and types of securities appropriate for the customer.

new construction program A real estate direct participation program that aims to provide capital appreciation from building new property.

New Housing Authority bond (NHA) A municipal special revenue bond backed by the U.S. government and issued by a local public housing authority to develop and improve low-income housing. *Syn.* Housing Authority bond; Public Housing Authority bond.

new issue market The securities market for shares in privately owned businesses that are raising capital by selling common stock to the public for the first time. *Syn.* primary market. *Related item(s):* initial public offering; secondary market.

New Issues Act *See* Securities Act of 1933.

New York Stock Exchange (NYSE) The largest stock exchange in the United States.

New York Stock Exchange Composite Index Index of common stocks listed on the NYSE, based on the price of each stock weighted by its total value of shares outstanding. *Syn.* NYSE Index.

NH *See* not held order.

NHA *See* New Housing Authority bond.

NIC *See* net interest cost.

no-load fund A mutual fund whose shares are sold without a commission or sales charge. The investment company distributes the shares directly. *Related item(s):* mutual fund; net asset value; sales load.

nominal owner The person in whose name securities are registered if that person is other than the beneficial owner. This is a brokerage firm's role when customer securities are registered in street name.

nominal quote A quotation on an inactively traded security that does not represent an actual offer to buy or sell, but is given for informational purposes only. *Related item(s):* bona fide quote; firm quote.

nominal yield The interest rate stated on the face of a bond that represents the percentage of interest the issuer pays on the bond's face value. *Syn.* coupon rate; stated yield. *Related item(s):* bond yield.

nonaccredited investor An investor not meeting the net worth requirements of Regulation D. Nonaccredited investors are counted for purposes of the 35-investor limitation for Regulation D private placements. *Related item(s):* accredited investor; private placement; Regulation D.

nonaffiliate A buyer of an unregistered public offering security who has no management or major ownership interest in the company being acquired. Nonaffiliates may sell this stock only after a specified holding period.

noncompetitive bid An order placed for Treasury bills in which the investor agrees to pay stop out price and, in return, is guaranteed that the order will be filled.

noncumulative preferred stock An equity security that does not have to pay any dividends in arrears to the holder. *Related item(s):* convertible preferred stock; cumulative preferred stock; preferred stock.

nondiscrimination In a qualified retirement plan, a formula for calculating contributions and benefits that must be applied uniformly so as to ensure that all employees receive fair and equitable treatment. *Related item(s):* qualified retirement plan.

nondiversified investment company A management company that does not meet the diversification requirements of the Investment Company Act of 1940. These companies are not restricted in the choice of securities or by the concentration of interest they have in those securities. *Related item(s):* diversified investment company; management company; mutual fund.

nonequity option A security representing the right to buy or sell an investment instrument other than a common stock at a specified price within a specified period. Examples of such investment instruments include foreign currencies, indexes, and interest rates. *Related item(s):* equity option; foreign currency option; index option; interest rate option; option.

nonmargin security A security that must be purchased in a cash account, that must be paid for in full, and that may not be used as collateral for a loan. Examples include put and call options, rights, insurance contracts, and new issues. *Related item(s):* margin security.

nonqualified retirement plan A corporate retirement plan that does not meet the standards set by the Employee Retirement Income Security Act of 1974. Contributions to a nonqualified plan are not tax deductible. *Related item(s):* qualified retirement plan.

nonrecourse financing Debt incurred for the purchase of an asset that pledges the asset as security for the debt but that does not hold the borrower personally liable. *Related item(s):* recourse financing.

nonsystematic risk Company-specific risk.

normal yield curve A chart showing long-term debt instruments having higher yields than short-term debt instruments. *Syn.* positive yield curve. *Related item(s):* flat yield curve; inverted yield curve; yield curve.

note A short-term debt security, usually maturing in five years or less. *Related item(s):* Treasury note.

not held order (NH) An order that gives the floor broker discretion as to the price and timing of the order's execution. Not held orders are often entered for large amounts of a security. *Syn.* market NH; market not held order.

notification *See* registration by filing.

NSCC *See* National Securities Clearing Corporation.

numbered account An account titled with something other than the customer's name. The title might be a number, a symbol, or a special title. The customer must sign a form designating account ownership.

NYSE *See* New York Stock Exchange.

NYSE Composite Index *See* New York Stock Exchange Composite Index.

NYSE maintenance call *See* margin maintenance call.

NYSE maintenance requirement *See* margin maintenance requirement.

O

OBO *See* order book official.

OCC *See* Options Clearing Corporation.

OCC Disclosure Document *See* options disclosure document.

odd lot An amount of a security that is less than the normal unit of trading for that security. Generally, an odd lot is fewer than 100 shares of stock or five bonds. *Related item(s):* round lot.

odd-lot theory A technical analysis theory based on the assumption that the small investor is always wrong. Therefore, if odd-lot sales are up—that is, small investors are selling stock—it is probably a good time to buy.

offer Under the Uniform Securities Act, any attempt to solicit a purchase or sale in a security for value. *Related item(s):* bid; public offering price; quotation, ask.

offering circular An abbreviated prospectus used by corporations issuing up to $50 million of stock.

official notice of sale The invitation to bid on a municipal bond issue; the invitation is sent to prospective underwriters and specifies, among other things, the date, time and place of sale, description of the issue, maturities, call provisions, and amount of good-faith deposit required.

official statement (OS) A document concerning a municipal issue that must be provided to every buyer. The document is prepared by the underwriter from information provided by the issuer; typically included are the offering terms, descriptions of the bonds and the issuer, the underwriting spread, fees received by brokers, initial offering price, and tax status.

OID *See* original issue discount bond.

oil and gas direct participation program A direct participation program formed to locate new oil and gas reserves, develop existing reserves, or generate income from producing wells. A high return is the primary objective of such a program. *Syn.* oil and gas limited partnership.

oil depletion allowance An accounting procedure that reduces the taxable portion of revenues from the sale of oil to compensate for the decreased supply of oil in the ground. Depletion is the natural resource counterpart of depreciation.

omnibus account An account opened in the name of an investment adviser or a broker-dealer for the benefit of its customers. The firm carrying the account does not receive disclosure of the individual customers' names or holdings and does not maintain records for the individual customers. *Syn.* special omnibus account.

open-end covenant A provision of a bond's trust indenture allowing the issuer to use the same collateral backing a bond as collateral for future bond issues. As a result, new creditors have the same claim on the collateral as existing creditors. *Related item(s):* closed-end covenant; junior lien debt.

open-end investment company *See* mutual fund.

opening purchase Entering the options market by buying calls or puts. *Related item(s):* closing sale; opening sale.

opening sale Entering the options market by selling calls or puts. *Related item(s):* closing purchase; opening purchase.

open-market operations The buying and selling of securities (primarily government or agency debt) by the Federal Open Market Committee to effect control of the money supply. These transactions increase or decrease the level of bank reserves available for lending.

open order *See* good til canceled order.

operating expenses (1) The day-to-day costs incurred in running a business. (2) In an oil and gas program, any production or leasehold expense incurred in the operation of a producing lease, including district expense; direct out-of-pocket expenses for labor, materials, and supplies; and those shares of taxes and transportation charges not borne by overriding royalty interests.

operating income The profit realized from one year of operation of a business.

operating ratio The ratio of operating expenses to net sales; the complement to the margin of profit ratio.

operations and maintenance fund The account from which are paid current operating and maintenance expenses on a facility financed by a municipal revenue bond. *Related item(s):* flow of funds.

operator The person who supervises and manages the exploration, drilling, mining, production, and leasehold operations of an oil and gas or mining direct participation program.

option A security that represents the right to buy or sell a specified amount of an underlying security—such as a stock, bond, or futures contract—at a specified price within a specified time. The purchaser acquires a right, and the seller assumes an obligation.

option agreement The document a customer must sign within 15 days of being approved for options trading. In it, the customer agrees to abide by the rules of the options exchanges and not to exceed position or exercise limits.

option contract adjustment An adjustment made automatically to the terms of an option on the ex-dividend date when a stock pays a stock dividend or if there is a stock split or a reverse split.

options account A customer account in which the customer has received approval to trade options.

Options Clearing Corporation (OCC) The organization that issues options, standardizes option contracts, and guarantees their performance. The OCC made secondary trading possible by creating fungible option contracts.

options disclosure document A publication of the Options Clearing Corporation that outlines the risks and rewards of investing in options. The document must be given to each customer at the time of opening an options account and must accompany any options sales literature sent to a customer. *Syn.* OCC Disclosure Document.

order book official (OBO) The title given to a specialist or market maker employed on the Pacific, Philadelphia, and Chicago Board Options exchanges.

order department The department within a brokerage firm that transmits orders to the proper market for execution and returns confirmations to the appropriate representative. *Syn.* order room; wire room.

order memorandum The form completed by a registered representative that contains customer instructions regarding an order's placement. The memorandum contains such information as the customer's name and account number, a description of the security, the type of transaction (e.g., buy, sell, or sell short), and any special instructions (such as time or price limits). *Syn.* order ticket.

order protection rule Under SEC Regulation NMS, this rule prohibits a trade-through.

order room *See* order department.

order ticket *See* order memorandum.

ordinary income Earnings other than capital gain.

organization and offering expense The cost of preparing a direct participation program for registration and subsequently offering and distributing it to the public; the cost includes sales commissions paid to broker-dealers.

original issue discount bond (OID) A corporate or municipal debt security issued at a discount from face value. The bond may or may not pay interest. The discount on a corporate OID bond is taxed as if accrued annually as ordinary income. The discount on a municipal OID bond is exempt from annual taxation; however, the discount is accrued for the purpose of calculating cost basis. *Related item(s):* zero-coupon bond.

OTC Bulletin Board An electronic quotation system for equity securities that are not listed on a national exchange or included in the Nasdaq system.

OTC margin security A security that is not traded on a national exchange but that has been designated by the Federal Reserve Board as eligible for trading on margin. The Fed publishes a list of such securities. *Related item(s):* margin security.

OTC market The security exchange system in which broker-dealers negotiate directly with one another rather than through an auction on an exchange floor. The trading takes place over computer and telephone networks that link brokers and dealers around the world. Both listed and OTC securities, as well as municipal and U.S. government securities, trade in the OTC market.

OTC Market Group, Inc. The publisher of compiled quotes from market makers in over-the-counter stocks and bonds.

OTC option An option contract that is not listed on an exchange. All contract terms are negotiated between buyer and seller. *Syn.* nonstandard option. *Related item(s):* listed option.

out of the money The term used to describe an option that has no intrinsic value, such as a call option when the stock is selling below the exercise price or a put option when the stock is selling above the exercise price. *Related item(s):* at the money; in the money; intrinsic value.

outstanding stock Equity securities issued by a corporation and in the hands of the public; issued stock that the issuer has not reacquired. *Related item(s):* treasury stock.

overbought A technical analysis term for a market in which more and stronger buying has occurred than the fundamentals justify. *Related item(s):* oversold.

overlapping debt A condition resulting when property in a municipality is subject to multiple taxing authorities or tax districts, each having tax collection powers and recourse to the residents of that municipality. *Related item(s):* coterminous.

overriding royalty interest A sharing arrangement whereby a person with a royalty interest in an oil and gas direct participation program takes no risks but receives a share of the revenues; the share is carved out of the working interest without liability for any costs of extraction. *Related item(s):* sharing arrangement.

oversold A technical analysis term for a market in which more and stronger selling has occurred than the fundamentals justify. *Related item(s):* overbought.

P

paid-in capital *See* capital surplus.

paid-in surplus *See* capital surplus.

par The dollar amount the issuer assigns to a security. For an equity security, par is usually a small dollar amount that bears no relationship to the security's market price. For a debt security, par is the amount repaid to the investor when the bond matures, usually $1,000. *Syn.* face value; principal; stated value. *Related item(s):* capital surplus; maturity date.

parity In an exchange market, a situation in which all brokers bidding have equal standing and the winning bid is awarded by a random drawing. *Related item(s):* precedence; priority.

parity price of common The dollar amount at which a common stock is equal in value to its corresponding convertible security. It is calculated by dividing the convertible security's market value by its conversion ratio.

parity price of convertible The dollar amount at which a convertible security is equal in value to its corresponding common stock. It is calculated by multiplying the market price of the common stock by its conversion ratio.

partial call The redemption by an issuer of a portion of an outstanding bond issue before the maturity date. *Related item(s):* catastrophe call; mandatory call.

participant (1) A person who advises stockholders in a proxy contest. (2) The holder of an interest in a direct participation program. *Related item(s):* limited partner.

participating preferred stock An equity security that offers the holder a share of corporate earnings remaining after all senior securities have been paid a fixed dividend. The payment is made in addition to the fixed dividend stated on the certificate and may be cumulative or noncumulative. *Related item(s):* convertible preferred stock; cumulative preferred stock; noncumulative preferred stock; preferred stock.

participation The provision of the Employee Retirement Income Security Act of 1974 requiring that all employees in a qualified retirement plan be covered within a reasonable time of their dates of hire.

partnership A form of business organization in which two or more individuals manage the business and are equally and personally liable for its debts.

partnership account An account that empowers the individual members of a partnership to act on the behalf of the partnership as a whole.

partnership management fee The amount payable to the general partners of a limited partnership or to other persons for managing the day-to-day partnership operations. *Syn.* program management fee; property management fee.

par value The dollar amount assigned to a security by the issuer. For an equity security, par value is usually a small dollar amount that bears no relationship to the security's market price. For a debt security, par value is the amount repaid to the investor when the bond matures, usually $1,000. *Syn.* face value; principal; stated value. *Related item(s):* capital surplus; discount bond; premium bond.

passive income Earnings derived from a rental property, limited partnership, or other enterprise in which the individual is not actively involved. Passive income, therefore, does not include earnings from wages or active business participation, nor does it include income from dividends, interest, and capital gains. *Related item(s):* passive loss; unearned income.

passive investor *See* limited partner.

passive loss A loss incurred through a rental property, limited partnership, or other enterprise in which the individual is not actively involved. Passive losses may be used to offset passive income only, not wage or portfolio income. *Related item(s):* passive income.

pass-through certificate A security representing an interest in a pool of conventional, VA, Farmers Home Administration, or other agency mortgages. The pool receives the principal and interest payments, which it passes through to each certificate holder. Payments may or may not be guaranteed. *Related item(s)*: Federal National Mortgage Association; Government National Mortgage Association.

pattern A repetitive series of price movements on a chart used by a technical analyst to predict future movements of the market.

payment date The day on which a declared dividend is paid to all stockholders owning shares on the record date.

payment period As defined by the Federal Reserve Board's Regulation T, the period corresponding to the regular way settlement period.

payout stage *See* distribution stage.

payroll deduction plan A retirement plan whereby an employee authorizes a deduction from his check on a regular basis. The plan may be qualified, such as a 401(k) plan, or nonqualified.

P/E *See* price-to-earnings ratio.

peak The end of a period of increasing business activity throughout the economy, one of the four stages of the business cycle. *Syn.* prosperity. *Related item(s)*: business cycle.

pension plan A contract between an individual and an employer, a labor union, a government entity, or another institution that provides for the distribution of pension benefits at retirement.

P/E ratio *See* price-to-earnings ratio.

percentage depletion A method of tax accounting for a direct participation program whereby a statutory percentage of gross income from the sale of a mineral resource is allowed as a tax-deductible expense. Percentage depletion is available to small producers only and not to purchasers of producing interests.

person As defined in securities law, an individual, a corporation, a partnership, an association, a fund, a joint stock company, an unincorporated organization, a trust, a government, or a political subdivision of a government.

personal income (PI) An individual's total earnings derived from wages, passive business enterprises, and investments. *Related item(s)*: disposable income.

phantom income In a limited partnership, taxable income that is not backed by a positive cash flow. *Related item(s)*: crossover point.

Pink—OTC Pink A weekly electronic publication compiled by the OTC Market Group, Inc., and containing interdealer wholesale quotations for over-the-counter stocks.

pipeline theory *See* conduit theory.

placement ratio A ratio compiled by *The Bond Buyer* indicating the number of new municipal issues that have sold within the last week. Syn. acceptance ratio.

plan custodian An institution retained by an investment company to perform clerical duties. The custodian's responsibilities include safeguarding plan assets, sending out customer confirmations, and issuing shares. *Related item(s)*: custodian; mutual fund custodian.

plus tick A security transaction's execution price that is above the previous execution price by a minimum amount. *Syn.* up tick. *Related item(s)*: minus tick; tick; zero-plus tick.

point A measure of a bond's price; $10 or 1% of the par value of $1,000. *Related item(s)*: basis point.

point-and-figure chart A tool used by technical analysts to track the effects of price reversals, or changes in the direction of prices, of a commodity over time. *Related item(s)*: bar chart; moving average chart.

POP *See* public offering price.

portfolio income Earnings from interest, dividends, and all nonbusiness investments. *Related item(s)*: earned income; passive income; unearned income.

portfolio manager The entity responsible for investing a mutual fund's assets, implementing its investment strategy, and managing day-to-day portfolio trading. *Syn.* fund manager.

position The amount of a security either owned (a long position) or owed (a short position) by an individual or a dealer. Dealers take long positions in specific securities to maintain inventories and thereby facilitate trading.

position limit The rule established by options exchanges that prohibits an investor from having a net long or short position of more than a specific number of contracts on the same side of the market.

positive yield curve *See* normal yield curve.

power of substitution *See* stock power.

precedence In an exchange market, the ranking of bids and offers according to the number of shares involved. *Related item(s)*: parity; priority.

preemptive right A stockholder's legal right to maintain her proportionate ownership by purchasing newly issued shares before the new stock is offered to the public. *Related item(s)*: right.

preferred dividend coverage ratio An indication of the safety of a corporation's preferred dividend payments. It is computed by dividing preferred dividends by net income.

preferred stock An equity security that represents ownership in a corporation. It is issued with a stated dividend, which must be paid before dividends are paid to common stockholders. It generally carries no voting rights. *Related item(s)*: callable preferred stock; convertible preferred stock; cumulative preferred stock.

preferred stock fund A mutual fund whose investment objective is to provide stable income with minimal capital risk. It invests in income-producing instruments such as preferred stock. *Related item(s)*: bond fund.

preliminary prospectus An abbreviated prospectus that is distributed while the SEC is reviewing an issuer's registration statement. It contains all of the essential facts about the forthcoming offering except the underwriting spread, final public offering price, and date on which the shares will be delivered. *Syn.* red herring.

premium (1) The amount of cash that an option buyer pays to an option seller. (2) The difference between the higher price paid for a security and the security's face amount at issue. *Related item(s):* discount.

premium bond A bond that sells at a higher price than its face value. *Related item(s):* discount bond; par value.

prerefunding *See* advance refunding.

presale order An order communicated to a syndicate manager before formation of the underwriting bid of a new municipal bond issue. If the syndicate wins the bid, the order takes the highest priority when orders are filled. *Related item(s):* designated order; group net order; member-at-the-takedown order.

price risk The potential that the value of a currency or commodity will change between the signing of a delivery contract and the time delivery is made. The futures markets serve to manage price risk.

price spread *See* vertical spread.

price-to-earnings ratio (P/E) A tool for comparing the prices of different common stocks by assessing how much the market is willing to pay for a share of each corporation's earnings. It is calculated by dividing the current market price of a stock by the earnings per share.

primary distribution *See* primary offering.

primary earnings per share *See* earnings per share.

primary dealer Large bank or brokerage firm designated by the Federal Reserve Board to bid at Treasury auctions.

primary market *See* new issue market.

primary offering An offering in which the proceeds of the underwriting go to the issuing corporation, agency, or municipality. The issuer seeks to increase its capitalization either by selling shares of stock, representing ownership, or by selling bonds, representing loans to the issuer. *Syn.* primary distribution.

prime rate The interest rate that commercial banks charge their prime or most creditworthy customers, generally large corporations.

principal A person who trades for his own account in the primary or secondary market. Also, a dealer.

principal transaction A transaction in which a broker-dealer either buys securities from customers and takes them into its own inventory or sells securities to customers from its inventory. *Related item(s):* agency transaction; agent; broker; dealer; principal.

priority In an exchange market, the ranking of bids and offers according to the first person to bid or offer at a given price. Therefore, only one individual or firm can have priority. *Related item(s):* parity; precedence.

prior lien bond A secured bond that takes precedence over other bonds secured by the same assets. *Related item(s):* mortgage bond.

private label CMO Collateralized mortgage obligations issued by investment banks or their subsidiaries, financial institutions, or home builders.

private placement An offering of new issue securities that complies with Regulation D of the Securities Act of 1933. According to Regulation D, a security generally is not required to be registered with the SEC if it is offered to no more than 35 nonaccredited investors or to an unlimited number of accredited investors. *Related item(s):* Regulation D.

productive well An oil or gas well that produces mineral resources that may be marketed commercially. *Related item(s):* dry hole.

profitability The ability to generate a level of income and gain in excess of expenses.

profit ratio *See* net profit ratio.

profit-sharing plan An employee benefit plan established and maintained by an employer whereby the employees receive a share of the business's profits. The money may be paid directly to the employees or deferred until retirement. A combination of both approaches is also possible.

progressive tax A tax that takes a larger percentage of the income of high-income earners than that of low-income earners. An example is the graduated income tax. *Related item(s):* regressive tax.

property dividend A distribution made by a corporation to its stockholders of securities it owns in other corporations or of its products. *Related item(s):* dividend.

prospectus *See* final prospectus.

Prospectus Act *See* Securities Act of 1933.

proxy A limited power of attorney from a stockholder authorizing another person to vote on stockholder issues according to the first stockholder's instructions. To vote on corporate matters, a stockholder must either attend the annual meeting or vote by proxy.

proxy department The department within a brokerage firm that is responsible for sending proxy statements to customers whose securities are held in the firm's name, and for mailing financial reports received from issuers to their stockholders.

prudent investor rule A legal maxim that restricts discretion in a fiduciary account to only those investments that a reasonable and prudent person might make.

Public Housing Authority bond (PHA) *See* New Housing Authority bond.

publicly traded fund *See* closed-end investment company.

public offering The sale of an issue of common stock, either by a corporation going public or by an offering of additional shares. *Related item(s):* initial public offering.

public offering price (POP) (1) The price of new shares that is established in the issuing corporation's prospectus. (2) The price to investors for mutual fund shares, equal to the net asset value plus the sales charge. *Related item(s)*: ask; bid; mutual fund; net asset value.

public purpose bond A municipal bond that is exempt from federal income tax as long as no more than 10% of the proceeds benefit private entities.

Public Securities Association (PSA) An organization of banks and broker-dealers that conduct business in mortgage-backed securities, money market securities, and securities issued by the U.S. government, government agencies, and municipalities.

purchasing power risk The potential that, because of inflation, a certain amount of money will not purchase as much in the future as it does today. *Syn.* inflation risk.

put (1) An option contract giving the owner the right to sell a certain amount of an underlying security at a specified price within a specified time. (2) The act of exercising a put option. *Related item(s)*: call.

put bond A debt security requiring the issuer to purchase the security at the holder's discretion or within a prescribed time. *Syn.* tender bond.

put buyer An investor who pays a premium for an option contract and receives, for a specified time, the right to sell the underlying security at a specified price. *Related item(s)*: call buyer; call writer; put writer.

put spread An option investor's position in which the investor buys a put on a particular security and writes a put on the same security but with a different expiration date, exercise price, or both.

put writer An investor who receives a premium and takes on, for a specified time, the obligation to buy the underlying security at a specified price at the put buyer's discretion. *Related item(s)*: call buyer; call writer; put buyer.

pyramiding A speculative strategy whereby an investor uses unrealized profits from a position held to increase the size of the position continuously but by ever-smaller amounts.

Q

qualification *See* registration by qualification.

qualified legal opinion The statement of a bond attorney affirming the validity of a new municipal bond issue but expressing reservations about its quality. *Related item(s)*: legal opinion of counsel; unqualified legal opinion.

qualified retirement plan A corporate retirement plan that meets the standards set by the Employee Retirement Income Security Act of 1974. Contributions to a qualified plan are tax deductible. *Syn.* approved plan. *Related item(s)*: individual retirement account; Keogh plan; nonqualified retirement plan.

quick assets A measure of a corporation's liquidity that takes into account the size of the unsold inventory. It is calculated by subtracting inventory from current assets, and it is used in the acid-test ratio. *Related item(s)*: acid-test ratio.

quick ratio *See* acid-test ratio.

quotation The price or bid a market maker or broker-dealer offers for a particular security. *Syn.* quote. *Related item(s)*: ask; bid; bond quote; stock quote.

quote *See* quotation.

R

RAN *See* revenue anticipation note.

random walk theory A market analysis theory that the past movement or direction of the price of a stock or market cannot be used to predict its future movement or direction.

range A security's low price and high price for a particular trading period, such as the close of a day's trading, the opening of a day's trading, or a day, month, or year. *Syn.* opening range.

rate covenant A provision of a municipal revenue bond's trust indenture that helps ensure the safety of the issue by specifying the rates to be charged the user of the facility. *Related item(s)*: insurance covenant; maintenance covenant.

rating An evaluation of a corporate or municipal bond's relative safety, according to the issuer's ability to repay principal and make interest payments. Bonds are rated by various organizations, such as Standard & Poor's and Moody's. Ratings range from AAA or Aaa (the highest) to C or D, which represents a company in default.

rating service A company, such as Moody's or Standard & Poor's, that rates various debt and preferred stock issues for safety of payment of principal, interest, or dividends. The issuing company or municipality pays a fee for the rating. *Related item(s)*: bond rating; rating.

ratio writing An option hedge position in which the investor writes more than one call option for every 100 shares of underlying stock that the investor owns. As a result, the investor has a partly covered position and a partly naked position.

raw land program A real estate direct participation program that aims to provide capital appreciation by investing in undeveloped land.

real estate investment trust (REIT) A corporation or trust that uses the pooled capital of many investors to invest in direct ownership of either income property or mortgage loans. These investments offer tax benefits in addition to interest and capital gains distributions.

real estate limited partnership A direct participation program formed to build new structures, generate income from existing property, or profit from the capital appreciation of undeveloped land. Growth potential, income distributions, and tax shelter are the most important benefits of such a program.

realized gain The amount a taxpayer earns when he sells an asset. *Related item(s):* unrealized gain.

reallowance A portion of the concession available to firms that sell shares in an offering but are not syndicate or selling group members.

recapitalization Changing the capital structure of a corporation by issuing, converting, or redeeming securities.

recapture The taxation as ordinary income of previously earned deductions or credits. Circumstances that may cause the IRS to require this tax to be paid include excess depreciation, premature sale of an asset, or disallowing of a previous tax benefit.

recession A general economic decline lasting from 6 to 18 months.

reciprocal immunity *See* doctrine of mutual reciprocity.

reclamation The right of the seller of a security to recover any loss incurred in a securities transaction owing to bad delivery or other irregularity in the settlement process.

reclassification The exchange by a corporation of one class of its securities for another class of its securities. This shifts ownership control among the stockholders and therefore falls under the purview of the SEC's Rule 145. *Related item(s):* Rule 145.

record date The date a corporation's board of directors establishes that determines which of its stockholders are entitled to receive dividends or rights distributions.

recourse financing Debt incurred for the purchase of an asset and that holds the borrower personally liable for the debt. *Related item(s):* nonrecourse financing.

recovery *See* expansion.

redeemable security A security that the issuer redeems upon the holder's request. Examples include shares in an open-end investment company and Treasury notes.

redemption The return of an investor's principal in a security, such as a bond, preferred stock, or mutual fund shares. By law, redemption of mutual fund shares must occur within seven days of receiving the investor's request for redemption.

redemption notice A published announcement that a corporation or a municipality is calling a certain issue of its bonds.

red herring *See* preliminary prospectus.

refinancing Issuing equity, the proceeds of which are used to retire debt.

refunding Retiring an outstanding bond issue at maturity using money from the sale of a new offering. *Related item(s):* advance refunding.

regional exchange A stock exchange that serves the financial community in a particular region of the country. These exchanges tend to focus on securities issued within their regions, but also offer trading in NYSE-listed securities.

regional fund *See* sector fund.

registered Describes a security that prints the owner's name on the certificate. The owner's name is stored in records kept by the issuer or a transfer agent.

registered as to principal only The term describing a bond that prints the owner's name on the certificate, but that has unregistered coupons payable to the bearer. *Syn.* partially registered. *Related item(s):* coupon bond; fully registered bond; registered.

Registered Options Principal (ROP) The officer or partner of a brokerage firm who approves, in writing, accounts in which options transactions are permitted.

registered principal An associated person of a member firm who manages or supervises the firm's investment banking or securities business. This includes any individual who trains associated persons and who solicits business.

Unless the member firm is a sole proprietorship, it must employ at least two registered principals, one of whom must be registered as a general securities principal and one of whom must be registered as a financial and operations principal. If the firm does options business with the public, it must employ at least one registered options principal.

registered representative (RR) An associated person engaged in the investment banking or securities business. This includes any individual who supervises, solicits, or conducts business in securities or who trains people to supervise, solicit, or conduct business in securities.

Anyone employed by a brokerage firm who is not a principal and who is not engaged in clerical or brokerage administration is subject to registration and exam licensing as a registered representative. *Syn.* account executive; stockbroker. *Related item(s):* associated person of a member.

registrar The independent organization or part of a corporation responsible for accounting for all of the issuer's outstanding stock and certifying that its bonds constitute legal debt.

registration by coordination A process that allows a security to be sold in a state. It is available to an issuer that files for the security's registration under the Securities Act of 1933 and files duplicates of the registration documents with the state administrator. The state registration becomes effective at the same time the federal registration statement becomes effective.

registration by filing A process that allows a security to be sold in a state. Previously referred to as *registration by notification*, it is available to an issuer who files for the security's registration under the Securities Act of 1933, meets minimum net worth and certain other requirements, and notifies the state of this eligibility by filing certain documents with the state administrator. The state registration becomes effective at the same time the federal registration statement becomes effective.

registration by notification *See* registration by filing.

registration by qualification A process that allows a security to be sold in a state. It is available to an issuer who files for the security's registration with the state administrator; meets minimum net worth, disclosure, and other requirements; and files appropriate registration fees. The state registration becomes effective when the legal document that discloses all pertinent information concerning an offering of a security and its issuer is filed. It is submitted to the SEC in accordance with the requirements of the Securities Act of 1933, and it forms the basis of the final prospectus distributed to investors.

regressive tax A tax that takes a larger percentage of the income of low-income earners than that of high-income earners. Examples include gasoline tax and cigarette tax. *Related item(s)*: progressive tax.

Reg T *See* Regulation T.

Reg T call *See* margin call.

regular way A settlement contract that calls for delivery and payment within a standard payment period from the date of the trade. The Uniform Practice Code sets the standard payment period. The type of security being traded determines the amount of time allowed for regular way settlement. *Related item(s)*: cash transaction; settlement date.

regulated investment company An investment company to which Subchapter M of the Internal Revenue Code grants special status that allows the flow-through of tax consequences on a distribution to shareholders. If 90% of its income is passed through to the shareholders, the company is not subject to tax on this income.

Regulation A+ Provides two offering tiers for small- and medium-sized companies that will allow the companies to raise capital in amounts substantially more than the $5 million previously allowed under Regulation A. There are two tiers: tier 1 for offerings of up to $20 million and tier 2 for offerings of up to $50 million.

Regulation D The provision of the Securities Act of 1933 that exempts from registration offerings sold to a maximum of 35 nonaccredited investors during a 12-month period. *Related item(s)*: private placement.

Regulation NMS (National Market System) A broad sweeping SEC regulation designed to bring trading and reporting uniformity to U.S. securities markets. *Related item(s)*: order protection rule; minimum increments rule.

Regulation SP Regulation enacted by the SEC to protect the privacy of customer information, particularly nonpublic personal information. Your firm must provide a privacy notice describing its privacy policies to customers whenever a new account is opened and annually thereafter. The notice must provide customers a reasonable means to opt out of the disclosure of the customer's nonpublic personal information to unaffiliated third parties.

Regulation T The Federal Reserve Board regulation that governs customer cash accounts and the amount of credit that brokerage firms and dealers may extend to customers for the purchase of securities. Regulation T currently sets the loan value of marginable securities at 50% and the payment deadline at two days beyond regular way settlement. *Syn.* Reg T. *Related item(s)*: Regulation U.

Regulation U The Federal Reserve Board regulation that governs loans by banks for the purchase of securities. Call loans are exempt from Regulation U. *Related item(s)*: broker's loan; call loan; Regulation T.

rehypothecation The pledging of a client's securities as collateral for a bank loan. Brokerage firms may rehypothecate up to 140% of the value of their customers' securities to finance margin loans to customers. *Related item(s)*: hypothecation.

reinstatement privilege A benefit offered by some mutual funds, allowing an investor to withdraw money from a fund account and then redeposit the money without paying a second sales charge.

REIT *See* real estate investment trust.

rejection The right of the buyer of a security to refuse to accept delivery in completion of a trade because the security does not meet the requirements of good delivery.

renewal and replacement fund The account that is used to fund major renewal projects and equipment replacements financed by a municipal revenue bond issue. *Related item(s)*: flow of funds.

reoffering price The price or yield at which a municipal security is sold to the public by the underwriters.

reorganization department The department within a brokerage firm that handles transactions that represent a change in the securities outstanding, such as trades relating to tender offers, bond calls, preferred stock redemptions, and mergers and acquisitions.

repo *See* repurchase agreement.

repurchase agreement A sale of securities with an attendant agreement to repurchase them at a higher price on an agreed-upon future date; the difference between the sale price and the repurchase price represents the interest earned by the investor. Repos are considered money market instruments and are used to raise short-term capital and as instruments of monetary policy. *Syn.* repo. *Related item(s)*: reverse repurchase agreement.

reserve maintenance fund The account that holds funds that supplement the general maintenance fund of a municipal revenue bond issue. *Related item(s)*: flow of funds.

reserve requirement The percentage of depositors' money that the Federal Reserve Board requires a commercial bank to keep on deposit in the form of cash or in its vault. *Syn.* reserves.

residual claim The right of a common stockholder to corporate assets in the event that the corporation ceases to exist. A common stockholder may claim assets only after the claims of all creditors and other security holders have been satisfied.

resistance level A technical analysis term describing the top of a stock's historical trading range. *Related item(s):* breakout; support level.

restricted account A margin account in which the equity is less than the Regulation T initial requirement. *Related item(s):* equity; initial margin requirement; margin account; retention requirement.

restricted security An unregistered, nonexempt security acquired either directly or indirectly from the issuer, or an affiliate of the issuer, in a transaction that does not involve a public offering. *Related item(s):* holding period; Rule 144.

retail communications FINRA defines this category of communications with the public as any written (including electronic) communication that is distributed or made available to more than 25 retail investors within any 30 calendar-day period. A retail investor is any person other than an institutional investor, regardless of whether the person has an account with the member firm or not.

retained earnings The amount of a corporation's net income that remains after all dividends have been paid to preferred and common stockholders. *Syn.* earned surplus; reinvested earnings.

retention requirement The provision of Regulation T that applies to the withdrawal of securities from a restricted account. The customer must deposit an amount equal to the unpaid portion of the securities being withdrawn, in order to reduce the debit balance. The retention requirement is the reciprocal of the initial margin requirement. *Related item(s):* restricted account.

retirement account A customer account established to provide retirement funds.

retiring bonds Ending an issuer's debt obligation by calling the outstanding bonds, by purchasing bonds in the open market, or by repaying bondholders the principal amount at maturity.

return on common equity A measure of a corporation's profitability, calculated by dividing after-tax income by common shareholders' equity.

return on equity A measure of a corporation's profitability, specifically its return on assets, calculated by dividing after-tax income by tangible assets.

return on investment (ROI) The profit or loss resulting from a security transaction, often expressed as an annual percentage rate.

revenue anticipation note (RAN) A short-term municipal debt security issued in anticipation of revenue to be received.

revenue bond A municipal debt issue whose interest and principal are payable only from the specific earnings of an income-producing public project. *Related item(s):*

double-barreled bond; general obligation bond; municipal bond; special revenue bond.

reverse churning The unsuitable practice of placing a client who trades infrequently in a fee-based account rather than a commission based account that would be more appropriate. Related item: churning

reverse repo *See* reverse repurchase agreement.

reverse repurchase agreement A purchase of securities with an attendant agreement to resell them at a higher price on an agreed-upon future date; the difference between the purchase price and the resale price represents the interest earned by the investor. The purchaser initiates the deal. *Syn.* reverse repo. *Related item(s):* repurchase agreement.

reverse split A reduction in the number of a corporation's shares outstanding that increases the par value of its stock or its earnings per share. The market value of the total number of shares remains the same. *Related item(s):* stock split.

reversionary working interest A sharing arrangement whereby the general partner of a direct participation program bears none of the program's costs and does not share in revenues until the limited partners receive payment plus a predetermined rate of return. *Syn.* subordinated interest; subordinated reversionary working interest. *Related item(s):* sharing arrangement.

right A security representing a stockholder's entitlement to the first opportunity to purchase new shares issued by the corporation at a predetermined price (normally less than the current market price) in proportion to the number of shares already owned. Rights are issued for a short time only, after which they expire. *Syn.* subscription right; subscription right certificate. *Related item(s):* preemptive right; rights offering.

right of accumulation A benefit offered by a mutual fund that allows the investor to qualify for reduced sales loads on additional purchases according to the fund account's total dollar value.

rights agent An issuing corporation's agent who is responsible for maintaining current records of the names of rights certificate owners.

rights offering An issue of new shares of stock accompanied by the opportunity for each stockholder to maintain a proportionate ownership by purchasing additional shares in the corporation before the shares are offered to the public. *Related item(s):* right.

risk arbitrage The purchase of stock in a company that is being acquired and the short sale of stock in the acquiring company to profit from the anticipated increase in the acquired corporation's shares and decrease in the acquiring corporation's shares.

riskless and simultaneous transaction The buying or selling by a broker-dealer of a security for its own account to fill an order previously received from a customer. Although the firm is technically acting as a principal in the trade, the transaction is relatively riskless because the purchase and sale are consummated almost simultaneously. *Syn.* riskless transaction.

ROI *See* return on investment.

rollover The transfer of funds from one qualified retirement plan to another qualified retirement plan. If this is not done within a specified time period, the funds are taxed as ordinary income.

ROP *See* Registered Options Principal.

round lot A security's normal unit of trading, which is generally 100 shares of stock or five bonds. *Related item(s):* odd lot.

royalty interest The right of a mineral rights owner to receive a share in the revenues generated by the resource if and when production begins. The royalty interest retained is free from production costs.

Rule 15c2-1 SEC rule governing the safekeeping of securities in customer margin accounts. It prohibits broker-dealers from (1) using a customer's securities in excess of the customer's aggregate indebtedness as collateral to secure a loan without written permission from the customer, and (2) commingling a customer's securities without written permission from the customer. *Related item(s):* rehypothecation.

Rule 144 SEC rule requiring that persons who hold control or restricted securities sell them only in limited quantities, and that all sales of restricted stock by control persons must be reported to the SEC by filing a Form 144, Notice of Proposed Sale of Securities. *Related item(s):* control security; restricted security.

Rule 145 SEC rule requiring that, whenever the stockholders of a publicly owned corporation are solicited to vote on or consent to a plan for reorganizing the corporation, full disclosure of all material facts must be made in a proxy statement or prospectus that must be in the hands of the stockholders before the announced voting date. *Related item(s):* reclassification.

Rule 147 SEC rule that provides exemption from the registration statement and prospectus requirements of the 1933 Act for securities offered and sold exclusively intrastate.

Rule 405 NYSE rule requiring that each member organization exercise due diligence to learn the essential facts about every customer. *Syn.* know your customer rule.

Rule 415 SEC rule governing shelf offerings. The rule allows an issuer to sell limited portions of a new issue over a three-year period. *Related item(s):* shelf offering.

Rule 504 SEC rule providing that an offering of less than $1 million during any 12-month period may be exempt from full registration. The rule does not restrict the number of accredited or nonaccredited purchasers.

Rule 505 SEC rule providing that an offering of $1 million to $5 million during any 12-month period may be exempt from full registration. The rule restricts the number of nonaccredited purchasers to 35 but does not restrict the number of accredited purchasers.

Rule 506 SEC rule providing that an offering of more than $5 million during any 12-month period may be exempt from full registration. The rule restricts the number of nonaccredited purchasers to 35 but does not restrict the number of accredited purchasers.

Rule G-1 MSRB rule that classifies as municipal securities dealers any separately identifiable departments of banks that engage in activities related to the municipal securities business. *Related item(s):* separately identifiable department or division.

Rule G-2 MSRB rule that sets professional qualification standards.

Rule G-3 MSRB rule governing the classification of municipal securities principals and representatives.

Rule G-6 MSRB rule governing the fidelity bond requirements for member broker-dealers.

Rule G-7 MSRB rule governing the documentation that must be kept on each associated person.

Rule G-10 MSRB rule requiring that an investor brochure be delivered in response to a customer complaint.

Rule G-11 MSRB rule governing the priority given to orders received for new issue municipal securities.

Rule G-12 MSRB rule governing the uniform practices for settling transactions between municipal securities firms.

Rule G-13 MSRB rule requiring broker-dealers to publish only bona fide quotations for municipal securities unless the quotations are identified as informational.

Rule G-15 MSRB rule governing the confirmation, clearance, and settlement of customer municipal securities transactions.

Rule G-16 MSRB rule requiring inspections to be conducted every 24 months to verify compliance.

Rule G-17 MSRB rule that sets ethical standards for conducting municipal securities business.

Rule G-18 MSRB rule requiring firms to make an effort to obtain the best price when executing municipal securities transactions for customers.

Rule G-19 MSRB rule governing discretionary accounts and the suitability of municipal securities recommendations and transactions.

Rule G-20 MSRB rule that sets a limit on the value of gifts and gratuities given by municipal securities firms.

Rule G-21 MSRB rule governing the advertising of municipal securities.

Rule G-22 MSRB rule requiring disclosures to customers of control relationships between municipal firms and issuers.

Rule G-23 MSRB rule that seeks to minimize conflicts of interest arising out of the activities of financial advisers that also act as municipal underwriters to the same issuer.

Rule G-24 MSRB rule prohibiting the misuse of confidential information about customers obtained by municipal securities firms acting in fiduciary capacities.

Rule G-25 MSRB rule prohibiting the improper use of assets by municipal securities firms and their representatives.

Rule G-27 MSRB rule requiring each municipal securities firm to designate a principal to supervise its municipal securities representatives.

Rule G-28 MSRB rule governing employee accounts held at other municipal securities firms.

Rule G-29 MSRB rule governing the availability of MSRB regulations.

Rule G-30 MSRB rule requiring that prices and commissions charged by municipal securities firms be fair and reasonable.

Rule G-31 MSRB rule prohibiting a municipal securities professional from soliciting business from an investment company portfolio in return for sales of that fund to its customers.

Rule G-32 MSRB rule requiring that customers receive a copy of the preliminary or final official statement when purchasing a new municipal issue.

Rule G-33 MSRB rule governing the calculation of accrued interest on municipal bonds using a 360-day year.

Rule G-37 MSRB rule prohibiting municipal securities dealers from underwriting securities issued under the authority of a public official to whom an associated person of the dealer has contributed money.

Rule G-39 MSRB rule requiring telemarketers calling on behalf of a firm to limit calls to between 8:00 am and 9:00 pm in the called person's time zone. The caller must disclose his name, the firm's name, the firm's telephone number or address, and the fact that he is calling to solicit the purchase of municipal bonds or investment services. The rule does not apply if the person called is an established customer.

Rule G-41 MSRB rule requiring municipal securities dealers to establish and implement an anti-money laundering compliance program designed to achieve and monitor ongoing compliance with the requirements of the Bank Secrecy Act.

S

sale *See* sell.

sales charge *See* commission.

sales literature Any written material a firm distributes to customers or the public in a controlled manner. Examples include circulars, research reports, form letters, market letters, performance reports, and text used for seminars. *Related item(s):* advertisement; market letter.

sales load The amount added to a mutual fund share's net asset value to arrive at the offering price. *Related item(s):* mutual fund; net asset value; no-load fund.

Sallie Mae *See* Student Loan Marketing Association.

S&P *See* Standard & Poor's Corporation.

S&P 100 *See* Standard & Poor's 100 Stock Index.

S&P 500 *See* Standard & Poor's Composite Index of 500 Stocks.

SAR See suspicious activity report.

savings bond A government debt security that is not negotiable or transferable and that may not be used as collateral. *Related item(s):* Series EE bond; Series HH bond.

scale A list of each of the scheduled maturities in a new serial bond issue. The list outlines the number of bonds, maturity dates, coupon rates, and yields. *Related item(s):* writing a scale.

SEC *See* Securities and Exchange Commission.

secondary distribution (1) A distribution, with a prospectus, that involves securities owned by major stockholders (typically founders or principal owners of a corporation). The sale proceeds go to the sellers of the stock, not to the issuer. *Syn.* registered secondary distribution. (2) A procedure for trading very large blocks of shares of stock whereby the trade is executed off the floor of an exchange after the market closes.

secondary market The market in which securities are bought and sold subsequent to their being sold to the public for the first time. *Related item(s):* new issue market.

secondary offering A sale of securities in which one or more major stockholders in a company sell all or a large portion of their holdings; the underwriting proceeds are paid to the stockholders rather than to the corporation. Typically, such an offering occurs when the founder of a business (and perhaps some of the original financial backers) determines that there is more to be gained by going public than by staying private. The offering does not increase the number of shares of stock outstanding. *Related item(s):* secondary distribution.

sector fund A mutual fund whose investment objective is to capitalize on the return potential provided by investing primarily in a particular industry or sector of the economy. *Syn.* industry fund; specialized fund.

secured bond A debt security backed by identifiable assets set aside as collateral. In the event that the issuer defaults on payment, the bondholders may lay claim to the collateral. *Related item(s):* debenture.

Securities Act of 1933 Federal legislation requiring the full and fair disclosure of all material information about the issuance of new securities. *Syn.* Act of 1933; Full Disclosure Act; New Issues Act; Prospectus Act; Trust in Securities Act; Truth in Securities Act.

Securities Acts Amendments of 1975 Federal legislation that established the Municipal Securities Rulemaking Board. *Related item(s):* Municipal Securities Rulemaking Board.

Securities and Exchange Commission (SEC) Commission created by Congress to regulate the securities markets and protect investors. It is composed of five commissioners appointed by the president of the United States and approved by the Senate. The SEC enforces, among other acts, the Securities Act of 1933, the Securities Exchange Act of 1934, the Trust Indenture Act of 1939, the Investment Company Act of 1940, and the Investment Advisers Act of 1940.

Securities Exchange Act of 1934 Federal legislation that established the Securities and Exchange Commission. The act aims to protect investors by regulating the exchanges, the over-the-counter market, the extension of credit by the Federal Reserve Board, broker-dealers, insider transactions, trading activities, client accounts, and net capital. *Syn.* Act of 1934; Exchange Act.

Securities Investor Protection Corporation (SIPC) A nonprofit membership corporation created by an act of Congress to protect clients of brokerage firms that are forced into bankruptcy. Membership is composed of all brokers and dealers registered under the Securities Exchange Act of 1934. SIPC provides brokerage firm customers up to $500,000 coverage for cash and securities held by the firms (although cash coverage is limited to $250,000).

securitization Pooling assets that may be smaller or less liquid into financial instruments, allowing them to be sold more easily to investors.

security Other than an insurance policy or a fixed annuity, any piece of securitized paper that can be traded for value. Under the Act of 1934, this includes any note, stock, bond, investment contract, debenture, certificate of interest in a profit-sharing or partnership agreement, certificate of deposit, collateral trust certificate, preorganization certificate, option on a security, or other instrument of investment commonly known as a *security*.

segregation Holding customer-owned securities separate from securities owned by other customers and securities owned by the brokerage firm. *Related item(s):* commingling.

selection risk The potential for loss on an investment owing to the particular security chosen performing poorly in spite of good overall market or industry performance.

self-regulatory organization (SRO) One of eight organizations accountable to the SEC for the enforcement of federal securities laws and the supervision of securities practices within an assigned field of jurisdiction. For example, the Financial Industry Regulatory Authority regulates trading on the NYSE and the over-the-counter market; the Municipal Securities Rulemaking Board supervises state and municipal securities; and certain exchanges, such as the Chicago Board Options Exchange, act as self-regulatory bodies to promote ethical conduct and standard trading practices.

sell To convey ownership of a security or another asset for money or value. This includes giving or delivering a security with or as a bonus for a purchase of securities, a gift of assessable stock, and selling or offering a warrant or right to purchase or subscribe to another security. Not included in the definition is a bona fide pledge or loan or a stock dividend if nothing of value is given by the stockholders for the dividend. *Syn.* sale.

seller *See* writer.

seller's option A settlement contract that calls for delivery and payment according to a number of days specified by the seller. *Related item(s):* buyer's option.

selling away An associated person engaging in private securities transactions without the employing broker-dealer's knowledge and consent. This violates the Conduct Rules.

selling concession *See* concession.

selling dividends (1) Inducing customers to buy mutual fund shares by implying that an upcoming distribution will benefit them. This practice is illegal. (2) Combining dividend and gains distributions when calculating current yield.

selling group Brokerage firms that help distribute securities in an offering but that are not members of the syndicate.

sell out The procedure that the seller of a security follows when the buyer fails to complete the contract by accepting delivery of the security. The seller closes the contract by selling the security in the open market and charging the account of the buyer for transaction fees and any loss caused by changes in the market. *Related item(s):* buy-in.

sell stop order An order to sell a security that is entered at a price below the current market price and that is triggered when the market price touches or goes through the sell stop price.

senior lien debt A bond issue that shares the same collateral as is backing other issues but that has a prior claim to the collateral in the event of default.

senior security A security that grants its holder a prior claim to the issuer's assets over the claims of another security's holders. For example, a bond is a senior security over common stock.

SEP *See* simplified employee pension plan.

separate account The account that holds funds paid by variable annuity contract holders. The funds are kept separate from the insurer's general account and are invested in a portfolio of securities that match the contract holders' objectives. *Related item(s):* accumulation unit; annuity; general account.

separately identifiable department or division A department of a bank that engages in the business of buying or selling municipal securities under the direct supervision of an officer of the bank. Such a department is classified by the Municipal Securities Rulemaking

Board as a municipal securities dealer and must comply with MSRB regulations. *Related item(s):* Rule G-1.

Separate Trading of Registered Interest and Principal of Securities (STRIPS) A zero-coupon bond issued and backed by the Treasury Department. *Related item(s):* zero-coupon bond.

SEP-IRA *See* simplified employee pension plan.

serial bond A debt security issued with a maturity schedule in which parts of the outstanding issue mature at intervals until the entire balance has been repaid. Most municipal bonds are serial bonds. *Related item(s):* maturity date; series bond.

series Options of the same class that have the same exercise price and the same expiration date. *Related item(s):* class; type.

Series 6 The investment company/variable contract products limited representative license, which entitles the holder to sell mutual funds and variable annuities and is used by many firms that sell primarily insurance-related products. The Series 6 can serve as the prerequisite for the Series 26 license.

Series 7 The general securities registered representative license, which entitles the holder to sell all types of securities products, with the exception of commodities futures (which requires a Series 3 license). The Series 7 is the most comprehensive of the FINRA representative licenses and serves as a prerequisite for most of the principals' examinations.

Series 24 The General Securities Principal License, which entitles the holder to supervise the business of a broker-dealer. A Series 7 or a Series 62 qualification is a prerequisite for this license.

Series 63 The uniform securities agent state law exam, which entitles the successful candidate to sell securities and give investment advice in those states that require Series 63 registration. *Related item(s):* blue-sky laws; Uniform Securities Act.

series bond A debt security issued in a series of public offerings spread over an extended time period. All the bonds in the series have the same priority claim against assets. *Related item(s):* serial bond.

Series EE bond A nonmarketable, interest-bearing U.S. government savings bond issued at a discount from par. Interest on Series EE bonds is exempt from state and local taxes. *Related item(s):* savings bond; Series HH bond.

Series HH bond A nonmarketable, interest-bearing U.S. government savings bond issued at par and purchased only by trading in Series EE bonds at maturity. Interest on Series HH bonds is exempt from state and local taxes. *Related item(s):* savings bond; Series EE bond.

settlement The completion of a trade through the delivery of a security or commodity and the payment of cash or other consideration.

settlement date The date on which ownership changes between buyer and seller. The Uniform Practice Code standardizes settlement provisions. *Related item(s):* cash transaction; regular way.

75-5-10 test The standard for judging whether an investment company qualifies as diversified under the Investment Company Act of 1940. Under this act, a diversified investment company must invest at least 75% of its total assets in cash, receivables, or invested securities and no more than 5% of its total assets in any one company's voting securities. In addition, no single investment may represent ownership of more than 10% of any one company's outstanding voting securities. *Related item(s):* diversified management company.

share identification An accounting method that identifies the specific shares selected for liquidation in the event that an investor wishes to liquidate shares. The difference between the buying and selling prices determines the investor's tax liability.

sharing arrangement A method of allocating the responsibility for expenses and the right to share in revenues among the sponsor and limited partners in a direct participation program. *Related item(s):* carried interest; disproportionate sharing; functional allocation; net operating profits interest; overriding royalty interest; reversionary working interest.

shelf offering An SEC provision allowing an issuer to register a new issue security without selling the entire issue at once. The issuer may sell limited portions of the issuer over a three-year period without reregistering the security or incurring penalties. *Related item(s):* Rule 415.

short The term used to describe the selling of a security, contract, or commodity that the seller does not own. For example, an investor who borrows shares of stock from a broker-dealer and sells them on the open market is said to have a *short position* in the stock. *Related item(s):* long.

short against the box The term used to describe the selling of a security, contract, or commodity that the seller owns but prefers not to deliver; frequently, this is done to defer taxation.

short-interest theory A technical analysis theory that examines the ratio of short sales to volume in a stock. Because the underlying stock must be purchased to close out the short positions, a high ratio is considered bullish.

short sale The sale of a security that the seller does not own, or any sale consummated by the delivery of a security borrowed by or for the account of the seller.

short straddle An option investor's position that results from selling a call and a put on the same stock with the same exercise price and expiration month. *Related item(s):* long straddle; spread; straddle.

short-term capital gain The profit realized on the sale of an asset that has been owned for 12 months or less. *Related item(s):* capital gain; capital loss; short-term capital loss.

short-term capital loss The loss incurred on the sale of a capital asset that has been owned for 12 months or less. *Related item(s):* capital gain; capital loss; short-term capital gain.

simplified arbitration An expedient method of settling disputes involving claims not exceeding $50,000, whereby a panel of arbitrators reviews the evidence and renders a decision. All awards are made within 30 business days. *Related item(s):* arbitration.

simplified employee pension plan (SEP) A qualified retirement plan designed for employers with 25 or fewer employees. Contributions made to each employee's individual retirement account grow tax deferred until retirement. *Related item(s):* individual retirement account.

single account An account in which only one individual has control over the investments and may transact business.

sinking fund An account established by an issuing corporation or municipality into which money is deposited regularly so that the issuer has the funds to redeem its bonds, debentures, or preferred stock.

SIPC *See* Securities Investor Protection Corporation.

SLD A message on the Consolidated Tape indicating that the sale being reported was not reported on time and is therefore out of sequence.

SLMA *See* Student Loan Marketing Association.

SMA *See* special memorandum account.

solvency The ability of a corporation both to meet its long-term fixed expenses and to have adequate money for long-term expansion and growth.

special assessment bond A municipal revenue bond funded by assessments only on property owners who benefit from the services or improvements provided by the proceeds of the bond issue. *Related item(s):* revenue bond.

specialist See designated market maker

specialist's book A journal in which a specialist (designated market maker) records the limit and stop orders that he holds for execution. The contents of the journal are confidential. *Syn.* limit order book. *Related item(s):* specialist.

specialized fund *See* sector fund.

special memorandum account (SMA) A notation on a customer's general or margin account indicating that funds are credited to the account on a memo basis; the account is used much like a line of credit with a bank. An SMA preserves the customer's right to use excess equity. *Syn.* special miscellaneous account.

special revenue bond A municipal revenue bond issued to finance a specific project. Examples include industrial development bonds, lease rental bonds, special tax bonds, and New Housing Authority bonds. *Related item(s):* revenue bond.

special situation fund A mutual fund whose objective is to capitalize on the profit potential of corporations in nonrecurring circumstances, such as those undergoing reorganizations or being considered as takeover candidates.

special tax bond A municipal revenue bond payable only from the proceeds of a tax on certain items, rather than an ad valorem tax. *Related item(s):* revenue bond.

speculation Trading a commodity or security with a higher-than-average risk in return for a higher-than-average profit potential. The trade is effected solely for the purpose of profiting from it and not as a means of hedging or protecting other positions.

speculator One who trades a commodity or security with a higher-than-average risk in return for a higher-than-average profit potential. *Related item(s):* speculation.

spin-off A type of divestiture where a parent company sells all the shares of a subsidiary or distributes new shares of a company or division it owns to create a new company.

split offering A public offering of securities that combines aspects of both a primary and a secondary offering. A portion of the issue is a primary offering, the proceeds of which go to the issuing corporation; the remainder of the issue is a secondary offering, the proceeds of which go to the selling stockholders. *Syn.* combined distribution. *Related item(s):* primary offering; secondary offering.

sponsor A person who is instrumental in organizing, selling, or managing a limited partnership.

spousal account A separate individual retirement account established for a nonworking spouse. Contributions to the account made by the working spouse grow tax deferred until withdrawal. *Related item(s):* individual retirement account.

spread In a quotation, the difference between a security's bid and ask prices.

spread order A customer order specifying two option contracts on the same underlying security and a price difference between them.

SRO *See* self-regulatory organization.

$\frac{s}{s}$ A symbol on the Consolidated Tape indicating that the stock in question sold in 10-share units.

stabilizing Bidding at or below the public offering price of a new issue security. Underwriting managers may enter stabilizing bids during the offering period to prevent the price from dropping sharply.

stagflation A period of high unemployment in the economy accompanied by a general rise in prices. *Related item(s):* deflation; inflation.

Standard & Poor's 100 Stock Index (S&P 100) A value-weighted index composed of 100 blue-chip stocks. The index is owned and compiled by Standard & Poor's Corporation. *Related item(s):* index; Standard & Poor's Corporation; Standard & Poor's Composite Index of 500 Stocks.

Standard & Poor's Composite Index of 500 Stocks (S&P 500) A value-weighted index that offers broad coverage of the securities market. It is composed of 400 industrial stocks, 40 financial stocks, 40 public utility stocks, and 20 transportation stocks. The index is owned and compiled by Standard & Poor's Corporation. *Related item(s):* index; Standard & Poor's Corporation; Standard & Poor's 100 Stock Index.

Standard & Poor's Corporation (S&P) A company that rates stocks and corporate and municipal bonds according to risk profiles and that produces and tracks the S&P indexes. The company also publishes a variety of financial and investment reports. *Related item(s):* bond rating; Moody's Investors Service; rating; Standard & Poor's 100 Stock Index; Standard & Poor's Composite Index of 500 Stocks.

standby underwriter An investment banker that agrees to purchase any part of an issue that has not been purchased by current stockholders through a rights offering. The firm exercises the remaining rights, maintains a trading market in the rights, and offers the stock acquired to the public. *Related item(s):* rights offering.

stated yield *See* nominal yield.

statutory disqualification Prohibiting a person from associating with a self-regulatory organization because the person has been expelled, barred, or suspended from association with a member of an SRO; has had his registration suspended, denied or revoked by the SEC; has been the cause of someone else being suspended, barred, or having their license revoked; has been convicted of certain crimes; or has falsified an application or a report that he must file with or on behalf of a membership organization.

statutory voting A voting procedure that permits stockholders to cast one vote per share owned for each position. The procedure tends to benefit majority stockholders. *Related item(s):* cumulative voting.

step-out well An oil or gas well or prospect adjacent to a field of proven reserves. *Related item(s):* developmental drilling program.

stock ahead The term used to describe the inability to fill a limit order at a specific price because other orders at the same price were entered previously.

stockbroker *See* registered representative.

stock certificate Written evidence of ownership in a corporation.

stock dividend *See* dividend.

stock loan agreement The document that an institutional customer must sign when the broker-dealer borrows stock from the customer's account; the document specifies the terms of the loan and the rights of both parties.

stock power A standard form that duplicates the back of a stock certificate and is used for transferring the stock to the new owner's name. A separate stock power is used if a security's registered owner does not have the certificate available for signature endorsement. *Syn.* irrevocable stock power; power of substitution. *Related item(s):* assignment.

stock quote A list of representative prices bid and asked for a stock during a particular trading day. Stocks are quoted in points, where one point equals $1. Stock quotes are listed in the financial press and most daily newspapers. *Related item(s):* bond quote.

stock split An increase in the number of a corporation's outstanding shares, which decreases its stock's par value. The market value of the total number of shares remains the same. The proportional reductions in orders held on the books for a split stock are calculated by dividing the stock's market price by the fraction that represents the split.

stop limit order A customer order that becomes a limit order when the market price of the security reaches or passes a specific price. *Related item(s):* limit order; stop order.

stop order (1) A directive from the SEC that suspends the sale of new issue securities to the public when fraud is suspected or filing materials are deficient. (2) A customer order that becomes a market order when the market price of the security reaches or passes a specific price. *Related item(s):* limit order; market order; stop limit order.

straddle An option investor's position that results from buying a call and a put or selling a call and a put on the same security with the same exercise price and expiration month. *Related item(s):* long straddle; short straddle; spread.

straight-line depreciation An accounting method used to recover the cost of a qualifying depreciable asset, whereby the owner writes off the cost of the asset in equal amounts each year over the asset's useful life.

strike price *See* exercise price.

striking price *See* exercise price.

stripped bond A debt obligation that has been stripped of its interest coupons by a brokerage firm, repackaged, and sold at a deep discount. It pays no interest but may be redeemed at maturity for the full face value. *Related item(s):* zero-coupon bond.

stripper well An oil well that produces fewer than 10 barrels per day.

STRIPS *See* Separate Trading of Registered Interest and Principal of Securities.

Student Loan Marketing Association (SLMA) A publicly owned corporation that purchases student loans from financial institutions and packages them for sale in the secondary market, thereby increasing the availability of money for educational loans. *Syn.* Sallie Mae.

subject quote A securities quotation that does not represent an actual offer to buy or sell but is tentative, subject to reconfirmation by the broker-dealer. *Related item(s):* bona fide quote; firm quote; nominal quote; workout quote.

subordinated debenture A debt obligation backed by the general credit of the issuing corporation that has claims to interest and principal subordinated to ordinary debentures and all other liabilities. *Related item(s):* debenture.

subordinated debt financing A form of long-term capitalization used by broker-dealers in which the claims of lenders are subordinated to the claims of other creditors. Subordinated financing is considered part of the broker-dealer's capital structure and is added to net worth when computing its net capital.

subordinated interest *See* reversionary working interest.

subordinated loan A loan to a broker-dealer in which the lender agrees to subordinate its claim to the claims of the firm's other creditors.

subordinated reversionary working interest *See* reversionary working interest.

sub-penny pricing Pricing increments of less than $.01 for stocks priced less than $1 as allowed under the minimum increment pricing rule under Regulation NMS. *Related item(s):* minimum increment pricing; Regulation NMS.

subscription agreement A statement signed by an investor indicating an offer to buy an interest in a direct participation program. In the statement, the investor agrees to grant power of attorney to the general partner and to abide by the limited partnership agreement. The sale is finalized when the subscription agreement is signed by the general partner.

subscription amount The total dollar amount that a participant in a direct participation program has invested.

subscription right *See* right.

suitability A determination made by a registered representative as to whether a particular security matches a customer's objectives and financial capability. The representative must have enough information about the customer to make this judgment. *Related item(s):* Rule 405.

Super Display Book (SDBK) The electronic order entry and processing system used by the New York Stock Exchange.

supplemental liquidity provider (SLP) An off-floor market maker who trades only for his proprietary account and may compete with the on-floor designated market maker in a stock listed on the NYSE. The SLP must maintain a bid or an offer in an assigned stock at least 5% of the trading day.

supply The total amount of a good or service available for purchase by consumers. *Related item(s):* demand.

supply-side theory An economic theory holding that bolstering an economy's ability to supply more goods is the most effective way to stimulate economic growth. Supply-side theorists advocate income tax reduction insofar as this increases private investment in corporations, facilities, and equipment.

support level A technical analysis term describing the bottom of a stock's historical trading range. *Related item(s):* breakout; resistance level.

suspicious activity report (SAR) A report filed by broker-dealers and financial institutions when investor behavior is detected that is commercially illogical and serves no apparent purpose. The filing threshold for a SAR is $5,000.

syndicate A group of investment bankers formed to handle the distribution and sale of a security on behalf of the issuer. Each syndicate member is responsible for the sale and distribution of a portion of the issue. *Syn.* underwriting syndicate. *Related item(s):* Eastern account; Western account.

syndicate manager *See* underwriting manager.

systematic risk The potential for a security to decrease in value owing to its inherent tendency to move together with all securities of the same type. Neither diversification nor any other investment strategy can eliminate this risk. *Related item(s):* market risk.

T

T Consolidated Tape market identifier for trades of exchange-listed securities executed over the counter.

takedown The discount from the public offering price at which a syndicate member buys new issue securities from the syndicate for sale to the public. *Related item(s):* concession.

TAN *See* tax anticipation note.

Tape *See* Consolidated Tape.

taxability The risk of the erosion of investment income through taxation.

taxable gain The portion of a sale or distribution of mutual fund shares subject to taxation.

tax and revenue anticipation note (TRAN) A short-term municipal debt security to be paid off from future tax receipts and revenues.

tax anticipation note (TAN) A short-term municipal or government debt security to be paid off from future tax receipts.

tax basis The amount that a limited partner has invested in a partnership.

tax credit An amount that can be subtracted from a tax liability, often in connection with real estate development, energy conservation, and research and development programs. Every dollar of tax credit reduces the amount of tax due, dollar for dollar. *Related item(s):* deduction.

tax-deferred annuity *See* tax-sheltered annuity.

tax-equivalent yield The rate of return a taxable bond must earn before taxes in order to equal the tax-exempt earnings on a municipal bond. This number varies with the investor's tax bracket.

taxes per capita *See* taxes per person.

taxes per person A measure of the tax burden of a municipality's population, calculated by dividing the municipality's tax receipts by its population. *Syn.* taxes per capita.

tax-exempt bond fund A mutual fund whose investment objective is to provide maximum tax-free income. It invests primarily in municipal bonds and short-term debt. *Syn.* tax-free bond fund.

tax-free bond fund *See* tax-exempt bond fund.

tax liability The amount of tax payable on earnings, usually calculated by subtracting standard and itemized deductions and personal exemptions from adjusted gross income, then multiplying by the tax rate. *Related item(s):* adjusted gross income.

tax preference item An element of income that receives favorable tax treatment. The item must be added to taxable income when computing alternative minimum tax. Tax preference items include accelerated depreciation on property, research and development costs, intangible drilling costs, tax-exempt interest on municipal private purpose bonds, and certain incentive stock options. *Related item(s):* alternative minimum tax.

tax-sheltered annuity (TSA) An insurance contract that entitles the holder to exclude all contributions from gross income in the year they are made. Tax payable on the earnings is deferred until the holder withdraws funds at retirement. TSAs are available to employees of public schools, church organizations, and other tax-exempt organizations. *Syn.* tax-deferred annuity.

T-bill *See* Treasury bill.

T-bond *See* Treasury bond.

T-call *See* margin call.

TDA *See* tax-sheltered annuity.

technical analysis A method of evaluating securities by analyzing statistics generated by market activity, such as past prices and volume. Technical analysts do not attempt to measure a security's intrinsic value. *Related item(s):* chartist; fundamental analysis.

technician *See* chartist.

Telephone Consumer Protection Act of 1991 (TCPA) Federal legislation restricting the use of telephone lines for solicitation purposes. A company soliciting sales via telephone, facsimile, or email must disclose its name and address to the called party and must not call any person who has requested not to be called.

tenants in common (TIC) A form of joint ownership of an account whereby a deceased tenant's fractional interest in the account is retained by his estate. *Related item(s):* joint tenants with right of survivorship.

tender offer An offer to buy securities for cash or for cash plus securities.

term bond *See* term maturity.

term maturity A repayment schedule for a bond issue in which the entire issue comes due on a single date. *Syn.* term bond. *Related item(s):* maturity date.

testimonial An endorsement of an investment or service by a celebrity or public opinion influencer. The use of testimonials in public communications is regulated by FINRA.

third market The exchange where listed securities are traded in the over-the-counter market.

third-party account (1) A customer account for which the owner has given power of attorney to a third party. (2) A customer account opened by an adult naming a minor as beneficial owner. (3) A customer account opened for another adult. This type of account is prohibited.

30-day visible supply *See* visible supply.

Thomson A municipal wire service offering Thomson Muni News and Thomson Muni Market Monitor (formerly Munifacts)

tick A minimum upward or downward movement in the price of a security. *Related item(s):* minus tick; plus tick.

ticker tape *See* Consolidated Tape.

TIGR *See* Treasury Investors Growth Receipt.

time deposit A sum of money left with a bank (or borrowed from a bank and left on deposit) that the depositing customer has agreed not to withdraw for a specified time period or without a specified amount of notice. *Related item(s):* demand deposit.

time spread *See* horizontal spread.

time value The amount an investor pays for an option above its intrinsic value; it reflects the amount of time left until expiration. The amount is calculated by subtracting the intrinsic value from the premium paid. *Related item(s):* intrinsic value.

timing risk The potential for an investor to incur a loss as a result of buying or selling a particular security at an unfavorable time.

T-note *See* Treasury note.

tombstone A printed advertisement that solicits indications of interest in a securities offering. The text is limited to basic information about the offering, such as the name of the issuer, type of security, names of the underwriters, and where a prospectus is available.

total capitalization The sum of a corporation's long-term debt, stock accounts, and capital in excess of par.

TRACE (Trade Reporting and Compliance Engine) FINRA-approved trade reporting system for corporate bonds trading in the OTC secondary market.

trade confirmation A printed document that contains details of a transaction, including the settlement date and amount of money due from or owed to a customer. It must be sent to the customer on or before the settlement date.

trade date The date on which a securities transaction is executed.

Trade Reporting and Compliance Engine (TRACE) FINRA-approved trade reporting system for corporate bonds trading in the OTC secondary market.

trade-through Generally, any time an order is executed through the price limit of another order that would have represented a better execution. Trade-throughs are prohibited under the order protection rule of Regulation NMS.

trading authorization *See* full trading authorization; limited trading authorization.

trading halt A pause in the trading of a particular security on one or more exchanges, usually in anticipation of a news announcement or to correct an order imbalance. During a trading halt, open orders may be canceled and options may be exercised.

TRAN *See* tax and revenue anticipation note.

tranche One of the classes of securities that form an issue of collateralized mortgage obligations. Each tranche is characterized by its interest rate, average maturity, risk level, and sensitivity to mortgage prepayments. Neither the rate of return nor the maturity date of a CMO tranche is guaranteed. *Related item(s):* collateralized mortgage obligation.

transfer agent A person or corporation responsible for recording the names and holdings of registered security owners, seeing that certificates are signed by the appropriate corporate officers, affixing the corporate seal, and delivering securities to the new owners.

transfer and hold in safekeeping A securities buy order settlement and delivery procedure whereby the securities bought are transferred to the customer's name but are held by the broker-dealer. *Related item(s):* hold in street name; transfer and ship.

transfer and ship A securities buy order settlement and delivery procedure whereby the securities bought are transferred to the customer's name and sent to the customer. *Related item(s):* hold in street name; transfer and hold in safekeeping.

Transportation Average *See* Dow Jones Transportation Average.

Treasury bill A marketable U.S. government debt security with a maturity of less than one year. Treasury bills are issued through a competitive bidding process at a discount from par; they have no fixed interest rate. *Syn.* T bill.

Treasury bond A marketable, fixed-interest U.S. government debt security with a maturity of more than 10 years. *Syn.* T bond.

Treasury Bond Receipt (TBR) One of several types of zero-coupon bonds issued by brokerage firms and collateralized by Treasury securities. *Related item(s):* Treasury receipt.

Treasury Investors Growth Receipt (TIGR) One of several types of zero-coupon bonds issued by brokerage firms and collateralized by Treasury securities. *Related item(s):* Treasury receipt.

Treasury note A marketable, fixed-interest U.S. government debt security with a maturity of between 2 and 10 years. *Syn.* T note.

Treasury receipt The generic term for a zero-coupon bond issued by a brokerage firm and collateralized by the Treasury securities a custodian holds in escrow for the investor.

treasury stock Equity securities that the issuing corporation has issued and repurchased from the public at the current market price. *Related item(s):* issued stock; outstanding stock.

trendline A tool used by technical analysts to trace a security's movement by connecting the reaction lows in an upward trend or the rally highs in a downward trend.

triangle On a technical analyst's trading activity chart, a pattern that shows a narrowing of the price range in which a security is trading. The left side of the triangle typically shows the widest range, and the right side narrows to a point. *Syn.* pennant. *Related item(s):* ascending triangle; descending triangle.

trough The end of a period of declining business activity throughout the economy, one of the four stages of the business cycle. *Related item(s):* business cycle.

true interest cost (TIC) A means of evaluating the competitive bids of prospective bond underwriting syndicates. Each syndicate provides a calculation of the coupon interest to be paid by the issuer over the life of the bond, taking into account the time value of money. *Related item(s):* net interest cost.

trust agreement *See* trust indenture.

trustee A person legally appointed to act on a beneficiary's behalf.

trust indenture A legal contract between a corporation and a trustee that represents its bondholders that details the terms of a debt issue. The terms include the rate of interest, maturity date, means of payment, and collateral. *Syn.* deed of trust; trust agreement.

Trust Indenture Act of 1939 The legislation requiring that certain publicly offered, nonexempt debt securities be registered under the Securities Act of 1933 and be issued under a trust indenture that protects the bondholders.

Trust in Securities Act *See* Securities Act of 1933.

Truth in Securities Act *See* Securities Act of 1933.

TSA *See* tax-sheltered annuity.

12b-1 asset-based fees An Investment Company Act of 1940 provision that allows a mutual fund to collect a fee for the promotion or sale of or another activity connected with the distribution of its shares. The fee must be reasonable (typically .25% to 1% of net assets managed).

two-dollar broker An exchange member that executes orders for other member firms when their floor brokers are especially busy. Two-dollar brokers charge a commission for their services; the amount of the commission is negotiated.

type A term that classifies an option as a call or a put. *Related item(s):* class; series.

U

UGMA *See* Uniform Gift to Minors Act.

UIT *See* unit investment trust.

uncovered *See* naked.

uncovered call writer *See* naked call writer.

uncovered put writer *See* naked put writer.

underlying securities The securities that are bought or sold when an option, right, or warrant is exercised.

underwriter An investment banker that works with an issuer to help bring a security to the market and sell it to the public.

underwriting The procedure by which investment bankers channel investment capital from investors to corporations and municipalities that are issuing securities.

underwriting compensation The amount paid to a broker-dealer firm for its involvement in offering and selling securities.

underwriting discount *See* underwriting spread.

underwriting manager The brokerage firm responsible for organizing a syndicate, preparing the issue, negotiating with the issuer and underwriters, and allocating stock to the selling group. *Syn.* manager of the syndicate; managing underwriter; syndicate manager. *Related item(s):* agreement among underwriters; syndicate.

underwriting spread The difference in price between the public offering price and the price an underwriter pays to the issuing corporation. The difference represents the profit available to the syndicate or selling group. *Syn.* underwriting discount; underwriting split.

underwriting syndicate *See* syndicate.

undivided account *See* Eastern account.

unearned income Income derived from investments and other sources not related to employment services. Examples of unearned income include interest from a savings account, bond interest, and dividends from stock. *Related item(s):* earned income; passive income; portfolio income.

Uniform Gift to Minors Act (UGMA) Legislation that permits a gift of money or securities to be given to a minor and held in a custodial account that an adult manages for the minor's benefit. Income and capital gains transferred to a minor's name are taxed at a lower rate. *Related item(s):* Uniform Transfers to Minors Act.

Uniform Securities Act (USA) Model legislation for securities industry regulation at the state level. Each state may adopt the legislation in its entirety, or it may adapt it (within limits) to suit its needs. *Related item(s):* blue-sky laws; Series 63.

Uniform Transfers to Minors Act (UTMA) Legislation adopted in some states that permits a gift of money or securities to be given to a minor and held in a custodial account that an adult manages for the minor's benefit until the minor reaches a certain age (not necessarily the age of majority). *Related item(s):* Uniform Gifts to Minors Act.

unit A share in the ownership of a direct participation program that entitles the investor to an interest in the program's net income, net loss, and distributions.

unit investment trust (UIT) An investment company that sells redeemable shares in a professionally selected portfolio of securities. It is organized under a trust indenture, not a corporate charter. *Related item(s):* fixed unit investment trust; unit of beneficial interest.

unit of beneficial interest A redeemable share in a unit investment trust, representing ownership of an undivided interest in the underlying portfolio. *Syn.* share of beneficial interest. *Related item(s):* unit investment trust.

unit refund annuity An insurance contract in which the insurance company makes monthly payments to the annuitant over the annuitant's lifetime. If the annuitant dies before receiving an amount equal to the account's value, the money remaining in the account goes to the annuitant's named beneficiary.

unqualified legal opinion The statement of a bond counsel affirming the compliance of a new municipal bond issue with municipal statutes and tax regulations and expressing no reservations about its validity. *Related item(s):* legal opinion of counsel; qualified legal opinion.

unrealized gain The amount by which a security appreciates in value before it is sold. Until it is sold, the investor does not actually possess the sale proceeds. *Related item(s):* realized gain.

unsecured bond *See* debenture.

uptick *See* plus tick.

USA *See* Uniform Securities Act.

U.S. government and agency bond fund A mutual fund whose investment objective is to provide current income while preserving safety of capital through investing in securities backed by the U.S. Treasury or issued by a government agency.

Utilities Average *See* Dow Jones Utilities Average.

UTMA *See* Uniform Transfers to Minors Act.

V

Value Line An investment advisory service that rates hundreds of stocks as to safety, timeliness, and projected price performance. *Related item(s):* Value Line Composite Index.

Value Line Composite Index A market index composed of 1,700 exchange and over-the-counter stocks. *Related item(s):* index; Value Line.

variable annuity An insurance contract in which, at the end of the accumulation stage, the insurance company guarantees a minimum total payment to the annuitant. The performance of a separate account, generally invested in equity securities, determines the amount of this total payment. *Related item(s):* accumulation stage; annuity; fixed annuity; separate account.

variable-rate demand note *See* variable-rate municipal note.

variable-rate demand obligation Municipal bonds issued with variable, or floating, rates of interest. These securities offer interest payments tied to the movements of another specified interest rate.

variable-rate municipal note A short-term municipal debt security issued when either general interest rates are expected to change or the length of time before permanent funding is received is uncertain. *Syn.* variable-rate demand note.

vertical spread The purchase and sale of two options on the same underlying security and with the same expiration date but with different exercise prices. *Syn.* money spread; price spread. *Related item(s):* spread.

vesting (1) An ERISA guideline stipulating that an employee must be entitled to his entire retirement benefits within a certain period of time, even if he no longer works for the employer. (2) The amount of time that an employee must work before retirement or before benefit plan contributions made by the employer become the employee's property without penalty. The IRS and the Employee Retirement Income Security Act of 1974 set minimum requirements for vesting in a qualified plan.

visible supply (1) The disclosure, published in *The Bond Buyer*, of the total dollar amount of municipal securities known to be coming to market within the next 30 days. (2) All supplies of goods and commodities that are readily deliverable.

VIX The volatility market index, known as the fear index, that measures investor expectation of implied volatility in the S&P 500.

volatility The magnitude and frequency of changes in the price of a security or commodity within a given time period.

volume of trading theory A technical analysis theory holding that the ratio of the number of shares traded to total outstanding shares indicates whether a market is strong or weak.

voluntary accumulation plan A mutual fund account into which the investor commits to depositing amounts on a regular basis in addition to the initial sum invested.

voting right A stockholder's right to vote for members of the board of directors and on matters of corporate policy—particularly the issuance of senior securities, stock splits, and substantial changes in the corporation's business. A variation of this right is extended to variable annuity contract holders and mutual fund shareholders, who may vote on material policy issues.

W

warrant A security that gives the holder the right to purchase securities from the warrant issuer at a stipulated subscription price. Warrants are usually long-term instruments with expiration dates years in the future.

wash sale Selling a security at a loss for tax purposes and, within 30 days before or after, purchasing the same or a substantially identical security. The IRS disallows the claimed loss. *Related item(s):* bond swap.

Western account A securities underwriting in which the agreement among underwriters states that each syndicate member will be liable only for the sale of the portion of the issue allocated to it. *Syn.* divided account. *Related item(s):* Eastern account; syndicate.

when-, as-, and if-issued security *See* when issued security.

when-issued contract A trade agreement regarding a security that has been authorized but is not yet physically available for delivery. The seller agrees to make delivery as soon as the security is ready, and the contract includes provisions for marking the price to the market and for calculating accrued interest.

when-issued security (WI) A securities issue that has been authorized and is sold to investors before the certificates are ready for delivery. Typically, such securities include new issue municipal bonds, stock splits, and Treasury securities. *Syn.* when-, as-, and if-issued security.

WI *See* when-issued security.

wildcatting *See* exploratory drilling program.

Wilshire 5,000 Equity Index A value-weighted market indicator composed of 5,000 exchange-listed and over-the-counter common stocks. It is the broadest measure of the market. *Related item(s):* index.

wire room *See* order department.

workable indication The price at which a municipal securities dealer is willing to purchase securities from another municipal dealer. The price may be revised if market conditions change.

working capital A measure of a corporation's liquidity; that is, its ability to transfer assets into cash to meet current short-term obligations. It is calculated by subtracting total current liabilities from total current assets.

working capital ratio *See* current ratio.

working interest An operating interest in a mineral-bearing property entitling the holder to a share of income from production and carrying the obligation to bear a corresponding share of all production costs.

workout quote A qualified quotation whereby a broker-dealer estimates the price on a trade that will require special handling owing to its size or to market conditions. *Related item(s):* bona fide quote; firm quote; nominal quote; subject quote.

writer The seller of an option contract. An option writer takes on the obligation to buy or sell the underlying security if and when the option buyer exercises the option. *Syn.* seller.

writing a scale The process by which a syndicate establishes the yield for each maturity in a new serial bond issue in order to arrive at its competitive bid. *Related item(s):* scale.

Y

yield The rate of return on an investment, usually expressed as an annual percentage rate. *Related item(s):* current yield; dividend yield; nominal yield.

yield-based option A security representing the right to receive, in cash, the difference between the current yield of an underlying U.S. government security and the strike price of the option. A yield-based option is used to speculate on or hedge against the risk associated with fluctuating interest rates; its strike price represents the anticipated yield of the underlying debt security.

yield curve A graphic representation of the actual or projected yields of fixed-income securities in relation to their maturities. *Related item(s):* flat yield curve; inverted yield curve.

yield to call (YTC) The rate of return on a bond that accounts for the difference between the bond's acquisition cost and its proceeds, including interest income, calculated to the earliest date that the bond may be called by the issuing corporation. *Related item(s):* bond yield.

yield to maturity (YTM) The rate of return on a bond that accounts for the difference between the bond's acquisition cost and its maturity proceeds, including interest income. *Related item(s):* bond yield.

YTC *See* yield to call.

YTM *See* yield to maturity.

Z

zero-coupon bond A corporate or municipal debt security traded at a deep discount from face value. The bond pays no interest; rather, it may be redeemed at maturity for its full face value. It may be issued at a discount, or it may be stripped of its coupons and repackaged.

zero-minus tick A security transaction's execution price that is equal to the price of the last sale but lower than the last different price. *Related item(s):* minus tick; plus tick; zero-plus tick.

zero-plus tick A security transaction's execution price that is equal to the price of the last sale but higher than the last different price. *Related item(s):* minus tick; plus tick; zero-minus tick.

Index

Notes

Notes

Notes

Notes

Notes

Notes

Notes